Learning GNU Emacs

Other Resources from O'Reilly

Related titles   Unix in a Nutshell   sed and awk
                     Learning the vi Editor   Essential CVS
                     GNU Emacs Pocket Reference   Version Control with
                                                      Subversion

oreilly.com   *oreilly.com* is more than a complete catalog of O'Reilly books. You'll also find links to news, events, articles, weblogs, sample chapters, and code examples.

oreillynet.com is the essential portal for developers interested in open and emerging technologies, including new platforms, programming languages, and operating systems.

Conferences   O'Reilly brings diverse innovators together to nurture the ideas that spark revolutionary industries. We specialize in documenting the latest tools and systems, translating the innovator's knowledge into useful skills for those in the trenches. Visit *conferences.oreilly.com* for our upcoming events.

Safari Bookshelf (*safari.oreilly.com*) is the premier online reference library for programmers and IT professionals. Conduct searches across more than 1,000 books. Subscribers can zero in on answers to time-critical questions in a matter of seconds. Read the books on your Bookshelf from cover to cover or simply flip to the page you need. Try it today with a free trial.

THIRD EDITION

Learning GNU Emacs

Debra Cameron, James Elliott,
Marc Loy, Eric Raymond, and Bill Rosenblatt

O'REILLY®

Beijing · Cambridge · Farnham · Köln · Paris · Sebastopol · Taipei · Tokyo

Learning GNU Emacs, Third Edition

by Debra Cameron, James Elliott, Marc Loy, Eric Raymond, and Bill Rosenblatt

Published by O'Reilly Media, Inc., 1005 Gravenstein Highway North, Sebastopol, CA 95472.

O'Reilly books may be purchased for educational, business, or sales promotional use. Online editions are also available for most titles (*safari.oreilly.com*). For more information, contact our corporate/institutional sales department: (800) 998-9938 or *corporate@oreilly.com*.

Editors:	Debra Cameron and Mike Loukides
Production Editor:	Jamie Peppard
Cover Designer:	Edie Freedman
Interior Designer:	Melanie Wang

Printing History:

October 1991:	First Edition.
April 1992:	Minor corrections.
September 1996:	Second Edition.
December 2004:	Third Edition.

 This book uses RepKover™, a durable and flexible lay-flat binding.

ISBN: 0-596-00648-9
ISBN13: 978-0-596-00648-8
[M]

Table of Contents

Preface . . . . **ix**

1. Emacs Basics **1**

Introducing Emacs!   1
Understanding Files and Buffers   3
A Word About Modes   3
Starting Emacs   5
About the Emacs Display   6
Emacs Commands   10
Opening a File   11
Saving Files   15
Leaving Emacs   15
Getting Help   16
Summary   18

2. Editing **20**

Moving the Cursor   22
Deleting Text   27
Marking Text to Delete, Move, or Copy   32
Emacs and the Clipboard   37
Editing Tricks and Shortcuts   39
Canceling Commands and Undoing Changes   41
Making Emacs Work the Way You Want   45

3. Search and Replace **49**

Different Kinds of Searches   49
Search and Replace   55

Checking Spelling Using Ispell   64
Word Abbreviations   74

4. Using Buffers, Windows, and Frames **82**
Understanding Buffers, Windows, and Frames   82
Working with Multiple Buffers   85
Working with Windows   88
Working with Frames   93
More About Buffers   95
More About Windows   102
Holding Your Place with Bookmarks   106

5. Emacs as a Work Environment **114**
Executing Commands in Shell Buffers   114
Using Dired, the Directory Editor   123
Printing from Emacs   140
Reading Manpages in Emacs   141
Using Time Management Tools   141

6. Writing Macros **150**
Defining a Macro   151
Tips for Creating Good Macros   154
A More Complicated Macro Example   155
Editing a Macro   157
The Macro Ring   160
Binding Your Macro to a Key   160
Naming, Saving, and Executing Your Macros   161
Building More Complicated Macros   161
Executing Macros on a Region   167
Beyond Macros   168

7. Simple Text Formatting and Specialized Editing **170**
Using Tabs   170
Indenting Text   176
Centering Text   186
Using Outline Mode   187
Rectangle Editing   194
Making Simple Drawings   204

8. Markup Language Support **218**
Comments   219
Font-Lock Mode   220
Writing HTML   220
Writing XML   243
Marking up Text for TEX and LATEX   258

9. Computer Language Support **263**
Emacs as an IDE   264
Writing Code   266
C and C++ Support   275
Java Support   284
The Java Development Environment for Emacs (JDEE)   285
Perl Support   294
SQL Support   296
The Lisp Modes   298

10. Customizing Emacs **306**
Using Custom   307
Modifying the .emacs File Directly   326
Modifying Fonts and Colors   330
Customizing Your Key Bindings   335
Setting Emacs Variables   339
Finding Emacs Lisp Packages   340
Starting Modes via Auto-Mode Customization   341
Making Emacs Work the Way You Think It Should   342

11. Emacs Lisp Programming **344**
Introduction to Lisp   345
Lisp Primitive Functions   353
Useful Built-in Emacs Functions   358
Building an Automatic Template System   374
Programming a Major Mode   381
Customizing Existing Modes   389
Building Your Own Lisp Library   395

12. Version Control **398**
The Uses of Version Control   398
Version Control Concepts   399

How VC Helps with Basic Operations 401
Editing Comment Buffers 403
VC Command Summary 403
VC Mode Indicators 404
Which Version Control System? 405
Individual VC Commands 405
Customizing VC 411
Extending VC 412
What VC Is Not 413
Using VC Effectively 413
Comparing with Ediff 414

13. **Platform-Specific Considerations** **421**
Emacs and Unix 421
Emacs and Mac OS X 427
Emacs and Windows 433

14. **The Help System** **440**
Using the Tutorial 440
Help Commands 441
Help with Complex Emacs Commands 445
Navigating Emacs Documentation 446
Completion 453

A. **Emacs Variables** **457**

B. **Emacs Lisp Packages** **464**

C. **Bugs and Bug Fixes** **470**

D. **Online Resources** **472**

E. **Quick Reference** **475**

Glossary **487**

Index **493**

Preface

Emacs is the most powerful text editor available today. Unlike most other editors (in particular, unlike the standard Unix editor, **vi**), Emacs is a complete working environment. No matter what you do, you can start Emacs in the morning, work all day and all night, and never leave it: you can use it to edit, rename, delete, and organize files; to compile programs; to run shell commands; and so on. Before windowing systems like X and Microsoft Windows became popular, Emacs often served as a complete windowing system of its own. All you needed was a terminal, and you could live within Emacs forever. Emacs is also infinitely flexible; you can write your own commands, change the keys that are associated with commands, and (if you are willing to take the time) do just about anything you want.

Why Read This Book?

Because it does so much, Emacs has a reputation for being extremely complicated. We don't think that's warranted; we teach you Emacs from the ground up, covering first the basics and then some of the more advanced features.

In this book, we have tried to reach as broad an audience as possible: from casual users to professional writers and web authors to programmers to system administrators. No matter what you do with Emacs, you will find it's easy to learn; after one or two sessions, you'll know the basics of editing any file. After you learn the basics, you can go on to learn about more advanced topics that provide the real benefits of using Emacs. These include:

- Using multiple windows and buffers so you can work on several files at once
- Customizing keyboard commands
- Tailoring Emacs to fit your work style
- Making Emacs your work environment where you can do all your everyday tasks, such as organizing files, compiling programs, and issuing shell commands
- Creating macros to streamline repetitive tasks

- Using Emacs to support programming in many languages (including C, C++, Lisp, Java, and Perl)
- Formatting files with various markup languages, such as HTML and XML
- Using word abbreviations to avoid spelling out long phrases or to correct common misspellings

Of course, many of the topics may not apply to you; some topics may be appropriate for a second reading but not for the first. Toward the end of the preface, we'll sketch several different ways to approach the book, depending on your interests and experience.

Which Emacs Is Which?

Numerous versions of Emacs are available, offering a wide range of features, but two are in widespread use today: GNU Emacs and XEmacs. (An exhaustive list of Emacs implementations can be found at *http://www.finseth.com/~fin/emacs.html*.) XEmacs was originally tailored for GUI usage and has a fairly wide user base, but lacks some of the features of GNU Emacs.*

This book covers GNU Emacs. Since its appearance, GNU Emacs has become the most popular, powerful, and flexible Emacs, and there's no reason to believe that this situation will change. If you know GNU Emacs, you will be able to adapt to any other Emacs implementation with no trouble; it's not so easy to go in the other direction.

This book, however, isn't limited to GNU Emacs users. Because of the similarities between different Emacs implementations, this book should help you get started with any Emacs editor. The basic keyboard commands change little from one editor to another—you'll find that **C-n** (for **Ctrl-n**) almost always means "move to the next line." Emacs editors tend to differ in the more advanced commands and features, but if you are using these more advanced facilities and you aren't using GNU Emacs, you should consider making the switch.

What's New in This Edition?

This third edition covers GNU Emacs 21, specifically 21.3 and even more specifically 21.3.5.† This new edition has been completely revised and expanded to cover new features and to meet the evolving needs of Emacs users.

---

* Quite a few issues come up in discussions of GNU Emacs versus XEmacs, with character encoding schemes, user interface differences, and copyright issues among them. We're not interested in taking sides in the battles between these emacsen.

† Typically we would not find the need to be quite so specific, but the user interface changed at Emacs 21.3.5; in particular you'll notice different toolbar icons if you have an earlier version.

Here are some of the highlights of what we've changed:

- User interface changes, including the addition of an icon-based toolbar, extensive changes to menus, and a more graphical interface (Chapter 1)
- How Emacs interacts with the operating system clipboard, including specific clipboard-related commands (Chapter 2)
- Dynamic abbreviations (Chapter 3)
- Expanded coverage of the directory editor, Dired, to help you organize and work with files more efficiently (Chapter 5)
- Changes to the way Emacs handles tabs and indentation and how to get Emacs to do what you want it to (Chapter 7)
- Artist mode for drawing with the mouse (Chapter 7)
- Inserting characters from other character sets in HTML files (Chapter 8)
- Using font-lock mode for coloring text for easier editing (Chapter 9)
- Expanded Java coverage, including how to install and use the Java Development Environment for Emacs (JDEE) (Chapter 9)
- Perl support with Cperl mode (Chapter 9)
- Managing changes to large, multiple file projects more effectively using etags (Chapter 9)
- Customizing Emacs through the interactive Custom interface or through the *.emacs* startup file (Chapter 10)
- Expanded coverage of how version control mode connects with a variety of change control systems, including CVS, RCS, Subversion, and SCCS (Chapter 12)
- A new chapter on platform-specific considerations, including details on how to install the latest version of Emacs on Unix, Windows, and Mac OS X (Chapter 13)

GNU Emacs and the Free Software Foundation

You don't need to know its history to use GNU Emacs, but its origins are an interesting part of computer history. The Free Software Foundation (FSF), which maintains and distributes GNU Emacs, has become an important part of computer culture.

A long time ago (1975) at MIT, Richard Stallman wrote the first Emacs editor. According to the folklore, the original Emacs editor was a set of macros for TECO, an almost incomprehensible and now obsolete line editor. The name Emacs stands for "Editing Macros." Tradition also has it that Emacs is a play on the name of a favorite ice cream store. Much has happened since 1975. TECO has slipped into deserved obscurity, and Emacs has been rewritten as an independent program. Several commercial versions of Emacs appeared, of which Unipress Emacs and CCA Emacs were the most important. For several years, these commercial implementations were the Emacs editors you were most likely to run across outside of the academic world.

Stallman's Emacs became prominent with the birth of the Free Software Foundation (FSF) and the GNU Project in 1984. GNU stands for "GNU's Not Unix" and refers to a complete Unix-like operating system (OS) that Stallman and his associates were building.

Stallman founded the FSF to guarantee that some software would always remain free. Note that *Free* does not necessarily mean cheap (you may have to pay a fee to cover the cost of distribution); it most definitely does mean liberated from restrictions about how it can be used and specifically how it can be shared.

Stallman is widely recognized as the founder of the free software movement, which was an important predecessor of the open source movement. Linux is now the most prominent example of open source software, and it falls under the GNU Public License or GPL (available online at *http://www.gnu.org/copyleft/gpl.html*). Stallman argues that much of Linux outside the kernel itself is GNU software and so he refers to it as GNU/Linux. All controversies aside, Stallman's contribution to the open source movement cannot be underestimated. GNU software and open source software distributed under the GPL are a mainstay for developers and computer users all over the world.

The FSF was created precisely to distribute programs under terms that encourage you to share, rather than hoard, software. The GPL is designed to prevent an unfortunately common practice—namely, a company taking public domain code, making a few modifications and bug fixes, and then copyrighting the modified version. Once a company does this, the program has essentially become private property and disappears from the public domain. Stallman formed the foundation because he finds this practice abhorrent. As he explains in the GNU Manifesto, "I cannot in good conscience sign a nondisclosure agreement or a software license agreement... So that I can continue to use computers without dishonor, I have decided to put together a sufficient body of free software so that I will be able to get along without any software that is not free." Elsewhere in the manifesto, Stallman calls sharing software the "fundamental act of friendship among programmers." Their software is free because it *can* be shared and will *always* be shareable—without restriction. FSF software is not under restrictive copyright laws, which Stallman objects to in principle. In fact, he coined the term *copyleft* to describe the FSF's sharable software base.*

---

* FSF programs such as Emacs are often distributed with commercial systems. Even in these cases, the General Public License guarantees your right to use and give away their programs without restriction. Of course, the license does not apply to other proprietary software with which GNU tools have been shipped.

Since GNU Emacs was first released, many other pieces of the GNU operating environment have fallen into place: C and C++ compilers (*gcc* and *g++*), a very powerful debugger (*gdb*), substitutes for **lex** and **yacc** (called *flex* and *bison*, respectively), a Unix shell (*bash*, which stands for "Bourne-Again Shell"), the Gimp (a graphics tool comparable to Adobe PhotoShop), GNOME (a desktop environment for Linux), and many other programs and libraries. Many important open source projects that originally used variants of the GPL or other licensing schemes have adopted the GPL as their license, including Python, Mozilla, and Zope. Author David Wheeler argues that all open source projects should release their software under a GPL-compatible license* (see *http://www.dwheeler.com/essays/gpl-compatible.html* for his views and some statistics about GPL'd software). With Linux, GNU tools, and other GPL'd software, it's possible to have a complete operating environment consistent with the values set forth by the FSF.

An Approach to Learning Emacs

This book is designed to get you started with Emacs as quickly as possible, whether you are an experienced computer user or a novice. The first two chapters give you the basics you need to know, and the rest of the book builds on these basics. After the first two chapters, you don't have to read the rest consecutively; you can skip to the topics that interest you. Additionally, the book is designed to give you just the level of hand-holding you want; you can either read the book in detail or skim it, looking for tables of commands and examples.

Here are some reading paths you could take:

If	Read
You are a casual user	Preface, Chapters 1–3, 14
You are a programmer or system administrator	Preface, Chapters 1–5, 9–12
You are a writer or production person	Preface, Chapters 1–3, 7, 8, 14
You want to customize Emacs	Chapter 10 and possibly Chapter 11
You write HTML or XML	Preface, Chapters 1–3, 8
You want to use operating system commands in Emacs	Chapter 5
You use Emacs on Windows or Mac OS X	Chapter 13

These reading paths are offered only as a guideline. Emacs is one gigantic, functionally rich editor. We've divided it up into digestible bites for you, so you don't have to

---

* GPL-compatible is a critical distinction for many organizations. As our reviewer Mike Trent points out, many organizations release their software under a modified GPL because the GPL's license is actually "viral." That is, if one line of GPL'd code appears in a project, the entire project must be GPL'd. This means corporations interested in protecting their assets but still wanting to share code with the open source community cannot use the GPL without some modification.

be put off by its size and scope. The best way to learn Emacs is incrementally; learn a little now, then learn more features as you get curious about them. If you need to do something and don't know how to do it in Emacs, Emacs probably already does it; if it doesn't, you can learn how to write a Lisp function to add it to Emacs (see Chapter 11 for details). The online help system is an excellent place to learn about new features on the fly; online help is discussed in Chapter 1 and in more detail in Chapter 14.

Here's a list of some features you might want to learn about on a rainy day:

- How to use multiple Emacs buffers, windows, and frames (Chapter 4)
- Word abbreviation mode (Chapter 3)
- Macros (Chapter 6)
- How to map function keys to Emacs commands (Chapter 10)
- How to issue (and edit) shell commands (Chapter 5)
- How to organize files in Emacs (Chapter 5)
- Using ediff to compare files (Chapter 12)

Here's a quick summary of what's in each chapter:

Chapter 1, *Emacs Basics*, tells you how to start Emacs and how to work with files. It also provides a quick introduction to the online help system.

Chapter 2, *Editing*, explains commands for moving around, copying and pasting text, and undoing changes. It also introduces very basic customization.

Chapter 3, *Search and Replace*, covers more editing features, including search and replace, word abbreviation mode, and spell checking.

Chapter 4, *Using Buffers, Windows, and Frames*, describes how to use multiple buffers and windows, both Emacs-style windows (that divide a single OS window) and traditional OS windows (which Emacs refers to as *frames*). It also discusses how to bookmark your place in large files.

Chapter 5, *Emacs as a Work Environment*, talks about issuing commands from within Emacs, working with files and directories, and using basic time management tools such as the calendar and diary.

Chapter 6, *Writing Macros*, discusses using macros to eliminate repetitive tasks.

Chapter 7, *Simple Text Formatting and Specialized Editing*, covers basic text formatting (such as tabs, indentation, and centering) as well as some of the more rarefied features, like outline mode and rectangle editing.

Chapter 8, *Markup Language Support*, describes Emacs support for HTML, XML, TEX and LaTeX.

Chapter 9, *Computer Language Support*, covers Emacs as a programming environment, including editing support for C, Java, Lisp, Perl, and SQL, as well as the interface to compilers and the Unix **make** utility. It also describes the Java Development Environment for Emacs (JDEE).

Chapter 10, *Customizing Emacs*, describes Emacs's customization facilities. The interactive Custom tool allows you to change variables without editing your startup file. The chapter also explains how to set up your *.emacs* customization file. It describes how to modify your display, keyboard commands, and editing environment as well as how to load Lisp packages for extra functionality.

Chapter 11, *Emacs Lisp Programming*, describes the basics of Emacs Lisp, the language you can use to further customize Emacs.

Chapter 12, *Version Control*, describes VC mode for version control and its interface to CVS, RCS, Subversion, and SCCS.

Chapter 13, *Platform-Specific Considerations,* discusses how to install Emacs on Unix, Windows, and Mac OS X. It also provides platform-specific information for Windows and Mac OS X.

Chapter 14, *The Help System*, describes Emacs's rich, comprehensive online help facilities.

Appendix A, *Emacs Variables*, lists many important Emacs variables, including all the variables mentioned in this book.

Appendix B, *Emacs Lisp Packages*, lists some of the most useful Lisp packages that come with Emacs.

Appendix C, *Bugs and Bug Fixes*, tells you how (and when) to report bugs you find in Emacs. It also describes how to contribute to the GNU Project, whether through code enhancements or monetarily.

Appendix D, *Online Resources*, gives a tour of some important Emacs-related web sites.

Appendix E, *Quick Reference*, provides brief descriptions of the most important Emacs commands discussed in this book.

The book concludes with a glossary that defines Emacs terms you'll encounter, an index, and a detachable quick reference card that summarizes important commands for easy access.

What We Haven't Included

GNU Emacs is a large and powerful editor; in this book, we give you only a sample of what it does. Many features have been left out, and more features are added all the time. Some topics, however, are not covered:

Compatibility modes
> GNU Emacs provides compatibility modes for **vi**, for example. We've left a discussion of these modes out. If you really want to use **vi** or another editor, do so. You're better off getting to know Emacs on its own terms rather than pretending it is something else.

Many programming language modes
> In this book, we discuss editing modes for C++, Java, Lisp, Perl, and SQL. There are many modes for other languages, including rare languages like Scheme. There's no way we could discuss everything.

Advanced Lisp programming
> GNU Emacs incorporates a complete Lisp interpreter. We give a very basic and brief introduction to Emacs Lisp; Chapter 11 should be enough to get you started, but it really only scratches the surface. We recommend the FSF's *Emacs Lisp Reference Manual*, now included in the Emacs distribution.

Using Emacs to access the Internet
> When our last edition came out, it was common to use Emacs to access Internet resources or read email. Now that isn't so common; better mailers, browsers, and other tools are commonly in use on all platforms.

Unicode support
> At present, Emacs is on its way to full Unicode support; that is the most important change slated for the next major release. At this writing, Unicode support is spotty.

Games and amusements
> GNU Emacs includes an eclectic bunch of games and amusements, including the ability to pipe random quotations from Zippy the Pinhead into the famous "Eliza" pseudopsychoanalyst. Emacs 21 includes a Games menu under Tools with several cool ways to waste time in Emacs (and it doesn't even include Emacs's version of pong, one of our favorites). Alas, we had to draw the line somewhere.

The Meta Key

Emacs commands consist of a modifier, such as **Control**, which you hold down as you would the **Shift** key, and a series of keystrokes. For example, **Control-x Control-s** saves a file.

The other modifier Emacs uses is the **Meta** key. Few keyboards have keys labeled **Meta**. Because of this, in previous editions of this book, we refused to talk about the **Meta** key and substituted **Esc** in all our instructions.

In this edition, we want you to learn where the **Meta** key is. Typically **Meta** keys are to the immediate left and right of the Space bar. On Linux and Windows keyboards, the **Alt** key is the **Meta** key. On Mac keyboards, the **Apple** key, often called **Command** is the **Meta** key by default.

Why learn about and use the **Meta** key? The reason is speed. We emphasize key bindings in this book. New users may find icons and menus helpful, but in the long run, learning how to keep your hands on the keyboard allows you to gain speed and boosts your productivity. The **Meta** key will help you gain that speed and make it easy for you to use Emacs help, which refers to **Meta**.

Depending on your style, you may still prefer to use **Esc** instead of **Meta**. Just bear in mind that with **Esc** you press and release the key, then press the next key.

Conventions Used in This Book

This section covers the conventions used in this book.

Keystroke Notation

Emacs commands consist of a modifier, such as **Ctrl** or **Meta**, followed by one or two characters. Commands shown in this book abbreviate **Ctrl** to **C** and **Meta** to **M**:

C-g
> Hold down the **Ctrl** key and press **g**.

M-x
> Hold down the **Meta** key and press **x**.

Sometimes **Meta** is followed by a literal hyphen character. In these cases, we spell out **Meta**:

Meta -
> Hold down the **Meta** key and press -.

To complete a command you may need to press **Enter**. (This key may be labeled **Return**.)

Enter
> Press the **Enter** key.

Esc
> Can be used as an alternative to **Meta**. Press **Esc**, *release it*, then press the next key.

A few mouse commands use the **Shift** key as a modifier, often in combination with the **Ctrl** key. This is abbreviated as:

S-right
> Hold down **Shift** and click the right mouse button.

C-S-right
> Hold down **Shift** and **Ctrl** and click the right mouse button.

All Emacs commands, even the simplest ones, have a full name; for example, **forward-word** is equivalent to the keystrokes **M-f**, and **forward-char** is equivalent to **C-f**. This tying of a command to a keystroke combination is called a key binding. Some commands have only full names, with no corresponding key binding.

When we discuss a command, we'll give both its full name and the keystrokes (if any) that you can type to invoke it.

Command Tables

To find a group of commands quickly, look for tables in each section that summarize commands. These tables are formatted like this:

Keystrokes	Command name	Action
C-n	next-line	Move to the next line.
C-x C-f *File → Open File*	find-file	Open a specified file.
(none)	yow	Print ineffable wisdom from the Pinhead in the minibuffer.

The first column shows the default key binding for the command, the second column shows the command's full name, and the third column describes what the command does. For example, pressing **C-n** (also known as the **next-line** command) moves the cursor to the next line in the file. Some commands, like **C-x C-f**, can also be reached through menus. If there is a menu option for a particular command, it is given in *italics* below the keystrokes for the command. For example, you can use the **find-file** command by typing **C-x C-f** or by selecting **Open File** from the **File** menu. Sometimes you'll see *(none)* in the keystrokes column, which doesn't mean you can't use the command, but rather that the command isn't bound to particular keystrokes. To use commands with no keystrokes, type **M-x**, followed by the command's full name, and press **Enter**. (Try typing **M-x pong Enter** sometime.)

Examples

Throughout the book, you'll find keystrokes to type, followed by a screenshot showing the results.

Type: **C-x C-f** *myfile*

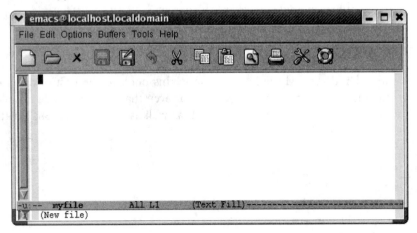

Use the **find-file** command to open a file or create a new file.

C-x C-f is in bold, indicating that this is exactly what you type. *myfile* is shown in constant width italics because you could substitute any filename you choose and need not type exactly what you see here.

Typically, these screenshots come from a Linux system. We also include screenshots taken on Mac OS X and Windows. When we show such screenshots, we include an indication of the platform in the caption for the screenshot.

Toward the end of the book, when we're discussing programming modes, customization, and Lisp programming, screenshots become rather unwieldy. We eventually use fewer of them. Instead, we may show one or two lines of text. If it's relevant, we show the cursor's position:

```
/* This is a c comment */
```

Font Usage

This book uses the following font conventions:

boldface
> Indicates operating system commands, Emacs keystrokes, command names, and variables.

italic
> Indicates filenames, URLs, and new terms when first introduced.

`constant width`
> Indicates buffer names, Lisp code, C code, Emacs messages, and other excerpts from programs.

`constant width italic`
> Indicates dummy parameters that you replace with an actual value. May also be shown sometimes in angle brackets (<filename>).

How to Contact Us

We have tested and verified the information in this book to the best of our ability, but you may find that features have changed (or even that we have made mistakes!). Please let us know about any errors you find, as well as your suggestions for future editions, by writing to:

> O'Reilly Media, Inc.
> 1005 Gravenstein Highway North
> Sebastopol, CA 95472
> 1-800-998-9938 (in the U.S. or Canada)
> 1-707-829-0515 (international/local)
> 1-707-829-0104 (FAX)

To ask technical questions or comment on the book, send email to:

bookquestions@oreilly.com

We have a web site for the book, where we'll list examples, errata, and any plans for future editions. You can access this page at:

http://www.oreilly.com/catalog/gnu3/

 When you see a Safari® enabled icon on the cover of your favorite technology book that means the book is avaialbe online through the O'Reilly Network Safari Bookshelf.

Safari offers a solution that's better than e-Books. It's a virtual library that let's you easily search thousands of top tech books, cut and paste code samples, download chapters, and find quick answers when you nee the most accurate, current information. Try it free at *http://safari.oreilly.com*.

For more information about this book and others, see the O'Reilly web site:

http://www.oreilly.com

You can also send questions about Emacs and suggestions about this book to *deb@oreilly.com*.

Acknowledgments

Debra Cameron: First, I would like to thank Duffy Craven for introducing me to Emacs. Second, I would like to thank my coauthors. Bill Rosenblatt was a tremendous help on the first edition of this book, and Eric Raymond worked with blinding speed and brilliance on the second, providing some input on the third as well. I would especially like to thank my coauthors Jim Elliott and Marc Loy, without whom, in all honesty, this third edition would never have been finished. Their constant encouragement, support, and hard work helped make this edition a reality. I would like to thank all the readers who wrote in with their suggestions, especially Russell Harris, Seema Kumar, and Hui Oulan. I would also like to thank Eric Pement, who pointed me to the very interesting TEI Emacs add-on, as well as the authors of that extended environment for Emacs, including Sebastian Rahtz and Syd Bauman. Personally, I would like to thank my husband Jim and my kids Meg, David, Beth, and Kevin for their patience and help during the revision of this book and also my friends Irene and Jacki for their support. Most of all, I would like to thank all the developers and hackers who continue to make GNU Emacs the most amazing piece of software I have ever worked with.

James Elliott: I have to thank Deb for asking me to help people learn about Emacs. I've long admired (and relied on) the editor and its ever-growing ecosystem of tools and extensions, as well as the philosophy and results of the Free Software Foundation. They represent a distillation of what makes computing an interesting and valuable field for me, and I am honored to be part of this project. Ironically, I have to also thank Deb for letting me take a big chunk of time off when my Hibernate book came into being.

Thanks are also due to Marc, both for initially introducing me to the fine folks at O'Reilly and for his help and input on this book. He ended up contributing more than he signed up for when I got pulled away in the middle. Nor should I forget my fine colleagues at GE's Corporate Research and Development Center in Niskayuna, New York who first introduced me to the mysteries of Emacs as an intern there. I'm indebted to Joe for his love and support. And let's hear it for the cast of thousands who have grown Emacs into what it is today!

Marc Loy: I have the occasionally lazy—no, let's say overworked—staff at the University of Southern California's computer labs to thank for getting me started on Emacs. They were out of **vi** cheat sheets when I sat down to write my first computer program. (I won't admit to the language I had to use.) I've been grateful for that happenstance ever since. I'd also like to thank Jim and Deb for their cheery outlook on things as we finished up this latest edition. As always, my sister Amy and my partner Ron remain constant forces for good in my world and make all the silliness (like politics) surrounding the fun stuff (like writing about Emacs) tolerable.

Eric Raymond: My thanks go first to the hacker community at large, all the people who created the rich tradition of Emacs Lisp programming that takes Emacs customization from elegant theoretical possibility to practical tool. I learned what I know partly from reading code written by the likes of Olin Shivers, Jamie Zawinski, Kyle Jones, Barry Warsaw, Roland McGrath, Richard Stallman himself (of course), and many others. Secondly, my thanks and warmest love go as always to my wife Catherine, who supported me on many levels while I worked on my bits of this book. Finally, my thanks and respect to the hip, professional, and clueful people at O'Reilly. They know how to produce a good book and how to treat an author right. They care, and it shows.

Bill Rosenblatt: I would like to thank the following people: Professor Richard Martin (Princeton Classics Department), for planting the seed in me that eventually turned writing from a chore to a pleasure; Intermetrics, Inc., for giving me little enough to do that I could fritter away my workdays delving into GNU Emacs; Hal Stern, for getting me this gig; Sandy Wise, for his help; Jessica Lustig, for her love and support; and most importantly, my grad-school housemates for putting up with a tied-up phone line at all hours of the day and night.

CHAPTER 1

Emacs Basics

Some of you out there are probably dying to get your hands on the keyboard and start typing. We won't try to stop you; turn to the section called "Starting Emacs" and you can go ahead. But do read the beginning of this chapter later when you're ready for a break. Emacs is much easier to learn if you understand some of the basic concepts involved, which we discuss in the following introduction.

Introducing Emacs!

GNU Emacs is one of the most commonly used text editors in the world today. Many users prefer Emacs to **vi** (Unix's standard editor) or to other GUI text editors. Why is Emacs so popular? It isn't the newest tool, and it's certainly not the prettiest. But it may well be the most useful tool you'll ever learn. We want to present what you need to know about Emacs to do useful work, in a way that lets you use it effectively. This book is a guide for Emacs users; it tries to satisfy the needs of many readers, ranging from casual users to programmers.

Our approach therefore isn't to tell you absolutely everything that Emacs does. It has many features and commands that this book doesn't describe. We don't think that's a problem; Emacs has a comprehensive online help facility that helps you figure out what these are. We focus our attention on describing how to get useful work done. After covering basic editing in the first three chapters, we describe how to use Emacs as a comprehensive working environment: how to boost productivity with multiple buffers and windows, how to give commands without leaving the editor, how to take advantage of special editing modes, how to use Emacs for editing special types of files (source files for various programming languages), and so on. We cover the most important commands and the most important editing modes. However, you should always keep one principle in mind: Emacs does many things well, but it isn't important for that reason. Emacs is important because of the integration of different things you need to do.

What does integration mean? A simple example will help. Assume that someone sends you a mail message describing a special command for accessing a new printer. You can fire up an Emacs shell, paste the command into Emacs, and execute it directly. If it works, you can edit your startup file to create an alias for the command. You can do all this without leaving the editor and without having to retype the command once. That's why Emacs is so powerful. It's more than just an editor; it's a complete environment that can change the way you work.

An initial word of advice, too. Many people think that Emacs is an extremely difficult editor to learn. We don't see why. Admittedly, it has a lot of features, and you probably will never use all of them. But any editor, no matter how simple or complex, has the same basic functions. If you can learn one, you can learn any of them. We'll give you the standard mnemonic devices that will help you remember commands (like "C-p means previous line"), but we really don't think even these are necessary. They get you over an initial hump in the learning process but don't make much difference in the long run. Learning to use an editor is basically a matter of learning finger habits: learning where to put your fingers to move to the previous line. If you experiment with Emacs and try typing a few of our examples, you'll quickly acquire these finger habits. And after you've acquired these habits, you'll never forget, any more than you'll forget how to ride a bicycle. After using Emacs for a day or two, we never had to think, "C-p means previous line." Our fingers just knew where to go. Once you're at this point, you're home. You can become creative with Emacs and start thinking about how to put its features to work for you. Emacs has extensive menus, but we still recommend learning the key bindings for commonly used commands. Good finger habits can make you an incredibly fast typist, and reaching from keyboard to mouse only slows you down.

The finger-habits approach also implies a different way of reading this book. Intellectually, it's possible to absorb a lot from one reading, but you can form only a few new habits each day. (Unless, of course, they're bad habits.) Chapter 2 covers most of the basic editing techniques you'll use. You may need to read it several times, with a slightly different focus each time. For example, Emacs gives you many different ways to move forward: you can move forward one character, one word, one line, one sentence, one paragraph, one page, and so on. All of these techniques are covered in Chapter 2. Start by learning how to move forward and backward, then gradually add more complex commands. Similarly, Emacs provides many different techniques for searching through a file, covered in Chapter 3. Don't feel obliged to learn them all at once; pick something, practice it, and move on to the next topic. No one will complain if you have to work through the first three chapters of our book several times before you're comfortable. Time spent developing good habits is time well spent.

Understanding Files and Buffers

You don't really edit files with Emacs. Instead, Emacs copies the contents of a file into a temporary buffer and you edit that. The file on disk doesn't change until you save the buffer. Like files, Emacs buffers have names. The name of a buffer is usually the same as the name of the file that you're editing. There are a few exceptions. Some buffers don't have associated files—for example, *scratch* is just a temporary practice buffer, like a scratchpad; the help facility displays help messages in a buffer named *Help*, which also isn't connected to a file.

A Word About Modes

Emacs achieves some of its famed versatility by having various editing modes in which it behaves slightly differently. The word mode may sound technical, but what it really means is that Emacs becomes sensitive to the task at hand. When you're writing, you often want features like word wrap so that you don't have to press **Enter** at the end of every line. When you're programming, the code must be formatted correctly depending on the language. For writing, there's text mode; for programming, there are modes for different languages, including C, Java, and Perl. Modes, then, allow Emacs to be the kind of editor you want for different tasks.

Text mode and Java mode are major modes. A buffer can be in only one major mode at a time; to exit a major mode, you have to enter another one. Table 1-1 lists some of the major modes, what they do, and where they're covered in this book.

Table 1-1. Major modes

Mode	Function
Fundamental mode	The default mode (Chapter 6)
Text mode	For writing text (Chapter 2)
View mode	For viewing files but not editing (Chapter 4)
Shell mode	For running a shell within Emacs (Chapter 5)
Outline mode	For writing outlines (Chapter 7)
Indented text mode	For indenting text automatically (Chapter 7)
Paragraph indent text mode	For indenting the first line of each paragraph (Chapter 7)
Picture mode	For creating ASCII drawings using the keyboard (Chapter 7)
HTML mode	For writing HTML (Chapter 8)
SGML mode	For writing SGML and XML (Chapter 8)
LaTeX mode	For formatting files for $\mathrm{T_EX}$ and $\mathrm{L\!A\!T_EX}$ (Chapter 8)
Compilation mode	For compiling programs (Chapter 9)
cc mode	For writing C, C++, and Java programs (Chapter 9)
Java mode	For writing Java programs (Chapter 9)

Table 1-1. Major modes (continued)

Mode	Function
Perl mode and Cperl mode	For writing Perl programs (Chapter 9)
SQL mode	For interacting with databases using SQL (Chapter 9)
Emacs Lisp mode	For writing Emacs Lisp functions (Chapters 9 and 11)
Lisp mode	For writing Lisp programs (Chapters 9 and 11)
Lisp interaction mode	For writing and evaluating Lisp expressions (Chapters 9 and 11)

Whenever you edit a file, Emacs attempts to put you into the correct major mode for what you're going to edit. If you edit a file that ends in *.c*, it puts you into cc mode. If you edit a file that ends in *.el*, it puts you in Lisp mode. Sometimes it looks at the contents of the file rather than just its name. If you edit a file formatted for TEX, Emacs puts you in LaTeX mode. If it cannot tell what mode you should be in, it puts you in fundamental mode, the most general of all. Because Emacs is extensible, add-in modes are also available; we talk about some in this book, though we do not list them in Table 1-1.

In addition to major modes there are also *minor modes*. These define a particular aspect of Emacs's behavior and can be turned on and off within a major mode. For example, auto-fill mode means that Emacs should do word wrap; when you type a long line, it should automatically make an appropriate line break. Table 1-2 lists some minor modes, what they do, and where they're covered in this book.

Table 1-2. Minor modes

Mode	Function
Auto-fill mode	Enables word wrap (Chapter 2).
Overwrite mode	Replaces characters as you type instead of inserting them (Chapter 2).
Auto-save mode	Saves your file automatically every so often in a special auto-save file (Chapter 2).
Isearch mode	For searching (Chapter 3).
Flyspell mode	For flyspell spell-checker (Chapter 3).
Flyspell prog mode	For spell-checking programs with flyspell (Chapter 3).
Abbrev mode	Allows you to use word abbreviations (Chapter 3).
Paragraph indent text mode	For indenting the first line of each paragraph (Chapter 7).
Refill mode	A mode in which Emacs attempts to fill paragraphs as you edit them (a bit experimental; mentioned in Chapter 2).
Artist mode	For creating ASCII drawings using the mouse (Chapter 7).

Table 1-2. Minor modes (continued)

Mode	Function
Outline mode	For writing outlines (Chapter 7).
SGML name entity mode	For inserting special characters in HTML, SGML, and XML documents (Chapter 8).
ISO accents mode	For inserting accented characters in text files.
Font lock mode	For highlighting text in colors and fonts to improve readability (separating, for example, comments from code visually) (Chapter 9).
Compilation mode	For compiling programs (Chapter 9).
Enriched mode	For saving text attributes (Chapter 10).
VC mode	For using various version control systems under Emacs (Chapter 12).
Info mode	A mode for reading Emacs's own documentation (Chapter 14).

You may have noticed that several modes, including paragraph indent text mode, outline mode, and compilation mode, are both major and minor modes. Each can be used alone—as a major mode—or with another major mode as a minor mode.

There are many other modes that we won't discuss, including modes for some obscure but interesting programming languages (like Modula-2). There are also some other modes that Emacs uses itself, like Dired mode for the directory editing feature (described in Chapter 5).

In addition, if you're good at Lisp programming, you can add your own modes. Emacs is almost infinitely extensible.

Starting Emacs

To start Emacs, simply click on the Emacs icon or type **emacs** on the command line and press Enter.*

---

* How you start Emacs may vary by platform. Linux has no icon on the desktop by default; Windows and Mac OS X do (if you've installed Emacs on these platforms). Note that Mac OS X comes with a version of GNU Emacs installed in */usr/bin*, and that is what runs by default when you start up Emacs using the Terminal application. You won't be able to use the mouse at all if you run Emacs in the Terminal application, and there are a number of other limitations as well. Better versions of GNU Emacs are available to you; see Chapter 13 for details.

Click on the Emacs icon or, from the command line, type: **emacs Enter**

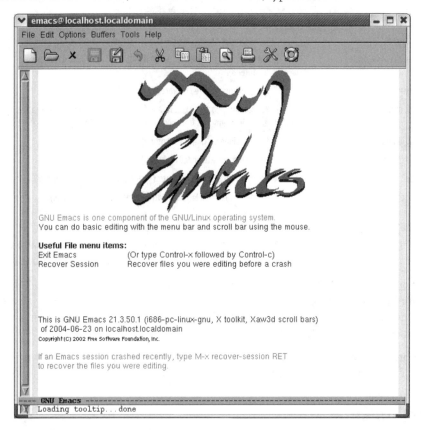

Starting Emacs.

You'll see a short message describing a few important menu items and the version of Emacs that you're running. It may appear as a graphical splash screen (like the one shown here) or a text splash screen. This message disappears as soon as you type the first character. Emacs then puts you in an (almost) empty buffer called *scratch*, an ideal place for you to experiment.

About the Emacs Display

When you enter Emacs, you see a large workspace near the top of the window where you do your editing. (See Figure 1-1.)

A *cursor* marks your position. The cursor is also called *point*, particularly among people who are more familiar with Emacs and in the online help system; therefore, it's useful to remember this term.

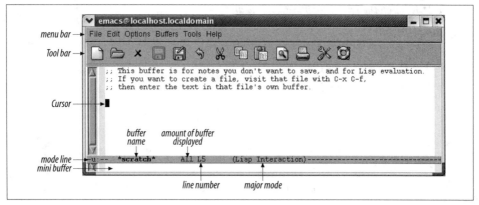

Figure 1-1. Understanding the Emacs display

You don't have to do anything special before you start typing. As long as you type alphanumeric characters and punctuation, Emacs inserts them into your buffer. The cursor indicates where Emacs inserts the new characters; it moves as you type. Unlike many editors (particularly **vi**), Emacs does not have separate modes for inserting text and giving commands. Try typing something right now, and you'll begin to see how easy Emacs is to use. (If you get stuck for any reason, just press **C-g**.)

The Toolbar

The toolbar is a new feature in Emacs 21. Its basic icons and their functions are listed in Table 1-3. Note that the toolbar is context sensitive; in some modes, such as the Info mode for reading the Emacs manual, the toolbar changes to provide browsing help. We'll discuss those icons when we cover the relevant modes.

Table 1-3. Icons on the Emacs toolbar

Icon	Function	Where to learn more
	Find a file or create a new file (supplying the filename).	This chapter
	Start the directory editor so you can manipulate files and folder.	Chapter 5
	Kill the current buffer.	Chapter 4
	Save current buffer in its associated file.	This chapter
	Save current buffer as a different file.	This chapter

Table 1-3. Icons on the Emacs toolbar (continued)

Icon	Function	Where to learn more
	Undo.	Chapter 2
	Cut text that comprises the current region.	Chapter 2
	Copy text in current region.	Chapter 2
	Paste cut or copied text.	Chapter 2
	Search for a string.	Chapter 3
	Print page (with headings).	Chapter 5
	Customize using interactive interface.	Chapter 10
	Start online help system.	Chapter 14

If you don't like the toolbar, you can hide it using a menu option (Options → Show/
Hide → Toolbar), and choosing Options → Save Options. For more information, see
"Making Emacs Work the Way You Want" at the end of Chapter 2.

The Menus

The menu bar menu lists the options File, Edit, Options, Buffers, Tools, and Help;
you can explore them to see what options are available.

In addition to navigating the menus using the mouse, Emacs now offers pop-up
menus. In the Emacs window, hold down **Ctrl** and click the right mouse button to
pop up the Edit menu.[*]

You can access menus without a mouse using the keyboard. In this case, using keyboard commands is much more efficient than menus, but for completeness, we'll
show you how to use the text-based menus. (If you prefer to use the mouse with
Emacs but have access only to a text interface, see Chapter 13 to learn how to download and install a version of Emacs that runs graphically on Unix, Linux, Mac OS X,
or Windows.)

---

[*] Emacs works best with a three-button mouse (more buttons are okay, too).

If your mouse does not work with the menus, press **F10** or **M-`** (a back quote, the single open quotation mark, located above the **Tab** key in the upper-left corner of many keyboards) to access them.

Press: **F10**

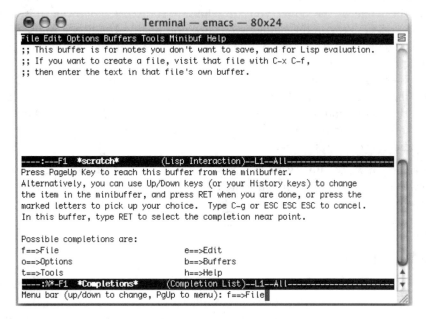

Using text-based menus (Emacs 21.2 on Mac OS X Terminal application).

You can select text-based menu options in three ways:

- You can press **Enter** to select the default option that appears in the minibuffer. If you want a different one, press the up or down arrow key until the option you want appears and press **Enter**.
- You can type the letter preceding the option in the *Completions* buffer. For example, type **f** to choose **File**.
- You can press **PgUp** to move to the *Completions* buffer, then use the arrow keys to move to the option you want. Press **Enter**. (On Mac OS X, press **Shift-PgUp** instead.)

After you select a menu option, choices for that menu appear. Repeat the process until you find the option you're looking for.

The Mode Line

Just above the bottom of the window (on the second-to-last line), Emacs prints a lot of information about what it's doing. This line is called the *mode line*. At the beginning of the mode line, you may see some information about the coding system that Emacs is using for the file; usually you'll see just --:, indicating that there is no unusual encoding scheme in place. Near the left edge of the mode line, you may see two asterisks (**). These asterisks indicate that you've modified whatever you're editing. If you haven't made any changes, the asterisks won't be there. Next, Emacs prints the name of the buffer you are editing (*scratch*). Following this, Emacs shows where you are in the buffer—your position relative to the rest of the file and what line you are on (L5 for line 5 in Figure 1-1). If you're at the beginning of the file, Emacs prints the word Top; if you're at the end, it prints Bot; if you're in the middle, it shows you a percentage (for example, 50% means you're looking at the midpoint); and if the entire file is visible, Emacs prints the word All. In parentheses following this is the editing mode or modes you are in, in this case Lisp Interaction is the major mode (no minor modes are active). The scrollbar on the side of the window also indicates your position in the file.*

You will often work with several buffers simultaneously. In this case, each buffer has its own mode line, and when you switch buffers, the mode line reflects the state of the current buffer. Don't worry about this for now; just remember that every buffer has a mode line to describe it.

The Minibuffer

Below the mode line is the *minibuffer*. This is the area where Emacs echoes the commands you enter and where you specify filenames for Emacs to find, values for search and replace, and so on. It is also where Emacs displays error messages. If you find yourself stuck in the minibuffer, press **C-g** to get out again.

Emacs Commands

You're about to start learning some Emacs commands, so let's discuss them a bit first. How do you give commands? Each command has a formal name, which (if you're fastidious) is the name of a Lisp routine. Some command names are quite long; you usually wouldn't want to type the whole thing. As a result, we need some way to abbreviate commands.

Emacs ties a command name to a short sequence of keystrokes. This tying of commands to keystrokes is known as *binding*. Even things you don't normally think about as commands, such as inserting the characters that you type, are handled through the binding mechanism. Keys like "A" are bound to the Emacs command **self-insert-command**, which inserts them into the buffer you are editing.† Most

---

* The scrollbar's location depends on the platform and windowing system you're using. Linux puts scrollbars on the left while Mac OS X and Windows put them on the right by default. Note also that the order of the information in the mode line is different if you run Emacs in a terminal window.

actions that you would normally think of as editor commands are bound to key-stroke sequences starting with **Ctrl** or **Meta**. Emacs also binds some commands to mouse clicks (alone or modified by **Shift** or **Ctrl**) and to options on menus.

The authors of Emacs try to bind the most frequently used commands to the key sequences that are the easiest to reach. Here are the varieties of key sequences you'll encounter:

- The most commonly used commands (such as cursor movement commands) are bound to **C-*n*** (where *n* is any character). To press **C-*n***, press and hold the **Ctrl** key and press *n*, then release both keys.

- Slightly less commonly used commands are bound to **M-*n***. To press **M-*n***, press and hold the **Meta** key (usually next to the space bar), then press *n*.

- Other commonly used commands are bound to **C-x *something*** (**C-x** followed by something else—one or more characters or another control sequence). Among other types of commands, file manipulation commands, like the ones you are about to learn, are generally bound to **C-x *something***.

- Some specialized commands are bound to **C-c *something***. These commands often relate to one of the more specialized modes, such as Java mode or HTML mode. You won't encounter them until later in this book.

- This list still doesn't take care of all the possibilities. You can get at the remaining commands by typing **M-x *long-command-name*** **Enter**. (This works for any command really, but the keystrokes are usually easier to learn.)

You can define your own key bindings, too, and you should do so if you find yourself using the long form of a command all the time. More on this topic in Chapter 10.

You can also access common commands through menus, but for maximum productivity, we recommend you learn the keystrokes, often given in parentheses following the menu option.

Opening a File

You can open a file by specifying the filename when you start Emacs from the command line or by typing **C-x C-f** (the long command name is **find-file**).

The paper icon on the toolbar also runs this command. In some applications, a similar icon simply creates a new, unnamed file (e.g., *Document1* in Word). Emacs expects you to provide a filename, as we'll see in a moment.

---

† In certain special editing modes, such as **dired-mode** for viewing and manipulating directories on your computer, the normal typing keys don't insert themselves. They are instead bound to special commands that do things like opening and renaming files. This flexibility in defining and changing *keymaps*, while it might seem somewhat arbitrary and overwhelming at first, is one of the great sources of power in Emacs.

Press: **C-x C-f**

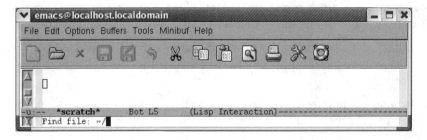

Emacs prompts you for a filename.

To press **C-x C-f**, hold down **Ctrl**, press **x** and then press **f**. Now release **Ctrl**.

After you press **C-x C-f**, Emacs uses the minibuffer to ask you for the filename. Whenever Emacs wants input from you, it puts the cursor in the minibuffer. When you're done typing in the minibuffer, press **Enter**.

Type: *newfile* **Enter**

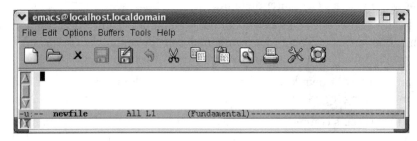

Emacs starts another buffer with the new file in it.

What if you try to read the same file twice? Instead of creating a new buffer, Emacs just moves you to the buffer the file is in.

You can also open a file in Emacs by dragging and dropping it on an Emacs window or on the Emacs icon.

Now is a good time to try typing if you haven't already done so. You may find yourself wanting to learn more about cursor movement and editing; that's fine. Feel free to skim the rest of this chapter and go on to Chapter 2. We recommend that you read the sections on saving files and exiting Emacs. There's also a table of commands at the end of this chapter for future reference. If you'd like to learn more about working with files as well as some shortcuts, stay with us through the rest of the chapter.

If You Read the Wrong File

If you happen to read the wrong file, an easy way to get the right file is by typing **C-x C-v** (for **find-alternate-file**). This command means "Read a different file instead of the one I just read." After typing **C-x C-v**, Emacs puts the name of the current file in the minibuffer; you can then correct a typo or the path, the most common reasons for finding the wrong file. Make the correction and press **Enter**. Emacs replaces the buffer's contents with the alternate file.

Letting Emacs Fill in the Blanks

Emacs has a very helpful feature known as completion. If you want an existing file, you need only type the first few letters of the name, enough to uniquely identify the filename. Press **Tab**, and Emacs completes the filename for you. For example, suppose you are trying to find a file called *dickens*.

Type: **C-x C-f di**

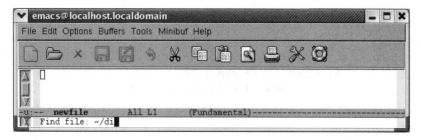

After **C-x C-f**, Emacs prompts you for the filename; type the first few letters.

Press: **Tab**

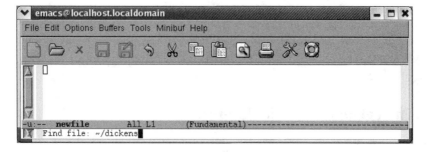

When you press **Tab**, Emacs fills in the rest of the filename.

Press: **Enter**

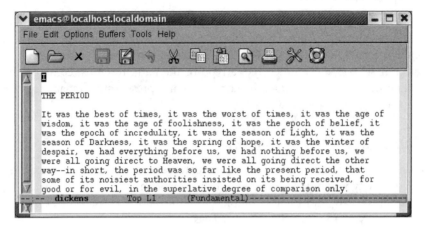

Emacs reads the file *dickens*.

If more than one file starts with *di*, Emacs displays a window with various files that start with that string. You select one by typing a few more characters (enough to identify your file as unique) and pressing **Tab** again. Or you can select one of the alternatives with the mouse or by pressing **PgUp** to move to the completions window, moving to the desired option, then pressing **Enter**.

Completion also works for long command names. It's a wonderful Emacs feature that can save you time—and show you some commands you might not know existed in the process. Chapter 14 provides more details on the glories of completion.

Inserting and Appending Files

If you want to insert one file into another, you simply move to the appropriate location in the file and type **C-x i**. (Yes, we know, we haven't told you how to move around in a file yet. Use the arrow keys for now and we'll teach you the "real" Emacs cursor movement commands in Chapter 2.) To append a file, move to the end of the file (**M->**) and type **C-x i**. As with **C-x C-f**, Emacs prompts you for the filename in the minibuffer.

How Emacs Chooses a Default Directory

When you use any command that asks for a filename (such as **C-x C-f**), Emacs displays a default directory in the minibuffer and asks you to type the rest of the filename. How does Emacs choose the default directory? The default directory is taken from the buffer that the cursor is currently in. If you are editing a file in your home directory when you type **C-x C-f**, Emacs assumes you want to edit another file in your home directory. If you are editing the file */sources/macros/html.macs* then Emacs makes the default directory */sources/macros*. If you want to find a file in another directory, edit the default directory that Emacs displays.

Saving Files

To save the file you are editing, type **C-x C-s**. Emacs writes the file. To let you know that the file was saved, it puts the message *Wrote filename* in the minibuffer. If you haven't made any changes to the file, Emacs puts the message No changes need to be saved in the minibuffer. You can also get to this option by pressing the diskette on the toolbar or choosing Save (current buffer) from the File menu.

If you decide to save something you've typed in the *scratch* buffer by typing **C-x C-s**, Emacs asks you for a filename. After you give it a filename, Emacs changes the mode line accordingly.

A related command is **write-file** (**C-x C-w**). It is the Emacs equivalent of the *Save As* option found on many applications' File menus. The **write-file** command asks you to type a new filename in the minibuffer. However, if you just press **Enter** instead of typing a new filename, **write-file** saves the file with its old name—just as **C-x C-s** would have done. (It does ask if you want to replace the current file with the one in this buffer, however.)

The **write-file** command is useful for editing files that you do not have permission to change. Use the **find-file** command to get the file you want into a buffer, and then use **write-file** to create your own private version, with a different name or path. This maneuver allows you to copy the file to one that you own and can change. Of course, the original file is not affected.

Leaving Emacs

To quit Emacs, type **C-x C-c** or close it like you would any other application. If you have made changes to a buffer, Emacs asks you if you want to save them.[*] If you type **y**, Emacs writes the file, then exits. If you type **n**, Emacs asks you to confirm that you want to abandon the changes you made by typing **yes** or **no** in full. If you type **no**, your normal Emacs session continues just as if you never attempted to exit. If you type **yes**, you exit Emacs and the changes you made during this session do not become permanent. Leaving without saving changes can be useful if you make changes you didn't intend to make.

---

[*] One exception to this rule is the *scratch* buffer. It's a scratchpad and Emacs assumes you were doodling, not doing serious artwork, so to speak. If you do any serious work in the *scratch* buffer, you must save it explicitly.

By the way, Emacs is picky about whether you type **y** or **yes**. Sometimes it wants one, sometimes the other. If it asks for a **y**, you can sometimes get away with typing **yes** but not vice versa. If it beeps and displays, Please answer yes or no, you didn't enter the whole word and it wants you to.

Getting Help

Emacs has extensive online help, which is discussed further in Chapter 14. You can enter help through the lifesaver icon on the toolbar or through the Help menu. Either method will show you a help menu, described later in this section. To enter help using the keyboard, press **C-h**. Pressing **C-h ?** gives you a list of options. Pressing **C-h t** starts a tutorial that is an excellent introduction to Emacs.

To get information about the meaning of a keystroke combination, press **C-h k** for **describe-key**. For example, if you type **C-h k C-x i**, Emacs displays a description of the **insert-file** command, which is bound to **C-x i**. Pressing **C-h f** (for **describe-function**) asks Emacs to describe a function (really just a command name, such as **find-file**). Essentially, **C-h k** and **C-h f** give you the same information; the difference is that with **C-h k**, you press a key whereas with **C-h f**, you type a command name.

Assume you want to find out about what **C-x i** does.

Type: **C-h k**

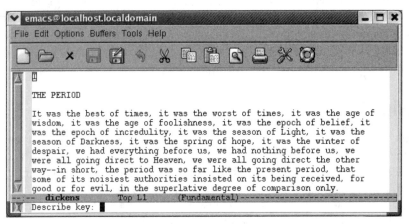

Asking for help about a keyboard command.

Type: **C-x i**

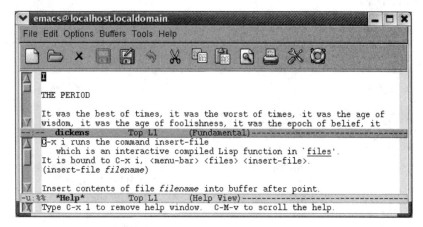

Emacs splits the screen to display help.

A few things to notice: the window is now split into two parts because you're look-ing at two separate buffers. Each buffer has its own mode line. The lower buffer is the *Help* buffer; it contains the information about the **insert-file** command. Emacs keeps the cursor in the dickens buffer because there's no good reason for you to edit the *Help* buffer.

You might also notice that in the text describing this command, Emacs calls the cur-sor *point*. This term is used throughout Emacs to refer to the cursor; you're bound to encounter it.

To make the *Help* buffer disappear, press **C-x 1** (we cover this command in Chapter 4).

The Help Menu

You can also use the Help menu to access help commands quickly, and you can get there either through the menu or through the lifesaver on the toolbar. On this menu, you find options we've discussed here: Emacs Tutorial, Describe → Describe Key, and Describe → Describe Function. It includes a host of interesting options, includ-ing access to the Emacs frequently asked questions (FAQ) file, a new search feature, and even an Emacs psychiatrist (you might tell it something like "Emacs is driving me over the edge today"). There's an interface to Info, Emacs's online documenta-tion. Simply choose Read the Emacs Manual to start Info.

In this section, we've given a very brief introduction to a few of the paths you can take in the help system. There are many more help facilities; they are described thor-oughly in Chapter 14. The help features we've described here should be enough to get you started; if you want to learn more, jump ahead to Chapter 14.

Summary

Now you know the basic commands for starting and stopping Emacs and for working with files. Chapter 2 builds on these commands to give you the skills you need for editing with Emacs. Table 1-4 summarizes the commands we covered in this chapter.

Table 1-4. File handling commands

Keystrokes	Command name	Action
C-x C-f *File → Open File*	find-file	Find file and read it in a new buffer.
C-x C-v	find-alternate-file	Read an alternate file, replacing the one read with **C-x C-f**.
C-x i *File → Insert File*	insert-file	Insert file at cursor position.
C-x C-s *File → Save (current buffer)*	save-buffer	Save file.
C-x C-w *File → Save Buffer As*	write-file	Write buffer contents to file.
C-x C-c *File → Exit Emacs*	save-buffers-kill-emacs	Exit Emacs.
C-h	help-command	Enter the online help system.
C-h f *Help → Describe Function*	describe-function	Gives online help for a given command name.
C-h k *Help → Describe Key*	describe-key	Gives online help for a given keystroke sequence.
C-h t *Help → Emacs Tutorial*	help-with-tutorial	Start the Emacs tutorial.
C-h i *Help → Browse Manuals*	info-goto-emacs-command-node	Start the Info documentation reader.

Problems You May Encounter

- **Emacs doesn't do what this book says or look like our screenshots**. Make sure that you have GNU Emacs 21.3.5 or later running by typing **M-x version Enter** or selecting Help → About Emacs. Read the section "Making Emacs Work the Way You Want" in Chapter 2. You may need to install a graphical version of Emacs if you are running in a terminal window; see Chapter 13 for details.

- **The toolbar icons are completely different**. The icons changed between Emacs 21.3.1 and Emacs 21.3.5. The older icons do the same thing; the newer ones are substantially better looking and more intuitive. Upgrade Emacs using instructions in Chapter 13.

- **You can't access menus using the mouse.** Use the text-based menus instead by pressing **F10** or **M-`**. Better yet, install a graphical version of Emacs using the instructions in Chapter 13.

- **PgUp** doesn't work properly when using text-based menus. **PgUp** is probably bound to some application-specific function, such as scrolling in the Mac OS X Terminal application. Press **Shift-PgUp**, **F10**, or **M-`** to access the menus.

- **You can't see a mode line or minibuffer.** Your Emacs window is bigger than your display. See Chapter 10 for information on how to get Emacs to start with a reasonable window size. As a temporary workaround, resize the window. (On some Windows systems, maximizing the window ironically makes it smaller, solving the problem.)

CHAPTER 2
Editing

Now that you know how to enter and exit Emacs as well as the basics of working with files, it's time to learn how to move around in and edit files. Emacs offers lots of ways to move around in files. At first, you might find it confusing that there are so many ways to do the same thing. Be patient—as you learn, the confusion will lessen, and you'll begin to appreciate the variety of Emacs commands. The more ways you learn, the fewer keystrokes you'll need to get to the part of the file you want to edit.

If you want to practice commands while you're reading—which will help you learn faster—start by typing a page or two from anything you happen to have handy; the newspaper is fine. That will give you some text to work with as you learn the editing skills described in this chapter. Don't worry if you make mistakes; just keep on typing. You can correct any mistakes after you learn the basic editing skills outlined here. Learning any editor is primarily a matter of forming certain finger habits rather than memorizing what the book says. You will learn the right finger habits only if you start typing.

When you are typing and you get to the right side of the display, you have two options. You can press **Enter** to go to the next line, or you can keep typing. If you type a long line and don't press **Enter**, Emacs waits until you reach the end of the display. Then it puts a curved arrow at the end of the line and one at the beginning of the next line as a visual indication that the next line is a continuation of the previous line (see Figure 2-1). If Emacs is run in a nongraphical environment, a backslash (\) is used instead.

Refill mode is a minor mode that keeps paragraphs neat as you edit them. It is not on by default. Look at the mode line. If the word Refill appears, you are in refill mode already. If not, you can turn it on for this buffer only by typing **M-x refill-mode Enter**. If you decide that you don't like refill mode, type **M-x refill-mode Enter** again. This command is like a light switch: it toggles refill mode on and off.

You may decide that you want to enter refill mode automatically whenever you edit. We'll describe how to do so at the end of this chapter.

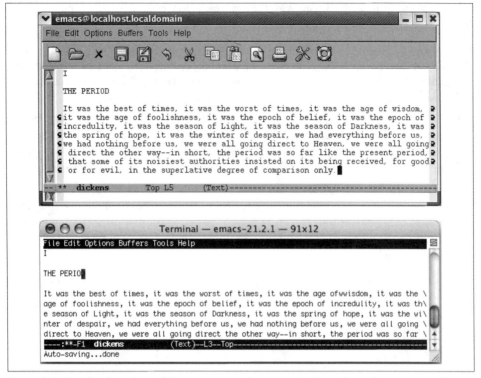

Figure 2-1. Graphical versions of Emacs use curved arrows to indicate that a line is continued; terminal versions use backslashes

In some contexts, refill mode can be annoying, and it is still a work in progress according to the Emacs manual. You may prefer auto-fill mode. You enter it in the same way; type **M-x auto-fill-mode Enter.** The word Fill appears on the mode line.

When you type paragraphs, auto-fill mode formats them. When you edit them, however, auto-fill mode does not automatically reformat them. You do that yourself using the **fill-paragraph** command, **M-q.**

If you turn on refill mode and then decide to use auto-fill mode, you still have to turn refill mode off explicitly by typing **M-x refill-mode Enter.** Otherwise, both modes appear on the mode line, and refill mode continues its merry automatic reformatting of paragraphs, ignoring the fact that auto-fill mode has been enabled.

Watch out for one important pitfall when reformatting paragraphs. In text mode, a paragraph is any text that is indented or has a blank line before and after it. If you have a file with no blank lines, Emacs thinks it is all one long paragraph. Typing **M-q** takes all the text, ignoring line breaks, and makes it one long paragraph. This command is a particular problem if you have a data file, a program, or if you just prefer to write files with no blank lines. Luckily, pressing **C-_** or **C-x u** (both for **undo**) magically puts things back the way they were. If you regularly create files with no blank lines, here are some suggestions:

- Instead of writing in text mode, use paragraph indent text mode. In this mode, a line that starts with any blank space is a new paragraph. Type **M-x paragraph-indent-text-mode** to start this mode; you'll see `Parindent` on the mode line. See Chapter 6 for more details.

- Use a specific mode rather than text mode for writing. For example, use HTML mode or LaTeX mode, described in Chapter 8, for editing files of these types. These special modes redefine what a paragraph means so that the **fill-paragraph** command works correctly. Otherwise, these modes are very similar to text mode.

- Instead of filling a paragraph, fill a marked section of text called a *region* (we'll discuss regions later in this chapter). Define the region you want to fill and press **M-x fill-region Enter**. This command takes a region and formats each individual paragraph within it.

Table 2-1 lists commands for filling text automatically and reformatting paragraphs with auto-fill mode.

Table 2-1. Text filling and reformatting commands

Keystrokes	Command name	Action
(none) [a]	**refill-mode**	Toggle refill mode, in which Emacs automatically reformats text.
(none) *Options → Word Wrap in Text Modes*	**auto-fill-mode**	Toggle auto-fill mode, in which Emacs formats paragraphs as you type them.
M-q	**fill-paragraph**	Reformat paragraph.
(none) *Edit → Fill*	**fill-region**	Reformat individual paragraphs within a region.

[a] Remember that *(none)* in the first column means that you type **M-x** followed by the command name in the second column, then press **Enter** to run the command. There are no default keystrokes. To use the **refill-mode** command, type **M-x refill-mode Enter**.

Moving the Cursor

The easiest way to move the cursor is to click the left button on your mouse or to press the arrow keys. However, it's a hassle to reach for a mouse all the time. Learn to use keyboard commands to move around so that you will ultimately achieve blinding speed and maximum productivity in Emacs.

To use Emacs commands to move the cursor forward one space, type **C-f** (**f** for "forward"). As you might guess, **C-b** moves the cursor backward. To move up, type **C-p** (for **previous-line**), and to move down, type **C-n** (for **next-line**). It's easier to memorize commands if you remember what the letters stand for.

Figure 2-2 illustrates how to move up, down, left, and right using Emacs commands.

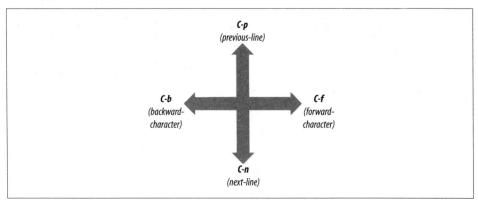

Figure 2-2. Basic cursor motion

If you're at the end of a line, **C-f** moves to the first character on the next line. Likewise, if you're at the beginning of a line, **C-b** moves to the last character of the previous line. If there's no place to go, Emacs beeps and displays the message `Beginning of buffer` or `End of buffer`.

Other Ways to Move the Cursor

Now we'll learn some more advanced ways to move the cursor. One common way is moving forward and backward by word: **M-f** moves *forward* a word; **M-b** moves *backward* a word. You can also move to the beginning or end of the line. **C-a** moves you to the beginning of the line (just like *a* is the beginning of the alphabet). **C-e** moves you to the *end* of the line. To move backward one sentence, type **M-a**; to move forward one sentence, type **M-e**. To move forward a whole paragraph at a time, type **M-}**; to move backward a paragraph, type **M-{**. If you're in the middle of a sentence or paragraph, moving back a sentence or paragraph actually takes you to the beginning of the current sentence or paragraph.

Figure 2-3 uses a few paragraphs of Victor Hugo's *Les Misérables* to show how you can move the cursor more than one character at a time.

You may have picked up on a pattern here. Notice the difference between commands starting with **Ctrl** and those starting with **Meta**. **Ctrl** commands generally move in smaller units than their associated **Meta** commands. For example, **C-b** moves the cursor backward one character, whereas **M-b** moves the cursor back one word. Likewise, **C-a** moves to the beginning of the line, whereas **M-a** moves to the beginning of a sentence.

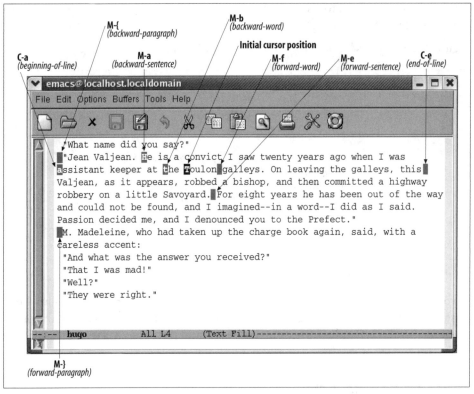

Figure 2-3. Moving the cursor more than one character at a time

There's one caveat about moving by sentence or paragraph. Emacs defines a sentence pretty strictly. You need *two* spaces after the final punctuation mark, unless you're at the end of the line. If there's only one space, Emacs won't recognize it. Similarly, moving backward and forward by paragraph involves understanding the Emacs definition of a paragraph. To Emacs (and to most of us), paragraphs are either indented with a tab or at least one space or have blank lines between them (block style). You can change these definitions, but first you have to understand how to use regular expressions, which are discussed briefly in Chapter 3 and in more depth in Chapter 11. Chapter 10 discusses how to change variables.

If your file has page breaks in it, you can move to the next page or previous page by typing **C-x]** (**forward-page**) or **C-x [** (**backward-page**). Similar to paragraph and sentence movement, moving by page involves the Emacs definition of what a page is. A variable called **page-delimiter** defines what constitutes a page break. If there are no Emacs-recognized page breaks in the file, Emacs regards the buffer as one very long page. In this case, the **forward-page** command takes you to the end of the buffer, and the **backward-page** command takes you to the beginning of the buffer.

In text mode, a page break is a formfeed character that tells the printer to move to the next page (to feed the next form or page through the printer, hence the term *formfeed*) before continuing to print. If you are in text mode and you want to insert page breaks in your file, type **C-q C-l** (the lowercase letter L). **C-q** is the **quoted-insert** command. It tells Emacs to put a **C-l** control character in your file, rather than interpreting **C-l** as the **recenter** command. A **C-l** character looks like two characters (^L), but it's really only one. (Try to erase one using **Del** and see what we mean.)

Moving a Screen (or More) at a Time

Like other graphical applications, you can use the scrollbar to move around in Emacs. Like most things in Emacs, in addition to using the mouse or scrollbar to move around, you should learn Emacs's own keyboard commands to maximize your productivity.

If you want to page through a file one screen at a time, use the **PgDown** key or type **C-v**. Emacs displays the next full screen from your file. It leaves a couple of lines from the previous screen at the top to give you a sense of context. Likewise, pressing **M-v** (or the **PgUp** key) shows you the previous screen. Together, **M-v** and **C-v** provide a convenient way to scroll through a file quickly.

Scrolling happens automatically if you type any motion command that takes you beyond the limits of the text currently displayed. For example, if you are on the last line of the screen and press **C-n**, Emacs scrolls forward. Similarly, if you are at the top of the screen and press **C-p**, Emacs scrolls backward.

You often want to move all the way to the beginning or the end of a file. Type **M->** or press **End** to go to the end of a buffer. To go to the beginning, type **M-<** or press **Home**. It may help you to remember that > points to the end of the buffer, and < points to the beginning of the buffer.

There are two more ways to move around that may come in handy. **M-x goto-line Enter *n* Enter** moves the cursor to line *n* of the file. Of course, Emacs starts counting lines from the beginning of the file. Likewise, **M-x goto-char Enter *n* Enter** goes to the *n*th character of the file, counting from the beginning. In both cases, *n* is a number.

For programmers, these commands are useful because many compilers give error messages like `Syntax error on line 356`. By using these commands, you can move easily to the location of your error. There are some more sophisticated ways to link Emacs with error reports from compilers and other programs. In addition, several other cursor motion commands are applicable only when you are editing programs (see Chapter 9 for details).

Repeating Commands

Now let's learn some efficiency tricks. Emacs lets you repeat any command as many times as you want to. First, you can repeat a command any number of times by pressing **M-n** before the command, where *n* is the number of times you want to repeat it. This command is called the **digit-argument** command.

You can give **M-n** a large argument if you want it to repeat the command many times. For example, let's say you are editing a large file of 1000 lines. If you typed **M-500 C-n**, the cursor would move down 500 lines, to the halfway point in the file. If you give **M-n** a larger argument than it can execute, it repeats the command as many times as possible and then stops.

There's another multiplier command you can use, too: **C-u** (the **universal-argument** command). You can give **C-u** an argument just like you do **M-n**. Typing either **M-5** or **C-u 5** repeats the command that follows five times. But unlike **M-n**, **C-u** doesn't need an argument to repeat commands. With no argument, **C-u** executes the next command four times. If you type **C-u C-u**, it executes the command 16 times. In this way, you can stack up **C-u**'s to make commands execute many times: 16, 64, 256, and so on.*

Centering the Display

C-l, the **recenter** command, puts the current line in the center of the window vertically. This feature is useful if you're typing at the bottom or the top of the display. Typing **C-l** quickly moves the material that you care about to the middle of the display, where it is easier to see the full context.

C-l also redraws the display, if for any reason it appears obscured or contains random characters. This doesn't happen as often as it used to when we used terminals, but it can be a handy thing to know about, especially if you find yourself using Emacs remotely in a terminal interface.

Table 2-2 lists cursor movement commands. If the command is mnemonic, the word to remember is given in *italics*.

Table 2-2. Cursor movement commands

Keystrokes	Command name	Action
C-f	forward-char	Move *forward* one character (right).
C-b	backward-char	Move *backward* one character (left).
C-p	previous-line	Move to *previous* line (up).

---

* Most often, you'll use **C-u** as we've described here. However, it doesn't always work as a multiplier; sometimes **C-u** modifies the command's function. Later in this chapter, you'll see one such case. However, if you're doing something where a multiplier makes sense, **C-u** is almost certain to work.

Table 2-2. Cursor movement commands (continued)

Keystrokes	Command name	Action
C-n	next-line	Move to *next* line (down).
M-f	forward-word	Move one word *forward*.
M-b	backward-word	Move one word *backward*.
C-a	beginning-of-line	Move to *beginning* of line.
C-e	end-of-line	Move to *end* of line.
M-e	forward-sentence	Move forward one sentence.
M-a	backward-sentence	Move backward one sentence.
M-}	forward-paragraph	Move forward one paragraph.
M-{	backward-paragraph	Move backward one paragraph.
C-v	scroll-up	Move forward one screen.
M-v	scroll-down	Move backward one screen.
C-x]	forward-page	Move forward one page.
C-x [	backward-page	Move backward one page.
M-<	beginning-of-buffer	Move to beginning of file.
M->	end-of-buffer	Move to end of file.
(none)	goto-line	Go to line *n* of file.
(none)	goto-char	Go to character *n* of file.
C-l	recenter	Redraw screen with current line in the center.
M-*n*	digit-argument	Repeat the next command *n* times.
C-u *n*	universal-argument	Repeat the next command *n* times (four times if you omit *n*).

Emacs Commands and Your Keyboard

You can access many Emacs commands by pressing standard keys on your keyboard, such as **PageDown** (to scroll down one screen) or **Home** (to go to the beginning of a buffer). Figure 2-4 shows a sample keyboard layout and what the keys do. Your keys may be in a slightly different place, but if you have a key with the same or a similar name, it should work. We say "should" because there are situations in which the keys won't work—for example, if you use Emacs on a remote machine. We recommend that you also learn the standard Emacs commands; they work on any keyboard, and they are often easier to reach once you learn them.

Deleting Text

Before you start practicing deletion commands, you might want to know the undo command, which is discussed fully later in this chapter. Typing **C-_** or **C-x u** undoes your last edit; typing **undo** again undoes the edit before that one, and so on.

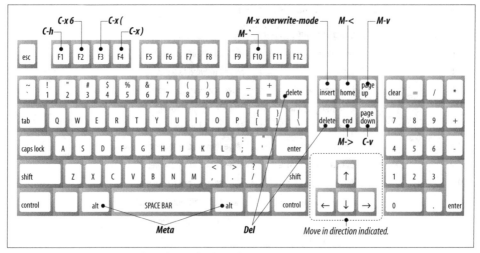

Figure 2-4. Emacs commands and your keyboard

Emacs provides many ways to delete text. The simplest way to delete text is to press the **Del** key, which deletes the character immediately to the left of the cursor. See Figure 2-4 for possible locations of the **Del** key on your keyboard. It is sometimes referred to as the **Backspace** key. **Del** is easiest to define by what it does: it deletes the previous character. If you're typing and you decide to erase the last character you typed, what key do you reach for? That's the key Emacs refers to as **Del**.

Emacs provides a number of other deletion commands—perhaps too many for your taste, although you'll eventually find a reason to use most of them. For example, **C-d** (for **delete-character**) deletes the character under the cursor. The command for deleting the next word is **M-d** (for **kill-word**). Once again, note how the **Meta** key augments the command: **C-d** operates on a character, and **M-d** operates on a word.

Emacs has commands to delete the next or previous word, sentence, and paragraph. By their names, you can guess what they do when you're between words, sentences, or paragraphs. If you're in the middle of an entity, however, they do something a little surprising: they delete a portion of the current word, sentence, or paragraph, backward or forward depending on whether the command deletes previous or next. For example, here's how **M-d** acts differently depending on where the cursor is.

If the cursor is here:	M-d makes this edit:
It was the w█rst of times	It was the w█of times
It was the █worst of times	It was the █of times
It was the wors█ of times	It was the wors█of times

Similarly, if you are in the middle of a word and ask Emacs to delete the previous word (**M-Del**, for **backward-kill-word**), it deletes from the cursor position back to the beginning of the current word.

If you want to delete an entire line or part of a line, use the command **C-k** (for **kill-line**). This command deletes everything from the cursor to the end of the line. Typing **C-k** on a blank line deletes the line itself. So, it usually takes two **C-k**'s to delete a line: one to delete the text and one to delete the resulting blank line. If you want to delete everything from the beginning of the line up to the cursor, try the more complex incantation **Meta - C-k** (i.e., hold down **Meta**, followed by a hyphen, and then **C-k**).

You can also use **C-k** to join two lines. If you're at the end of a line, **C-k** deletes the newline character, effectively making two lines into one long line.

The Kill Ring

By now you may have noticed that some deletion commands in Emacs are called *kill* commands, such as **kill-region**, **kill-word**, and the like. In Emacs, killing is not fatal, but in fact, quite the opposite. Text that has been killed is not gone forever but is hidden in an area called the *kill ring*. The kill ring, though it sounds somewhat like a violent gang, is an internal storage area where Emacs puts things you've copied or deleted. Do not confuse the kill ring with the system clipboard, which allows for copying and pasting between applications. We'll cover how Emacs relates to the system clipboard later in this chapter.

You can get back what you've deleted by typing **C-y** (for **yank**).[*] Conveniently, if you kill several lines in succession, Emacs collects them into a single item and places the whole unit into the kill ring; a single **C-y** command will bring everything back. In the following example, we'll use **C-k** four times to delete the first two lines of *A Tale of Two Cities*. (Remember: the first **C-k** deletes the text; the second **C-k** deletes the remaining blank line.) Then we'll use a single **C-y** to bring everything back.

---

[*] You may be used to pressing **C-v** to paste in all applications if you are a Linux or Windows user. Emacs has options to change its default paste, cut, and copy commands to the familiar C-v, C-x, and C-c. See "Making Emacs Work the Way You Want" for details. Also, a quick warning to **vi** users who are learning Emacs: **vi** also uses the term *yank*, but its meaning is almost the exact opposite. Don't let this confuse you.

Initial state:

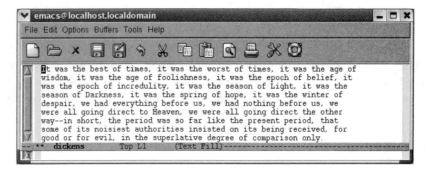

The cursor is in upper-left corner.

Type: **C-k C-k C-k C-k**

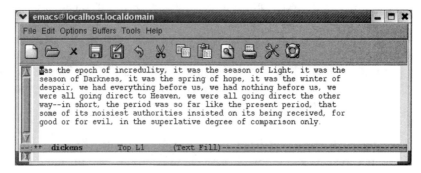

You have deleted the first two lines with **C-k**.

Type: **C-y**

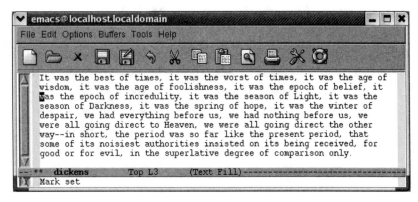

You got everything back with a single command.

What exactly goes into the kill ring? Everything you delete with **C-k** in addition to everything you delete with **C-w** and everything you copy with **M-w** (two commands that you'll learn shortly) go into the kill ring. Words, sentences, and paragraphs that you delete with **M-d**, **M-Del**, and their relatives also go into the kill ring. In addition, text that you delete with **C-u** followed by either **Del** or **C-d** goes into the kill ring. About the only thing that Emacs doesn't save in the kill ring is single characters, deleted with **Del** or **C-d**. (If you need to, you can get this type of deletion back using the **undo** command, bound to both **C-_** and **C-x u**.)

Emacs is clever about what it puts into the kill ring: when it is assembling a big block of text from a group of deletions, it always assembles the text correctly. For example, you can type a few **M-d**'s, followed by some **M-Del**'s, with a couple of **C-k**'s thrown in. When you type **C-y**, Emacs yanks all the text that you've deleted in the proper order.

However, there's one thing you have to watch out for. Emacs stops assembling these blocks of text as soon as you give any command that *isn't* a kill command. For example, if you type **C-k**, then delete a single character with **C-d**, then type another **C-k**, you've broken the chain. Emacs doesn't consider deletion of a single character with **C-d** a "kill" command; it's just a deletion and it isn't stored. In this case, you haven't made a single chain of kill commands; you've made two chains. Later, we'll see how to get the older killed text back.

Table 2-3 summarizes the commands for deleting, killing, and yanking text, including options from the **Edit** menu.

Table 2-3. Deletion commands

Keystrokes	Command name	Action
C-d	delete-char	Delete character under cursor.
Del	delete-backward-char	Delete previous character.
M-d	kill-word	Delete next word.
M-Del	backward-kill-word	Delete previous word.
C-k	kill-line	Delete from cursor to end of line.
M-k	kill-sentence	Delete next sentence.
C-x Del	backward-kill-sentence	Delete previous sentence.
C-y	yank	Restore what you've deleted.
C-w *Edit → Cut*	kill-region	Delete a marked region (see next section).
(none)	kill-paragraph	Delete next paragraph.
(none)	backward-kill-paragraph	Delete previous paragraph.

Marking Text to Delete, Move, or Copy

What if the text you want to delete is just a phrase? Or half a paragraph? Or several paragraphs? In Emacs, you select text by defining an area called a *region*. You can mark regions with the mouse or by using the keyboard. What happens with the mouse is a bit complicated, so we describe it later in this chapter, following our discussion of the system clipboard.

To define a region using the keyboard, you use a secondary pointer called a *mark*. Some versions of Emacs display the mark on the screen; unfortunately, in GNU Emacs, the mark is invisible.

You set the mark at one end of the region by pressing **C-Space** or **C-@**, then move the cursor to the other end of the region. (The cursor is sometimes also referred to as *point*. There is one minor but important difference between the cursor and the point, however. The cursor is on top of a character; in Emacs, the point is actually in between the character the cursor is on and the previous character. As we said, this difference is minor, but it helps you to visualize where the cursor should be when you mark a region.) Figure 2-5 illustrates point, mark, and region.

Let's mark a sample region. In this example, we remove the phrase "it was the worst of times." First, we find the beginning of the phrase. Then we set the mark, move forward to the end of the phrase, and cut.

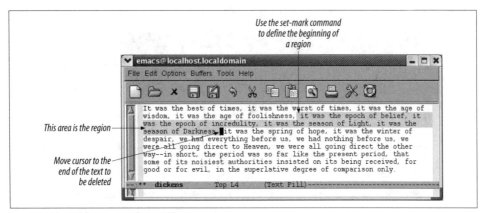

Use the set-mark command
to define the beginning of
a region

This area is the region

Move cursor to the
end of the text to
be deleted

Figure 2-5. Point, mark, and region

Move to the beginning of "it" and press **C-Space.**

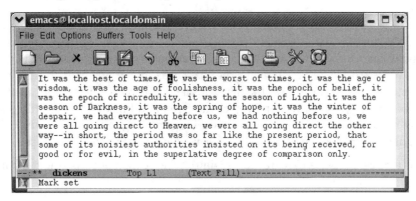

Set the mark; **Mark set** appears in the minibuffer.

Move to the "i" in "it was the age of wisdom." Because the point is really just before the "i," this placement will be just right.

Move to the "i" in "it was the age of wisdom"

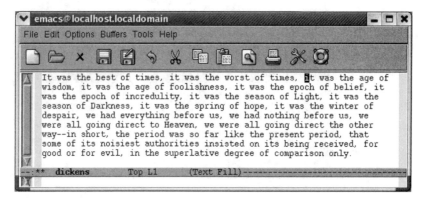

The point is at the end of the region to be marked.

Now the region is marked. If the region is not highlighted, you'll want to make sure it is marked correctly before giving the delete command. Press **C-x C-x** (for **exchange-point-and-mark**); this command swaps the locations of the mark and the point. If the cursor moves to where you thought the mark was, the region is marked correctly. Especially because you can't see the mark, it's a good habit to check its location using **C-x C-x** before deleting a region. People who have used Emacs for years still forget to set the mark and then make a deletion without knowing what they've just deleted. (The undo command, bound to **C-_** and **C-x u**, comes in handy in such a case.)

To cut the region, press **C-w** (for **kill-region**). (The scissors icon on the toolbar also works.)

Press: **C-w**

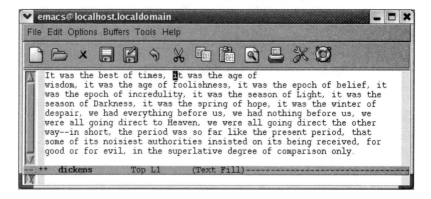

C-w cuts the region.

If you're not sure of what you deleted, just press **C-_** to undo it. The text is still marked, and you can delete it again with **C-w** if you want to. To move text, mark it, press **C-w** to cut the region, then move the cursor to the place you want to insert the text, and press **C-y**. If you yank the text back into the wrong location, just type **C-_** to undo it, then move to the place you really wanted to put the text, and press **C-y** again.

When you're defining a region, you normally set the mark at one end and then move the cursor to the other end of the region. A few shortcuts are helpful in some of the most common situations. To mark a paragraph, press **M-h**. This sets the mark at the end of the paragraph and places the cursor at the beginning automatically. Similarly, **C-x h** (for **mark-whole-buffer**) marks the entire buffer; the cursor goes to the beginning, and the mark is placed at the end. Finally, **C-x C-p** marks the current page, with *pages* being defined by the **C-l** character if you are in text mode. Of course, marking a paragraph, page, or buffer is usually only the prelude to some other operation, like killing (**C-w**).

Copying Text

To copy text, mark a region, then press **M-w** (for **kill-ring-save**; the toolbar icon with two pieces of paper also runs this command). Move the cursor to the place where you want to insert the copied text and press **C-y**. Copying text is exactly the same as killing it, except that Emacs doesn't delete anything. The text you have copied is placed in the kill ring, so you can use **C-y** to access it as often as you like.

One advantage to **M-w** is that it works on read-only files and buffers. For example, if you wanted to create a file of Emacs hints, you could use **M-w** to copy some text from online help into one of your buffers.

Here are the steps for some common deletion tasks.

To mark a region:

1. Move the cursor to the beginning of the area you want to delete.
2. Press **C-Space**. Emacs displays the message **Mark set**.
3. Move the cursor to the end of the region you want to delete.

To delete a region:

1. Mark the region to be deleted.
2. Press **C-w** to delete the region.

To move text:

1. Delete the text you want to move using the procedures for marking and deleting a region.
2. Move the cursor where you want to insert the text.
3. Press **C-y**. Emacs inserts the text you deleted.

To copy text:

1. Mark the region you want to copy.
2. Press **M-w** to copy the text.
3. Move the cursor where you want to insert the copied text and press **C-y**. Emacs inserts the text you copied.

Recovering Earlier Deletions

Earlier we mentioned the kill ring, a temporary storage area in which Emacs saves the stuff you delete. So far, we've assumed that you're interested in resurrecting what you've most recently killed. However, the kill ring does a lot more. It actually stores your last 30 deletions. We've seen that **C-y** restores the text you deleted most recently. Typing **M-y** deletes the text you just yanked and gets the next most recent text from the kill ring.

Here's how it works. In Table 2-4, assume that you've just killed the words "most recent." **C-y** retrieves these words from the kill ring. When you press **M-y**, Emacs gets rid of "most recent" and gets the next entry from the kill ring ("second-last").

Table 2-4. The kill ring in action

Keystrokes	Action
C-y	This was the most recent deletion.
M-y	This was the second-last deletion.
M-y	This was the third-last deletion.
M-y	This was the fourth-last deletion.

You can keep on typing **M-y**, retrieving successively more ancient deletions, until you reach the end of the kill ring (at which point it cycles back to the most recently killed text; that's why it's called a *ring*).

Thirty deletions by default is a nice size—far more generous than most programs offer. But you can enlarge or reduce the size of the kill ring if you wish, using a variable called **kill-ring-max**. To experiment, give the command: **M-x set-variable Enter kill-ring-max Enter *new-value* Enter** (where *new-value* is a number).

Selecting and Pasting

Using the menus, you can access text from the kill ring in a more straightforward way: by choosing Edit → Select and Paste. A menu showing deletions appears, with the most recent ones on top. To show you as many deletions as possible, each line in the window represents a separate deletion. So if you've killed a large region, say 500 lines, you see only the beginning of the first line of that deletion, ellipses, and the end of the deletion. Your selection is pasted into the buffer at the cursor position.

Table 2-5 summarizes commands for working with regions.

Table 2-5. Commands for working with regions

Keystrokes	Command name	Action
C-@ or C- Space	set-mark-command	Mark the beginning (or end) of a region.
C-x C-x	exchange-point-and-mark	Exchange location of cursor and mark.
C-w	kill-region	Delete the region.
C-y	yank	Paste most recently killed or copied text.
M-w	kill-ring-save	Copy the region (so it can be pasted with **C-y**).
M-h	mark-paragraph	Mark paragraph.
C-x C-p	mark-page	Mark page.
C-x h	mark-whole-buffer	Mark buffer.
M-y	yank-pop	After **C-y**, pastes earlier deletion.

Emacs and the Clipboard

Emacs 21 plays well with the clipboard, though it still may not do what you want it to in some cases. Let's dig into this in a little more detail.

Placing Text on the Clipboard

By default, text that you cut or copy using icons on the toolbar or options on the Edit menu is placed on the clipboard and is accessible to other applications.

Unfortunately, Emacs diverges by platform on this issue. Normally we save platform-specific issues for Chapter 13, but cutting and pasting is such a vital operation that we must describe the differences here.

On Windows and Mac OS X (but not on Linux) any text you cut or copy using **C-w** or **M-w** is also copied to the clipboard.

On Windows and Mac OS X, simply selecting text with the mouse places it on the clipboard. (This doesn't work on Linux.). Most applications require you to highlight text, then issue a copy command. Emacs doesn't. Table 2-6 shows how this works on various platforms.

Table 2-6. Selecting text with the mouse

	Linux	Windows	Mac OS X graphical	Mac OS X terminal
Sends to clipboard?	no	yes	yes	no[a]
Sends to kill ring?	yes	yes	yes	no

a You can make this happen if you highlight the text and then press ⌘-C. Simply high-lighting the text doesn't copy it to the clipboard.

To send text to the clipboard on Linux, select it with the mouse (or mark it as a region), then click on the cut or copy toolbar icon or menu option. You can also use the clipboard-specific commands listed in Table 2-8 on any platform.

Retrieving Text from the Clipboard

As we mentioned, in other applications, you typically cut and paste by selecting text, then issuing a copy command. How do you then paste that text into Emacs?

Not surprisingly, the paste icon on the toolbar and the associated option on the Edit menu do this in most cases (see Table 2-7; Emacs on Mac OS X disables both the icon and the option inappropriately; the associated command name **clipboard-yank** works, however). **C-y** inserts text from the clipboard too. Additionally, an easy mouse gesture works on most platforms: simply click the middle mouse button or mouse wheel in the Emacs window to paste from the clipboard. The caveat here is that you must have a mouse with a middle button.

Table 2-7. Pasting from the clipboard

	Linux	Windows	Mac OS X graphical	Mac OS X terminal
C-y pastes?	yes	yes	yes	no[a]
Toolbar paste icon pastes?	yes	yes	no	no
Edit → Paste option pastes?	yes	yes	no	no
Middle mouse button pastes?	yes	yes	yes	no
M-x clipboard-yank pastes?	yes	yes	yes	no

[a] ⌘-v pasttes from the clipboard.

Another issue with cutting and pasting is encoding. Encoding is a complex topic in Emacs; full Unicode support is slated for Emacs 22. At this point, we can only point you to a variable that may help you resolve cut-and-paste related encoding issues: **set-clipboard-coding-system**.

If you're interested in the clipboard, you may want to change Emacs' keys for cutting and pasting to the more universal **C-x**, **C-c**, and **C-v**. See "Making Emacs Work the Way You Want" later in this chapter for more details.

Table 2-8 summarizes clipboard-related commands.

Table 2-8. Clipboard commands

Keystrokes	Command name	Action
(none)	**clipboard-kill-region**	Cut region and place both in kill ring and on system clipboard.
(none)	**clipboard-yank**	Paste text from clipboard.
(none)	**clipboard-kill-ring-save**	Copy text to clipboard.

Editing Tricks and Shortcuts

Now that you've learned the basics of editing—moving the cursor to the right position, deleting, copying, and moving text—you can learn some tricks that make editing easier.

Fixing Transpositions

The most common typo involves the transposition of two letters, and most typos are noticed immediately after you make them. Pressing **C-t** transposes two letters, to put them in the right order:

Before C-t	After C-t
the best of timse, it	the best of times, it

To transpose two letters, put the cursor on the second of the two letters to be transposed. Press **C-t**. (If you often transpose letters, word abbreviation mode, discussed in Chapter 3, cleans up typos automatically.)

You can also transpose two words, lines, paragraphs, or sentences. To transpose two words, put the cursor between the two words and press **M-t**. After Emacs has finished, the cursor follows the second of the two (transposed) words:

Before M-t	After M-t
one three two	one two three

Interestingly, Emacs moves words, but not punctuation. Let's say that two names are reversed:

Before M-t	After M-t
Charles, Dickens	Dickens, Charles

To transpose two lines, put the cursor anywhere on the second of the two and press **C-x C-t**. Emacs moves the second before the first:

Before C-x C-t	After C-x C-t
second line	first line
first line	second line
third line	third line

Table 2-9 summarizes the transposition commands.

Table 2-9. Transposition commands

Keystrokes	Command name	Action
C-t	transpose-chars	Transpose two letters.
M-t	transpose-words	Transpose two words.
C-x C-t	transpose-lines	Transpose two lines.
(none)	transpose-sentences	Transpose two sentences.
(none)	transpose-paragraphs	Transpose two paragraphs.

Changing Capitalization

Mistakes in capitalization are also common and annoying typing errors. Emacs has some special commands for fixing capitalization. To capitalize the first letter of any word, put the cursor on the first letter and press **M-c**. To put a word in lowercase, press **M-l**. To put a word in uppercase, press **M-u**. The key bindings here are mnemonic: **Meta** followed by **c** for capitalize, **l** for lowercase, and **u** for uppercase. Note that if the cursor is in the middle of a word, Emacs takes action only from the character under the cursor to the end of the word. You can easily use **M-l** to lowercase the second half of a word, and so on.

If you notice that the word you just typed is incorrect, you can use the same commands prefaced by **Meta-** (press and hold **Meta** followed by a hyphen). This corrects the previous word without moving the cursor. If the cursor is positioned in the middle of a word, using **Meta-** before a command causes it to work on the first part of the word (the part preceding the cursor), rather than the part following the cursor.

For example, starting with **abcd**e**fghij**:

If you press:	You'll get:
Meta - u	abcdEFGHIJ
Meta - M-u	ABCDefghij
M-c	abcdEfghij
Meta - M-c	Abcdefghij

Table 2-10 summarizes the capitalization commands.

Table 2-10. Capitalization commands

Keystrokes	Command name	Action
M-c	capitalize-word	Capitalize first letter of word.
M-u	upcase-word	Uppercase word.
M-l	downcase-word	Lowercase word.

Table 2-10. *Capitalization commands (continued)*

Keystrokes	Command name	Action
Meta - M-c	negative-argument; capitalize-word	Capitalize previous word.
Meta - M-u	negative-argument; upcase-word	Uppercase previous word.
Meta - M-l	negative-argument; downcase-word	Lowercase previous word.

Overwrite Mode

You may be used to typing over old text rather than having to delete it. There is a certain satisfaction in destroying some really bad text in this way. You can do this in Emacs, too, by entering a minor mode called overwrite mode. When you're in overwrite mode, any new text you type wipes out the text that's underneath. When you're not in overwrite mode (i.e., in normal Emacs), any new text you type is inserted at the cursor position and any subsequent text is pushed to the right. (Other software may refer to this as insert mode; because it is the way GNU Emacs normally behaves, it doesn't have a name here.)

To enter overwrite mode, press the **Insert** key.* **Ovwrt** should appear on the mode line. If this doesn't work (or if you don't have an **Insert** key), type **M-x overwrite-mode Enter**. You can turn off overwrite mode by typing **M-x overwrite-mode Enter** again. Using Emacs's command completion, simply type **M-x ov** and press **Enter**. This is enough of a unique string to tell Emacs you want to toggle overwrite mode. Completion, one of the best shortcuts in Emacs, is discussed further in Chapter 14.

Canceling Commands and Undoing Changes

Sometimes you start a command by accident or change your mind about it. Don't worry: with Emacs, you can quit in the middle or undo it.

Canceling Commands

When you want to cancel any command that's in progress, press **C-g**. The word **Quit** appears in the command area. This command is helpful when you are stuck in the minibuffer and didn't really mean to go there. Depending on what you were doing, you may have to press **C-g** a few times.

Undoing Changes

What happens if you make a mistake while you're editing? You can undo your changes by pressing **C-_** or **C-x u** (for **undo**; conveniently, the toolbar also has an

---

* On a Mac keyboard, we found that the **Help** key, to the left of **Home**, toggles overwrite mode.

undo icon, a curved left arrow). By typing **undo** repeatedly, you can gradually work your way back to a point before your mistake.* Although the **undo** command is very powerful, saving your file frequently, if not compulsively, is nevertheless a good idea. We usually save a file whenever we stop typing—even if only for a few seconds. Train your fingers to press **C-x C-s** whenever you pause; it's a good habit to form.

If you're used to typing **C-z** to undo, you can easily change Emacs's behavior to match your habits. See "Making Emacs Work the Way You Want" at the end of this chapter for information on CUA mode.

What if you'd like to redo a command after you type **undo**? There is no formal *redo* command, but you can use **undo** in the following way. Just move the cursor in any direction, and type **C-_** or **C-x u** again. Emacs redoes the last command you undid. You can repeat it to redo previous **undo**s.

Although **undo** is an important command, it can be slow if you want to undo a large number of changes. Table 2-11 summarizes three methods for undoing changes and circumstances in which you might want to use them.

Table 2-11. Methods for undoing changes

If you:	Use this command:
Don't like the recent changes you've made and want to undo them one by one	C-_ *or* C-x u (undo)
Want to undo all changes made since you last saved the file	M-x revert-buffer Enter
Want to go back to an earlier version of the file (the file as it was when you started this editing session)	C-x C-f *filename*~ Enter C-x C-w *filename* Enter

We've already talked about undoing changes with **undo**; next we describe how to revert a buffer from a file and how to go back to an earlier version.

Reverting a Buffer from a File

If the **undo** command isn't useful, there's another way to restore a file to an earlier state. If you want to get the file back to the state that is stored on disk, type **M-x revert-buffer Enter**. Emacs asks the following question:

```
Revert buffer from file filename? (yes or no)
```

The filename is the name of your original file. Type **yes** if you want to restore the file, or **no** if you've changed your mind. Emacs copies the file stored on disk into the buffer, conveniently forgetting everything that happened since the last time you

---

* If you find that you repeat the undo command frequently, it's worth getting fluent with **C-_**. It's true that this requires holding down **Ctrl** and **Shift** at the same time, but once you've got that down, pressing _ repeatedly is much easier than typing **C-x u** again and again.

saved the file. Although this command is called **revert-buffer**, note that it can revert only buffers associated with files.

Going Back to a Previous Version: Backup Files

The first time you save a file during an editing session, Emacs creates a backup file. If something disastrous happens, and the other techniques for undoing changes won't help you, you can always return to the backup file. The name of the backup file is the same as the name of the file you're editing, with a tilde (~) added. For example, if you are editing the file *text*, the backup file is *text~*.

Emacs doesn't provide any special commands for restoring a buffer from the backup copy. The easiest way to do this is to edit the backup copy and then save it as the real file. For example, if you were working with a file called *text*, you could: exit Emacs by typing **C-x C-c**, then start Emacs again by typing **emacs *text~***. After the backup file is displayed, save it as the real file by typing **C-x C-w *text* Enter**. As a safeguard, Emacs asks you before it writes over the original file:

```
File text exists; overwrite? (y or n)
```

Type **y** to overwrite the original file with the backup file.

GNU Emacs also has a numbered backup facility. If you turn on numbered backups, Emacs creates a backup file (with the suffix *~n~*) every time you save your file. *n* increments with each successive save. If you are nervous about deleting older versions, it might be worth using: you can keep all of your old versions forever, if you want to. However, numbered backups can also waste disk space; a happy medium may be to tell Emacs to keep the last *n* versions, where *n* is the number of versions you want to keep. The variables that control numbered backups are described in Appendix A. If you are interested in full-blown version control, check out VC mode, discussed in Chapter 12. Table 2-12 summarizes the commands for stopping commands and undoing changes.

Table 2-12. Stopping and undoing commands

Keystrokes	Command name	Action
C-g	keyboard-quit	Abort current command.
C-x u	advertised-undo[a]	Undo last edit (can be done repeatedly).
C-_ *Edit → Undo*	undo	Undo last edit (can be done repeatedly).
(*none*)	revert-buffer	Restore buffer to the state it was in when the file was last saved (or auto-saved).

[a] There is no real difference between **undo** and **advertised-undo**. They work the same way.

Recovering Lost Changes

We've just discussed how to eliminate changes you don't want to keep; getting back changes you've lost is a different kind of problem. You might lose changes if the power goes out momentarily or if the computer you're working on suddenly freezes or is turned off accidentally. You might also lose changes if you exit Emacs abnormally. Luckily, Emacs, being the watchful editor that it is, saves your file for you every so often in *auto-save files*. If you watch carefully, you'll see the message **Auto saving** in the minibuffer from time to time. Using auto-save files, you can get back most, if not all, of your changes. The name of an auto-save file is the same as the name of the file you are editing, with a sharp (#) added to the beginning and the end. For example, if you are editing the file *text*, its auto-save file is *#text#*.

To recover text from an auto-save file, type **M-x recover-file Enter**. Emacs opens a window that lists both the file and its associated auto-save file so that you can compare the time at which they were created, their size, and so forth. Emacs asks you the following question:

```
Recover auto-save file #text#? (yes or no)
```

Type **yes** to confirm that you want to copy the contents of the auto-save file into the current file or **no** if you change your mind. (If you are unsure, you might want to use **C-x C-f** to read the auto-save file *#text#* into a buffer first and look it over carefully before using the **recover-file** command. If you really want to compare the differences between the two versions, see "Comparing Files Between Windows" in Chapter 4.)

When does Emacs create auto-save files? Emacs creates an auto-save file every few hundred keystrokes or if Emacs is terminated abnormally.* You can change the frequency with which Emacs creates auto-save files by changing the variable **auto-save-interval**. By default, Emacs creates an auto-save file every 300 keystrokes. For more information on changing variable values, see Chapter 10.

There's one more important fact to know about Emacs and auto-save files. If you delete a large portion of a file, Emacs stops auto-saving the file and displays a message telling you so. To make Emacs start auto-saving again, save the file with **C-x C-s** or type **M-1 M-x auto-save Enter** (that's the number 1).

Now you've learned enough commands for most of the editing you'll do with Emacs. At this point, you may want to learn how to make Emacs turn on certain features like auto-fill mode automatically, so you don't have to turn them on every time you enter Emacs. The next section provides a brief introduction to customization; this topic is covered in much greater detail in Chapter 10.

---

* We should say that Emacs *tries* to do this. In some cases, Emacs can't, and there is really no guarantee. Power surges and OS crashes are examples of times where things happen so fast that Emacs may not be able to create an auto-save file. But we are surprised at how often it manages to do so.

Making Emacs Work the Way You Want

If you've been reading straight through this book, you may have started a list of things you'd like to change about Emacs, such as

- Hiding the toolbar
- Changing Emacs cut and paste commands to **C-x**, **C-c**, and **C-v**
- Turning on text mode and a fill mode so Emacs does word wrap
- Changing the way some of the keys work

We're going to tell you how to give Emacs the to-do list, a list of options to turn on each time you enter Emacs. These options are defined in an initialization file called *.emacs*. Initialization files run automatically. Some run when you start up your computer. Others, like *.emacs*, run when you start up an associated software program. So *.emacs* runs automatically when you start Emacs and turns on whatever options the file defines. Emacs doesn't need this file to run; its only purpose is to make Emacs work the way you want it to.

The *.emacs* file consists of Lisp statements. If you're not a Lisp programmer, you can think of each line as an incantation that follows a certain pattern; you need to type it exactly.

Emacs now has another way to handle customization: an interactive interface called Custom that writes Lisp for you and automatically inserts it in your *.emacs* file. The Custom interface is discussed in Chapter 10, but we'll show you an even faster method for common options.

When you want to add a line to your *.emacs* file directly, take these steps:

1. Enter Emacs (if you're not already there).
2. Type **C-x C-f ~/.emacs Enter**.
3. Type the line to be added exactly as shown in this book and press Enter.
4. Press **C-x C-s** to save the *.emacs* file.
5. Press **C-x C-c** to exit Emacs.
6. Restart Emacs to have the line take effect.

If you make a minor typing mistake (such as forgetting a single quotation mark or a parenthesis), you are likely to get an error message that says `Error in init file` when you restart Emacs. Simply edit the *.emacs* file again, checking the line you added against the place you got it from, whether from this book or another user's *.emacs* file. Usually, you can find the error if you look hard enough; if not, find someone who has a *.emacs* file (and preferably understands Lisp) and ask for help. Make the changes, save the file, and restart Emacs.

What if you make a change that essentially keeps Emacs from being able to start? You can still exit Emacs, rename the file, edit it, then save it as *.emacs* and try again.

Hiding the Toolbar

New users may find the toolbar helpful. Others may not. It's easy to hide it by selecting Options → Show/Hide → Toolbar, and then Options → Save Options.

When Emacs sets options for you through Custom (and this is what it is doing even when you use the Options menu), it writes your *.emacs* file. If you already have a *.emacs* file, it appends to it. Custom essentially groups all of its settings in one part of the file, and it is commented to indicate that you should not change it manually. Here's the *.emacs* file that we created by selecting this option:

```
(custom-set-variables
  ;; custom-set-variables was added by Custom.
  ;; If you edit it by hand, you could mess it up, so be careful.
  ;; Your init file should contain only one such instance.
  ;; If there is more than one, they won't work right.
  '(tool-bar-mode nil nil (tool-bar)))
(custom-set-faces
  ;; custom-set-faces was added by Custom.
  ;; If you edit it by hand, you could mess it up, so be careful.
  ;; Your init file should contain only one such instance.
  ;; If there is more than one, they won't work right.
  )
```

This may seem a bit bulky, but as we'll see in the next section, Emacs adds this section only once and then augments it when you set more options either through the options menu or directly through the Custom interface. Also note that this auto-generated Lisp is certainly less clean than Lisp statements you'll typically see in *.emacs* files. That's another reason not to edit Custom's work directly.

Turning On CUA Mode for C-x, C-c, and C-v to Cut, Copy, and Paste

If you're new to Emacs, you might be used to the Common User Access (CUA) conventions for cutting, copying, and pasting, **C-x**, **C-c**, and **C-v** respectively. You might reach for **C-z** for undo. CUA mode was once an add-on mode that you had to install separately, but it became so popular that it is now part of Emacs. It's coded in a clever way that doesn't interfere with Emacs keystrokes that are prefixed with **C-x** and **C-c**. Details on CUA mode can be found in Chapter 13.

You can turn this feature on through the Options menu to try it out. Simply choose Options → C-x/C-c/C-v cut and paste (CUA). After you select this option, a check mark appears next to it on the Options menu. To keep it for subsequent sections, select Save Options from the Options menu. Emacs writes your *.emacs* file for you. If you turned off the toolbar and then set this option, your *.emacs* file would look like this (note that the line relating to CUA mode is bold so you can see the difference from the previous example):

```
(custom-set-variables
  ;; custom-set-variables was added by Custom.
```

```
;; If you edit it by hand, you could mess it up, so be careful.
;; Your init file should contain only one such instance.
;; If there is more than one, they won't work right.
'(cua-mode t nil (cua-base))
'(tool-bar-mode nil nil (tool-bar)))
(custom-set-faces
   ;; custom-set-faces was added by Custom.
   ;; If you edit it by hand, you could mess it up, so be careful.
   ;; Your init file should contain only one such instance.
   ;; If there is more than one, they won't work right.
)
```

Interestingly, Emacs happily writes the *.emacs* file even if it is open at the time. You can watch Emacs change the file if you have it open when you choose Save Options.

Turning On Text Mode and Auto-Fill Mode Automatically

To make text mode the default major mode and start auto-fill mode automatically each time you enter Emacs, add these lines to your *.emacs* file:

```
(setq default-major-mode 'text-mode)
(add-hook 'text-mode-hook  'turn-on-auto-fill)
```

The first line tells Emacs to make text mode the default major mode; in other words, "Turn on text mode unless I tell you otherwise." The second line turns on auto-fill mode whenever you are in text mode. Alternatively, selecting Options → Word Wrap in Text Modes, and then Options → Save Options adds auto-fill mode to your *.emacs* file directly. It doesn't make text mode the default major mode, however.

If you prefer refill mode, replace the second line of code with this line:

```
(add-hook 'text-mode-hook (lambda () (refill-mode 1)))
```

Remapping Keys

Another major use of the *.emacs* file is to redefine things about Emacs that irritate you. You may have ergonomic concerns about Emacs; more than one person has aggravated carpal tunnel syndrome using the default bindings. You may simply be used to reaching for certain keys for certain functions and would rather change Emacs than your habits. Whatever the case, this section gives a brief introduction to key remapping; for more details, see Chapter 10.

If you use the default bindings (rather than CUA mode), you may use **C-x u** for undo.* (Undo is such a common command that it's easy to type **C-x C-u** by mistake when you undo repeatedly. Unfortunately, **C-x C-u** is a disabled command for

---

* You could use **C-_** for undo instead and then you wouldn't need to read this section. We recommend that you read it anyway because you might find another annoying key mapping that you want to change and this section tells a bit about how to do so.

upcase-region. If you type **C-x C-u**, an annoying message about enabling the command pops up.

If you don't anticipate a big need for upcasing regions, you can redefine **C-x C-u** so that it also runs **undo**. To do so, add this line to your *.emacs* file:

```
(define-key global-map "\C-x\C-u" 'undo)
```

After making this change, typing **C-x C-u** runs undo, just as **C-x u** does.

Emacs customization is extremely powerful, and you can make Emacs work just the way you want it to. A far more extensive treatment of customization is found in Chapter 10. This brief introduction is meant to whet your appetite and to make it possible for you to add lines to your *.emacs* file as we mention potential customizations throughout the book.

The next chapter covers topics such as the many searches offered by Emacs, including query-replace, as well as spell checking and word abbreviation mode (often used to correct typos automatically). If you want to learn about these features, go on to the next chapter. From here on, you can take a selective approach to reading this book, picking and choosing whatever you want to learn about; you don't need to read the rest of the book sequentially.

Problems You May Encounter

- **You get an error message when you start Emacs after changing the *.emacs* file.** The message appears only briefly; press **M-p** to view it again. Edit your *.emacs* file, checking the lines you added carefully against their source for minor typographical errors. Something as simple as a missing hyphen or apostrophe can cause this error. Fix the error, save the file, exit Emacs, and reenter. In extreme cases (the *.emacs* file is so messed up that Emacs won't even let you edit it), exit Emacs, rename the *.emacs* file, and then start Emacs and edit it again to fix it. Rename it back to *.emacs* and start again.

- **Paragraphs are not reformatted properly.** This seems to relate to window size. Try resizing the window horizontally until paragraphs format properly.

CHAPTER 3

Search and Replace

The commands we discussed in the first two chapters are enough to get you started, but they're certainly not enough to do any serious editing. If you're using Emacs for anything longer than a few paragraphs, you'll want the support this chapter describes. In this chapter, we cover the various ways that Emacs lets you search for and replace text. Emacs provides the traditional search and replace facilities you would expect in any editor; it also provides several important variants, including incremental searches, regular expression searches, and query-replace. We also cover spell-checking here, because it is a type of replacement (errors are sought and replaced with corrections). Finally, we cover word abbreviation mode; this feature is a type of automatic replacement that can be a real timesaver.

Different Kinds of Searches

While you're editing, you frequently want to find something you've already typed. Rather than hunt through the file trying to find what you're looking for, virtually all editors provide some kind of search feature that lets you look for a particular text string. Emacs is no exception to the rule. It supplies a search command—in fact, it provides a dizzying array of search commands. Here's a quick summary of the different kinds of searches that are available:

Simple search
> You give Emacs a search string, and it finds the next occurrence. You will find this search in almost any editor.

Incremental search
> With incremental search, Emacs starts to search the file as soon as you type the first character of a search string. It continues to search as you type more characters.

Word search
> A word search is like a simple search, except that Emacs searches only for full words and phrases. For example, if you are searching for the word *hat*, you don't have to worry about finding the word *that*. A word search is also useful when you need to find a phrase that is spread across two lines.

Regular expression search

> To search for patterns, you can use a regular expression search. For example, if you wanted to find all instances of **B1** and **B2**, you could search for them using the regular expression **B[12]**. However, regular expressions can be extremely complex. We'll give a brief introduction to this topic here; it is discussed more fully in Chapter 11.

Incremental regular expression search

> This search procedure is a combination of an incremental search and a regular expression search.

You can search forward or backward. Searches can be either case-sensitive, meaning that Emacs considers upper- and lowercase letters to be different (i.e., the words *This* and *this* are different) or case-insensitive, in which upper- and lowercase are not differentiated (i.e., *This* and *this* are equivalent). By default, searches are case-insensitive, with upper- and lowercase letters considered to be the same. One exception: if you type any uppercase letters, Emacs makes the whole search string case-sensitive; it assumes you are looking for something precise since you've made the extra effort to type some letters in uppercase.

Replacement operations are closely related to searches. As with searches, Emacs offers you several different flavors:

Simple search and replace

> In this procedure, Emacs replaces all occurrences of one string with another. Usually, this is too radical a solution and can have unintended results. Try query-replace instead.

Query-replace

> With query-replace, Emacs conditionally replaces a string throughout a file. Emacs finds all occurrences of the search string, and for each one it asks you whether or not to perform the replacement. This type of replacement is useful if you need to change some, but not all, instances of a word or phrase throughout a file.

Regular expression replace

> Regular expression replacement uses the powerful pattern matching facility of the same name to find strings and replace them.

So now you know what you'll be looking at. Don't be intimidated by the wealth of searches that are available. In practice, you'll probably settle on one search command and one replace command and use these for 99 percent of your work. For example, we use incremental search and query-replace most of the time. If you're a writer, you may use word search all the time; if you're a programmer, you might want a regular expression search. If you're just beginning, you may want to learn incremental search and read the rest of this chapter later. However, if you know what's available, you'll be able to make use of the other search commands when they become useful.

Incremental Search

Incremental search starts to work from the moment you type the first character of the search string. Many users like the efficiency of incremental searches, and they like the highlighting as well. Emacs highlights all occurrences of the search string in aqua blue (if your display supports it) and uses purple to highlight the string at the cursor position (the current match).

Type: **C-s m**

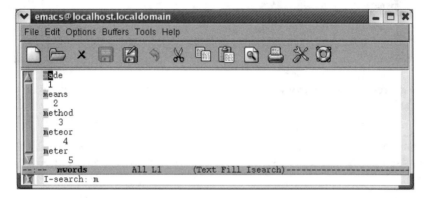

Emacs highlights all the words that start with m.

To start an incremental search, type **C-s** and then type the text you want to find. Emacs temporarily enters Isearch mode. Notice how this search works: Emacs looks for each character as soon as you type it. For example, if you are searching for the word *meter*, in an incremental search Emacs finds the next *m* as soon as you type the *m*; it finds the next *me* as soon as you type the *e*; it finds the *met* as soon as you type the *t*; and so on. Sooner or later, you either find what you want, or Emacs is unable to find anything. If you find what you want, press **Enter**; doing so stops the search at the current place in the file. If Emacs can't find anything that matches your search string, it prints the message Search failed at the bottom of your screen and then it beeps.

Here's what happens when we search for the word *meter*; the numbers show how the cursor moves with each new letter in the search string.

Type: **C-s meter**

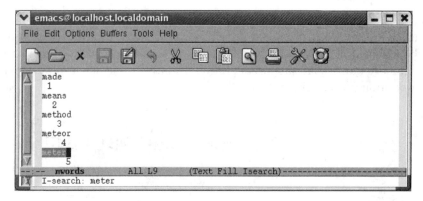

Emacs moves the cursor from one position to another as you type the letters of the search string.

In this incremental search, Emacs moves the cursor from position 1 to 2, to 3, and so on, as you type the search string *meter*. Also, note that Isearch appears on the mode line.

What happens if you find the string you're looking for but not the right occurrence of the string? Let's say you're searching for the word *eschatology* and you find the word, but you're still not in the right place. Simply press **C-s** again to find the next occurrence of the current search string. Emacs uses the same search string; you don't have to retype it.

Remember to press **Enter** when you've found the text you want. Forgetting to stop the search (by pressing **Enter** or with any other cursor movement command) is a common mistake: you type a few things, and suddenly Emacs is off looking at some completely different part of the file. What has happened? Emacs thinks you're still searching, and it has just added the characters you've typed to the search string.

If you type a letter in your search string incorrectly, press **Del**: Emacs moves back to the first instance of the reduced string in the file. If you keep pressing **Del** to delete characters from the search string, you'll see Emacs cycle back through the file to previous matches.

To cancel a search (that is, to give up searching), type **C-g**. This command brings you back to the place where the search began.

To search backward through a file, use **C-r**, which works exactly like **C-s** except that it searches in the opposite direction. It puts the cursor at the beginning of the text you find. Just as you can do when repeating **C-s**, you can press **C-r** to make the search go in the other direction without retyping the search string.

To avoid typing your search string, you can copy text from the buffer into the search string. To copy text from the cursor position through the next space or punctuation mark into the search string, type **C-s C-w** (it may help to think of **C-s C-w** as "*search a word*"). To copy text from the cursor to the end of the line into the search string, type **C-s C-y**. Notice that the text that is yanked is always converted to lowercase; this conversion ensures that the search will be case-insensitive. You can also copy text from the kill ring to the search string by typing **C-s M-y**. After you've given this command, you can press **M-p** to see previous items from the kill ring. **M-n** takes you to the next item if you've gone back with **M-p**.

Once you're in an incremental search, certain keys (such as **Enter** and **Del**) have different functions than they normally do. This situation may sound confusing, but it's actually fairly easy to get used to. Table 3-1 shows a summary of key functions during incremental search.

Table 3-1. Incremental search commands

Keystrokes	Command name	Action
C-s *Edit → Search → Incremental Search → Forward String*	isearch-forward	Start incremental search forward; follow by search string. Also, find next occurrence (forward) of search string.
C-r *Edit → Search → Incremental Search → Backward String*	isearch-backward	Start incremental search backward; follow by search string. Also, find next occurrence (backward) of search string.
Enter	isearch-exit	In an incremental search , exit the search.
C-g	keyboard-quit	In an incremental search , cancel the search.
Del	isearch-delete-char	In an incremental search, delete character from search string.
C-s C-w	isearch-yank-word	Start an incremental search with the word the cursor is on as the search string.
C-s C-y	isearch-yank-line	Start an incremental search with the text from the cursor position to the end of the line as the search string.
C-s M-y	isearch-yank-kill	Start an incremental search with text from the kill ring as the search string.
C-s C-s	isearch-repeat-forward	Repeat previous search.
C-r C-r	isearch-repeat-backward	Repeat previous search backward.

Simple Searches

Emacs also offers a simple, or nonincremental, search. To use a more straightforward search, type **C-s Enter**. Type the search string, press **Enter**, and Emacs begins the search. Simply press **C-s** again to repeat the search. To start a nonincremental search backwards through the file, press **C-r Enter**. Again, you type the search string and press **Enter** to begin the search.

The search icon on the toolbar (a magnifying glass over paper) and the Edit → Search → String Forward option run the same kind of a search. The prompt is slightly different. **C-s Enter** prompts you with Search: in the minibuffer while the toolbar icon and the menu option prompt with Search for string:. This is a minor difference; the searches are virtually identical otherwise.

Table 3-2 summarizes the simple search commands.

Table 3-2. Simple search commands

Keystrokes	Action
C-s Enter *searchstring* **Enter** *Edit → Search → String Forward*	Start nonincremental search forward.
C-s	Repeat search forward.
C-r Enter *searchstring* **Enter** *Edit → Search → String Backwards*	Start nonincremental search backward.
C-r	Repeat search backward.

Word Search

If you're searching for a phrase and you know it's in the file but you can't find it with incremental search, try word search. (You probably can't find your phrase with incremental search because the phrase has a line break in it.) Word search is a nonincremental search that ignores line breaks, spaces, and punctuation. It also requires that your search string match entire words in the file.

To do a word search, type **C-s Enter C-w** (for **word-search-forward**). The prompt Word search appears in the minibuffer. (Don't be put off by the prompts that appear along the way: you'll see an I-search prompt after typing **C-s** and a Search prompt after pressing **Enter**. Ignore these.) Type the search string and press **Enter**. Emacs searches for the given string. To do a word search backwards, type **C-r Enter C-w** instead. For example, assume that you have the following text, with the cursor at the beginning:

```
He said, "All good elephants are wise, aren't they?"
She answered, "Some are smarter than others, but we
think this is socially conditioned."
```

The command **C-s Enter C-w they she Enter** positions the cursor after the word *She*. This command looks complicated, but it's really nothing more than a word search (**C-s Enter C-w**) for the word *they*, followed by the word *she*. It ignores the punctuation (?") and the newline between *they* and *she*.

Assume that you're looking for the word *the*. You don't want to bother with *thence*, *there*, *theater*, *thesis*, *blithe*, or any other word that happens to contain the letters *the*. In this situation, neither an incremental search nor a simple search is very useful—you need a word search. If you're writing a paper, word search is often exactly what you need. It is the *only* one of the three basic search commands that allows you to find what you want even if the phrase is split between two lines.

Now that you've seen the three most commonly used searches, you might want to experiment and see which you find most useful.

Search and Replace

Search and replace definitely go together, like coffee and cream. Let's say you're working on a new software application and at the last possible moment, the Marketing Department decides to change the product's name.

Tere's a press release for Whirligig, an email service that periodically reminds you to make healthy lifestyle changes like exercising, drinking water, and taking vitamins. The level of harassment or, as the marketing department says, encouragement, can be set by the user. Whirligig isn't really the most descriptive name, so at the last minute the Marketing Department changes it to HealthBug.

Simple Search and Replace Operations

Assume you're in the situation we just described. You want to replace every occurrence of one string with another. You know that Whirligig is never correct, and there is absolutely no ambiguity about how you want to replace it. When you want to replace every instance of a given string, you can use a simple command that tells Emacs to do just that. Type **M-x replace-string Enter**, then type the search string and press **Enter**. Now type the replacement string and press **Enter** again. Emacs replaces all occurrences in the file from the cursor position onward. If you want to search and replace throughout the file, press **M-<** to go to the beginning of the file before typing this command. Here's a quick example of using **replace-string**.

Initial state:

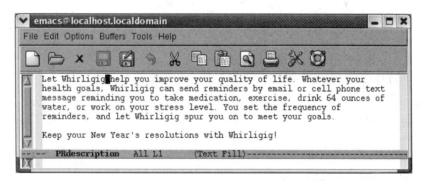

Whirligig appears four times, but the cursor is positioned after the first instance.

Now we'll do the replacement.

Type: **M-x replace-string Enter Whirligig Enter HealthBug Enter**

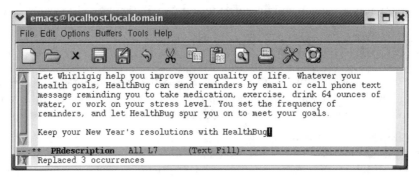

Emacs replaces all instances from the cursor position onward.

The replacement occurs only from the cursor position onward; *Whirligig* in the first sentence is still incorrect. We'll work with this example again in a moment.

Query-Replace

Few search and replace situations are as straightforward as those we've described. Often you're not sure that you want to replace every appearance of your search string: a global replacement can be reckless. If you want to decide whether to replace the string on a case-by-case basis, use a query-replace, which allows you to change a string conditionally throughout a file. After Emacs finds an occurrence of the search string, it asks whether it should replace it, and you respond accordingly.

To use query-replace, go to the beginning of the buffer using **M-<** and then type **M-%**. The prompt Query replace: appears in the minibuffer. Type the search string and press **Enter**. Now this appears:

    Query replace *searchstring* with:

Type the replacement string and press **Enter**. So far, this procedure is almost identical to a **replace-string** operation; only the prompts are different.

Emacs now searches for the first occurrence of the search string. When it finds one, a new prompt appears:

    Query replacing *searchstring* with *newstring*

Before performing the replacement, Emacs waits for a response to tell it what to do. Table 3-3 lists the possible responses and their results.

Table 3-3. Responses during query-replace

Keystrokes	Action
Space or **y**	Replace *searchstring* with *newstring* and go to the next instance of the string.

Table 3-3. Responses during query-replace (continued)

Keystrokes	Action
Del or **n**	Don't replace; move to next instance.
.	Replace the current instance and quit.
,	Replace and let me see the result before moving on. (Press **Space** or **y** to move on.)
!	Replace all the rest and don't ask.
^	Back up to the previous instance.
Enter or **q**	Exit query-replace.
E	Modify the replacement string.
C-r	Enter a recursive edit (discussed in detail later).
C-w	Delete this instance and enter a recursive edit (so you can make a custom replacement).
C-M-c	Exit recursive edit and resume query-replace.
C-]	Exit recursive edit and exit query-replace.

This list seems like a lot of keystrokes to remember, but you can get away with knowing two or three. Most of the time you'll respond to the prompt by pressing **Space**, telling Emacs to perform the replacement and go on to the next instance, or **n** to skip this replacement and go on to the next instance. If you're not too sure what will happen, enter a comma (,); Emacs makes the replacement but doesn't go on until you press **Space**. After performing the first few replaces, you may realize that there's no need to inspect every change individually. Typing an exclamation mark (!) tells Emacs to go ahead and finish the job without bothering you anymore. If you remember these keystrokes, you're all set.

How does this work in practice? Let's revisit our previous example, assuming that we want to change *Whirligig* to *HealthBug* throughout (and that we didn't save the changes we made with **replace-string**).

Type: **M-< M-% Whirligig Enter HealthBug Enter**

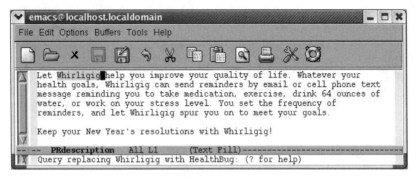

You're ready to replace the first occurrence; press **Space** to go on.

Press: **Space**

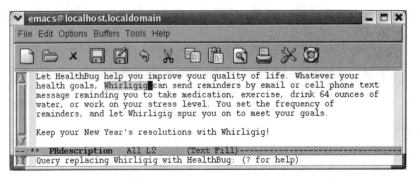

When you press **Space**, Emacs replaces the first word; the query-replace operation then moves to the second word.

This procedure continues until you reach the end of the file. As we've said, typing **!** fixes the rest of the file.

In Table 3-3, you might have noticed that several keys, such as **Space**, have special-ized meanings while the replacement is in progress. In practice, using these keys for a different function is not confusing, though it might sound bad on paper. You might want to try a query-replace on a practice file to get the hang of using the different responses. If you are easily amused, you might enjoy opening the Emacs FAQ, sav-ing it as another file, then replacing Emacs throughout.

Repeating Query-Replaces (and Other Complex Commands)

Now that you've learned the basics of query-replace, let's talk about a shortcut that applies not only in query-replace but anywhere in Emacs: repeating complex com-mands, with slight modifications. We often exit a query-replace by mistake or decide that the replacement we really wanted was just slightly different. Do we have to type it all again? No. Simply go the beginning of the file and press **C-x Esc Esc**. The last complex command you typed appears. If it's not the one you want, type **M-p** to see the previous command (do this as many times as necessary; **M-n** goes to the next command). For example, let's go to the beginning of the file and repeat the query-replace we just carried out.

Type: **M-<** followed by **C-x Esc Esc**

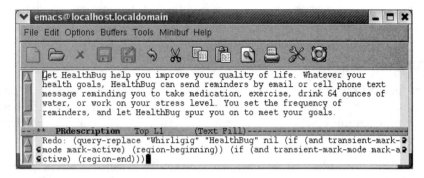

Emacs puts the last complex command in the minibuffer; in fact it looks more complex than we remember it.

When we press **M-<**, we move to the beginning of the file; when we press **C-x Esc Esc**, the last complex command is displayed. Emacs speaks to itself in dark words, but we can still see that this is the command that we want.

This is the right command, so we don't have to press **M-p** to see a previous command. If we wanted to, we could change the query-replace strings before pressing **Enter**. In this case, the Marketing Department has once again changed the product's name from HealthBug (since bug could be construed as pest) to HealthBot (neutral, but a bit less descriptive in our opinion). Our earlier query replace changed Whirligig to HealthBug. We need to modify this command so it replaces *Bug* with *Bot*.

In the minibuffer, change *Whirligig* to *Bug* and *HealthBug* to *Bot* and press **Enter.**

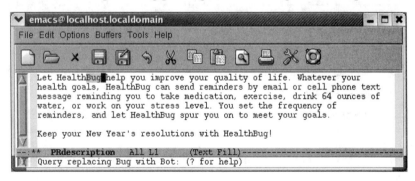

Pressing **Enter** executes the command again with the modified search and replacement strings.

As we mentioned, **C-x Esc Esc** works for any command involving input in the minibuffer, not just query-replace. But we use this feature most frequently in query-replace. It is also good for repeating keyboard macros (see Chapter 6).

Recursive Editing

When you do a query-replace, you inevitably see something else you want to change in the file. Try it a few times—you'll see what we mean! We typically try to remember the problem until we're done, then get frustrated when we forget exactly what and where the problem was.

Fortunately, Emacs provides an easier way. It allows you to start a recursive edit while you're in the middle of a query-replace. By starting a recursive edit, you effectively put query-replace on hold while you make any other desired edits. When you exit the recursive edit, the query-replace resumes where you left off.

To start a recursive edit while in query-replace, press **C-r**. (Note that like many other key bindings, **C-r** has a different meaning in query-replace than it does in standard Emacs.) When you start a recursive edit, square brackets ([ ]) appear on the mode line. Let's go back, one more time, to our public relations piece. You've used query-replace to find the first Bug to change to Bot, and you are about to press **Space** to fix it, when you remember that the lawyers said that the "64 ounces of water" statement was too specific and could be construed as giving medical advice. A quick recursive edit saves the day.

Type: **C-r**

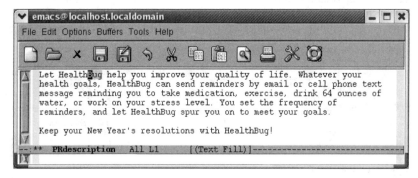

Notice the square brackets around (Text Fill), indicating a recursive edit in progress.

Now do any editing you want to; you are in an editing mode just like standard Emacs. Move down to the third line and delete "64 ounces of." When you want to resume the query-replace, press **C-M-c**. This command tells Emacs to leave the recursive edit and reactivate the query-replace. Emacs moves back to the point where you were when you started the recursive edit. You can then continue making replacements just as if nothing had happened.

Delete "64 ounces of," then type **C-M-c**

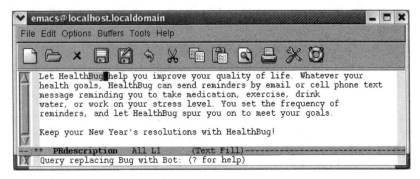

Emacs goes back to query-replace and you press **Space** to fix the next Bug.

If you decide to exit the recursive edit and cancel the query-replace in one fell swoop, you can type **C-]** (for **abort-recursive-edit**) or **M-x top-level Enter** rather than **C-M-c**.

In fact, you can start a recursive edit at any time, not just when you're in a query-replace. The command **M-x recursive-edit Enter** puts you into a recursive edit; **C-M-c** takes you out of the recursive edit and brings you back to what you were doing before. You can even have recursive edits within recursive edits, although the possibility for confusion increases with each new level.

Are Emacs Searches Case-Sensitive?

By default, Emacs searches are not case-sensitive. Look at the Options menu and you'll see that the option Case-Insensitive Search is the only option that is checked by default.

What does this mean in practical terms? If you search for the word *random*, the search finds *random*, *Random*, and *RANDOM*, as well as oddities like *RanDoM* and *rANdOM*. When doing replacements, Emacs pays attention to the form of the word being replaced and replaces it with the same case. If you replaced *random* with *tandem*, *Random* would be replaced with *Tandem*, and *RANDOM* would be replaced with *TANDEM*. If you mix capitalization, the replacement string appears just as you type it. *healthbug* would be replaced with *HealthBug* if that was the case in the replacement string. In other words, the default search and replacement operations usually do what you want: they find a search string regardless of its case and adjust the replacement appropriately for its context. However, sometimes you need finer control.

The variable **case-fold-search** determines whether searches are case-sensitive. It applies to all searches: incremental searches, word searches, searches within search-and-replace operations, and so on. By default, **case-fold-search** is set to **t**, which means "ignore case unless the user types in mixed or uppercase." This sensible default is usually just what you want. But if you need case-sensitive searches, the Case-Insensitive Search option on the Options menu provides an easy way to experiment with this variable.

Likewise, if you don't want Emacs to adjust the case of your replacement strings, you can set the variable **case-replace**. Again, its value is **t** (for "true") by default, which means "adjust the case of a replacement string to match the original text"—that is, capitalize the replacement if the original word was capitalized and so on. Setting this variable to **nil** means "never adjust the case of the replacement string; always put it in exactly as I typed it." To change the value of **case-replace**, type **M-x set-variable Enter case-replace Enter nil Enter** (there's no menu option for this variable).

Both the menu option and the **set-variable** command change the behavior of Emacs only temporarily. If you start a new editing session, you'll be back to the default behavior. This is probably what you want, because searching separately for capitalized and lowercase words is inconvenient.

You can set the value for the Case-Insensitive Search option permanently by selecting Save Options from the Options menu or by adding this line to your *.emacs* file:

```
(setq-default case-fold-search nil)  ; require exact matches
```

To set **case-replace** permanently, add the following line to your *.emacs* file. You'll need to restart Emacs to have the change take effect.

```
(setq-default case-replace nil)      ; never change case when replacing
```

You could change these variables through Emacs's interactive customization facility, Custom, instead (see Chapter 10).

Regular Expressions for Search and Replacement Operations

Sometimes none of the simpler searches described in this chapter are adequate. Regular expressions allow you to build searches with strings that contain various wildcards.

Table 3-4 shows some of the characters you can use in creating a regular expression.

Table 3-4. Characters for creating regular expressions

Character(s)	Match
^	Matches the beginning of a line.
$	Matches the end of a line.
.	Matches any single character (like ? in filenames).

Table 3-4. Characters for creating regular expressions (continued)

Character(s)	Match
.*	Matches any group of zero or more characters (. matches any character and * matches zero or more of the previous character).
\<	Matches the beginning of a word.
\>	Matches the end of a word.
[]	Matches any character specified within the brackets; for example, [a-z] matches any alphabetic character.
\s, \S	Matches any whitespace character: space, a newline, a tab, a carriage return, a formfeed, or a backspace; \S matches any character except whitespace.
\d, \D	Matches any single digit, 0-9; \D matches any character but a digit.
\w, \W	Matches any "word" character (upper- and lowercase letters, digits, and the underscore character); \W matches any character but these.

If you do a regular expression search for **^word$**, you would find instances of *word* on a line by itself. The **^** says that the **w** must be the first character on the line, the **$** says that the **d** must be the last character.

If you wanted to find all words starting with *beg* and ending with the letter *s*, you could use **beg[a-z]*s** as your regular expression. This would find the words *begins*, *begets*, and *begonias*, in addition to really odd words like *shibegrees* and *altbegaslia*. If you don't want these mutants—that is, if you really want words that begin with *beg* and end with *s*, use **\<beg[a-z]*s\>**. The **\<** is a special sequence that matches the beginning of a word; **\>** matches the end of a word. If you wanted to find the words *beg*, *big*, and *bag*; but not *begonias*, and certainly not any strange words with *beg* on the inside, you would use **\<b[a-z]g\>** as the regular expression.

To search for a **^**, **$**, **.**, *****, **[**, **]**, or any number of other special characters, you obviously can't use the character itself. Put a backslash (\) first—i.e., to search for a period, search for \. For example, to search for the electronic mail address':

    howie@mcds.com

the regular expression would be:

    howie@mcds\.com

This is a barebones introduction to regular expressions; see Chapter 11 for more details and *Mastering Regular Expressions* by Jeffrey Friedl (O'Reilly) for a book-length treatment of this topic.

You can use regular expressions in incremental searches and in query-replace. Table 3-5 lists the commands you use for regular expression searches. Although they are initiated with slightly different commands, the searches are the same as those described earlier in this chapter.

Table 3-5. Regular expression search commands

Keystrokes	Command name	Action
C-M-s Enter *Edit → Search → Regexp Forward*	**re-search-forward**	Search for a regular expression forward.
C-M-r Enter *Edit → Search → Regexp Backwards*	**re-search-backward**	Search for a regular expression backward.
C-M-s *Edit → Search → Incremental Search →* *Forward Regexp*	**isearch-forward-regexp**	Search incrementally forward for a regular expression.
C-M-r *Edit → Search → Incremental Search →* *Backward Regexp*	**isearch-backward-regexp**	Search incrementally backward for a regular expression.
C-M-% *Edit → Replace → Replace Regexp*	**query-replace-regexp**	Query-replace a regular expression.
(none)	**replace-regexp**	Globally replace a regular expression unconditionally (use with caution).

Checking Spelling Using Ispell

Emacs includes two spell-checking interfaces: to the Unix spell checker, spell, and to Ispell, which many people, including us, prefer. We say "interfaces" because Emacs does not include the executables for either of these spell-checkers. Because Ispell is superior and runs on a variety of platforms, we'll cover only Ispell here. If you attempt to run Ispell and it is not available, you'll have to install it. Chapter 13 provides details on installing Ispell on Windows and on Mac OS X.

A further enhancement to Ispell is Flyspell, a command that highlights misspelled words on the fly. If you have Ispell installed, you'll have Flyspell support as well.

Checking a Buffer

Ispell includes options to check a buffer, a region, the comments in a program, or a single word. After you type the command telling Ispell what area you want to check, it works the same way for all these options. We'll describe **ispell-buffer** here. If all the words are spelled correctly, Ispell displays the message, Spell-checking done. If Ispell finds a misspelled word, a screen like the following appears. Let's spell-check a hastily typed passage from Homer's *Odyssey*.

Type: **Esc x ispell-buffer Enter**

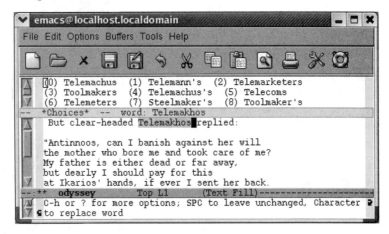

Ispell finds the first unrecognized word in the buffer.

Ispell moves to the first unrecognized word, in this case a proper name correctly spelled (except for the proper accent marks). At the top of the screen, Ispell opens a small window that displays alternative spellings, numbered starting with 0. The minibuffer says `C-h or ? for more options`, `SPC to leave unchanged`, `character to replace word`. In this case, we have a properly spelled name, so press **i** to ask Ispell to insert it into your private dictionary, which is kept in a file called *.ispell_<language>* in your home directory,* where *language* is the *language* you are using (English by default). If this file doesn't exist, Ispell creates it without complaint and later asks you if you want to save it. To insert the word in the dictionary in lowercase, press **u** and Ispell lowercases the word and then puts it into your dictionary. Of course, because this is a proper name, we insert it as it appears in the passage.

---

* Your default dictionary might be called something else entirely, like *.aspell.language.pws*. If you run the command **ispell-check-version**, you'll see that although Ispell is supposedly running, it's really Aspell behind the scenes.

Press **i**:

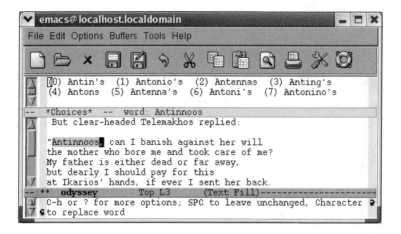

Ispell moves to the next unrecognized word, another proper name.

We insert a few more proper names and move along to the first real misspelling, *pwers*.

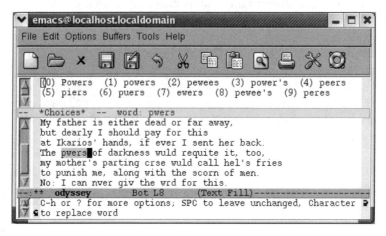

Ispell finds *pwers* misspelled.

Ispell opens a window at the top of the screen listing choices for a replacement. Usually one of its top few choices is correct.

To select *powers*, press: **1**

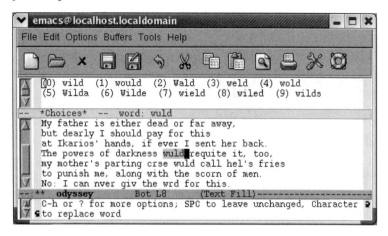

Ispell replaces the word and goes on to the next misspelling.

If one of the words that Ispell lists at the top of the screen is correct, you type the number, and Ispell makes the replacement. To replace a word yourself, press **r**. After you type the corrected word, Ispell replaces it. If you press **R** instead, Ispell starts a query-replace through which you can correct all cases of the misspelling in this buffer.

Instead of replacing the word, you may simply want Ispell to skip over it. To skip this occurrence of a misspelled word, press **Space**. To ignore a misspelled word for the rest of the session for all buffers, press **a** (for accept). Uppercase **A** has one subtle difference: it tells Ispell to accept the word for this session but only in this buffer.

If you can see that something more complicated is wrong, you can start a recursive edit by typing **C-r**. Fix the error and type **C-M-c** to exit the recursive edit and resume Ispell. (You may recall that we discussed recursive editing earlier in this chapter.)

Our passage repeatedly spells *would* incorrectly and typing the character beside the correct word only replaces a single incidence, so a better choice would be to type **R** to query-replace the word throughout the buffer.

Type: **R**

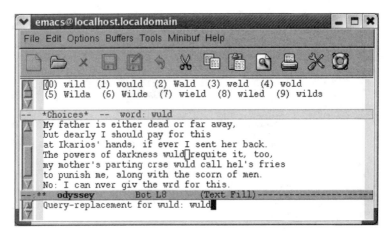

Ispell asks for the correction for *wuld*.

Change *wuld* to *would* and press **Enter**.

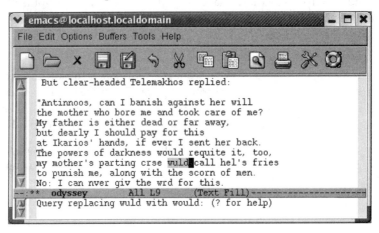

Ispell starts a query-replace.

We want to replace all occurrences of the misspelled word, so we'll type **!**, which, as you might recall, means "replace them all without asking."

Type ! then **y** when prompted about saving your personal dictionary.

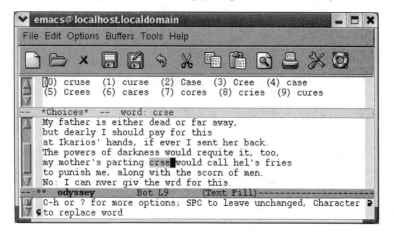

Emacs moves to the "next" misspelling, *crse*.

Ispell replaces the words, then goes on to the next misspelling, *crse*. Note that this misspelling occurs before the second incorrect *wuld*. Because we already query-replaced *wuld* with *would*, Ispell had to move backward to find the next misspelling.

Remember that Ispell, like all spellcheckers, corrects only true misspellings. If a misspelling forms another word, Ispell will leave it alone. It's up to you to change *fries* to *fires* in this passage.

Different forms of the same word must be corrected separately. For example, if you misspell *receive*, *receives*, and *receiving* by reversing the *i* and the *e*, you must change each misspelled word.

Checking a Single Word

Sometimes when you are typing, you'll say, "That doesn't look right." To check the word the cursor is on, type **M-$** (for **ispell-word**). Ispell checks the spelling of the word and displays *word*: ok if the word is spelled correctly. If the word is incorrect, Ispell displays a window with the options discussed earlier.

Completing a Word

You might start typing a word and then wonder, "How is that spelled?" This is where **ispell-complete-word** comes in. You're typing a word and you get stuck. Type **M-Tab** (for **ispell-complete-word**) and you get a list of choices. After typing *occur*, you use this command to find out the answer.

Type: **occur M-Tab**

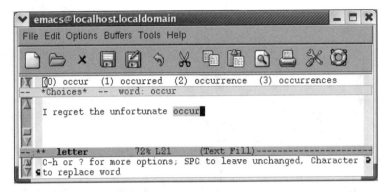

Ispell choices appear at the top of the screen.

To select *occurrence*, type: **2**

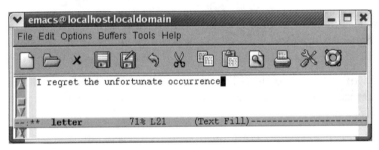

Ispell completes the word for you.

This feature varies in its helpfulness. In this case the replacement needed was shown. It won't always work that way, but you can always simply spell it wrong and then use **ispell-buffer** to fix it.

Spellchecking on the Fly with Flyspell

Flyspell highlights misspelled words as you type. You can also use it to check existing text. The commands for doing this are different.

To check text as you type, enter Flyspell mode by typing **M-x flyspell-mode Enter**. Fly appears on the mode line. If you set up Emacs to enter Flyspell mode automatically, your text is always spell-checked "on the fly." An alternative to Flyspell mode is Flyspell prog mode. In this mode, designed for programmers, Emacs highlights misspellings only in comments or strings. To enter it, type **M-x flyspell-prog-mode Enter**.

To check existing text, you run **M-x flyspell-buffer Enter**. This command is like **ispell-buffer**; it spell-checks the entire buffer. Flyspell's interface is different; it underlines all the words it suspects are misspelled and gives you a pop-up menu of alternatives.

The best way to check out Flyspell mode is to turn it on and type some misspelled text to see it in action. No matter whether you enter Flyspell mode or run **flyspell-buffer**, you correct errors in the same way. We'll demonstrate **flyspell-buffer** on our misspelled *odyssey* file. Because it's an existing file (not a new file we're typing), we need to issue the **flyspell-buffer** command.

Type: **Esc x flyspell-buffer Enter**

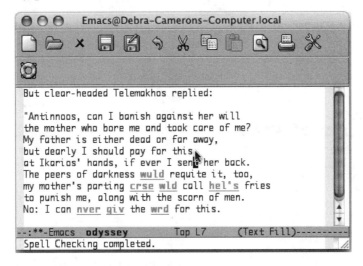

Flyspell highlights misspelled words (Mac OS X).

Flyspell highlights misspelled words in red. Words that are repeatedly misspelled are highlighted in yellow. Note that it doesn't highlight the proper names we inserted in the dictionary earlier using Ispell; Flyspell checks to see whether words are in your personal dictionary before highlighting them as errors.

You move to a misspelled word and press the middle mouse button to display a pop-up menu of possible replacements. (This implies that you have a three-button mouse, and, to be honest, you need one to make Flyspell work properly.) You select a replacement using the mouse.

Move the cursor to *crse* and press the middle mouse button.

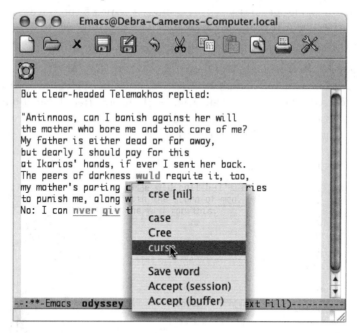

Flyspell displays a pop-up window of alternatives; you choose one with the mouse (Mac OS X).

Choose *curse* with the mouse.

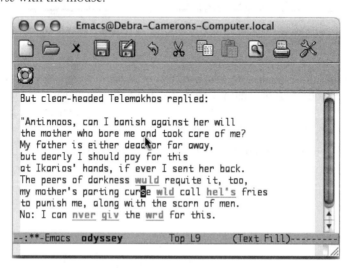

Emacs inserts the correct replacement (Mac OS X).

Ispell inserts new words in the dictionary. Flyspell takes it a step further, creating word abbreviations for words that you misspell. In essence, a word abbreviation tells Emacs, in this case, that *wrd* is just an abbreviation for *word*, and that therefore Emacs should replace it automatically. If you turn on word abbreviation mode, described in the next section, chronic misspellings that Flyspell encounters will be automatically corrected.

How can you tell Flyspell is using word abbreviations? When you exit a session in which you've used Flyspell, you see a prompt that says, Save abbrevs in ~/.abbrev_ defs (y or n). This automatic correction won't occur without turning on word abbreviation mode, whether in your startup or manually. Read the section on this topic in this chapter for more details.

What do you do if you encounter a word that's spelled correctly but that Flyspell doesn't recognize? You could insert it in your Ispell dictionary if it's a word you use frequently. The Save word option on the Flyspell pop-up menu handles this. For a temporary fix, the options Accept buffer and Accept session tell Flyspell to accept a word for the current buffer or for all buffers in the current Emacs session automatically. Of course, if it's a word you use frequently, you may want to insert it in the Ispell dictionary to keep Flyspell from flagging it each time.

To enter flyspell mode automatically, add this line to your *.emacs* file:

```
(setq-default flyspell-mode t)
```

Table 3-6 summarizes the Ispell and Flyspell commands.

Table 3-6. Spell-checking commands

Keystrokes	Command name	Action
M-$ *Tools → Spell Checking →* *Spell-Check Word*	**ispell-word**	Check the word the cursor is on or the word following the cursor.
(none) *Tools → Spell Checking →* *Spell-Check Region*	**ispell-region**	Check spelling of the region.
(none) *Tools → Spell Checking →* *Spell-Check Buffer*	**ispell-buffer**	Check spelling of the buffer.
(none) *Tools → Spell Checking →* *Spell-Check Message*	**ispell-message**	Check spelling of the body of a mail message.
(none) *Tools → Spell Checking →* *Spell-Check Comments*	**ispell-comments-and-strings**	Check spelling of comments and strings in a program.
C-u M-$ *Tools → Spell Checking →* *Continue Spell-Checking*	**ispell-continue**	Resume Ispell; it works only if stopped Ispell with **C-g**.

Table 3-6. Spell-checking commands (continued)

Keystrokes	Command name	Action
(none)	ispell-kill-ispell	Kill the Ispell process, which continues to run in the background after it is invoked.
M-Tab *Tools → Spell Checking →* *Complete Word*	ispell-complete-word	In text mode, list possible completions for the current word.
(none) *Tools → Spell Checking →* *Automatic Spell-Checking (Flyspell)*	flyspell-mode	Enter the Flyspell minor mode, in which incorrectly spelled words are highlighted.
(none)	flyspell-buffer	Spell-check the current buffer, underlining all mis-spelled words. Use middle mouse button to correct.

Word Abbreviations

Word abbreviation mode and dynamic abbreviations are two features that lazy typists will love. The authors proudly include themselves in that category, so you'll be in good company if you choose to explore these features. Dynamic abbreviations are less complex, so we'll discuss them first.

Dynamic Abbreviations

Let's say that you are a scientist writing a paper on invertebrates. You're likely to have many long technical words in your paper, and if you're like us, you get tired of typing long words.

Dynamic abbreviations come to the rescue. After you've typed a long word once, you can simply type a few letters and give the command **M-/** (for **dabbrev-expand**). Emacs inserts the nearest word that starts with that string.

Type: **In M-/**

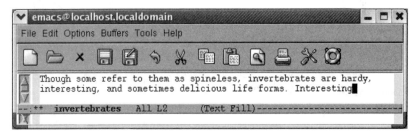

Emacs inserts the last word starting with *in*, in this case, *interesting*.

Interesting was not the word we were hoping for; it's *invertebrates* we wanted. Without moving the cursor, type **M-/** again.

Type: **M-/**

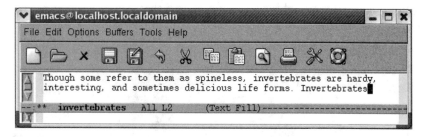

Emacs inserts the word *Invertebrates*, which is what we wanted.

The word being expanded need not be earlier in the file to be considered nearest. Emacs looks behind and ahead of the cursor position to find words it can expand. If there are eligible words that are equidistant above and below the cursor position both, Emacs selects the word that is above as the expansion.

Earlier we talked about completing a word with Ispell. Dynamic abbreviations are a bit different. When you complete a word, the word probably isn't in the buffer (yet). When you use a dynamic abbreviation, you simply don't want to type a word you typed earlier and you're asking Emacs to do it for you.

Using dynamic abbreviations doesn't require entering a special minor mode, as standard word abbreviations do. They are simply an aid for the tired typist. Word abbreviation mode has some other advantages, though, such as the ability to create an abbreviation for a phrase or a habitual typo, as we will see next.

Word Abbreviation Mode

Word abbreviation mode lets you define abbreviations for special words and phrases. You can use it in many ways. Traditionally, abbreviation mode is used so that you don't have to type long words or phrases in their entirety. For example, let's say you are writing a contract that repeatedly references the National Institute of Standards and Technology, and you are not allowed to use an acronym. Rather than typing the full name, you can define the abbreviation *nist*. Once you have set up this definition, Emacs inserts the full name whenever you type the abbreviation *nist*, followed by a space, tab, or punctuation mark. Emacs watches for you to type an abbreviation, then expands it automatically for you.

Before showing you how to get into word abbreviation mode and define your abbreviation list, we'll start with an example. Our favorite nontraditional use for word abbreviation mode is to correct misspellings as you type.* Almost everyone has a dozen or so words that they habitually type incorrectly because of worn neural pathways. You can simply tell Emacs that these misspellings are "abbreviations" for the correct versions, and Emacs fixes the misspellings every time you type them; you may not even notice that you typed the word wrong before Emacs fixes it. So assume that you've entered word abbreviation mode, and that you've defined *receive* as an abbreviation for *recieve*; now, as you're typing, you make an innocent mistake.

Type: **You will recieve**

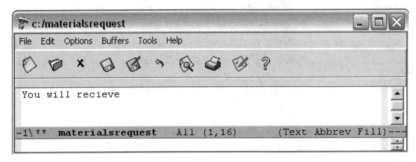

You type the offending word but haven't yet pressed **Space**, which will cue Emacs to correct it (Windows).

Type: **Space the materials you requested shortly**

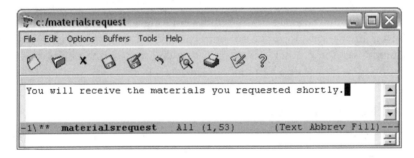

Emacs corrects the word automatically after you press **Space**; you need not stop typing or even be aware that a mistake has been made and corrected (Windows).

Besides the convenience of being able to invent abbreviations for phrases that you frequently type, you can see that setting up a short list of abbreviations for common misspellings could reduce the time it takes to proofread files and reduce the number of common typing errors.

---

* Once upon a time this use of word abbreviation mode was nontraditional; these days Flyspell, described earlier, automatically defines misspellings as abbreviations.

When you define abbreviations, never use abbreviations that are words in their own right or Emacs may expand the word when you don't want it to, because expansion takes place without asking. For example, if you frequently write about the World Association for Replicant Technology, don't define an abbreviation of *wart*, or you won't be able to write about the difficulties of handling toads. (If you use the word *wart* so infrequently that you think the convenience of the acronym warrants it, you can use **C-_** to undo the abbreviation when you really want to type *wart*.)

Emacs knows the abbreviations exactly as you define them. If you define *recieve* as an abbreviation for *receive*, you must also define *recieves*, *recieving*, and *recieved* as abbreviations to cover all the forms of the word you might misspell.

Before you go ahead and define some abbreviations, here's one more basic fact you should know. Emacs classifies abbreviations according to which modes they work in. Global abbreviations work in all modes; local abbreviations work only in the mode in which they were defined. For example, if you want abbreviations to work only in text mode and not in C mode, define them as *local* while you are in text mode. If you want abbreviations to work in any mode, define them as *global*. Remember: abbreviations are local to modes, not to files or buffers.

Emacs also provides an inverse method for defining abbreviations. This method is called *inverse* because you type the abbreviation and then the definition. Some commands (which we won't discuss) let you type the definition and then the abbreviation, but they require some tricky key sequences to let Emacs know how many words preceding the cursor are part of the abbreviation. The inverse method is easier and it works whether the definition for the abbreviation is one word or ten words.

Trying word abbreviations for one session

Usually, if you go to the trouble of defining a word abbreviation, you will use it in more than one Emacs session. But if you'd like to try out abbreviation mode to see if you want to incorporate it into your startup, use the following procedure.

To define word abbreviations for this buffer and session:

1. Enter word abbreviation mode by typing **M-x abbrev-mode Enter**. Abbrev appears on the mode line. For a global abbreviation, type the abbreviation you want to use and type **C-x a i g** or **C-x a -** (for **add-inverse-global**). (For a local abbreviation, type **C-x a i l** for **add-inverse-local** instead.) Emacs then asks you for the expansion.

2. Type the definition for the abbreviation and press **Enter**. Emacs then expands the abbreviation and will do so each time you type it followed by a space or punctuation mark.

3. When you exit Emacs. it asks if you want to save the abbreviations in *.abbrev_ defs*. Type **y** if you want to save them.

4. The abbreviations you've defined will work only in buffers where you enter abbrev mode.

If you find that you like using word abbreviation mode, you may want to make it part of your startup, as described in the following section.

Making word abbreviations part of your startup

Once you become hooked on using abbreviation mode, it's easiest to incorporate it into your *.emacs* file. This procedure creates a permanent file of your word abbreviations that is loaded every time you start Emacs. You can also delete abbreviations from this file; we'll discuss how to do so in the next section.

To define word abbreviations and make them part of your startup:

1. Add these lines to your *.emacs* file:

   ```
   (setq-default abbrev-mode t)
   (read-abbrev-file "~/.abbrev_defs")
   (setq save-abbrevs t)
   ```

2. Save the *.emacs* file and reenter Emacs. Abbrev appears on the mode line. You may get an error message saying Emacs can't load your abbrev file (understandable if you haven't created the file yet). Ignore this error message; it won't happen again.

3. Type an abbreviation and type **C-x a i g** or **C-x a -** following the abbreviation. These commands create a global abbreviation; if you want to create a local abbreviation instead, type **C-x a i l**. Emacs asks you for the expansion.

4. Type the definition for the abbreviation and press **Enter**. Emacs expands the abbreviation and will do so each time you type it followed by a space or punctuation mark. You can define as many abbreviations as you want to by repeating Steps 3 and 4.

5. Type **C-x C-c** to exit Emacs. Emacs asks if you want to save the abbreviations in *.abbrev_defs*.

6. Type **y** to save your abbreviations.

After you define some abbreviations and save them, Emacs loads the abbreviations file automatically. When you define word abbreviations in subsequent sessions, Emacs asks again whether you want to save the abbreviations file. Respond with a **y** to save the new abbreviations you've defined and have them take effect automatically.

Deleting a word abbreviation

If you use word abbreviations frequently, you may define an abbreviation and later change your mind. You can edit the word abbreviation list by typing **M-x edit-abbrevs Enter**. You can see (but not edit) the list by typing **M-x list-abbrevs Enter**.

After the list is displayed, use **C-k** (or any other editing commands) to delete the abbreviations you don't want to use. Because Emacs itself formats this list, don't try to edit lines or add new lines; deleting is about the only operation that's safe. Here's how the abbreviations look when you edit word abbreviations. The file is divided into different sections based on whether the abbreviations are global or local to a particular mode:

```
(text-mode-abbrev-table)

(lisp-mode-abbrev-table)

(fundamental-mode-abbrev-table)

(global-abbrev-table)

"iwthout"1      "without"
"prhase" 1      "phrase"
"teh"    1      "the"
"fo"     1      "of"
"eamcs"  2      "Emacs"
"wrok"   1      "work"
"aslo"   1      "also"
"sotred" 1      "stored"
"inforamtion"1"information"
"esc"    6      "Esc"
"taht"   1      "that"
"chatper"1      "chapter"
"adn"    1      "and"
"iwth"   1      "with"
"chpater"1      "chapter"
"loaction"1"location"
"recieve"1      "receive"
"wart"   1      "World Association for Replicant Technology"
```

The file is divided into sections by mode. We defined global abbreviations in this case; any abbreviations Flyspell (described earlier in this chapter) creates are local abbreviations and would be listed under the mode in which they were defined.

In this buffer, the first column lists the abbreviations (in this case, mostly misspellings). The second column is for internal record keeping; you don't need to concern yourself with it. The third column provides the definitions of the abbreviations, the word or phrase that Emacs substitutes whenever it sees the abbreviation.

To delete any abbreviation, delete the line for that abbreviation and save the file by typing **M-x write-abbrev-file**. You can move back to the buffer you were editing before by typing **C-x b** (a command for working with multiple buffers, discussed in Chapter 4).

Disabling word abbreviations

You can get rid of word abbreviations completely in one of two ways. First, you can type **M-x kill-all-abbrevs Enter**. This command disables word abbreviations for the current session.

Second, you can delete the file the abbreviations are in. If you made word abbreviations part of your startup, delete the **read-abbrev-file** line from your *.emacs* file.

Abbreviations and capitalization

Usually, Emacs capitalizes abbreviations exactly the way you want. If you run into special situations with abbreviations and capitalization, however, you may wantl to know what's going on behind the scenes. Here are the rules:

- If the abbreviation's definition contains any uppercase letters, Emacs always inserts the definition without changing anything. For example, if you define *ora* as an abbreviation for *O'Reilly Media*, *O'Reilly* will always be capitalized exactly as shown.
- If the abbreviation's definition is all lowercase, Emacs capitalizes according to the following rules:
  - If you type all of the letters of the abbreviation in lowercase, Emacs inserts the definition in lowercase.
  - If you type any of the letters of the abbreviation in uppercase, Emacs capitalizes the first letter of the first word.
  - If you type all of the letters of the abbreviation in uppercase, Emacs capitalizes the first letter of every word, unless the variable **abbrev-all-caps** is set to **t**; in this case, it capitalizes all letters.

Table 3-7 shows some examples.

Table 3-7. Word abbreviation capitalization

Abbreviation	Definition	You type:	Expands to:	Because:
lc	lamb chop	lc	lamb chop	*lc* is lowercase, so *lamb chop* is lowercase.
lc	lamb chop	Lc	Lamb chop	There's one capital in *Lc*, so *Lamb* is capitalized.
lc	lamb chop	lC	Lamb chop	There's one capital in *lC*, so *Lamb* is capitalized.
lc	lamb chop	LC	Lamb Chop	*LC* is all capitals, so both words are capitalized.
lc	Lamb Chop	lc	Lamb Chop	Capitals in the definition are always unchanged.
lc	Lamb Chop	LC	Lamb Chop	Capitals in the definition are always unchanged.

You don't need to remember the rules, but looking them over may help you out if you can't understand how Emacs is capitalizing. In our experience, defining abbreviations in lowercase circumvents most capitalization problems.

Table 3-8 summarizes word abbreviation commands.

Table 3-8. Word abbreviation commands

Keystrokes	Command name	Action
M-/	dabbrev-expand	Complete this word based on the nearest word that starts with this string (press M-/ again if that's not the word you want).
(none)	abbrev-mode	Enter (or exit) word abbreviation mode.
C-x a - or C-x a i g	inverse-add-global-abbrev	After typing the global abbreviation, type the definition.
C-x a i l	inverse-add-mode-abbrev	After typing the local abbreviation, type the definition.
(none)	unexpand-abbrev	Undo the last word abbreviation.
(none)	write-abbrev-file	Write the word abbreviation file.
(none)	edit-abbrevs	Edit the word abbreviations.
(none)	list-abbrevs	View the word abbreviations.
(none)	kill-all-abbrevs	Kill abbreviations for this session.

Problems You May Encounter

- **You search for a string you can see on the screen, and Emacs can't find it.** The most probable explanation is that Emacs is taking into account line breaks and punctuation, and you're not including these in the search string. Use word search, which ignores any line breaks or punctuation, to find the string.

- **You get a message that says,** Searching for program: No such file or directory ispell. You don't have Ispell installed. Ispell is external to Emacs; see Chapter 13 for details on installing Ispell on Mac OS X and Windows.

- **You can't see the pop-up menu in Flyspell.** You activate this pop-up menu by pointing the mouse at a given word and pressing the middle mouse button. Essentially, you need a three-button mouse to run Flyspell.

CHAPTER 4

Using Buffers, Windows, and Frames

One of the most universally useful features of Emacs is the ability to edit multiple buffers at once and to display more than one buffer using windows and frames. The commands for doing this are simple; you learn only a few commands and yet experience a tremendous boost in productivity. The more you use multiple buffers, frames, and windows, the more uses you'll think of for them.

In this chapter, we discuss how to use buffers, windows, and frames. First we cover the most commonly used commands, then, in the case of buffers and windows, move on to some more esoteric commands. At the end of the chapter, we discuss bookmarks, a method for marking your place in a file.

Understanding Buffers, Windows, and Frames

Conceptually, Emacs is different from most applications in two important ways. First, its window terminology is different. Second, Emacs buffers are not tied to windows or frames, unlike most applications.

Windows Versus Frames

Let's get our terms straight first. GUI windows are not Emacs windows. Emacs calls GUI windows *frames*. In part, this terminology is necessary because Emacs predates GUIs and is still often used on terminals without GUI windows. Emacs windows are split screens. We've seen them already; for example, when you ask for keyboard help, you see it displayed in a *Help* buffer at the bottom of your screen. Figures 4-1 and 4-2 show Emacs frames and Emacs windows. In Figure 4-1, we see our dickens and odyssey buffers in two separate frames. Figure 4-2 shows a single frame displaying two Emacs windows, one on top of the other, showing these two files.

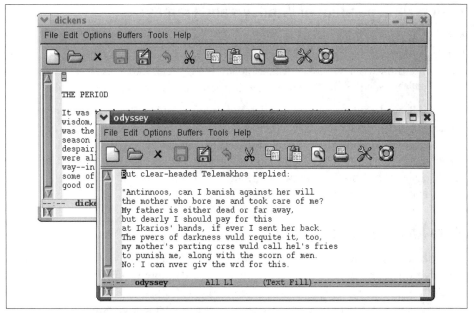

Figure 4-1. Editing dickens and odyssey in Emacs frames

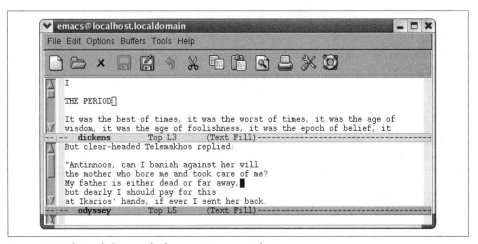

Figure 4-2. Editing dickens and odyssey in Emacs windows

From now on, when we say frame, we mean a separate GUI window. When we say window, we mean a portion of the current Emacs display. And from a practical standpoint, we emphasize that this is not an either-or proposition. Even if you prefer multiple frames, you will still use Emacs-style windows sometimes. Emacs itself will see to that.

Buffers: Independent of Windows and Frames

Now what about buffers? Essentially, both windows and frames are ways to display a buffer, which, as defined in Chapter 1, may contain a copy of a file or not. Buffers may contain files. They may be Emacs-generated buffers, like *Messages*, *scratch*, or *Help*. Or they may be buffers that you create but haven't written to a file.

Most GUI applications tie certain files to certain GUI windows or, in Emacspeak, frames. Emacs's detachment of buffers from their display (whether a split display or a separate frame) is more powerful and flexible. To be honest, most of the time we prefer using a single Emacs frame and switching between buffers using **C-x b**. It's much easier than mousing between frames or dealing with a split screen, though each has its advantages in some situations.

More About Buffers

How do you know how many buffers are active in Emacs and what they are? There are three ways: the buffer list (which appears in a window when you type **C-x C-b**), the Buffers menu (which lists active buffers and commands for navigating them), and the Buffer pop-up menu (accessed by holding down **Ctrl** and clicking the left mouse button, which lists buffers by mode).

Emacs creates its own specialized buffers. The names for these internal buffers generally have the format *buffer name*. *Help*, *scratch*, and *Buffer List* are just a few of the buffers that Emacs creates.

When you start Emacs, it generates two buffers:

```
*Messages*
*scratch*
```

Messages is a buffer where Emacs accumulates messages from its startup and from the minibuffer. *scratch* is just what it sounds like: a temporary scratchpad where you can type. It won't be saved unless you explicitly write it to a file using **C-x C-w**.

Of course, typically you edit files with Emacs. These files are then copied into buffers of the same name. If you ask for help, you'll also have a *Help* buffer.

The number of buffers you can have really has no limit. Most of the time, only one or two buffers are displayed, but even if you can't see them, all the buffers you create in an Emacs session are still active. You can think of them as a stack of pages, with the one being displayed as the top page. At any time, you can turn to another page (another buffer), or you can create a new page.

Each buffer has an associated major mode that determines much about how Emacs behaves in that buffer. For example, text mode, designed for writing text, behaves differently from Lisp mode, which is designed for writing Lisp programs.

You can display multiple buffers in separate windows or frames or both. The important thing to remember is that all the buffers you create are active even if they are not currently displayed.

Working with Multiple Buffers

If you want to create a buffer that contains a file, simply type **C-x C-f** to find the file. Emacs automatically creates a second buffer and moves you there. If you already have a copy of the file in a buffer, **C-x C-f** just moves you to the existing buffer. This move is sensible and probably really what you want anyhow; if **C-x C-f** read the file from disk every time, you could end up with many versions of the same file that were each slightly different. If the filename you give **C-x C-f** doesn't exist, Emacs assumes you want to create a new file by that name and moves you to a blank buffer.

Switching Buffers

C-x C-f is always followed by a filename. The command for moving between buffers, **C-x b**, is followed by a buffer name. Did you realize that the mode line doesn't display filenames but only buffer names? Some versions of Emacs show both, but GNU Emacs shows only the buffer name. The buffer name and the filename, if any, are the same unless you change them (see the section "Renaming Buffers," later in this chapter).

To move between the buffers, type **C-x b**. Emacs shows you a default buffer name. Press **Enter** if that's the buffer you want, or type the first few characters of the correct buffer name and press **Tab**. Emacs fills in the rest of the name. Now press **Enter** to move to the buffer.

You can do the following with **C-x b**:

If you type C-x b followed by:	Emacs:
A new buffer name	Creates a new buffer that isn't connected with a file and moves there.
The name of an existing buffer	Moves you to the buffer (it doesn't matter whether the buffer is connected with a file or not).

If you want to create a second (or third or fourth, etc.) empty buffer, type **C-x b**. Emacs asks for a buffer name. You can use any name, for example, **practice**, and press **Enter**. Emacs creates the buffer and moves you there. For example, assume you've been working on your tried-and-true dickens buffer. But you'd like something new, so you start a new buffer to play with some prose from James Joyce.

Type: **C-x b joyce**

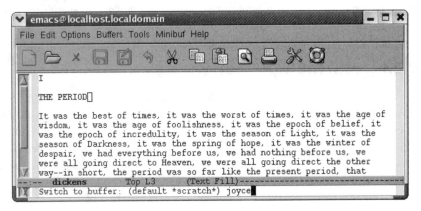

You typed a new buffer name.

Type: **Enter**

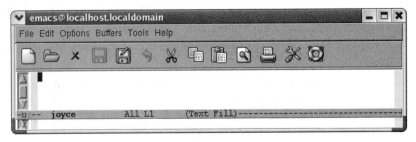

Now you have a new buffer named joyce to type in.

This procedure isn't all that different from using **C-x C-f**; about the only difference is that the new buffer, joyce, isn't yet associated with a file. Therefore, if you quit Emacs, the editor won't ask you whether or not you want to save it.

C-x b is especially useful if you don't know the name of the file you are working with. Assume you're working with some obscure file with an unusual name such as *.saves-5175-pcp832913pcs.nrockv01.ky.roadrunner.com*. Now assume that you accidentally do something that makes this buffer disappear from your screen. How do you get *.saves-5175-pcp832913pcs.nrockv01.ky.roadrunner.com* back onto the screen? Do you need to remember the entire name or even a part of it? No. Before doing anything else, just type **C-x b**. The default buffer is the buffer that most recently disappeared; type **Enter** and you'll see it again.

Alternatively, the Buffer Menu popup lists buffers by major mode, and you can choose one. Hold down **Ctrl** and click the left mouse button to see a pop-up menu of your current buffers. (The Buffers menu at the top of the screen also shows all current buffers.)

Hold down **Ctrl** and click the left mouse button.

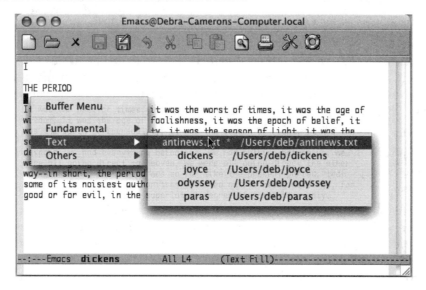

Emacs displays a pop-up menu of current buffers by mode (Mac OS X).

To cycle through all the buffers you have, type **C-x** → to go to the next buffer (in the buffer list) or **C-x** ← to go to the previous buffer. (Don't hold down Ctrl while you press the arrow key or Emacs beeps unhappily.)

Deleting Buffers

It's easy to create buffers, and just as easy to delete them when you want to. You may want to delete buffers if you feel your Emacs session is getting cluttered with too many buffers. Perhaps you started out working on a set of five buffers and now want to do something with another five. Getting rid of the first set of buffers makes it a bit easier to keep things straight. Deleting a buffer can also be a useful emergency escape. For example, some replacement operation may have had disastrous results. You can kill the buffer and choose not to save the changes, then read the file again.

Deleting a buffer doesn't delete the underlying file nor is it the same as not displaying a buffer. Buffers that are not displayed are still active whereas deleted buffers are no longer part of your Emacs session. Using the analogy of a stack of pages, deleting a buffer is like taking a page out of the current stack of buffers you are editing and filing it away.

Deleting buffers doesn't put you at risk of losing changes, either. If you've changed the buffer (and the buffer is associated with a file), Emacs asks if you want to save your changes before the buffer is deleted. You will lose changes to any buffers that aren't connected to files, but you probably don't care about these buffers.

Deleting a buffer is such a basic operation that it is on the Emacs toolbar, the X symbol. Now let's learn how to do it from the keyboard to increase your fluency in Emacs.

To delete a buffer, type **C-x k** (for **kill-buffer**). Emacs shows the name of the buffer currently displayed; press **Enter** to delete it or type another buffer name if the one being displayed is not the one you want to delete, then press **Enter**. If you've made changes that you haven't yet saved, Emacs displays the following message:

        Buffer *buffer name* modified. Kill anyway? (yes or no).

To ditch your changes, type **yes**, and Emacs kills the buffer. To stop the buffer deletion process, type **no**. You can then type **C-x C-s** to save the buffer, followed by **C-x k** to kill it.

You can also have Emacs ask you about deleting each buffer, and you can decide whether to kill each one individually. Type **M-x kill-some-buffers** to weed out unneeded buffers this way. Emacs displays the name of each buffer and whether or not it was modified, then asks whether you want to kill it. Emacs offers to kill each and every buffer, including the buffers it creates automatically, like *scratch* and *Messages*. If you kill all the buffers in your session, Emacs creates a new *scratch* buffer; after all, something has to display on the screen!

Working with Windows

Windows are areas on the screen in which Emacs displays the buffers that you are editing. You can have multiple windows on the screen at one time, each displaying a different buffer or different parts of the same buffer. Granted, the more windows you have, the smaller each one is; unlike GUI windows, Emacs windows can't overlap, so as you add more windows, the older ones shrink. The screen is like a pie; you can cut it into many pieces, but the more pieces you cut, the smaller they have to be. You can place windows side-by-side, one on top of the other, or mix them. Each window has its own mode line that identifies the buffer name, the modes you're running, and your position in the buffer. To make it clear where one window begins and another ends, mode lines are usually shaded.

As we've said, windows are not buffers. In fact, you can have more than one window on the same buffer. Doing so is often helpful if you want to look at different parts of a large file simultaneously. You can even have the same part of the buffer displayed in two windows, and any change you make in one window is reflected in the other.

The difference between buffers and windows becomes important when you think about marking, cutting, and pasting text. Marks are associated with buffers, not with windows, and each buffer can have only one mark. If you go to another window on the same buffer and set the mark, Emacs moves the mark to the new location, forgetting the place you set it last.

As for cursors, you have only one cursor, and the cursor's location determines the active window. However, although there is only one cursor at a time, each window does keep track of your current editing location separately—that is, you can move the cursor from one window to another, do some editing, jump back to the first window, and be in the same place. A window's notion of your current position (whether or not the cursor is in the window) is called the *point*. Each window has its own point. It's easy to use the terms *point* and *cursor* interchangeably—but we'll try to be specific.

You can create horizontal windows or vertical windows or both, but personally we place vertical windows with the more advanced esoterica near the end of the chapter. Here we'll discuss creating horizontal windows, finding a file in a new window, and deleting windows.

Creating Horizontal Windows

The most commonly used window command is **C-x 2** (for **split-window-vertically**). This command splits the current window into two, horizontally oriented windows. You can repeat this command to split the screen into more horizontal windows.

Initial state:

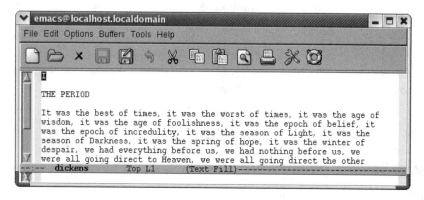

Editing our trusty dickens buffer.

Type: **C-x 2**

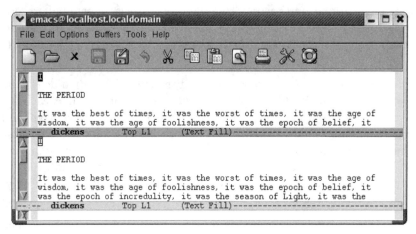

The screen is divided into two horizontal windows; the mode line demarcates each window.

You can also have Emacs set up windows for you when you start a session. If you want to edit two files in horizontal windows, specify their filenames when you start Emacs at a command prompt. For example, if you wanted to edit *dickens* and *joyce*, you would type **emacs dickens joyce** and Emacs would display these files in two horizontal windows. If you try this with more than two files, Emacs displays two horizontal windows, with a file in one and a list of buffers in the other.

A number of the "other window" commands are just the ordinary command with a *4* inserted in it. For example, to find a file in another window, type **C-x 4 f**. (If only one window is currently open, Emacs opens another one.) To select a different buffer in another window, type **C-x 4 b**. Many users find these commands preferable to the normal **C-x C-f** and **C-x b** commands because they save you a step: you need not move to the window, give a command, and move back.

Once you've got multiple windows open, it's helpful to be able to scroll them without moving there. To scroll the other window, type **C-M-v**.

Moving Between Windows

To move from one window to another, type **C-x o** (**o** stands for *other* in this command). If you have more than two windows displayed, Emacs moves from one to the next. There's no way to specify which window to move to, so you may have to type **C-x o** a few times to get to the one you want if you have more than two windows displayed. (You can also click your mouse in a window if you're using the GUI version.)

Now that you can create windows and can move between them, what else can you do? Practically anything. With our two windows on *dickens* open, one on top of the other. Initially, both of these windows are looking at the same file.

Type: **C-x 2**

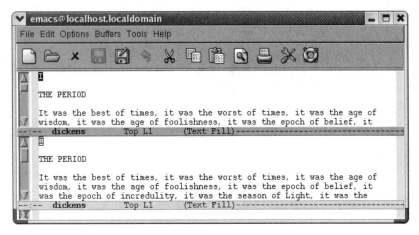

Two windows open on dickens.

We can give any editing commands we want within either window. We can move back and forth in one window without affecting the other. Let's see what happens if we want to edit another file.

Type: **C-x C-f blake**

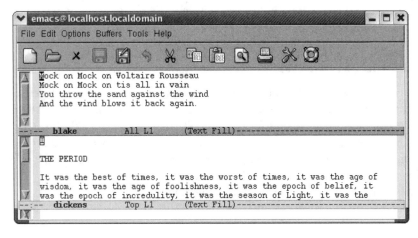

Now you have two windows, two buffers, and two files.

By using **C-x o**, we can edit one file and then the other. We can kill text from one buffer and yank it back in another. For example, let's move the first line of Blake's poem to the top of the dickens buffer.

Type: **C-k C-k C-x o M-< C-y Enter**

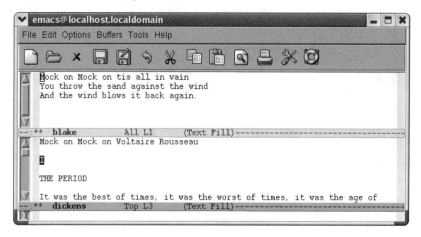

The Blake text has been yanked into the dickens buffer.

Editing with multiple buffers in separate windows is particularly useful if, for example, you want to copy material from one file to another or if you want to read a file containing reference material while editing another. Programmers often need to look at several different files at the same time—for example, a header file and a code file, or a function call site and the routine that's being called. Once you get used to the commands for moving between different windows, you may spend most of your time with two or three windows on your screen.

Getting Rid of Windows

Deleting a window only means that it isn't displayed anymore; it doesn't delete any of the information or any of your unsaved changes. The underlying buffer is still there, and you can switch to it using **C-x b**. To delete the window you're in, type **C-x 0** (zero). If you want to delete all windows but the one you're working on, type **C-x 1** (one), meaning "make this my one and only window." As you'd expect, the remaining window "grows" to fill up the rest of the space. You can also delete all windows on a certain buffer by typing: **M-x delete-windows-on Enter** *buffername* **Enter**.

Working with Frames

By now you know that Emacs calls GUI windows "frames." In this section, we'll cover how to create frames, navigate between frames, and delete frames.

Creating a New Frame

To open a new frame, type **C-x 5 2** (for **make-frame**). Emacs makes a new frame containing the current buffer and puts it on top of the current frame.

If your new frame completely overlaps your current frame, you may need to size the new frame to tell them apart. For a more convenient solution, add these lines to your *.emacs* file:

```
(setq initial-frame-alist '((top . 10) (left . 30)
                            (width . 90) (height . 50)))
(setq default-frame-alist '((width . 80) (height . 45)))
```

These lines set up sizes for the width and height of Emacs frames. The first frame is the size set in **initial-frame-alist** (in this example, 90 characters wide by 50 lines high with top and left defining an inset), and subsequent frames, specified by **default-frame-alist**, will be 80 characters wide and 45 lines high. Depending on your display, you can make these numbers smaller or larger.

Here we edit a bit of Henry James.

Type: **C-x 5 2**

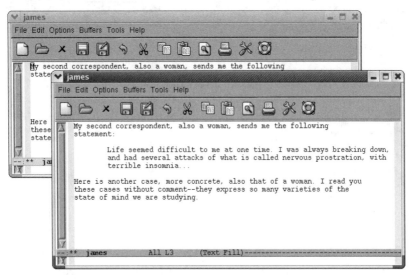

Emacs opens a new frame titled james

Frame Names

Note the title of your new frame. The first frame in your session, your initial Emacs frame, displays Emacs@*system name* at the top (or Emacs's best guess at the system name). Any other frames you create display the buffer name at the top. In fact, once you have multiple frames, *all frames* display the buffer name as their title. If you delete all frames but one, the title once again reverts to Emacs@*system name*.

Let's say we want to open a frame on our dickens buffer.

Type: **C-x 5 f dickens Enter**

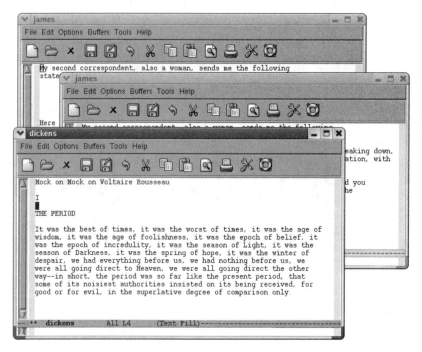

Emacs opens a new frame on dickens.

If you type **C-x b** to move to another buffer, the name at the top of the frame changes to the new buffer's name (and on Linux, it shows the path as well). To move to a buffer and put it in a new frame, type **C-x 5 b**. You might have guessed that one.

Moving Between Frames

You can move between frames in several ways. You can use the mouse to select a frame or press **C-x 5 o** to go to another frame. To see a list of current frames, select **Frames** from the **Buffers** menu. (If you have only one frame, the **Frames** option does not appear on this menu.)

Deleting and Minimizing Frames

To get rid of a frame, press **C-x 5 0**. Emacs deletes the frame you are in. Deleting a frame, like deleting a window, affects only the display. The underlying buffer is still active, and you can move to it by typing **C-x b**.

If you try to use **C-x 5 0** to delete the only frame that is left, Emacs won't do it. To exit Emacs, type **C-x C-c** or close the frame as you would any other GUI window using the mouse.

To minimize a frame, either minimize it in the usual way or press **C-z**. Table 4-1 summarizes the frame commands.

Table 4-1. Frame commands

Keystrokes	Command name	Action
C-x 5 o *Buffers → Frames*	other-frame	Move to other frame.
C-x 5 0 *File → Delete Frame*	delete-frame	Delete current frame.
C-x 5 2 *File → New Frame*	make-frame	Create a new frame on the current buffer.
C-x 5 f	find-file-other-frame	Find file in a new frame.
C-x 5 r	find-file-read-only-other-frame	Finds a file in a new frame, but it is read-only.
C-x 5 b	switch-to-buffer-other-frame	Make frame and display other buffer in it.

More About Buffers

In this section, we'll learn about saving multiple buffers, renaming buffers, read-only buffers, and operations you can do with the buffer list—not only a useful tool but a good introduction to the principles you'll encounter in the directory editor, Dired, covered in Chapter 5.

Saving Multiple Buffers

You know about saving buffers individually by typing **C-x C-s**. Once you're using multiple buffers, you should also know that you can save them all at once by typing **C-x s** (for **save-some-buffers**). Emacs asks you if you want to save each buffer that is connected with a file (it doesn't offer to save new buffers you've created but have not associated with a file and, of course, it doesn't save its own internal buffers). For each buffer, you can answer **y** to save it or **n** not to. You can also type **!** to save all the buffers without asking. If you want to save this buffer and no more, type a period (.). If you want to cancel the command and not save the current buffer, press **q** (of course, any buffers you saved before pressing **q** are already saved; **q** does not undo those). You may want to look at the buffer before deciding whether to save it; if so, type **C-r**. Emacs enters view mode, allowing you to look at the buffer but not make changes. Press **q** to exit view mode and continue saving buffers.

Renaming Buffers

When you are editing a file, the buffer takes on the name of the file. If you have long filenames, you may find it convenient to rename buffers to shorter names (this renaming doesn't affect the filename, just the buffer name). This feature is mostly useful on versions of Emacs that don't offer good completion capabilities; in GNU Emacs, whenever you have to type a buffer name, you just type the first few unique letters and press **Tab** to have Emacs complete the name for you. In some circumstances, you may want to rename buffers.

To rename a buffer, type **M-x rename-buffer**. Emacs asks for the new name; type it and press **Enter**. The new name is displayed on the mode line. Renaming buffers comes in particularly handy in shell mode, described in Chapter 5. You start one command shell, and then rename the buffer and start another, in this way running as many shells as you have use for simultaneously.

As mentioned earlier, in GNU Emacs only the buffer name is displayed on the mode line, rather than the buffer name and the filename. Even if you rename a buffer that contains a file, Emacs remembers the connection between buffer and file, which you can see if you save the file (**C-x C-s**) or display the buffer list (described later in the chapter).

What if you have two buffers with the same name? Let's say you are editing a file called *outline* from your home directory and another file called *outline* from one of your subdirectories. Both buffers are called `outline`, but Emacs differentiates them by appending `<2>` to the name of the second buffer. (You can tell which is which by looking at the buffer list, discussed later in this chapter.) Emacs offers an option that adds a directory to buffers in this situation: select Use Directory in Buffer Names from the Options menu. Let's say you've turned on this option and are editing a file called *.localized*; Emacs will call this buffer simply `.localized`. Now you find a second file of the same name from a subdirectory. Instead of calling this buffer `.localized<2>`, Emacs names the buffer *directory/*`.localized`, making it easy for you to tell the buffers apart at a glance. This option has some limitations. It shows only the parent directory, not the full path, and it shows directory names only if multiple buffers have the same name.

We wish it would go a bit further and provide the option of including the directory on the mode line for all buffers.

One word of advice: if you have a lot of buffers with names like proposal, proposal <2>, and proposal<3> around, you're probably forgetting to edit the directory when you ask for a file. If you try to find a file but get the directory wrong, Emacs assumes you want to start a new file. For example, let's say you want to edit the file ~/work/proposal, but instead ask for the file ~/novel/proposal. Since ~/novel/proposal doesn't exist, Emacs creates a new, empty buffer named proposal. If you correct your mistake (**C-x C-f ~/work/ proposal**), Emacs renames your buffers accordingly: your empty buffer proposal is associated with ~/novel/proposal; the buffer you want is named proposal<2>.

Here's a hint for dealing with the very common mistake of finding the wrong file. If you notice that you've found the wrong file with **C-x C-f**, use **C-x C-v** to replace it with the one you want. **C-x C-v** finds a file, but instead of making a new buffer, it replaces the file in the current buffer. It means "get me the file I really meant to find instead of this one." Using this command circumvents the problem of having unnecessary numbered buffers (i.e., proposal, proposal<2>, and so on) lying around.

Read-Only Buffers

While you're working, you may need to read some file that you don't want to change: you just want to browse through it and look at its contents. Of course, it is easy to touch the keyboard accidentally and make spurious modifications. We've discussed several ways to restore the original file, but it would be better to prevent this from happening at all. How?

You can make any buffer read-only by pressing **C-x C-q**. Try this on a practice buffer and you'll notice that two percent signs (%%) appear on the left side of the mode line, in the same place where asterisks (**) appear if you've changed a buffer. The percent signs indicate that the buffer is read-only.* If you try to type in a read-only buffer, Emacs just beeps at you and displays an error message (Buffer is read-only) in the minibuffer. What happens when you change your mind and want to start editing the read-only buffer again? Just type **C-x C-q** again. This command toggles the buffer's read-only status—that is, typing **C-x C-q** repeatedly makes the buffer alternate between read-only and read-write.

Of course, toggling read-only status doesn't change the permissions on a file. If you are editing a buffer containing someone else's file, **C-x C-q** does not change the read-only status. One way to edit someone else's file is to make a copy of your own using the **write-file** command, and then make changes. Let's say you want to

---

* The exception to the rule that ** means changed and %% means read-only is the *scratch* buffer. Because Emacs doesn't warn you if you kill the *scratch* buffer, even if it is changed, it wants to give you some indication that there are unsaved changes. Instead of %%, the *scratch* buffer puts %* on the mode line.

change a proposal that is owned by someone else. Read the file, write the file as one you own using **C-x C-w**, then change it from read-only to writable status by pressing **C-x C-q**. None of this, of course, modifies the original file; it just gives you a copy to work with. If you want to move a minor amount of text from a read-only file to another, you can mark the text then press **M-w** to copy it. Move to the place you want to put the text and press **C-y** to paste it.

You can open a file as read-only in a new window by typing **C-x 4 r** or in a new frame by typing **C-x 5 r**. This is one of a number of commands in which *4* means window and *5* means frame.

Getting a List of Buffers

Because you can create an unlimited number of buffers in an Emacs session, you can have so many buffers going that you can't remember them all. At any point, you can get a list of your buffers (yes, we know you know how to do that by holding down **Ctrl** and clicking the left mouse button, but this is a little different). This list provides you with important information—for example, whether you've changed the buffer since you last saved it.

If you press **C-x C-b**, Emacs lists your buffers. It creates a new *Buffer List* window on the screen, which shows you all the buffers.

Type: **C-x C-b**

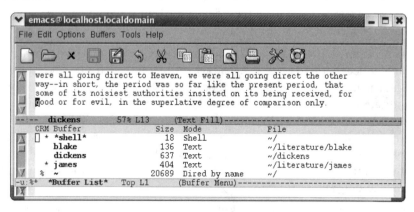

Emacs displays a list of buffers.

You can use this list as an informational display ("these are my buffers") or you can actually work with buffers from this list, as covered in the next section.

Figure 4-3 shows what each of the symbols in the buffer list means.

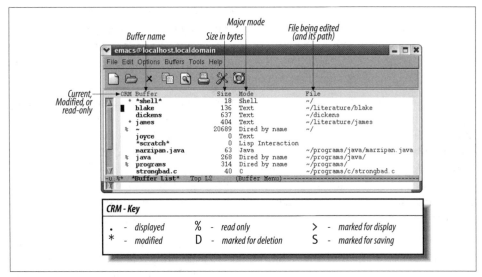

Figure 4-3. Understanding the buffer list

Working with the Buffer List

The buffer list is more than a display. From the buffer list, you can display, delete, and save buffers. To move to the buffer list window, type **C-x o**. Emacs puts the cursor in the first column. For a particular buffer, press **n** or **C-n** to move down a line or **p** or **C-p** to move up a line. You can also press **Space** to move down to the next line and **Del** to move up. (The up and down arrow keys work, too.) This array of up and down choices may seem confusing, but multiple bindings are given to make it easy to move up and down without consulting a book like this one.

You use a set of one-character commands to work with the buffers that are listed. To delete a buffer, go to the line for the buffer you want to delete and type **d** or **k**. The letter D appears in the first column. You can mark as many buffers for deletion as you want to. The buffers aren't deleted immediately; when you're finished marking buffers, press **x** (which stands for "execute") to delete them. If any of the buffers you want to delete are connected with files, Emacs asks if you want to save the changes before doing anything. (Note that it does not ask you about buffers that aren't connected with files, so be sure to save any that you want before deleting them.)

If you change your mind about deleting a buffer before typing **x**, you can unmark the buffer by going to the appropriate line and typing **u**. As a convenience, the **Del** key also unmarks the previous buffer in the list. Why would you do this? Simple: **d** automatically moves you down one line. If you mark a file for deletion and immediately change your mind, you can press a single **Del** rather than moving to the previous line and typing **u** for *unmark*).

To save a buffer, go to the line for the buffer you want to save and press **s**. The letter S appears in the first column. Press **x** when you really want to save the buffer. Therefore, you can look at the buffer list, choose which buffers you want to delete and which you want to save, and then type **x** to do everything at once. Again, you can press **u** or **Del** to cancel saves if you change your mind.

One command that affects a buffer immediately when you type it is tilde (**~**). Typing ~ marks a buffer as unmodified. In effect, this symbol tells Emacs not to save changes automatically (since the buffer is unmodified, Emacs has no reason to save changes with its auto-save feature). Of course, if you have made changes, the changes are still in the buffer; it's just that you're in essence "lying" to Emacs to say that no changes have been made. Also, if you change the buffer again after marking it unmodified, Emacs once again knows it has been modified and saves it automatically in a backup file. The backup filename (not coincidentally) has the format *filename~*.

You can change a buffer's status from read-write to read-only and back again by pressing **%**. Pressing **%** changes the buffer's status immediately. Percentage signs appear on the mode line when a buffer is read-only. When you are editing, you can toggle a buffer between read-write and read-only by pressing **C-x C-q**, as we discussed earlier.

You can also use the buffer list to display multiple buffers in windows. To display one of the buffers in a full screen, move the cursor into the buffer list's window; use **C-n** and **C-p** to move to the line for the buffer that you want, and press **1** (the number one). Emacs displays the buffer in a full-screen window.

If you want to display one of the buffers in place of the buffer list, you can press **f**. To put a buffer in another window (i.e., one not occupied by the buffer list), type **o**. Emacs displays the buffer in the other window and puts the cursor there. Pressing **C-o** has a slightly different result; Emacs displays the buffer in another window but doesn't put the cursor there.

One final buffer display command remains. You can ask Emacs to display multiple buffers and have Emacs create windows for them dynamically. To select buffers to be displayed in windows, press **m** (for *mark*) next to the buffers you want. Emacs displays a > next to the buffers you mark with **m**. To tell Emacs to display the buffers you've marked, press **v**. Emacs makes horizontal windows to display the buffers you've chosen.

To get rid of the *Buffer List* window, type **C-x 0** if you are in the buffer list window or **C-x 1** (the number one) if you are in another window. Table 4-2 shows a summary of buffer manipulation commands.

Table 4-2. Buffer manipulation commands

Keystrokes	Command name	Action
C-x b *Buffers → Select Named Buffer*	**switch-to-buffer**	Move to the buffer specified.
C-x → *Buffers → Next Buffer*	**next-buffer**	Move to the next buffer in the buffer list.
C-x ← *Buffers → Previous Buffer*	**previous-buffer**	Move to the previous buffer in the buffer list.
C-x C-b *Buffers → List All Buffers*	**list-buffers**	Display the buffer list.
C-x k	**kill-buffer**	Delete the buffer specified.
(none)	**kill-some-buffers**	Ask about deleting each buffer.
(none)	**rename-buffer**	Change the buffer's name to the name specified.
C-x s	**save-some-buffers**	Ask whether you want to save each modified buffer.

Table 4-3 summarizes the commands for working with the buffer list.

Table 4-3. Buffer list commands

Keystrokes	Action	Occurs
C-n, Space, n, or ↓	Move to the next buffer in the list (i.e., down one line).	Immediately
C-p, p, or ↑	Move to the previous buffer in the list (i.e., up one line).	Immediately
d	Mark buffer for deletion.	When you press **x**
k	Mark buffer for deletion.	When you press **x**
s	Save buffer.	When you press **x**
u	Unmark buffer.	Immediately
x	Execute other one-letter commands on all marked buffers.	Immediately
Del	Unmark the previous buffer in the list; if there is no mark, move up one line.	Immediately
~	Mark buffer as unmodified.	Immediately
%	Toggle read-only status of buffer.	Immediately
1	Display buffer in a full screen.	Immediately
2	Display this buffer and the next one in horizontal windows.	Immediately
f	Replace buffer list with this buffer.	Immediately
o	Replace other window with this buffer.	Immediately
m	Mark buffers to be displayed in windows.	When you press **v**
v	Display buffers marked with **m**; Emacs makes as many windows as needed.	Immediately
q	Quit buffer list.	Immediately

More About Windows

Depending on your requirements, you may want to work with side-by-side windows in addition to or instead of horizontal windows. For finer control, you may want to know how to size windows (and because they're not GUI windows, you can't do that with the mouse).* You may also want to know how to compare files between windows, a good feature for basic file comparison.

Creating Vertical or Side-by-Side Windows

To split the window vertically into two side-by-side windows, type **C-x 3**. You can execute this step repeatedly to create more side-by-side windows.

Type: **C-x 3**

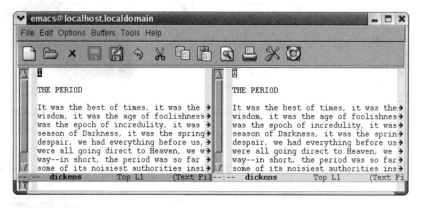

Emacs creates two vertical windows.

When you create multiple vertical windows, Emacs usually doesn't have enough room to display a full line of text. Because vertical windows don't usually show full lines of text, a right arrow (on graphical implementations) or a dollar sign (on terminal-based implementations) at the end of a line tells you the line is continued.

To see the rest of the line, you need to know how to scroll text to the left and right. To push the text currently being displayed to the left (so you can see what's on the right), type **C-x <**. Left arrows or dollar signs are displayed on the left side of the window to indicate that there is more text to the left. To push the text being displayed to the right (so you can see what's on the left), type **C-x >**. You can use these commands whenever one of your lines is too wide, which can happen with or without windows.

---

* It's true that you can't resize Emacs windows using the mouse. But if you resize an Emacs frame, it does impact the size of the windows, even eliminating windows at times if the frame cannot display all the windows. Of course, as always, eliminating a window doesn't impact the underlying buffer.

Navigating Windows

How do you move between windows? As we mentioned earlier, **C-x o** moves you to the "next" window. But how does Emacs determine what that is?

The best way to express it is to say that Emacs moves through the windows in natural reading order, from left to right, then down, and again from left to right. In Figure 4-4, buffer names are numbered to show you how Emacs moves from one window to the next.

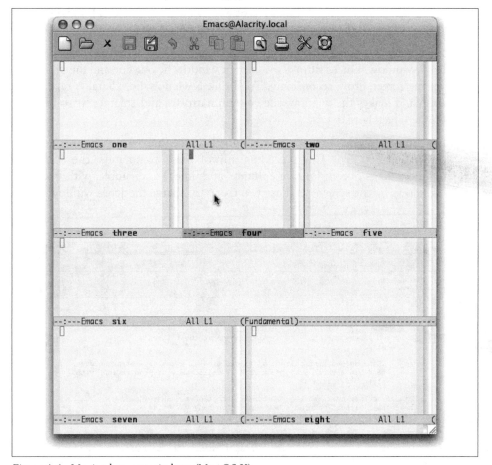

Figure 4-4. Moving between windows (Mac OS X)

Alternatively, you can simply select the window you want using the mouse.

Enlarging and Shrinking Windows

Emacs always splits windows into two equal parts. Such a split is often good enough, but sometimes it's not, particularly if you become a window aficionado. When you have four or five or six windows on your screen at once, controlling each window's size becomes important. Otherwise, the windows you are most interested in will eventually become too small, and useful editing is almost impossible when you can see only five or six lines from a file. If you want to make the window you're working on taller, type **C-x ^**. Emacs lengthens the current window and makes the one below it smaller, accordingly. To make the current window wider, type **C-x }**. Emacs makes this window wider, at the expense of the one to the right of it.

To make windows smaller, you can shrink them. To shrink a window vertically, type **M-x shrink-window**. Emacs shrinks the current window by one line and the other windows on the screen grow accordingly. To shrink a window horizontally, type **C-x {**. This command makes the window one column narrower and enlarges the other windows on the screen horizontally.

Usually you want to work in larger increments than one line or one column at a time, however. When you type **C-u** preceding any of these commands, the command works in increments of four lines or columns at a time. For example, with two horizontal windows on the screen, let's use **C-u C-x ^** to enlarge the james window.

Type: **C-u C-x ^**

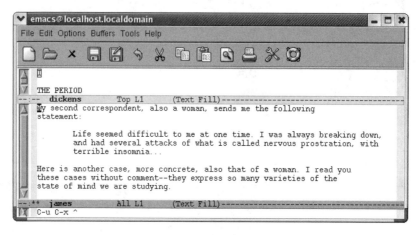

Emacs makes the current window larger.

As you would expect, when you make the window larger, it automatically fills with more text from the buffer. There are shortcuts to sizing windows as well. If you have a very small buffer—for example, a one-line buffer containing the vocabulary-building word for the day and its definition—you can shrink the window to the size of the buffer by typing **C-x -** (for **shrink-window-if-larger-than-buffer**). If the buffer is larger than the window, this command does nothing. Typing **C-x +** (for **balance-windows**) creates windows of equal size again. (This latter command is also useful if you have an odd number of windows; **C-x +** divides the display equally among them.)

Limits on Window Size

Windows in Emacs can be as big as your screen. There's a limit to how small windows can be, however, and this limit is specified by the variables **window-min-height** (whose default is four lines) and **window-min-width** (whose default is ten characters). If you enlarge other windows to the point that their counterparts become less than ten characters wide or four lines high, Emacs deletes the smaller windows. You can set these variables to other values if you want to; more information on setting variables is found in Chapter 10.

Comparing Files Between Windows

Especially if you're looking for minute differences between large files, the **compare-windows** command comes in handy. To use **compare-windows**, you must first have the buffers you want to compare in two windows, either side by side or horizontally. Go to the beginning of each buffer, then type **M-x compare-windows**. Emacs scrolls each buffer to the place where the discrepancy is. It places the point in each buffer at the place of the discrepancy, so using **C-x o** to move the cursor between buffers will show you exactly where the files differ.[*]

Of course, this maneuver finds only the first difference between the two buffers. Finding the second, third, and so on, is a bit tricky. The **compare-windows** command works only if the point in both buffers is in exactly the same place. Therefore, you need to move past the discrepancy in both buffers before you can type **M-x compare-windows** again. The Unix **diff** command provides a more comprehensive (although somewhat awkward looking) way to find the differences between two files. Emacs also provides an interface to **Ediff**, with options on the Compare menu (a submenu of the Tools menu). Ediff is far more comprehensive; see Chapter 12 for details.

Table 4-4 summarizes the window commands discussed in this chapter.

Table 4-4. Window commands

Keystrokes	Command name	Action
C-x 2 *File → Split Window*	split-window-vertically	Divide current window into two windows, one above the other.
C-x 3	split-window-horizontally	Divide current window into two side-by-side windows.

---

[*] You can have more than two windows on the screen, but only two are compared: the one the cursor is in and the next window (remember that the next window is either to the right or down if there is no window to the right).

Table 4-4. Window commands (continued)

Keystrokes	Command name	Action
C-x >	scroll-right	Scroll the window right.
C-x <	scroll-left	Scroll the window left.
C-x o	other-window	Move to the other window; if there are several, move to the next window (see "Navigating Windows").
C-x 0	delete-window	Delete the current window.
C-x 1 *File → Unsplit Windows*	delete-other-windows	Delete all windows but this one.
(none)	delete-windows-on	Delete all windows on a given buffer.
C-x ^	enlarge-window	Make window taller.
(none)	shrink-window	Make window shorter.
C-x }	enlarge-window-horizontally	Make window wider.
C-x {	shrink-window-horizontally	Make window narrower.
C-x -	shrink-window-if-larger-than-buffer	Make window smaller if buffer is smaller than window.
C-x +	balance-windows	Make windows the same size.
C-M-v	scroll-other-window	Scroll other window.
C-x 4 f	find-file-other-window	Find a file in the other window.
C-x 4 b	switch-to-buffer-other-window	Select a buffer in the other window.
(none) *Tools → Compare (Ediff) →* *This Window and Next Window*	compare-windows	Compare this window with the next window and show the first difference.

Holding Your Place with Bookmarks

Once you start working with multiple files, remembering just where you were in each one becomes harder. Bookmarks provide a convenient way of marking your place in a file, a place you can easily return to. You might, for example, be working with a file that has a long pathname. Rather than retype the pathname each time you start Emacs, you could just jump to a bookmark you've named *current project* by having Emacs find the file and put the cursor wherever you set the bookmark.

Bookmarks make the process of finding your place in any file easier. Particularly if you are working on a project several directories down from your home directory or in a totally different filesystem, putting bookmarks in the file makes it easy to get back there.

When you create a bookmark, Emacs creates a bookmark file in your home directory, called *.emacs.bmk*. It saves any new bookmarks in this file automatically when you exit Emacs.

Bookmarks are stored by user. If you and others access the same online documentation set, you can hold your place with your bookmark and they can hold their places with theirs, never interfering with each other's reading.

From the Edit menu, you can access the Bookmarks menu, which lists all the bookmark commands you'll probably ever need. We feel the menu interface for bookmarks is particularly well developed; even if you don't normally use menus, you might want to make an exception in this case. (At least until you learn the commands. Bookmarks are addictive, and when you use them frequently, the commands are easier to type than to reach by menu.)

Setting Bookmarks

To place a bookmark at the cursor position, type **C-x r m** (for **bookmark-set**). Emacs asks for a bookmark name, which can be virtually any length (practically speaking, as long as the width of your display) and can include spaces (so current project or Moore proposal's greatest flaw or Othello Act 2 Scene 4 would all be fine). Emacs also puts a default bookmark in parentheses, suggesting the filename if you haven't used a bookmark during this session (in which case it uses the bookmark name). Either press **Enter** to accept the default or type a bookmark name and then press **Enter**. You now have a bookmark you can jump to at any time, in any Emacs session.

One subtlety: if you give a new bookmark the same name as an old one, Emacs assumes you just want to move the bookmark, even if it was formerly in another file. So remember to make bookmark names unique unless you are really trying to move them.

Moving to a Bookmark

To move to a bookmark, press **C-x r b** (for **bookmark-jump**). Type the bookmark's name, or type the first few letters and press **Tab**. Emacs either finishes the bookmark's name or gives you a window of possible choices. Press **Enter** after the bookmark's name appears. Emacs retrieves the file and places the cursor at the bookmark location; the file is retrieved no matter how complicated its path is.

With menus, there's an easier way to move to a bookmark. When you select Edit → Bookmarks → Jump to Bookmark, Emacs displays a window of available bookmarks. Select the bookmark you want, and Emacs displays the file with the cursor in the bookmark's position. This is useful if you have set many bookmarks, but we prefer to stick with the keyboard as much as possible.

Renaming and Deleting Bookmarks

You may find that you made the name of your bookmark too generic; current project may be too vague if you are juggling projects and the one in your hand is the current one. To rename a bookmark, type **M-x bookmark-rename**. If you do the renaming from the keyboard, Emacs prompts Old bookmark name: and you type the old name and press **Enter**. (If you use the menus, you select the old name from a window instead.) Then Emacs asks, New name: and you type the new name and press **Enter**, all very straightforwardly. Renaming a bookmark does just that and nothing else: it doesn't change the bookmark's location or its contents; it simply changes its name.

To delete a bookmark, press **M-x bookmark-delete**. Type the name of the bookmark to delete or select it with the mouse. Deleting a bookmark doesn't in any way affect the file that was marked.

This discussion brings up an interesting question. What happens if you delete text in a file in which you've put a bookmark? Because a bookmark points to a position in a file and not to a piece of text, the bookmark stays in the same place after the text is deleted, just as the cursor remains in the same place after you delete several paragraphs. This fact is more intuitive than it sounds. You don't delete bookmarks by deleting marked text. Let's say you have a file with four lines. You bookmark the third line, then later delete lines two through four. When you jump to that bookmark again, it appears after the first line, the end of the file.

Inserting text works the same way. Bookmarks point to a position in a file, not to text. If you insert a new line before the third line, the bookmark remains at the point in the file where you set it, in this case, the beginning of the new line. If you move text around, the bookmark points to the same location in the file, the line and column where you set it.

What happens if you delete a file that has a bookmark in it? If you delete the whole file or even rename it and then try to access a bookmark attached to the file, Emacs gives you the following error message:

    filename *nonexistent. Relocate* "bookmark name"*? (y or n)*

If you press **y**, you can give a new path to the file, which works well if you really just renamed or moved the file but didn't delete it. If you press **n**, however, Emacs gives you a message, along with some advice:

    Bookmark not relocated, consider removing it

In other words, Emacs argues that no one needs bookmarks to nonexistent files, and we're inclined to agree.

Working with a List of Bookmarks

Remember the buffer list we discussed earlier in this chapter? Bookmarks have a similar list with one-letter commands that allow you to work with all your bookmarks at once.

To work with a list of bookmarks, type **C-x r l** (the lowercase letter "L"). The *Bookmark List* buffer appears.

Type: **C-x r l**

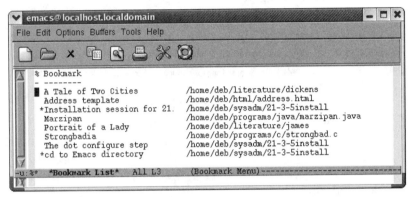

Emacs displays a list of bookmarks and the path to the associated files.

If you press **Enter**, **f**, or **j**, Emacs displays the bookmarked file with the cursor in the bookmarked location. From the bookmark list, press **d** to mark bookmarks for deletion, then **x** to delete them (unlike in the buffer list, in the bookmark list, deleting is the only reason you need the **x** command). If you change your mind, press **Del** to remove the **d** before you press **x**. Pressing **r** renames a bookmark, and Emacs prompts you for the new name. To save all the bookmarks, press **s**. You can mark several bookmarks and then display their associated files by typing **m** next to the bookmarks. A > appears beside bookmarks you've marked. When you've marked all you want, type **v** (for *view*) and Emacs pulls up the files associated with the bookmarks and displays them in multiple windows (with the cursor at the bookmarked location, of course). If you just want to move to one bookmarked file, you can press **v** without marking the bookmark first.

You can change the display of the bookmark list slightly by pressing **t**. By default, the list shows a bookmark's name, followed by the complete path to the file with which it is associated. If you press **t** (for *toggle*), only the bookmark names appear.

Table 4-5 summarizes the bookmark list commands. It includes a few commands relating to annotations; we'll cover these in the next section.

Table 4-5. Commands for editing the bookmark list

Command	Action
Enter, **f**, or **j**	Go to the bookmark on the current line.
C-o or **o**	Open the bookmark on the current line in another window; **o** moves the cursor to that window; **C-o** keeps the cursor in the current window.
d, **C-d**, or **k**	Flag bookmark for deletion.
r	Rename bookmark.
s	Save all bookmarks listed.
m	Mark bookmarks to be displayed in multiple windows.
v	Display marked bookmarks or the one the cursor is on if none are marked.
t	Toggle display of paths to files associated with bookmarks.
w	In the minibuffer, display location of file associated with bookmark.
x	Delete bookmarks flagged for deletion.
u	Remove mark from bookmark.
Del	Remove mark from bookmark on previous line or move to the previous line (if there is no mark).
q	Exit bookmark list.
Space or **n**	Move down a line.
p	Move up a line.
l	Load a bookmark file (other than the default).
A	Display all annotations.
a	Display annotation for current bookmark.
e	Edit (or create) annotation for the current bookmark.

Annotating Bookmarks

You can add annotations to your bookmarks. These annotations can provide any type of information you want: details about the file in question, what you are doing with it, documentation for someone else on your project to review when looking at your files, or really anything you want.

Annotations are most easily added from the bookmark list itself. Open the bookmark list using **C-x r l**, then move to the line of the bookmark you want to annotate. Type **e**, the command to edit an annotation.

From the bookmark list, type: **e**

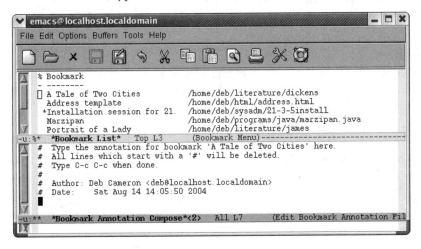

Emacs opens a *Bookmark Annotation Compose* window.

Emacs provides some guidance in this buffer about what to do. It says that all lines that start with a comment mark (#) will be deleted and that you press **C-c C-c** to save and exit the annotations buffer.

The annotation includes lines that are commented out and won't become part of the annotation, but if you'd like to keep the Author and Date lines (logical portions of an annotation), just uncomment those lines by deleting the initial #. You then add any annotation you would like and press **C-c C-c** to exit the window.

Annotations exhibit a couple of behaviors that are at least annoying if not bugs. First, Emacs defines a # as the default fill prefix. You must either change that (see Chapter 6 for details) or delete the initial # if Emacs inserts it. Second, and more critically, Emacs doesn't automatically save annotations when you exit Emacs. If you set a bookmark, Emacs saves the bookmarks file automatically (and in fact without asking). If you set an annotation but do not add or move a bookmark during the session, you must save the bookmarks file manually by typing **M-x bookmark-save**.

After you add an annotation, Emacs puts an asterisk (*) before the bookmark name as a visual indication that the bookmark has been annotated. To display an annotation for the current bookmark, press **a**. To display all annotations, press **A**.

When you jump to a bookmark or move to a bookmarked file from the bookmark list, annotations are automatically displayed in another window (but don't edit them in this window; you must use the procedure described earlier). If you open the bookmarked file some other way (using **C-x C-f**, for example), annotations are not displayed.

A Few More Bookmark Commands

In addition to those we've discussed, there are a few more esoteric bookmark commands. These include **bookmark-insert**, which inserts the text of the bookmarked file at the cursor position; **bookmark-write**, which prompts for a new filename in which to save bookmarks; and **bookmark-load**, to load these separate bookmark files. These commands are less useful than the others, but you may think of some clever uses we have not.

Table 4-6 summarizes bookmark commands.

Table 4-6. Bookmark commands

Keystrokes	Command name	Action
C-x r m *Edit → Bookmarks →* *Set Bookmark*	**bookmark-set**	Set a bookmark at the current cursor position.
C-x r b *Edit → Bookmarks →* *Jump to Bookmark*	**bookmark-jump**	Jump to a bookmark.
(none) *Edit → Bookmarks →* *Rename Bookmark*	**bookmark-rename**	Rename a bookmark.
(none) *Edit → Bookmarks →* *Delete Bookmark*	**bookmark-delete**	Delete a bookmark.
(none) *Edit → Bookmarks →* *Save Bookmarks*	**bookmark-save**	Save all bookmarks in default file.
C-x r l *Edit → Bookmarks →* *Edit Bookmark List*	**bookmark-menu-list**	Move to *Bookmark List* buffer.
(none) *Edit → Bookmarks →* *Insert Contents*	**bookmark-insert**	Insert full text of file associated with a given bookmark.
(none) *Edit → Bookmarks →* *Save Bookmarks As*	**bookmark-write**	Save all bookmarks in a specified file.
(none) *Edit → Bookmarks →* *Load a Bookmark File*	**bookmark-load**	Load bookmarks from specified file.
(none) *Edit → Bookmarks →* *Insert Location*	**bookmark-insert-location**	Insert the path to a given bookmark at the cursor position.

Now that you know how to work with multiple buffers, frames, and windows, why not read the next chapter to discover some of the things you can do with them? Some, like using the directory editor and working with the command line from within Emacs, have been alluded to in this chapter.

CHAPTER 5

Emacs as a Work Environment

Many of the everyday things you do from a command prompt can be done from within Emacs. You can execute commands, work with directories, and print files—all without leaving Emacs. Changing tasks is as simple as jumping between buffers.

What's important about this? Of course, it's nice to be able to move between tasks easily. What's even more important is that you have the same editing environment no matter what you're doing: you can use all of the Emacs editing commands to work on a file, give shell commands, then start up Dired, the directory editor, to do some file maintenance. It is simple to move text from one window to another. You can execute a command and then use Emacs commands to cut and paste the results into a file. If you're trying to compile a program and keep getting error messages, you can save the interactive session as a file and confer with someone about the problem. Despite the many advantages of modern window systems, Emacs often provides the best way to integrate the many kinds of work you do daily.

Much of the information in this chapter involves integration between Emacs and the operating system. Emacs is most commonly a Unix editor, so forgive us for a bias in that direction. But we are happy to report that for users of GNU Emacs on other platforms, integration with the operating system is still available; you can use shell mode to run commands and can edit directories with Dired. There's no reason to leave Emacs no matter what your platform is.

Executing Commands in Shell Buffers

One of the most important features of Emacs is its ability to run a command shell in a buffer. Once you have started a shell buffer, you can do all of your normal command-line work within Emacs. What does this buy you?

- You don't have to leave Emacs to get a command prompt. If you want to print or compile a file that you're editing, you can do it immediately.
- You can use Emacs editing features to write your commands.

- You can use Emacs editing features to "back up" through your command list, copy an old command, modify it, and execute it again.
- You can save your shell buffer, keeping a transcript of your editing session—which automatically includes the output from every command that you ran. For debugging or remembering commands you run infrequently, this can be invaluable.
- You can copy output from commands into a file or into another command.
- You can save complex commands in a file and insert the file at the prompt, rather than retyping the command.

As you get used to working within Emacs, you will undoubtedly discover more and more ways to put shell mode to use.

In this section, we discuss shell mode. Later in this chapter, we discuss directory editing, printing, and calendar and diary features for doing simple time management in Emacs. Right now, we'll start with a simple variation on shell mode, a feature that lets you execute commands one at a time.

Running One Command at a Time

To run a command while you're in an Emacs session, type **M-!**. Emacs asks for the command you want to run. Type the command and press **Enter**. Emacs then opens a window called *Shell Command Output* where it displays the results of your command.

Type: **M-!**

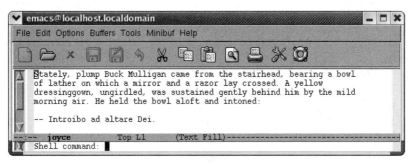

Emacs prompts you for a command to execute.

Type: **diff joyce joyce2**

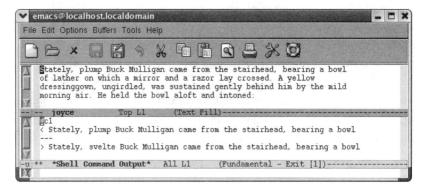

Emacs executes the **diff** command and puts the output into a *Shell Command Output* buffer.

Because the output from the **diff** command is in a buffer, you can edit it, save it, or do anything else you would like with it. Of course, if the operating system has no **diff** command or cannot access it for some reason, this command fails.

An interesting twist to the shell command facility is that you can use a region of a buffer rather than a traditional file as input to the command. For example, let's say we want to sort a phone list. First, we put the cursor somewhere in the list (say, on the first character of Liam), then we give the **mark-paragraph** command (**M-h**). This command defines the phone list as a region, with the cursor at the beginning of the paragraph and the mark at the end.

In the following example, the shaded area shows the extent of the region we want to sort. After selecting a region, we press **M-|** (for **shell-command-on-region**); Emacs prompts for the shell command to run.

Type: **M-h M-|**

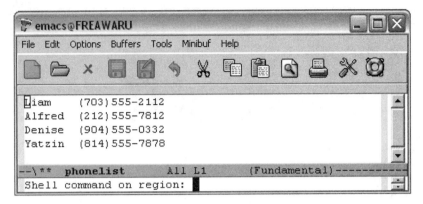

Emacs prompts you for a command to execute (Windows).

Now we give the command **sort** without specifying any input file. Emacs is taking care of the input for us.

Type: **sort Enter**

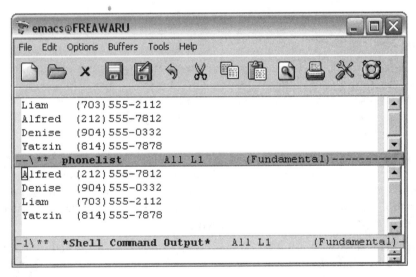

Emacs runs a sort on the region (Windows).

Emacs has sorted the phone list (i.e., everything within the region).

A useful variation for **M-!** puts the output directly into the current buffer, rather than into a *Shell Command Output* buffer. To do so, precede the command with **C-u**: for example, **C-u M-!** runs a shell command and puts the output in the current buffer.

Type: **C-u M-! ls -la Enter**

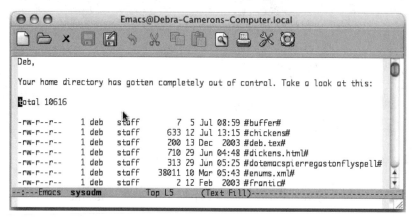

Emacs runs **ls** and inserts the result at your current location (Mac OS X).

Using Shell Mode

Now we're ready to discuss shell mode, the interactive facility for running commands. To start a shell buffer, type **M-x shell Enter**. This creates a buffer named *shell*. You see the prompt for your shell within this buffer. (This defaults to your usual shell; you can substitute another shell to use in Emacs. See "Which shell?" later in this chapter.)

For the most part, shell mode is exactly like the normal command interface, except that you can use Emacs to edit the commands as you type them. You can copy commands from one place to another, copy the results into a file, save the whole shell buffer to a file, and so on. Note in Figure 5-1 that Emacs has added a few items to the menu bar (Complete, In/Out, and Signals).

A few tricks are worth knowing, though. For example, you normally interrupt a command by typing **C-c**. If you type **C-c** in shell mode, Emacs thinks that the **C-c** is part of a command meant for it, because many Emacs commands start with **C-c**. Therefore, you have to type **C-c C-c** to terminate the current job. Likewise, under Unix, you type **C-c C-z** to stop a job, instead of **C-z**, and **C-c C-d** instead of **C-d**,

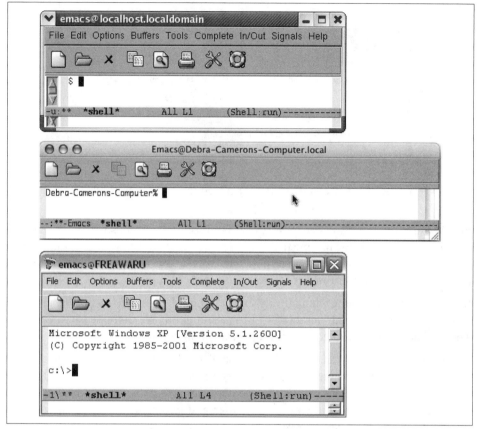

Figure 5-1. Shell buffers for Linux, Mac OS X, and Windows

and so on. (**C-c C-d** is not strictly necessary because Emacs understands **C-d** in context. If you're at the end of the buffer, **C-d** means "end of file"; if you're anywhere else, it deletes a character.) Alternatively, you can select options from the **Signals** menu rather than using control characters, if desired (for example, selecting **EOF** instead of typing **C-d**).

Shell mode also provides a few convenient shortcuts. The command **M-p** retrieves the last shell command you typed, no matter how far back in the buffer it is. Typing successive **M-p**'s brings back earlier commands.

Type: **M-p**

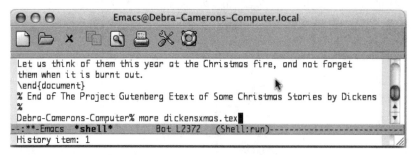

M-p retrieves the last command, even if it isn't on the screen (Mac OS X).

In this example, the previous command was **more dickensxmas.tex**. It's no longer on the screen; its output has pushed it off the top. **M-p** (for **comint-previous-input**) retrieves the command, but doesn't execute it; you can edit the command before pressing **Enter**. To find subsequent commands, type **M-n**.

If these commands sound familiar to you, they should. They are history commands, which are identical to the minibuffer history commands we discussed in Chapter 3. The **In/Out** menu is devoted to working with command history.

Enter and **Tab** have special functions in shell mode. Pressing **Enter** executes the command on the line where the cursor is, even if you move the cursor up to the line of an earlier command you want to execute again. When you press **Enter**, Emacs copies the command to the end of the buffer and executes it. Of course, you can modify the command before pressing **Enter**.

Pressing **Tab** puts the Emacs completion feature into action; use completion for operating system commands, filenames, and variables. Note that the completion of system commands works best on Unix implementations like Linux and Mac OS X; Emacs doesn't seem to find all the possible Windows commands, for example.

If you type a command that produces a lot of output, cluttering up your session, there's an easy way to get rid of it. Type **C-c C-o** (for **comint-kill-output**).

Type: **C-c C-o**

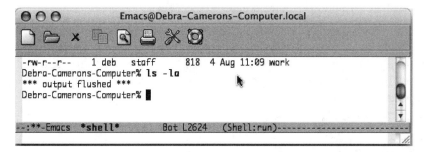

C-c C-o automatically deletes the output from the last command (Mac OS X).

The previous command (**ls-la**) remains on the screen, but its output, a long list of files, is deleted. **C-c C-o** can delete output from only the most recent command; it can't delete output from your previous commands.

Another useful command for shell mode is **C-c C-r** (for **comint-show-output**). This command is useful if a command produces a lot of output and causes the first few lines of output to scroll off the screen. **C-c C-r** repositions the window so the first line of output from your last command is at the top of the window. If you want to see the end of the output instead, type **C-c C-e** (for **comint-show-maximum-output**); this command moves the last line of the input to the bottom of the window.

When you're writing a book, moving by paragraphs makes sense, but when you're using a shell, moving by output group is more helpful. An *output group* consists of a command and its output. To move to the previous output group, type **C-c C-p**. To move to the next output group, type **C-c C-n**.

An advantage of shell mode is that you can start a command and then edit another buffer while the command runs. The shell buffer doesn't need to be onscreen; just type **M-x shell** to get the buffer back again.

You can have multiple shell buffers running at once; just use the command **M-x rename-uniquely** to rename your shell buffer. You can start another shell buffer, and another, and another—as many as you need to juggle all your tasks.

Which shell?

Normally, Emacs uses your default shell in shell mode. Under Windows that's *cmd.exe* (the familiar **C:\>** prompt or a close relative).* But Unix has a wide variety of available

---

* You do have choices under Windows as well, thanks to Cygwin (*http://cygwin.com/*). For example, if you wanted to run Cygwin's bash, you'll find helpful information on how to set that up on Ngai Kim Hoong's page on that topic at *http://www.khngai.com/emacs/cygwin.php*.

shells, including the GNU Project's **bash** and the zed shell, **zsh**. Whatever shell you normally use, that's what Emacs starts when you enter shell mode.

How does Emacs know which shell to start? First, it looks at the variable **shell-file-name**. Then it looks for a Unix environment variable named **ESHELL**. Finally it looks for an environment variable named **SHELL**. If you want to run another particular shell (for example, the zed shell) when you're in Emacs, you can add the following command to your *.emacs* file:

```
(setq shell-file-name "/bin/zsh")
```

When Emacs starts an interactive shell, it runs an additional initialization file after your shell's normal startup files. The name of this file is *.emacs_shell-name*, where *shell-name* is the name of the shell you want to use in Emacs. It must be located in your home directory. For example, if you use the C shell, you can add Emacs-only startup commands by placing them in the file *.emacs_csh*. Let's say that when you're in Emacs, you want to change the prompt to **emacs:%** and you want an environment variable called **WITHIN_EDITOR** to be set to **T**. Here's the contents of your *.emacs_csh* file:

```
set prompt="emacs:% "
setenv WITHIN_EDITOR T
```

Within a shell buffer, Emacs also sets the environment variable **EMACS** to **t**, and sets your terminal type (the **TERM** variable) to **emacs**.

Making passwords invisible in shell mode

By default, shell mode displays everything you type and that includes passwords—not a good situation if someone is peering over your shoulder. There is a way around this problem, however. Before you type the password, type **M-x send-invisible**. Emacs asks for the nonechoed text. When you type a character, Emacs puts an asterisk in the minibuffer. Press **Enter** and Emacs enters the password without displaying it. To have Emacs hide passwords as you type them, add the following two lines to your *.emacs* file:

```
(add-hook 'comint-output-filter-functions
    'comint-watch-for-password-prompt)
```

Emacs asks for nonechoed text in the minibuffer whenever a password prompt appears on the screen, making sure that the password is never displayed. Table 5-1 summarizes shell mode commands.

Table 5-1. Shell mode commands

Keystrokes	Command name	Action
(none)	**shell**	Enter shell mode.
C-c C-c *Signals → BREAK*	**comint-interrupt-subjob**	Interrupt current job; equivalent to **C-c**.

Table 5-1. Shell mode commands (continued)

Keystrokes	Command name	Action
C-d	comint-delchar-or-maybe-eof	Send EOF character if at end of buffer; delete a character elsewhere.
C-c C-d *Signals → EOF*	comint-send-eof	Send EOF character.
C-c C-u	comint-kill-input	Erase current line; equivalent to **C-u** in Unix shells.
C-c C-z *Signals → STOP*	comint-stop-subjob	Suspend or stop a job; **C-z** in Unix shells.
M-p *In/Out → Previous Input*	comint-previous-input	Retrieve previous commands (can be repeated to find earlier commands).
M-n *In/Out → Next Input*	comint-next-input	Retrieve subsequent commands (can be repeated to find more recent commands).
Enter	comint-send-input	Send input on current line.
Tab	comint-dynamic-complete	Complete current command, filename, or variable name.
C-c C-o *In/Out → Delete Current Output Group*	comint-kill-output	Delete output from last command.
C-c C-r	comint-show-output	Move first line of output to top of window.
C-c C-e *In/Out → Show Maximum Output*	comint-show-maximum-output	Move last line of output to bottom of window.
C-c C-p *In/Out → Backward Output Group*	comint-previous-prompt	Move to previous command.
C-c C-n *In/Out → Forward Output Group*	comint-next-prompt	Move to next command.

Using Dired, the Directory Editor

Dired is one of the most interesting features of Emacs. With Dired, you can look at a listing of all the files in a directory, delete them, rename them, copy them, and perform almost all basic file operations. More important, Dired can make you more productive. For example, you can work with groups of files, deleting, moving, compressing, or even query-replacing strings in them.

There are several ways to start directory editing. If you're not in Emacs, invoke Emacs with a directory name as an argument, for example:

```
% emacs literature
```

Emacs starts up editing the directory *literature*: you'll see a single window that contains a listing of the *literature* directory. You can also start the directory editor by using **C-x C-f** (or any other command for visiting a file) and naming a directory, rather than a file. For example, typing **C-x C-f literature** gets you ready to edit the *literature* directory. Typing **C-x d** (for **dired**) or selecting the folder icon on the toolbar also starts Dired; you then specify a directory name. Finally, dragging a folder onto the Emacs window also starts Dired.*

No matter how you start the editor, the result is the same.

Type: **C-x C-f literature Enter**

A basic directory editor display.

As you can see, Dired's display is similar to what you see if you type **ls -l** at a Unix shell prompt. The permissions associated with the file, the owner, the group name, the size of the file, and the date last modified all precede the filename. All files and directories are listed, including those whose names start with a dot. The cursor starts out on a filename, rather than in the first column.

Also, if your display supports colors (unfortunately this book doesn't), you'll see that directories are blue, backup and auto-save files are tan, and symbolic links are purple. Colors are a function of font-lock mode. If you don't see colors in your directory listing, type **M-x font-lock-mode Enter** or add the following line to your *.emacs* file:

```
(global-font-lock-mode t)
```

By default, the list is sorted by filename, but you can sort it by date instead. Look at the mode line. It says (Dired by name). To change the order of the display, type **s** (for **dired-sort-toggle-or-edit**). This command puts the newest files at the top of the list, solving the "Where's that file I worked on yesterday?" problem quite easily. The mode line says (Dired by date). Typing **s** again toggles the sort, putting it back in alphabetical order.

---

* The one exception to this is running Emacs in the Mac OS X Terminal application, which has its own drag-and-drop behavior. In the terminal—and thus in Emacs running in the terminal window—dragging and dropping a folder inserts the complete pathname of that folder rather than opening the folder in Dired.

If you remember the commands used to edit the buffer list (from Chapter 4), you will find that they are almost identical to the directory editor commands. You can do many additional things, but the basic commands are the same.

 Remember, in the directory editor you are working directly with files, not with buffers. When you delete a file using Dired, it's gone permanently.

There are several ways to move around in Dired. The commands **Space**, **C-n**, and **n** all move you to the next file in the list. **Del**, **C-p**, and **p** all move you to the previous file. Arrow keys and **PgUp** and **PgDown** work as well. You can also use any of the search commands (incremental search, word search, and so on) to find a particular file.

Viewing and Editing Files

When you look at a directory listing, you may want to get a quick look at the files. Dired's **v** command does just this: put the cursor on the file you want to view and press **v** (for **dired-view-file**). Emacs displays the file in view mode.* This is a read-only mode, so you can't modify the file. Press **C-c** or **q** to return to the directory listing. While you're viewing the file, you can use **s** to start an incremental search, or press **Enter** to scroll the display down one line. Typing **=** tells you what line the cursor is on. There are a number of shortcuts for other Emacs commands (like marking text), but frankly, the regular commands work correctly. There's no reason to remember a special set of commands when the ones you already know work.

If you want to edit a file from the Dired buffer, move to the line the file is on and press **Enter** (a variety of other keystrokes work as well, such as **f** for find or **e** for edit). Emacs finds the file and you can edit it. This is a completely normal editing buffer: you can make any changes you want, save them, visit other files, and so on. Typing **C-x b** followed by the name of the directory you were working in moves you back to the Dired buffer. Or you can use the buffer menu (**C-x C-b**) to find and display the Dired buffer.

Viewing and editing files is nice, but you already know how to do that—right? You're waiting for the interesting stuff: how to delete files.

---

* What if it's a file that shouldn't be viewed in Emacs, like a JPG or a PDF? In this case, the variable **dired-view-command-alist** associates viewers with file extensions. The defaults for this command work on Linux, but require some tweaking on other platforms. See Chapter 10 for an example of using Custom to change this variable for Mac OS X and Windows.

Deleting, Copying, and Renaming Files

As we've said, file deletion is almost identical to buffer deletion with the buffer list. If you learned how to delete buffers, you know the basics of deleting files with Dired. First, you flag a file for deletion by moving to the file's name and typing **d**. Doing this places a **D** on the left margin and moves the cursor to the next file in the list. You can flag as many files as you want. You can change your mind at this point and type **u** to undelete the file. At some later time, you type **x** to delete the files (more on this in a minute). The following screen shows what the Dired buffer looks like when you flag a few files for deletion.

Type: **d d d**

Three files flagged for deletion (Windows).

As we mentioned, you can type **u** at any time to remove the deletion flags from the files. Typing **u** moves you to the next file in the list, and, if it is marked, unmarks it. You can also use **Del** to unmark. This command undeletes the *previous* file in the list and then moves up one line.

Because Emacs generates backup files and, at times, auto-save files, you may want to delete them from time to time. Emacs offers shortcut commands to flag such files. Typing **#** flags all the auto-save files (files whose names start and end with **#**) for deletion. Emacs flags them with D. Typing **~** flags all the backup files (whose names end with **~**) for deletion. You can remove the flags from backup files you want to keep, for example, the backup copies of files you've recently worked on.

When you really want files to be deleted from disk, press **x**. Emacs displays the names of all the files flagged for deletion and asks you if you want to delete them.

Type: **x**

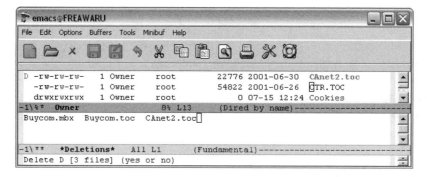

Emacs asks you to confirm the deletion by typing **yes** (Windows).

Type **yes** to delete them all or type **no** to return to the Dired buffer without deleting any of them.

This is the usual way of deleting files, but if you want a file deleted right away, type an uppercase **D**. Emacs asks if you want to delete the file **(yes or no)**. Type **yes** to delete the file immediately or **no** to change your mind. In Dired, this is one of a number of cases in which the lowercase letter (like **d** to flag for deletion) and the uppercase letter (like **D** to delete immediately) have a different meaning.

To copy a file in Dired, type **C** next to it (it must be a capital C). Emacs asks for the name of the file you want to copy to. Type the name and press **Enter**. Emacs says, `Copied: 1 file`. To copy several files in the list, preface the C with a number. For example, typing **3C** would copy this file and the next two files. (See "Working with Groups of Files" later in this chapter for fancier ways to select a group of files to operate on.)

To rename a file with Dired (similar to the Unix **mv** command), type **R** next to the filename. Emacs asks what the new name should be. Type it and press **Enter**. Emacs says, `Moved: 1 file`.

If you move files between platforms, you can wind up with some filenames in uppercase and some in lowercase. Files moving from older versions of Windows may be in all caps, for example. Simply mark the files in question by typing **m**, then press **%l** for lowercase or **%u** for uppercase. Voilà—painless case consistency.

Compressing and Uncompressing Files

Compressing files saves disk space, and Dired provides an easy way to do it. Put the cursor on the line of the file you want to compress and press **Z** (for **dired-do-compress**). Emacs asks the following:

```
Compress or uncompress filename? (y or n)
```

Emacs compresses the file if it's not compressed and uncompresses it if it is.* Press **y** to compress or uncompress the current file. Compression happens immediately, so you can watch both the extension and file size change as Emacs compresses the file.

What about editing compressed files? Although it's not on by default, Emacs has an automatic compression/decompression mode called auto-compress mode. To enter it for this session, type **M-x auto-compress-mode Enter**, which turns automatic compression on. To enable auto-compression automatically, add this line to your *.emacs* file:

```
(auto-compression-mode   1)
```

Comparing Files

In Chapter 4, we discussed comparing files in two windows. Emacs provides a way to do this using the **diff** command in Dired. Set the mark on the file you want **diff** to compare, put the cursor on the other file, then type =. Emacs compares the two files and opens a window with a *diff* buffer containing the output from the command.

Emacs has a separate option for comparing a file to its backup file. Put the cursor on the file you want to compare with its backup and type **M-=**. Emacs displays a *diff* buffer showing the differences between the two files.

If you are serious about version control, you may want to check out Chapter 12, which discusses version control as well as the GNU tool **ediff**.

Running Shell Commands on Files

While Dired's implementation of **diff** is useful (and there are implementations of **chmod**, **grep**, and **find** as well), in a more general sense, you can perform any command on a file by pressing an exclamation point (!). For example, let's alphabetize the phone list file using the **sort** command.

---

* Emacs understands only **compress** and **gzip** formats, not ZIP or other proprietary file compression algorithms. When you uncompress files, Emacs recognizes and correctly uncompresses files with the following suffixes: *.z*, *.Z*, or *.gz*. When you compress files, Emacs uses **gzip**, resulting in files that end in *.gz*.

Move to the *phone* file and press !

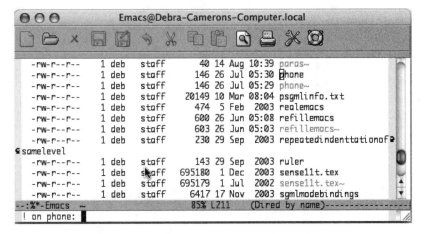

Emacs asks what command you want to run (Mac OS X).

Type: **sort**

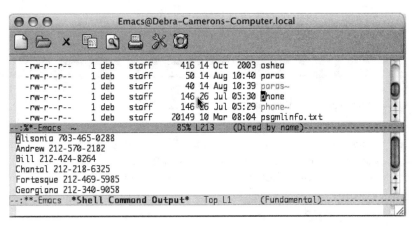

Emacs displays the output from the command in a separate window (Mac OS X).

Usually, asterisks (*) and question marks are used as wildcards in commands. In Dired, they have a special meaning. An asterisk means "use the file I'm on or the files I've marked"; that way you don't have to type filenames explicitly. When multiple files are marked, a question mark means to run this command separately on each file.

In a slightly more complex example, you might have a command with more than one file as an argument. For example, you might want to make a new file out of the sorted phone list.

Move the cursor to the *phone* file, then type: !

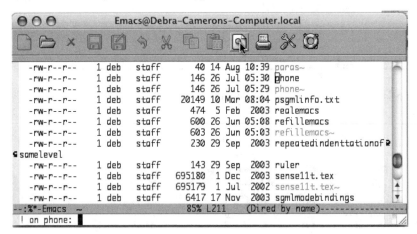

Emacs asks what command you want to run (Mac OS X).

Now tell Emacs you want to sort your *phone* file and put the output in a new file called *phonesorted*. The cursor is on the *phone* file, so you don't need to type its name in the command. Substitute an asterisk (*) for the name of the file:

Type: **sort** * > **phonesorted**

The operating system sorts the *phone* file and puts the output into the new file *phonesorted* (Mac OS X).

We created the file, but it doesn't appear on the display, which is not automatically updated in this case. To see the *phonesorted* file, type **g**.

Type: **g**

Emacs updates the Dired display, showing the file *phonesorted* (Mac OS X).

Dired is frankly inconsistent about whether you type **g** before the display is updated. Some commands, as we'll see shortly, update the display immediately. Others, such as running shell commands on files, do not (Emacs really doesn't know what shell commands it's running or their effect on the display). A good rule of thumb is to type **g** if you don't see what you expect to see.

Working with Groups of Files

So far we've talked about working with one file at a time; any commands you give apply to the file the cursor is on. Working with multiple files is a better illustration of the real power of Dired. You can organize your directories in a flash once you learn a few shortcuts. First let's talk about some ways to select files, and then we'll talk about what we can do with the selected files.

Selecting files

So far we've primarily talked about flagging files for deletion. When you want to do something else with a group of files, you first mark them with an asterisk. Pressing **m** marks the file the cursor is on; an asterisk appears where you normally see a D. Typing **3m** marks this file and the next two files. Once you mark files with an asterisk, Emacs assumes that any command you issue is meant for these files. So if you have three files marked with an asterisk and press **Z** to compress, Emacs assumes you want to compress those three files. After the compression, the files remain marked with asterisks. So how do you get rid of the asterisks when you're done with these files?

To remove the asterisks, you press **M-Del** (for **dired-unmark-all-files**). Emacs asks which marks to remove. Press **Enter**, and Emacs removes all the marks.

Sometimes it's easier to mark the files you don't want to work with than those you do. Pressing **t** toggles the marks, marking all unmarked files and removing marks from those previously marked.

Selecting likely candidates for deletion

Marking files sequentially is simple but, in all honesty, it's not very powerful. Emacs provides commands for selecting types of files that you often want to get rid of when you're cleaning up a directory: backup files, auto-save files, and so-called garbage files.

Auto-save files are created when a session terminates abnormally; they have the format *#filename#*. Backup files which Emacs creates periodically, have the format *filename~*. To mark these files in Dired, type # or ~ respectively.

Emacs also has an option that automatically selects "garbage" files. By default, this includes files with the following extensions: *.log*, *.toc*, *.dvi*, *.bak*, *.orig*, and *.rej*. Garbage files are defined by a regular expression, which is contained in the variable **dired-garbage-files-regexp**; you can change the value of this variable to define garbage files as you see fit (after all, one man's junk is another man's treasure).

Selecting files by type

Dired provides commands for selecting executable files, directories, and symbolic links. To select executable files, type * *. To select directories, type * /. Typing * @ marks symbolic links.

Using regular expressions to choose files

Often you want to select related files and either archive them, move them, compress them, or just delete them. Typically, you use wildcards to select multiple files. In Dired, you use regular expressions. To mark a group of files whose filenames match a regular expression, press **%** followed by **m** to mark them with an asterisk.

For example, let's mark all the files that start with *ch*. Remembering the quick lesson on regular expressions from Chapter 3, **^** finds the beginning of a word, so the regular expression **^ch** would mark all the files that start with *ch*.

Type: **%m**

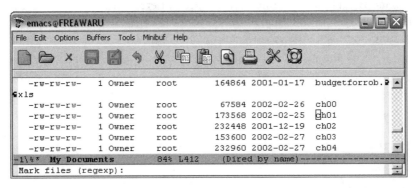

Emacs asks for a regular expression so that it can mark the files (Windows).

Type: ^ch **Enter**

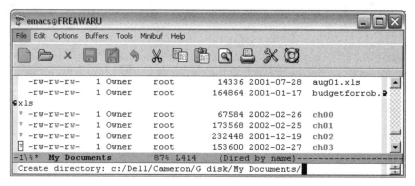

Emacs marks all the files starting with *ch* and tells you how many it marked.

Sometimes it's more useful to mark files whose *contents* match a given regular expression. To mark files that contain a certain regular expression, type **% g**, followed by the regular expression to match (think *g* for *grep* if you're familiar with *grep*).

Now that we've got the files marked, let's talk about what to do with them.

Operating on groups of files

In the course of daily work, a directory can get cluttered with many different kinds of files. Eventually, you need to make subdirectories to organize the files by project, then move the files to those subdirectories. You can do both these things from within Dired.

Let's say that the *ch* files are chapters from a novel you work on in your spare time. We need a subdirectory called *novel* to store the files in. You can create a directory by typing + (for **dired-create-directory**).

Type: +

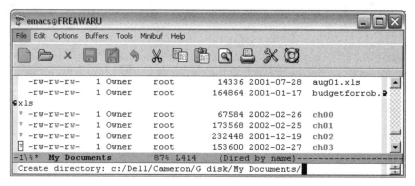

Emacs asks for a directory name (Windows).

Type: **novel Enter**

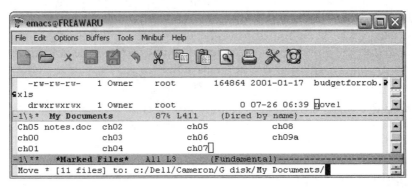

Emacs creates the directory and displays it on the screen (Windows).

Now let's move the *ch* files we marked into the new directory. We'll use the rename command, **R**. This command, like the Unix **mv** command, is used for renaming files and for moving them. Because we have marked more than one file with an asterisk, when we type **R**, Emacs assumes we mean to move the marked files.

Type: **R**

Emacs asks where you want to move the marked files to (Windows).

Type: **novel Enter**

```
 emacs@FREAWARU                                            _ □ ✕

 File  Edit  Options  Buffers  Tools  Operate  Mark  Regexp  Immediate  Subdir  Help

   🗋  📂  ✕  🗐  🔍  🖨  🛠  📷

    -rw-rw-rw-  1 Owner    root      14336 2001-07-28  aug01.xls        ▲
    -rw-rw-rw-  1 Owner    root     164864 2001-01-17  budgetforrob.🄿
 🄻xls
    drwxrwxrwx  1 Owner    root          0 07-26 06:39  novel
    -rw-rw-rw-  1 Owner    root      16384 2001-08-01  convergencefi🄿
 🄻g.xls
    -rw-rw-rw-  1 Owner    root      14336 2000-07-20  checkbook.xls   ▼
 -1\%*  My Documents       89% L410     (Dired by name)----------------
 Move: 11 files                                                      ≑
```

Emacs moves the files (Windows).

Now you can see that the files have moved. Marking files by regular expression allows you to work with a select group of files quickly.

One of the more interesting things you can do with a group of files is perform a query-replace on all of them with a single command. On large projects, a last-minute change often forces arduous searching and replacing of certain text in each file. First, select the files you want to include in the query-replace, then press **Q** (for **dired-do-query-replace**). Put in the search string, then the replacement string (the strings can be plain text or a regular expression) and Emacs starts a query-replace that moves you through each file sequentially. Here's the only hitch: if you interrupt the query-replace with a recursive edit, you can't restart it without going back to the Dired buffer.

Another interesting command is searching across files for a given regular expression. To do this, mark the files, then press **A**. Emacs stops at the first match; press **M-,** to move to the next match.

Navigating Directories

Often when you are cleaning up directories, you're moving files between them, organizing subdirectories, and the like. This naturally involves a lot of moving among directories.

To move to the parent directory of the one you're in, press **^**. To move to the next directory in the buffer, press **>**; pressing **<**, not surprisingly, moves you to the previous directory in the buffer.

Sometimes it's more convenient to edit a directory and its subdirectories in the same buffer. To insert a subdirectory in the current Dired buffer, move to it and press **i**.

Emacs inserts the subdirectory at the end of the buffer. If you insert more subdirectories in this fashion, they will appear in alphabetical order at the end of the buffer.

As you can see, much of your file maintenance and cleanup can be done easily from within Dired. Table 5-2 summarizes Dired commands, some of which we haven't fully discussed. There's more to learn about Dired,* but now that you know the basics, you can experiment on your own.

Table 5-2. Dired commands

Keystrokes	Command name	Action
C-x d *File → Open Directory*	**dired**	Start Dired.
A *Operate → Search Files*	**dired-do-search**	Do a regular expression search on marked files; stops at first match; **M-,** finds next match.
B *Operate → Byte-compile*	**dired-do-byte-compile**	Byte-compile file.
C *Operate → Copy to*	**dired-do-copy**	Copy file.
d *Mark → Flag*	**dired-flag-file-deletion**	Flag for deletion.
D *Operate → Delete*	**dired-do-delete**	Query for immediate deletion.
e *Immediate → Find This File*	**dired-find-file**	Edit file.
f	**dired-advertised-find-file**	Find (so you can edit).
g *Immediate → Refresh*	**revert-buffer**	Reread the directory from disk.
G *Operate → Change Group*	**dired-do-chgrp**	Change group permissions.
h	**describe-mode**	Display descriptive help text for Dired.
H *Operate → Hardlink to ...*	**dired-do-hardlink**	Create a hard link to this file; Emacs asks you to name the hard link (not all OSes support hard links).
i *Subdir → Insert This Subdir ...*	**dired-maybe-insert-subdir**	Add a listing of this subdirectory to the current dired buffer; if it's already there, just move to it.
k	**dired-do-kill-lines**	Remove line from display (don't delete file).
L *Operate → Load*	**dired-do-load**	Load file.

---

* And if all the Dired features aren't enough, there's Dired-x, an add-in module that includes other features such as omitting unimportant files from the listing, finding files mentioned in any buffer, and additional variables and means of marking files. For more details, see the Info text on this subject (type **C-h i** to get to the Info menu).

Table 5-2. Dired commands (continued)

Keystrokes	Command name	Action
m or * m *Mark → Mark*	dired-mark	Mark with *.
M *Operate → Change Mode*	dired-do-chmod	Use **chmod** command on this file.
n	dired-next-line	Move to next line.
o *Immediate →* *Find in Other Window*	dired-find-file-other-window	Find file in another window; move there.
C-o *Immediate →* *Display in Other Window*	dired-display-file	Find file in another window; don't move there.
O *Operate → Change Owner*	dired-do-chown	Change ownership of file.
p	dired-previous-line	Move up a line.
P *Operate → Print*	dired-do-print	Print file.
q	quit-window	Quit Dired.
Q *Operate →* *Query Replace in Files*	dired-do-query-replace	Query replace string in marked files.
R *Operate → Rename to*	dired-do-rename	Rename file.
S *Operate → Symlink to*	dired-do-symlink	Create a symbolic link to this file; Emacs asks you to name the symbolic link.
s	dired-sort-toggle-or-edit	Sort the Dired display by date or by filename (toggles between these).
t *Mark → Toggle Marks*	dired-toggle-marks	Toggle marks on files and directories; pressing **t** once marks all unmarked files and directories; pressing **t** again restores original marks.
u *Mark → Unmark*	dired-unmark	Remove mark.
v *Immediate → View This File*	dired-view-file	View file (read-only).
w	dired-copy-filename-as-kill	Copy filename into the kill ring; if multiple files are marked, copy names of all marked files to kill ring.
x	dired-do-flagged-delete	Delete files flagged with **D**.
y	dired-show-file-type	Display information on the type of the file using the **file** command.
Z *Operate → Compress*	dired-do-compress	Compress or uncompress file.
~ *Mark → Flag Backup Files*	dired-flag-backup-files	Flag backup files for deletion; **C-u ~** removes flags.

Table 5-2. Dired commands (continued)

Keystrokes	Command name	Action
# *Mark → Flag Auto-save Files*	**dired-flag-auto-save-files**	Flag auto-save files for deletion; **C-u** # removes flags.
& *Mark → Flag Garbage Files*	**dired-flag-garbage-files**	Flag "garbage" files for deletion.
. *Mark → Mark Old Backups*	**dired-clean-directory**	Flag numbered backups for deletion (if any).
= *Immediate → Diff*	**dired-diff**	Compare this file to another file (the one at the mark).
M-= *Immediate →* *Compare With Backup*	**dired-backup-diff**	Compare this file with its backup file.
! or X *Operate → Shell Command*	**dired-do-shell-command**	Ask for shell command to execute on the current file or marked files.
+ *Immediate → Create Directory*	**dired-create-directory**	Create a directory.
> *Subdir → Next Dirline*	**dired-next-dirline**	Move to next directory.
< *Subdir → Prev Dirline*	**dired-prev-dirline**	Move to previous directory.
^	**dired-up-directory**	Find the parent directory in a new Dired buffer.
$ *Subdir → Hide/Unhide Subdir*	**dired-hide-subdir**	Hide or show the current directory or subdirectory.
M-$ *Subdir → Hide All*	**dired-hide-all**	Hide all subdirectories, leaving only their names; repeat command to show.
C-M-n *Subdir → Next Subdir*	**dired-next-subdir**	Move to next subdirectory (if you've inserted sub-directories using **i**).
C-M-p *Subdir → Prev Subdir*	**dired-prev-subdir**	Move to previous subdirectory (if you've inserted subdirectories using **i**).
C-M-u *Subdir → Tree Up*	**dired-tree-up**	If you've inserted subdirectories using **i**, move to the parent directory in this buffer.
C-M-d *Subdir → Tree Down*	**dired-tree-down**	If you've inserted subdirectories using **i**, move to the first subdirectory for this directory in this buffer.
* c *Mark → Change Marks*	**dired-change-marks**	Change marks on specified files, for example, from * (generic mark) to **D** (flagged for deletion).
*! or M-Del *Mark → Unmark All*	**dired-unmark-all-files**	Remove all marks from all files.
* * *Mark → Mark Executables*	**dired-mark-executables**	Mark executables; **C-u** * unmarks.
* / *Mark → Mark Directories*	**dired-mark-directories**	Mark directories; **C-u** / unmarks.

Table 5-2. Dired commands (continued)

Keystrokes	Command name	Action
* @ *Mark → Mark Symlinks*	**dired-mark-symlinks**	Mark symlinks; **C-u** * @ unmarks.
M-} *Mark → Next Marked*	**dired-next-marked-file**	Move to the next file marked with * or **D**.
M-{ *Mark → Previous Marked*	**dired-prev-marked-file**	Move to previous file marked with * or **D**.
% d *Regexp → Flag*	**dired-flag-files-regexp**	Flag for deletion files that match regular expression.
% g *Regexp → Mark Containing*	**dired-mark-files-containing-regexp**	Mark files whose contents match regular expression.
% l *Regexp → Downcase*	**dired-downcase**	Lowercase marked files.
% R *Regexp → Mark*	**dired-do-rename-regexp**	Rename files with filenames that match regular expression.
% u *Regexp → Upcase*	**dired-upcase**	Uppercase marked files.

Printing from Emacs

Emacs offers several commands for printing buffers and regions. To print a buffer with page numbers and headers for the filename, type **M-x print-buffer Enter**. This command sends the buffer to **pr** (a program that does simple formatting for listings), followed by **lpr** (which sends the listing to the printer). If you want to print the file directly, without the headers and page numbers that **pr** provides, give the command **M-x lpr-buffer Enter**. You can also use these commands to print a selected portion of a file. First define a region by setting a mark at one end and moving the cursor to the other end. Then give the command **M-x print-region Enter** (or **M-x lpr-region Enter**).

The **lpr-buffer** and **lpr-region** commands always check the variable **lpr-switches** to determine whether any options should be passed to the Unix **lpr** command. These options are used to request a particular printer and for many other purposes; see the manpage for **lpr** for more information. For example, if you want to use the printer named lpt1 whenever you print from Emacs, you would want to set **lpr-switches** to -Plpt1. To do so, add the following line to your *.emacs* file:

```
(setq lpr-switches '("-Plpt1"))
```

Note the single quote preceding, and the parentheses surrounding, the string "-Plpt1". This is just weird-but-necessary Lisp syntax; see Chapter 11 for more details.

You can also print from Dired. To print the file the cursor is on, type **P**. Emacs puts the default printing command in the minibuffer, and you can modify it.

Emacs also includes commands to print a buffer as a PostScript file. If you have formatted text in the file, you can print the buffer with those attributes by typing **M-x ps-print-buffer-with-faces**.

Table 5-3 provides a summary of commands for printing.

Table 5-3. Printing commands

Keystrokes	Action
M-x print-buffer *File → Print Buffer*	Print the buffer (similar to Unix **pr** | **lpr**).
M-x print-region *File → Print Region*	Print the region (similar to Unix **pr** | **lpr**).
M-x lpr-buffer	Print buffer with no page numbers (similar to Unix **lpr**).
M-x lpr-region	Print region with no page numbers (similar to Unix **lpr**).
P *Operate → Print*	From Dired, put the default print command in the minibuffer; you can change it or press **Enter** to execute it.
M-x ps-print-buffer-with-faces *File → Postscript Print Buffer*	Print the buffer with text attributes.
M-x ps-print-region-with-faces *File → Postscript Print Region*	Print the region with text attributes.

Reading Manpages in Emacs

You can read Unix online documentation (called *manpages*) from within Emacs by typing **M-x man** or by selecting **Man** from the **Help** menu.[*] This command creates a buffer with a formatted manpage in it, which you can scroll through (or copy from) using Emacs commands. Simply type: **M-x man Enter** *Unix-command-name* **Enter**.

For the Unix command name, you can use either a simple name, like **ls**, or a manpage section name like **ttytab(5)**.

The advantage of using the **man** command is that you can scroll through the manpage easier than you can in some terminal applications or shell windows. Also, if you try to view manpages in shell mode, they may come out garbled if the settings aren't right, whereas **man** gives you clean text.

Using Time Management Tools

Emacs is a natural place to organize all your work. It won't replace your Palm or other handheld, but ongoing work in this area may help you sync your favorite

---

[*] This feature works on Linux, but not on Windows. To make it work on Mac OS X, set `shell-file-name` to `/bin/sh`.

device with your Emacs-based schedule. Here we cover the main features that Emacs itself offers—the calendar and the diary.

Displaying the Calendar

To display the calendar, type **M-x calendar**. Emacs displays a calendar window with three months: last month, this month, and next month.

Type: **M-x calendar**

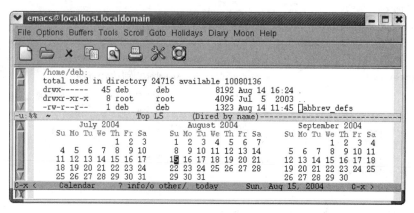

Emacs puts the cursor on today's date and displays the date on the mode line. There's no room to write on the calendar; that's what the diary is for, which we'll discuss shortly.

By default, weeks start on Sunday. If you'd like them to start on Monday instead, type **M-x set-variable calendar-week-start Enter 1 Enter**. You enter the calendar again to have this take effect. If you'd like to have the calendar always start on Monday, add this line to your *.emacs* file:

```
(setq calendar-week-start-day 1)
```

If you'd like to see the calendar each time you start Emacs, you can add this line to your *.emacs* file:

```
(calendar)
```

Moving in the calendar

When you're in the calendar, Emacs sensibly moves by day rather than by character. **C-f** moves you to the next day; **C-b** moves you to the previous day. **C-n** moves you to the same day of the next week; **C-p** moves you back a week. The arrow keys work the same way. **M-}** and **M-{** move forward and backward by month, and **C-x [** and **C-x]** move forward and backward by year. **C-v** scrolls forward by three months; **M-v** scrolls back three months.

The movement commands just discussed move you relative to the cursor position. If you're on Tuesday and you press **C-n**, you'll move to next Tuesday. If you're on January 25 and press **M-}** you'll move to February 25. If you're on August 15, 2004 and press **C-x [**, you'll move to August 15, 2003.

Other commands move to the beginning or the end of the week, month, or year. **C-a** and **C-e** move to the beginning and end of the week, **M-a** moves to the beginning of the month, and **M-<** moves to the beginning of the year. Table 5-4 summarizes these calendar movement commands.

To go to a particular date, press **g d**. Emacs asks for the year, then the month, and then the day. Emacs moves you to the day selected (this command is well-suited for answering that all-important question, "On what day of the week does my birthday fall in 2020?").

Table 5-4. Calendar movement commands

Keystrokes	Command name	Action
(none) *Tools → Display Calendar*	**calendar**	Display the calendar.
. *Goto → Today*	**calendar-goto-today**	Move to today's date.
C-f	**calendar-forward-day**	Move forward a day.
C-b	**calendar-backward-day**	Move backward a day.
C-n	**calendar-forward-week**	Move forward a week.
C-p	**calendar-backward-week**	Move backward a week.
M-}	**calendar-forward-month**	Move forward one month.
M-{	**calendar-backward-month**	Move backward a month.
C-x] *Scroll → Forward 1 Year*	**calendar-forward-year**	Move forward a year.
C-x [*Scroll → Backward 1 Year*	**calendar-backward-year**	Move backward a year.
C-a *Goto → Beginning of Week*	**calendar-beginning-of-week**	Move to the beginning of the week.
C-e *Goto → End of Week*	**calendar-end-of-week**	Move to the end of the week.
M-a *Goto → Beginning of Month*	**calendar-beginning-of-month**	Move to the beginning of the month.
M-e *Goto → End of Month*	**calendar-end-of-month**	Move to the end of the month.
M-< *Goto → Beginning of Year*	**calendar-beginning-of-year**	Move to the beginning of the year.

Table 5-4. Calendar movement commands (continued)

Keystrokes	Command name	Action
M-> *Goto → End of Year*	calendar-end-of-year	Move to the end of the year.
g d *Goto → Other Date*	calendar-goto-date	Go to the specified date.
o	calendar-other-month	Put the specified month in the middle of the display.
C-x < *Scroll → Forward 1 Month*	scroll-calendar-left	Scroll forward one month.
C-x > *Scroll → Backward 1 Month*	scroll-calendar-right	Scroll backward one month.
C-v *Scroll → Forward 3 Months*	scroll-calendar-left-three- months	Scroll forward three months.
M-v *Scroll → Forward 3 Months*	scroll-calendar-right-three- months	Scroll backward three months.
Space	scroll-other-window	Scroll another window.

Displaying holidays

Let's move to a topic everyone is interested in: holidays. To display the holidays for the part of the calendar you are looking at, type **a** (for **list-calendar-holidays**) or select **3 Months** from the **Holidays** menu.

Type: **a**

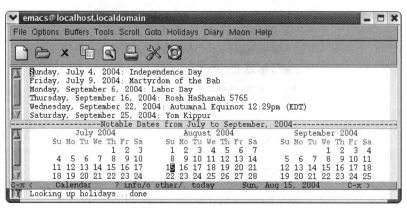

Emacs lists holidays for the time period shown.

As you can see, Emacs knows about a fairly wide variety of holidays or, as it calls them, "notable dates." If you are somewhere else on the calendar but want to see holidays surrounding the current month, type **M-x holidays**. Emacs lists them. To see whether today is a holiday, type **h** or select **One Day** from the **Holidays** menu.

Typing **x** marks holidays in a special way, typically highlighting them in pink. If the display doesn't support this, Emacs puts an asterisk to the right of the date. Typing **u** removes the marks.

We have taught you only the bare bones of the calendar commands. Emacs offers to tell you sunrise and sunset and phases of the moon. You can choose other calendars, like the Islamic calendar, the Hebrew calendar, the Mayan calendar, or even the French Revolutionary calendar. But we will leave these for you to explore.

More calendar commands are used in the context of the diary, discussed next.

Using the Diary

The diary, closely related to the calendar, allows you to make notes about certain dates. You can enter a full daily schedule or just mark major events. The level of detail is entirely up to you.

Creating a diary file

To use the diary, you must have a *diary* file that contains notations about important events or things to do. It can remind you to back up your system every Thursday, that you get paid every two weeks, that you're on vacation during the first two weeks in July, or that your mother's birthday is August 6.

The file must be called *diary* and must exist in your home directory. In this file, you insert lines—or have Emacs write lines for you—that note dates you want to remember. The *diary* file need not be all in one format and need not be sorted in any particular order. Date formats can be mixed: December 19, 2004 could be 12/19/04, Dec 19 04, or dec 19 2004. Here are a few lines from a *diary* file to illustrate what we mean.

```
11/14 My birthday
July 17 2004 Company picnic
March 18 2004 Annual report due
January 8 2004 Hair appointment
&Saturday Tea with Queen Elizabeth
Friday Payday
```

If you don't specify a year, Emacs assumes you want to mark that date every year, as in birthdays. If you don't specify a date but only the day of the week (as in tea with the queen on Saturday), Emacs displays the diary entry every Saturday. Putting an ampersand (&) before an entry tells Emacs not to mark it on the calendar (you don't want every Saturday marked, and you may not want everyone to know that you hang around with the royal family).

Date formats can be mixed, but the choice to use European date format (DD/MM/YYYY or 9 October 2004) versus the default American format (MM/DD/YYYY or

October 9, 2004) must be made before you create the *diary* file. To specify European date format, add this line to your *.emacs* file:

```
(setq european-calendar-style 't)
```

Adding diary entries

You can write your own entries or have Emacs help you put them in. To have Emacs help you, go to the calendar by typing **M-x calendar**. Then press **g d** to specify the date you want to move to. Press **i d** (for **insert-diary-entry**). Emacs moves you to the diary window with the date written out. You can then make a diary entry next to the date. If your entry spans more than one line, begin the second and subsequent lines with a single space, so that Emacs understands it's a continuation. After you make the notation about the date, Emacs leaves you in the diary buffer so you can make more entries. Type **C-x b** to move to another buffer.

The **insert-diary-entry** command assumes you want to make a single, one-time entry. To create a recurring entry, you need a few more commands. To insert a weekly entry, type **i w**. Emacs moves you to the diary buffer with the day of the week written out. Type the weekly activity (such as a staff meeting), and save the *diary* file. To insert an annual entry, type **i y**. Emacs moves you to the diary buffer with the day and month written out; type the annual event. There is a more specific command for anniversaries. Type **i a** to add an anniversary; this entry includes the year (though we have not seen a function that uses this information for any particular purpose, such as counting which anniversary this is).

You can also put in *cyclic* diary entries, entries that occur at regular intervals, like reminders to change the oil in your car every three months. To do so, move to the date you changed your oil last and type **i c**. Emacs says, Repeat every how many days: and you type the number of days between oil changes. Emacs writes a Lisp function to handle this and puts it in the diary buffer. You can then make a notation next to the Lisp function, such as a note that tells you to change the oil. The entry that Emacs inserts looks like this (we put the part about changing the oil in ourselves):

```
%%(diary-cyclic 90 12 23 2004) Change the oil
```

The entry says that every 90 days, counting from the day we inserted the entry, December 23, 2004, we should change the oil in our car.

You can mark a block of dates, as in the case of a week-long conference or a vacation. Put the cursor on the first date and press **C-Space** to set the mark.[*] Move (using calendar movement commands like **C-f**, **C-n**, and so on) to the second date and press

---

[*] If you normally use another binding for the **set-mark** command or if you typically spell out that command, you'll run into a problem marking regions in the calendar. In the calendar, **C-Space** and **C-@** run **calendar-set-mark** rather than **set-mark**, so that regions are marked by time rather than just across the screen. To mark regions correctly in the calendar (linearly by time rather than simply across the screen), you must type **C-Space**, **C-@**, or **M-x calendar-set-mark** to set the mark.

i b. Emacs moves you to the diary buffer and inserts an incantation that marks the week on your calendar. Make a notation following the Lisp function Emacs inserts. The entry will look something like this:

```
%%(diary-block 3 15 2004 3 20 2004) Trip to Alabama
```

This entry indicates that from March 15 to March 20, we'll go on a trip to Alabama.

What if you want to note that you have to file your expense report on the fifteenth of every month? Emacs accepts the asterisk wildcard (*) for the month, as you will see when you type **i m** (for **insert-monthly-diary-entry**). Emacs inserts an asterisk in place of the month, followed by the day, as in * **15** for something scheduled for the fifteenth of each month. As always, you make a note following the entry.

Now that you see how Emacs constructs diary entries, you can try writing some of your own based on what Emacs has done. After all, the *diary* file is like any other Emacs file; you can make changes, add lines, and delete lines at will. The only requirement is that you save the file when you're through. Now let's see how to display diary entries on the appropriate dates.

Displaying diary entries

If you want to review the diary entries for a given date, press **d** from the calendar. In order to see the whole *diary* file, press **s** from the calendar. If you want today's diary entries to display automatically when you start Emacs, add this line to your *.emacs* file:

```
(diary)
```

That way, when you start up Emacs on a day for which there is a diary entry, the diary entry displays automatically. For example, let's say you marked your best friend's birthday some time ago, and today is the day. When you start Emacs, the screen would look like this:

You start Emacs.

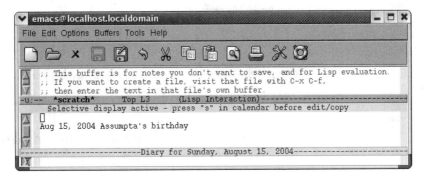

Emacs displays the diary entry for your friend's birthday.

If there are no diary entries for a given day, the diary is not displayed. If you start Emacs with two files so that you are editing in two windows, the diary is also not displayed.

If you have already put in a (**calendar**) entry in your *.emacs* file to have the calendar displayed automatically, the calendar supersedes the diary, and you'll have to remove the calendar if you prefer to see the diary instead.

To mark dates with diary entries in red, press **m** from the calendar. To remove the marks, press **u**. (This command removes highlighting for diary entries as well as for holidays.)

Table 5-5 summarizes the calendar and diary commands.

Table 5-5. Holiday and diary commands

Keystrokes	Command name	Action
p d	calendar-print-day-of-year	Display the day of the year this is (for example, Day 364 of 365).
p o	calendar-print-other-dates	Display information about this date for all calendars.
Space	scroll-other-window	Scroll the other window.
q	exit-calendar	Quit calendar.
a *Holidays → For Window*	list-calendar-holidays	Display holidays for calendar period shown.
h *Holidays → For Cursor Date*	calendar-cursor-holidays	In the minibuffer, display holiday information for the day the cursor is on.
x *Holidays → Mark*	mark-calendar-holidays	Display holidays in a different typeface, color, or with an asterisk beside them.
u *Holidays → Unmark Calendar*	calendar-unmark	Remove marks for holidays and diary entries (opposite of **x** command).
i w *Diary → Insert Weekly*	insert-weekly-diary-entry	Add a weekly entry based on the day of the week.
i y *Diary → Insert Yearly*	insert-yearly-diary-entry	Add an annual entry.
i d *Diary → Insert Daily*	insert-diary-entry	Add an entry for a particular day.
i m *Diary → Insert Monthly*	insert-monthly-diary-entry	Add an entry for the day of the month.
i c *Diary → Insert Cyclic*	insert-cyclic-diary-entry	Add an entry to recur every *n* days.
i a *Diary → Insert Anniversary*	insert-anniversary-diary-entry	Add an annual entry (the year is included for reference).
i b *Diary → Insert Block*	insert-block-diary-entry	Add a block entry.
m	mark-diary-entries	Display diary entries in a different typeface, color, or with a plus sign beside them.

Table 5-5. Holiday and diary commands (continued)

Keystrokes	Command name	Action
d	view-diary-entries	Display diary entries for the current date.
s *Diary → Show All*	show-all-diary-entries	Display *diary* file.
M-=	calendar-count-days-region	Count the number of days in a region.
M *Moon → Lunar Phases*	calendar-phases-of-moon	Display phases of the moon for a three-month period.
S	calendar-sunrise-sunset	Given longitude and latitude, display sunrise and sunset times for the current date.
C-Space or C-@	calendar-set-mark	Mark regions by time rather than horizontally.

Problems You May Encounter

- **In shell mode on Mac OS X, Emacs says, "Warning: no access to tty (Bad file descriptor). Thus no job control in this shell."** This happens with the graphical version of Emacs, not with the version run from the Mac OS X Terminal application. If you change to a different shell using the instructions under "Which shell?" earlier in this chapter, the error goes away.

- **Some commands don't work on Mac OS X.** The graphical version of Mac OS X fails to find some operating system commands, especially when invoking them through **M-!** (for **shell-command**). Change to a different shell; see "Which shell?" earlier in this chapter for details. Another problem is that some Unix commands are not available by default on Mac OS X. Try them in the Mac Terminal application to see if they work at all before trying them in shell mode. To increase Mac OS X's Unix functionality, use Fink (*http://fink.sourceforge.net*) to download a wide variety of Unix commands and software for Mac OS X.

- **Some commands don't work on Windows.** This chapter describes many commands that have no Windows equivalent. The Windows port of Emacs works well for most Dired functions, the calendar, and the diary. To get Unix command functionality under Windows, install Cygwin (*http://cygwin.com*).

- **Printing does not work from Windows on USB printers.** Many USB printers do not support printing from the command line. This problem is not specific to Emacs.

CHAPTER 6
Writing Macros

What is a macro? In Emacs, a *macro* is simply a group of recorded keystrokes you can play back over and over again. Macros are a great way to save yourself repetitive work. For example, let's say you want to delete the third column of a table. Normally, you would go to the first line; move over to the third column; delete it; then go to the second line; give the same set of commands; and so on, until you finish, your fingers wear out, or you get too bored. Emacs lets you record the keystrokes you used to work on the first line of the table, and then "play these back" repeatedly until the job is done.*

Any command or action you do within Emacs, from typing text to editing to switching buffers, can be done within a macro. The key to using macros well is, not too surprisingly, recognizing when you're doing repetitive work: sensing that you have pressed more or less the same sequence of keys several times in a row. Once you learn to recognize repetitious work, you have a good feel for when to use macros. The next talent that you'll need is, given that you've recognized a cycle of "almost identical" keystrokes, figuring out how to make that cycle *precisely identical*—that is, figuring out a set of keystrokes that, if repeated, will do exactly what you want. Neither of these skills is particularly difficult; with a little practice, you'll be using macros all the time.

If this sounds like lazy man's programming, it is: macros give you a simple way to do very complicated things without learning Lisp and without learning any customization tricks. If the task you build the macro for is something you have to do frequently, you can save macros and load them when you want to use them. In this way, you can build up a set of convenient macros that become your own editing commands. Even if you don't write Lisp, you're not limited to the commands Emacs gives you; you can make your own!

---

* You could delete the third column of a table by marking it as a rectangle, as described in Chapter 7. But bear with us for the sake of making this point: when you find yourself doing repetitive work, macros are the tool to remember.

What you use macros for will depend on the kind of work you do in Emacs. We've used macros to:

- Mark up text for formatting.
- Copy headings from one buffer to another to create an outline.
- Perform complex search-and-replace type operations that query-replace can't quite handle.
- Create index entries.
- Reformat files that were imported from another application.
- Edit tables.
- Compile, run, and test the output from a program with a single command.
- Manipulate and clean large datasets.

You'll be able to think of many more things to do with macros after you learn the few basic commands you need to use them.

A Macro Revolution

In this book, we almost never emphasize which version of Emacs we're talking about. Macros, specifically changes to macros in Emacs 21.3.5, have forced our hand. Macros underwent a major overhaul in 21.3.5. Although some of the core key bindings still work the same way, the keyboard macro functionality was radically expanded. If you are running an earlier version of Emacs, we encourage you to install the latest version (see Chapter 13) or go to the web site for this book, *http://www.oreilly.com/catalog/gnu3/*, which includes a link to an earlier version of this chapter.

Defining a Macro

To start defining a macro, press **F3** or **C-x** (.[*] The abbreviation Def appears on the mode line, showing that you are in macro definition mode. In this mode, Emacs records all the keystrokes that you type, whether they are commands or literal text, so that you can replay them later. To end the macro, press **F4** or **C-x**); you leave macro definition mode, and Emacs stops recording your keystrokes. Emacs also stops recording your keystrokes automatically if an error occurs or if you press **C-g**.

---

[*] Mac OS X users may have bound **F3** and **F4**, used in defining and executing macros, to another key. These users should press **Option-F3** and **Option-F4** to get the same functionality.

While you're defining a macro, Emacs acts on your keystrokes as well as recording them: that is, anything you type while in macro definition mode is treated as a regular command and executed. While you're defining a macro, you're doing completely normal editing. That way you can see that the macro does exactly what you want it to, and you can cancel it (with **C-g**) if you notice that the macro isn't really quite what you want.

To execute your macro, press **F4** or **C-x e**. Emacs then replays your keystrokes exactly. (You can see that **F4** has two different functions relating to macros: to end a macro definition and, after it's defined, to execute the macro.)

This macro is referred to as the "last" keyboard macro, with last here meaning most recent. Only one macro is the last keyboard macro. A macro ring, much like the kill ring, allows you to access a number of macros during an Emacs session.

Table 6-1 shows the steps required to define and execute a macro. This macro takes a list of names in the ordinary First Name Last Name order and changes it to the frequently needed Last Name, First Name order.

Table 6-1. Steps for creating name transposition macro

Keystrokes	Action
F3 *or* **C-x (**	Start the macro; Def appears on the mode line.
C-a	Move to the beginning of the current line.
M-f	Move forward a word.
,	Type a comma.
M-t	Transpose first and last.
C-n	Move to the next line.
F4 *or* **C-x)**	End the macro definition.

Define the macro using the keystrokes given in Table 6-1.

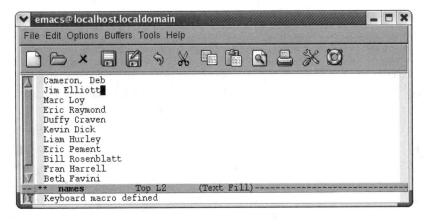

In defining the macro, you transposed the names on the first line, leaving the cursor on the second line.

Now let's be brave and assume the macro works; we'll try repeating it five times by prefacing the command to execute a macro with **M-5**. Of course, in real life, you'd be better off trying it once before doing anything so bold.

Type **M-5 F4** or **M-5 C-x e**

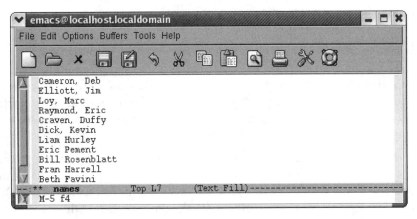

Now we've done the first six lines: one by defining the macro and five more by executing it.

The macro works well, so we can finish the rest of the buffer with confidence: type **M-100**, then **C-x e** or **F4**. Emacs stops automatically when you reach the end of the buffer, so it doesn't matter if you repeat the macro more times than necessary.

Here are a few points to remember:

- Don't forget to press **F4** or **C-x)** when you've finished the macro. If you try to execute a macro before it has been defined, Emacs complains and forgets the macro's definition.
- **C-g** terminates a macro, causing Emacs to forget its definition.
- Virtually any error automatically terminates a macro. If Emacs beeps at you, you have to start over.
- Emacs executes the keystrokes *exactly* as you type them, with no intelligence whatsoever. Avoid making assumptions like, "Of course I'll be at the beginning (or end) of the line when I execute the macro."

If you invoke a macro and it does the wrong thing, you can use **C-_** to undo it. Emacs is smart enough to realize that "undo the last command" means "undo the entire macro" rather than "undo the last command within the macro." However, if you repeat a macro multiple times using **M-*n***, **C-_** undoes only the last instance of the macro, not all the instances.

Tips for Creating Good Macros

It's easy to learn how to record and reuse your keystrokes. However, when you're starting out, you make a few mistakes: you create a macro, use it, and then find out that it doesn't do exactly what you thought. With a little care, it's easy to make your macros more useful and less vulnerable to mistakes.

Good macros work in all situations. Therefore, within a macro, you should use commands that are absolute rather than relative. For example, if you write a macro that puts a formatting string around the word the cursor is on, you want the macro to work no matter how long the word is. Therefore, you would use an absolute command such as **M-f** (for **forward-word**) rather than a few **C-f**s to move forward one character at a time. Similarly, commands such as **C-e** and **C-a** are good for finding the beginning or end of a line rather than moving the cursor forward or backward.

Often, macros start with a search command that brings you to the place in the file you want the macro to start. It's a good idea to type the search argument (as in **C-s** *searchstring*) rather than using the command to repeat the last search (**C-s C-s**). You may have changed the search string between the time you define the macro and the time you execute it, and **C-s C-s** remembers only what the last search string was.

It is often a good idea to add extra commands (typically **C-a** and **C-e**) that aren't strictly necessary, just to make sure that you're positioned correctly on the line. The fewer assumptions that a macro makes, the better it works. So, if a sequence of commands works correctly only if you start at the end of the line, start the macro with **C-e**, even if you already "know" that you want to give the command only when you're at the end of the line.

Finally, while we're reciting rules and cautions, here's one more: keep in mind that you probably want to execute macros repeatedly. With a little foresight, you'll be able to create macros that can be executed in long chains without problems.

In general, good macros have three parts:

- They find the place you want the macro to start working (often using search).
- They do the work that needs to be done on the text.
- They prepare themselves to repeat.

How can a macro prepare itself to repeat? For example, assume that you're writing a macro to delete the third column of a table. After deleting the column, the macro should position itself at the beginning of the next line (or wherever it needs to be) so you don't have to reposition the cursor before reusing it.

Here's a slightly more complex example. If you start a macro with a search, you have to make sure that the end of the macro moves the cursor past the last spot you searched for. If you don't, the macro will keep finding the same place in the file and never go on to the next occurrence of what you're searching for. As a general rule, if your macro operates on a line of text, it should end by moving to the beginning of the next line. Remember that your goal is to create a sequence of keystrokes that can be executed many times in a row, with no interruption.

A More Complicated Macro Example

Sometimes you may want to find all the references to a particular topic in a file. Table 6-2 lists steps for creating a macro that takes takes every sentence in the buffer that contains the word *Emacs* and copies it to another buffer. If you try this macro, you'll need to type some text about Emacs into a buffer. You can also get a test file to work with by opening the Emacs *NEWS* file (using **C-h n**), then writing it to a file (**C-x C-w NEWS**). This buffer is in view mode by default; change to text mode by typing **M-x text-mode Enter**.

Table 6-2. *Steps for macro that creates a buffer of Emacs references*

Keystrokes	Action
F3 *or* C-x (	Start macro definition; Def appears on the mode line.
C-s emacs	Find the word Emacs.
Enter	Stop the search after it is successful; if the search is unsuccessful, it rings the bell and stops the macro.
M-a	Move to the beginning of the sentence.[a]
C-Space	Set the mark.
M-e	Move to the end of the sentence.
M-w	Copy the sentence to the kill ring.

Table 6-2. Steps for macro that creates a buffer of Emacs references (continued)

Keystrokes	Action
C-x b emacsrefs Enter	Move to a buffer called emacsrefs.
C-y	Insert the sentence.
Enter	Start the next sentence on a new line.
C-x b Enter	Move back to the original buffer.
F4 *or* C-x)	End the macro definition; Def is removed from the mode line.

a M-a's definition of a "sentence" is controlled by the variable **sentence-end**, which is a fairly complex regular expression. By default, a sentence ends with a period, question mark, or exclamation mark, optionally followed by a quotation mark or parenthesis (including brackets or braces), and followed by two or more spaces or a newline.

Now, assume that you've already constructed the macro outlined in Table 6-2 and that you can invoke it with **F4**. The following screen shows what happens when you run it five times and then display the emacsrefs buffer.

Type: **M-5 F4** or **M-5 C-x e**, followed by **C-x b Enter**

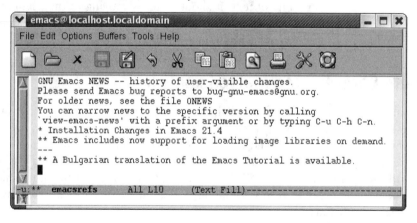

By executing the macro repeatedly, we've created a buffer that contains references to the Emacs editor.

As in the previous example, you can jump back and forth between an unlimited number of buffers while defining a macro. Macros don't need to be confined to one buffer. Macros that work with several buffers are more difficult to debug; when several buffers are involved, it becomes harder for you to keep track of where the cursor and the mark are. It is also easy to make mistaken assumptions about what buffer you're visiting; hence, it's a good idea to specify the buffer name explicitly. However, after you get accustomed to working with macros and multiple buffers, you'll be amazed at how much work you can do with almost no effort.

Windows are sometimes useful in macros, but, again, you have to watch out. It's better to start a macro with one window on the screen, have the macro open other windows, and finally close all but one window (**C-x 1**). If you write a macro with two windows on the screen and later try to execute it with four windows on the screen, the results will be unpredictable at best! In general, moving to a named buffer, **C-x b** *buffername*, is preferable to moving to the "other" window using **C-x o** (too vague to be generally useful). The other window could be anything—a *Help* buffer, *Completion* buffer, *shell* buffer, and so on. Moving to a named buffer always gets you to the right place, no matter how (or whether) the buffer is displayed.

Editing a Macro

You can edit a macro and make changes to it in a few different ways. For this example, we chose an all-purpose editing command, **edit-kbd-macro**, which is bound to **C-x C-k e**. Several macro editing commands are available, but this one works for all types of macros, so it's good to learn.

Our macro could use a bit of tweaking. First of all, finding references to Emacs in our copy of the Emacs *NEWS* file is pretty lame. Perhaps we're interested in using a mouse more frequently with Emacs and would like to know about changes to that part of the interface. We'll edit the macro to search for the word *mouse*. We'll also modify it so it marks a paragraph rather than a sentence since a sentence doesn't really provide enough context to be helpful.

Let's start editing the macro.

Type: **C-x C-k e**

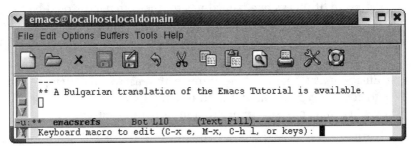

Emacs prompts you for the type of macro to edit.

Emacs asks you if you want to edit the last keyboard macro (**C-x e**), a named macro (**M-x**), the last 100 keystrokes as a macro, termed "lossage" (**C-h l**), or keys (meaning the keystrokes you bound a macro to). Yes, that's a lot of choices, and later in the chapter we describe named macros and binding macros to keys (you can experiment on your own with creating a macro from lossage). For now, just choose **C-x e** to edit the last keyboard macro.

Type: **C-x e**

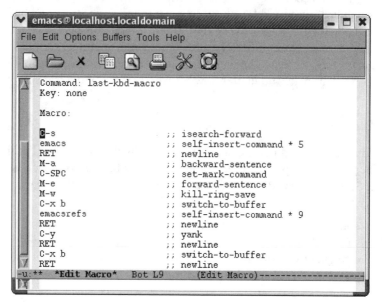

Emacs opens an *Edit Macro* buffer.

Notice two fields near the top of this buffer, Command: and Key:. Right now, Command: says last-kbd-macro. If this were a named macro, the command would be the name you gave your macro. Additionally, for frequent use, you can bind your macro to a key, at which point the Key: field lists the keystrokes to execute this macro. Right now it says none because we haven't defined any keystrokes yet.

Note that Emacs inserts comments all through the macro. It's attempting to map keystrokes to commands. You do not need to update these comments or add comments if you add commands to your macro; Emacs does that itself.

To tweak our macro, we change the search string on the second line from *emacs* to *mouse*. Note that we can just press **C-k** to wipe out the line and type mouse. Now change **M-a** to **M-{** and **M-e** to **M-}**. We change the buffer name from emacsrefs to mouseinfo.

We've made the edits from the previous paragraph. The screen looks like this:

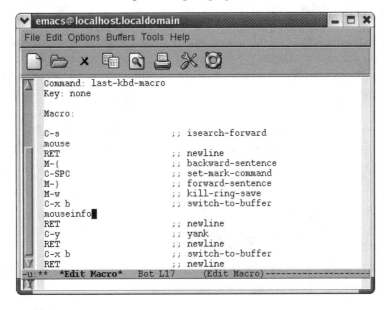

A modified macro that captures information about using a mouse in Emacs.

To exit the macro editing buffer, we have to type **C-c C-c** and go back to our NEWS buffer. Let's do that and then execute the macro again to see what happens.

Type: **C-c C-c C-x b Enter M-< M-5 F4 C-x b Enter M-<**

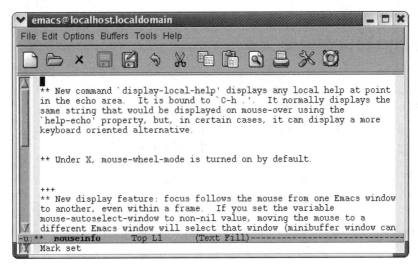

The mouseinfo buffer shows paragraphs from our copied *NEWS* file that mention the mouse.

The Macro Ring

Although our latest macro is interesting, it's not really a general purpose macro. It is a temporary solution to a one-time problem. It saves you some work, but it isn't general enough to save and use again. On the other hand, our macro to transpose names is generally useful. We'd like to use it again. We'd like to bind it to a key. But it is no longer the "latest" keyboard macro.

As we mentioned earlier, Emacs has a macro ring much like the infamous kill ring. It's useful in the case we've just described, but it's also useful because of the fragility of the macro definition process. You create a macro and make a wrong move that rings the bell, and your macro is canceled. It's fairly easy to create a macro that does nothing. Perhaps the macro that you just created was wonderful, and this new non-functional nothing macro has supplanted it. Again, the macro ring is the solution. To delete a macro from the ring, type **C-x C-k C-d** (for **kmacro-delete-ring-head**). This deletes the most recently defined keyboard macro.

What if you want to swap the positions of two macros? Instead, type **C-x C-k C-t** (for **kmacro-swap-ring**). This transposes macros 1 and 2.

In a more general sense, you can cycle to the previously defined macro by typing **C-c C-k C-p** (for **kmacro-cycle-ring-previous**). To move the ring the other way, type **C-x C-k C-n** (for **kmacro-cycle-ring-next**). The familiar **C-p** for previous and **C-n** for next bindings are appended to the general macro keyboard prefix **C-x C-k**.

Before we can work with the transpose names macro, we must either define it again or, if you've been working through our examples, type **C-x C-k C-p** to move to the previous macro.

Binding Your Macro to a Key

Binding a macro to a key is easy. The key sequences **C-x C-k 0** through **9** and capital **A** through **Z** are reserved for user macro bindings. You can choose one that strikes you as mnemonic for your macro.

For example, to bind our transpose names macro to **C-x C-k T**, type **C-x C-k b**. Emacs prompts for the key binding. Type **C-x C-k T Enter**. Emacs confirms, Keyboard macro bound to C-x C-k T. Binding a macro command to a key in this way works for only one session. We want to keep this macro, so read on to find out how to make this binding permanent.

Naming, Saving, and Executing Your Macros

In this section, we'll describe how to save macros so that you can use them in different editing sessions. To save a macro, bind it permanently to a key, and load it in subsequent Emacs sessions, follow these steps:

1. Define the macro, if you haven't already.

2. Type **C-x C-k n** (for **name-last-kbd-macro**). Now type a name for your macro and press **Enter**. A non-Emacs sounding name is best so that Emacs doesn't confuse it with one of its own commands. Once you've executed this command, Emacs remembers the macro for the rest of the editing session. To use it again, type the command **M-x *name*** (where *name* is the name you've chosen). Emacs treats your named macro like one of its own commands; it shows up in completion lists if you press **Tab** after typing a few letters of the name.

3. If you want to save the macro definition permanently, you must insert the macro definition into a file. This could be your *.emacs* file or a macro file that you load through your *.emacs* file. Type **C-x C-f** *filename* **Enter** to find the file into which to insert the definition and move to the end of it by typing **M->**.

4. Type **M-x insert-kbd-macro Enter** *macroname* **Enter**. Emacs inserts Lisp code that represents your macro.

5. Add a line to *.emacs* make the key binding permanent. For example, if we called our macro **transpose-names** and bound it to **C-x C-k T**, we would add this line to our *.emacs* file (or other macro definition file):

   ```
   (global-set-key "\C-x\C-kT" 'transpose-names)
   ```

6. If you save the macro in some other file, it won't be loaded automatically. For example, let's say that you have defined a macro called **transpose-names** and placed it in the file *html.macs*, in the directory *~/macros*. Add this line to your *.emacs* file to load your macros automatically:

   ```
   (load-file "~/macros/html.macs")
   ```

7. Save the *.emacs* file and, if different, the file in which you inserted your macro. Exit and restart Emacs. You can now execute this macro either by typing **M-x transpose-names Enter** or by pressing **C-x C-k T**.

Building More Complicated Macros

So far, we've covered the basics of writing, executing, and saving keyboard macros. Now let's discuss a couple of more advanced features Emacs lets you add to your macros: pausing a macro for keyboard input and inserting a query in a macro.

Pausing a Macro for Keyboard Input

Sometimes it's useful to pause a macro briefly so you can type something. For example, if you write a lot of letters, you could have a macro that prints out a template and then pauses for you to fill in variables (such as the date and the recipient's name). You can perform this task (and similar tasks) by inserting a recursive edit into a macro. A recursive edit is just a fancy way to say, "Stop and let me type a while, then pick up the macro where I left off."

When you're defining a macro, type **C-u C-x q** at the point where you want the recursive edit to occur. Emacs enters a recursive edit. (You can tell you're in a recursive edit because square brackets appear on the mode line; you'll see them in the screenshots later in this section.) Nothing you type during the recursive edit becomes a part of the macro. You can type whatever you want to and then press **C-M-c** to exit the recursive edit. Notice how the square brackets disappear when you type **C-M-c**. When the square brackets are no longer on the screen, you have left the recursive edit. Anything you type at this point becomes part of the macro. You can put as many pauses in your macros as you want to.

Example

Here's an example of a macro that puts a business letter template on the screen and uses recursive edits to let you type your return address, the recipient's name and address, and the date. Because the brackets on the mode line are a pretty subtle clue to what you are going to type, we'll give the user of this macro explicit instructions about what to type. Table 6-3 provides these instructions.

Table 6-3. Steps for creating a business letter macro

Keystrokes	Action
F3 *or* **C-x (**	Start keyboard macro definition.
M-5 Enter	Put in 5 blank lines.
Type your address and press C-M-c	Display Type your address and press C-M-c on the screen.
C-a	Move to the beginning of the line.
C-u C-x q	Enter a recursive edit, during which the keystrokes you type are not recorded as part of the macro.
C-M-c	Exit the recursive edit.
C-e	Move to the end of the line.
M-5 Enter	Move the cursor down 5 lines.
Type recipient name and address and press C-M-c	Display Type recipient name and address and press C-M-c on the screen.
C-a	Move to the beginning of the line.
C-u C-x q	Enter a recursive edit.
C-M-c	Exit the recursive edit.

Table 6-3. Steps for creating a business letter macro (continued)

Keystrokes	Action
C-e	Move to the end of the line.
M-5 Enter	Move the cursor down 5 lines.
Type date and press C-M-c	Display Type date and press C-M-c on the screen.
C-a	Move to the beginning of the line
C-u C-x q	Enter a recursive edit.
C-M-c	Exit the recursive edit.
C-e	Move to the end of the line.
M-5 Enter	Move the cursor down 5 lines.
Dear Space	Display **Dear** on the screen.
F4 *or* C-x)	End keyboard macro definition.

The following screens show what the macro defined in Table 6-3 looks like when you run it.

Type: **F4**

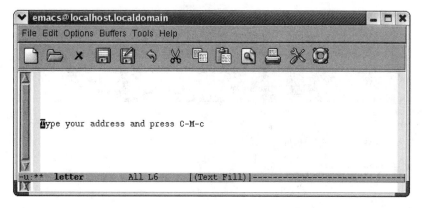

The macro pauses so that you can type your address.

Type your address and press: **C-M-c**

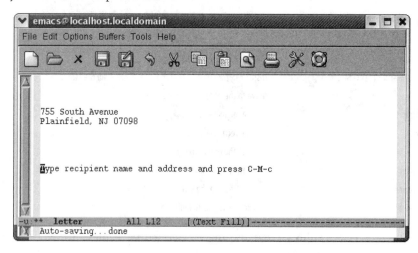

The macro pauses so you can type the recipient's name and address.

Type the recipient's name and address and press: **C-M-c**

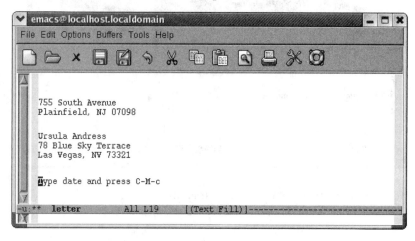

The macro pauses so you can type the date.

Type the date and press: **C-M-c**

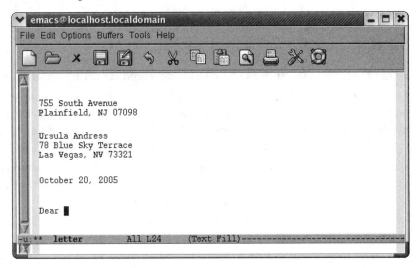

The macro finishes by typing the opening for the letter.

Now the macro has finished editing; you can type the recipient's name and then the body of the letter, and of course you can go back and edit any of the information you've already filled in.

Adding a Query to a Macro

The more complex the task your macro performs, the more difficult it is to make the macro general enough to work in every case. Although macros can do a lot of things, they aren't programs: you can't have **if** statements, loops, and the other things you associate with a program. In particular, a macro can't get input from the user and then take some action on the basis of that input.

However, one feature lets a macro get input, in a limited way, from the user. You can create a macro that queries the user while it is running; it works much like a query-replace. To create this kind of a macro, type **C-x q** when you reach the point in the macro definition where you want the macro to query the user. Nothing happens immediately; go on defining the macro as you normally would.

Things get interesting later, when you execute the macro. When it gets to the point in the macro where you typed **C-x q**, Emacs prints a query in the minibuffer:

```
Proceed with macro? (y, n, RET, C-l, C-r)
```

The responses listed here are analogous to those in query-replace:

- Pressing **y** means to continue and go on to the next repetition, if any.
- Pressing **n** means to stop executing the macro but go on to the next repetition, if any.
- Pressing **Enter** means to stop executing the macro and cancel any repetitions.
- Pressing **C-r** starts a recursive edit, which lets you do any editing or moving around you may want to and then resume the macro when you exit the recursive edit. To exit a recursive edit, press **C-M-c**. Emacs again asks if you want to proceed with the macro, and you type **y** for yes or **n** or **Enter** for no.
- Pressing **C-l** puts the line the cursor is on in the middle of the screen (this is good for getting a feel for the context). Similar to **C-r**, Emacs again asks if you want to proceed with the macro, and you have to answer **y**, **n**, or **Enter**.
- Pressing **C-g** (although not listed as an option) cancels the query and the macro; it is similar to pressing **Enter**.

Example

Let's say that you write a macro that copies comments from a program to another buffer. The comments in our program are preceded by a slash, so you start the macro with a search for a slash. However, not all comments are worth copying. Following the search with a query lets you decide case by case whether the search has found a comment you want to copy. Table 6-4 shows a macro to copy comments to another buffer.

Table 6-4. Comment-copying macro with a query

Keystrokes	Action
F3	Start the macro definition.
C-s /	Search for a slash.
Enter	Stop the search when it is successful.
C-x q	Insert a query in the macro; Emacs asks you if you want to proceed at this point when you run the macro.
M-f	Move forward one word.
M-b	Move to the beginning of this word.
C-Space	Set the mark.
C-e	Move to the end of the line.
C-f	Move forward one character.
M-w	Copy the comment to the kill ring.

Table 6-4. Comment-copying macro with a query (continued)

Keystrokes	Action
C-x b comments	Move to a buffer called comments.
C-y	Insert the comment in the buffer.
C-x b	Move back to the original buffer.
F4	End the macro definition.

Executing Macros on a Region

A special command lets you execute a macro on each line in a region. How frequently do you encounter an email with text that you want to yank, but that is quoted several indentation levels? Of course, we can think of several ways to delete the indentation quickly, but a line-oriented macro is a quick approach too. You define the macro and execute it on a region by typing **C-x C-k r** (for **apply-macro-to-region-lines**). Remember that earlier we said that macros should set themselves up to repeat? This command is different because it expects to work on one line at a time. You don't want to set it up to repeat by moving to the next line; it does that automatically.

Table 6-5 shows a quick line-oriented macro that deletes indentation marks from text quoted in an email or newsgroup message.

Table 6-5. Macro for deleting indentation marks

Keystrokes	Action
F3	Start the macro definition.
C-a	Move to the beginning of the line.
M-f	Move forward one word.
M-b	Move to the beginning of this word.
C-Space	Set the mark.
C-a	Move to the beginning of the line.
C-w	Delete the extraneous indentation characters.
F4	End the macro definition.

Initial state:

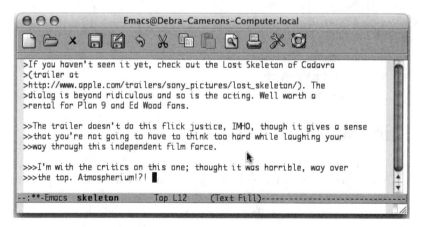

Text indented at various levels (Mac OS X).

Mark the text as a region, move to the beginning of the region, then type: **C-x C-k r**

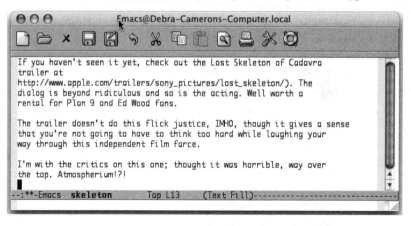

Indentation is deleted (Mac OS X).

Beyond Macros

Macros are an important tool for streamlining repetitive editing. They let you write your own commands for performing complex tasks without needing to know anything more than you already know: the basic Emacs commands for moving around and manipulating text. Even if you're an Emacs novice, you should be able to use macros with little difficulty.

However, Emacs is almost infinitely flexible, and macros cannot do everything. In many situations, there's no substitute for writing a Lisp function that does exactly what you want. If you know Lisp or would like to learn some, you can write your own Lisp functions to do more complex tasks than keyboard macros can handle. Chapter 11 covers the basics of writing Lisp functions.

Table 6-6 summarizes macro commands.

Table 6-6. Macro commands

Keystrokes	Command name	Action
C-x (	kmacro-start-macro	Start macro definition.
F3	kmacro-start-macro-or-insert-counter	Start macro definition. If pressed while defining a macro, insert a counter.
C-x)	kmacro-end-macro	End macro definition.
F4	kmacro-end-or-call-macro	End macro definition (if definition is in progress) or invoke last keyboard macro.
C-x e	kmacro-end-and-call-macro	Execute last keyboard macro defined. Can type **e** to repeat macro.
C-x C-k n	name-last-kbd-macro	Name the last macro you created (before saving it).
(*none*)	insert-kbd-macro	Insert the macro you named into a file.
(*none*)	*macroname*	Execute a named keyboard macro.
C-x q	kbd-macro-query	Insert a query in a macro definition.
C-u C-x q	(none)	Insert a recursive edit in a macro definition.
C-M-c	exit-recursive-edit	Exit a recursive edit.
C-x C-k b	kmacro-bind-to-key	Bind a macro to a key (**C-x C-k 0-9** and **A-Z** are reserved for macro bindings). Lasts for current session only.
C-x C-k Space	kmacro-step-edit-macro	Edit a macro while stepping through it (in our opinion, the interface is overly complex).
C-x C-k l	kmacro-edit-lossage	Turn the last 100 keystrokes into a keyboard macro. If any mouse clicks are among the last 100 keystrokes, does not work.
C-x C-k e	edit-kbd-macro	Edit a keyboard macro by typing C-x e for the last keyboard macro defined, M-x for a named macro, C-h l for lossage, or keystrokes for a macro bound to a key.
C-x C-k Enter	kmacro-edit-macro	Edit the last keyboard macro.
C-x C-k C-e	kmacro-edit-macro-repeat	Edit the last keyboard macro again.
C-x C-k C-t	kmacro-swap-ring	Transpose last keyboard macro with previous keyboard macro.
C-x C-k C-d	kmacro-delete-ring-head	Delete last keyboard macro from the macro ring.
C-x C-k C-p	kmacro-cycle-ring-previous	Move to the previous macro in the macro ring.
C-x C-k C-n	kmacro-cycle-ring-next	Move to the next macro in the macro ring.
C-x C-k r	apply-macro-to-region-lines	Apply this macro to each line in a region.

CHAPTER 7

Simple Text Formatting and Specialized Editing

Emacs is fundamentally a text editor, rather than a word processor: it is a tool that creates files containing exactly what you see on the screen rather than a tool that makes text files look beautiful when printed. However, Emacs does give you the capability to do the following:

- Indent text using tabs and other indentation tricks.

- Center words, lines, and paragraphs of text.

- Hide and show portions of a document using outline mode, which gives you a feel for a document's overall structure. Outline mode can make it easier to go from rough outline, to detailed outline, to rough draft, to the final product.

- Edit by column rather than by line (especially helpful when you create or change tables or work with column-oriented datasets), referred to in Emacs as *rectangle editing*.

- Create simple pictures using keyboard characters or the mouse.

Much of this chapter, though, focuses on some fairly simple stuff: tabs and indenting text. We describe Emacs's behavior in primarily two major modes: fundamental mode and text mode. If you are a developer, you'll probably want to write code in a mode appropriate to the language you're using; see Chapter 9 for details. If you use a markup language like HTML, see Chapter 8 for additional relevant information.

Using Tabs

Tabs provide an easy way to do some simple formatting. While we were revising this book, we found that the way Emacs handles tabs has changed a great deal. This section describes first how Emacs works by default and then discusses what you can do to change the default behavior to meet your needs.

How Emacs 21 Handles Tabs by Default

If you open a new file in text mode, tabs are set every eight spaces by default. (Programming modes have their own indentation behavior; see Chapter 9 for details.)

Press **Tab**.

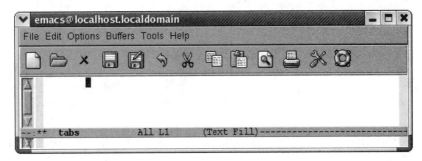

Pressing **Tab** in text mode or fundamental mode inserts a tab character that moves the cursor forward eight columns by default.

Watch what happens when we type a sentence. The default tab stops change automatically.

Type: **It was the best of times Enter Tab Tab**

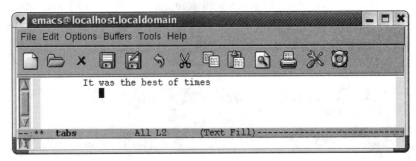

Pressing **Tab** twice moves the cursor under the word *was*, clearly less than eight columns.

Every time you press **Tab**, Emacs moves the cursor under the next word. This is the behavior that many people expect when writing code. Neatly lined up code is easier to read.

As we experimented with this feature, we would tab across under each word, and press **Enter**. What happens next is surprising if you are not expecting it. Emacs considers that newline to be the only character you typed on the line, so pressing **Tab** on a subsequent line brings you nearly to the end of the line.

Press **Tab** repeatedly to the end of the window, press **Enter**, then press **Tab** once.

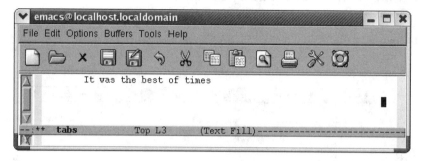

Emacs moves the cursor to the column where you pressed **Enter**.

If you press **Enter** but don't press **Tab** at all, the indentation level moves back to the left margin.

Changing tabs to align with each word can be helpful, if, for example, you're typing tables. However, the default tab behavior may not be helpful to you in all situations. If you are interested in changing the default behavior, read on and we'll describe how to get Emacs to do what you want it to do.

Changing Tab Stops

By default (and if text is not lining up with some previous line of text), tabs are set every eight characters. Emacs allows you to change the positions of the tab stops. To change the tab stops, type **M-x edit-tab-stops**. A *Tab Stops* buffer appears.

Type: **M-x edit-tab-stops**

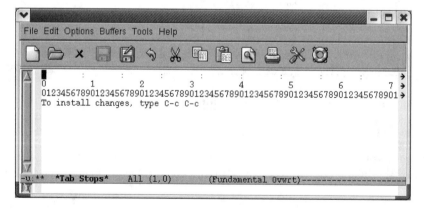

You now see a tab stop ruler; colons show the locations of tab stops.

The colons in the first line of the display show you where tab stops are currently located. The next two lines form a ruler that shows each character position on the line. To insert a tab, use **C-f** to move to the desired column, and then type a colon (:). To delete a tab, move to the desired tab, and press **Space**. The *Tab Stops* buffer is in overwrite mode, so these changes won't change the position of other tabs. Make sure that you do all your editing in the first line of the display. Changes made to the other lines won't have any effect.

When you're satisfied with the tab stops, press **C-c C-c** to install them. If you don't make any changes, press **C-c C-c** to exit the buffer. If you make some changes and then decide you don't want them after all, kill the buffer by typing **C-x k Enter**. The default tab stops remain in effect.

If you press **C-c C-c** to install them, the new tab settings affect all buffers that you create but remain in effect for this Emacs session only.

Again, it may well appear to you that this feature doesn't work as you would expect. Because Emacs's default behavior tries to align with preceding lines, changing tab stops really affects only the first line of any buffer.

In this example, we set the first tab at column 51, pressed **C-c C-c** to install the tab stops, and started a new buffer. Pressing **Tab** at the beginning of the buffer moves the cursor immediately to column 51. That works fine.

Press **Tab** once.

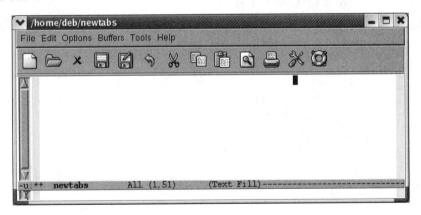

Cursor moves to column 51.

Now we press **Tab** a few more times, followed by **Enter** to move to a new line.

When we press **Tab** on the second line, Emacs views the newline as the only item on the last line. Pressing **Tab** moves us right to the end of the line.

Press **Tab** on the next line.

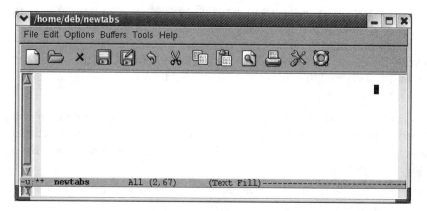

Emacs moves to the end of the line.

As you can see, changing tab stops in this way is of limited efficacy if you're going to add blank lines between rows of your table or whatever you're typing. You'd have to work around this by adding blank lines after typing the whole table, perhaps using a macro as described in Chapter 6.

What if You Want Literal Tabs?

Let's say that all this tab finery is getting on your nerves. You don't want context-sensitive indenting; you don't even want to change tab stops. There is a way to make Emacs treat tabs just like a regular old typewriter did, moving over eight characters at a time.[*]

To insert rigid, typewriter-style tabs, press **C-q Tab**. In theory, this should insert a tab character into the file, which would look like ^I. In practice, it moves the cursor forward rigidly eight columns.

---

[*] You can't change tab stops with this method, but you can change tab width. We'll cover this shortly.

Type: **C-q Tab**

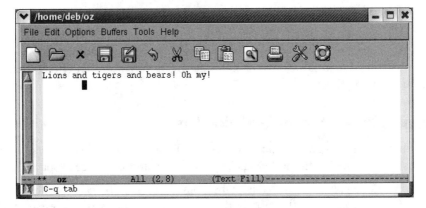

The cursor moves eight columns forward and does not align with the text in the previous line.

C-q Tab does in fact insert a tab character in the file. You can check that by erasing it with a single press of the **Del** key.

Changing Tab Width

One problem with tabs is that there is no universal definition of what a tab means. In *vi*, the default tab width is four columns versus eight columns in Emacs. Further, Unix generally favors eight columns for tabs while some operating systems tend to use four spaces. Emacs uses eight columns by default no matter what platform it's running on. If you view another user's file in Emacs, Emacs interprets the tabs as eight columns each, throwing things off. For this reason, you might want to set your tab default to four columns by adding this line to your *.emacs* file:

```
(setq-default tab-width 4)
```

You have to press **C-q Tab** to have the modified tab width take effect.

Tabs and Spaces

Another characteristic of Emacs's default behavior is the fact that it may insert a combination of tabs and spaces when you press **Tab**. Try to erase a few "tabs" and you'll see that often it isn't one character, but the equivalent number of spaces or a combination of tabs and spaces. Of course, this largely depends on the tab stops compared to setting of the tab-width variable. If you set tab stops that are multiples of six while you have a tab-width of 4 or 8, Emacs is going to have to use a combination of tabs and spaces to achieve the desired tab stops.

If you want Emacs to insert spaces for indentation rather than tab characters, add this line to your *.emacs* file:

```
(setq-default indent-tabs-mode nil)
```

With this setting, Emacs inserts only spaces when you press **Tab**. Pressing **C-q Tab** instead inserts a literal tab character. It's safe to say you won't enter tab characters accidentally with this setting.

Changing Tabs to Spaces (and Vice Versa)

We've just talked about a way to make sure that Emacs inserts spaces instead of tabs. But what if you inherit a file and it has tabs that you want to change to spaces?

Emacs provides a command to banish tabs from your files. You can use tabs for editing and then convert all of the tabs to the appropriate number of spaces so that the appearance of your file doesn't change. Unlike tabs, a space is almost always well defined. The command for eliminating tabs is **M-x untabify**. There's a corresponding command to convert spaces into tabs: **tabify**. However, we trust that you'll take our advice and forget about it.

The **untabify** command works on a region. Therefore, to use it, you must put the mark somewhere in the buffer (preferably at the beginning), move to some other place in the buffer (preferably the end), and type **M-x untabify Enter**. The command **C-x h** (for **mark-whole-buffer**) automatically puts the cursor at the beginning of the buffer and the mark at the end. It makes untabification a bit easier because you can do it all at once with the simple sequence **C-x h M-x untabify Enter**.

Table 7-1 shows the tab commands we've covered in this section.

Table 7-1. Tab commands

Keystrokes	Command name	Action
(none)	edit-tab-stops	Open a buffer called *Tab Stops* where you can change the tab settings.
(none)	untabify	Change all tabs into the equivalent number of spaces.
(none)	tabify	Change groups of three or more spaces to tabs where possible without affecting the text placement.

Indenting Text

Emacs provides the ability to indent paragraphs, like a block quote in a paper. It also allows you to use a paragraph style that indents just the first line of a paragraph. This section describes indentation-related commands, including how to change the margins for the current session.

Before we start, make sure you're in text mode. Look at the mode line and, if the word Text is displayed, you are in text mode. If not, type **M-x text-mode Enter** to enter text mode.

Indenting Paragraphs

Let's say you're writing a paper and want to include some indented block quotes. Emacs's default behavior makes this a no-brainer.* After you finish your first paragraph, use tabs or spaces to indent to the desired level and start typing the quote. Emacs automatically fills the paragraph and the quote correctly, as shown in the following screen.

Some indented text:

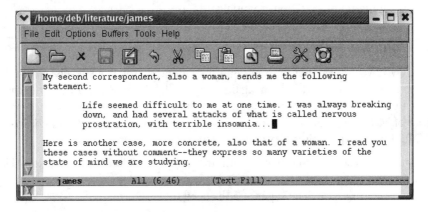

Emacs indents the text properly and fills it correctly in auto-fill mode.

What if an indented quote has multiple paragraphs? You could just press **Enter** and then **Tab** again at the beginning of subsequent paragraphs or you could press **C-j** (for **newline-and-indent**). Pressing **C-j** twice gives you a blank line between paragraphs.

Indenting the First Line of a Paragraph

Some people prefer paragraphs in which the first line is indented. Knowing about the intricacies of tabs, you might be concerned that pressing **Tab** to indent the opening line of your paragraph will incite Emacs to indent the whole paragraph as you continue typing. And it would, to be honest.

---

* Once upon a time, you had to enter indented text mode explicitly to get the behavior we describe here. Now it is on by default in text mode.

Emacs provides a special mode for this purpose: paragraph indent text mode. It's also available as a minor mode. Enter either **M-x paragraph-indent-text-mode** or **M-x paragraph-ident-minor-mode** respectively. If you run the major mode, Emacs displays Parindent on the mode line.

When you press **Tab** to start a paragraph, Emacs inserts a tab's worth of space. When you start a new paragraph, you don't have to skip a line in between and pressing **Tab** to start that second paragraph yields again a tab's worth of space, not aligning with the second word of the previous line as Emacs would do in text mode or fundamental mode.

Pressing **M-q** reformats paragraphs without mushing them all together. If you prefer indented paragraphs, this mode is exactly what you want. When you need to indent a block quote, you may want to temporarily enter text mode to make it easier and add your paragraph indentations manually.

Filling Indented Paragraphs

Let's say you've got a paper with paragraphs indented at various levels. What if you edit them and need to fill them again? Especially if there are no blank lines in between paragraphs, **M-q** munges all the text into one big (nonindented) paragraph. Instead of **M-q**, mark the region in question and use a special fill command: **M-x fill-individual-paragraphs**. Emacs preserves each paragraph's indentation.

Let's contrast these two commands with an example. We'll use our previous Henry James example, but delete the lines between paragraphs to show what happens if you use **M-q** in this case. These paragraphs need to be reformatted.

Initial state:

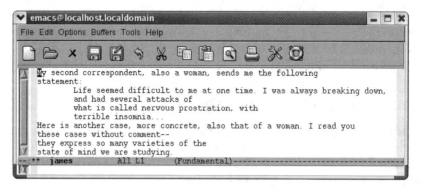

Some sample paragraphs from Henry James, in need of reformatting.

Type: **M-q**

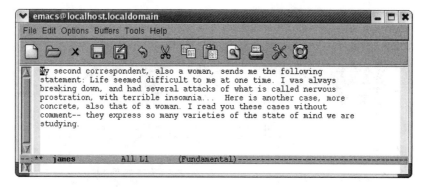

Emacs munges it all into one large paragraph.

We'll undo that command, mark the buffer as a region, and use the **fill-individual-paragraphs** command.

Type: **C- _ C-x h M-x fill-individual-paragraphs Enter**

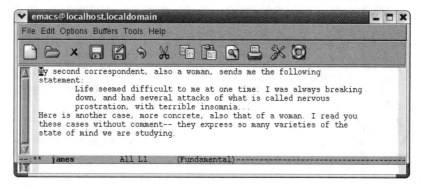

Emacs refills the paragraphs properly.

Indenting regions

What if you have already typed your text without indentation and want to indent it later? Two commands can handle this, depending on how far you want to indent the region.

The **indent-region** command, bound to **C-M-**, can indent a region one level easily. If you want to indent two levels, it is unpredictable. (This command is designed for indenting code.)

Here's an example. The second paragraph is marked as a region.

Type: **C-M-**

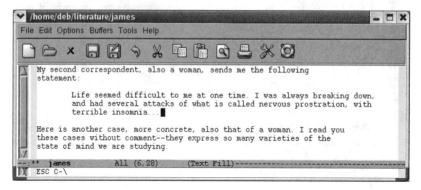

Emacs indents the paragraph one level.

You decide that's not far enough.

Type: **C-M-**

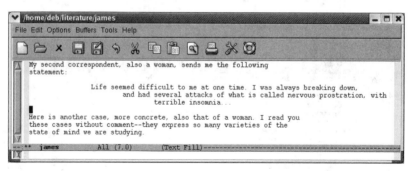

Emacs creates a stairstep hanging indent.

So you can see that this works fine if you're indenting one level. If you try this with multiple paragraphs of different indentation levels, **indent-region** pulls them all to the right, aligning them with the least indented paragraph, probably not what you intended. If you write code, however, this command is great for cleaning up messy indentation.

The other option is to mark the region and type **C-x Tab** (for **indent-rigidly**). By default, this command indents only one space, so if you want to indent further, you need to give it an argument. For example, to indent the previous paragraph 15 spaces:

Mark the region then type: **M-15 C-x Tab**

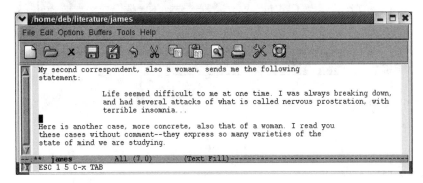

Emacs indents the paragraph 15 spaces.

Although arguably it can be a pain to supply an argument, **indent-rigidly** uniformly indents text, leaving indented paragraphs indented. If you find yourself wanting to indent whole files, you may actually want to change the margin settings, as described in the next section.

Other indentation tricks

Whenever you are using indentation, you can use **M-m** (for **back-to-indentation**) to move to the first nonblank character on a line. On a line that's not indented, this command simply moves you to the beginning of the line. In other words, **M-m** brings you to the "logical" beginning of the line, which is what you usually mean when you type **C-a**.

Another indentation command is **C-M-o** (for **split-line**). You can use this command to create a stairstep effect. Move the cursor to the text that you want to put on the next line and press **C-M-o**. Note that there must be some text following the cursor in order for this command to work properly; if you try it at the end of a line, it does nothing.

Initial state:

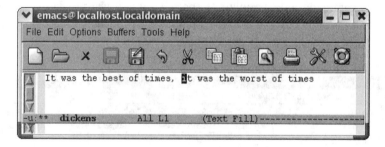

We want to split this line.

Type: **C-M-o**

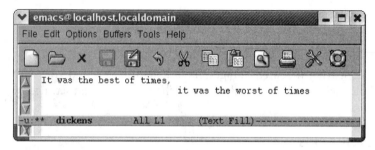

C-M-o splits the line at the cursor position.

Changing Margins

Emacs is not a word processor, but it does have a few commands that change left and right indentation for a buffer for the current session. First, mark the whole buffer using **C-x h**. You can then gchange the indention using **M-x** followed by one of the following commands:

increase-left-margin
decrease-left-margin
increase-right-margin
decrease-right-margin

These commands are also available through the Edit menu. Choose Edit → Text Properties → Indentation to see the options.

Unless you supply a numeric argument using **C-u** or **M-*n*** preceding these commands, Emacs increases or decreases the margins by the number of characters in the variable **standard-indent**, which defaults to 4. If auto-fill mode is on, Emacs also reformats the paragraphs automatically.

Margin settings remain in effect for the current session and the current buffer only. Although the values don't persist to another session, any text that is indented using this method remains indented when you reopen the file. If you open the file again and add some text, however, it is not indented; you have to set the margins again.

These commands work best in cases where you want to change the margin for the whole buffer. If you define a smaller region, the commands work but if you type more paragraphs, the margin settings persist whether you want them to or not. These commands work fine if you've completed the file and then decide to change the indentation.

Alternatively, you can set and save margins using enriched mode, a minor mode that allows Emacs to save text properties, including margin settings and font changes. See Chapter 10 for more details on enriched mode.

Using Fill Prefixes

Fill prefixes are a way of putting a certain string of characters at the beginning of each line in a paragraph or a file. Developers will immediately think of comments as a potential fill prefix. When writing email or newsposts, email programs often insert a string to help readers distinguish the threads of a discussion. For those of us writing text files, fill prefixes can be used to insert whitespace in paragraphs or any relevant string of characters.

The term *fill prefix* comes from the fact that Emacs calls word wrap *auto-fill mode*; in other words, a fill prefix is a string that Emacs should insert at the beginning of each line (or "prefix" each line with) when doing word wrap.

To use fill prefixes, it's best to be in auto-fill mode. If your mode line says `Fill` on it, you're already in auto-fill mode. If it doesn't, type **M-x auto-fill-mode Enter**.

Now let's assume that you want to indent a letter. For the first line of the letter, type your indentation by hand—say, eight spaces. Then type **C-x .** (for **set-fill-prefix**). Emacs displays the message: `fill prefix " "` in the minibuffer. Then start typing normally. Whenever you type past the right margin and Emacs breaks a line for you, it automatically inserts your eight-space indentation at the beginning of the line.

Here's a slightly more exciting example. There's no reason that fill prefixes must to be spaces; they can be anything you choose. Assume that you're sending an email message to your friends to announce a unique event and you want an eye-catching fill prefix.

Type: **Elephant Riding Party!!! C-x .**

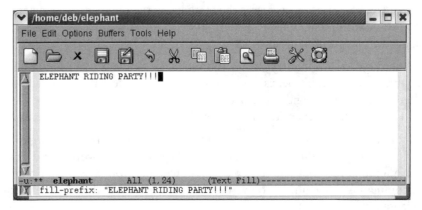

Type the prefix, then **C-x .** to set it.

Once you've set the prefix, you can type your message normally.

Type: **The time ... the zoo.**

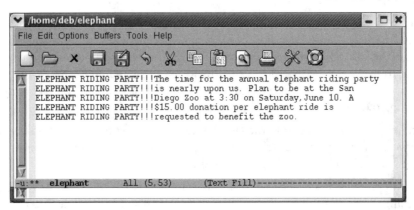

Emacs inserts the fill prefix at the beginning of each line of the message.

You had to type "Elephant Riding Party!!!" only once; Emacs inserted the rest automatically. Here are some things you might want to know about fill prefixes:

- Emacs never applies the fill prefix to the first line of a paragraph. You obviously can't apply it to the first line of the first paragraph (you have to type it somewhere). But Emacs can't apply it to the first line of *any* paragraph. In other words, if the "elephant riding" message had two paragraphs, you'd have to type (or yank) the phrase "Elephant Riding Party!!!" at the beginning of the second paragraph.

However, you don't need to set the fill prefix again. Emacs supplies your prefix for all lines but the first in subsequent paragraphs. It just gets confused about the initial line of any paragraph.

- Once you've started using a fill prefix, how do you turn it off? There's no special command. All you do is put the cursor at the left margin and type **C-x .** to define a new, empty fill prefix.

- You can edit paragraphs with fill prefixes, then reformat them with **M-q**, as long as the fill prefix is still defined. If you have cleared the fill prefix, Emacs reformats the paragraph without regard to the fill prefix. If you need to reformat your paragraphs later, after you've canceled the fill prefix, define it again and then type **M-q**.

Table 7-2 lists the indentation commands we've discussed.

Table 7-2. Indentation commands

Keystrokes	Command name	Action
C-j	**newline-and-indent**	Move to the next line and indent to the current level.
(none)	**paragraph-indent-text-mode**	A major mode for writing paragraphs with indented first lines and no blank lines between paragraphs.
(none)	**paragraph-indent-minor-mode**	The minor mode equivalent of paragraph-indent-text mode.
(none)	**fill-individual-paragraphs**	Reformat indented paragraphs, preserving indentation.
C-x Tab	**indent-rigidly**	Indent one column; preface with **C-u** or **M-n** to specify multiple columns.
C-M-	**indent-region**	Indent a region to match the first line in the region.
M-m	**back-to-indentation**	Move the cursor to the first non-whitespace character on a line.
C-M-o	**split-line**	Split the line at the cursor position and indent it to the column of the cursor position.
(none) *Edit → Text Properties →* *Indentation → Indent More*	**increase-left-margin**	Increase the left indentation level for the buffer by four characters by default.
(none) *Edit → Text Properties →* *Indentation → Indent Less*	**decrease-left-margin**	Decrease the left indentation level for the buffer by four characters by default.
(none) *Edit → Text Properties →* *ndentation → Indent Right More*	**decrease-right-margin**	Decrease the right indentation level for the buffer by four characters by default.
(none) *Edit → Text Properties →* *Indentation → Indent Left More*	**increase-right-margin**	Increase the right indentation level for the buffer by four characters by default.
C-x .	**set-fill-prefix**	Use the information up to the cursor column as a prefix to each line of the paragraph; typing this command in column 1 cancels the fill prefix.

Centering Text

Another common formatting task is centering text. For example, you might want to center the title of a document or individual headings within a document. Emacs provides commands to center lines, paragraphs, and regions.

In text mode, you can center a line by simply typing the line you want to center (or moving anywhere on an existing line), and then pressing **M-s**.

Type: **Annual Report**

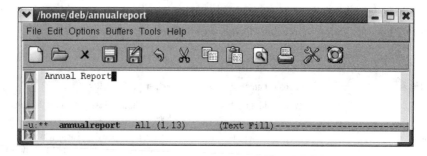

You type the document's title.

Type: **M-s**

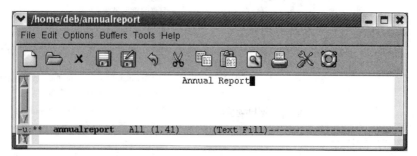

Emacs centers the line.

You can also center paragraphs and regions. In both cases, Emacs does line-by-line centering rather than block centering. To center a paragraph, use the command **M-S** (for **center-paragraph**); to center a region, use **M-x center-region**. For example, let's say you want to center the following quotation.

Type: **M-S**

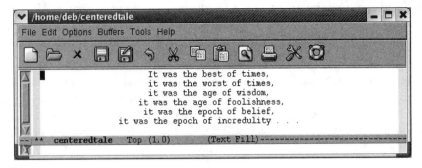

Text is now centered.

In this case, line-by-line centering looks rather artistic. But there are times when you might wish Emacs did block centering. You can replicate this effect by using the **indent-rigidly** command, discussed earlier in this chapter. You just have to play with the indentation to see how far the block of text should be indented to look centered.

There's one more choice for centering. You can change justification by choosing Edit → Text Properties → Justification → Center. This command works on whatever text is selected.

Table 7-3 lists the commands used to center text.

Table 7-3. Centering commands

Keystrokes	Command name	Action
M-s	center-line	Center the line the cursor is on.
M-S	center-paragraph	Center the paragraph the cursor is on.
(none)	center-region	Center the currently defined region.
(none) Edit → Text Properties → Justification → Center	set-justification-center	Center selected text.

Using Outline Mode

When you're writing something, whether it's a book, a long paper, or a technical specification, getting a sense of organization as you go along is frequently difficult. Without a sense of structure, it is hard to expand an outline smoothly into a longer paper or to reorganize a paper as you go along. The words get in the way of your headings, making it hard to see the forest for the trees.

Outline mode provides a built-in solution to this problem. This mode gives you the ability to hide or display text selectively, based on its relationship to the structure of your document. For example, you can hide all of your document's text except for its headings, thereby giving you a feel for the document's shape. When you're looking at the headings, you can focus on structure without being concerned about individual paragraphs. When you've solved your structural problems, you can make the text reappear.

Outline mode is more useful for documents with several levels of headings (or for long programs) than for plain outlines containing very little text. The longer a document is, the harder it is to get a quick feel for the overall structure; it is in such a situation that outline mode's ability to hide and show portions of the text comes in handy.

Outline mode requires you to follow some special conventions in your outline or document. Figure 7-1 shows an outline in traditional format and the same outline prepared for outline mode. On the left, we show a "traditional" outline; on the right, we show the same outline, after being prepared for outline mode:

Traditional outline	Outline mode
All about the Universe	All about the Universe
I. Preface	*Preface
A. Scope of book	**Scope of book
This book is all-inclusive	This book is all-inclusive
B. Intended audience	**Intended audience
Universe dwellers	Universe dwellers
II. Chapter 1	*Chapter 1
A. Universe basics	**Universe basics

Figure 7-1. *Traditional Outline versus Outline Mode*

Whereas traditional outlines use a hierarchical scheme of Roman numerals, uppercase letters, numbers, and lowercase letters for heading levels 1 through 4, outline mode by default expects to see one asterisk (*) for a first-level heading, two for a second-level heading, and so on. Lines that don't start with an *, such as "This book is all-inclusive," are referred to as *body* lines. Notice that Emacs expects to see the asterisk in the first column. You can use traditional outline indentation, provided that the asterisks start in the first column.*

---

* Of course, after the document is complete, you'll want to remove the asterisks. You can use a query-replace to change the asterisk-style headers into headers that are appropriate for your preferred formatting style. Find the lowest-level heading and do its replacement first. If you have third-level headings, replace all occurrences of *** with the mark-up for a third-level heading, then move on to second-level headings, and finally first-level headings. Be careful on first-level headings, though; there may well be asterisks in the file that are unrelated to headings; preface the asterisk with **C-q C-j** to ensure that you get an asterisk that starts on a new line. Another approach is to use Eric Pement's awk scripts. The script at *http://www.student.northpark.edu/pemente/awk/outline_classic11.awk.txt* converts an outline mode outline to a classic outline while the script at *http://www.student.northpark.edu/pemente/awk/outline_numbered11.awk.txt* converts to a numbered outline.

The sample outline has only two body lines. As we developed the book, though, we'd gradually add more and more body: "This book is all-inclusive" would be replaced by a substantial chunk of the preface, and other body lines later in the outline would turn into the text for Chapter 1. When used properly, outline mode removes the distinction between outlining and writing. As your outline grows and becomes more detailed, it can gradually become your paper.

Entering Outline Mode

To start outline mode, type **M-x outline-mode Enter**. Outline appears on the mode line. (Outline mode is also available as a minor mode; we'll discuss that later in this section.)

After you are in outline mode, you can use special commands to move quickly from one part of the outline to another. **C-c C-n** moves to the next heading or subheading; **C-c C-p** moves to the previous one. **C-c C-f** moves to the next heading of the same level, so you can use this command to move from one first-level heading to another throughout the outline, or from one second-level heading to another within a given entry. **C-c C-b** moves backward to the previous heading of the same level. If you want to move from a second-level heading to its first-level heading, up a level in the outline structure, you type **C-c C-u**. (If you are on a first-level heading already, **C-c C-u** beeps because it can't move to a higher level.) Figure 7-2 illustrates how these cursor commands would work on our sample outline.

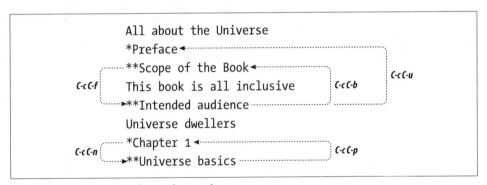

Figure 7-2. *Moving around in outline mode*

These commands make it easy to solve a lot of organizational problems. If you often think, "I know I'm writing about widgets, but I can't remember the bigger point I'm trying to make," type **C-c C-u** to get to the next higher level of the outline. If you want to figure out how widgets relate to the other topics within the section, use **C-c C-b** and **C-c C-f** to move backward and forward to your other headings.

Hiding and Showing Text

The most important feature of outline mode is the ability to selectively hide or show different portions of your text. The ability to see a skeletal view of a long document with outline mode is its best feature; it's much easier to evaluate the structure of a document when you can hide everything but the headings and see whether it is coherent or in need of some reorganization.

Although it sounds like something out of a detective novel, the **hide-body** command, **C-c C-t**, hides all the body (or text) lines but leaves all the headings (lines that begin with an asterisk) visible. Wherever Emacs hides text, it places an ellipsis (...) on the corresponding heading line. The ellipsis tells you that some hidden text is present. The buffer itself is *not* modified; you'll notice, if you watch the left side of the mode line, that the asterisks that indicate a modified buffer don't appear. If you save a file and exit while some text is hidden, Emacs saves the hidden text along with what you see displayed; hiding text in no way implies losing text. The next time you read the file, Emacs shows all text that was hidden.

Using the **hide-body** command is a good way to get a feel for the structure of a long document. You can then type **C-c C-t** and see only the headings without the text. For example, let's start with the simple outline we gave above and hide the body.

Type: **C-c C-t**

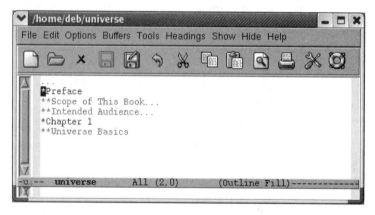

The body is hidden; ellipses show us where body lines are.

To show all the hidden text in a file, whether headings or body, type **C-c C-a** (for **show-all**). These commands, **hide-body** and **show-all**, work on the outline as a whole. A command similar to **hide-body** is **hide-sublevels**, **C-c C-q**. This command shows only first-level headers, giving you a feel for the major sections in the document you're working on.

Type: **C-c C-q**

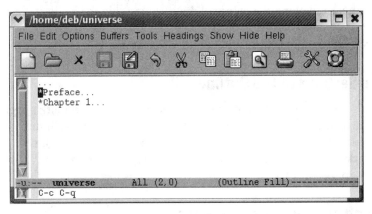

Only first-level headers appear.

Editing While Text Is Hidden

Now that you know how to hide and show text, let's discuss some of the properties of hidden text. Editing a document while some of it is hidden is often useful—it's a great way to make major changes in document structure—but there are some dangers that you should be aware of. Let's say you've hidden all text with outline mode and only the headings are showing, giving you a true "outline" of your document. If you move a heading that has hidden text and headings associated with it, everything that is hidden moves when you move the visible text. Later, when you "show" all of the document, the hidden text appears in its new location—underneath the heading that you moved. Similarly, if you delete a heading, you delete all hidden text as well.

This feature makes moving blocks of text easy. However, there are some things to watch out for. If you delete the ellipsis following an entry, Emacs deletes the hidden information as well. To its credit, Emacs tries to keep you from doing this; it does not allow you to delete the ellipsis using the **Del** key or using normal cursor commands like **C-b** to move the cursor onto it. However, if you're persistent you can delete the ellipses (and the text it represents) using, for example, **C-k**. If you do so, Emacs deletes the hidden text. Typing **C-y** yanks the hidden text that you killed when you deleted the ellipsis; the **undo** command, **C-_**, restores the ellipsis. Our advice is to display text before deleting it so you can see what you're doing. On the other hand, when you are moving sections of an outline around, it is helpful to do sowhile text is hidden so you can keep the structure in mind.

Be careful when moving hidden text to a buffer that's not in outline mode. Let's say that your outline ends with a heading followed by an ellipsis. When marking that section to move to another buffer, make sure the region includes the newline following the ellipsis (for example, move to the beginning of the next line). If you simply place the cursor following the ellipsis, Emacs copies only the header, not the hidden text. We're not sure why. Moving past the newline copies the body as well as the heading correctly, and pasting it into a buffer in text mode shows all the hidden text.

Marking Sections of the Outline

When you're moving text around, it's convenient to be able to mark a section of the outline and then move it or promote or demote it a level, as we'll discuss next. To mark a section of the outline (the current heading and its children), type **C-c @** (for **outline-mark-subtree**). You can then cut or paste the section you've marked. You might want to type **C-x C-x** to verify that the region is marked correctly.

Promoting and Demoting Sections

Often as you're writing, you find that a certain heading should really be promoted or demoted a level. To promote a heading, type **C-c C-^**. To demote it a level, **C-c C-v**. (Note the clever attempt to make the key bindings indicate that you're moving headings up or down a level using ^ and v.) This automatically changes the markings for the heading in question. In other words, promoting a second-level heading removes an asterisk, making it a first-level heading. You'll find the commands to move to the next and previous headings, **C-c C-n** and **C-c C-p**, helpful when you are promoting and demoting sections.

But what if you want to demote not just a heading but a subtree? Or even the entire outline? At the moment, you'd have to write a Lisp function to do that (or use someone else's). Several functions like this have been written by gurus and posted online, but none are part of Emacs at this writing. We hope this function is incorporated soon.

Using Outline Minor Mode

Outline mode is also available as a minor mode so that you can use it subordinately to your favorite major mode. To start outline mode as a minor mode, type **M-x outline-minor-mode**; Outl appears on the mode line. In some ways, this mode is less convenient; rather than the simple **C-c** prefix you use for most outline mode commands, in outline minor mode, you must preface all commands with **C-c @** instead, to avoid interfering with the usual **C-c** commands of the major mode. So, if you want to move down to the next heading (the **C-c C-n** command in outline mode), you would type **C-c @ C-n** instead.

Please note that mixing outline major mode and outline minor mode is not only redundant but can be dangerous. Turning on the minor mode while the major mode is on can confuse Emacs. Exit outline mode, then enter outline minor mode if you wish.

Table 7-4 summarizes outline mode commands. In the next section, we discuss another specialized editing method: editing with rectangles.

Table 7-4. Outline mode commands

Keystrokes	Command name	Action
(none)	outline-mode	Toggle outline mode.
C-c C-n *Headings → Next*	outline-next-visible-heading	Move to the next heading.
C-c C-p *Headings → Previous*	outline-previous-visible-heading	Move to the previous heading.
C-c C-f *Headings →* *Next Same Level*	outline-forward-same-level	Move to the next heading of the same level.
C-c C-b *Headings →* *Previous Same Level*	outline-backward-same-level	Move to the previous heading of same level.
C-c C-u *Headings → Up*	outline-up-heading	Move up one heading level.
C-c C-t *Hide → Hide Body*	hide-body	Hide all body lines.
C-c C-a *Show → Show All*	show-all	Show everything that's hidden.
C-c C-q *Hide → Hide Sublevels*	hide-sublevels	Display first level headers only.
C-c C-o *Hide → Hide Other*	hide-other	Hide all text and headings outside the current sub-tree. First level headers show.
C-c @	outline-mark-subtree	Mark the current header and all sublevels.
C-c C-^	outline-promote	Promote the current heading one level.
C-c C-v	outline-demote	Demote the current heading one level.
C-c C-d *Hide → Hide Subtree*	hide-subtree	Hide subheads and body associated with a given heading.
C-c C-c *Hide → Hide Entry*	hide-entry	Hide the body associated with a particular heading (not subheads and their bodies).
C-c C-l *Hide → Hide Leaves*	hide-leaves	Hide the body of a particular heading and the bodies of all its subheads.
C-c C-s *Show → Show Subtree*	show-subtree	Show the subheads and text associated with a given heading.
C-c C-e *Show → Show Entry*	show-entry	Show the body associated with a particular heading (not subheads and their bodies).
C-c C-k *Show → Show Branches*	show-branches	Show the body of a heading and bodies of all its sub-heads.
C-c Tab *Show → Show Children*	show-children	Show the next level of subheads associated with a particular heading (none of body text).

Rectangle Editing

When you mark regions to move or delete, they always cover the full width of the window. Editing by region is fine for most of the work that you do in Emacs. But what if you wanted to edit a table? Regions cover the full width of the window, so they can't handle columns. Emacs offers another way to define areas to delete, copy, and move around: using *rectangles*. Rectangles are just what they sound like: rectangular areas that you define and manipulate using special rectangle editing commands. Editing with rectangles is useful whenever you want to move or delete vertical columns of information; for instance, moving a column of a table or rearranging fields in a dataset.

For example, let's say you want to edit the following table, moving the "Hours" column to the right side. There's no way to do this using regions, but it's easy to do if you learn some rectangle editing commands.

Initial state:

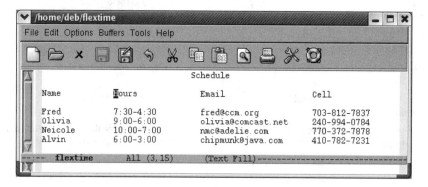

A flextime schedule.

You define a rectangle the same way you define a region; the commands you use after marking the area tell Emacs whether you want to work with a region or a rectangle. (This is a good time to let go of your mouse and use keyboard commands for marking the text. Highlighting remains horizontal when you're working with rectangles and will only confuse you as you begin to think rectangularly. Of course, there's nothing wrong with using the mouse to move the cursor quickly; just don't use it to highlight text.)

Before we start working with these columns, select the buffer with **C-x h** and untabify it by typing **M-x untabify**. Rectangle editing works best with files that do not contain tab characters.

To define a rectangle, move the cursor to the upper-left corner and set the mark by pressing **C-Space**, then move the cursor to the lower-right corner of the rectangle.

Once you're at the lower-right corner of the rectangle, move one character farther. Why move one character farther? Remember that when you define a region, the character that the cursor is on *isn't* part of the region. (The character that the mark is on *is* part of the region.)

Let's define a rectangle that covers the second column of our table.

Move to the H in Hours and type **C-Space**

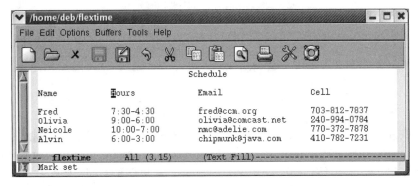

The mark is set at the upper-left corner of the rectangle to be moved.

Move the cursor to the space following the bottom-right corner of the rectangle, the c in chipmunk.

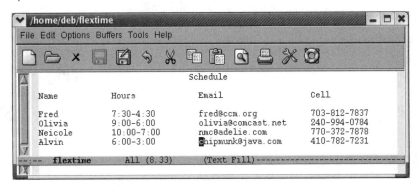

The cursor follows the bottom-right corner of the rectangle.

Now that the rectangle is marked, we want to delete it and then move it. The command to delete a rectangle so you can retrieve it elsewhere is **C-x r k** (for **kill-rectangle**).

Type: **C-x r k**

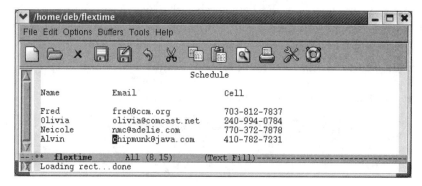

The rectangle is deleted; it's in a special rectangle kill buffer.

Once again, when you mark a rectangle, you put the cursor on the upper-left corner, set the mark, then move to the lower-right corner of the rectangle and over one more space. Emacs expects rectangles to be rectangles. If necessary, it pads an area with spaces to make up the straight line on the right side.

You can move anywhere on the screen and reinsert the rectangle last killed with the **yank-rectangle** command, **C-x r y**. To put the "Hours" column on the right side of the table, we move the cursor following the cell phone column.

Place the cursor following Cell and press **M-10 Space** to move to a good location to paste the "Hours" column:

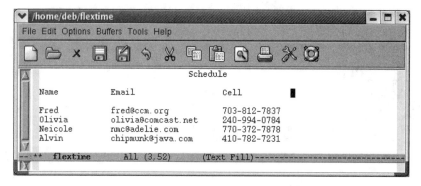

Move the cursor to where we want to reinsert the rectangle.

Type: **C-x r y**

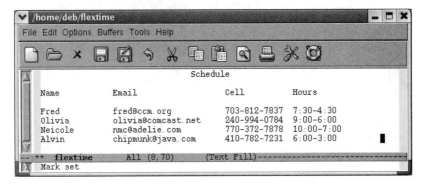

Emacs inserts the rectangle we killed earlier.

Emacs inserts the rectangle exactly where you tell it to. We moved past the cell phone column and then added some space between the cell phone and hours columns. Otherwise, Emacs would have blithely inserted the hours column into the middle of the cell phone column. Note that there's no equivalent of the kill ring for rectangles. You can yank only the most recent rectangle.[*]

Killing and yanking rectangles requires practice. Once you get the hang of the procedure, it is an easy way to edit tables and other column-dependent material.

A few other commands create blank rectangles. For example, let's say we want to put four more spaces between the cell phone and hours columns. To do this, we set the mark, move to the bottom of the column, move forward four spaces, then type **C-x r o** (for **open-rectangle**). This command inserts a blank rectangle and pushes the remaining text to the right.

---

[*] You can, however, store rectangles in registers, providing the effective equivalent of the kill ring. More on this shortly.

Move the cursor to the H in Hours and type **C-Space**

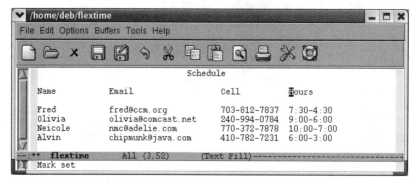

Emacs sets the mark at the upper-left corner of the rectangle.

Now we need to define the amount of space we want to insert. Move down to the bottom of the rectangle (the "Alvin" line) and then move to the hyphen between 6:00 and 3:00.

Move the cursor following 6:00.

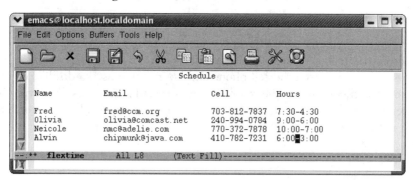

The lower right corner of the rectangle is defined.

Finally, type **C-x r o** to add the new space to the table.

Type **C-x r o**

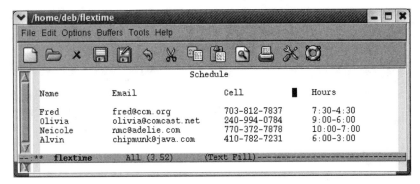

Emacs inserts a blank rectangle that is four spaces wide. It moves the rest of the table to the right.

The **clear-rectangle** command wipes out text, leaving a blank rectangle in its place. It's just as though you had erased a column on a blackboard. Like the blackboard column, the text column that is wiped out is gone, not stored in the rectangle kill buffer. To continue with our example, let's say that after reviewing the schedule, all those involved agreed that they'd rather not have their cell phones listed.

Move the cursor to the C in Cell and type **C-space.**

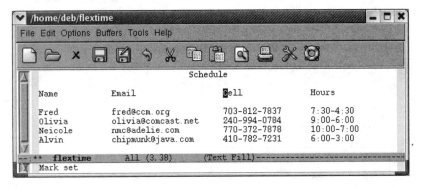

The upper-left corner of the rectangle to be cleared is marked.

Move to the space following the last phone number and type: **C-x r c**

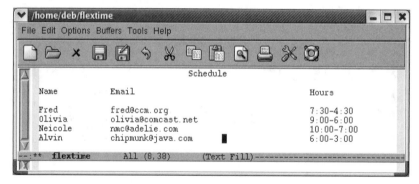

The **clear-rectangle** command removes the "Cell Phone" column and leaves a blank space in its place.

As you can see, the spacing of our table still isn't perfect; you'd probably want to use the **delete-rectangle** command* to delete the extra space between the second and the third columns. To delete the blank space without storing it, start by moving the cursor to the space following the longest email address and press **C-Space** to set the mark, then move to the opposite corner of the box you want to delete and type **C-x r d**.

On the header line, move to the column after the longest email address and press **C-Space**

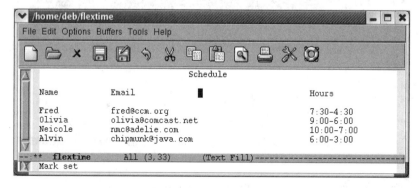

The upper-left corner of the rectangle to be deleted is marked.

---

* Like all Emacs delete commands, **delete-rectangle** doesn't store what you delete in the kill ring.

Move a few spaces before 6:00 on the last line and type **C-x r d**

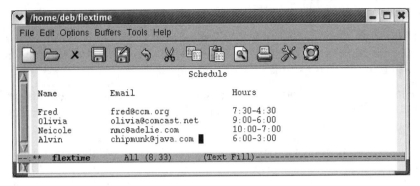

The **delete-rectangle** command deletes the blank space.

If you're doing some really fancy table editing, being able to store several rectangles is helpful. That way, you can have every column as a rectangle, as well as having a rectangle for the exact amount of blank space to put between each column. You can store rectangles in registers by typing **C-x r r** *r* where *r* is any alphanumeric character, including punctuation. To insert a rectangle you've stored, type **C-x r i** *r*. Registers don't persist between sessions.

Table 7-5 lists rectangle commands.

Table 7-5. Rectangle commands

Keystrokes	Command name	Action
C-x r k	kill-rectangle	Delete a rectangle and store it.
C-x r d	delete-rectangle	Delete a rectangle and do not store it.
C-x r y	yank-rectangle	Insert the last rectangle killed.
C-x r c	clear-rectangle	Using spaces, blank out the area marked as a rectangle and do not store it.
C-x r o	open-rectangle	Insert a blank rectangle in the area marked.
C-x r r r	copy-rectangle-to-register	Copy rectangle to register r (where r is any character) .
C-x r i r	insert-register	Insert rectangle from register r (where r is any character).
(none)	delete-whitespace-rectangle	If a rectangle includes initial whitespace, deletes it, narrowing rectangle.
C-x r t string Enter	string-rectangle	Change contents of marked rectangle to *string* (if *string* is narrower or wider than rectangle, dimensions change accordingly).
(none)	string-insert-rectangle	Prompts for string and inserts rectangle.

CUA Rectangle Editing

If you are familiar with CUA mode, which is part of Emacs starting with 21.3.5, you may know that it provides cut and paste key sequences familiar to Windows users, as in **C-x** to cut and **C-v** to paste (see Chapter 13). The second most commonly touted feature of CUA mode is its superior rectangle support.

We've just looked at a myriad of rectangle commands. CUA's rectangle support is far simpler. By learning essentially one command, you can cut and paste rectangles in CUA mode.

Unfortunately at present, CUA mode support is standard but not nuanced on Emacs 21. 3.5. You either take the whole enchilada or you don't. To turn it on, select C-x/C-c/C-v cut and paste (CUA) from the Options menu. If you don't generally like to use the CUA keybindings for cut and paste, you might turn this option on only when you are doing rectangle editing.

To select a rectangle, type **Shift-Enter**. Emacs starts to highlight in a dark pink color by default. You extend the highlighting with normal cursor movement keys (the mouse does not work at present).

Move to the C in Cell and type: **Shift-Enter**

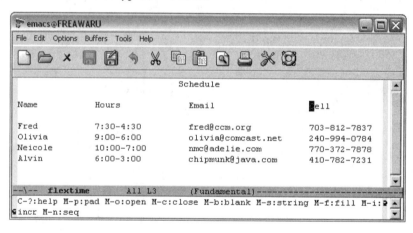

The upper-left corner of our rectangle is marked (Windows).

The minibuffer displays an array of CUA mode rectangle commands. For now, we'll just mark the rectangle and experiment with one of these commands momentarily.

Move the cursor to the last number in Alvin's phone number.

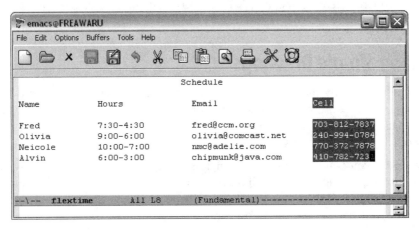

The rectangle is marked (Windows).

Note that the marked rectangle isn't strictly rectangular in shape. The phone numbers form a true rectangle, but in order to create a rectangle that includes the column header, we need to ask CUA mode to "pad" the rectangle using **M-p**, one of the commands listed in the minibuffer earlier.

Type: **M-p**

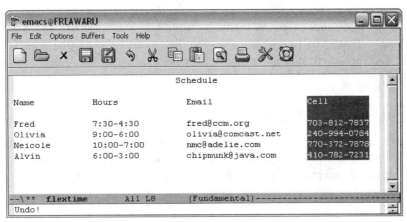

The pad command makes this a true rectangle (Windows).

We can now cut or paste the rectangle using **C-x** or **C-v** respectively. This is just a taste of the CUA mode rectangle commands. You can explore more of them on your own. We thought you should be aware of this method as an alternative to the more keyboard-intensive rectangle commands that have been part of Emacs for many years.

Making Simple Drawings

Emacs is not, by any means, a graphics package, but it does provide some limited drawing capabilities. Emacs includes a picture mode that allows you to draw simple pictures using keyboard characters; it also includes artist mode, which enables you to draw quickly using the mouse.

Why would you want to draw with Emacs? Well, Emacs is useful for inserting a quick drawing or diagram in a mail message, something that most graphics packages can't do. It's also good for making block diagrams, timing diagrams (for electrical engineers), timelines, and other simple drawings.

Don't overlook this simple facility! We have seen many papers that were carefully formatted with a simple star-and-bar diagram dropped in the middle. Sure, you can use a graphics package to create a much nicer drawing, but if that's not your area of expertise, an Emacs ASCII drawing might be just the ticket.* We discuss picture mode first and then artist mode.

Picture mode turns the area being edited into a kind of drawing board consisting of columns and rows. In picture mode, you can create simple pictures (such as the one in Figure 7-3) using keyboard characters without having them "rearranged" by the word-wrap capabilities of auto-fill mode, for example.

To enter picture mode, type **M-x edit-picture**. The word Picture appears on the mode line, followed by the default drawing direction (more on that shortly). Typing **C-c C-c** exits picture mode and returns you to whatever major mode you were in before.

Drawing in Picture Mode

In picture mode, you can "draw" with any character in any of eight directions. Although you can draw in eight directions, only one direction is available at a time; this direction is referred to as the *default direction*. When you first enter picture mode, the default direction is right, meaning that if you press the hyphen key four

---

* A number of online groups are dedicated to ASCII art. Of course, all such art requires that you use a mono-space font for proper viewing. Newsgroups such as *alt.ascii.art* and web sites such as the Ascii Art Dictionary (*http://www.ascii-art.de/*) provide a good introduction.

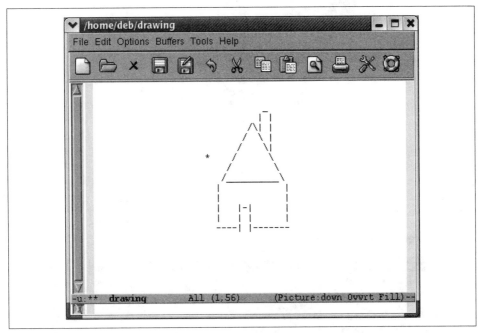

Figure 7-3. Drawing in picture mode

times, you would draw a line to the right, as follows: ----. The default direction is displayed on the mode line, like this:

```
(Picture: right)
```

By typing special commands that change the default direction, you can draw in seven other directions as well. For example, **C-c** \ makes the default direction "southeast;" the mode line would then read (Picture: se). If you typed four hyphens in this direction, they would look like stair steps:

```
  -
    -
      -
        -
```

Figure 7-4 illustrates the commands for setting various directions as the default in picture mode.

Picture mode tries to make these commands easy to remember, and it doesn't do too badly: for example, **C-c** ^ points upward, **C-c-`** arguably points to the northwest, and so on. If you can come up with a good mnemonic device for **C-c** . let us know! Maybe you can think of it as "dot for down."

After you set a default direction, pressing any character repeatedly draws a line of characters in that direction. Give it a try in a scratch buffer, using the commands in the figure to change the default direction. Try drawing a box.*

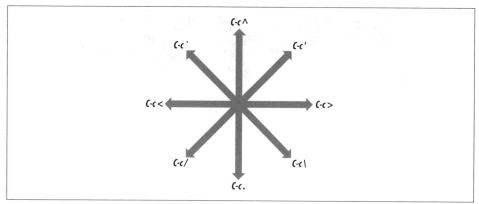

Figure 7-4. Moving around in picture mode

Type: **M-x picture-mode**

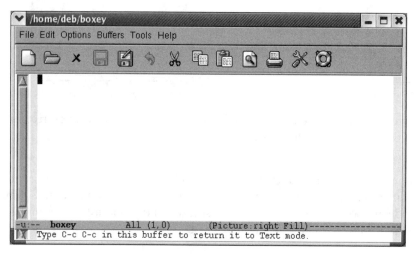

Putting the buffer into picture mode, default direction "right."

---

* Other commands can accomplish this task more quickly, but bear with us for the sake of a simple example. For example, this little exercise could be accomplished with a single mouse drag in artist mode. Picture mode also offers a quick command for drawing a rectangle, **C-c C-r**.

Type: **Tab M-20 -**

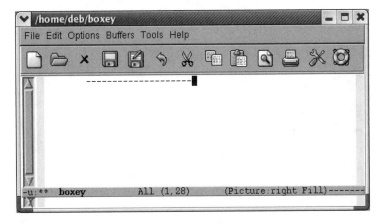

Emacs draws a line to the right. Next, we'll change the default direction to down, and use | for the right side of the square.

Type: **C-c . M-5** |

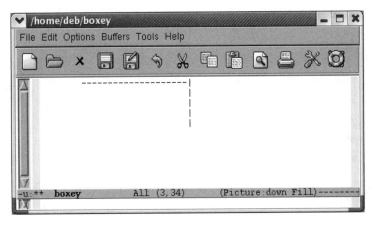

Emacs draws a line down. Now we'll set the default direction to "left," then draw the bottom of the square.

Type: **C-c < M-20 -**

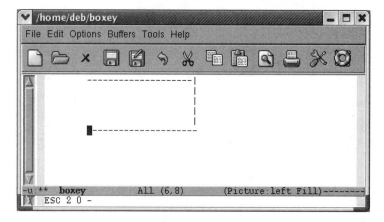

Emacs draws a line to the left. Next, use **C-c ^** to set the default direction to "up," and then draw vertical bars back to the starting point.

Type: **C-c ^ M-5 |**

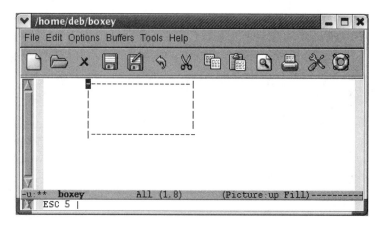

Emacs draws a line up that completes the box.

Editing in Picture Mode

By now, you should have a basic understanding of what picture mode can do for you. It's one of the more complicated minor modes because it redefines what many of the major editing keys do—and with good reason. The editing techniques you use for most ASCII files just won't work well for pictures. You don't really want to insert characters; the standard insert mode would prevent you from editing effectively, because any character you type distorts the rest of the line. Therefore, picture mode implicitly changes to overwrite mode. Many other features are redefined—some in insignificant ways, others in more substantial ways.

Therefore, to do justice to picture mode, we have to revisit most of the basic editing concepts. Please bear with us, or skip this section if you aren't interested in pictures. Let's start at the beginning: basic cursor motion.

Cursor motion in picture mode

Picture mode makes some small but important changes in the basic cursor commands. There's an easy way to summarize these changes: in picture mode the buffer becomes a grid of rows and columns. For example, consider what **C-f** does in most other modes: it moves forward through the file, one character at a time. Typing **C-f** repeatedly moves the cursor to the left, then at the end of the line, it jumps to the first character on the next line. picture mode, **C-f** means "move to the right." When you reach the end of the line in picture mode, **C-f** doesn't wrap to the next line; it continues adding characters to the current line.

C-p and **C-n** become vertical "up" and "down" commands, respectively. Try editing some sample text, moving to the end of a line, and typing **C-p**. Normally, as you type **C-p**, the cursor stays at the end of the line; if the previous line is short, the cursor moves to the left when it goes up. In picture mode, **C-p** and **C-n** always move up (or down) in a straight line.

You can get to every place you need to go with **C-f**, **C-b**, **C-p**, and **C-n**. The arrow keys work too, but you may want to know the cursor movement commands for moving in the default direction as well, so you can also go sideways when it's faster. **C-c C-f** moves you forward in the default direction (so "forward" here could mean to the left, right, up, or down, as well as all directions in between). **C-c C-b** moves you backward in the default direction. (Moving "up" or "down" relative to the default direction isn't defined.)

For example, let's say you had drawn the house shown in Figure 7-1 and you wanted to move the cursor down the left side of the roof. You would set the default direction to "southwest" by typing **C-c /**. If the cursor were on the top shingle on the left side of the roof, typing **C-c C-f** would move you down the left side of the roof and typing **C-f** would move you to the top-right shingle, as shown in Figure 7-5.

Inserting blank lines

As you continue to work in picture mode, you'll find a few more surprises. Pressing **Enter** in picture mode moves you to the beginning of the next line, without inserting a blank line—on the assumption that you probably don't want to change

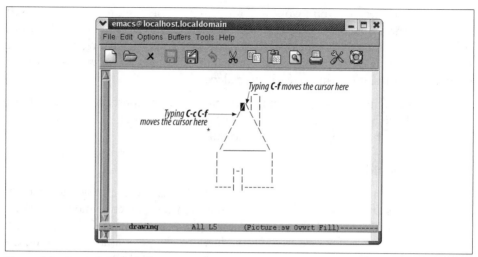

Figure 7-5. Using the default direction versus typical cursor movement commands

the relationship between lines. If you want to insert a new line, type **C-o**; an empty line appears beneath the current line, and the cursor does not move. For example, the cursor is initially on the 0 in the first line. If we want to open another line between the two, we type **C-o**.

Initial state:

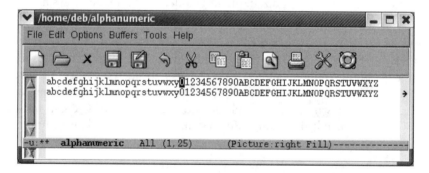

Initial text; the cursor is on the 0 in the first line.

Type: **C-o**

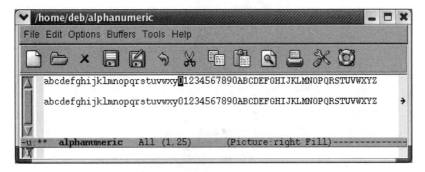

C-o opens a new line but doesn't move the cursor.

One of the more difficult things to do in picture mode is to type a standard carriage return that breaks a line in the middle. You can move to a point in the middle of a line, type **C-k** to kill the right-hand portion, type **C-o** to insert a blank line; type **Enter** to move to the beginning of this blank line, and type **C-y** to yank the right-hand part of the line back. Or you can use the **split-line** command (**C-M-o**), and then delete the blank space at the beginning of the new line.

Deletion isn't quite the same, either. In picture mode **C-c C-d** is the delete character command that you're used to: it deletes the character under the cursor and moves the rest of the line to the left. An unadorned **C-d** deletes the character under the cursor, replacing it with a space. **Del** deletes the character to the left of the cursor, replacing it with a space.

Table 7-6 contrasts the picture mode commands with their normal text mode behavior.

Table 7-6. Picture mode v. text mode

Keystrokes	In text mode	In picture mode	Picture mode alternative
Enter	Insert a blank line.	Move the cursor to the beginning of the next line.	**C-o** inserts blank lines.
C-d	Delete the character and move the text to left.	Replace the character with **Space** and don't move.	**C-c C-d** is like **C-d** in text mode.
Space	Move the text to the right and insert a space.	Move the cursor to the right and delete any character you space over.	None; go back to text mode to insert blank spaces.
C-k	Erase the text on the current line; pressing **C-k** twice deletes a line.	Erase the text on the current line; it doesn't delete the line.	To delete a line, go back to text mode or use **delete-rectangle**.
Tab	Insert **tabs** and move the remaining text to the right.	Move the cursor across the screen but don't affect the underlying text.	To insert a tab's worth of space, go back to text mode.

Table 7-6. Picture mode v. text mode (continued)

Keystrokes	In text mode	In picture mode	Picture mode alternative
C-n	Move to the next line.	Move down, staying in the same column.	(none)
C-p	Move to the previous line.	Move up, staying in the same column.	(none)
C-f	Move one character forward in the file.	Move one character to the right.	(none)
C-b	Move one character backward in the file.	Move one character to the left; stop at the beginning of the line.	(none)

If you want to insert a block of blank space, you can use a rectangle command such as **open-rectangle**. See the discussion of this command earlier in this chapter for more information. Also, if you want to insert blank space at the end of a line, you can use **C-f**.

To perform some tasks, you may find it easier to switch back temporarily to the mode you're used to. **C-c C-c** moves you back to the mode you were in before you entered picture mode. Make any necessary changes, then enter picture mode again by typing **M-x picture-mode**.

If you want to move something you've drawn, the easiest way is to use rectangles, as described earlier in this chapter.

Tabs are also different in picture mode. By default, picture mode interprets the following characters as tab stops if they appear by themselves on a line: exclamation point (!), hyphen (-) and tilde (~). If these characters appear on a line and the user presses tab on the next line, these characters are presumed to denote tab stops. You can change this behavior by setting the variable **picture-tab-chars** to other characters. If the characters appear with normal text, they are not interpreted as tab stops. To use these characters as tab stops, press **Esc-Tab** (for **picture-tab-search**).

Table 7-7 summarizes the commands for editing in picture mode.

Table 7-7. Picture mode commands

Keystrokes	Command name	Action
(none)	picture-mode or edit-picture	Enter picture mode.
C-c C-c	picture-mode-exit	Exit picture mode and return to the previous mode.
C-c ^	picture-movement-up	Set the default drawing direction to up.
C-c .	picture-movement-down	Set the default drawing direction to down.
C-c >	picture-movement-right	Set the default drawing direction to right.
C-c <	picture-movement-left	Set the default drawing direction to left.

Table 7-7. Picture mode commands (continued)

Keystrokes	Command name	Action
C-c `	picture-movement-nw	Set the default drawing direction to northwest.
C-c '	picture-movement-ne	Set the default drawing direction to northeast.
C-c /	picture-movement-sw	Set the default drawing direction to southwest.
C-c \	picture-movement-se	Set the default drawing direction to southeast.
C-c C-f	picture-motion	Move the cursor forward in the default drawing direction.
C-c C-b	picture-motion-reverse	Move the cursor backward in the default drawing direction.
C-f	picture-forward-column	Move the cursor to the right one character.
C-b	picture-backward-column	Move the cursor to the left one character.
C-n	picture-move-down	Move the cursor down one character.
C-p	picture-move-up	Move the cursor up one character.
C-d	picture-clear-column	Blank out the character under the cursor; doesn't move remaining text to the left.
C-c C-d	delete-char	Delete the character under the cursor and move the remaining text to the left.
C-k	picture-clear-line	Delete the text on the current line; the line is not deleted if used twice.
C-o	picture-open-line	Insert a blank line.
C-c C-w r	picture-clear-rectangle-to-register	Clear the rectangle and save it in register r.
C-u C-c C-w r	picture-clear-rectangle-to-register	Delete the rectangle and save it in register r.
C-c C-x r	picture-yank-rectangle-from-register	Insert the rectangle saved in register r at the cursor position.
C-c C-r	picture-draw-rectangle	Draw a rectangle around current region.
C-c C-y	picture-yank-rectangle	Paste rectangle.
C-c C-k	picture-clear-rectangle	Erase rectangle.
C-c Tab	picture-set-tab-stops	Set tab stops applicable only in picture mode (!, -, and ~ denote tab stops by default).
M-Tab	picture-tab-search	Move to the next picture mode tab.

Drawing with the Mouse Using Artist

We would be remiss if we didn't introduce you to artist mode, an easy way to create ASCII art using the mouse. (You can also use keyboard commands, but trust us—you won't want to.)

Artist mode is a minor mode related to picture mode, so you use them together. For example, you might draw using artist mode, then edit the picture in picture mode. Or you might choose to use artist mode alone for your creations.

We're going to give you a taste of artist mode; you can perfect your skills in your spare time. When you start artist mode, picture mode starts automatically.

Type: **M-x artist-mode**

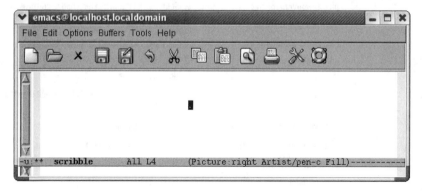

Artist appears on the mode line, as does Picture.

When you start artist mode, pen drawing is selected by default.

Hold down the left mouse button and move around to scribble.

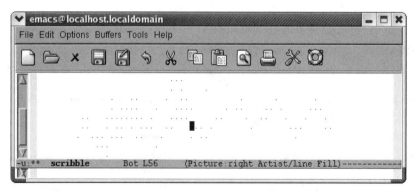

A random scribble.

With the pen, you can draw freestyle. Hold down the middle mouse button and a menu appears, with Drawing, Edit, and Settings submenus. The Drawing menu offers a variety of shapes from which to choose. Now that we've scribbled, let's create some graffiti using the spray can.

Select Spray Can from the Drawing menu, then spray the screen by holding down the left mouse button and moving the mouse.

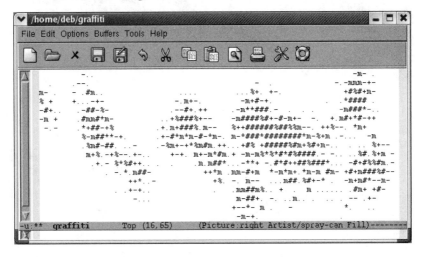

A random spray.

We aren't going to go deep into artist mode, but we would like to give you a flavor of the basic drawing choices. You can draw rectangles (our personal favorite), ellipses, lines (which strive to be straight), and poly-lines (which strive to be polygon-angular). Figure 7-5 shows a representative sample of shapes. With practice, you can create complex drawings and edit them, either using the mouse or using standard picture mode commands.

For rectangles, lines, and ellipses, hold down the left mouse and pull them to the size and, in the case of lines, angle you prefer. (Ellipses are made of straight lines, so use your imagination; this is ASCII art after all.) For poly-lines, draw a line by holding down the left mouse button, then release it. Move the mouse away from that line to the next corner of the polygon and click. Emacs draws a line connecting the two points. Poly-lines allow you to create polygons quickly.

Table 7-8 provides an overview of artist commands. Artist works very well with the mouse and the middle-button mouse menu; if you're mouse-averse, you'll prefer picture mode.

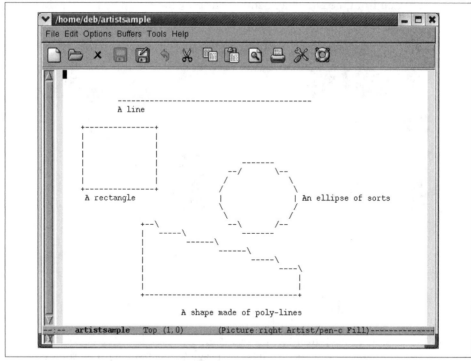

Figure 7-6. A representative sample of artist shapes

Table 7-8. Artist mode commands

Keystrokes	Command name	Action
(none)	artist-mode	Enter artist mode.
C-c C-c	artist-mode-off	Exit artist mode.
C-f	artist-forward-char	Move to the right one character (at end of line, keep adding characters to current line).
C-b	artist-backward-char	Move to the left one character (at beginning of line, does nothing).
C-n	artist-next-line	Move down a column (at end of buffer, keep adding lines to the buffer).
C-p	artist-previous-line	Move up a column (at first line of buffer moves to first position in file, then does nothing).
C-c C-a C-o *or* Mouse-2	artist-select-operation	Select an operation (press Tab to see a list).
C-c C-a f´ *Artist menu → Edit →* *Flood-fill*	artist-select-op-flood-fill	Select flood fill as the operation.
C-c C-a C-k *Artist menu → Edit → Cut*	artist-select-op-cut-rectangle	Draw a rectangle around an area, then cut.

Table 7-8. Artist mode commands (continued)

Keystrokes	Command name	Action
C-c C-a M-w *Artist menu →* *Edit → Copy*	artist-select-op-copy-rectangle	Draw a rectangle around an area, then copy.
C-c C-a C-y *Artist menu → Edit → Paste*	artist-select-op-paste	Paste what you copied wherever you click the mouse.
C-c C-a v *Artist menu → Drawing →* *Vaporize*	artist-select-op-vaporize-line	Erase a line you select (literal line; not a line in the file).
C-c C-a C-d *Artist menu →* *Drawing → Erase*	artist-select-op-erase-char	Set operation to erase (use the mouse as your eraser).
C-c C-a S *Artist menu → Drawing →* *Spray-can*	artist-select-op-spray-can	Set operation to spray can.
C-c C-a e *Artist menu → Drawing →* *Ellipse*	artist-select-op-ellipse	Draw ellipses.
C-c C-a p *Artist menu → Drawing →* *Poly-line*	artist-select-op-poly-line	Draws poly-lines
C-c C-a r *Artist menu → Drawing →* *Rectangle*	artist-select-op-rectangle	Draw rectangles.
C-c C-a l *Artist menu → Drawing →* *Line*	artist-select-op-line	Draw lines.
C-c C-a C-r *Artist menu → Settings →* *Rubber banding*	artist-toggle-rubber-banding	If on (the default), show shape while stretching; if not, mark end-points.
C-c C-a C-l *Artist menu → Settings →* *Set Line*	artist-select-line-char	Select character to use when drawing lines (- is the default).
C-c C-a C-f *Artist menu → Settings →* *Set Fill*	artist-select-fill-char	Select character to fill shapes with (Space is the default).

Problems You May Encounter

- **Artist mode says you can't change to another shape while drawing.** Exit artist mode and then reenter. Before drawing anything, click the mouse's middle button to display the pop-up menu and select the desired shape from the Drawing menu.

CHAPTER 8
Markup Language Support

It's true that many of the people who use Emacs are developers, writing code, tweaking it, recompiling it, and just generally enjoying the services of an amazingly extensible work environment. A variety of people, including developers, need to produce text for publication, whether internally, online, or in book format. This chapter describes the markup language support that Emacs offers, a topic relevant to both information publishers and developers, as more and more development work uses variants of the Extensible Markup Language, XML.

Choosing a format for producing documents isn't all that straightforward these days, especially if you eschew Microsoft Word. Some people write HTML, and Emacs offers a few options for this. HTML gives you some control over formatting but displays differently on various browsers. Of course, it is important as the *lingua franca* of the Web.

Other text publishing options include the TEX family. TEX (pronounced "tek") is a formatter that was developed by Donald Knuth for generating books. LATEX (pronounced "lay-tek") is a set of TEX commands created by Leslie Lamport. With TEX and LATEX, you can produce very precisely formatted text with equations, interesting fonts, graphics, headers and footers, and the like. Whether using filters or features of the program itself, you can publish TEX documents in a variety of formats.

Another option for publishing text—as well as programming—is XML. XML, when combined with a Document Type Definition (DTD) or schema, enables you to write text once and publish it in a variety of formats. Extensible Style Language (XSL) is also important in this regard. Because the standards are still being defined, organizations involved in document production may choose an established XML dialect, such as DocBook, as their publication format. XML at this point provides less precise control over format, but maximizes flexibility.

XML bridges the programming and publishing worlds, and what you do with XML will in part determine what tools you use and what support you need. We discuss a few options for writing XML in Emacs, including psgml mode and Jim Clark's nxml mode, which uses Relax NG schemas rather than DTDs for validation.

Some word processors and other tools integrate formatting and editing. These tools are often called WYSIWYG (what you see is what you get) tools. What's the advantage of using Emacs versus a WYSIWYG tool? Well, whether you're writing LATEX, XML, or HTML, you can be crystal clear about what's in the file and how it's structured if you use Emacs. Save a Microsoft Word file as HTML and then open the resulting file in Emacs. Word bloats the file with additional tags and formatting that is not strictly required. In terms of output, the streamlined and straightforward code you picture in your mind's eye when viewing a page is definitely not what you get, an ironic consequence of using a WYSIWYG tool like Word to create markup files. Chances are, if you've read this far, you're planning to use Emacs anyway, so we won't belabor the point.

In this chapter, we talk about these markup modes:

- For writing HTML, Emacs HTML mode (a subset of SGML mode) and the add-on HTML helper mode are discussed.
- For writing XML, Emacs SGML mode and the add-on modes psgml mode and nxml mode are described in brief.
- For writing LATEX documents, Emacs LaTeX mode is discussed.

These major modes help you insert formatting commands, or markup, into your text. While the amount of help that Emacs offers varies, using the mode designed for your text formatter will streamline your work.

At this point we must insert a caveat. We provide a barebones introduction to the markup modes described in this chapter. What we say here will get you started, but not much more than that. Entire books could be and have been written about using each of the markup tools described here. Now that that's out of the way, let's talk about a few features that are important in all the modes: comment handling and font-lock mode.

Comments

All the modes described in this chapter share a feature with the programming language modes such as Java mode and Lisp mode, which we discuss in Chapter 9. All these modes understand comments and use a single command, **M-;** (for **indent-for-comment**) to insert the appropriate comment syntax. Table 8-1 lists the comment syntax for the tools in this chapter.

Table 8-1. Comments in markup modes

If you type M-; in:	Emacs inserts:
HTML mode	<!-- -->
HTML helper mode	<!-- -->
SGML mode	<!-- -->

Table 8-1. Comments in markup modes (continued)

If you type M-; in:	Emacs inserts:
nxml mode	`<!-- -->`
psgml mode	`<!-- -->`
LaTeX mode	`%% (on blank lines)`
	`% (on lines with content)`

Font-Lock Mode

Font-lock mode is discussed primarily in Chapter 9; it's designed for coloring code to make it easier to read. But the fact is that it works well in other modes too, like the Buffer List (Chapter 4), Dired (Chapter 5), and in all the markup modes described in this chapter.

To turn on font lock mode, choose Syntax Highlighting from the Options menu. If you decide you want to turn it on for every session, select Save Options from the Options menu and Emacs writes your *.emacs* file.

For more details on font-lock mode, see Chapter 9.

Writing HTML

Without doubt, the most commonly used markup language today is hypertext markup language (HTML), used for creating web pages. HTML consists of text with tags that define characteristics about the text. HTML is not hard to write, and you could use Emacs or any other editor to write the tags and the text. An HTML tag generally looks like this:

```
<tagname>text being tagged</tagname>
```

For your convenience, several modes are available for writing HTML in Emacs, including HTML mode, HTML helper mode, html menus, and a variety of SGML* tools including sgml mode and psgml mode. Of these tools, we've chosen to describe HTML mode, a variant of sgml mode, which is included in GNU Emacs, and HTML helper mode, which is a popular add-on. If you are writing XHTML, a stricter version of HTML that can be validated, you should consider XHTML mode, described briefly in this section, or psgml mode, covered later in the XML section of this chapter.

Serious web developers may want to investigate some of the cutting edge development going on to make Emacs even more powerful. Check out HTMLModeDeluxe (*http://www.emacswiki.org/cgi-bin/wiki/HtmlModeDeluxe*) and the Emacs WebDev Environment by Darren Brierton (*http://www.dzr-web.com/people/darren/projects/emacs-webdev*).

---

* SGML stands for standardized general markup language. Both XML and HTML are descendants of SGML.

Both of these tools support mmm mode (where mmm stands for "multiple major modes"). Using this feature, the cursor changes major mode depending on the section of the page you are editing. When you edit a script, the mode changes automatically to support that type of authoring. Both are excellent tools for building complex web pages.

In the following sections, we are not going to teach you to write HTML. (For more information on writing HTML, see *HTML and XHTML: The Definitive Guide* by Chuck Musciano and Bill Kennedy, O'Reilly) Rather, we're going to teach you the rudiments of using HTML mode and HTML helper mode to help you create HTML documents.

Using HTML Mode

To start HTML mode, type **M-x html-mode** (or simply open an HTML file). Most authors use a standard template when they write HTML. You may already have one. If you don't, HTML mode is happy to supply one for you. Simply start by typing **C-c C-t** (for **sgml-tag**) or by selecting Insert Tag from the SGML menu. If you enter the <html> tag that signifies the start of an HTML document, Emacs inserts a basic template in your buffer.

Type: **C-c C-t html Enter**

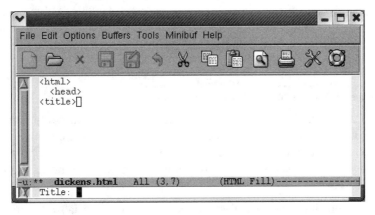

Emacs prompts for a title.

Type: **A Tale of Two Cities Enter**

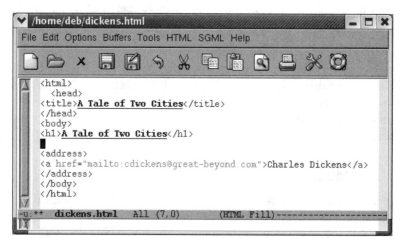

Emacs inserts an HTML template.

Note that Emacs automatically creates a first-level header that is equal to the title you entered. It also inserts a hyperlink so that readers can email you. Depending on your spam tolerance, you may want to delete that line. Also, Emacs is just guessing at your name and email address. You can set these explicitly by adding two lines to your *.emacs* file. Change Mr. Dickens' information to settings appropriate for you.

```
(setq user-mail-address "cdickens@great-beyond.com")
(setq user-full-name "Charles Dickens")
```

You could approach HTML mode in a couple of ways. You could learn the key bindings for various tags, or you could simply use the **sgml-tag** command for everything. It depends how many bindings you want to learn. A mixed approach may be best, where you learn keystrokes for the most common tags and use **sgml-tag** for less common tags.

Key bindings are intuitive in HTML mode. Like most specialized editing modes, many functions are bound to **C-c C-*something***. We've seen **C-c C-t** to insert a tag. You won't be too surprised to find that to move forward to the next tag you type **C-c**

C-f and to move back to the previous tag you type **C-c C-b**. To insert an `<href>` tag, type **C-c C-h**. You see what we mean.

HTML mode is designed for writing HTML, not XHTML. XHTML is stricter, requiring all tags to have a closing tag. The common `<p>` tag is a salient example. HTML authors would never use the closing tag `</p>` that XHTML requires. HTML mode inserts a lone `<p>` tag even when given a command, such as **sgml-tag**, that normally inserts a tag pair. If you want to write XHTML, use XHTML mode instead. Emacs starts this mode itself if your file contains a reference to an XHTML document type definition. Other than completion of tags, XHTML mode is very similar to HTML mode described here.[*]

Being able to hide the tags is a helpful feature. To hide HTML tags, type **C-c Tab**; use the same command to display the tags again. Let's say that we've inserted some of our *dickens* file into the *dickens.html* file we were just working with.

Initial state:

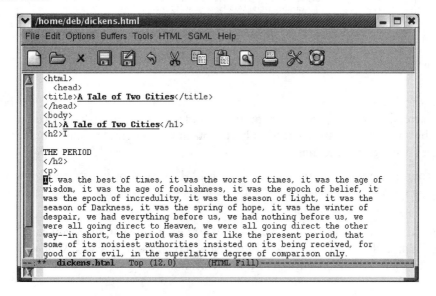

dickens.html with tags showing.

---

[*] At this writing, there is no way to enter XHTML mode explicitly. If your file looks like an XHTML file, Emacs puts you in that mode automatically.

Type: **C-c Tab**

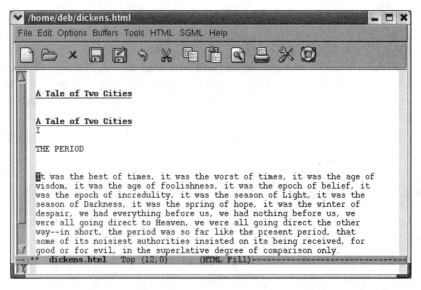

Emacs hides the tags.

You can keep typing text, concentrating on what you're writing rather than being distracted by the markup. Emacs protects you from deleting tags when you're writing by making hidden text read-only. If you move the cursor onto a hidden tag, Emacs displays it in the minibuffer.

Of course, the whole purpose of writing HTML is to display it in a web browser. Typing **C-c C-v** (for **browse-url-of-buffer**) opens the default web browser to view the web page you're writing.

If you'd like to look at the file in a web browser each time you save, you can turn on a function called **html-autoview-mode**, invoked by pressing **C-c C-s**. When you save the file, Emacs automatically opens it in the default browser.

Character encoding in HTML mode

What if you want to include special characters or characters from other character sets in your web page? The short answer is that you can enter a character's encoding explicitly. For example, to enter a capital U with an umlaut, you can type Ü. Many characters can also be represented as named entities, which are certainly easier to remember than numbers. For example, the named entity for a capital U with an umlaut is Ü.

But HTML mode does provide more support than this. We'll take the simplest case first. Let's say you can create a character with your keyboard; for a common case,

---

take the ampersand, a character that must be encoded since it has a special meaning in HTML. Type **C-c C-n & Enter**. Emacs inserts the entity for an ampersand, &. You can insert entities for a wide variety of keyboard characters this way.

But let's say that you are inserting characters that are not on your keyboard. For example, perhaps you are in the U.S. writing up a list of contributors from Europe and many of their names have accent marks. The ISO Latin-1 character set will handle this.

If you have a keyboard that already emits Latin-1 characters and Latin-1 is your default coding system for keyboard input, inserting such characters is relatively straightforward. Simply press **C-c 8** to turn on a minor mode called SGML name entity mode. Emacs says `sgml name entity mode is now on`.* **C-c 8** toggles this state. Type Latin-1 characters as you normally would and Emacs inserts the named entities associated with those characters.

For those of us with other keyboard encodings, however, there's a bit more to do. To get bindings to insert entities into your HTML file, we discuss two options. The first is ISO accents mode. This mode provides support, as the name implies, for accented text. Whether you're typing umlauts, cedillas, circumflexes, acute, or grave marks, ISO accents mode is up to the task. The other option is to use the **C-x 8** prefix to insert a wide range of entities, including currency signs, mathematical symbols, and copyright signs (as well as all the accented characters ISO accents mode supports).

Using ISO accents mode. To use ISO accents mode to insert entities in your file, type **C-c 8** to turn on SGML name entity mode, then **M-x iso-accents-mode Enter** to turn on that mode. In ISO accents mode, certain characters (including /, ~, ', ", `, and ^) are interpreted as prefixes to create accented characters. SGML name entity mode captures these keystrokes and automatically inserts the appropriate HTML entity. For example, typing 'a produces the HTML entity for á, á. For specific key bindings, see Table 8-2.

Using the C-x 8 prefix. You can also insert a wide range of entities using **C-x 8** after you do some setup.† First enter SGML name entity mode by typing **C-c 8**. Next specify Latin-1 as your character set by typing **C-x Enter k latin-1 Enter**. You can then enter a large number of entities by typing commands prefixed with **C-x 8**. For example, to insert the entity for a yen symbol, type **C-x 8 Y**. Watch the minibuffer. The literal character will appear in the minibuffer as the entity is inserted. Both ISO accents mode and the **C-x 8** prefixes allow you to type a single undo command (**C-_**) to translate the entity back into the literal character.

---

* Pay no attention to the fact that this is called SGML versus HTML name entity mode. Since HTML mode is derived from SGML mode, many commands that work with HTML have sgml in their names. Also, note that the command is called **sgml-name-8bit-mode**, a clear discrepancy with the minibuffer message.

† For some reason, perhaps the way SGML name entity mode is programmed, you can insert these entities only using key bindings. The mode fails to trap the equivalent commands and translate them into entities. For this reason, we focus on key bindings.

Table 8-2 provides a list of accented characters and the bindings that help insert them. Table 8-3 lists other named entities including punctuation marks and symbols.

Table 8-2. Bindings for inserting entities for accented characters[a]

C-x 8 prefix keystrokes	ISO accents mode shortcut	Character entity	Character displayed in browser
C-x 8 "	"	&acute;	´
C-x 8 ' a	' a	&aacute;	á
C-x 8 ' A	' A	&Aacute;	Á
C-x 8 ' e	' e	&eacute;	é
C-x 8 ' E	' E	&Eacute;	É
C-x 8 ' i	' i	&iacute;	í
C-x 8 ' I	' I	&Iacute;	Í
C-x 8 ' o	' o	&oacute;	ó
C-x 8 ' O	' O	&Oacute;	Ó
C-x 8 ' u	' u	&uacute;	ú
C-x 8 ' U	' U	&Uacute;	Ú
C-x 8 ' y	' y	&yacute;	ý
C-x 8 ' Y	' Y	&Yacute;	ÿ
C-x 8 ` a	` a	&agrave;	à
C-x 8 ` A	` A	&Agrave;	À
C-x 8 ` e	` e	&egrave;	è
C-x 8 ` E	` E	&Egrave;	È
C-x 8 ` i	` i	&igrave;	ì
C-x 8 ` I	` I	&Igrave;	Ì
C-x 8 ` o	` o	&ograve;	ò
C-x 8 ` O	` O	&Ograve;	Ò
C-x 8 ` u	` u	&ugrave;	ù
C-x 8 ` U	` U	&Ugrave;	Ù
C-x 8 ^ a	^ a	&acirc;	â
C-x 8 ^ A	^ A	&Acirc;	Â
C-x 8 ^ e	^ e	&ecirc;	ê
C-x 8 ^ E	^ E	&Ecirc;	Ê
C-x 8 ^ i	^ i	&icirc;	î
C-x 8 ^ I	^ I	&Icirc;	Î
C-x 8 ^ o	^ o	&ocirc;	ô
C-x 8 ^ O	^ O	&Ocirc;	Ô
C-x 8 ^ u	^ u	&ucirc;	û
C-x 8 ^ U	^ U	&Ucirc;	Û
C-x 8 " "	" "	&uml;	¨

Table 8-2. Bindings for inserting entities for accented characters[a] (continued)

C-x 8 prefix keystrokes	ISO accents mode shortcut	Character entity	Character displayed in browser
C-x 8 " a	" a	&auml;	ä
C-x 8 " A	" A	&Auml;	Ä
C-x 8 " e	" e	&euml;	ë
C-x 8 " E	" E	&Euml;	Ë
C-x 8 " i	" i	&iuml;	ï
C-x 8 " I	" I	&Iuml;	Ï
C-x 8 " o	" o	&ouml;	ö
C-x 8 " O	" O	&Ouml;	Ö
C-x 8 " u	" u	&uuml;	ü
C-x 8 " U	" U	&Uuml;	Ü
C-x 8 " s	" s	&szlig;	ß
C-x 8 " y	" y	&yuml;	ÿ
C-x 8 " Y	" Y	&Yuml;	Ÿ
C-x 8 ~ ~		&not;	¬
C-x 8 ~ a	~ a	&atilde;	ã
C-x 8 ~ A	~ A	&Atilde;	Ã
C-x 8 ~ d	~ d	&eth;	ð
C-x 8 ~ D	~ D	&ETH;	Ð
C-x 8 ~ n	~ n	&ntilde;	ñ
C-x 8 ~ N	~ N	&Ntilde;	Ñ
C-x 8 ~ o	~ o	&otilde;	õ
C-x 8 ~ O	~ O	&Otilde;	Õ
C-x 8 ~ t	~ t	&thorn;	þ
C-x 8 ~ T	~ T	&THORN;	Þ
C-x 8 / /		&divide;	÷
C-x 8 o	/ /	&ring;	°
C-x 8 / a	/ a	&aring;	å
C-x 8 / A	/ A	&Aring;	Å
C-x 8 / e	/ e	&aelig;	æ
C-x 8 / E	/ E	&AElig;	Æ
C-x 8 / o	/ o	&oslash;	ø
C-x 8 / O	/ O	&Oslash;	Ø
C-x 8 , ,	~ ~	&cedil;	¸
C-x 8 , c	~ c	&ccedil;	ç
C-x 8 , C	~ C	&Ccedil;	Ç

[a] For instructions on making these bindings work properly, read this section carefully.

Table 8-3. Bindings for inserting entities for punctuation and symbols

C-x 8 prefix keystrokes	Character entity	Character displayed in browser
C-x 8 1 / 2	&frac12;	½
C-x 8 1 / 4	&frac14;	¼
C-x 8 3 / 4	&frac34;	¾
C-x 8 SPC		nonbreaking space
C-x 8 !	&iexcl;	¡
C-x 8 $	&curren;	¤
C-x 8 +	&plusmn;	±
C-x 8 -	&shy;	soft hyphen
C-x 8 .	&middot;	·
C-x 8 <	&laquo;	«
C-x 8 =	&macr;	¯
C-x 8 >	&raquo;	»
C-x 8 ?	&iquest;	¿
C-x 8 |	&brvbar;	¦
C-x 8 c	&cent;	¢
C-x 8 C	&copy;	©
C-x 8 L	&pound;	£
C-x 8 P	&para;	¶
C-x 8 R	&reg;	®
C-x 8 S	&sect;	§
C-x 8 u	&micro;	µ
C-x 8 x	&#215;	×
C-x 8 Y	&yen;	¥
C-x 8 ^ 1	&sup1;	1
C-x 8 ^ 2	&sup2;	2
C-x 8 ^ 3	&sup3;	3
C-x 8 _ a	&ordf;	a
C-x 8 _ o	&ordm;	o

Table 8-4 lists HTML mode commands.

Table 8-4. HTML mode commands

Keystrokes	Command name	Action
(none)	**html-mode**	Enter HTML mode.
C-c C-t *SGML → Insert Tag*	**sgml-tag**	Inserts a tag, prompting for attributes. If you enter **html** as the tag name, inserts a template html file.

Table 8-4. HTML mode commands (continued)

Keystrokes	Command name	Action
C-c Tab *SGML → Toggle Tag Visibility*	**sgml-tags-invisible**	Hides or shows the tags in the file.
C-c C-v *SGML → View Buffer Contents*	**browse-url-of-buffer**	Display buffer in default browser.
C-c C-s	**html-autoview- mode**	If this mode is on (this command toggles it), display file in browser each time it is saved in Emacs.
C-c 8	**sgml-name-8bit-mode**	If turned on, certain keystrokes for inserting Latin-1 characters are captured and replaced with the appropriate entities. See "Character encoding in HTML mode" for details.
C-c C-f *SGML → Forward Tag*	**sgml-skip-tag-forward**	Move forward to the next tag of the same level.
C-c C-b *SGML → Backward Tag*	**sgml-skip-tag-backward**	Move backward to previous tag of the same level.
C-c Del *or* **C-c C-d** *SGML → Delete Tag*	**sgml-delete-tag**	With cursor on or before a tag, deletes tag or tag pair.
C-c 1	**html-headline-1**	Insert an <h1>.
C-c 2	**html-headline-2**	Insert an <h2>.
C-c 3	**html-headline-3**	Insert an <h3>.
C-c 4	**html-headline-4**	Insert an <h4>.
C-c 5	**html-headline-5**	Insert an <h5>.
C-c 6	**html-headline-6**	Insert an <h6> (useful for footnote text) .
C-c Enter	**html-paragraph**	Insert <p> tag.
C-c C-c h *HTML → Href Anchor*	**html-href-anchor**	Insert a hyperlink.
C-c C-c n *HTML → Name Anchor*	**html-name-anchor**	Insert an anchor so that a link can be created to the anchored part of the page.
C-c C-c u *HTML → Unordered List*	**html-unordered-list**	Create a bulleted list.
C-c C-c o *HTML → Ordered List*	**html-ordered-list**	Create a numbered list.
C-c C-c l *HTML → List Item*	**html-list-item**	Add an item to a list.
C-c C-c i *HTML → Image*	**html-image**	Insert <img src=""> and position cursor for you to enter filename of image.
C-c C-j *HTML → Line Break*	**html-line**	Insert a line break ( ).
C-c C-c - *HTML → Horizontal Rule*	**html-horizontal-rule**	Insert a horizontal rule (<hr>).

Table 8-4. HTML mode commands (continued)

Keystrokes	Command name	Action
C-c C-r	html-radio-buttons	Insert a group of radio buttons. Emacs prompts for a name for the group, then repeatedly for value, whether it should be checked, and associated text. Press **C-g** to complete the group.
C-c C-c c *HTML → Checkboxes*	html-checkboxes	Insert a group of checkboxes. Emacs prompts for a name for the group, then repeatedly for value, whether it should be checked, and associated text. Press **C-g** to complete the group.
C-c ? *SGML → Describe Tag*	sgml-tag-help	Provide brief verbal description of tag at cursor position.

Using HTML Helper Mode

HTML helper mode, written by Nelson Minar and now maintained by Gian Uberto Lauri, offers great flexibility in writing HTML. You can enable various hand-holding features depending on your level of expertise and preferences.

Why would you choose HTML helper mode over Emacs's own HTML mode? Although HTML mode makes it easy to write basic HTML, it provides little support for programmatic, interactive web pages. HTML helper mode supports ASP, JSP (and JDE, the Java Development Environment, discussed in Chapter 9), and PHP, to name a few more advanced features. If you're writing HTML in Emacs, you're likely to be a developer of such pages rather than a more text-oriented author. For this reason, HTML helper mode continues to be popular among Emacs users.

Html helper mode is not part of Emacs by default. You can download it from its homepage at *http://www.nongnu.org/baol-hth*. Download the file into a directory such as *~/elisp*, move to that directory, and then type:

```
% tar xvzf html-helper-mode.tar.gz
```

The system unpacks the *tar* file for you. (Of course, if you are installing on Windows, you can simply use WinZip to decompress and unpack the file.) The *tar* file contains several components, including:

- *html-helper-mode.el*—the Lisp file for HTML helper mode
- *hhm-changelog*—changes that have been made
- *hhm-config.el*—a Lisp file that allows Emacs customization to work[*]

---

[*] The version we downloaded in August 2004 marked this file as alpha code, so don't be surprised if you find bugs. Visit the file to see if its status has changed.

Starting HTML helper mode

Before you can start HTML helper mode, you have to load it into Emacs. (For a complete discussion of this topic, see "Building Your Own Lisp Library" in Chapter 11; we describe it briefly here.) Begin by typing **M-x load-file Enter**. Emacs asks which file to load and you enter **~/elisp/html-helper-mode.el** and press **Enter**, adjusting the path to reflect the location where you installed *html-helper-mode.el*. You enter the mode by typing **M-x html-helper-mode Enter**. HTML helper appears on the mode line.

Making HTML helper mode part of your startup is easier. Put the following lines in your *.emacs* file:

```
(setq load-path (cons "~/elisp " load-path))
(autoload 'html-helper-mode "html-helper-mode" "Yay HTML" t)
```

In the first line, insert the complete path for the directory in which *html-helper-mode.el* is located in quotation marks, replacing *~/elisp* to the correct value for your system. The second line tells Emacs to load HTML helper mode automatically when you start Emacs.

If you want to use HTML helper mode for editing HTML files by default, add this line to *.emacs* as well:

```
(setq auto-mode-alist (cons '("\\.html?$" . html-helper-mode) auto-mode-alist))
```

If you edit other types of files with HTML helper mode, you may want to add lines to include all the types of files you edit. Adding more lines is the easiest way. For example, to make HTML helper mode the default for PHP files, add this line to *.emacs*:

```
(setq auto-mode-alist (cons '("\\.php$" . html-helper-mode) auto-mode-alist))
```

A brief tour of HTML helper mode

The main reason people like HTML helper mode is that it provides easy menu access to a wide variety of options. Realizing that having a crowded menu with many submenus could overwhelm new users, the authors created an option called Turn on Novice Menu. Selecting this option from the HTML menu provides a barebones menu, as shown in Figure 8-1. Novice HTML writers can use these options to create a basic HTML document without worrying about what forms, JSPs, PHP, and the like mean.

Selecting Turn on Expert Menu from the HTML menu returns the larger menu with its numerous submenus, as shown in Figure 8-2.

Inserting an HTML template

HTML helper mode inserts a template for you every time you create a new HTML file.

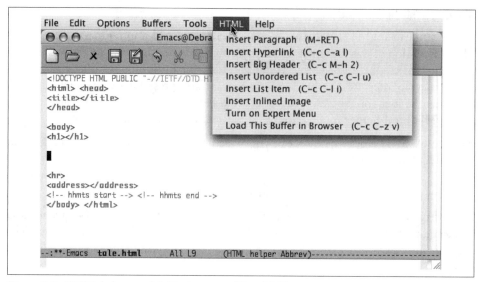

Figure 8-1. HTML helper mode's Novice menu (Mac OS X)

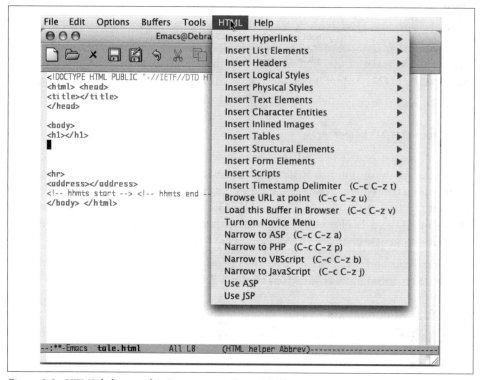

Figure 8-2. HTML helper mode's Expert menu (Mac OS X)

Type: **C-x C-f new.html**

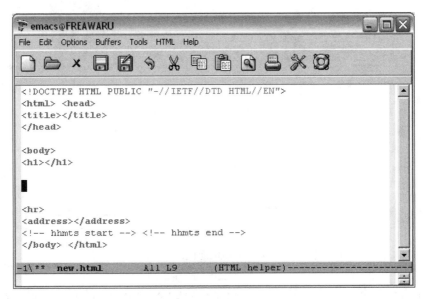

HTML helper mode inserts a template with all the basic elements needed for a valid HTML document (Windows).

The template contains all the basic HTML elements. The entire document is surrounded by <html></html> tags. Then the head and the body are separated. Following an <hr> tag that tells the browser to insert a horizontal line, called a horizontal rule, the <address> tag leaves a place for the author to put in his or her email address. In these days of spam, it's unlikely you'll want to do that. (You can leave the <address> tag blank or delete it.)

If you do want to include an email address, enter a line like this in your *.emacs* file (substituting your own email address, of course):

```
(setq html-helper-address-string
  "<a href=\"mailto:cdickens@great-beyond.com \">Charles Dickens</a>")
```

Type: **C-x C-f newfile.html**

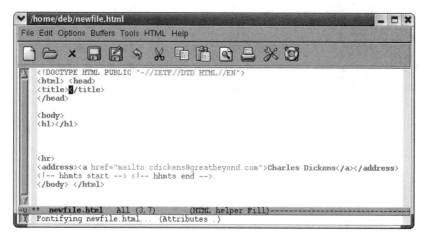

Emacs inserts the HTML template, including the address.

Normally you begin filling out the template by entering title and a level-one header (these are often the same). You can then begin writing paragraphs of text. Before you start typing, press **M-Enter**. Emacs inserts <p></p> and positions the cursor between them. You can see from the ending paragraph tag that HTML helper mode is working toward XHTML compliance.

Type: **M-Enter**

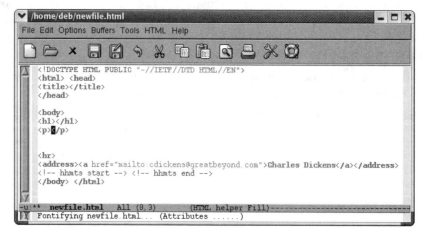

Emacs positions the cursor between <p> and </p> so you can start insert text.

Putting tags around a region

When editing HTML files, you often spend a lot of time marking up existing text. If you preface any of the tag commands with **C-u**, Emacs inserts the tags around a region rather than putting them at the cursor position.* To demonstrate, we'll start a new HTML file and insert text from our *dickens* file.

Type: **C-x C-f ataleoftwocities.html**

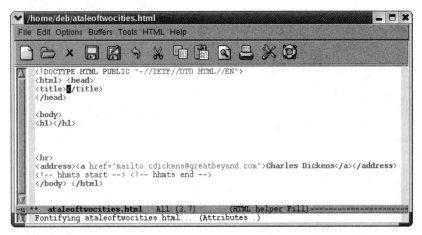

Emacs inserts the HTML template.

---

* For this to work, you must invoke the command through the keyboard, either using its key binding or its command name. Using a menu option doesn't work.

Move the cursor past the `<h1>` pair and type **C-x C-i dickens**.

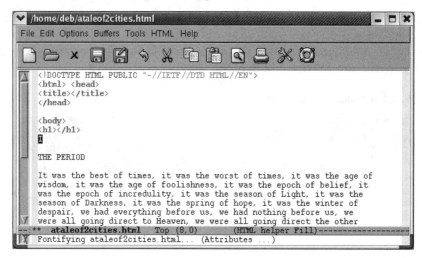

Emacs inserts the *dickens* text file, to which we can add HTML tags.

If you were really doing this properly, you'd type something like "A Tale of Two Cities, Chapter 1" as the title and the first-level header. But for now, you just want to see how to mark up a region of existing text. Begin by marking the Dickens paragraph as a region and type **C-u M-Enter**.

Type: **M-h C-u M-Enter**.

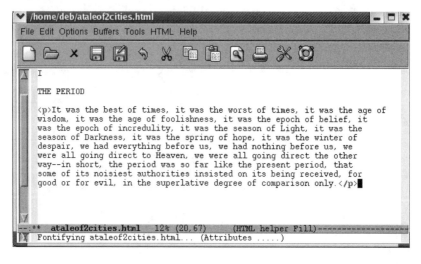

Emacs inserts opening and closing paragraph tags.

Using completion

HTML helper mode supports completion. You type the beginning of a tag and press **M-Tab** (for **tempo-complete-tag**).* If there's more than one possibility, a window of possible completions appears. Let's say you are working on a bulleted list.

Type: **<olM-Tab**

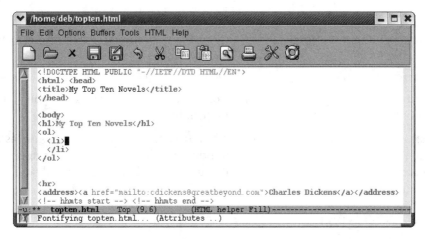

Emacs inserts the tags to begin and end the list and the tag for one list item.

Note, however, that completion is sometimes case-sensitive. For example, typing **<s M-Tab** shows the following completions:

```
<select            <span class=
<span style =      <strike>
<strong>           <samp>
```

Notice that the <script> tag is missing. But if you try typing **<S M-Tab**, the script tag and its attributes are inserted, as in:

```
<SCRIPT TYPE="text/javascript">
</SCRIPT>
```

The distinction between upper- and lowercase shows that HTML helper mode is moving toward XHTML compliance, but hasn't quite arrived. XHTML requires that all tags be lowercase. On the positive side, note that the attribute is in quotation marks, another XHTML requirement.

---

* If **M-Tab** is trapped by the operating system to switch between applications (it is on Red Hat Linux), type **Esc Tab** instead.

Turning on prompting

Some HTML tags require you to input certain attributes. For example, when you enter a hyperlink, you have to specify the URL of the link and the text that the user will select. If you type **C-c C-a l** (the lowercase letter "L") to enter a link, HTML helper mode inserts:

```
<a href=""></a>
```

with the cursor on the second quotation mark so you can type in the URL. HTML helper mode offers additional help if you turn on prompting. Add this line to your *.emacs* file:

```
(setq tempo-interactive t)
```

Note that HTML helper mode prompts only for required attributes; if you want to input optional attributes, you have to add them by hand.

Whether you consider prompting useful or intrusive is a matter of personal taste. If you are a beginning HTML author, prompting may help you remember to enter all the necessary information for each tag. If you find you don't like it, simply delete the line you added to the *.emacs* file.

Character encoding in HTML helper mode

HTML helper mode supports entry of only the most common character entities. However, it does make it easy to insert these entities. Simply type **C-c** before the character in question. For example, type **C-c <** to enter the escape code for a less-than sign (<).

Character entities are also available by selecting HTML → Insert Character Entities.

Table 8-5 lists bindings for inserting character entities in HTML helper mode.

Table 8-5. Inserting character entities in HTML helper mode

Keystrokes	Command name	Character entity	Character rendered on web page
C-c >	tempo-template-html-greater-than	&gt;	>
C-c <	tempo-template-html-less-than	&lt;	<
C-c &	tempo-template-html-ampersand	&amp;	&
C-c u	tempo-template-html-u`-(&ù)	&ugrave;	ù
C-c i	tempo-template-html-i`-(&ì)	&igrave;	ì
C-c o	tempo-template-html-o`-(&ò)	&ograve;	ò
C-c E	tempo-template-html-e'-(&é)	&eacute;	é
C-c e	tempo-template-html-e`-(&è)	&egrave;	è
C-c a	tempo-template-html-a`-(&à)	&agrave;	à
C-c SPC	tempo-template-html-nonbreaking-space		nonbreaking space

Table 8-5. Inserting character entities in HTML helper mode (continued)

Keystrokes	Command name	Character entity	Character rendered on web page
C-c -	tempo-template-html-soft-hyphen	&shy;	soft hyphen
C-c @	tempo-template-html-copyright	&copy;	©
C-c $	tempo-template-html-registered	&reg;	®
C-c "	tempo-template-html-quotation-mark	&quot;	"
C-c #	tempo-template-html-ascii-code	Enter the 3-digit code for the desired character	specified character

Table 8-6 lists the key bindings for HTML helper mode. There are key bindings for advanced HTML features such as forms as well as for some of the HTML 3.0 features. Some tags would normally appear on different lines (for example, in the case of a list); in this table, they are shown on one line.

Table 8-6. HTML helper mode commands

Keystrokes	Command name	Action
C-u	universal-argument	When used before any other tag command, insert tags around a region.
M-Tab	tempo-complete-tag	Complete the current tag.
C-c C-z v HTML → Load This Buffer in Browser	browse-url-of-file	Display this file in the default browser.
C-c C-z u HTML → Browse URL at Point	browse-url-default-browser	Load the URL at point in default browser.
C-c M-h 1 HTML → Insert Headers → Header 1	tempo-template-html-header-1	Insert <h1></h1>.
C-c M-h 2 HTML → Insert Headers → Header 2	tempo-template-html-header-2	Insert <h2></h2>.
C-c M-h 3 HTML → Insert Headers → Header 3	tempo-template-html-header-3	Insert <h3></h3>.
C-c M-h 4 HTML → Insert Headers → Header 4	tempo-template-html-header-4	Insert <h4></h4>.
C-c M-h 5 HTML → Insert Headers → Header 5	tempo-template-html-header-5	Insert <h5></h5>.
C-c M-h 6 HTML → Insert Headers → Header 6	tempo-template-html-header-6	Insert <h6></h6>.
M-Enter HTML → Insert Text Elements → Paragraph	tempo-template-html-paragraph	Insert <p></p>.
C-c C-a l HTML → Insert Hyperlinks → Hyperlink	tempo-template-html-hyperlink	Insert <a href=""></a>.

Table 8-6. HTML helper mode commands (continued)

Keystrokes	Command name	Action
C-c C-a n *HTML → Insert Hyperlinks → Target*	**tempo-template-html-link-target**	Insert `<a name=""></a>`.
C-c Enter *HTML → Insert Text Elements →* *Line Break*	**tempo-template-html-line-break**	Insert a literal line break, ` `.
C-c = *HTML → Insert Text Elements →* *Horizontal Line*	**tempo-template-html-horizontal-line**	Insert a horizontal rule, `<hr>`.
C-c C-z t *HTML → Insert Timestamp Delimiter*	**html-helper-insert-timestamp-delimiter-at-point**	Insert timestamp delimiters.
C-c C-h t *HTML → Insert Structural* *Elements → Title*	**tempo-template-html-title**	Insert `<title></title>`.
C-c Tab a *HTML → Insert Inlined Images →* *Image*	**tempo-template-html-image**	Insert `<img src="">`.
C-c C-l u *HTML → Insert List Elements →* *Unordered List*	**tempo-template-html-unor-dered-list**	Insert `<ul><li></li></ul>`.
C-c C-l o *HTML → Insert List Elements →* *Ordered List*	**tempo-template-html-ordered-list**	Insert `<ol><li></li></ol>`.
C-c C-l t *HTML → Insert List Elements →* *Definition Item*	**tempo-template-html-definition-item**	Insert `<dt><dd>`.
C-c C-l l *HTML → Insert List Elements →* *List Item*	**tempo-template-html-item**	Insert `<li></li>`.
C-c C-l d *HTML → Insert List Elements →* *Definition List*	**tempo-template-html-definition-list**	Insert `<dl><dt><dd></dl>`.
C-c C-l m *HTML → Insert List Elements →* *Menu List*	**tempo-template-html-menu-list**	Insert `<menu><li></li></menu>`.
C-c C-l r *HTML → Insert List Elements →* *Directory List*	**tempo-template-html-directorylist**	Insert `<dir><li></li></dir>`.
C-c C-l i *HTML → Insert List Elements →* *List Item*	**html-helper-smart-insert-item**	Insert `<li></li>`.
C-c C-f z *HTML → Insert Form Elements →* *Rest Form*	**tempo-template-html-reset-form**	Insert `<input type="RESET">`.

Table 8-6. HTML helper mode commands (continued)

Keystrokes	Command name	Action
C-c C-f b *HTML → Insert Form Elements →* *Button*	tempo-template-html-button	Insert `<input type="BUTTON">`.
C-c C-f m *HTML → Insert Form Elements →* *Submit Form*	tempo-template-html- submit- form	Insert `<input type="SUBMIT">`.
C-c C-f s *HTML → Insert Form Elements →* *Selections*	tempo-template-html-selections	Insert `<select><option></select>`.
C-c C-f o *HTML → Insert Form Elements →* *Option*	tempo-template-html-option	Insert `<option>`.
C-c C-f v *HTML → Insert Form Elements →* *Option with Value*	tempo-template-html-option- with-value	Insert `<option value="">`.
C-c C-f i *HTML → Insert Form Elements →* *Image Field*	tempo-template-html-input- image-field	Insert `<input type="IMAGE">`.
C-c C-f r *HTML → Insert Form Elements →* *Radiobutton*	tempo-template-html-input- radiobutton	Insert `<input type="RADIO">`.
C-c C-f c *HTML → Insert Form Elements →* *Checkbox*	tempo-template-html-checkbox	Insert `<input type="CHECKBOX">`.
C-c C-f p *HTML → Insert Form Elements →* *Text Area*	tempo-template-html-text-area	Insert `<textarea></textarea>`.
C-c C-f f *HTML → Insert Form Elements →* *Form*	tempo-template-html-form	Insert `<form></form>`.
C-c C-f t´ *HTML → Insert Form Elements →* *Text Field*	tempo-template-html-text-field	Insert `<input type="TEXT">`.
C-c C-f h *HTML → Insert Form Elements →* *Hidden Field*	tempo-template-html-hidden- field	Insert `<input type="HIDDEN">`.
C-c M-l s *HTML → Insert Logical Styles → Strong*	tempo-template-html-strong	Insert `<strong></strong>`.
C-c M-l e *HTML → Insert Logical Styles →* *Emphasized*	tempo-template-html-empha- sized	Insert `<em></em>`.
C-c M-l b *HTML → Insert Logical Styles →* *Blockquote*	tempo-template-html-block- quote	Insert `<blockquote></blockquote>`.

Table 8-6. HTML helper mode commands (continued)

Keystrokes	Command name	Action
C-c M-l p *HTML → Insert Logical Styles →* *Preformatted*	**tempo-template-html-prefor-matted**	Insert `<pre></pre>`.
C-c C-p s *HTML → Insert Physical Styles →* *Strikethru*	**tempo-template-html-strikethru**	Insert `<s></s>`.
C-c C-p f *HTML → Insert Physical Styles → Fixed*	**tempo-template-html-fixed**	Insert `<tt></tt>`.
C-c C-p u *HTML → Insert Physical Styles →* *Underline*	**tempo-template-html-underline**	Insert `<u></u>`.
C-c C-p i *HTML → Insert Physical Styles → Italic*	**tempo-template-html-italic**	Insert `<i></i>`.
C-c C-p b *HTML → Insert Physical Styles → Bold*	**tempo-template-html-bold**	Insert `<b></b>`.
C-c C-p c *HTML → Insert Physical Styles →* *Center*	**tempo-template-html-center**	Insert `<center></center>`.
C-c C-p l *HTML → Insert Physical Styles →* *Spanning Class*	**tempo-template-html-spanning-class**	Insert `<span class=""></span>`.
C-c C-p 5 *HTML → Insert Physical Styles →* *Spanning Style*	**tempo-template-html-spanning-style**	Insert `<span style=""></span>`.
C-c C-s a *HTML → Insert Logical Styles →* *Address*	**tempo-template-html-address**	Insert `<address></address>`.
C-c M-l d *HTML → Insert Logical Styles →* *Definition*	**tempo-template-html-definition**	Insert `<dfn></dfn>`.
C-c M-l v *HTML → Insert Logical Styles →* *Variable*	**tempo-template-html-variable**	Insert `<var></var>`.
C-c M-l k *HTML → Insert Logical Styles →* *Keyboard Input*	**tempo-template-html-keyboard**	Insert `<kbd></kbd>`.
C-c M-l r *HTML → Insert Logical Styles →* *Citation*	**tempo-template-html-citation**	Insert `<cite></cite>`.
C-c M-l x *HTML → Insert Logical Styles →* *Sample*	**tempo-template-html-sample**	Insert `<samp></samp>`.
C-c M-l c *HTML → Insert Logical Styles → Code*	**tempo-template-html-code**	Insert `<code></code>`.

Table 8-6. HTML helper mode commands (continued)

Keystrokes	Command name	Action
C-c C-h b *HTML → Insert Structural Elements → Base*	**tempo-template-html-base**	Insert `<base href="">`.
C-c C-h l *HTML → Insert Structural Elements → Link*	**tempo-template-html-link**	Insert `<link href="">`.
C-c C-h m *HTML → Insert Structural Elements → Meta Name*	**tempo-template-html-meta-name**	Insert `<meta content="">`.
C-c C-h n *HTML → Insert Structural Elements → Nextid*	**tempo-template-html-nextid**	Insert `<nextid>`.
C-c C-h i *HTML → Insert Structural Elements → Isindex*	**tempo-template-html-isindex**	Insert `<isindex>`.
C-c C-h B *HTML → Insert Structural Elements → Body*	**tempo-template-html-body**	Insert `<body></body>`.
C-c C-h H *HTML → Insert Structural Elements → Head*	**tempo-template-html-head**	Insert `<head></head>`.
C-c C-t t *HTML → Insert Tables → Table*	**tempo-template-html-table**	Insert `<table></table>`.
C-c C-t p *HTML → Insert Tables → html table caption*	**tempo-template-html-html-table-caption**	Insert `<caption></caption>`.
C-c C-t d *HTML → Insert Tables → Table Data*	**tempo-template-html-table-data**	Insert `<TD></TD>`.
C-c C-t h *HTML → Insert Tables → Table Header*	**tempo-template-html-table-header**	Insert `<TH></TH>`.
C-c C-t r *HTML → Insert Tables → Table Row*	**tempo-template-html-table-row**	Insert `<TR></TR>`.

Writing XML

Writing XML involves entering structured information that complies with a document type definition or schema. Even within Emacs, the XML support you receive varies. At the low end of the spectrum, there is plain vanilla Fundamental mode. It provides simply a screen where you type. Specialized modes like SGML mode provide support for entering tags, as we saw earlier in our discussion of HTML mode, a derivative of SGML mode. But neither of these approaches help you parse or validate XML (SGML mode has a command for validating, but it is tricky to set up correctly). More advanced Lisp packages, though currently not included in Emacs, are available to provide these functions. These add-on packages provide validation against DTDs or schemas, parsing capabilities, and, typically, an array of standard DTDs and schema definitions. In Emacs, these tools primarily work in conjunction with one of two major modes. psgml mode validates XML (and SGML) against DTDs. The newer nxml mode validates against RELAX NG schemas. We cover both of these options in this section. Before we go into detail on those modes, however, let's look briefly what Emacs has built-in with SGML mode.

Writing XML with SGML Mode

Emacs's own SGML mode provides support for entering tags. We covered much of this earlier under HTML mode, so we provide just one brief example here. Inserting, hiding, and showing tags are especially helpful features provided by SGML mode.

Let's look at a chapter on enumerated types by *Java in a Nutshell* author David Flanagan. This chapter uses the DocBook DTD.

Initial state:

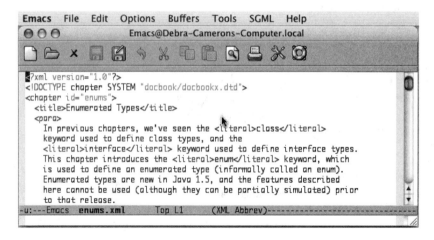

Editing a document that uses the DocBook DTD (Mac OS X).

Note that Emacs displays XML on the mode line. XML mode in this context is a sub-set of SGML mode. Actually, despite this name, all the commands in this mode start with sgml, not xml. The menu of relevant commands is called SGML as well. Emacs doesn't pretend to have extensive XML support.

We want to insert a paragraph before the first paragraph.

Add a blank line following the title and type: **C-c C-t**

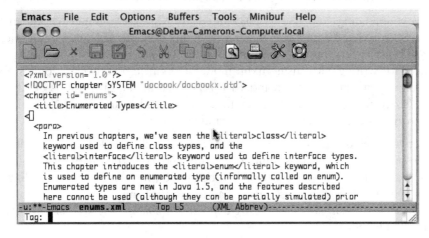

Emacs inserts an open angle bracket and prompts for the tag name (Mac OS X).

Type: **para Enter**

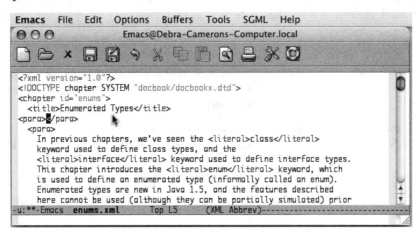

Emacs inserts opening and closing paragraph tags (Mac OS X).

Note that Emacs is not following our indentation style. We can correct it by moving to the beginning of the line and pressing **Tab**. See Table 8-4 earlier in this chapter for details on SGML mode commands.

TEI Emacs: XML Authoring for Linux and Windows

The Text Encoding Initiative (TEI) wanted an XML authoring environment for Emacs, so it created (the somewhat misleadingly named) TEI Emacs.* Despite its name, TEI Emacs does not include Emacs itself. Rather, it creates an authoring environment for writing XML using nxml mode or psgml mode. It incorporates XSLT tools, along with most of the standard DTDs, such as the three forms of XHTML DTDs (strict, frameset, and transitional), DocBook DTDs, and more. Naturally, the TEI's own DTDs and schemas are also included.

The active development of this tool and its careful packaging led us to describe this tool despite the fact that it is limited to Linux and Windows at this writing.† You should have Emacs 21.3 already installed before you install this tool. Installing TEI Emacs is trivial. The Windows version has an installer, and Linux users follow simple instructions at *http://www.tei-c.org/Software/tei-emacs/*, the web site for downloading TEI Emacs.

Writing XHTML Using nxml Mode

James Clark, an XML pioneer, wrote nxml mode to provide Emacs support for his schema standard RELAX NG. For details on the standard, visit *http://www.relaxng.org/* or pick up a copy of *RELAX NG* by Eric van der Vlist (O'Reilly). The important thing about nxml mode is that it validates text as you type instead of making validation and debugging separate steps.

If you did not install TEI Emacs, you can download nxml mode and its schemas from *http://thaiopensource.com/download/*. If you decide to become an active nxml mode user, you may want to join a related Yahoo Group discussion list (see *http://groups.yahoo.com/group/emacs-nxml-mode/*).

In this section, we change our running HTML example to XHTML, first using a RELAX NG schema and nxml mode. Open *dickens.html*, then enter nxml mode.

---

* We'd like to thank Emacs guru Eric Pement for pointing out TEI Emacs to Deb.

† We sincerely hope that this support will be extended to Mac OS X as well, providing developers and writers on that platform the benefits of this tool's capabilities. Meanwhile, Mac users may want to install nxml mode from *http://thaiopensource.com/download/* and psgml mode from *http://www.lysator.liu.se/projects/about_psgml.html*.

Type: **C-x C-f dickens.html Enter M-x nxml-mode Enter**

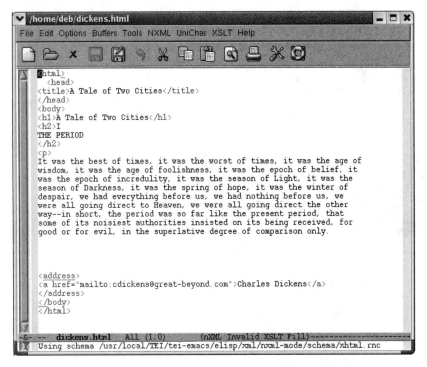

Editing *dickens.html* in nxml mode.

nxml mode tells you what schema it is using in the minibuffer. It's smart enough to know that its XHTML schema is best for this purpose.

The mode line tells us that this file is currently invalid. Emacs highlights errors with red underscores. Let's deal with these errors one at a time.

Move the cursor to the red underscore at the end of the html tag.

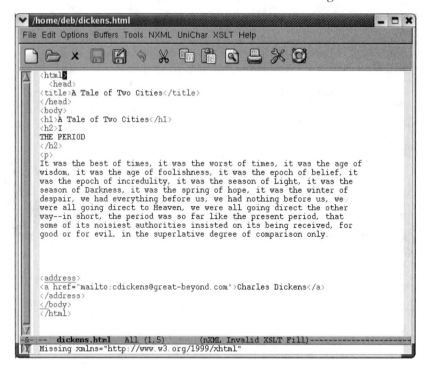

The minibuffer describes what's missing.

Editing XHTML with a schema requires a namespace definition in the <html> tag. nxml mode knows what we need. This is a good time to use nxml's completion feature to let it supply the details for us. **C-Enter** completes the current tag.

Type: **Space xmlns=" C-Enter**

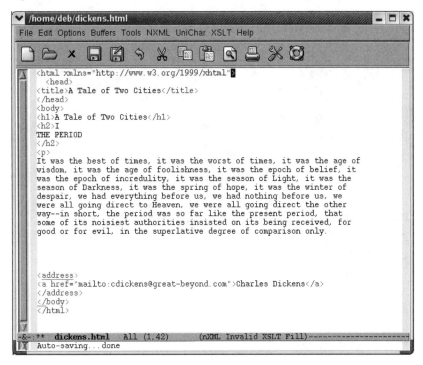

Emacs inserts the rest of the namespace declaration.

The mode line tells us that this file is still invalid. Moving to the underlined address tag gives us a fairly cryptic reason; it says, Element not allowed in this context. Let's move down to the closing body tag to see if that error provides any more insight into the problem.

Move to </body>.

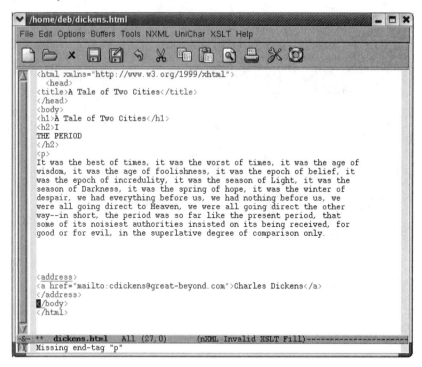

The minibuffer says `Missing end-tag "p"`.

This message provides a clue. Although HTML authors are not accustomed to adding closing tags to paragraphs, XHTML requires them. Let's insert a closing tag after our paragraph.

Move to the line following the Dickens paragraph and type: **</**

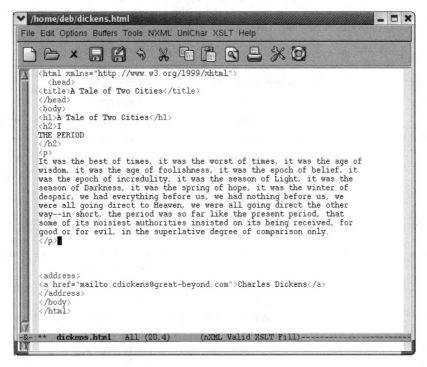

Emacs inserts a closing tag.

Note that just typing **</** was adequate to insert a closing tag for the current element. We don't need to type **C-Enter** to invoke completion. That's because in nxml mode, slash is bound to **nxml-electric-slash**. It automatically completes the nearest open element, another shortcut for us.

A similar command is **C-c C-f** (for **nxml-finish-element**). With **C-c C-f**, you don't have to type anything; it inserts the relevant closing tag for you.

Look at the mode line now. It says valid. Using nxml mode, it's not too tough to take an HTML file and change it to valid XHTML.

Validating text as you type it is a key feature of nxml mode. It's validating against a schema. To specify a different schema, type **C-c C-s** (for **rng-set-schema-and-validate**). The minibuffer prompts for the file where the schema resides. A number of schemas can be found online at *http://www.relaxng.org/#schemas*. You can also convert DTDs to schemas using tools listed on that page.

Your menus vary depending on whether you install nxml mode directly or whether you use TEI's version. TEI provides support for encoded characters using the UniChar menu. It also provides extensive XSLT support. TEI's NXML menu includes some TEI skeletons as well as nxml mode options. Nxml mode installed from *thaiopensource.org* includes an XML menu with options for setting the schema and customizing the mode. Table 8-7 lists some of the commands available in nxml mode.

Table 8-7. Nxml mode commands

Keystrokes	Command name	Action
C-Enter	nxml-complete	Complete the current tag.
/	nxml-electric-slash	Add a closing tag for the last open element.
C-c C-n	rng-next-error	Move to the next error.
C-c C-l	rng-save-schema-location	Creates (or updates) a file called *schemas.xml* in your home directory. This file associates schemas with files.
C-c C-s	rng-set-schema-and-validate	Set the schema and validate against it.
C-c C-a	rng-auto-set-schema	Set the schema automatically according to the contents of the file.
C-c C-w	rng-what-schema	Show in the minibuffer the current schema associated with this file.
C-c C-v	rng-validate-mode	Toggles whether the mode line indicates that the file is valid or invalid.
C-c C-u	nxml-insert-named-char	Insert a named character; press **Tab** to see a list.
(none)	nxml-insert-xml-declaration	Insert an XML declaration at the beginning of the file.
C-c Tab	nxml-balanced-close-start-tag-inline	Insert the ending tag for the starting tag you are typing, putting the ending tag on the current line.
C-c C-b	nxml-balanced-close-start-tag-block	Insert the ending tag for the starting tag you are typing, putting the ending tag on a separate line.
C-c C-f	nxml-finish-element	Finish the current element.
M-h	nxml-mark-paragraph	Mark the current paragraph.
M-}	nxml-forward-paragraph	Move forward one paragraph.
M-{	nxml-backward-paragraph	Move back one paragraph.
C-M-p	nxml-backward-element	Move back one element.
C-M-n	nxml-forward-element	Move forward one element.
C-M-d	nxml-down-element	Move down one element (if nested).
C-M-u	nxml-backward-up-element	Move up one element (if nested).

Using psgml Mode

Lennart Stafflin's psgml mode has been around for a while. It is more robust than Emacs's own SGML mode, but, like any add-on, you have to install it in order to use it. Either install TEI Emacs as described earlier or download psgml mode from *http://www.lysator.liu.se/projects/about_psgml.html* and follow the installation instructions there. TEI Emacs includes a functioning psgml mode, so if you've installed TEI Emacs, your setup work is done.

psgml mode consists of two parts: sgml-mode for writing SGML and xml-mode for writing XML (and in our case XHTML).

To start psgml mode to edit our XHTML file, type **M-x xml-mode**.

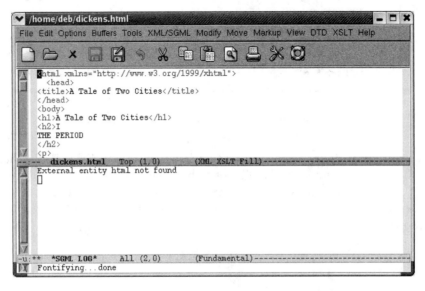

XML appears on the mode line and an *SGML LOG* window opens. If you are using TEI Emacs, XSLT appears on the mode line along with XML.

The *SGML LOG* window displays messages about this session. (If it doesn't appear immediately, click on the first character in the file.) The log buffer complains that it could not find an external entity called html. This file has been changed to work with the XHTML RELAX NG schema. psgml mode expects it to conform to an XHTML DTD. To get started with the (minimal) work needed to undertake the transformation from a schema-based file to a DTD-based file, we ask psgml to normalize the buffer.

Type: **M-x sgml-normalize** or select Normalize from the Modify menu

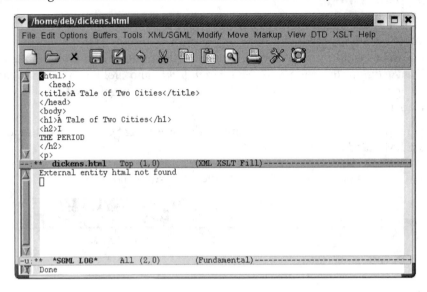

psgml mode eliminates the namespace declaration in the <html> tag.

More needs to be done, however. The first statements in an XHTML file include an XML statement and a DOCTYPE entry that identifies the DTD this document should be validated against. One of the nice things about TEI Emacs is that it includes a variety of DTDs. (Users of standard psgml mode don't have this feature; sorry.*)

---

* A straightforward introduction to setting up a complete environment for psgml mode can be found at *http://openacs.org/doc/openacs-5-0-0/psgml-mode.html*.

At the beginning of the file, select DTD → Insert DTD → XHTML Transitional.

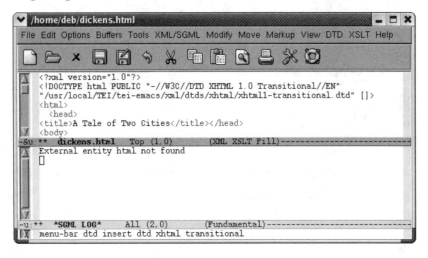

Emacs inserts the two required elements for us.

That's all it takes to make this file a well-formed XHTML file. psgml mode allows for validation against the DTD. Let's validate it using **C-c C-v** to make sure it's okay.

Type: **C-c C-v**

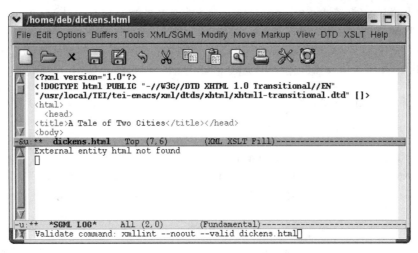

psgml mode inserts the default validate command in the minibuffer; press **Enter** to run it.

Press **Enter** and type **y** to save the buffer when prompted

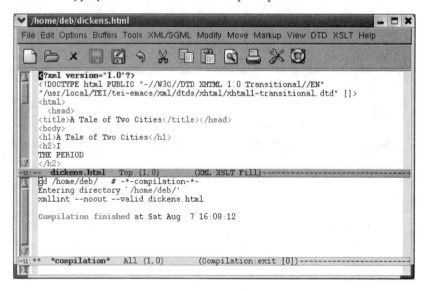

The *compilation* buffer indicates (somewhat cryptically) that the document is valid.

Of course, typical documents are far more complex than this one. Options on the View menu provide selective hiding and showing of elements, including an option to hide all tags, allowing you to focus on the content of the file instead.

psgml mode also offers numerous options. If you are running TEI Emacs, you'll find the File Options and User Options submenus on the XML/SGML menu. If you've installed psgml mode standalone, you'll find them on the SGML menu. Table 8-8 summarizes some of the psgml commands.

Table 8-8. Bindings in psgml mode

Keystrokes	Command name	Action
C-M-Space	sgml-mark-element	Mark the current element.
M-Tab	sgml-complete	Complete the current tag.
C-M-t	sgml-transpose-element	Transpose two elements.
C-M-h	sgml-mark-current-element	Mark the current element.
C-M-k *Modify → Kill Element*	sgml-kill-element	Delete the current element (and any child elements).
C-M-u *Move → Backward Up Element*	sgml-backward-up-element	Move up to the parent element for this element.
C-M-d *Move → Down Element*	sgml-down-element	Move down to the next child element.

Table 8-8. Bindings in psgml mode (continued)

Keystrokes	Command name	Action
C-M-b *Move → Backward Element*	**sgml-backward-element**	Move to the previous element.
C-M-f *Move → Forward Element*	**sgml-forward-element**	Move to the next element.
C-M-e **Move → End of Element**	**sgml-end-of-element**	Move to the end of the current element.
C-M-a *Move → Beginning of Element*	**sgml-beginning-of-element**	Move to the beginning of the current element.
C-c C-w *SGML → What Element*	**sgml-what-element**	Similar to sgml-position but describes hierarchy in terms of tags versus content (for example, start-tag in title in head in html).
C-c C-v *SGML → Validate*	**sgml-validate**	Insert validation command in the minibuffer so you can modify it if necessary before pressing Enter to execute it.
C-c C-t *SGML → List Valid Tags*	**sgml-list-valid-tags**	List tags that are valid in the current context.
C-c C-q *Modify → Fill Element*	**sgml-fill-element**	Fill element according to the mode's indentation rules.
C-c C-o *Move → Next Trouble Spot*	**sgml-next-trouble-spot**	Find the next problem spot and display the problem in the minibuffer.
C-c C-n *Move → Up Element*	**sgml-up-element**	Move to the parent element.
C-c Enter	**sgml-split-element**	Split current element.
C-c C-l *SGML → Show/Hide Warning Log*	**sgml-show-or-clear-log**	Display or delete the SGML LOG buffer (menu option name is misleading).
C-c C-k *Modify → Kill Markup*	**sgml-kill-markup**	Delete current tag.
C-c / *Markup → End Current Element*	**sgml-insert-end-tag**	Insert closing tag for current tag.
C-c - *Modify → Untag Element*	**sgml-untag-element**	Delete the current tag pair.
C-c # *Modify → Make Character Reference*	**sgml-make-character-reference**	Change character under the cursor to the equivalent entity.
C-c C-f C-e *View → Fold Element*	**sgml-fold-element**	Hide the current element and its children if any.
C-c C-u C-e *View → Unfold Element*	**sgml-unfold-element**	Show the current element and its children if any.
C-c C-f C-s *View → Fold Subelement*	**sgml-fold-subelement**	Hide subelements.
C-c C-f C-r *View → Fold Region*	**sgml-fold-region**	Hide the region.

Table 8-8. Bindings in psgml mode (continued)

Keystrokes	Command name	Action
C-c C-u C-a *View → Unfold All*	**sgml-unfold-all**	Show all hidden tags and text.

Marking up Text for TEX and LATEX

GNU Emacs provides excellent support for marking up TEX files. Most people today use LATEX, which is written in TEX and provides more control over formatting. As a result, we'll talk about LaTeX mode here.

Before we launch into this discussion, we assume that you have set up LATEX on your platform. On Red Hat Linux, it's set up by default. Windows and Mac OS X users must install and configure LATEX before proceeding.*

Emacs attempts to guess whether you're editing a TEX or LATEX file and enter the appropriate mode. You can force LaTeX mode if Emacs doesn't enter it automatically by typing **M-x latex-mode Enter**.

Matching Braces

LATEX commands often take the form \keyword{text}. LaTeX mode doesn't try to figure out if you're using the "right" keywords since the language is extensible and you may have defined your own keywords. It does, however, provide support for avoiding the most common error: mismatched curly braces and dollar signs.

In LATEX, curly braces ({}) and dollar signs ($$) should always appear in pairs; Emacs checks to make sure that each opening brace or dollar sign has a counterpart. When you type a closing brace or dollar sign, the cursor moves quickly to its counterpart (provided that it is on the screen; it shows the context in the minibuffer if it is not), then back again.

Emacs generates braces in matching pairs. The command **C-c {** inserts opening and closing braces and positions the cursor for typing between the braces.

Typing **C-c }** moves you past the right brace. It always finds the correct closing brace, given your current position. If there is no closing brace, you get an error message that says Scan error: Unbalanced parentheses. You also get this error message if you type **C-c }** while the cursor is in a section that is not surrounded by braces, which can be a little confusing.

---

* TEI Emacs, mentioned earlier in this chapter, automatically sets up the environment for you and adds more features including Auctex, a complete authoring environment that supports many TEX variants as well as bibcite/bibtex for generating bibliographies. However, LaTeX mode under TEI Emacs appears to be a different beast from Emacs LaTeX mode, and we do not describe it here.

To check for mismatched curly braces and dollar signs, type **M-x tex-validate-buffer Enter**. This command checks the entire buffer for unbalanced parentheses, curly braces, dollar signs, and the like. (If you have a large file, you might want to validate a region instead using **M-x tex-validate-region Enter**). If it finds any errors, Emacs displays an *Occur* buffer with Mismatches: at the top and a list of lines on which it found errors. You can then easily move to each line that contains an error with **M-x goto-line**.

Sometimes a mismatched parenthesis early in the buffer can start a chain reaction of "errors" through the rest of the file. If you suspect that one of the corrections you make may have fixed most of the remaining errors, simply run **tex-validate-buffer** again.

When you're stepping through errors, **C-c }** provides a good way to check where the closing brace for a given opening brace is. Position the cursor right after the opening brace and press **C-c }**.

Quotation Marks and Paragraphing

LaTeX mode also has features for handling quotation marks and paragraph separation. Typing a quotation mark (") causes Emacs to simulate left and right quotation marks. Left quotation marks are represented as two backtick characters (``) while right quotation marks are represented as two apostrophes (''). (Left and right quotation marks are not part of the standard ASCII character set.) If you need to type a literal quotation mark for any reason, simply use the quote-character command preceding the quotation mark, like this: **C-q "**.

Command Pairs

LaTeX mode provides support for inserting command pairs. To insert a command pair, type **C-c C-o** (for **latex-insert-block**). Emacs prompts for the block name, and then for associated options. For example, type **C-c C-o Enter document Enter Enter** (the second **Enter** indicates no options). Emacs inserts the command pair and positions the cursor between them:

```
\begin{document}
█
\end{document}
```

You can use this command to mark up a text file after you write it. If you mark a region, you can type **C-c C-o** to wrap a command pair around that region.

A related command is **C-c C-e** (for **latex-close-block**). In this case, you type an opening command, press **C-c C-e**, and Emacs inserts the corresponding closing command.

These commands work with any keyword, regardless of what it is. Emacs can't check to make sure that it's a valid LATEX keyword or even that it's been defined. For example, if you type **\begin{eating} C-c C-e**, Emacs inserts **\end{eating}**. It's up to you to make sure you use valid keywords.

Processing and Printing Text

In addition to marking up files for LATEX, you can process files, see your errors (if any), and invoke a viewer, all without leaving Emacs. To process a file, just type **C-c C-f** (for **tex-file**).* Emacs saves the file before processing it. Messages that would appear on screen are channeled to a buffer called *tex-shell*, which Emacs displays on your screen. If the buffer isn't on the screen, typing **C-c C-l** (for **tex-recenter-output-buffer**) automatically displays it.

To demonstrate, let's try processing *dickens.tex*, a very basic file indeed.

Type: **C-c C-f**

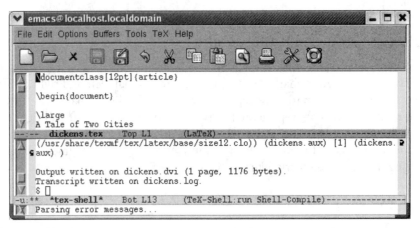

Processing a LATEX file displays a special *tex-shell* buffer.

This command generates a *.dvi* file, which is an intermediate, device-independent file. You can view the resulting file by typing **C-c C-v**. On Linux, the default viewer is *xdvi*. Pressing **C-c C-v** displays the output in an *xdvi* window.

---

* If you don't have your TEX environment set up properly (and it isn't by default on Mac OS X, for example), this command hangs or crashes Emacs (pressing **C-g** may help; in one author's case it did and in another's it didn't). Try the *latex* command at a shell prompt to see if the command exists before attempting to process a file using Emacs.

Type: **C-c C-v**

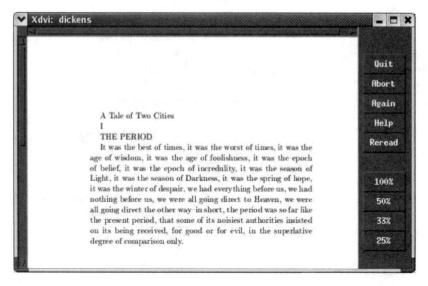

Output displayed by *xdvi*.

To print the *.dvi* file, give the command **C-c C-p** (for **tex-print**); this formats the *.dvi* file and sends it to your default printer. **C-c C-q** (**tex-show-print-queue**) displays the print queue so you know when to go to the printer to look for your processed output.

Two important variables tell Emacs how to print a TEX, file. You need to know about them if **C-c C-p** or **C-c C-q** doesn't work correctly; if these commands don't work, the configuration of TEX, on your system may be nonstandard, or the print and print queue commands are slightly different. The variable **tex-dvi-print-command** determines the command that is used to print a *.dvi* file; its default is **lpr -d**. For print queues, the command used to show the print queue is controlled by the **tex-show-queue-command** variable. By default, **tex-show-queue-command** is set to **lpq**.

Table 8-9 summarizes TeX and LaTeX mode commands.

Table 8-9. TeX and LaTeX mode commands

Keystrokes	Command name	Action
(none)	**tex-mode**	Enter TeX or LaTeX mode according to file's contents.
(none)	**plain-tex-mode**	Enter TeX mode.
(none)	**latex-mode**	Enter LaTeX mode.
C-j	**tex-terminate-paragraph**	Insert two hard returns (standard end of paragraph) and check syntax of paragraph.
C-c{	**tex-insert-braces**	Insert two braces and put cursor between them.

Table 8-9. TeX and LaTeX mode commands (continued)

Keystrokes	Command name	Action
C-c }	up-list	If you are between braces, position the cursor following the closing brace.
(none) *TeX → Validate Buffer*	tex-validate-buffer	Check buffer for syntax errors.
(none) *TeX → Validate Region*	tex-validate-region	Check the region for syntax errors.
C-c C-f *TeX → TeX File*	tex-file	Saves the current file, then processes it.
C-c C-b *TeX → TeX Buffer*	tex-buffer	Process buffer.[a]
C-c C-l *TeX → TeX Recenter*	tex-recenter-output-buffer	Put the message shell on the screen, showing (at least) the last error message.
C-c C-k *TeX → TeX Kill*	tex-kill-job	Kill processing.
C-c C-p *TeX → TeX Print*	tex-print	Print output.
C-c C-q *TeX → Show Print Queue*	tex-show-print-queue	Show print queue.
C-c C-e	latex-close-block	Provide closing element of a command pair.
(none)	tex-close-latex-block	Provide closing element of a command pair.
C-c Tab' *TeX → BibTeX File*	tex-bibtex-file	Process the current file using BibTeX, a system for creating bibliographies automatically.
C-c C-v *TeX → TeX View*	tex-view	View *.dvi* output.
(none) *TeX → TeX Print (alt printer)*	tex-alt-print	Print *.dvi* file using an alternative printer defined by the variable **tex-alt-dvi-print-command**.
C-c C-o	latex-insert-block	Insert a block (prompts for block name and options).
C-c C-u	tex-goto-last-unclosed-latex-block	Look backward in the file to find the nearest unclosed block and move the cursor there.
M-Enter	latex-insert-item	Insert \item.
(none)	latex-split-block	Insert an end to the current block and the beginning of a new one.
"	tex-insert-quote	Insert TeX-style quotation marks.

[a] Using **tex-buffer** gives the resulting *.dvi* file a long and strange filename that includes your domain name. We recommend using **C-c C-f** (for **tex-file**) instead.

CHAPTER 9

Computer Language Support

As many programmers know, the task of programming usually breaks down into a cycle of think-write-debug. If you have used Unix (or various other operating systems) for programming, you have probably become accustomed to using separate tools for each phase of the cycle, for example, a text editor for writing, a compiler for compiling, and the operating system itself for running programs. You would undoubtedly find an environment much more productive if the boundaries between the cycle phases—and the tools that support them—were erased.

Emacs provides considerable support for writing, running, and debugging programs written in a wide variety of languages, and it integrates this support into a smooth framework. You never have to leave Emacs when developing programs, so you will find it easier to concentrate on the actual programming task (i.e., the "think" part of the cycle) because you won't have to spend lots of time going from one tool to another.

When you write code, you can use one of Emacs's *programming language modes*; these turn Emacs into a spiffy syntax-directed or language-sensitive editor that knows about the syntax of the language. That makes it easier for you to write code in a uniform, easy-to-read, customizable style. Language modes exist for several different programming languages.

Emacs also supports running and debugging programs. Shell mode (see Chapter 5) and multiple windows (see Chapter 4) allow you to run your code while editing it. Emacs has a powerful facility for interfacing to many compilers and the Unix **make** command: Emacs can interpret compilers' error messages and visit files where errors occur at the appropriate line number. Indeed, many tools (such as the Java build tool, **ant**) include command-line options to format their output in an Emacs-friendly way.

In this chapter, we cover the features of language modes in general such as compiling and debugging programs, comments, indentation, and syntax highlighting. We also spend a bit of time upfront looking at the **etags** facility, which is a great help to programmers who work on large, multifile projects. These features apply to all language modes. We then delve into Emacs's support for various languages, including C, C++, Java, Perl, SQL, and Lisp.

Emacs as an IDE

Emacs provides a number of features that appeal to developers. You can edit code quickly with font support and auto-completion of function and variable names; you can compile the program and even run a debugger all without leaving your "editor." While you don't have some of the graphical tools commonly found in commercial integrated development environments (IDEs), almost every other feature of those IDEs can be found in Emacs—for every language you could imagine working in.

Of course, there will always be occasions when you need to view your documents without the bells and whistles some language modes attach. You can always switch to plain text (**M-x text-mode**) or, more to the point, fundamental mode (**M-x fundamental-mode**).

Compiling and Debugging

As mentioned at the beginning of this chapter, Emacs's support for programmers does not end when you are done writing the code. A typical strategy for using Emacs when working on a large programming project is to log in, go to the directory where your source files reside, and invoke Emacs on the source files (e.g., **emacs Makefile myproj*.[ch]** for C programmers). While you are editing your code, you can compile it using the commands described later—as you will see, you need not even worry about saving your changes. You can also test your compiled code in a shell using shell mode (see Chapter 5). The bottom line is that you should rarely—if ever—have to leave Emacs throughout your session.

Emacs provides an interface to compilers and the Unix **make** utility that is more direct and powerful than shell mode. At the heart of this facility is the command **M-x compile Enter**. This command causes a series of events to occur. First, it prompts you for a compilation command. The default command is **make -k**,* but if you type another command, that new command becomes the default for subsequent invocations during your Emacs session. You can change the default by setting the variable **compile-command** in your *.emacs* file. For example, to use the Java build tool **ant** as your default compile command, just add this line:

```
(setq 'compile-command "ant -emacs")
```

---

* The **-k** option overrides **make**'s default of stopping after a job returns an error. Instead, **make** continues on branches of the dependency tree that do not depend on the branch where the error occurred.

After you have typed the command, Emacs offers to save all unsaved file buffers, thus relieving you of the responsibility of making sure your changes have been saved. It then creates a buffer called *compilation* and an associated window. It runs the compilation command (as a subprocess, just like the shell in shell mode), with output going to the *compilation* buffer. While the command runs, the minibuffer says Compiling: run; it says exit when the compile job finishes.

Now the fun begins. If the compilation resulted in an error, you can type **C-x `** (for **next-error**; this is a backquote, not a single quote). Emacs reads the first error message, figures out the file and line number of the error, and visits the file at that line number. After you have corrected the error, you can type **C-x `** again to visit subsequent error locations. Each time you type **C-x `**, Emacs scrolls the *compilation* window so that the current error message appears at the top.

To start at the first error message again, type **C-x `** with a prefix argument (i.e., **C-u C-x `**). A nice thing about **C-x `** is that you can use it as soon as an error is encountered; you do not have to wait for the compilation to finish.

The mode of the *compilation* buffer (compilation mode) supports a few other useful commands for navigating through the error messages as summarized in Table 9-1.

Table 9-1. Compilation mode commands

Keystrokes	Command name	Action
C-x `	next-error	Move to the next error message and visit the corresponding source code.
M-n	compilation-next-error	Move to the next error message.
M-p	compilation-previous-error	Move to the previous error message.
C-c C-c	compilation-goto-error	Visit the source code for the current error message.
Space	scroll-down	Scroll down one screen.
Del	scroll-up	Scroll up one screen.

Space and **Del** are handy screen-scrolling commands found in various read-only Emacs modes.

Note that **M-n** and **M-p** do not visit the source code corresponding to the error message; they simply allow you to move easily through error messages that may take up more than one line each. However, you can visit the source code from any error message by typing **C-c C-c**.

How does Emacs interpret the error message? It uses the variable **compilation-error-regexp-alist**, which is a list of regular expressions designed to match the error messages of a wide variety of C and C++ compilers and the **lint** C code checking program.* It should also work with compilers for languages for which Emacs has language modes,

---

* Unfortunately, Emacs won't understand error messages generated by **make** itself, such as those due to syntax errors in your *Makefile*.

such as Java, Fortran, Ada, and Modula-2. Emacs tries to parse (analyze) an error message with each of the regular expressions in the list until it finds one that extracts the filename and line number where the error occurred.

There is a chance that the error message parser won't work with certain compilers, especially if you are using Emacs on a non-Unix system. You can find out by trying **M-x compile** on some code that you know contains an error; if you type **C-x `**, and Emacs claims that there are no more errors, the **next-error** feature does not work with your compiler.

If the parser doesn't work for you, you may want to try adding a regular expression to **compilation-error-regexp-alist** that fits your compiler's error message format. We'll show you an example of this in Chapter 11.

The **compile** package also includes similar support for the Unix **grep** (search files) command, thus effectively giving Emacs a multifile search capability. If you type **M-x grep**, you are prompted for arguments to send to **grep**—that is, a search pattern and filename(s). Emacs runs **grep** with the -n option, which tells it to print filenames and line numbers of matching lines.* The same happens as with **M-x compile**; you can type **C-x `** to have Emacs visit the next matched line in its file.

Writing Code

We have already seen various examples of Emacs modes, including text mode (see Chapter 2) and shell mode (see Chapter 5). Special functionality like the buffer list (see Chapter 4) and Dired (see Chapter 5) are actually modes as well. All modes have two basic components: an Emacs Lisp *package* that implements the mode and a *function* that invokes it.

Language Modes

The version of Emacs on which this book is based (21.3.5) comes with language modes for Ada, assembly, awk, C, C++, Common Lisp, Fortran, ICON, Java, Lisp, MIM, Modula-2, Objective-C, Pascal, Pike, Perl, PROLOG, Python, Scheme, SGML, Simula, and SQL; future versions will undoubtedly add more. Many—but not all—of the language modes are "hooked" into Emacs so that if you visit a file with the proper filename suffix, you will automatically be put in the correct mode. To find out whether Emacs does this for the language you use, look up your language in the table of Emacs Lisp packages in Appendix B. If one or more suffixes is listed in the right-hand column, Emacs invokes the mode for files with those suffixes.

---

* If **grep -n** is run on only one file, it just prints line numbers; Emacs forces it to print the filename as well in this case by appending the dummy file */dev/null* to the **grep** command.

However, if no suffix is listed (or if your compiler supports a different suffix than the ones listed), you can set up Emacs to invoke the mode automatically when you visit your source files. You need to do two things: first, look again at the right-hand column in the package table entry for your language, and you will find the name of the function that invokes the mode (e.g., **ada-mode**, **modula-2-mode**). Second, you insert code in your *.emacs* file that tells Emacs to automatically load the proper package whenever you visit a file with the suffix for the language in question.

You need to write two lines of code for this customization. The first uses the **autoload** function, which tells Emacs where to look for commands it doesn't already know about. It sets up an association between a function and the package that implements the function so that when the function is invoked for the first time, Emacs loads the package to get the code. In our case, we need to create an association between a function that invokes a language mode and the package that implements the mode. This shows the format of **autoload**:

```
(autoload 'function "filename" "description" t)
```

Note the single quote preceding function and the double quotes around filename and description; for more details on this Lisp syntax, see Chapter 11. If you are a PHP programmer, for example, you can grab the latest Emacs PHP mode from *http://sourceforge.net/projects/php-mode/* online. You would then put the following line in your *.emacs* file:

```
(autoload 'php-mode "php-mode" "PHP editing mode." t)
```

This tells Emacs to load the *PHP* package when the function **php-mode** is invoked for the first time.

The second line of code completes the picture by creating an association between the suffix for source files in your language and the mode-invoking function so that the function is automatically invoked when you visit a file with the proper suffix. This involves the Emacs global variable **auto-mode-alist**, covered in Chapter 10; it is a list of associations that Emacs uses to put visited files in modes according to their names. To create such an association for PHP mode so that Emacs puts all files with the suffix *.php* in that mode, add this line to your *.emacs* file:

```
(setq auto-mode-alist (cons '("\\.php$" . php-mode) auto-mode-alist))
```

This Lisp code sets up the following chain of events when you visit a file whose suffix indicates source code in your programming language. Let's say you visit the file *pgm.php*. Emacs reads the file, then finds an entry corresponding to the *.php* suffix in the **auto-mode-alist** and tries to invoke the associated function **php-mode**. It notices that the function **php-mode** doesn't exist, but that there is an **autoload** association between it and the *PHP* package. It loads that package and, finding the **php-mode** command, runs it. After this, your buffer is in PHP mode.

For some interpreted languages like Perl and Python, you will also want to update the **interpreter-mode-alist global** variable:

```
(setq interpreter-mode-alist
      (cons '("python" . python-mode)
            interpreter-mode-alist))
```

If your script file begins with the Unix interpreter prefix #!, Emacs checks that line to determine what language you are using. That can be especially helpful when the script file does not have a telltale extension like *.py* or *.pl*.

Syntax

Although language modes differ in exact functionality, they all support the same basic concepts. The most important of these involves knowledge of the *syntax* of the language in question—its characters, vocabulary, and certain aspects of its grammar. We have already seen that Emacs handles some syntactic aspects of human language. When you edit regular text, Emacs knows about words, sentences, and paragraphs: you can move the cursor and delete text with respect to those units. It also knows about certain kinds of punctuation, such as parentheses: when you type a right parenthesis, it "flashes" the matching left parenthesis by moving the cursor there for a second and then returning.* This is a convenient way of ensuring that your parentheses match correctly.

Emacs has knowledge about programming language syntax that is analogous to its knowledge of human language syntax. In general, it keeps track of the following basic syntactic elements:

- *Words*, which correspond to *identifiers* and *numbers* in most programming languages.
- *Punctuation*, which includes such things as *operators* (e.g., +, -, <, and >) and *statement separators* (e.g., semicolons).
- *Strings*, which are strings of characters to be taken literally and surrounded by *delimiters* (such as quotation marks).
- *Parentheses*, which can include such things as square brackets ([and]) and curly braces ({ and }) as well as regular parentheses.
- *Whitespace*, such as spaces and tabs, which are to be ignored.
- *Comments*, which are strings of characters to be ignored and surrounded by delimiters that depend on the language (e.g., /* and */ for C, // and a newline for C++ and Java, or semicolon (;) and a newline for Lisp).

---

* Actually, there is a limit to how far back (in characters) Emacs searches for a matching open parenthesis: this is the value of the variable **blink-matching-paren-distance**, which defaults to 25,600. The duration of the "flash" is also configurable: it's the value (in seconds) of **blink-matching-delay**, whose default value is 1.

Emacs keeps this information internally in the form of *syntax tables*; like keymaps (as described in Chapter 10), Emacs has a *global* syntax table used for all buffers, as well a *local* table for each buffer, which varies according to the mode the buffer is in. You can view the syntax table for the current buffer by typing **C-h s** (for **describe-syntax**). In addition, language modes know about more advanced language-dependent syntactic concepts like statements, statement blocks, functions, subroutines, Lisp syntactic expressions, and so on.

Comments

All programming languages have comment syntax, so Emacs provides a few features that deal with comments in general; these are made language-specific in each language mode. The universal comment command for all language modes is **M-;** (for **indent-for-comment**).* When you type **M-;**, Emacs moves to a column equal to the value of the variable **comment-column**; if the text on the line goes past that column, it moves to one space past the last text character. It then inserts a comment delimiter (or a pair of opening and closing delimiters, as in /* and */ for C) and puts the cursor after the opening delimiter.

For example, if you want to add a comment to a statement, put the cursor anywhere on the line containing that statement and type **M-;**. The result is

```
    result += y;            /* █*/
```

You can then type your comment in between the delimiters. If you were to do the same thing on a longer line of code, say,

```
    q_i = term_arr[i].num_docs / total_docs;
```

the result would be

```
    q_i = term_arr[i].num_docs / total_docs; /* █*/
```

You can customize the variable **comment-column**, of course, by putting the appropriate code in your *.emacs* file. This is the most useful way if you want to do it permanently. But if you want to reset **comment-column** temporarily within the current buffer, you can just move the cursor to where you want the comment column to be and type **C-x ;** (for **set-comment-column**). Note that this command affects only the value of **comment-column** in the current buffer; its value in other buffers—even other buffers in the same mode—is not changed.

When you are typing a comment and want to continue it on the next line, **M-j** (for **indent-new-comment-line**) does it. This command starts a new comment on the next line (though some language modes allow you to customize it so that it continues the

---

* The key binding is mnemonic for Lisp programmers because comments in Lisp start with semicolons.

same comment instead). Say you have typed in the text of the comment for this statement, and the cursor is at the end of the text:

```
result += y;                    /* add the multiplicand█*/
```

You want to extend the comment to another line. If you type **M-j**, you get the following:

```
result += y;                    /* add the multiplicand*/
                                /* █*/
```

You can type the second line of your comment. You can also use **M-j** to split existing comment text into two lines. Assume your cursor is positioned like this:

```
result += y;                    /* add the█multiplicand */
```

If you type **M-j** now, the result is:

```
result += y;                    /* add the */
                                /* █ultiplicand */
```

If you want to comment out a section of your code, you can use the **comment-region** command (not bound to keystrokes except in certain language modes). Assume you have code that looks like this:

```
this = is (a);
section (of, source, code);
that += (takes[up]->a * number);
of (lines);
```

If you define a region in the usual way and type **M-x comment-region**, the result is:

```
/*      this = is (a); */
/*      section (of, source, code); */
/*      that += (takes[up]->a * number); */
/*      of (lines); */
```

You can easily get rid of *single-line* comments by typing **M-x kill-comment Enter**, which deletes any comment on the current line. The cursor does not have to be within the comment. Each language mode has special features relating to comments in the particular language, usually including variables that let you customize commenting style.

Indenting Code

In addition to syntactic knowledge, Emacs language modes contain various features to help you produce nicely formatted code. These features implement standards of indentation, commenting, and other aspects of programming style, thus ensuring consistency and readability, getting comments to line up, and so on. Perhaps more importantly, they relieve you of the tiresome burden of supplying correct indentation and even of remembering what the current indentation is. The nicest thing about these standards is that they are usually customizable.

We have already seen that, in text mode, you can type **C-j** instead of **Enter**, at the end of a line, and Emacs indents the next line properly for you. This indentation is controlled by the variable **left-margin**, whose value is the column to indent to. Much the same thing happens in programming language modes, but the process is more flexible and complex.

As in text mode, **C-j** indents the next line properly in language modes. You can also indent any line properly after it has been typed by pressing **Tab** with the cursor anywhere on the line.

Some language modes have extra functionality attached to characters that terminate statements—like semicolons or right curly braces—so that when you type them, Emacs automatically indents the current line. Emacs documentation calls this behavior *electric*. Most language modes also have sets of variables that control indentation style (and that you can customize).

Table 9-2 lists a few other commands relating to indentation that work according to the rules set up for the language in question.

Table 9-2. Basic indentation commands

Keystrokes	Command name	Action
C-M-\	indent-region	Indent each line between the cursor and mark.
M-m	back-to-indentation	Move to the first nonblank character on the line.
M-^	delete-indentation	Join this line to the previous one.

The following is an example of what **C-M-** does. This example is in C, and subsequent examples refer to it. The concepts in all examples in this section are applicable to most other languages; we cover analogous Lisp and Java features in the sections on modes for those languages.

Suppose you have the following C code:

```
int times (x, y)
int x, y;
{
int i;
int result = 0;

for (i = 0; i < x; i++)
{
result += y;
}
}
```

If you set mark at the beginning of this code, put the cursor at the end, and type **C-M-**, Emacs formats it like this:

```
int times (x, y)
     int x, y;
{
  int i;
  int result = 0;
```

```
    for (i = 0; i < x; i++)
      {
        result += y;
      }
  }
```

C-M-\ is also handy for indenting an entire file according to your particular indentation style: you can just type **C-x h** (for **mark-whole-buffer**) followed by **C-M-**.

M-m is handy for moving to the beginning of the actual code on a line. For example, assume your cursor is positioned like this:

```
    int result = 0;
```

If you type **M-m**, it moves to the beginning of the **int**:

```
    int result = 0;
```

As an example of **M-^**, let's say you want the opening curly brace for the **for** statement to appear on the same line as the **for**. Put the cursor anywhere on the line with the opening curly brace, type **M-^**, and the code looks like this:

```
    for (i = 0; i < x; i++) {
        result += y;
    }
```

Language modes usually provide additional indentation commands that relate to specific features of the language. Having covered the general language mode concepts, we want to show you a few other general utilities: **etags** and font-lock mode. The **etags** facility helps programmers who work on large, multifile programs. All language modes can also take advantage of font-lock mode to make development more efficient.

etags

Another general feature of Emacs that applies to programmers is the **etags** facility.[*] **etags** works with code in many other languages as well, including Fortran, Java, Perl, Pascal, LATEX, Lisp, and many assembly languages. If you work on large, multifile projects, you will find **etags** to be an enormous help.

etags is basically a multifile search facility that knows about C and Perl function definitions as well as searching in general. With it, you can find a function anywhere in an entire directory without having to remember in which file the function is defined, and you can do searches and query-replaces that span multiple files. **etags** uses *tag tables*, which contain lists of function names for each file in a directory along with information on where the functions' definitions are located within the files. Many of the commands associated with **etags** involve regular expressions (see Chapter 11) in search strings.

---

[*] **etags** is also a platform-specific feature. The **etags** facility is available on Unix platforms, including Mac OS X.

To use **etags**, you must first invoke the separate **etags** program in your current directory to create the tag table. Its arguments are the files for which you want tag information. The usual way to invoke it is **etags** *.[ch], that is, building a tag table from all files ending in *.c* or *.h*. (That's for you C programmers; other languages would use their appropriate extensions, of course.) You can run **etags** from shell mode or with the command **M-!** (for **shell-command**). The output of **etags** is the file *TAGS*, which is the tag table. When you are writing code, you can update your tag table to reflect new files and function definitions by invoking **etags** again.

After you have created the tag table, you need to make it known to Emacs. To do this, type **M-x visit-tags-table Enter**. This prompts you for the name of the tag table file; the default is *TAGS* in the current directory, as you would expect. After you execute this step, you can use the various Emacs tags commands.

The most important tag command is **M-.** (for **find-tag**). This command prompts you for a string to use in searching the tag table for a function whose name contains the string. Supply the search string, and Emacs visits the file containing the matching function name in the current window and goes to the first line of the function's definition. A variation of **M-.** is **C-x 4 .** (for **find-tag-other-window**), which uses another window instead of replacing the text in your current window.

A nice feature of **M-.** is that it picks up the word the cursor is on and uses it as the default search string. For example, if your cursor is anywhere on the string **my_function**, **M-.** uses **my_function** as the default. Thus, when you are looking at a C statement that calls a function, you can type **M-.** to see the code for that function.

If you have multiple functions with the same name, **M-.** finds the function in the file whose name comes first in alphabetical order. To find the others, you can use the command **M-,** (for **tags-loop-continue**) to find the next one (or complain if there are no more). This feature is especially useful if your directory contains more than one program, that is, if there is more than one function called *main*. **M-,** also has other uses, as we will see.

You can use the tag table to search for more than just function definitions. The command **M-x tags-search Enter** prompts for a regular expression; it searches through all files listed in the tag table (such as, all *.c* and *.h* files) for any occurrence of the regular expression, whether it is a function name or not. This capability is similar to the **grep** facility discussed earlier in this chapter. After you have invoked **tags-search**, you can find additional matches by typing **M-,**.

There is also an analogous query-replace capability. The command **M-x tags-query-replace Enter** does a regular expression query-replace (see Chapter 3) on all files listed in the tag table. As with the regular **query-replace-regexp** command, if you precede **tags-query-replace** with a prefix argument (i.e., **C-u M-x tags-query-replace Enter**), Emacs replaces only matches that are whole words. This feature is useful, for example, if you want to replace occurrences of **printf** without disturbing occurrences of **fprintf**. If you exit a **tags-query-replace** with **Esc** or **C-g**, you can resume it later by typing **M-,**.

The command **M-x tags-apropos** rounds out the search facilities of **etags**. If you give it a regular expression argument, it opens a *Tags List* buffer that contains a list of all tags in the tag table (including names of files as well as functions) that match the regular expression. For example, if you want to find out the names of output routines in a multiple-file C program, you could invoke **tags-apropos** with the argument **print** or **write**.

Finally, you can type **M-x list-tags Enter** to list all the tags in the table—that is, all the functions—for a given C file. Supply the filename at the prompt, and you get a *Tags List* buffer showing the names of functions defined in that file along with their return types (if any). Note that if you move your cursor to this list, you can use **M-.** to look at the actual code for the function. **M-.** picks up the word the cursor is on as the default function name, so you can just move the cursor to the name of the function you want to see and press **M-.** followed by **Enter** to see it.

Fonts and Font-lock Mode

There's one last common feature to mention. The use of fonts to help present code is very popular—so popular, in fact, that it is now universal. Unlike the indentation and formatting supported by the various language modes, nothing in the code itself changes. But when you're in font-lock mode, your program certainly *looks* different.

You can turn on this feature for any language mode with **M-x font-lock-mode** to see for yourself. Keywords get a particular color; comments get a different color and are often italicized; strings and literals get yet another color. It can aid quick browsing of code. Many people come to depend on it much the way they rely on proper indentation. If you become one of those people, you'll want to make it the default for all language sessions. You can add the following line to your *.emacs* file to achieve this aim:

```
;; Turn on font-locking globally
(global-font-lock-mode t)
```

The colors and styles used are customizable if you don't like the defaults. **M-x list-faces-display** produces a list of the named faces Emacs knows about. You'll see something similar to the screen shown in Figure 9-1.

Of course, in real life, the colors and bold and whatnot should be more pronounced. You'll also see quite a few more faces. You can modify any of those faces with either **M-x modify-face** (a simple prompted "wizard" approach) or **M-x customize-face** (the big fancy interactive approach). You can also add lines to your *.emacs* file for your favorite customizations. Here's an example:

```
'(font-lock-comment-face
  (((class color) (background light))
    (:foreground "Firebrick" :slant italic)))))
```

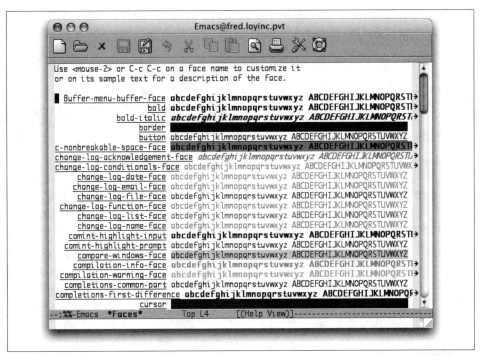

Figure 9-1. Fonts available for customization in Emacs

Note that not all displays support all of the possible variations of bold, italic, underline, colors, and so on. This is a classic case of "your mileage may vary." Still, with the ability to customize it all yourself, you should be able to find a combination that works well on your system.

The remaining sections in this chapter deal with several of the language-specific modes including JDEE, a suite of packages devoted to the world of Java development in Emacs.

You need not read all of these sections if you are interested in only one or two of the languages. If you program in another language for which Emacs has a mode, you may want to read one of the following sections to get the "flavor" of a language mode; all language modes have the same basic concepts, so this should get you off to a good start. Indeed, many language modes use another mode as a base. For example, Java mode is really just an extension of C mode.

C and C++ Support

Emacs automatically enters C mode when you visit a file whose suffix is *.c, .h, .y* (for **yacc** grammars), or *.lex* (**lex** specification files). Emacs invokes C++ mode when you visit a file whose suffix is *.C, .H, .cc, .hh, .cpp, .cxx, .hxx, .c++*, or *.h++*. You can also put any file in C mode manually by typing **M-x c-mode Enter**. Similarly, you can use **c++-mode** to put a buffer into C++ mode.

Both C and C++ modes are implemented in the same Emacs Lisp package, called **cc-mode**,* which also includes a mode for the Objective-C language used in Mac OS X. C mode understands both ANSI C and the older Kernighan and Ritchie C syntax. We describe C mode functions, but you should assume that everything also applies to C++ mode. C++ mode has a small number of additional features, which we describe at the end of this section.

We should also note that the Emacs mode for Perl is derived from an older version of C mode. If you program in Perl, you will find that virtually all of the motion, indentation, and formatting commands in C mode apply equally to Perl mode, with **perl-** replacing **c-** in their names. Emacs invokes Perl mode on files with suffix *.pl*. (However, to be honest we prefer CPerl mode, discussed later in this chapter.)

In C mode, Emacs understands the syntax elements described earlier in this chapter. The characters semicolon (;), colon (:), comma (,) curly braces ({ and }), and pound sign (#, for C preprocessor commands) are all electric, meaning that Emacs automatically indents the current line when you type them. It also actively uses the font options when you have font-lock mode turned on.

Motion Commands

In addition to the standard Emacs commands for words and sentences (which are mainly useful only inside multiline comments), C mode contains advanced commands that know about statements, functions,† and preprocessor conditionals. A summary of these commands appears in Table 9-3.

Table 9-3. Advanced C motion commands

Keystrokes	Command name	Action
M-a	c-beginning-of-statement	Move to the beginning of the current statement.
M-e	c-end-of-statement	Move to the end of the current statement.
M-q	c-fill-paragraph	If in comment, fill the paragraph, preserving indentations and decorations.
C-M-a	beginning-of-defun	Move to the beginning of the body of the function surrounding the point.
C-M-e	end-of-defun	Move to the end of the function.
C-M-h	c-mark-function	Put the cursor at the beginning of the function, the mark at the end.
C-c C-q	c-indent-defun	Indent the entire function according to indentation style.

---

* We know! There is no **M-x cc-mode**. It can be confusing. Just try to remember that the modes are named directly after the language they support.

† The function commands have "defun" in their names because they are actually adaptations of analogous commands in Lisp mode; a defun is a function definition in Lisp.

Table 9-3. Advanced C motion commands (continued)

Keystrokes	Command name	Action
C-c C-u	c-up-conditional	Move to the beginning of the current preprocessor conditional.
C-c C-p	c-backward-conditional	Move to the previous preprocessor conditional.
C-c C-n	c-forward-conditional	Move to the next preprocessor conditional.

Notice that the statement motion commands have the same key bindings as **backward-sentence** and **forward-sentence**, respectively. In fact, they act as sentence commands if you use them within a C comment.

Similarly, **M-q** is normally the **fill-paragraph** command; C mode augments it with the ability to preserve indentations and decorative characters at the beginnings of lines. For example, if your cursor is anywhere in this comment:

```
/* This is
 * a
 * comment paragraph with wildly differing right
 *  margins.
 * It goes on      for a while,
 * then stops.
 */
```

typing **M-q** has this result:

```
/* This is a comment paragraph with wildly differing right margins.
 * It goes on for a while, then stops. */
```

You will find that the preprocessor conditional motion commands are a godsend if you have to slog through someone else's voluminous code. Especially if you're faced with code built to run on a variety of systems—like Emacs itself—often the most important question you need answered is, "What code is actually compiled?"

With **C-c C-u**, you can tell instantly what preprocessor conditional governs the code in question. Consider this code block:

```
#define LUCYX
#define BADEXIT -1

#ifdef LUCYX
    ...
    *ptyv = open ("/dev/ptc", O_RDWR | O_NDELAY, 0);
    if (fd < 0)
        return BADEXIT;
    ...
#else
    ...
    fprintf (stderr, "You can't do that on this system!");
    ...
#endif
```

Imagine that the ellipses (...) represent hundreds of lines of code. Now suppose you are trying to determine under what conditions the file */dev/ptc* is opened. If your cursor is on that line of code, you can type **C-c C-u**, and the cursor moves to the line **#ifdef LUCYX**—telling you that the code is compiled if you're on a LUCYX system. If you want to skip the code that would not be compiled and go directly to the end of the conditional, type **C-c C-n**. We will see another command that is useful for dealing with C preprocessor code later in this section.

C statement and statement block delimiter characters are bound to commands that, in addition to inserting the appropriate character, also provide proper indentation. These characters are {, }, ;, and : (for labels and **switch** cases). For example, if you are closing out a statement block or function body, you can press **C-j** (or **Enter**) and type }, and Emacs lines it up with its matching {. This eliminates the need for you to scroll back through the code to find out what column the { is in.

Because } is a parenthesis-type character, Emacs attempts to "flash" a matching { when you type }. If the matching { is outside of the text displayed in your window, Emacs instead prints the line containing the { in the minibuffer. Furthermore, if only whitespace (blanks or tabs) follows the { on its line, Emacs also prints a **^J** (for **C-j**) followed by the next line, thus giving a better idea of the context of the {.

Recall the "times" example earlier in this chapter. Let's say you are typing in a } to end the function, and the { that begins the function body is off-screen. There is no code on the line following the beginning {, so you see the following in the minibuffer after you type }:

```
Matches {^J  int i;
```

Customizing Code Indentation Style

Coding style in C—or any programming language for that matter—is a very personal thing. C programmers learn from various books or by referring to various different pieces of other people's code; eventually they evolve a personal style that may or may not conform to those that they learned from.

C mode provides a rich set of features for customizing its indentation behavior that mirrors this way of learning the language. At the simplest level, you can choose a coding style by name. Then, if you're not satisfied, you can customize your chosen style or even create your own from scratch. The latter tasks, however, require a fair amount of Emacs Lisp programming knowledge (see Chapter 11) and perhaps a bit of bravery.

You can choose a named coding style with the command **M-x c-set-style**. This command prompts you for the name of the style you want. The easiest thing to do at this point is to type **Tab**, the completion character (see Chapter 14), which brings up a *Completions* window that lists all of the choices. Type one of them and press **Enter** to select it.

By default, Emacs comes loaded with the styles shown in Table 9-4.

Table 9-4. Built-in cc-mode indentation styles

Style	Description
bsd	Style used in code for BSD-derived versions of Unix.
cc-mode	The default coding style, from which all others are derived .
ellemtel	Style used in C++ documentation from Ellemtel Telecommunication Systems Laboratories in Sweden .
gnu	Style used in C code for Emacs itself and other GNU-related programs .
java	Style used in Java code (the default for Java mode).
k&r	Style of the classic text on C, Kernighan and Ritchie's *The C Programming Language* .
linux	Style used in C code that is part of the Linux kernel.
python	Style used in python extensions.
stroustrup	C++ coding style of the standard reference work, Bjarne Stroustrup's *The C++ Programming Language* .
user	Customizations you make to *.emacs* or via Custom (see Chapter 10). All other styles inherit these customizations if you set them.
whitesmith	Style used in Whitesmith Ltd.'s documentation for their C and C++ compilers .

To show how some of these styles work, let's start with the C function example from earlier in this chapter:

```
int times (x, y)
int x, y;
{
int i;
int result = 0;

for (i = 0; i < x; i++)
{
result += y;
}
}
```

If you define a region around this code and you type **C-M-** (for **indent-region**), Emacs reformats the code in the default style like this:

```
int times (x, y)
    int x, y;
{
    int i;
    int result = 0;

    for (i = 0; i < x; i++)
    {
        result += y;
    }
}
```

If you type **C-c .** (for **c-set-style**), enter **k&r**, and then repeat the reformatting, the code looks like this:

```
int times (x, y)
```

```
int x, y;
{
    int i;
    int result = 0;

    for (i = 0; i < x; i++)
    {
        result += y;
    }
}
```

Or, if you want to switch to GNU-style indentation, choose the style **gnu** and refor-mat. The result is:

```
int times (x, y)
    int x, y;
{
  int i;
  int result = 0;

  for (i = 0; i < x; i++)
    {
      result += y;
    }
}
```

Once you decide on a coding style, you can set it up permanently by putting a line in your *.emacs* file that looks like this:

```
(add-hook 'c-mode-hook
        '(lambda ()
          (c-set-style "stylename")))
```

Unfortunately, we'll have to wait until Chapter 11 to understand exactly what this code does. For now, make sure that you insert a single quote (') before the (lambda in the second line.

Each coding style contains subtleties that makes it nontrivial for Emacs to imple-ment. Older versions of Emacs did this by defining several variables that controlled various indentation levels; these were not easy to work with and, frankly, did not really cover 100 percent of the nuances of each style. The current version of C mode, in contrast, uses a considerably larger set of variables—too large, in fact, for anyone other than hardy Emacs Lisp hackers to deal with.

Therefore, C mode keeps track of groups of these variables and their values under named styles. One huge variable, called **c-style-alist**, contains all of the styles and their associated information. You can customize this beast either by changing values of variables within existing styles or by adding a style of your own. For further details, look in the file *cc-mode.el* in your system's Emacs Lisp directory (see Chapter 11).

Additional C and C++ Mode Features

C mode contains a number of other useful features, ranging from the generally useful to the arcanely obscure. Perhaps the most interesting of these are two ways of adding additional electric functionality to certain keystrokes, called *auto-newline* and *hungry-delete-key*.*

When auto-newline is enabled, it causes Emacs to add a newline character and indent the new line properly whenever you type a semicolon (;), curly brace ({ or }), or, at certain times, comma (,) or colon (:). These features can save you some time and help you format your code in a consistent style.

Auto-newline is off by default. To turn it on, type **C-c C-a** for **c-toggle-auto-state**. (Repeat the same command to turn it off again.) You will see the **(C)** in the mode line change to **(C/a)** as an indication. As an example of how it works, try typing in the code for our times( ) function. Type the first two lines up to the **y** on the second line:

```
int times (x, y)
int x, y▮
```

Now press the semicolon; notice that Emacs inserts a newline and brings you down to the next line:

```
int times (x, y)
int x, y;
▮
```

Type the opening curly brace, and it happens again:

```
int times (x, y)
int x, y;
{
   ▮
```

Of course, the number of spaces Emacs indents after you type the { depends on the indentation style you are using.

The other optional electric feature, **hungry-delete-key**, is also off by default. To toggle it on, type **C-c C-d** (for **c-toggle-hungry-state**). You will see the **(C)** on the mode line change to **(C/h)**, or if you have **auto-newline** turned on, from **(C/a)** to **(C/ah)**.

Turning on **hungry-delete-key** empowers the **Del** key to delete all whitespace to the left of the point. To go back to the previous example, assume you just typed the open curly brace. Then, if you press **Del**, Emacs deletes everything back to the curly brace:

```
int times (x, y)
int x, y;
{▮
```

---

* These emulate **electric-c-mode** in the old Gosling Emacs.

You can toggle the states of both **auto-newline** and **hungry-delete-key** with the command **C-c C-t** (for **c-toggle-auto-hungry-state**).

If you want either of these features on by default when you invoke Emacs, you can put lines like the following in your *.emacs* file:

```
(add-hook 'c-mode-hook
    '(lambda ()
        (c-toggle-auto-state)))
```

If you want to combine this customization with another C mode customization, such as the indentation style in the previous example, you need to combine the lines of Emacs Lisp code as follows:

```
(add-hook 'c-mode-hook
    '(lambda ()
        (c-set-style "stylename")
        (c-toggle-auto-state)))
```

Again, we will see what this hook construct means in "Customizing Existing Modes" in Chapter 11.

C mode also provides support for comments; earlier in the chapter, we saw examples of this support. There is, however, another feature. You can customize **M-j** (for **indent-new-comment-line**) so that Emacs continues the same comment on the next line instead of creating a new pair of delimiters. The variable **comment-multi-line** controls this feature: if it is set to **nil** (the default), Emacs generates a new comment on the next line, as in the example from earlier in the chapter:

```
result += y;                /* add the multiplicand */
                            /* █/
```

This outcome is the result of typing **M-j** after **multiplicand**, and it shows that the cursor is positioned so that you can type the text of the second comment line. However, if you set **comment-multi-line** to **t** (or any value other than **nil**), you get this outcome instead:

```
result += y;                /* add the multiplicand
                            █/
```

The final feature we'll cover is **C-c C-e**, (for **c-macro-expand**). Like the conditional compilation motion commands (e.g., **C-c C-u** for **c-up-conditional**), **c-macro-expand** helps you answer the often difficult question, "What code actually gets compiled?" when your source code contains a morass of preprocessor directives.

To use **c-macro-expand**, you must first define a region. Then, when you type **C-c C-e**, it takes the code within the region, passes it through the actual C preprocessor, and places the output in a window called *Macroexpansion*.

To see how this procedure works, let's go back to the code example from earlier in this chapter that contains C preprocessor directives:

```
#define LUCYX
#define BADEXIT -1
```

```
#ifdef LUCYX
    *ptyv = open ("/dev/ptc", O_RDWR | O_NDELAY, 0);
    if (fd < 0)
        return BADEXIT;
#else
    fprintf (stderr, "You can't do that on this system!");
#endif
```

If you define a region around this chunk of code and type **C-c C-e**, you see following the message:

```
Invoking /lib/cpp -C on region...
```

followed by this:

```
done
```

Then you see a *Macroexpansion* window that contains this result:

```
    *ptyv = open ("/dev/ptc", O_RDWR | O_NDELAY, 0);
    if (fd < 0)
        return -1;
```

If you want to use **c-macro-expand** with a different C preprocessor command, instead of the default **/lib/cpp -C** (the **-C** option means "preserve comments in the output"), you can set the variable **c-macro-preprocessor**. For example, if you want to use an experimental preprocessor whose filename is */usr/local/lib/cpp*, put the following line in your *.emacs* file:

```
(setq c-macro-preprocessor "/usr/local/lib/cpp -C")
```

It's highly recommended that you keep the **-C** option for not deleting comments in your code.

C++ Mode Differences

As we mentioned before, C++ mode uses the same Emacs Lisp package as C mode. When you're in C++ mode, Emacs understands C++ syntax, as opposed to C (or Objective-C) syntax. That results in differences in how some of the commands discussed here behave, but in ways that are not noticeable to the user.

There are few apparent differences between C++ and C mode. The most important is the Emacs Lisp code you need to put in your *.emacs* file to customize C++ mode: instead of **c-mode-hook**, you use **c++-mode-hook**. For example, if you want C++ mode's indentation style set to **Stroustrup** with automatic newlines instead of the default style, put the following in your *.emacs* file:

```
(add-hook 'c++-mode-hook
    '(lambda ()
        (c-set-style "Stroustrup")
        (c-toggle-auto-state)))
```

Notice that you can set hooks for C mode and C++ mode separately this way, so that if you program in both languages, you can set up separate indentation styles for each.

C++ mode provides an additional command: **C-c :** (for **c-scope-operator**). This command inserts the C++ double colon (::) scope operator. It's necessary because the colon (:) is normally bound to electric functionality that can reindent the line when you don't want that done. The scope operator can appear virtually anywhere in C++ code whereas the single colon usually denotes a *case* label, which requires special indentation. The **C-c :** command may seem somewhat clumsy, but it's a necessary workaround to a syntactic clash in the C++ language.

Finally, both C and C++ mode contain the commands **c-forward-into-nomenclature** and **c-backward-into-nomenclature**, which aren't bound to any keystrokes by default. These are like **forward-word** and **backward-word**, respectively, but they treat capital letters in the middle of words as if they were starting new words. For example, they treat *ThisVariableName* as if it were three separate words while the standard **forward-word** and **backward-word** commands treat it as one word. *ThisTypeOfVariableName* is a style used by C++ programmers, as opposed to *this_type_of_variable_name*, which is somehow more endemic to old-school C code.

C++ programmers may want to bind **c-forward-into-nomenclature** and **c-backward-into-nomenclature** to the keystrokes normally bound to the standard word motion commands. We show you how to do this in "Customizing Existing Modes" in Chapter 11.

We've covered the main features of C and C++ modes, but actually these modes include many more features, most of them quite obscure or intended only for hard-core Emacs Lisp–adept customizers. Look in the Emacs Lisp package **cc-mode.el**—and the ever-expanding list of **cc-** helper packages—for more details.

Java Support

As we mentioned earlier, recent versions of Emacs come with support for Java built-in (Java mode is based on cc-mode). We'll explore Java mode briefly and then take a more in-depth look at the Java Development Environment for Emacs (JDEE).

Java Mode

Java mode shares all of the formatting and font features mentioned above, but understands the Java language specifically. You get thrown into Java mode when opening any *.java* file.

When working in Java mode, you have exactly the same features available as you do in C mode. Syntax highlighting handles Java keywords and syntax when font-lock mode is turned on. You can navigate Java commands using **M-a** and **M-e**. When commenting out a region, it uses the C++ style **//** comments.

You'll notice a small augmentation in the indent alignment commands if you choose to spread your **throws** or **extends** clauses over multiple lines. For example, consider the following method declaration:

```
public Object getNetResource(String host, int port, String resName)
throws IllegalArgumentException,
IOException,
SQLException,
FileNotFoundException
{
```

If you mark the region and run **M-C-** to indent the region, it uses a special alignment for the exception list:

```
public Object getNetResource(String host, int port, String resName)
    throws IllegalArgumentException,
           IOException,
           SQLException,
           FileNotFoundException
{
```

It all works like it is supposed to—just with Java as the language at the core of the action. However, for more than casual Java editing, you should read the next section on the JDEE.

The Java Development Environment for Emacs (JDEE)

While you can certainly get started right away with the built-in Java mode, if you do more than occasional Java programming, you might want to venture into the world of Paul Kinnucan's Java Development Environment for Emacs (JDEE). It takes Emacs into the realm of Java IDE. You won't find a GUI builder, but everything else is in place and ready to roll.

Getting Started

You can pick up the latest version of the JDEE online from *http://jdee.sunsite.dk/*.[*] This site is essential to getting the JDEE up and running. You'll find all sorts of tips and tricks and full user documentation on all of the bells and whistles is available.

---

[*] Before we take you through the installation process, we should mention two caveats. XEmacs has the JDEE built-in, though it is often out-of-date. TEI-Emacs, an add-on for Linux and Windows described in Chapter 8, also includes the JDEE.

Before you can install the JDEE, you'll need the following components:

Collection of Emacs Development Environment Tools (CEDET)
  Available on SourceForge (*http://cedet.sourceforge.net/*) or by following the links from the JDEE home page. This collection is quite popular as a foundation for more interesting programmer tools. You may already have a sufficient version installed, but it's best to get the latest release.

The JDEE Emacs Lisp library package
  Available as a separate download from the JDEE site.

One or more JDKs
  While technically not required for editing files in Emacs, a JDK is required to take advantage of any of the compilation or debugging features of the JDEE. You'll also have to register each JDK you plan to use, but more on that later.

Installing CEDET

Installing CEDET is fairly straightforward if you have a **make** command available. (For Windows users, you'll want to have the Cygnus Unix Distribution installed. It gives you access to a large subset of Unix tools which will come in handy far beyond the installation of the JDEE.)

After you download the CEDET distribution from SourceForge, unpack it wherever you want it to reside. Open a terminal window (or start a Cygwin bash terminal on Windows) and change to the directory where you unpacked the distribution. From there you should be able to run the following command:

```
shell$ make EMACS=/path/to/emacs
```

That process will probably take a few minutes to complete. The Lisp files will be compiled for you.

When the **make** command completes, you should be in good shape. The last step for CEDET is to update your *.emacs* file:

```
;; Turn on CEDET's fun parts
(setq semantic-load-turn-useful-things-on t)
;; Load CEDET
(load-file "/path-to-cedet/common/cedet.el")
```

Installing the ELisp Library

Installing the ELisp library package from the JDEE site is also straightforward. Unpack the downloaded file wherever you like, but before you run the **make** command, you'll need to edit the *Makefile* and configure the entries outlined in Table 9-5 to match your system.

Table 9-5. JDEE Makefile entries

Makefile entry	Example	Description
prefix	/usr/local	The top-level directory for any shared or info directories.
datadir	$(prefix)/share	The directory where your main Emacs directory is located.
locallisppath	$(datadir)/emacs/site-lisp	The directory where any local Lisp files should be installed.
ELIBDIR	$(locallisppath)/elib	The directory where the elib Lisp files will go.
EMACS	/usr/bin/emacs	The command to start Emacs. This can be a fully qualified path or simply "emacs" to reach the default version found on your system.

Run the **make** command with the **install** option to get everything set up:

```
shell$ make install
```

The last step for the ELisp library is to make sure the Emacs defaults acknowledge the new package. You simply need to add the new directory to your **load-path** variable, as described next.

The ELisp library actually provides a simple template file that matches where you installed the package. After the **make** process completes, you should have an *elib_startup.el* file in the directory where you ran the **make** command. That file contains the line you'll need to add to your *.emacs* file or you can merge it with the system *default.el* file for everyone to use. (The *default.el* file is often found in your *site-lisp* directory. Chapter 11 has more details.)

Installing the JDEE

Five basic steps are required to install the JDEE on your system:

1. Get the necessary prerequisites downloaded and installed.
2. Update the load path (*.emacs*).
3. Set the JDEE to load at startup (*.emacs*).
4. Compile JDEE *.el* files (optional).
5. Register your JDKs (optional).

The previous section covered the first step. Make sure you take care of those prerequisites before continuing. The next steps can be handled in your *.emacs* file. The JDEE site proposes the following entries as a minimal setup; we excerpt them here (with one or two small tweaks) for easy reference.

```
;; This .emacs file illustrates the minimal setup
;; required to run the JDEE.

;; Set the debug option to enable a backtrace when a
;; problem occurs.
(setq debug-on-error t)
```

```
;; Update the Emacs load-path to include the path to
;; the JDEE and its require packages. This code assumes
;; that you have installed the packages in the
;; /usr/local/emacs/site-lisp directory.  Adjust appropriately.
(add-to-list 'load-path
  (expand-file-name "/usr/local/emacs/site-lisp/jde/lisp"))
(add-to-list 'load-path
  (expand-file-name "/usr/local/emacs/site-lisp/semantic"))
(add-to-list 'load-path
  (expand-file-name "/usr/local/emacs/site-lisp/speedbar"))
(add-to-list 'load-path
  (expand-file-name "/usr/local/emacs/site-lisp/eieio"))
(add-to-list 'load-path
  (expand-file-name "/usr/local/emacs/site-lisp/elib"))


;; If you want Emacs to defer loading the JDEE until you open a
;; Java file, edit the following line
(setq defer-loading-jde nil)
;; to read:
;;
;;   (setq defer-loading-jde t)
;;

(if defer-loading-jde
    (progn
      (autoload 'jde-mode "jde" "JDE mode." t)
      (setq auto-mode-alist
        (append
         '(("\\.java\\'" . jde-mode))
         auto-mode-alist)))
  (require 'jde))


;; Set the basic indentation for Java source files
;; to two spaces.
(add-hook 'jde-mode-hook
          '(lambda ()
             (setq c-basic-offset 2)))

;; Include the following only if you want to run
;; bash as your shell.

;; Set up Emacs to run bash as its primary shell.
(setq shell-file-name "bash")
(setq shell-command-switch "-c")
(setq explicit-shell-file-name shell-file-name)
(setenv "SHELL" shell-file-name)
(setq explicit-sh-args '("-login" "-i"))
(if (boundp 'w32-quote-process-args)
  (setq w32-quote-process-args ?\")) ;; Include only for MS Windows.
```

Of course, you'll need to make sure the paths in the add-to-list 'load-path lines
match the actual directories you're using.

Compiling the JDEE Lisp files is not required, but as noted in "Byte-Compiling Lisp Files" in Chapter 11, it's a good idea and speeds up several operations including general startup times. The JDEE makes this step simple. After you have it installed, start Emacs and run **M-x jde-compile-jde**. You run this command only once, so it is definitely worthwhile.

Registering Your Java Tools

The last step we need to cover is registering your Java development kits. This is not strictly necessary, but you don't want to skip this step. It is especially handy if you work in an environment where you have to test multiple versions of the JDK. With all of your kits registered in the JDEE, you can switch between versions with a simple variable change.

To register a JDK, use the **M-x customize-variable** command. The variable you need to customize is **jde-jdk-registry**. That will land you in the interactive customization screen. You can select the **INS** (insert) button to add the version number and path of your JDK. You can repeat that process for as many JDKs as you want to register. See Figure 9-2 for a list of such entries on a Mac OS X system.

Be sure to hit the State button and save this state for future sessions. You can click the Finish button when you're done or just close the buffer.

After you have your JDKs registered, you can switch to the active version using that same **M-x customize-variable** command. This time, edit the **jde-jdk** variable. You'll be prompted to choose one of the registered versions. You may or may not want to save this decision for future sessions. In any case, this variable can be edited at any time.

JDK tools.jar problems

The compilation feature requires access to the *tools.jar* file (or the equivalents built-in to some JDKs). If the JDEE compile command fails with an error message about not being able to find the *tools.jar* file, your best bet is to customize the JDEE variable **jde-global-classpath**. Make sure that variable includes the *tools.jar* file.

For some systems that do not have a *tools.jar* file*, you can steal that file from another machine, but usually you just need to get your classpath and registry entries set up correctly. Customizing the variables in Table 9-6 should get you compiling and running without too much effort.

---

* For Mac OS X users, the classes normally found in *tools.jar* are already a permanent part of the standard *classes.jar* so they are always available—even though *tools.jar* isn't in any of the library locations.

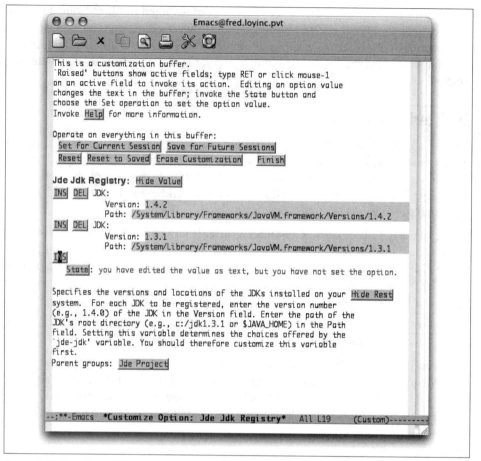

Figure 9-2. Inserting JDK entries in a Custom list

Table 9-6. JDEE variables to customize

JDEE variable	Sample values
jde-global-classpath	/usr/local/j2se:.
jde-jdk-registry	Version = 1.4.2 Path = /usr/local/j2se

Whew! That was a lot of work. But the good news is that once you've made it through the installation process, you have all the spiffy features of the JDEE forever at your command. So let's get on with the features!

Editing with the JDEE

First off, you're still in Emacs, so the usual motion commands described for Java mode (and C mode) still apply. But the JDEE adds two really great features to your editing cycle: command completion and class browsing.

The idea behind command completion is that the JDEE can (usually) predict which methods and variables are valid choices to make at certain points in your Java program. For example, if you start typing **System.** in your program, there are a finite number of choices for what follows that period. JDEE can display a list of those choices.

The command to show your list of completions is **C-c C-v C-.** (for **jde-complete**), which defaults to showing you a menu of completions. (You can change that behavior by customizing the **jde-complete-function** variable.) The completions are generated by looking at all of the classes listed in the **jde-global-classpath** variable (or the CLASSPATH environment variable if no global classpath was defined).

The class browser can be accessed quickly from the JDE menu and launches a Bean-Shell browser for the class your cursor was on. It's like a context-sensitive documentation tool, but a bit more powerful. Figure 9-3 shows what you get when starting the browser while your cursor is on the word *System*.

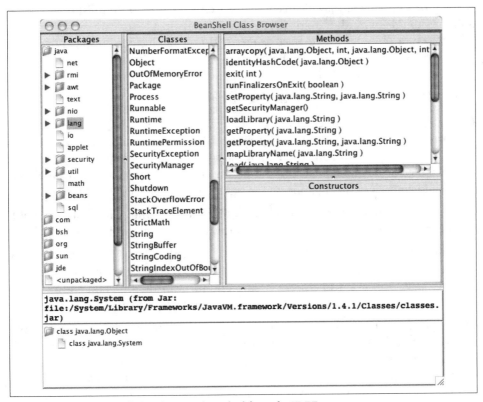

Figure 9-3. The BeanShell class browser launched from the JDEE

You can also launch the class browser with the **M-x jde-browse-class-at-point** command.

One other edit-time feature worth pointing out is the Code Generation item in the JDE menu. It has some great timesavers built-in, as shown in Table 9-7.

Table 9-7. Code Generation menu options

Keystrokes	Menu option (M-x command)	Action
C-c C-v C-l (lowercase L)	Println Wizard (jde-gen-println)	Prompts for the contents to print and inserts a complete System.out.println( ) method for you.
C-c C-v C-z	Import Class (jde-import-find-and-import)	Prompts for the (simple) class name to import and automatically adds the proper import line to the top of your file.
C-c C-v i	Implement Interface (jde-wiz-implement-interface)	Prompts you for the name of the interface to implement. Adds any missing import statements (including dependent imports, such as imports required for method arguments). Provides commented skeletons for each of the methods in the interface.

Other helpers are available from the JDE menu. Generate Get/Set Pairs in particular is great for working with JavaBeans design patterns. Just create your list of attributes and then run the wizard. It even checks to see if you already have an existing get/set pair. If you do, it notes that get/set pair as "existing" and keeps on trucking so you can use the wizard to update existing classes.

Compiling and Running with the JDEE

Compiling the current buffer can be done quickly with the **C-c C-v C-c** command. Any errors show up in the compilation buffer. That compilation buffer also allows you to navigate quickly to any errors that the compiler finds. Simply move your cursor to the error in question (using the normal motion commands) and hit **Enter**. You'll find yourself in the right file on the right line number. Very handy indeed.

Note that you can also run **ant** builds with **M-x jde-ant-build**. Check out the JDEE documentation or the help for various **jde-ant** variables for more information.

Running a simple program that has its own main( ) method is easy: just press **C-c C-v C-r**. That command executes the current buffer (by opening an execution buffer named **fully.qualified.ClassName**). Any output from the program shows in the buffer. You can move around in the buffer just as you would in a normal text buffer.

Of course, if you are working on anything other than a simple test class, you'll probably be in a package. Java's use of the classpaths rarely leaves room for being at the "bottom" of a package hierarchy. For example, in the package com.oreilly.demo, you want to start execution from the same directory that contains the *com* directory, not from the *demo* directory that contains the actual Java files. Regrettably, the *demo* directory is the default.

You can edit the following variables to make executing in larger projects a bit more convenient:

jde-run-working-directory
> The directory in which execution starts

jde-run-application-class
> The fully qualified name of the class that contains the `main( )` method to execute

With those values set, you should be able to run your application from any buffer, regardless of what directory the file you're editing happens to be in.

Another fun note about running your application through the JDEE: if any stack traces appear because of exceptions, you can navigate those traces by using the **C-c C-v C-[** and **C-c C-v C-]** commands (up and down, respectively). Again, Emacs makes it possible to manage quite a large portion of a development project all from one interface.

Debugging with the JDEE

A crucial element in any good IDE is its debugger. The JDEE allows you to stay in the Emacs realm while interacting with the **jdb** process. The JDEE also comes with its own debugger, the JDEbug application. JDEbug is more powerful but requires more setup effort.

> Before we touch anything, you need to make sure that your classes are compiled with support for debugging. Otherwise, many things will appear broken when you run the debugger.
>
> To add debug support when you compile, you run the **javac** command with the **–g** option. With the JDEE you can also use the variable **jde-compile-option-debug** to hold all the variations for debugging you like. If you customize this variable through Custom (see Chapter 10), just choose the "all" option for which debugging information to include. (Optionally, you can be more specific and select from the three types of debug information: Lines, Variables, and Source.)

We'll look at the **jdb** route just to get you started. You can start the debug session by typing **M-x jde-jdb**. The same variables that control the starting directory and main application class are used for debugging purposes.

After you have launched the debugger, you can control the debug process in a number of ways.

- Interact directly with the **jdb** process in the *debug* buffer. Here you can type any command that you would normally give when running **jdb**.
- Use the Jdb menu. You have all the usual debug options available: step into/over, continue, toggle breakpoint, and so on. This is a bit more limited than the first approach, but easier to manage if you're new to **jdb**.
- Use keyboard commands while you're in your source buffer. These commands are even more limited than the menu options, but give you really quick access to

the most common tasks (namely stepping and break points). Table 9-8 shows the commands that are available while you're in a source buffer.

Table 9-8. JDEE debugger controls

Keystrokes	Menu item	JDB command
C-c C-a C-s	Step Into	step
C-c C-a C-n	Step Over	next
C-c C-a C-c	Continue	cont
C-c C-a C-b	Toggle Breakpoint	stop in/stop at/clear
C-c C-a C-p	Display Expression	print
C-c C-a C-d	Display Object	dump

Figure 9-4 shows a simple application running in debug mode. Notice the small black triangle to the left of the Java source code in the upper buffer. That's the debug cursor that lets you know where you are in the file. It tracks the commands you issue, whether by directly entering **jdb** commands, by menu option, or through the keyboard.

Learning More about the JDEE

Clearly, there is a lot more to the JDEE than we can cover here. The package you download comes with some good documentation and several user guides for the basic JDEE and various options like the debuggers. The JDEE web site, at *http://jdee.sunsite.dk*, is a great source of information, too. As you would expect from an Emacs package, you can customize everything. Those customizations are stored in your *.emacs* file so you can tweak them by hand (or at least peek at them).

The best approach is to install the JDEE and start coding with it. If you find yourself saying "There should be a way to do X," get out the documentation. Chances are there is a way to do X—usually with more options than you could hope for!

Perl Support

Emacs has Perl support. Indeed, much like Perl itself, there are multiple ways to get things done—in this case, multiple Perl modes: the classic Perl mode (which comes up by default) and the more popular CPerl mode.

You should have a version of CPerl mode built right in, but you can also pick up the latest release from CPAN (the Comprehensive Perl Archive Network) online at *http://www.cpan.org*.

You can add one of the following pairs of lines to your *.emacs* file to make sure CPerl mode is invoked rather than Perl mode

Figure 9-4. Debugging a Java application with jdb

```
;; load cperl-mode for perl files
(fset 'perl-mode 'cperl-mode)

;; or maybe use an alias
(defalias 'perl-mode 'cperl-mode)
```

CPerl mode is mostly like **cc-mode** with respect to motion and other programming language features. It also includes fun debug operations. You can start the debugger with **M-x cperl-db**. You'll be prompted to verify the debugger command and then be dropped into a split-screen mode. One buffer allows you to drive the normal **perldb** environment with all the regular commands you're accustomed to using in the Perl debugger.

The other buffer shows your script and follows along as you work through the debugger. It tracks the line you're about to execute as you issue commands in the other buffer. It's amazing how quickly you grow to depend on having such tools available while you're developing scripts. It is worth trying out if you've never done it before.

Perl Caveats

A big reason we wanted to mention Perl mode here is to highlight a few caveats. Perl is an amazingly expressive language much more akin to the idioms found in human languages than just about any other computer language out there. That expressiveness can cause problems—especially when considering the expressiveness of regular expressions.

Perl supports all sorts of "funny" variable names like **$'** and **$/**. CPerl mode boasts the use of a syntax table to help understand most of Perl's odd and occasionally disruptive verbiage. The older Perl mode has no such trick up its sleeves and suffers under many circumstances in the font-lock and indentation realms. This is one of the main reasons to make the leap into CPerl mode.

Even with that syntax table, though, you'll probably find some combinations of variables and strings that give Emacs headaches. Sometimes restructuring your code will help, sometimes not. The important thing to remember is that it won't harm your program at all. It might make things a bit less readable, but the script itself should run just fine. And if it doesn't, you can always launch the debugger to find out why!

Here are some parting *.emacs* thoughts for you Perl programmers. These lines select **cperl-mode** as the default and make sure the syntax highlighting is turned on. These lines also turn on *folding* (**outline-minor-mode** in the snippet below). Folding allows you to "hide" chunks of your code, such as functions where the body of the function is "folded" into the name. That can make it easier to get a grip on everything that is going on in the file. Try it—it can become addictive!

```
;; Turn on highlighting globally
(global-font-lock-mode t)

;; automatically load cperl-mode for perl files
(fset 'perl-mode 'cperl-mode)

;; show only the toplevel nodes when loading a file
(add-hook 'cperl-mode-hook 'hide-body)

;; outline minor mode with cperl
(add-hook 'cperl-mode-hook 'outline-minor-mode)

;; Change the prefix for outline commands from C-c @ to C-c C-o
(setq outline-minor-mode-prefix "\C-co")

(load-file "cperl-mode.el")
```

SQL Support

For you database folks out there, you can even run interactive SQL sessions through Emacs. You can navigate through your SQL command history using normal motion

---

commands and even create complex SQL statements in any buffer and then shuttle them off to the interactive area for debugging.

Prerequisites

Before we get started with SQL queries, you do need to have a few things in place. Most of the SQL interaction modes require an actual client application for their particular database. For example, we use the MySQL server. We have to install the MySQL client programs (mysql, at a minimum) on any system where we want to use SQL mode. Even though the MySQL version of SQL mode is built-in, we still need access to a real client. This is true for every type of database you expect to access.

And speaking of communicating with the database, you must also have the basics of communication taken care of. You need to have network access to the server in question. You also need to have a valid username and password for connecting to that server. A good rule before jumping into SQL mode in Emacs is to make sure you can connect and interact with your database server from your machine. If it works from a terminal window or other client application, you can make it work in Emacs.

One last thing to remember: the various SQL modes in Emacs are just helpers, so you can't do anything with them that you couldn't do with your normal database client. You won't magically have access to that restricted table with everyone's salaries. Sorry. Even so, it's just more convenient to stay in Emacs when possible, so let's forge ahead.

Modes of Operation

You'll find two modes of operation for dealing with SQL. The interactive mode lets you communicate directly with a database server and run commands and view their output immediately. The editing mode allows you to build up (and edit) more complex commands. If you want, you can have the editing buffer send parts of itself to the interactive session for testing and verification.

Interactive mode

Start the interactive mode by typing **M-x sql-mysql** (or rather, your own variant of the interactive modes shown in Table 9-9).

Table 9-9. Commands for entering database-specific SQL modes

sql-db2	sql-linter	sql-postgres
sql-informix	sql-ms (Microsoft)	sql-solid
sql-ingres	sql-mysql	sql-sqlite
sql-interbase	sql-oracle	sql-sybase

You'll be prompted for things like your username and password, the database or catalog to use, and the server to contact. Remember the prerequisites, though; many modes require that you have a normal command-line client available. The mode simply supplies an intelligent layer on top of those clients.

After you get connected, just type normal SQL commands that your server understands. Most interactive clients have some type of "end-of-line" marker to let the system know when to send a completed command. In MySQL, for example, you can end statements with a semicolon (;) or the \g sequence.

Emacs keeps these commands in a history buffer for you so that you can revisit them. **M-p** and **M-n** allow you navigate to previous and next commands respectively. (**C-p** and **C-n** simply allow you to move around in the buffer as you would expect.)

Editing mode

You can also put a buffer directly into SQL mode with **M-x sql-mode**. This provides some assistance for motion and composition of SQL statements, but mostly it's there to let you build complex statements and then ship them to the interactive buffer for execution. Table 9-10 shows how to send various segments of the buffer to the database.

Table 9-10. SQL mode send commands

Keystroke	Command name	Action
C-c C-c	sql-send-paragraph	Send the paragraph the cursor is on. A paragraph is defined by the particular database client. For the **sql-mysql** process, for example, a paragraph begins with a statement like select or update and ends with a semicolon. Any number of lines can intervene.
C-c C-r	sql-send-region	Send the marked region.
C-c C-b	sql-send-buffer	Send the entire buffer.

The output of all of these send commands shows up in your interactive buffer. Nothing changes in the editing buffer so you should feel free to experiment. That's what these modes are here for!

The Lisp Modes

Emacs has three Lisp modes, listed here by their command names:

emacs-lisp-mode
> Used for editing Emacs Lisp code, as covered in Chapter 11 (filename *.emacs* or suffix *.el*).

lisp-mode
> Used for editing Lisp code intended for another Lisp system (suffix *.l* or *.lisp*).

lisp-interaction-mode
> Used for editing and running Emacs Lisp code.

All three modes have the same basic functionality; they differ only in the support they give to running Lisp code.

All three Lisp modes understand the basic syntax elements common to all language modes. In addition, they have various commands that apply to the more advanced syntactic concepts of S-expressions, lists, and defuns. An *S-expression* (or syntactic expression) is any syntactically correct Lisp expression, be it an atom (number, symbol, variable, etc.), or parenthesized list. *Lists* are special cases of S-expressions, and *defuns* (function definitions) are special cases of lists. Several commands deal with these syntactic concepts; you will most likely become comfortable with a subset of them.

Table 9-11 shows the commands that handle S-expressions.

Table 9-11. S-expression commands

Keystrokes	Command name	Action
C-M-b	backward-sexp	Move backward by one S-expression.
C-M-f	forward-sexp	Move forward by one S-expression.
C-M-t	transpose-sexps	Transpose the two S-expressions around the cursor.
C-M-@	mark-sexp	Set mark to the end of the current S-expression; set the cursor to the beginning.
C-M-k	kill-sexp	Delete the S-expression following the cursor.
(none)	backward-kill-sexp	Delete the S-expression preceding the cursor.

Since an S-expression can be a wide variety of things, the actions of commands that handle S-expressions are determined by where your cursor is when you invoke them. If your cursor is on a (or on a space preceding one, the S-expression in question is taken to be the list that starts with that (. If your cursor is on some other character such as a letter or number (or preceding whitespace), the S-expression is taken to be an atom (symbol, variable, or constant).

For example, suppose your cursor is in this position:

    (mary bob█(dave (pete)) ed)

If you type **C-M-f**, the cursor moves like this:

    (mary bob (dave (pete))█ed)

That is, the cursor moves forward past the S-expression (**dave (pete)**), which is a list. However, say your cursor is positioned like this:

    (mary█bob (dave (pete)) ed)

When you type **C-M-f**, it moves here:

    (mary bob█(dave (pete)) ed)

In this case, the S-expression is the atom **bob**.

The commands moving in lists are shown in Table 9-12.

Table 9-12. Commands for moving in lists

Keystrokes	Command name	Action
C-M-n	forward-list	Move forward by one list.
C-M-p	backward-list	Move backward by one list.
C-M-d	down-list	Move forward and down one parenthesis level.
(none)	up-list	Move forward out of one parenthesis level.
C-M-u	backward-up-list	Move backward out of one parenthesis level.

As a mnemonic device, you can think of lists as analogous to lines and S-expressions as analogous to characters; thus, **C-n** and **C-p** appear in list motion commands, whereas **C-f** and **C-b** appear in S-expression motion commands. **C-M-n** and **C-M-p** work similarly to **C-M-f** and **C-M-b**, respectively, except that you must position the cursor so that there is a list in front or back of it to move across—that is, there must be an opening or closing parenthesis on, after, or before the cursor. If there is no parenthesis, Emacs signals an error. For example, if your cursor is positioned like this:

```
(fred bob (dave (pete)) ed)
```

and you type **C-M-n**, Emacs complains with the message:

```
Containing expression ends prematurely
```

However, if your cursor is here:

```
(fred bob (dave (pete)) ed)
```

the "next list" is actually (**dave (pete)**), and the cursor ends up like this if you type **C-M-n**:

```
(fred bob (dave (pete)) ed)
```

The commands for moving up or down lists enable you to get inside or outside them. For example, say your cursor is here:

```
(fred bob (dave (pete)) ed)
```

typing **C-M-d** moves the cursor here:

```
(fred bob (dave (pete)) ed)
```

This is the result because **fred** is the next level down after its enclosing list. Typing **C-M-d** again has this result:

```
(fred bob (dave (pete)) ed)
```

You are now inside the list (**dave (pete)**). At this point, typing **C-M-u** does the opposite of what **C-M-d** does: it moves the cursor back and outside of the two lists. But if you type **M-x up-list Enter**, you will move forward as well as out, resulting in this:

```
(fred bob (dave (pete)) ed)
```

The commands for defuns listed in Table 9-13 are more straightforward.

Table 9-13. Commands for working with functions

Keystrokes	Command name	Action
C-M-a	beginning-of-defun	Move to the beginning of the current function.
C-M-e	end-of-defun	Move to the end of the current function.
C-M-h	mark-defun	Put the cursor at the beginning of the function, put the mark at the end.

These commands work properly only when the (**defun** that starts the current function is at the beginning of a line.

Indentation in Lisp Modes

The Lisp modes provide "flashing" of matching left parentheses; if the matching parenthesis is outside of the current window, the line it is on appears in the minibuffer. The Lisp modes also provide indentation via the **Tab** key and **C-j** for **newline-and-indent** (except in Lisp interaction mode, described later in this chapter). The indentation style supported by the Lisp modes "knows" a lot about Lisp keywords and list syntax; unfortunately, it is not easily customized.*

Here is an example, a Lisp equivalent of the "times" C function shown earlier in the chapter, that illustrates the indentation style:

```
(defun times (x y)
  (let ((i 0)
        (result 0))
    (while (< i x)
      (setq result (+ result y)
            i (1+ i)))
    result))
```

The basic indentation value is 2; this value is used whenever code on the next line goes down a level in nesting. For example, the body of the function, after the line containing **defun**, is indented by 2. The (**while...** and **result**)) lines are indented by 2 with respect to the **let** because they are the body of the block **let** introduces.

Things like **defun**, **let**, and **while** are function calls, even though they act like keywords. The indentation convention for function calls is that if there are arguments on lines after the line where the function name and first argument appear, the additional arguments line up with the first one. In other words, this has the form:

```
(function-name arg1
               arg2
               arg3
               ...)
```

---

* The indentation style is bound up in the Emacs Lisp code for Lisp mode. If you are an experienced Lisp hacker, you can examine the code for **lisp-mode.el** in the Emacs Lisp directory and determine how to customize indentation the way you wish. A good place to start looking is the function **lisp-indent-line**.

The multiple arguments to **setq** in the preceding function provide another example of this.

However, the indentation of the line (**result 0**) shows that something a bit different happens with lists that are not function calls. The list in question is actually ((**i** 0) (**result** 0)), which is a list with two elements (both of which are also lists). The indentation style supported by the Lisp modes lines up these two elements.

Even though keyword-like terms such as **let** and **while** are actually function calls, the Lisp modes "understand" these functions to the extent that special indentation conventions are set up for them. For example, if we were to put the condition for the while-loop on a separate line and press **Tab** to indent it properly, the result would be:

```
(while
    (< i x)
    (setq result (+ result y)
          i (1+ i)))
```

Similar things happen with **if** and **cond** control structures; Chapter 11 contains properly indented examples.

Another remark about indentation conventions: the Lisp modes are geared toward a style in which multiple right parentheses are put on the same line immediately following each other, instead of on separate lines. For example, the line **i** (**1+ i**)) contains right parentheses that close off the **1+** function, the **setq**, and the **while** respectively. If you prefer, you can put your closing parentheses on separate lines, but if you press **Tab** to indent them, they won't line up properly with their matching open parentheses; you have to indent them manually.

In addition to the **Tab** and **C-j** commands for indentation, the Lisp modes support the command **C-M-q** (for **indent-sexp**), which indents every line in the S-expression just following the cursor. You can use this command, for example, to indent an entire function definition: just put the cursor right before the **defun** and type **C-M-q**.

Comments in Lisp Modes

Comments in the Lisp modes are handled by the universal comment command **M-;**, which indents out to **comment-column** (or, if there is text at that column, one space past the last character), inserts a semicolon, and puts the cursor just past it. If you want a comment to occupy an entire line (or to start anywhere other than at **comment-column**), you must move to where you want the comment to start and type the semicolon yourself. Note that if you press **Tab** on any line that contains only a comment, the comment moves out to **comment-column**. To get around this, use two or more semicolons; doing so causes **Tab** to leave the comments where they are. The Lisp modes also support the other comment commands discussed earlier in the chapter, including **M-j** to extend a comment to another line and **M-x kill-comment Enter** to get rid of a single-line comment. These features are common to all three Lisp modes; next, we discuss the features unique to each.

Emacs Lisp Mode Differences

Emacs Lisp mode was designed to be used with code meant to run within Emacs itself, so it facilitates running the code you type. Lisp is an interpreted (as opposed to purely compiled) language, so it is possible to blur the line between the write and run/debug phases of Lisp programming; Emacs Lisp mode takes some advantage of this opportunity, whereas Lisp interaction mode goes even further, as we'll see later. In Emacs Lisp mode, the command **C-M-x** (**eval-defun**) picks up the function definition around or after the cursor and evaluates it, meaning that it parses the function and stores it so that Emacs "knows" about the function when you invoke it.

Emacs Lisp mode also includes the command **M-Tab** (for **lisp-complete-symbol**),* which performs completion on the symbol (variable, function name, etc.) preceding the cursor, as described in Chapter 14. Thus, you can type the shortest unambiguous prefix for the symbol, followed by **M-Tab**, and Emacs tries to complete the symbol's name for you as far as it can. If it completes the symbol name, you can go on with whatever you are doing. If it doesn't, you haven't provided an unambiguous prefix. You can type more characters (to disambiguate further), or you can type **M-Tab** again, and a help window showing the choices pops up. Then you can type more characters and complete the symbol yourself, or you can try for completion again.

Lisp Mode Differences

Lisp mode (as opposed to Emacs Lisp mode) is meant for use with Lisp processors other than the Emacs Lisp interpreter. Therefore it includes a couple of commands for interfacing to an external Lisp interpreter. The Lisp mode command **C-c C-z** (**run-lisp**) starts up your system's Lisp interpreter as a subprocess and creates the *lisp* buffer (with an associated window) for input and output.† If a Lisp subprocess already exists, **C-c C-z** uses it rather than creating a second one. You can send function definitions to the Lisp subprocess by putting the cursor anywhere within a function's definition and using **C-M-x**, which in this case stands for **lisp-send-defun**. This procedure causes the functions you define to become known to the Lisp interpreter so that you can invoke them later.

---

* This key binding may not work on all platforms. If it is intercepted by the operating system (as it is on Red Hat Linux), type **Esc Tab** instead (remember to release **Esc** before you press **Tab**).

† This Lisp mode command (**run-lisp**) was designed to run with the franz Lisp system on BSD Unix systems, though it should work with other Lisp interpreters.

Working with Lisp Fragments

Emacs Lisp mode is probably the best thing to use if you are editing entire files of Emacs Lisp code, for example, if you are programming your own mode (as described in Chapter 11) or modifying an existing one. However, if you are editing "little" pieces of Lisp code (for example, making additions or modifications to your *.emacs* file), Emacs has more powerful features you can use that further blur the line between writing and running code.

Commands for evaluating a line of Lisp

The first of these is the command **M-:** (for **eval-expression**). This command enables you to type a one-line Lisp expression of any kind in the minibuffer; the expression is evaluated, and the result is printed in the minibuffer. This is an excellent, quick way to check the values of Emacs variables and to experiment with "internal" Emacs functions that aren't bound to keys or that require arguments. You can use the symbol completion command **M-Tab** while you are using **eval-expression**.

Unfortunately (or fortunately, depending on your point of view), Emacs doesn't normally let you use **eval-expression**. If you try pressing **M-:**, you will see the message loading novice... in the minibuffer. Then a window pops up with a message on the order of, "You didn't really mean to type that, did you?" You get three options: press **Space** to try the command only once, **y** to try it and enable it for future use with no questions asked, or **n** to do nothing.

If you want to use **eval-expression**, type **y**. This command actually results in the following line being put in your *.emacs* file:

```
(put 'eval-expression 'disabled nil)
```

If you are a knowledgeable Lisp programmer, you will understand that this addition sets the property **disabled** of the symbol **eval-expression** to **nil**. In other words, Emacs considers certain commands to be verboten to novice users and thus allows commands to be disabled. If you want to skip this entire procedure and just use **eval-expression**, simply put the above line in your *.emacs* file yourself (make sure you include the single quotes).

Another feature that helps you exercise Emacs Lisp code is **C-x C-e** (for **eval-last-sexp**). This command runs the line of Lisp that your cursor is on and prints its value in the minibuffer. **C-x C-e** is handy for testing single lines of code in an Emacs Lisp file.

Using Lisp interaction mode

An even more powerful feature is Lisp interaction mode. This is the mode the default buffer *scratch* is in. Filenames with no suffixes normally cause Emacs to go into Lisp interaction mode, though you can change this using the variable **auto-mode-alist**, described earlier in this chapter and in more detail in Chapter 10. You can also put any buffer in Lisp interaction mode by typing **M-x lisp-interaction-mode Enter**;

to create an extra Lisp interaction buffer, just type **C-x b** (for **switch-to-buffer**), supply a buffer name, and put it in Lisp interaction mode.

Lisp interaction mode is identical to Emacs Lisp mode except for one important feature: **C-j** is bound to the command **eval-print-last-sexp**. This command takes the S-expression just before point, evaluates it, and prints the result in the buffer. To get the usual **newline-and-indent** functionality attached to **C-j** in other modes, you must press **Enter**, followed by **Tab**.

Remember that an S-expression is any syntactically valid expression in Lisp. Therefore, you can use **C-j** in Lisp interaction mode to check the values of variables, enter function definitions, run functions, and so on. For example, if you type **auto-save-interval** and press **C-j**, the value of that variable (300 by default) appears. If you type a **defun** and press **C-j** after the last right parenthesis, Emacs stores the function defined (for future invocation) and prints its name; in this case, **C-j** is similar to **C-M-x** (for **eval-defun**) except that the cursor must be after (as opposed to before or in the middle of) the function being defined. If you invoke a function, Emacs evaluates (runs) the expression and responds with whatever value the function returns.

C-j in Lisp interaction mode gives you an excellent way to play with, incrementally develop, and debug Emacs Lisp code, and since Emacs Lisp is "true" Lisp, it is even useful for developing some bits of code for other Lisp systems.

CHAPTER 10
Customizing Emacs

As you have probably noticed throughout this book, Emacs is very powerful and very flexible. You can take advantage of that power and flexibility to configure Emacs to match your work style and preferences. We'll look at several of the most common customization tasks and also look at a few resources for more in-depth coverage than we can provide here.

You can customize Emacs in three ways: using Custom, the interactive interface; using the Options menu, which is really a backdoor to Custom; and directly by adding lines of Lisp to your *.emacs* file. This chapter covers all three of these methods.

No matter what method you use, though, the *.emacs* startup file is modified. Custom modifies it for you when you save settings through that interface. The Options menu invokes Custom behind the scenes; when you choose Save Options, Custom again modifies *.emacs*. Throughout the book, we have been providing lines for you to add to *.emacs* directly so you could adjust Emacs to your preferences.

Before we get started, we should say that the very easiest way to customize Emacs is by selecting an option from the Options menu and choosing Save Options. This menu is designed to provide easy access to changing frequently used options. For example, you may not like the Toolbar and its icons, feeling that such graphical cod-swallop is beneath an Emacs user. You can hide the toolbar through the Show/Hide option on the Options menu. Choosing Save Options modifies *.emacs* so the toolbar is hidden every time you start Emacs. And if you miss the toolbar someday, you can get it back the very same way.

After describing customization methods, this chapter goes on to discuss several generic issues relating to customization, including how to change fonts and colors, modify your key bindings, set Emacs variables, find Lisp packages to load, start modes automatically based on file suffixes, and inhibit any global customization files that may be interfering with your own *.emacs* settings.

Using Custom

Emacs now ships with a quirky graphical-but-not interface that allows you to customize most aspects of Emacs without knowing the gory details. This feature, known as Custom, can be accessed by typing **M-x custom** or by clicking the tools icon on the toolbar.

Type: **M-x custom Enter**

Emacs displays the startup buffer for Custom (Mac OS X).

Navigating Custom

You can move around in a given Custom screen much the way you do in any other part of Emacs. All of the basic cursor movement commands like **C-n** and **C-p** work just as they should. But that's only part of the story in Custom. To accomplish anything useful, you need to activate special words and phrases. Those bits of text in grey boxes that look like buttons are the words and phrases in question.

To activate one of these buttons, click on the button with the mouse or position your cursor inside its borders and press **Enter**. Figure 10-1 highlights these options.

When you finish looking at a screen, if you are not interested in changing anything, you can type **C-x k** to kill the current buffer and go back to the previous screen. You can also activate the Finish button in the common header set discussed next.

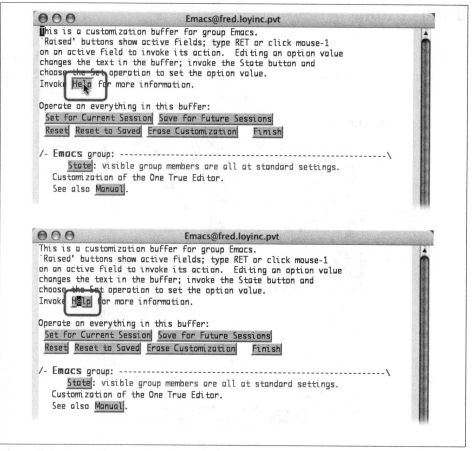

Figure 10-1. Custom button activation using the mouse cursor (top) and the keyboard cursor (bottom) (Mac OS X)

Common Options

At the top of each page in Custom is a common set of buttons shown in Figure 10-2. These options affect the entire buffer.

From here you can perform any of the following tasks:

Set for Current Session
> Make immediate changes that last for the duration of this session but will be reset the next time you start Emacs.

Save for Future Sessions
> Make immediate changes that last for the duration of this session and will also be in place the next time you start Emacs. These changes are stored in your *.emacs* file.

Reset
> Switch back to the previous values (previous to your current changes, anyway).

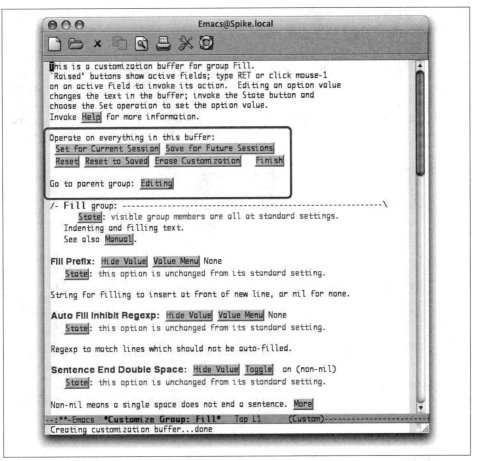

This is a customization buffer for group Fill.
'Raised' buttons show active fields; type RET or click mouse-1
on an active field to invoke its action. Editing an option value
changes the text in the buffer; invoke the State button and
choose the Set operation to set the option value.
Invoke Help for more information.

Operate on everything in this buffer:
 Set for Current Session Save for Future Sessions
 Reset Reset to Saved Erase Customization   Finish

Go to parent group: Editing

/- Fill group: --\
        State: visible group members are all at standard settings.
     Indenting and filling text.
     See also Manual.

Fill Prefix: Hide Value Value Menu None
     State: this option is unchanged from its standard setting.

String for filling to insert at front of new line, or nil for none.

Auto Fill Inhibit Regexp: Hide Value Value Menu None
     State: this option is unchanged from its standard setting.

Regexp to match lines which should not be auto-filled.

Sentence End Double Space: Hide Value Toggle on (non-nil)
     State: this option is unchanged from its standard setting.

Non-nil means a single space does not end a sentence. More
--:**-Emacs *Customize Group: Fill* Top L1   (Custom)---------------
Creating customization buffer...done

Figure 10-2. The actions common to all pages in Custom (Mac OS X)

Reset to Saved

> Switch back to the previously saved values. In this case, "saved" means saved for future sessions. If you haven't made (and subsequently saved) any customizations to a variable, this option has no effect.

Erase Customization

> This option pretty much does what it says. Any customizations made by Custom, whether for this or future sessions, are removed. Your own personal entries in your *.emacs* file should remain intact, but it's always a good idea to make a backup before deleting any information.

Finish

> Close this buffer and return to the previous customization buffer or back to the buffer from which you launched Custom. Note that you can also press the **q** key to activate Finish from anywhere in a Custom buffer.

These options are useful when you modify more than one option on a page and want to save them all at once (and in the same way).

Custom corrals options into customization groups, which are set up in a hierarchy of parent and child groups. To go to the parent group for the group you're looking at, choose the button for the parent group in question following the Go to parent group: prompt. To make it easier to find things, a group might have more than one parent. For example, the I18n (internationalization) group has two parents, Environment and Editing, as shown in Figure 10-3.

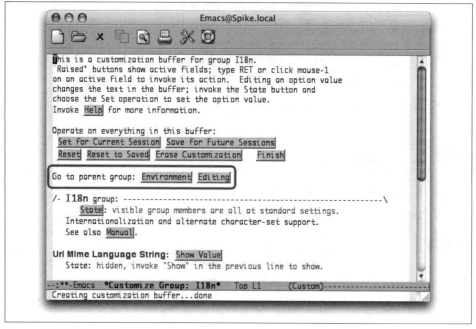

Figure 10-3. Custom's Go to parent group prompt

Choosing Go to parent group is much like choosing Finish but without closing the buffer. It's a useful option if you're just poking around looking for related variables. We'll show you better ways to find particular features to customize later in this chapter.

Customizing with Custom

After you learn your way around, you can tackle customizing Emacs. Each screen of Custom lists variables and other settings. You can edit the value of any variable in the grey text field to the right of variable's name. The current value should be listed. Just delete the current value and type the new value.

Changing a value, however, is not the last step you have to take. You need to save the change before it will take effect. You use the State button to save the change (as mentioned earlier, to save all the values on a page in the same way, you can use the options near the top of the screen). As with other parts of Custom, you can use your mouse or the keyboard. Clicking the left mouse button on State should bring up the list shown in Figure 10-4. Depending on the variable and the change you made (if any), you may or may not have all of the options available.

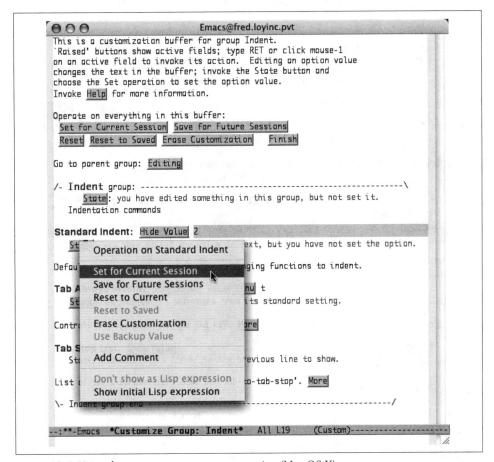

Figure 10-4. Using the mouse to save or reset an option (Mac OS X)

Of course, you can also activate the State button by placing your cursor on it and pressing **Enter**. That should create a second window with effectively the same options you get when using the mouse. Figure 10-5 shows the options you see using the **Enter** key to select State. This list is dynamic, showing only options that are available to you. (It won't show any options if you haven't changed anything yet, but it beeps with an error.)

When using the mouse, simply select the desired choice from the list. When using the text approach, type the number (or other character) corresponding to your

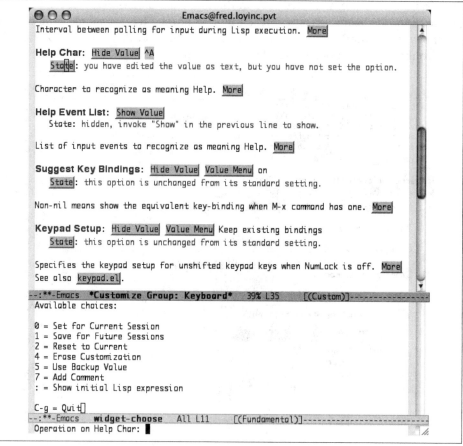

Figure 10-5. Using the keyboard to save or reset an option (Mac OS X)

desired choice. The options available are similar to those that apply to the entire buffer. You'll see the familiar save and reset options along with a few new ones:

Set for Current Session

Same as the global option. Saves the new value for the duration of this session.

Save for Future Sessions

Same as the global option. Applies this value immediately and updates your *.emacs* file so the new value is used whenever you start Emacs.

Reset to Current

Goes back to the current value for the variable. Any unsaved changes are thrown out, but changes saved—even just for this session—count as "current" changes.

Erase Customization

Same as the global option. Any changes to the variable are removed and *.emacs* is updated if needed.

Use Backup Value

Goes back to the value saved before the "current" value was set. In other words, revert to the value replaced by the most recent save.

Add Comment

You can add your own comments to the variable to help you remember why you made this change. Comments last as long as the saved change. Changes made only for the current session keep the comment only for the current session (not often useful). Comments added to changes that you save for future sessions show up on this screen in those future sessions. Erasing the customized value also erases comments.

If you make a mistake or supply a value that is not appropriate for the variable, you get a brief error message in the minibuffer. As with other utilities that grew up in the world of Unix, no news is good news. If you don't see any error messages, your change was successfully saved.

An Abbrev Mode Example

Word abbreviation mode is a wonderful way to correct typos on the fly. But it can't work that way unless it is turned on. Let's use Custom to turn on word abbreviation mode (discussed in Chapter 3).

Type: **M-x custom Enter**

Main customization screen.

Click on the Go to Group button next to Editing group

The Editing group.

Click on the Go to Group button next to Abbreviations group

The Abbreviations group.

Click on the Go to Group button next to Abbrev Mode group

The Abbrev Mode group.

Finally, we're at a screen where we can set the option! Notice that the first content line, Abbrev Mode group, says next to the State button `visible group members are all at standard settings`. Also note that Abbrev Mode, near the bottom of the screen, says `this option is unchanged from its standard setting`.

We'll turn on the Abbrev Mode option by pressing the Toggle button.

Click Toggle next to Abbrev Mode

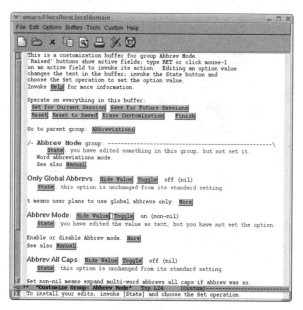

Abbrev mode is set to on.

The text near Abbrev Mode group now says, You have edited something in this group, but not set it. The text near the Abbrev Mode option says, you have edited the value as text, but you have not set the option. These are clear hints that we must take one more step to set this option. And if those weren't hints enough, the minibuffer explicitly instructs, To install your edits, invoke [State] and choose the Set operation. We could click on the State button next to the option, but it's just as convenient (if not more convenient) to click on the Save For Future Sessions option near the top of the screen. This saves all options we've changed in the buffer, which in our case is just one option.

Near the top of the screen, click on Save for Future Sessions

Emacs tells you that it wrote the *.emacs* file.

Next to the Abbrev Mode group it now says, `something in this group has been set and saved`. Next to the Abbrev Mode option it says, `this option has been set and saved`. Note also that `Abbrev` appears on the mode line now; we have indeed successfully turned on word abbreviation mode. Click Finish repeatedly to kill all the Custom buffers.

Congratulations; you're on your way to customizing Emacs. You should spend some time wandering around in the various groups Custom offers to get a sense of the things you can control. We'll look at the popular topics of customizing fonts, colors, and keyboard mappings in later sections. But Custom offers a much wider variety of areas to tweak. Don't be afraid to look around. You can always use the Reset option to undo something that doesn't behave the way you expected or wanted.

The Options Menu

You can also access Custom through a bit of a back door: the Options menu. Figure 10-6 shows the Options menu. There are three key entries at this top level:

Show/Hide
　　Allows you to turn on (and off) several features of Emacs including the menu bar and toolbar.

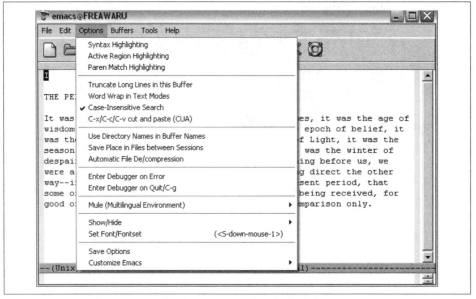

Figure 10-6. The Options menu (Windows)

Save Options
> A quick shortcut to saving any changes you make to Emacs through the Options menu.

Customize Emacs
> A submenu that allows you to tweak common items such as fonts and variables as well as helping you browse and search through the options available to Custom.

A Dired Example

Let's tackle another Custom example with the help of the Options menu. Dired (discussed in Chapter 5) has many customizable features. One such feature is the **dired-view-command-alist** variable. This is a list of helper applications that allow you to open various kinds of files. This feature can be quite handy for viewing binary files such as images or PDF files. This list of helper applications is tailored to Linux. If you want to use other applications or you're on a Windows or Mac system, you'll need to customize this variable.

Before you customize this option, you need to open a directory or simply type **C-x d** to enter Dired. Next, from the Options → Customize Emacs menu, select the Specific Option item.

Choose Options → Customize Emacs → Specific Option

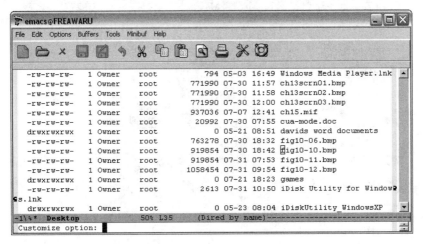

The minibuffer prompts for a specific option to customize (Windows).

The minibuffer prompts for an option name. We want to customize **dired-view-command-alist**.

Type: **dired-view-command-alist Enter**

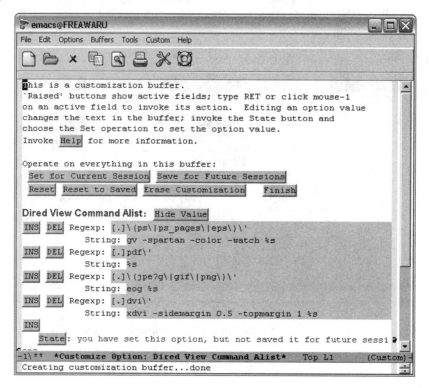

Editing a list entry in Custom (Windows).

You should see the familiar Custom options for saving and resetting the values along with the value of the **dired-view-command-alist** variable. For this particular variable, we have a list of entries for common file types including PostScript files, PDF documents, and images. To alter one of the existing entries, simply move to the String line and edit the text in grey to launch the application you would like to use. (You can also alter the filename pattern by editing the text in the Regexp line.) For example, PDF documents can be viewed with the open command in Mac OS X, so we could change that line as shown in Figure 10-7. In fact, on Mac OS X, you can use the generic open command for just about every type of file. On Windows it is even easier. Simply enter **%s** as the string, and Windows uses its default application to open that file type.

If you don't use DVI documents, you can get rid of that association using the DEL button shown in Figure 10-8.

You can also add new document types and viewers by clicking on any of the INS buttons. (The order of the associations isn't important for this particular variable, but it

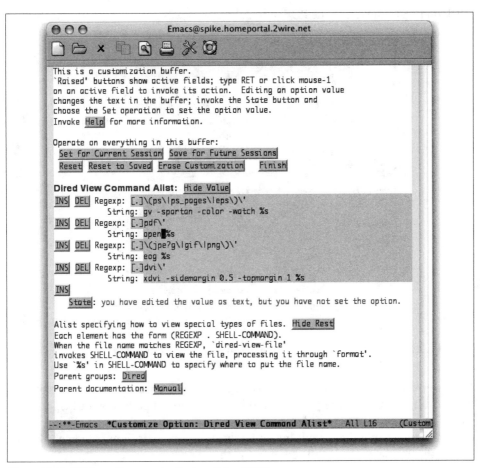

Figure 10-7. Editing a list entry in Custom (Mac OS X)

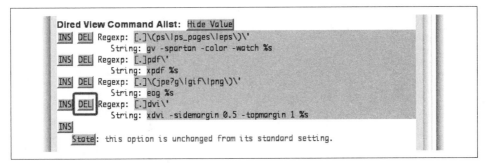

Figure 10-8. Deleting a list entry in Custom (Mac OS X)

might matter for other lists.) To insert a new association *before* the PDF entry, activate the INS button to the left of the PDF entry.

Click on INS to the left of the PDF entry.

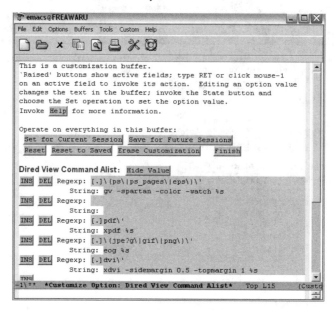

The first step in adding a new item to a list in Custom (Windows).

Now you can add an association for playing MP3 files on a PC by editing both the Regexp and String lines. Note that you'd have to supply a path to your helper application (winamp in this example) that matched your system. As mentioned earlier, if winamp was already the default helper application for MP3s, you could simply type **%s** for the String instead of the complete path to winamp.

Type **[.]mp3\\'** for the Regexp and **c:\apps\media\winamp.exe %s** for the String:

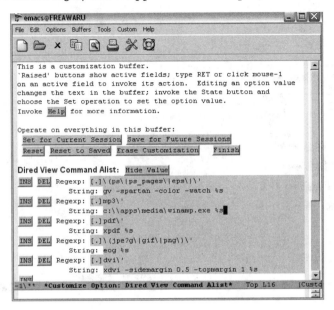

The second step in adding a new item (Windows).

You may have noticed the Save Changes option in the Options menu. This menu item saves changes you make through the Options menu. For example, you can modify such settings as whether or not the toolbar is visible or the Save Place in Files between Sessions option. It does not save changes you have made through Custom— even if you launched Custom from one of the Options → Customize Emacs submenu items. You'll still need to use the normal Custom options to save those changes.

For our Dired variable example, then, you'll need to select one of the Save options available. In this case, we'll save it for the current session only.

Click on Set for Current Session

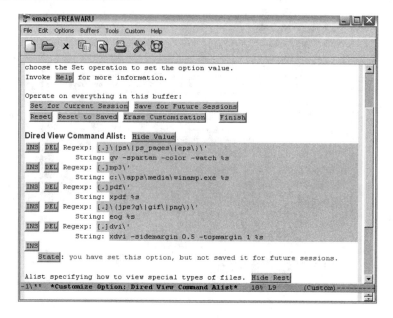

Saving changes for this session only (Windows).

When you're done saving your changes, you can exit the buffer as usual by clicking the Finish button, typing **q**, or typing **C-x k** to kill the buffer.

But Where Is the Variable I Want?

One of the biggest stumbling blocks to using Custom is knowing where a particular variable is located. Custom has a lot of groups and subgroups—and they aren't always intuitive. There are two quick ways to "search" for a specific variable. You can press **Tab** to use the completion feature in the minibuffer or you can browse through the entire Custom hierarchy.

To use the completion approach, type **M-x customize-option** or select Options → Customize Emacs → Specific Option. You'll see Customize Option: in the minibuffer. You can type a string like *font* and then hit the **Tab** key to see what variables start with that string.

You can also create a custom buffer with options matching a regular expression with **M-x customize-apropos** (or Options → Customize Emacs → Options Matching Regexp). You can type in a regular expression (or a simple string) and Custom builds a new buffer with all groups containing matching options.

If you want to browse the hierarchy to see the related groups of variables in a reasonably compact view, select Options → Customize Emacs → Browse Customization Groups. That should land you on a screen similar to Figure 10-9.

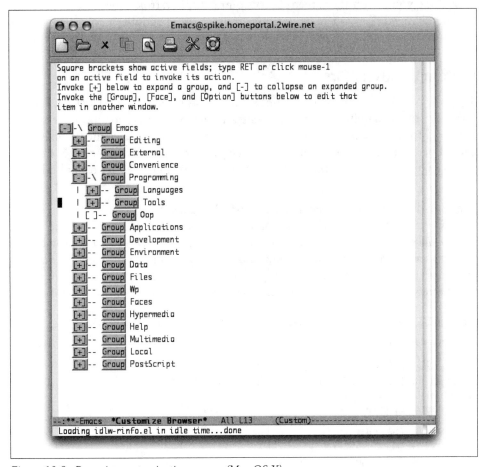

Figure 10-9. Browsing customization groups (Mac OS X)

You can activate the [+] and [-] buttons just like you do other Custom buttons (click on them with your mouse or move the keyboard cursor to them and press **Enter**.) This allows you to browse the entire set of Custom groups and subgroups. After you find the variable you're looking for, click on the Option button next to the variable or click on the Group button for the variable's parent group if you want to edit multiple variables in the group.

Modifying the .emacs File Directly

It's possible to customize Emacs in just about any way you can imagine. Almost everything you see on the screen, every command, keystroke, message, and so on, can be changed. As you may imagine, most customizations involve the Emacs startup file *.emacs*.

Custom Versus .emacs

The previous section discussed the interactive customization tool, Custom, but left out some of the details on what happens any time you "save for future sessions." Custom places the configuration information in your *.emacs* file. Some things simply cannot be done through Custom (yet). Once you get familiar with the types of statements that go into your *.emacs* file, you may also just find it easier to add a line or two directly.

We should emphasize that using Custom or editing *.emacs* by hand is not an either-or proposition. When you save options via Custom, it adds its settings to the end of your *.emacs* file and warns you not to edit them by hand. Despite this prohibition, you can easily add your own customizations to the beginning of that file. To illustrate this, Example 10-1 shows a sample *.emacs* file for Mac OS X that shows edits made directly by the user as well as sections added by Custom (shown in bold)

Example 10-1. A .emacs file for Mac OS X with lines added by the user and by Custom

```
(setq mac-command-key-is-meta nil)
(diary)
(setq load-path (cons "~/elisp" load-path))
(autoload 'html-helper-mode "html-helper-mode" "Yay HTML" t)
(setq html-helper-build-new-buffer t)
(setq auto-mode-alist (cons '("\.html$" . html-helper-mode) auto-mode-alist))
(setq-default indent-tabs-mode nil)
(setq-default tab-width 15)
(setq-default abbrev-mode t)
(read-abbrev-file "~/.abbrev_defs")
(setq save-abbrevs t)
(fset 'boldword
   [?\C-  escape ?f ?\C-x ?\C-x ?< ?b ?> ?\C-x ?\C-x ?< ?/ ?b ?>])
(fset 'italword
   [?\C-  escape ?f ?\C-x ?\C-x ?< ?e ?m backspace backspace ?i ?> ?\C-x ?\C-x ?< ?/ ?i ?>
])
(global-set-key "\C-x\C-kI" 'italword)
(setq shell-file-name "/bin/zsh")
(add-hook 'comint-output-filter-functions
   'comint-watch-for-password-prompt)
(custom-set-variables
  ;; custom-set-variables was added by Custom.
  ;; If you edit it by hand, you could mess it up, so be careful.
  ;; Your init file should contain only one such instance.
```

```
  ;; If there is more than one, they won't work right.
 '(global-font-lock-mode t nil (font-core))
 '(text-mode-hook (quote (turn-on-auto-fill text-mode-hook-identify))))
(custom-set-faces
  ;; custom-set-faces was added by Custom.
  ;; If you edit it by hand, you could mess it up, so be careful.
  ;; Your init file should contain only one such instance.
  ;; If there is more than one, they won't work right.
 )
```

Will the real .emacs please stand up?

You might have a bit of trouble finding the right *.emacs* file to work with when you're first starting out. Emacs actually looks for a variety of startup files. In order, they are:

.emacs.elc

> The byte-compiled Lisp version or your startup file. This is not editable, but can make startup quicker if you have a big, complex startup file.

.emacs.el

> The more formal name for your startup file. You can use Lisp commands to customize and initialize your entire Emacs environment.

.emacs

> The common name for the startup file. Exactly like the *.emacs.el* file, just without the *.el* extension. Both are editable.

As soon as Emacs finds one of these files, that's it; then it's on to the next step in startup. You can't have a *.emacs.elc* for the big customizations and then a separate *.emacs* for the last few. Sorry!

For all you Emacs users on Microsoft Windows-based systems, you might bump into a variation of this file that begins with an underscore (_) rather than a dot (.). In the past, the Windows filesystem required something before the first dot, so *.emacs* was an invalid filename. Consequently, *_emacs* was adopted. The same order and notes about the *.elc* and *.el* variants applies. In modern versions of Windows, *.emacs* is a valid filename and the dot variations take precedence over the underscore versions.

Basic .emacs Statements

Some changes require a knowledge of Emacs Lisp programming (see Chapter 11); others are simple enough without such knowledge. In this chapter, we cover a variety of useful customizations that require no programming knowledge. For now, however, you need to know this: every Emacs command corresponds to a Lisp *function*, which has the form:

```
(function-name arguments)
```

For example, if you want to move the cursor forward by a word, you type **M-f**. What you are actually doing is running the Lisp function:

```
(forward-word 1)
```

Caveat editor

Two important comments concerning *.emacs* files are in order. First, if you are inserting code into your *.emacs* file, you may end up putting in something that causes Emacs to fail or behave strangely. If this happens, you can invoke Emacs without running your *.emacs* file: simply invoke Emacs with the command-line option **-q**, and Emacs will not run your *.emacs* file. (Chapter 13 gives instructions for starting Emacs from the command-line on Windows and Mac OS X.) You can then examine the file to figure out what went wrong.

The other comment is perhaps the most important piece of advice we can give you concerning customizing your Emacs environment: *steal mercilessly from other users*. In particular, if you are dealing with a messy situation involving a configuration problem or a subtle point about some specialized mode, it is possible that some other user has solved the problem(s) already. This is not dishonest or subversive in any way; rather, it is *encouraged* by the makers of GNU Emacs, who would rather software be shared than kept to oneself. Emacs even provides an easy way to try out other users' *.emacs* files: invoke Emacs with the option **-u *username***, and *username*'s *.emacs* file will run instead of yours. (Of course, this works only with users on multiuser systems.)

In fact, numerous example *.emacs* files are available on the Web. (Check out "the very unofficial" *.emacs* site, *http://www.dotemacs.de/*.)

A Sample .emacs File

Here's a quick example of a (very) simple *.emacs* file:

```
;; Turn on font-lock mode to color text in certain modes
(global-font-lock-mode t)

;; Make sure spaces are used when indenting code
(setq-default indent-tabs-mode nil)
```

The lines beginning with two semicolons are comments. They're meant to help you understand what is being configured. Sometimes they also list possible values or the previous value. You can say anything you want in a comment—as long as it fits on one line. If you need to spill over onto a second or third line, just begin each successive line with ;;.

Blank lines are ignored. Every other line (that's not blank or a comment) is considered part of a Lisp program that is executed to configure your Emacs session. In this example, we first call the **global-font-lock-mode** function with an argument of **t** (true, or "on"). Next we make sure that using the **Tab** key when writing code doesn't actually insert a tab character but uses spaces instead. (This is a good thing to do when writing code—otherwise your code can come out very messy on systems that use a different tab width.) We use the **setq-default** function to assign the **indent-tabs-mode** a **nil** (false or "off") value. Using **setq-default** has the advantage of setting the default value only— modes that choose to override this value may still do so.

If you're a seasoned Lisp programmer, you can do anything you would normally have access to in Lisp. There are certainly particular functions and variables you need to know about to be effective, but it is just a Lisp program.

For the rest of us, this file mostly consists of blocks of Lisp found on the Internet or on a colleague's computer. You edit in your personal values and hope it all works. Really. If you use Custom to manage all of your configuration changes, you don't even have to look at *.emacs* unless you want to add your own lines at the beginning of the file or look at what Custom has done.

Editing .emacs

The great thing about configuring a text editor is that you can use the editor itself to make the changes. You can visit the *.emacs* file just as you would any other file. The only thing to watch out for is where you are. Some folks put backup copies of this file in strange places. You want to edit the file that came from your home directory. If you're unsure of where you are, you can use the full name *~/.emacs* which Emacs translates to the proper directory.

Note also that *.emacs* is not required. If you haven't had any reason to customize Emacs, it might not exist. But you should feel free to create it when you're ready to start tailoring your environment. (Making your first change via Custom will also create *.emacs* if it doesn't exist.)

The best way to deal with this file really is to find an example file and make small changes to it. Use those **;;** comments liberally. If you're going to change a line in your *.emacs* file, make a copy of it first:

```
;; Turn off font-lock
;;(global-font-lock-mode t)
(global-font-lock-mode nil)
```

That way you can easily get back to a known, working version of your *.emacs* file. If things get really bad, just start over. Rename your current *.emacs* file and then copy and paste small chunks of it at a time.

For changes required by modules and other packages, the documentation for those modules usually includes example lines for insertion into your *.emacs*. For example, the JDEE site includes a sample *.emacs* file that can be used as-is or appended to an existing file. (And if you want to get fancy, you can leave the JDEE sample in a separate file and simply include a **load-file** call from your *.emacs* file. More on **load-file** can be found in the Elisp documentation.)

Saving .emacs

You save your *.emacs* just as you normally save any file. To test any changes you've made, though, you'll have to do one of two things. The sure-fire method is to quit Emacs and launch it again. If everything comes up the way you expected, you're good to go.

You can also run **M-x load-file**. You'll be prompted for the name of the file. Just type in ~/**.emacs Enter** and you should be able to check your changes.

> Be careful here: it's entirely possible that something in your current session will interact with your new *.emacs* file. For example, if you have already set a default value for a variable, commenting out that line of your *.emacs* file will not remove the value unless you also remove the default value by hand. If you've got a fairly simple configuration, though, you should be fine. Reloading *.emacs* is certainly faster that restarting Emacs!

Either way, once you have verified that your configuration works the way you want, you can forget about this file. Until you want to make more changes, of course!

Modifying Fonts and Colors

Emacs on certain platforms (Windows, Mac OS X, and Unix) can display text in multiple fixed-width fonts. It doesn't yet handle proportional-spacing fonts well, although future releases are expected to address that issue. Emacs can display text in as many combinations of foreground and background colors as your system supports. We'll take a look at your options for changing fonts. You can make quick, interactive changes in any buffer. You can also customize the fonts and colors used by automatic highlight features such as Isearch and font-lock mode.

And just in case you want to use Emacs to edit rudimentary styled-text documents, we'll also look at how to save and load files that have font and color enriched text.

Changing Fonts Interactively

Both Custom and the Edit menu in Emacs provide you with a way to change the current font and color by picking a new one from the Text Properties menu.

To understand the Text Properties menu, you'll find it useful to know that Emacs thinks internally in terms of *faces*. A face is a font and color combination. The Text Properties menu presents you with a small set of premixed faces and the option to specify others by name.

We'll go into more detail about faces, how to name them, and the related Lisp programming constructs later in this chapter. For now, consider simply that every character in a buffer may have a different face invisibly associated with it (though in practice it would be quite surprising if face changes were that frequent!).

Holding down the **Shift** key while clicking the left mouse button takes you to a menu of fonts. Selecting one of these instantly changes the Emacs font for the current frame and redisplays the frame. This is an easy way to experiment with different fonts to see how well they trade screen space for readability on your display.

Automatic Highlighting and Coloring

A number of modules in Emacs feature text highlighting and syntax coloring. The various programming and markup language modes (Lisp mode, Java mode, HTML mode, and so on) have such highlighting. How you customize those fonts and colors depends heavily on the individual module.

Isearch

The Isearch facility in Emacs has undergone a few changes as it has matured. It uses font faces and coloring to highlight a document when you search for words or expressions. You may find the default choices a bit, well, stark. You can customize the group by typing **M-x customize-group** Enter **isearch-faces** Enter to change them.

Incidentally, you might just try changing the face it uses to highlight the secondary matches, so that it's less intrusive.

Buffer highlighting

The easiest way to use fonts and colors is to load the Lisp package *font-lock.el* (included with the Emacs distribution). This mode tries to highlight interesting features of your text buffers using color and different faces. As an example, try picking out comments in C and Lisp buffers, and painting them in a color that contrasts with the basic black of the code.

```
;; Turn on font lock mode every time Emacs initializes a buffer
;; for Lisp or C.
;;
(add-hook 'emacs-lisp-mode-hook 'turn-on-font-lock)
(add-hook 'c-mode-hook 'turn-on-font-lock)
```

Font-lock mode tends to be especially helpful for colorizing programming language code or outline mode text but also gives useful results for HTML files and Dired buffers. In fact, we find it useful in so you may want to turn it on globally instead, as we did in "A Sample *.emacs* file" earlier in this chapter. If you want more examples using font-lock mode, refer back to Chapter 9 on some of the various programming language modes supported by Emacs.

Customizing Fonts Through Custom

Now that you know how to work with Custom, you can also go that route to edit and alter fonts and colors. The easy way to get started in Custom is to run **M-x customize-group** and enter **faces** for the group name. (Figure 10-10 shows a sample of the groups you'll see.)

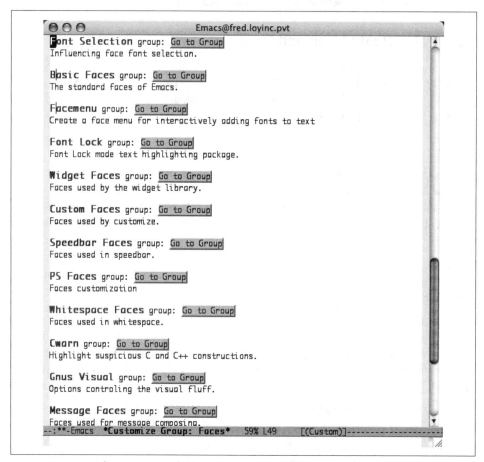

Figure 10-10. Font face groups available in Custom (Mac OS X)

Changing Colors

But what if you just want to change the default foreground and background colors? Well, that turns out to be quite simple. You can use the **M-x set-foreground-color** and **M-x set-background-color** commands to pick simple colors (based on their names such as black, white, yellow, blue, red, etc.). Be careful, though, because Emacs has no qualms about letting you set these values to garish—or even impossible—combinations! While black text on a black background may provide some level of security from anyone peeking over your shoulder, it's not the most productive combination in the long run.

To see the range of colors available, run **M-x set-foreground-color**. When it prompts you for a color, just press Tab to get a completion list of the possible colors—you should get quite a few! These names can also be typed into the foreground and background fields (or any other color-based field) in Custom.

You can also use Custom to control all aspects (including the foreground and background colors) of the "default" font. Figure 10-11 shows the Custom screen for just that font after switching the colors to green and black.

Figure 10-11. Changes to the default font colors effectively set the foreground and background colors for Emacs (Mac OS X)

You can go through the usual channels discussed previously to customize this face, or come here directly with **M-x customize-face** and then enter **default** at the prompt.

Changing the cursor color

Don't forget about the cursor! You can also use **set-cursor-color** to change the color of the cursor. That can be especially useful if you want a black background—the default black cursor can easily get lost.

Saving Font- and Color-Enriched Text

The astute reader will have noticed that, although the highlighting machinery allows us to set up enriched text in a buffer, we haven't shown a way to save text properties along with text between sessions. This is a significant issue. As long as there is no way to save properties along with text, all the font and color machinery remains little more than a display hack, good for decorating buffers but adding little to Emacs's editing power.

What's needed to remedy this situation is a way for text properties to be saved in an expanded text-markup form and restored into text properties when the file is next edited.

At the time of this writing, experimental code to support this is included with Emacs. A library called *enriched-mode* supports saving text properties into the MIME enriched-text format specified by the Internet standards document RFC 1896, and can parse files in that format into Emacs buffers with equivalent text and text properties.

Although this mode is quite usable as is, much design and development still needs to be done before the capabilities enriched mode supports are mature and well integrated with other Emacs modes. By the time you read this, there may be several such libraries, each supporting a different enriched format such as HTML. Eventually modes like these should enable Emacs to support WYSIWYG and even multimedia editing.

To enter enriched mode, type **M-x enriched-mode**. Enriched appears on the mode line. Emacs may ask if you want to make newlines between paragraphs hard. (This is because Emacs reformats the paragraphs when you change margin settings.) Type **y**.

You can use several font commands to decorate your text. Most begin with the **M-g** prefix. Table 10-1 lists some of the more common options. If you like using the menus, you can also select the options in Table 10-1 using the Edit → Text Properties → Face menu.

Table 10-1. Enriched mode font commands

Command	Font selected
M-g d	default
M-g b	bold
M-g i	italic
M-g l	bold-italic
M-g u	underline
M-g o	other (allows you to pick a font face by name)

The commands listed in Table 10-1 apply to the currently marked text. We used a number of these commands to produce the simple text example shown in Figure 10-12.

Saving enriched text

When you save enriched text, Emacs marks up the document with XML-like tags. Emacs will happily read the document back in, although not many other applications will know what to do with the tags. Still, as you can see below, the tags are straightforward and would allow custom applications such as CGI scripts for the Web to parse them quickly.

```
Content-Type: text/enriched
Text-Width: 70
```

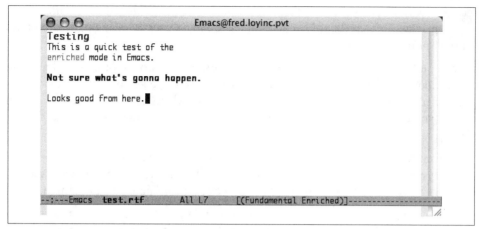

Figure 10-12. An enriched text example (Mac OS X)

```
<x-color><param>blue</param>Testing</x-color>

This is a quick test of the

<x-color><param>red</param>enriched</x-color> mode in Emacs.


<bold>Not sure what's gonna happen.</bold>


Looks good from here.
```

But, you can't rely too much on enriched mode yet. For example note the Testing title line. It doesn't appear to contain any information about the size of the font—which is definitely larger if you look at Figure 10-11. Sure enough, killing the buffer and reloading the file loses the size value. The text is still blue and the content is available, but some of the formatting has been lost.

The moral is a classic one: be careful. If you have serious enriched text needs, Emacs is probably not the tool to use (at least not yet). Many of the various word processors out there will do a much better job. But if you just need some basic enhancements to documents that only you or other Emacs users will view, enriched mode is just the ticket.

Customizing Your Key Bindings

Perhaps the most common things that Emacs users want to customize are the keystrokes that cause commands to run. Keystrokes are associated with commands via *key bindings*.

Actually, every keystroke runs a command in Emacs. Printable character keys (letters, numerals, punctuation, and spaces) run the **self-insert-command**, which merely causes the key just pressed to be inserted at the cursor in the current buffer. (You could play a nasty April Fool's joke on a naïve Emacs user by changing the bindings of their printable characters.)

The default set of key bindings is adequate for most purposes, of course, but there are various cases in which you may want to add or change key bindings. Emacs contains literally hundreds of commands, only some of which have key bindings. As you know, you can access those that don't have bindings by typing **M-x** *command-name* **Enter**.

If, however, you intend to use an unbound command often, you may want to bind it to a keystroke sequence for convenience. You may want to set special keys, such as arrow, numeric keypad, or function keys, to perform commands you use often.

The other important concept you need to know now is that of a *keymap*, which is a collection of key bindings. The most basic default key bindings in Emacs are kept in a keymap called **global-map**. There is also the concept of a *local* keymap, which is specific to a single buffer. Local keymaps are used to implement commands in modes (like C mode, text mode, shell mode, etc.), and each such mode has its own keymap it installs as the local map when invoked. When you type a key, Emacs first looks it up in the current buffer's local map (if any). If it doesn't find an entry there, it looks in **global-map**. If an entry for the key is found, its associated command is run.

What happens with commands that are bound to multiple keystrokes, as in **C-x k** for **kill-buffer**? The answer is that the keys **C-x**, **Esc**, and **C-c** are actually bound to special internal functions that cause Emacs to wait for another key to be pressed and then to look up that key's binding in another map; they also cause messages like **C-x-** to appear in the minibuffer if more than a second passes before the next key is pressed. The additional keymaps for **C-x** and **Esc** are called **ctl-x-map** and **esc-map**,[*] respectively; **C-c** is reserved for local keymaps associated with modes like C mode and shell mode.

For example, when you type **Esc d** or **M-d**, Emacs looks it up in the buffer's local keymap. We will assume it doesn't find an entry there. Then Emacs searches **global-map**; there it finds an entry for **Esc** with a special function (called **ESC-prefix**) that waits for the next keystroke and uses **esc-map** to determine which command to execute. When you type **d**, **ESC-prefix** looks up the entry for **d** in **esc-map**, finds **kill-word**, and runs it.

You can create your own key bindings by adding entries in keymaps (or overriding existing ones). Three functions are available for doing this: **define-key**, **global-set-key**, and **local-set-key**. Their forms are:

```
(define-key keymap "keystroke" 'command-name)
(global-set-key "keystroke" 'command-name)
(local-set-key "keystroke" 'command-name)
```

---

[*] You can use **Meta** in place of **Esc**, but the bindings are still stored in the **esc-map**.

Notice the double quotes around *keystroke* and the single quote preceding *command-name*. This is Lisp syntax; for more details, see Chapter 11. The *keystroke* is one or more characters, either printable or special characters. For the latter, use the conventions in Table 10-2.

Table 10-2. Special character conventions

Special character	Definition
\C-x	C-x (where x is any letter)
\C-[or \e	Esc
\M	Meta
\C-j or \n	Newline
\C-m or \r	Enter
\C-i or \t	Tab

Thus, the string **abc\C-a\ndef** is equal to **abc**, **C-a**, **newline**, and **def**, all concatenated into one string. Note that control characters are case-insensitive—that is, **\C-A** is the same thing as **\C-a**. However, the characters that follow control characters may be case-sensitive; **\C-ae** could be different from **\C-aE**, for example.

The function **define-key** is the most general because it can be used to bind keys in any keymap. **global-set-key** binds keys in the global map only; since there is only one **global-map**, (**global-set-key** ...) is the same as (**define-key global-map** ...). The function **local-set-key** binds keys in the local map of the current buffer; it is useful only for specifying temporary key bindings during an Emacs session.

Here is an example of a simple keyboard customization. Let's say you are writing code in a programming language. You compile it and get error messages that contain the line number of the error, and you want to go to that line in the source file to correct the error.[*] You would want to use the **goto-line** command, which is not bound by default to any keystroke. Say you want to bind it to **C-x l**. The command to put into your *.emacs* file is

```
(global-set-key "\C-xl" 'goto-line)
```

This binds the **l** slot in **ctl-x-map** to the function **goto-line** globally—that is, in all modes. Alternatively, you can use either of the following:

```
(define-key global-map "\C-xl" 'goto-line)
(define-key ctl-x-map "l" 'goto-line)
```

These commands have the same effect but aren't really any more efficient or better. And really, you shouldn't have to know that the keymap for **C-x** is called **ctl-x-map**. We'll stick to showing the **global-set-key** approach for the remaining examples, but

---

[*] There is a better way of dealing with this situation, which we will cover in the next chapter.

remember that you have **define-key** available for situations where setting the global key is not appropriate, such as when adding a mode-specific keystroke.

Other examples of key rebindings include binding **C-x ?** to **help-command** and **C-h** to **backward-char**. These key rebindings are shown below:

```
(global-set-key "\C-x?" 'help-command)
(global-set-key "\C-h" 'backward-char)
```

Notice that these could also be done as

```
(define-key ctl-x-map "?" 'help-command)
(define-key global-map "\C-h" 'backward-char)
```

After you put a key binding (or any other code) in your *.emacs* file, you need to "run" (or evaluate) the file for the change to take effect. The command for this is **M-x eval-current-buffer Enter**. Even better, you could press **C-x C-e**, which (as we will see in the next chapter) causes only the single line of Lisp code that your cursor is on to run. If you don't do either of these, the changes won't take effect until the next time you invoke Emacs.

Special Keys

A more complicated keyboard customization task is binding commands to special keys, such as arrow, numeric keypad, or function keys, on your keyboard. This level of customization takes some work, but if you like using special keys, it is well worth the effort.

Most of the special keys have reasonable names, but using them with the set key functions discussed above requires using a slightly different syntax. The name of the key appears inside square brackets rather than inside double quotes. For example, you could bind the **goto-line** command to the function key F5 like this:

```
(global-set-key [f5] 'goto-line)
```

And you can certainly use modifiers with your special keys. Control-Alt-F5 can be bound like this:

```
(global-set-key [C-A-f5] 'goto-line)
```

Table 10-3 lists the names of some common special keys.

Table 10-3. Special key ELisp names

ELisp Name	Key	ELisp Name	Key
DEL or backspace	Backspace	kp-0 .. kp-9	Keypad numbers 0 through 9
delete	Delete key	kp-enter	Enter key on the number pad
down	Down arrow key	left	Left arrow key
end	End key	next	Page Down

Table 10-3. Special key ELisp names (continued)

ELisp Name	Key	ELisp Name	Key
f1 .. f35	Function keys F1 through F35	prior	Page Up
home	Home key	right	Right arrow key
help	Help key	up	Up arrow key

Unsetting Key Bindings

You can also remove a particular key binding with the **global-unset-key** and **define-key** commands. For example, the following lines will both remove the **goto-line** command bindings from our previous examples:

```
(global-unset-key [f5])
(define-key ctl-x-map "l" nil)
```

Of course, you don't need to unset any bindings if you plan to replace them with something else. But this can be useful if you have a common "typo" key that you don't want firing off when you type it by mistake.

Setting Emacs Variables

Now we will get into ways to affect Emacs' behavior—not just its user interface. The easiest way to do so is by setting variables that control various things. We already saw examples of this like **auto-save-interval** in Chapter 2. To set the value of a variable, use the **setq** function in your *.emacs*, as in:

```
(setq auto-save-interval 800)
```

Although **auto-save-interval** takes an *integer* (number) value, many Emacs variables take true or false values, called *Boolean* in computer parlance. In Emacs Lisp, **t** is the true value, and **nil** is the false value, although in most cases, anything other than **nil** is taken to mean true. Emacs variables can take other types of values, and here is how to specify them:

- *Strings* of characters are surrounded by double quotes. We saw examples of strings in the arguments to key binding commands earlier in this chapter.

- *Characters* are specified like strings but with a **?** preceding them, and they are not surrounded by double quotes. Thus, **?x** and **?\C-c** are character values **x** and **C-c**, respectively.

- *Symbols* are given by a single quote followed by a symbol name—for example, **'never** (see the variable **version-control** in Appendix A).

A list of useful Emacs variables, grouped by category, appears in Appendix A, with descriptions and default values. Emacs has more than 2,500 variables—many more than are covered in Appendix A. If there is something about Emacs that you want to customize, a variable probably controls the feature (especially if what you want to change involves a number or a true-or-false condition). To find out whether any variables relate to what you want to do, you can use the **apropos-variable** command described in Chapter 14 to look for variables and their descriptions.

Several Emacs variables can have different values for each buffer (*local* values, in Emacs parlance) as well as a *default* value. Such variables assume their default values in buffers where the local values are not specified. A common example is starting a new text document. The local value for the **left-margin** variable has not been set, so Emacs uses the default value for **left-margin**. You can change the local value in this buffer if you like. But start a new document in a new buffer and you'll find that **left-margin** is back to the default value—because the second buffer's local value has not been set.

As you might expect, you can set both the default and local values of such variables. When you set the value of a variable such as **left-margin** or **case-fold-search** with **setq**, you are actually setting the local value. The way to set default values is to use **setq-default** instead of **setq**, as in:

```
(setq-default left-margin 4)
```

Unfortunately, there is no general way to tell whether a variable has just one global value or has default and local values (except, of course, by looking at the Lisp code for the mode). Therefore the best strategy is to use a plain **setq**, *unless* you find from experience that a particular variable doesn't seem to take on the value you **setq** it to—in which case you should use **setq-default**. For example, if you put the line:

```
(setq case-fold-search nil)
```

in your *.emacs* file, you will find that Emacs still ignores case differences in search commands as if this variable were still **t**; instead, you should use **setq-default**.

Finding Emacs Lisp Packages

Emacs contains lots of Lisp code; in fact, as we will see in Chapter 11, the majority of Emacs' built-in functionality is written in Lisp. Emacs also comes with several extra Lisp *packages* (also known as *libraries*) that you can bring in (or *load*) to add more features. Lisp packages are being added to Emacs all the time, and sometimes your system administrator will add packages obtained from sources other than the Free Software Foundation.

Appendix B lists the most useful *built-in* Lisp packages, along with explanations of how to use them. You can also get information about which packages are available on your system by typing **C-h p** (for **finder-by-keyword**). Briefly, the built-in packages do the following kinds of things:

- Support programming in C, Lisp, Perl, Java, and several other languages (see Chapter 9).
- Support text processing with TEX, LATEX, XML, and HTML (see Chapter 8).

- Emulate other editors (**vi**, **EDT**, and Gosling Emacs).
- Interface to operating system utilities, such as the shell (see Chapter 5).
- Provide editing support functions, such as spell checking (see Chapter 3) and outline editing (see Chapter 7) as well as text sorting, command history editing, Emacs variable setting (see Appendix A), and much more.
- Play various games and provide other forms of amusement.

See Appendix B for more details.

Starting Modes via Auto-Mode Customization

The tables in Appendix B list several major modes that are automatically invoked when you visit a file whose name ends in the appropriate suffix. Look for "suffix" in the right-hand columns of the tables to see many of the associations between file-name suffixes and major modes that Emacs sets up by default. These associations are contained in the special Emacs variable **auto-mode-alist**. **auto-mode-alist** is a list of pairs (*regexp . mode*), where *regexp* is a regular expression (see Chapters 3 and 11) and *mode* is the name of a function that invokes a major mode. When Emacs visits a file, it searches this list (from the beginning) for a regular expression that matches the file's suffix. If it finds one, it runs the associated mode function. Notice that *any* part of a file's name—not just its suffix—can actually be associated with a major mode.

You can add your own associations to **auto-mode-alist**, although the syntax is weird if you are not used to Lisp (see Chapter 11 for the gory details). If you are programming in the Ada language, and your Ada compiler expects files with suffix *.ada*, you can get Emacs to put your files in Ada mode whenever you visit them by putting the following line in your *.emacs* file:

```
(setq auto-mode-alist (cons '("\\.ada$" . ada-mode) auto-mode-alist))
```

Make sure you include the single quote after the term cons and the dot between "\\.ada$" and ada-mode. The notation '(x . y) is just Lisp syntax for "make x and y a pair." The string "\\.ada$" is a regular expression that means "anything with . *ada* at the end of it," that is, $ matches the end of the string (as opposed to the end of the line, which is what it matches during regular expression search and replace). The entire line of Lisp basically means "add the pair ("\\.ada$", 'ada-mode) to the front of the auto-mode-alist." Note that, because Emacs searches **auto-mode-alist** from the beginning and stops when it finds a match, you can use the above **cons** construct to override existing mode associations.[*]

---

[*] Lisp programmers will understand that there are other ways to add to **auto-mode-alist**, such as **append**.

As another example, let's say you save certain mail messages in files whose names begin with *msg-*, and you want to edit these files in text mode. Here is the way to do it:

```
(setq auto-mode-alist (cons '("^msg-" . text-mode) auto-mode-alist))
```

Notice that in this case we are matching the *beginning*, rather than the end, of the filename. The regular expression operator (^) means beginning of string, so the entire regular expression means "anything beginning with msg-."

Finally, if the name of a file you are editing does not match any of the regular expressions in **auto-mode-alist**, Emacs puts it into the mode whose name is the value of the variable **default-major-mode**. This mode is normally fundamental mode, a basic mode without special functionality. However, many people like to set their default mode to text mode, accomplished by adding a line like this to *.emacs*:

```
(setq default-major-mode 'text-mode)
```

Although we have covered many useful ways to customize Emacs in this chapter, we have really only scratched the surface. To find out more, turn to Chapter 11 and find out about Lisp programming, the key to getting Emacs to do just about anything you want.

Making Emacs Work the Way You Think It Should

Emacs not only has per-user customizations; it can also have sitewide customizations. If Emacs isn't doing what you expect it to, you might want to try inhibiting any global customization file by starting Emacs with no customization.

You can do that by using one of these command-line options when you invoke Emacs.

- **--no-init-file**, **-q**   *load neither ~/.emacs nor default.el*
- **--no-site-file**   *do not load site-start.el*

If you normally start Emacs from an icon, it's helpful to learn how to start it from the command-line for cases like this. (You may also want to use the –debug option sometime to help you figure out what's wrong with your *.emacs* file if it is messed up following a change.) Chapter 13 describes how to start Emacs from the command-line for Mac OS X and Windows users.

You can also inhibit global initialization by creating a one-line *.emacs* file in your home directory. It should look exactly like this:

```
(setq inhibit-default-init t) ; no global initialization
```

Start Emacs again. This file prevents Emacs from reading its global initialization file.

There's still one awkward situation: what if you're sitting down at someone else's system? You start Emacs, and all of a sudden you're faced with someone else's "private" key bindings and features. Even in this situation, there's a solution:

- Try using the command **emacs -q**. The **-q** option tells Emacs not to read the user's *.emacs* file before starting. By doing this, you'll avoid the user's private customizations.

- Let's say that after this step, you still don't have your own customizations. If you want to make Emacs read your *.emacs* file, even when you're using someone else's account, give the command **emacs -u *yourname***. For example: **emacs -u deb** starts Emacs with the user Deb's initialization file (*/home/deb/.emacs*).

The -u option may not work unless you're on a network where users have a shared home directory structure. It assumes either that you have the same home directory on every system, or that you have a different home directory on every system and an up-to-date *.emacs* file in all of your home directories.

If all that fails, fear not. You have more options. Let's take the worst case scenario: you're on someone else's system and you can't start Emacs from the command line. Go ahead and start Emacs. You can temporarily overwrite the other user's key bindings by loading up your own key bindings file in a buffer and running it with **M-x eval-buffer**.

You probably should make a separate file with key bindings and other variable options rather than using your *.emacs* file. That's because many times your *.emacs* file will have requests to load libraries that exist on a path that works only from your own system. If you find yourself jumping to a lot of different machines, it's worth the effort to create a portable "rebinding" file and put it somewhere accessible like a web page or a shared file server. Then you can evaluate it manually from your current Emacs.

CHAPTER 11

Emacs Lisp Programming

If you have been using Emacs for a while and have been taking advantage of some of its more advanced features, chances are that you have thought of something useful that Emacs doesn't do. Although Emacs has hundreds of built-in commands, dozens of packages and modes, and so on, everyone eventually runs into some functionality that Emacs doesn't have. Whatever feature you find missing, you can program using Emacs Lisp.

Before you dive in, however, note that this chapter is not for everyone. It is intended for people who have already become comfortable using Emacs and who have a fair bit of programming experience, though not necessarily with Lisp *per se*. If you have no such experience, you may want to skip this chapter; if there is something specific you would like Emacs to do, you might try to find a friendly Emacs Lisp hacker to help you write the necessary code. Or, if you're a little adventurous, you could skim enough to find the file-template example and learn how to install it—it gives you some useful features.

Readers who are building their Lisp skills but don't necessarily want to read the whole chapter might also want to look for the "Treasure Trove of Examples" section in the middle for a useful tool that can help jumpstart their exploration of the Emacs libraries.

Note that we do not cover Lisp in its entirety in this chapter. That would require another large, dense book. Instead, we cover the basics of the language and other features that are often useful in writing Emacs code. If you wish to go beyond this chapter, refer to the *GNU Emacs Lisp Reference Manual*, distributed with Emacs (choose Help → More Manuals → Introduction to Lisp and Emacs Lisp Reference) for details about the specific Lisp features in Emacs. You may also turn to any of the various Lisp textbooks[*] available for a solid grounding in the language itself.

---

[*] We recommend *Lisp* by Patrick Henry Winston and Berthold Klaus Paul Horn (Addison Wesley).

Emacs Lisp is a full-blown Lisp implementation;* thus it is more than the usual macro or script language found in many text editors. (One of the authors has written a small expert system entirely in Emacs Lisp.) In fact, you could even think of Emacs itself as a Lisp system with lots of built-in functions, many of which happen to pertain to text manipulation, window management, file I/O, and other features useful to text editing. The source code for Emacs, written in C, implements the Lisp interpreter, Lisp primitives, and only the most basic commands for text editing; a large layer of built-in Lisp code and libraries on top of that implements the rest of Emacs's functionality. A current version of Emacs comes with close to 250,000 lines of Lisp.

This chapter starts with an introduction to the aspects of Lisp that resemble common programming languages like Java and Perl. These features are enough to enable you to write many Emacs commands. Then we deal with how to interface Lisp code with Emacs so that the functions you write can become Emacs commands. We will see various built-in Lisp functions that are useful for writing your own Emacs commands, including those that use regular expressions; we give an explanation of regular expressions that extends the introduction in Chapter 3 and is oriented toward Lisp programming. We then return to the basics of Lisp for a little while, covering the unique features of the language that have to do with lists, and show how this chapter's concepts fit together by presenting a file template system you can install and use in your own programming or writing projects.

Finally we show you how to program a simple major mode, illustrating that this "summit" of Emacs Lisp programming isn't so hard to scale. After that, you will see how easy it is to customize Emacs's built-in major modes without having to change (or even look at) the code that implements them. We finish the chapter by describing how to build your own library of Lisp packages.

Introduction to Lisp

You may have heard of Lisp as a language for artificial intelligence (AI). If you aren't into AI, don't worry. Lisp may have an unusual syntax, but many of its basic features are just like those of more conventional languages you may have seen, such as Java or Perl. We emphasize such features in this chapter. After introducing the basic Lisp concepts, we proceed by building up various example functions that you can actually use in Emacs. In order to try out the examples, you should be familiar with Emacs Lisp mode and Lisp interaction mode, which were discussed in Chapter 9.

---

* Experienced Lisp programmers should note that Emacs Lisp most closely resembles MacLisp, with a few Common Lisp features added. More complete Common Lisp emulation can be had by loading the package cl (see Appendix B).

Basic Lisp Entities

The basic elements in Lisp you need to be familiar with are functions, variables, and atoms. Functions are the only *program units* in Lisp; they cover the notions of procedures, subroutines, programs, and even operators in other languages.

Functions are defined as lists of the above entities, usually as lists of calls to other, existing functions. All functions have *return values* (as with Perl functions and non-void Java methods); a function's return value is simply the value of the last item in the list, usually the value returned by the last function called. A function call within another function is equivalent to a *statement* in other languages, and we use statement interchangeably with function call in this chapter. Here is the syntax for function:

```
(function-name argument1 argument2 ...)
```

which is equivalent to this:

```
method_name (argument1, argument2, ...);
```

in Java. This syntax is used for all functions, including those equivalent to arithmetic or comparison operators in other languages. For example, in order to add 2 and 4 in Java or Perl, you would use the expression 2 + 4, whereas in Lisp you would use the following:

```
(+ 2 4)
```

Similarly, where you would use 4 >= 2 (greater than or equal to), the Lisp equivalent is:

```
(>= 4 2)
```

Variables in Lisp are similar to those in any other language, except that they do not have *types*. A Lisp variable can assume any type of value (values themselves do have types, but variables don't impose restrictions on what they can hold).

Atoms are values of any type, including integers, floating point (real) numbers, characters, strings, Boolean truth values, symbols, and special Emacs types such as buffers, windows, and processes. The syntax for various kinds of atoms is:

- **Integers** are what you would expect: signed whole numbers in the range -2^{27} to $2^{27}-1$.

- **Floating point numbers** are real numbers that you can represent with decimal points and scientific notation (with lowercase "e" for the power of 10). For example, the number 5489 can be written 5489, 5.489e3, 548.9e1, and so on.

- **Characters** are preceded by a question mark, for example, ?a. **Esc**, **Newline**, and **Tab** are abbreviated \e, \n, and \t respectively; other control characters are denoted with the prefix \C-, so that (for example) **C-a** is denoted as ?\C-a.[*]

---

[*] Integers are also allowed where characters are expected. The ASCII code is used on most machines. For example, the number 65 is interpreted as the character A on such a machine.

- **Strings** are surrounded by double quotes; quote marks and backslashes within strings need to be preceded by a backslash. For example, `"Jane said, \"See Dick run.\""` is a legal string. Strings can be split across multiple lines without any special syntax. Everything until the closing quote, including all the line breaks, is part of the string value.

- **Booleans** use `t` for true and `nil` for false, though most of the time, if a Boolean value is expected, any non-`nil` value is assumed to mean true. `nil` is also used as a null or nonvalue in various situations, as we will see.

- **Symbols** are names of things in Lisp, for example, names of variables or functions. Sometimes it is important to refer to the *name* of something instead of its value, and this is done by preceding the name with a single quote (`'`). For example, the **define-key** function, described in Chapter 10, uses the *name* of the command (as a symbol) rather than the command itself.

A simple example that ties many of these basic Lisp concepts together is the function **setq**.[*] As you may have figured out from previous chapters, **setq** is a way of assigning values to variables, as in

```
(setq auto-save-interval 800)
```

Notice that **setq** is a function, unlike in other languages in which special syntax such as = or := is used for assignment. **setq** takes two arguments: a variable name and a value. In this example, the variable **auto-save-interval** (the number of keystrokes between auto-saves) is set to the value 800.

setq can actually be used to assign values to multiple variables, as in

```
(setq thisvar thisvalue
      thatvar thatvalue
      theothervar theothervalue)
```

The return value of **setq** is simply the last value assigned, in this case *theothervalue*. You can set the values of variables in other ways, as we'll see, but **setq** is the most widely applicable.

Defining Functions

Now it's time for an example of a simple function definition. Start Emacs without any arguments; this puts you into the *scratch* buffer, an empty buffer in Lisp interaction mode (see Chapter 9), so that you can actually try this and subsequent examples.

Before we get to the example, however, some more comments on Lisp syntax are necessary. First, you will notice that the dash (-) is used as a "break" character to

---

[*] We hope that Lisp purists will forgive us for calling **setq** a function, for the sake of simplicity, rather than a *form*, which it technically is.

separate words in names of variables, functions, and so on. This practice is simply a widely used Lisp programming convention; thus the dash takes the place of the underscore (_) in languages like C and Ada. A more important issue has to do with all of the parentheses in Lisp code. Lisp is an *old* language that was designed before anyone gave much thought to language syntax (it was still considered amazing that you could use any language other than the native processor's binary instruction set), so its syntax is not exactly programmer-friendly. Yet Lisp's heavy use of lists—and thus its heavy use of parentheses—has its advantages, as we'll see toward the end of this chapter.

The main problem a programmer faces is how to keep all the parentheses balanced properly. Compounding this problem is the usual programming convention of putting multiple right parentheses at the end of a line, rather than the more readable technique of placing each right parenthesis directly below its matching left parenthesis. Your best defense against this is the support the Emacs Lisp modes give you, particularly the **Tab** key for proper indentation and the flash-matching-parenthesis feature.

Now we're ready for our example function. Suppose you are a student or journalist who needs to keep track of the number of words in a paper or story you are writing. Emacs has no built-in way of counting the number of words in a buffer, so we'll write a Lisp function that does the job:

```
1  (defun count-words-buffer ( )
2    (let ((count 0))
3      (save-excursion
4        (goto-char (point-min))
5        (while (< (point) (point-max))
6          (forward-word 1)
7          (setq count (1+ count)))
8        (message "buffer contains %d words." count))))
```

Let's go through this function line by line and see what it does. (Of course, if you are trying this in Emacs, don't type the line numbers in.)

The **defun** on line 1 defines the function by its name and arguments. Notice that **defun** is itself a function—one that, when called, defines a new function. (**defun** returns the name of the function defined, as a symbol.) The function's arguments appear as a list of names inside parentheses; in this case, the function has no arguments. Arguments can be made *optional* by preceding them with the keyword **&optional**. If an argument is optional and not supplied when the function is called, its value is assumed to be nil.

Line 2 contains a **let** construct, whose general form is:

```
(let ((var1 value1) (var2 value2) ... )
  statement-block)
```

The first thing **let** does is define the variables var1, var2, etc., and set them to the initial values value1, value2, etc. Then **let** executes the *statement block*, which is a sequence of function calls or values, just like the body of a function.

It is useful to think of **let** as doing three things:

- Defining (or declaring) a list of variables
- Setting the variables to initial values, as if with **setq**
- Creating a block in which the variables are known; the **let** block is known as the *scope* of the variables

If a **let** is used to define a variable, its value can be reset later within the **let** block with **setq**. Furthermore, a variable defined with **let** can have the same name as a global variable; all **setq**s on that variable within the **let** block act on the local variable, leaving the global variable undisturbed. However, a **setq** on a variable that is not defined with a **let** affects the global environment. It is advisable to avoid using global variables as much as possible because their names might conflict with those of existing global variables and therefore your changes might have unexpected and inexplicable side effects later on.

So, in our example function, we use **let** to define the local variable **count** and initialize it to 0. As we will see, this variable is used as a loop counter.

Lines 3 through 8 are the statements within the **let** block. The first of these calls the built-in Emacs function **save-excursion**, which is a way of being polite. The function is going to move the cursor around the buffer, so we don't want to disorient the user by jumping them to a strange place in their file just because they asked for a word count. Calling **save-excursion** tells Emacs to remember the location of cursor at the beginning of the function, and go back there after executing any statements in its body. Notice how **save-excursion** is providing us with capability similar to **let**; you can think of it as a way of making the cursor location itself a local variable.

Line 4 calls **goto-char**. The argument to **goto-char** is a (nested) function call to the built-in function **point-min**. As we have mentioned before, *point* is Emacs's internal name for the position of the cursor, and we'll refer to the cursor as point throughout the remainder of this chapter. **point-min** returns the value of the first character position in the current buffer, which is almost always 1; then, **goto-char** is called with the value 1, which has the effect of moving point to the beginning of the buffer.

The next line sets up a **while** loop; Java and Perl have a similar construct. The **while** construct has the general form

```
(while condition    statement-block)
```

Like **let** and **save-excursion**, **while** sets up another statement block. **condition** is a value (an atom, a variable, or a function returning a value). This value is tested; if it is nil, the condition is considered to be false, and the **while** loop terminates. If the value is other than nil, the condition is considered to be true, the statement block gets executed, the condition is tested again, and the process repeats.

Of course, it is possible to write an infinite loop. If you write a Lisp function with a **while** loop and try running it, and your Emacs session hangs, chances are that you have made this all-too-common mistake; just type **C-g** to abort it.

In our sample function, the condition is the function <, which is a less-than function with two arguments, analogous to the < operator in Java or Perl. The first argument is another function that returns the current character position of point; the second argument returns the maximum character position in the buffer, that is, the length of the buffer. The function < (and other relational functions) return a Boolean value, t or nil.

The loop's statement block consists of two statements. Line 6 moves point forward one word (i.e., as if you had typed **M-f**). Line 7 increments the loop counter by 1; the function 1+ is shorthand for (+ 1 variable-name). Notice that the third right parenthesis on line 7 matches the left parenthesis preceding **while**. So, the **while** loop causes Emacs to go through the current buffer a word at a time while counting the words.

The final statement in the function uses the built-in function **message** to print a message in the minibuffer saying how many words the buffer contains. The form of the **message** function will be familiar to C programmers. The first argument to **message** is a format string, which contains text and special formatting instructions of the form %x, where x is one of a few possible letters. For each of these instructions, in the order in which they appear in the format string, message reads the next argument and tries to interpret it according to the letter after the percent sign. Table 11-1 lists meanings for the letters in the format string.

Table 11-1. Message format strings

Format string	Meaning
%s	String or symbol
%c	Character
%d	Integer
%e	Floating point in scientific notation
%f	Floating point in decimal-point notation
%g	Floating point in whichever format yields the shortest string

For example:

```
(message "\"%s\" is a string, %d is a number, and %c is a character"
         "hi there" 142 ?q)
```

causes the message:

```
"hi there" is a string, 142 is a number, and q is a character
```

to appear in the minibuffer. This is analogous to the C code:

```
printf ("\"%s\" is a string, %d is a number, and %c is a character\n",
        "hi there", 142, 'q');
```

The floating-point-format characters are a bit more complicated. They assume a certain number of significant digits unless you tell them otherwise. For example, the following:

```
(message "This book was printed in %f, also known as %e." 2004 2004)
```

yields this:

```
This book was printed in 2004.000000, also known as 2.004000e+03.
```

But you can control the number of digits after the decimal point by inserting a period and the number of digits desired between the % and the e, f, or g. For example, this:

```
(message "This book was printed in %.3e, also known as %.0f." 2004 2004)
```

prints in the minibuffer:

```
This book was printed in 2.004e+03, also known as 2004.
```

Turning Lisp Functions into Emacs Commands

The **count-words-buffer** function that we've just finished works, but it still isn't as convenient to use as the Emacs commands you work with daily. If you have typed it in, try it yourself. First you need to get Emacs to evaluate the lines you typed in, thereby actually defining the function. To do this, move your cursor to just after the last closing parenthesis in the function and type **C-j** (or **Linefeed**)—the "evaluate" key in Lisp interaction mode—to tell Emacs to perform the function definition. You should see the name of the function appear again in the buffer; the return value of the **defun** function is the symbol that has been defined. (If instead you get an error message, double check that your function looks exactly like the example and that you haven't typed in the line numbers, and try again.)

Once the function is defined, you can execute it by typing **(count-words-buffer)** on its own line in your Lisp interaction window, and once again typing **C-j** after the closing parenthesis.

Now that you can execute the function correctly from a Lisp interaction window, try executing the function with **M-x**, as with any other Emacs command. Try typing **M-x count-words-buffer Enter**: you will get the error message [No match]. (You can type **C-g** to cancel this failed attempt.) You get this error message because you need to "register" a function with Emacs to make it available for interactive use. The function to do this is **interactive**, which has the form:

```
(interactive "prompt-string")
```

This statement should be the first in a function, that is, right after the line containing the **defun** and the documentation string (which we will cover shortly). Using **interactive** causes Emacs to register the function as a command and to prompt the user for the arguments declared in the **defun** statement. The prompt string is optional.

The prompt string has a special format: for each argument you want to prompt the user for, you provide a section of prompt string. The sections are separated by newlines (\n). The first letter of each section is a code for the type of argument you want. There are many choices; the most commonly used are listed in Table 11-2.

Table 11-2. Argument codes for interactive functions

Code	User is prompted for:
b	Name of an existing buffer
e	Event (mouse action or function key press)
f	Name of an existing file
n	Number (integer)
s	String
	Most of these have uppercase variations
B	Name of a buffer that may not exist
F	Name of a file that may not exist
N	Number, unless command is invoked with a prefix argument, in which case use the prefix argument and skip this prompt
S	Symbol

With the **b** and **f** options, Emacs signals an error if the buffer or file given does not already exist. Another useful option to **interactive** is **r**, which we will see later. There are many other option letters; consult the documentation for function **interactive** for the details. The rest of each section is the actual prompt that appears in the minibuffer.

The way **interactive** is used to fill in function arguments is somewhat complicated and best explained through an example. A simple example is in the function **goto-percent**, which we will see shortly. It contains the statement

```
(interactive "nPercent: ")
```

The n in the prompt string tells Emacs to prompt for an integer; the string `Percent:` appears in the minibuffer.

As a slightly more complicated example, let's say we want to write our own version of the **replace-string** command. Here's how we would do the prompting:

```
(defun replace-string (from to)
  (interactive "sReplace string: \nsReplace string %s with: ")
  ...)
```

The prompt string consists of two sections, `sReplace string:` and `sReplace string %s with:`, separated by a Newline. The initial s in each means that a string is expected; the `%s` is a formatting operator (as in the previous **message** function) that Emacs replaces with the user's response to the first prompt. When applying formatting operators in a prompt, it is as if **message** has been called with a list of all responses read so far, so the first formatting operator is applied to the first response, and so on.

When this command is invoked, first the prompt `Replace string:` appears in the minibuffer. Assume the user types **fred** in response. After the user presses **Enter**, the prompt `Replace fred with:` appears. The user types the replacement string and presses **Enter** again.

The two strings the user types are used as values of the function arguments **from** and **to** (in that order), and the command runs to completion. Thus, **interactive** supplies values to the function's arguments in the order of the sections of the prompt string.

The use of **interactive** does not preclude calling the function from other Lisp code; in this case, the calling function needs to supply values for all arguments. For example, if we were interested in calling our version of **replace-string** from another Lisp function that needs to replace all occurrences of "Bill" with "Deb" in a file, we would use

```
(replace-string "Bill" "Deb")
```

The function is not being called interactively in this case, so the **interactive** statement has no effect; the argument **from** is set to "Bill," and **to** is set to "Deb."

Getting back to our **count-words-buffer** command: it has no arguments, so its **interactive** command does not need a prompt string. The final modification we want to make to our command is to add a *documentation string* (or *doc string* for short), which is shown by online help facilities such as **describe-function** (**C-h f**). Doc strings are normal Lisp strings; they are optional and can be arbitrarily many lines long, although, by convention, the first line is a terse, complete sentence summarizing the command's functionality. Remember that any double quotes inside a string need to be preceded by backslashes.

With all of the fixes taken into account, the complete function looks like this:

```
(defun count-words-buffer ()
  "Count the number of words in the current buffer;
print a message in the minibuffer with the result."
  (interactive)
  (save-excursion
    (let ((count 0))
      (goto-char (point-min))
      (while (< (point) (point-max))
        (forward-word 1)
        (setq count (1+ count)))
      (message "buffer contains %d words." count))))
```

Lisp Primitive Functions

Now that you've seen how to write a working command, we'll discuss Lisp's primitive functions. These are the building blocks from which you'll build your functions. As mentioned above, Lisp uses functions where other languages would use operators, that is, for arithmetic, comparison, and logic. Table 11-3 shows some Lisp primitive functions that are equivalent to these operators.

Table 11-3. Lisp primitive functions

Arithmetic	+, -, *, /
	% (remainder)
	1+ (increment)
	1- (decrement)
	max, min
Comparison	>, <, >=, <=
	/= (not equal)
	= (for numbers and characters)
	equal (for strings and other complex objects)
Logic	and, or, not

All the arithmetic functions except 1+, 1-, and % can take arbitrarily many arguments, as can and and or. An arithmetic function returns floating point values only if at least one argument is a floating point number, so for example, (/ 7.0 4) returns 1.75, and (/ 7 4) returns 1. Notice that integer division truncates the remainder.

It may seem inefficient or syntactically ugly to use functions for everything. However, one of the main merits of Lisp is that the core of the language is small and easy to interpret efficiently. In addition, the syntax is not as much of a problem if you have support tools such as Emacs's Lisp modes to help you.

Statement Blocks

We have seen that a statement block can be defined using the **let** function. We also saw that **while** and **save-excursion** include statement blocks. Other important constructs also define statement blocks: **progn** and other forms of **let**.

progn, the most basic, has the form:

```
(progn
  statement-block)
```

progn is a simple way of making a block of statements look like a single one, somewhat like the curly braces of Java or the begin and end of Pascal. The value returned by **progn** is the value returned by the last statement in the block. **progn** is especially useful with control structures like **if** (see the following discussion) that, unlike **while**, do not include statement blocks.

The **let** function has other forms as well. The simplest is:

```
(let (var1 var2 ...)
  statement-block)
```

In this case, instead of a list of (var value) pairs, there is simply a list of variable names. As with the other form of let, these become local variables accessible in the statement block. However, instead of initializing them to given values, they are all just initialized to **nil**. You can actually mix both forms within the same **let** statement, for example:

```
(let (var1 (var2 value2) var3 ...)
  statement-block)
```

In the form of **let** we saw first, the initial values for the local variables can be function calls (remember that all functions return values). All such functions are evaluated before any values are assigned to variables. However, there may be cases in which you want the values of some local variables to be available for computing the values of others. This is where **let***, the final version of **let**, comes in. **let*** steps through its assignments in order, assigning each local variable a value before moving on to the next.

For example, let's say we want to write a function **goto-percent** that allows you to go to a place in the current buffer expressed as a percentage of the text in the buffer. Here is one way to write this function:

```
(defun goto-percent (pct)
  (interactive "nGoto percent: ")
  (let* ((size (point-max))
         (charpos (/ (* size pct) 100)))
    (goto-char charpos)))
```

As we saw earlier, the **interactive** function is used to prompt users for values of arguments. In this case, it prompts for the integer value of the argument **pct**. Then the **let*** function initializes **size** to the size of the buffer in characters, then uses that value to compute the character position **charpos** that is **pct** (percent) of the buffer's size. Finally, the call of **goto-char** causes point to be moved to that character position in the current window.

The important thing to notice is that if we had used **let** instead of **let***, the value of **size** would not be available when computing the value of **charpos**. **let*** can also be used in the (var1 var2 ...) format, just like **let**, but there wouldn't be any point in doing so.

We should also note that a more efficient way to write **goto-percent** is this:

```
(defun goto-percent (pct)
  (interactive "nPercent: ")
  (goto-char (/ (* pct (point-max)) 100)))
```

Control Structures

We already saw that the **while** function acts as a control structure like similar statements in other languages. There are two other important control structures in Lisp: **if** and **cond**.

The **if** function has the form:

```
(if condition true-case false-block)
```

Here, the condition is evaluated; if it is non-**nil**, *true-case* is evaluated; if **nil**, *false-block* is evaluated. Note that *true-case* is a single statement whereas *false-block* is a statement block; *false-block* is optional.

As an example, let's suppose we're writing a function that performs some complicated series of edits to a buffer and then reports how many changes it made. We're perfectionists, so we want the status report to be properly pluralized, that is to say "made 53 changes" or "made 1 change." This is a common enough programming need that we decide to write a general-purpose function to do it so that we can use it in other projects too.

The function takes two arguments: the word to be pluralized (if necessary) and the count to be displayed (which determines whether it's necessary).

```
(defun pluralize (word count)
  (if (= count 1)
      word
    (concat word "s")))
```

The condition in the **if** clause tests to see if **count** is equal to 1. If so, the first statement gets executed. Remember that the "true" part of the **if** function is only one statement, so **progn** would be necessary to make a statement block if we wanted to do more than one thing. In this case, we have the opposite extreme; our "true" part is a single variable, **word**. Although this looks strange, it is actually a very common Lisp idiom and worth getting used to. When the condition block is true, the value of **word** is evaluated, and this value becomes the value of the entire **if** statement. Because that's the last statement in our function, it is the value returned by **pluralize**. Note that this is exactly the result we want when **count** is 1: the value of **word** is returned unchanged.

The remaining portion of the **if** statement is evaluated when the condition is false, which is to say, when **count** has a value other than 1. This results in a call to the built-in **concat** function, which concatenates all its arguments into a single string. In this case it adds an "s" at the end of the word we've passed in. Again, the result of this concatenation becomes the result of the **if** statement and the result of our **pluralize** function.

If you type it in and try it out, you'll see results like this:

```
(pluralize "goat" 5)
"goats"
```

```
(pluralize "change" 1)
"change"
```

Of course, this function can be tripped up easily enough. You may have tried something like this already:

```
(pluralize "mouse" 5)
"mouses"
```

To fix this, we'd need to be able to tell the function to use an alternate plural form for tricky words. But it would be nice if the simple cases could remain as simple as they are now. This is a good opportunity to use an optional parameter. If necessary, we supply the plural form to use; if we don't supply one, the function acts as it did in its first incarnation. Here's how we'd achieve that:

```
(defun pluralize (word count &optional plural)
  (if (= count 1)
      word
    (if (null plural)
        (concat word "s")
      plural)))
```

The "else" part of our code has become another **if** statement. It uses the **null** function to check whether we were given the **plural** parameter or not. If **plural** was omitted, it has the value **nil** and the **null** function returns **t** if its argument is **nil**. So this logic reads "if **b** was missing, just add an **s** to **word**; otherwise return the special **plural** value we were given."

This gives us results like this:

```
(pluralize "mouse" 5)
"mouses"
(pluralize "mouse" 5 "mice")
"mice"
(pluralize "mouse" 1 "mice")
"mouse"
```

A more general conditional control structure is the **cond** function, which has the following form:

```
(cond
  (condition1    statement-block1)
  (condition2    statement-block2)
  ...)
```

Java and Perl programmers can think of this as a sequence of *if then else if then else if…*, or as a kind of generalized switch statement. The conditions are evaluated in order, and when one of them evaluates to non-nil, the corresponding statement block is executed; the **cond** function terminates and returns the last value in that statement block.*

We can use **cond** to give a more folksy feel to our hypothetical status reporter now that it's pluralizing nicely. Instead of reporting an actual numeric value for the number of changes, we could have it say *no*, *one*, *two*, or *many* as appropriate. Again we'll write a general function to do this:

```
(defun how-many (count)
  (cond ((zerop count) "no")
```

---

* Statement blocks are actually optional; some programmers like to omit the final statement block, leaving the final "condition" as an "otherwise" clause to be executed if all of the preceding conditions evaluate to nil. If the statement block is omitted, the value returned by cond is simply the value of the condition.

```
((= count 1) "one")
((= count 2) "two")
(t "many")))
```

The first conditional expression introduces a new primitive Lisp function, **zerop**. It checks whether its argument is zero, and returns t (true) when it is. So when **count** is zero, the **cond** statement takes this first branch, and our function returns the value **no**. This strange function name bears a little explanation. It is pronounced "zero-pee" and is short for "zero predicate." In the realm of mathematical logic from which Lisp evolved, a predicate is a function that returns true or false based on some attribute of its argument. Lisp has a wide variety of similar predicate functions, with structurally related names. When you run into the next one, you'll understand it. (Of course, you might now expect the **null** function we introduced in the previous example to be called "**nilp**" instead. Nobody's perfectly consistent.)

The next two conditional expressions in the **cond** statement check if **count** is 1 or 2 and cause it to return "one" or "two" as appropriate. We could have written the first one using the same structure, but then we'd have missed out on an opportunity for a digression into Lisp trivia!

The last conditional expression is simply the atom **t** (true), which means its body is executed whenever all the preceding expressions failed. It returns the value **many**. Executing this function gives us results like these:

```
(how-many 1)
"one"
(how-many 0)
"no"
(how-many 3)
"many"
```

Combining these two helper functions into a mechanism to report the change count for our fancy command is easy.

```
(defun report-change-count (count)
  (message "Made %s %s." (how-many count) (pluralize "change" count)))
```

We get results like these:

```
(report-change-count 0)
"Made no changes."
(report-change-count 1)
"Made one change."
(report-change-count 1329)
"Made many changes."
```

Useful Built-in Emacs Functions

Many of the Emacs functions that exist and that you may write involve searching and manipulating the text in a buffer. Such functions are particularly useful in specialized modes, like the programming language modes described in Chapter 9. Many built-in Emacs functions relate to text in strings and buffers; the most interesting ones take advantage of Emacs's regular expression facility, which we introduced in Chapter 3.

We first describe the basic functions relating to buffers and strings that don't use regular expressions. Afterwards, we discuss regular expressions in more depth than was the case in Chapter 3, concentrating on the features that are most useful to Lisp programmers, and we describe the functions that Emacs makes available for dealing with regular expressions.

Buffers, Text, and Regions

Table 11-4 shows some basic Emacs functions relating to buffers, text, and strings that are only useful to Lisp programmers and thus aren't bound to keystrokes. We already saw a couple of them in the **count-words-buffer** example. Notice that some of these are predicates, and their names reflect this.

Table 11-4. Buffer and text functions

Function	Value or action
point	Character position of point.
mark	Character position of mark.
point-min	Minimum character position (usually 1).
point-max	Maximum character position (usually size of buffer).
bolp	Whether point is at the beginning of the line (**t** or **nil**).
eolp	Whether point is at the end of the line.
bobp	Whether point is at the beginning of the buffer.
eobp	Whether point is at the end of the buffer.
insert	Insert any number of arguments (strings or characters) into the buffer after point.
number-to-string	Convert a numerical argument to a string.
string-to-number	Convert a string argument to a number (integer or floating point).
char-to-string	Convert a character argument to a string.
substring	Given a string and two integer indices *start* and *end*, return the substring starting after *start* and ending before *end*. Indices start at 0. For example, (substring "appropriate" 2 5) returns "pro".
aref	Array indexing function that can be used to return individual characters from strings; takes an integer argument and returns the character as an integer, using the ASCII code (on most machines). For example, (aref "appropriate" 3) returns 114, the ASCII code for r.

Many functions not included in the previous table deal with buffers and text, including some that you should be familiar with as user commands. Several commonly used Emacs functions use *regions*, which are areas of text within a buffer. When you are using Emacs, you delineate regions by setting the mark and moving the cursor. However, region-oriented functions (such as **kill-region**, **indent-region**, and **shell-command-on-region**—really, any function with *region* in its name) are actually more flexible when used within Emacs Lisp code. They typically take two integer arguments that are used as the character positions of the boundaries for the region on which they operate. These arguments default to the values of point and mark when the functions are called interactively.

Obviously, allowing point and mark as interactive defaults is a more general (and thus more desirable) approach than one in which only point and mark can be used to delineate regions. The **r** option to the **interactive** function makes it possible. For example, if we wanted to write the function **translate-region-into-German**, here is how we would start:

```
(defun translate-region-into-German (start end)
  (interactive "r")
  ...
```

The **r** option to **interactive** fills in the two arguments **start** and **end** when the function is called interactively, but if it is called from other Lisp code, both arguments must be supplied. The usual way to do this is like this:

```
(translate-region-into-German (point) (mark))
```

But you need not call it in this way. If you wanted to use this function to write another function called **translate-buffer-into-German**, you would only need to write the following as a "wrapper":

```
(defun translate-buffer-into-German ()
  (translate-region-into-German (point-min) (point-max)))
```

In fact, it is best to *avoid* using point and mark within Lisp code unless doing so is really necessary; use local variables instead. Try not to write Lisp functions as lists of commands a user would invoke; that sort of behavior is better suited to macros (see Chapter 6).

Regular Expressions

Regular expressions (regexps) provide much more powerful ways of dealing with text. Although most beginning Emacs users tend to avoid commands that use regexps, like **replace-regexp** and **re-search-forward**, regular expressions are widely used within Lisp code. Such modes as Dired and the programming language modes would be unthinkable without them. Regular expressions require time and patience to become comfortable with, but doing so is well worth the effort for Lisp programmers, because they are one of the most powerful features of Emacs, and many things are not practical to implement in any other way.

One trick that can be useful when you are experimenting with regular expressions and trying to get the hang of them is to type some text into a scratch buffer that corresponds to what you're trying to match, and then use **isearch-forward-regexp** (**C-M-s**) to build up the regular expression. The interactive, immediate feedback of an incremental search can show you the pieces of the regular expression in action in a way that is completely unique to Emacs.

We introduce the various features of regular expressions by way of a few examples of search-and-replace situations; such examples are easy to explain without introducing lots of extraneous details. Afterward, we describe Lisp functions that go beyond simple search-and-replace capabilities with regular expressions. The following are examples of searching and replacing tasks that the normal search/replace commands can't handle or handle poorly:

- You are developing code in C, and you want to combine the functionality of the functions read and readfile into a new function called get. You want to replace all references to these functions with references to the new one.

- You are writing a *troff* document using outline mode, as described in Chapter 7. In outline mode, headers of document sections have lines that start with one or more asterisks. You want to write a function called **remove-outline-marks** to get rid of these asterisks so that you can run *troff* on your file.

- You want to change all occurrences of *program* in a document, including *programs* and *program's*, to *module/modules/module's*, without changing *programming* to *moduleming* or *programmer* to *modulemer*.

- You are working on documentation for some C software that is being rewritten in Java. You want to change all the filenames in the documentation from *<filename>.c* to *<filename>.java*, since *.java* is the extension the *javac* compiler uses.

- You just installed a new C++ compiler that prints error messages in German. You want to modify the Emacs **compile** package so that it can parse the error messages correctly (see the end of Chapter 9).

We will soon show how to use regular expressions to deal with these examples, which we refer to by number. Note that this discussion of regular expressions, although more comprehensive than that in Chapter 3, does not cover every feature; those that it doesn't cover are redundant with other features or relate to concepts that are beyond the scope of this book. It is also important to note that the regular expression syntax described here is for use with Lisp strings only; there is an important difference between the regexp syntax for Lisp strings and the regexp syntax for user commands (like **replace-regexp**), as we will see.

Basic operators

Regular expressions began as an idea in theoretical computer science, but they have found their way into many nooks and crannies of everyday, practical computing. The syntax used to represent them may vary, but the concepts are much the same everywhere. You probably already know a subset of regular expression notation: the wildcard characters used by the Unix shell or Windows command prompt to match filenames. The Emacs notation is a bit different; it is similar to those used by the language Perl, editors like *ed* and *vi* and Unix software tools like *lex* and *grep*. So let's start with the Emacs regular expression operators that resemble Unix shell wildcard character, which are listed in Table 11-5.

Table 11-5. Basic regular expression operators

Emacs operator	Equivalent	Function
.	?	Matches any character.
.*	*	Matches any string.
[abc]	[abc]	Matches a, b, or c.
[a-z]	[a-z]	Matches any lowercase letter.

For example, to match all filenames beginning with *program* in the Unix shell, you would specify program*. In Emacs, you would say program.*. To match all filenames beginning with *a* through *e* in the shell, you would use [a-e]* or [abcde]*; in Emacs, it's [a-e].* or [abcde].*. In other words, the dash within the brackets specifies a *range* of characters.[*] We will provide more on ranges and bracketed character sets shortly.

To specify a character that is used as a regular expression operator, you need to precede it with a double-backslash, as in * to match an asterisk. Why a double backslash? The reason has to do with the way Emacs Lisp reads and decodes strings. When Emacs reads a string in a Lisp program, it decodes the backslash-escaped characters and thus turns double backslashes into single backslashes. If the string is being used as a regular expression—that is, if it is being passed to a function that expects a regular expression argument—that function uses the single backslash as part of the regular expression syntax. For example, given the following line of Lisp:

```
(replace-regexp "fred\\*" "bob*")
```

the Lisp interpreter decodes the string fred* as fred* and passes it to the **replace-regexp** command. The **replace-regexp** command understands fred* to mean fred followed by a (literal) asterisk. Notice, however, that the second argument to **replace-regexp** is not a regular expression, so there is no need to backslash-escape the asterisk in bob* at all. Also notice that if you were to invoke the this as a user command, you would not need to double the backslash, that is, you would type **M-x replace-regexp Enter** followed by **fred*** and **bob***. Emacs decodes strings read from the minibuffer differently.

---

[*] Emacs uses ASCII codes (on most machines) to build ranges, but you shouldn't depend on this fact; it is better to stick to dependable things, like all-lowercase or all-uppercase alphabet subsets or [0-9] for digits, and avoid potentially nonportable items, like [A-z] and ranges involving punctuation characters.

The * regular expression operator in Emacs (by itself) actually means something different from the * in the Unix shell: it means "zero or more occurrences of whatever is before the *." Thus, because . matches any character, .* means "zero or more occurrences of any character," that is, any string at all, including the empty string. Anything can precede a *: for example, read* matches "rea" followed by zero or more d's; file[0-9]* matches "file" followed by zero or more digits.

Two operators are closely related to *. The first is +, which matches one or more occurrences of whatever precedes it. Thus, read+ matches "read" and "readdddd" but not "rea," and file[0-9]+ requires that there be at least one digit after "file." The second is ?, which matches zero or one occurrence of whatever precedes it (i.e., makes it optional). html? matches "htm" or "html," and file[0-9]? matches "file" followed by one optional digit.

Before we move on to other operators, a few more comments about character sets and ranges are in order. First, you can specify more than one range within a single character set. The set [A-Za-z] can thus be used to specify all alphabetic characters; this is better than the nonportable [A-z]. Combining ranges with lists of characters in sets is also possible; for example, [A-Za-z_] means all alphabetic characters plus underscore, that is, all characters allowed in the names of identifiers in C. If you give ^ as the first character in a set, it acts as a "not" operator; the set matches all characters that aren't the characters after the ^. For example, [^A-Za-z] matches all nonalphabetic characters.

A ^ anywhere other than first in a character set has no special meaning; it's just the caret character. Conversely, - has no special meaning if it is given first in the set; the same is true for]. However, we don't recommend that you use this shortcut; instead, you should double-backslash-escape these characters just to be on the safe side. A double backslash preceding a nonspecial character usually means just that character—but watch it! A few letters and punctuation characters are used as regular expression operators, some of which are covered in the following section. We list "booby trap" characters that become operators when double-backslash-escaped later. The ^ character has a different meaning when used outside of ranges, as we'll see soon.

Grouping and alternation

If you want to get *, +, or ? to operate on more than one character, you can use the \\(and \\) operators for grouping. Notice that, in this case (and others to follow), the backslashes are part of the operator. (All of the nonbasic regular expression operators include backslashes so as to avoid making too many characters "special." This is the most profound way in which Emacs regular expressions differ from those used in other environments, like Perl, so it's something to which you'll need to pay careful attention.) As we saw before, these characters need to be double-backslash-escaped so that Emacs decodes them properly. If one of the basic operators immediately follows \\), it works on the entire group inside the \\(and \\). For example, \\(read\\)* matches the empty string, "read," "readread," and so on, and read\\(file\\)? matches "read" or "readfile." Now we can handle Example 1, the first of the examples given at the beginning of this section, with the following Lisp code:

```
(replace-regexp "read\\(file\\)?" "get")
```

The alternation operator \\| is a "one or the other" operator; it matches either whatever precedes it or whatever comes after it. \\| treats parenthesized groups differently from the basic operators. Instead of requiring parenthesized groups to work with subexpressions of more than one character, its "power" goes out to the left and right as far as possible, until it reaches the beginning or end of the regexp, a \\(, a \\), or another \\|. Some examples should make this clearer:

- read\\|get matches "read" or "get"
- readfile\\|read\\|get matches "readfile", "read," or "get"
- \\(read\\|get\\)file matches "readfile" or "getfile"

In the first example, the effect of the \\| extends to both ends of the regular expression. In the second, the effect of the first \\| extends to the beginning of the regexp on the left and to the second \\| on the right. In the third, it extends to the backslash-parentheses.

Context

Another important category of regular expression operators has to do with specifying the *context* of a string, that is, the text around it. In Chapter 3 we saw the **word-search** commands, which are invoked as options within incremental search. These are special cases of context specification; in this case, the context is word-separation characters, for example, spaces or punctuation, on both sides of the string.

The simplest context operators for regular expressions are ^ and $, two more basic operators that are used at the beginning and end of regular expressions respectively. The ^ operator causes the rest of the regular expression to match only if it is at the beginning of a line; $ causes the regular expression preceding it to match only if it is at the end of a line. In Example 2, we need a function that matches occurrences of one or more asterisks at the beginning of a line; this will do it:

```
(defun remove-outline-marks ()
  "Remove section header marks created in outline-mode."
  (interactive)
  (replace-regexp "^\\*+" ""))
```

This function finds lines that begin with one or more asterisks (the * is a literal asterisk and the + means "one or more"), and it replaces the asterisk(s) with the empty string "", thus deleting them.

Note that ^ and $ can't be used in the middle of regular expressions that are intended to match strings that span more than one line. Instead, you can put \n (for Newline)

---

in your regular expressions to match such strings. Another such character you may want to use is \t for Tab. When ^ and $ are used with regular expression searches on strings instead of buffers, they match beginning- and end-of-string, respectively; the function **string-match**, described later in this chapter, can be used to do regular expression search on strings.

Here is a real-life example of a complex regular expression that covers the operators we have seen so far: **sentence-end**, a variable Emacs uses to recognize the ends of sentences for sentence motion commands like **forward-sentence** (**M-e**). Its value is:

```
"[.?!][]\"')}]*\\($\\|\t\\|  \\)[ \t\n]*"
```

Let's look at this piece by piece. The first character set, [.?!], matches a period, question mark, or exclamation mark (the first two of these are regular expression operators, but they have no special meaning within character sets). The next part, []\"')}]*, consists of a character set containing right bracket, double quote, single quote, right parenthesis, and right curly brace. A * follows the set, meaning that zero or more occurrences of any of the characters in the set matches. So far, then, this regexp matches a sentence-ending punctuation mark followed by zero or more ending quotes, parentheses, or curly braces. Next, there is the group \\($\\|\t\\| \\), which matches any of the three alternatives $ (end of line), Tab, or two spaces. Finally, [\t\n]* matches zero or more spaces, tabs, or newlines. Thus the sentence-ending characters can be followed by end-of-line or a combination of spaces (at least two), tabs, and newlines.

There are other context operators besides ^ and $; two of them can be used to make regular expression search act like word search. The operators \\< and \\> match the beginning and end of a word, respectively. With these we can go part of the way toward solving Example 3. The regular expression \\<program\\> matches "program" but not "programmer" or "programming" (it also won't match "micropro-gram"). So far so good; however, it won't match "program's" or "programs." For this, we need a more complex regular expression:

```
\\<program\\('s\\|s\\)?\\>
```

This expression means, "a word beginning with *program* followed optionally by apostrophe s or just s." This does the trick as far as matching the right words goes.

Retrieving portions of matches

There is still one piece missing: the ability to replace "program" with "module" while leaving any s or 's untouched. This leads to the final regular expression feature we will cover here: the ability to retrieve portions of the matched string for later use. The preceding regular expression is indeed the correct one to give as the search string for **replace-regexp**. As for the replace string, the answer is module\\1; in other words, the required Lisp code is:

```
(replace-regexp "\\<program\\('s\\|s\\)?\\>" "module\\1")
```

The \\1 means, in effect, "substitute the portion of the matched string that matched the subexpression inside the \\(and \\)." It is the only regular-expression-related operator that can be used in replacements. In this case, it means to use 's in the replace string if the match was "program's," s if the match was "programs," or nothing if the match was just "program." The result is the correct substitution of "module" for "program," "modules" for "programs," and "module's" for "program's."

Another example of this feature solves Example 4. To match filenames *<filename>.c* and replace them with *<filename>.java*, use the Lisp code:

```
(replace-regexp "\\([a-zA-Z0-9_]+\\)\\.c" "\\1.java")
```

Remember that \\. means a literal dot (.). Note also that the filename pattern (which matches a series of one or more alphanumerics or underscores) was surrounded by \\(and \\) in the search string for the sole purpose of retrieving it later with \\1.

Actually, the \\1 operator is only a special case of a more powerful facility (as you may have guessed). In general, if you surround a portion of a regular expression with \\(and \\), the string matching the parenthesized subexpression is saved. When you specify the replace string, you can retrieve the saved substrings with *n*, where *n* is the number of the parenthesized subexpression from left to right, starting with 1. Parenthesized expressions can be nested; their corresponding *n* numbers are assigned in order of their \\(delimiter from left to right.

Lisp code that takes full advantage of this feature tends to contain complicated regular expressions. The best example of this in Emacs's own Lisp code is **compilation-error-regexp-alist**, the list of regular expressions the **compile** package (discussed in Chapter 9) uses to parse error messages from compilers. Here is an excerpt, adapted from the Emacs source code (it's become much too long to reproduce in its entirety; see below for some hints on how to find the actual file to study in its full glory):

```
(defvar compilation-error-regexp-alist
  '(
    ;; NOTE!  See also grep-regexp-alist, below.

    ;; 4.3BSD grep, cc, lint pass 1:
    ;;  /usr/src/foo/foo.c(8): warning: w may be used before set
    ;; or GNU utilities:
    ;;   foo.c:8: error message
    ;; or HP-UX 7.0 fc:
    ;;   foo.f        :16    some horrible error message
    ;; or GNU utilities with column (GNAT 1.82):
    ;;    foo.adb:2:1: Unit name does not match file name
    ;; or with column and program name:
    ;;    jade:dbcommon.dsl:133:17:E: missing argument for function call
    ;;
    ;; We'll insist that the number be followed by a colon or closing
    ;; paren, because otherwise this matches just about anything
    ;; containing a number with spaces around it.
```

```
    ;; We insist on a non-digit in the file name
    ;; so that we don't mistake the file name for a command name
    ;; and take the line number as the file name.
    ("\\([a-zA-Z][-a-zA-Z._0-9]+: ?\\)?\
\\([a-zA-Z]?:?[^:( \t\n]*[^:( \t\n0-9][^:( \t\n]*\\)[:(][ \t]*\\([0-9]+\\)\
\\([) \t]\\|:\\(\\([0-9]+:\\)\\)\\|[0-9]*[^:0-9]\\)\\)" 2 3 6)

;; Microsoft C/C++:
    ;;  keyboard.c(537) : warning C4005: 'min' : macro redefinition
    ;;  d:\tmp\test.c(23) : error C2143: syntax error : missing ';' before 'if'
    ;; This used to be less selective and allow characters other than
    ;; parens around the line number, but that caused confusion for
    ;; GNU-style error messages.
    ;; This used to reject spaces and dashes in file names,
    ;; but they are valid now; so I made it more strict about the error
    ;; message that follows.
    ("\\(\\(\\([a-zA-Z]:\\)?[^:(\t\n]+\\)(\\(\\([0-9]+\\)\\)) \
: \\(error\\|warning\\) C[0-9]+:" 1 3)

;; Caml compiler:
    ;;  File "foobar.ml", lines 5-8, characters 20-155: blah blah
    ("^File \"\\([^,\" \n\t]+\\)\", lines? \\([0-9]+\\)[-0-9]*, characters? \
\\([0-9]+\\)" 1 2 3)

;; Cray C compiler error messages
    ("\\(cc\\| cft\\)-[0-9]+ c\\(c\\|f77\\): ERROR \\([^,\n]+, \\)* File = \
\\([^,\n]+\\), Line = \\([0-9]+\\)" 4 5)

;; Perl -w:
    ;; syntax error at automake line 922, near "':'"
    ;; Perl debugging traces
    ;; store::odrecall('File_A', 'x2') called at store.pm line 90
    (".* at \\([^ \n]+\\) line \\([0-9]+\\)[,.\n]" 1 2)

    ;; See http://ant.apache.org/faq.html
    ;; Ant Java: works for jikes
    ("^\\s-*\\[[^]]*\\]\\s-*\\(.+\\):\\([0-9]+\\):\\([0-9]+\\):[0-9]+:[0-9]\
+:" 1 2 3)

    ;; Ant Java: works for javac
    ("^\\s-*\\[[^]]*\\]\\s-*\\(.+\\):\\([0-9]+\\):" 1 2)
)
```

This is a list of elements that have at least three parts each: a regular expression and two numbers. The regular expression matches error messages in the format used by a particular compiler or tool. The first number tells Emacs which of the matched subexpressions contains the filename in the error message; the second number designates which of the subexpressions contains the line number. (There can also be additional parts at the end: a third number giving the position of the column number of the error, if any, and any number of format strings used to generate the true filename from the piece found in the error message, if needed. For more details about these, look at the actual file, as described below.)

For example, the element in the list dealing with Perl contains the regular expression:

```
".* at \\([^ \n]+\\) line \\([0-9]+\\)[,.\n]"
```

followed by 1 and 2, meaning that the first parenthesized subexpression contains the filename and the second contains the line number. So if you have Perl's warnings turned on—you always do, of course—you might get an error message such as this:

```
syntax error at monthly_orders.pl line 1822, near "$"
```

The regular expression ignores everything up to *at*. Then it finds *monthly_orders.pl*, the filename, as the match to the first subexpression "[^ \n]+" (one or more non-blank, nonnewline characters), and it finds 1822, the line number, as the match to the second subexpression "[0-9]+" (one or more digits).

For the most part, these regular expressions are documented pretty well in their definitions. Understanding them in depth can still be a challenge, and writing them even more so! Suppose we want to tackle Example 5 by adding an element to this list for our new C++ compiler that prints error messages in German. In particular, it prints error messages like this:

```
Fehler auf Zeile linenum in filename: text of error message
```

Here is the element we would add to **compilation-error-regexp-alist**:

```
("Fehler auf Zeile \\([0-9]+\\) in \\([^: \t]+\\):" 2 1)
```

In this case, the second parenthesized subexpression matches the filename, and the first matches the line number.

To add this to **compilation-error-regexp-alist**, we need to put this line in *.emacs*:

```
(setq compilation-error-regexp-alist
  (cons '("Fehler auf Zeile \\([0-9]+\\) in \\([^: \t]+\\):" 2 1)
    compilation-error-regexp-alist))
```

Notice how this example resembles our example (from Chapter 9) of adding support for a new language mode to **auto-mode-alist**.

Regular expression operator summary

Table 11-6 concludes our discussion of regular expression operators with a reference list of all the operators covered.

Table 11-6. Regular expression operators

Operator	Function
.	Match any character.
*	Match 0 or more occurrences of preceding char or group.
+	Match 1 or more occurrences of preceding char or group.

Table 11-6. Regular expression operators (continued)

Operator	Function
?	Match 0 or 1 occurrences of preceding char or group.
[...]	Set of characters; see below.
\\(	Begin a group.
\\)	End a group.
\\|	Match the subexpression before or after \\|.
^	At beginning of regexp, match beginning of line or string.
$	At end of regexp, match end of line or string.
\n	Match Newline within a regexp.
\t	Match Tab within a regexp.
\\<	Match beginning of word.
\\>	Match end of word.
The following operators are meaningful within character sets:	
^	At beginning of set, treat set as chars not to match.
- *(dash)*	Specify range of characters.
The following is also meaningful in regexp replace strings:	
\\n	Substitute portion of match within the *n*th \\(and \\), counting from left \\(to right, starting with 1.

Finally, the following characters are operators (not discussed here) when double-backslash-escaped: b, B, c, C, w, W, s, S, =, _, ', and `. Thus, these are "booby traps" when double-backslash-escaped. Some of these behave similarly to the character class aliases you may have encountered in Perl and Java regular expressions.

A Treasure Trove of Examples

As mentioned above, the full **auto-mode-alist** has a lot more entries and documentation than fit in this book. The *compile.el* module in which it is defined also contains functions that use it. One of the best ways to learn how to use Emacs Lisp (as well as discovering things you might not have even realized you can do) is to browse through the implementations of standard modules that are similar to what you're trying to achieve, or that are simply interesting. But how do you find them?

The manual way is to look at the value of the variable **load-path**. This is the variable Emacs consults when it needs to load a library file itself, so any library you're looking for must be in one of these directories. (This variable is discussed further in the final section of this chapter.) The problem, as you will see if you look at the current value of the variable, is that it contains a large number of directories for you to wade through, which would be pretty tedious each time you're curious about a library. (An easy way to see the variable's value is through Help's "Describe variable" feature, **C-h v**.)

One of the authors wrote the command listed in Example 11-1 to address this problem and uses it regularly to easily snoop on the source files that make much of Emacs run. If you don't want to type this entire function into your *.emacs* by hand, you can download it from this book's web site, *http://www.oreilly.com/catalog/gnu3*.

Example 11-1. find-library-file

```
(defun find-library-file (library)
  "Takes a single argument LIBRARY, being a library file to search for.
Searches for LIBRARY directly (in case relative to current directory,
or absolute) and then searches directories in load-path in order.  It
will test LIBRARY with no added extension, then with .el, and finally
with .elc.  If a file is found in the search, it is visited.  If none
is found, an error is signaled.  Note that order of extension searching
is reversed from that of the load function."
  (interactive "sFind library file: ")
  (let ((path (cons "" load-path)) exact match elc test found)
    (while (and (not match) path)
      (setq test (concat (car path) "/" library)
            match (if (condition-case nil
                          (file-readable-p test)
                        (error nil))
                      test)
            path (cdr path)))
    (setq path (cons "" load-path))
    (or match
        (while (and (not elc) path)
          (setq test (concat (car path) "/" library ".elc")
                elc (if (condition-case nil
                            (file-readable-p test)
                          (error nil))
                        test)
                path (cdr path))))
    (setq path (cons "" load-path))
    (while (and (not match) path)
      (setq test (concat (car path) "/" library ".el")
            match (if (condition-case nil
                          (file-readable-p test)
                        (error nil))
                      test)
            path (cdr path)))
    (setq found (or match elc))
    (if found
        (progn
          (find-file found)
          (and match elc
               (message "(library file %s exists)" elc)
               (sit-for 1))
          (message "Found library file %s" found))
      (error "Library file \"%s\" not found." library))))
```

Once this command is defined, you can visit any library's implementation by typing **M-x find-library file Enter** *libraryname* **Enter**. If you use it as often as this author does, you too may find it worth binding to a key sequence. We won't present a detailed discussion of how this function works because it goes a bit deeper than this chapter, but if you're curious about what some of the functions do, you can put your cursor in the function name in a Lisp buffer and use the Help system's "Describe function" (**C-h f**) feature to get more information about it.

If you find that most of the time when you ask for a library, you end up with a file containing a lot of cryptic numeric codes and no comments, check if the filename ends in *.elc*. If that is usually what you end up with, it means that only the byte-compiled versions of the libraries (see the discussion at the end of this chapter) have been installed on your system. Ask your system administrator if you can get the source installed; that's an important part of being able to learn and tweak the Emacs Lisp environment.

Functions That Use Regular Expressions

The functions **re-search-forward**, **re-search-backward**, **replace-regexp**, **query-replace-regexp**, **highlight-regexp**, **isearch-forward-regexp**, and **isearch-backward-regexp** are all user commands that use regular expressions, and they can all be used within Lisp code (though it is hard to imagine incremental search being used within Lisp code). The section on customizing major modes later in this chapter contains an example function that uses **re-search-forward**. To find other commands that use regexps you can use the "apropos" help feature (**C-h a regexp Enter**).

Other such functions aren't available as user commands. Perhaps the most widely used one is **looking-at**. This function takes a regular expression argument and does the following: it returns t if the text after point matches the regular expression (nil otherwise); if there was a match, it saves the pieces surrounded by \\(and \\) for future use, as seen earlier. The function **string-match** is similar: it takes two arguments, a regexp and a string. It returns the starting index of the portion of the string that matches the regexp, or nil if there is no match.

The functions **match-beginning** and **match-end** can be used to retrieve the saved portions of the matched string. Each takes as an argument the number of the matched expression (as in \\n in **replace-regexp** replace strings) and returns the character position in the buffer that marks the beginning (for **match-beginning**) or end (for **match-end**) of the matched string. With the argument 0, the character position that marks the beginning/end of the entire string matched by the regular expression is returned.

Two more functions are needed to make the above useful: we need to know how to convert the text in a buffer to a string. No problem: **buffer-string** returns the entire buffer as a string; **buffer-substring** takes two integer arguments, marking the beginning and end positions of the substring desired, and returns the substring.

With these functions, we can write a bit of Lisp code that returns a string containing the portion of the buffer that matches the *n*th parenthesized subexpression:

```
(buffer-substring (match-beginning n (match-end n)))
```

In fact, this construct is used so often that Emacs has a built-in function, **match-string**, that acts as a shorthand; (match-string *n*) returns the same result as in the previous example.

An example should show how this capability works. Assume you are writing the Lisp code that parses compiler error messages, as in our previous example. Your code goes through each element in **compilation-error-regexp-alist**, checking if the text in a buffer matches the regular expression. If it matches, your code needs to extract the filename and the line number, visit the file, and go to the line number.

Although the code for going down each element in the list is beyond what we have learned so far, the routine basically looks like this:

```
for each element in compilation-error-regexp-alist
  (let ((regexp the regexp in the element)
        (file-subexp the number of the filename subexpression)
        (line-subexp the number of the line number subexpression))
    (if (looking-at regexp)
        (let ((filename (match-string file-subexp))
              (linenum (match-string line-subexp)))
          (find-file-other-window filename)
          (goto-line linenum))
      (otherwise, try the next element in the list))))
```

The second **let** extracts the filename from the buffer from the beginning to the end of the match to the file-subexp-th subexpression, and it extracts the line number similarly from the line-subexp-th subexpression (and converts it from a string to a number). Then the code visits the file (in another window, not the same one as the error message buffer) and goes to the line number where the error occurred.

The code for the calculator mode later in this chapter contains a few other examples of **looking-at**, **match-beginning**, and **match-end**.

Finding Other Built-in Functions

Emacs contains hundreds of built-in functions that may be of use to you in writing Lisp code. Yet finding which one to use for a given purpose is not so hard.

The first thing to realize is that you will often need to use functions that are already accessible as keyboard commands. You can use these by finding out what their function names are via the **C-h k** (for **describe-key**) command (see Chapter 14). This gives the command's full documentation, as opposed to **C-h c** (for **describe-key-briefly**), which gives only the command's name. Be careful: in a few cases, some common keyboard commands require an argument when used as Lisp functions. An example is **forward-word**; to get the equivalent of typing **M-f**, you have to use (forward-word 1).

Another powerful tool for getting the right function for the job is the **command-apropos** (**C-h a**) help function. Given a regular expression, this help function searches for all commands that match it and display their key bindings (if any) and documentation in a *Help* window. This can be a great help if you are trying to find a command that does a certain "basic" thing. For example, if you want to know about commands that operate on words, type **C-h a** followed by *word*, and you will see documentation on about a dozen and a half commands having to do with words.

The limitation with **command-apropos** is that it gives information only on functions that can be used as keyboard commands. Even more powerful is **apropos**, which is not accessible via any of the help keys (you must type **M-x apropos Enter**). Given a regular expression, **apropos** displays all functions, variables, and other symbols that match it. Be warned, though: **apropos** can take a long time to run and can generate very long lists if you use it with a general enough concept (such as *buffer*).

You should be able to use the **apropos** commands on a small number of well-chosen keywords and find the function(s) you need. Because, if a function seems general and basic enough, the chances are excellent that Emacs has it built-in.

After you find the function you are interested in, you may find that the documentation that **apropos** prints does not give you enough information about what the function does, its arguments, how to use it, or whatever. The best thing to do at this point is to search Emacs's Lisp source code for examples of the function's use. "A Treasure Trove of Examples" earlier in this chapter provides ways of finding out the names of directories Emacs loads libraries from and an easy way of looking at a library once you know its name. To search the contents of the library files you'll need to use *grep* or some other search facility to find examples, then edit the files found to look at the surrounding context. If you're ambitious you could put together the examples and concepts we've discussed so far to write an extension of the **find-library-file** command that searches the *contents* of the library files in each directory on the load path! Although most of Emacs's built-in Lisp code is not profusely documented, the examples of function use that it provides should be helpful—and may even give you ideas for your own functions.

By now, you should have a framework of Emacs Lisp that should be sufficient for writing many useful Emacs commands. We have covered examples of various kinds of functions, both Lisp primitives and built-in Emacs functions. You should be able to extrapolate many others from the ones given in this chapter along with help techniques such as those just provided. In other words, you are well on your way to becoming a fluent Emacs Lisp programmer. To test yourself, start with the code for **count-words-buffer** and try writing the following functions:

count-lines-buffer
> Print the number of lines in the buffer.

count-words-region
> Print the number of words in a region.

what-line
> Print the number of the line point is currently on.

Building an Automatic Template System

You're probably starting to see how all these tools can be put together in really powerful ways. Most of the rest of the chapter consists of examples of building relatively real and useful new features for Emacs. You can use them as learning tools for how to build your own, and you may be able to use them as-is, or with a little tweaking, in your own daily work.

The example we're about to look at is something that one of the authors developed over a decade ago to help with the tedium of creating new files in development projects where a certain amount of structure and standard documentation were always needed. Many coding and writing projects have this characteristic; each file needs some boilerplate, but it needs to be adjusted to the details of the file. Emacs turned out to be very much up to the task of automating a lot of the drudge work, and this template system has been heavily used ever since.

Most of the code in this example should already make sense to you. A couple of aspects that will be explained more thoroughly in the next section about programming a major mode. In particular, don't worry too much yet about exactly what a "hook" function is, or **funcall**. For now it's sufficient to know that the **file-not-found-hook** allows us to run code when the user uses **find-file** to open a file that doesn't exist yet (exactly the time at which we'd like to offer our template services).

Before launching into the code, it's worth looking at an example of it in action. You'd set up your template by creating a file named *file-template-java* at the top level of a Java project directory hierarchy, containing something like the code shown in Example 11-2.

Example 11-2. file-template-java

```
/* %filename%
 * Created on %date%
 *
 * (c) 2004 MyCorp, etc. etc.
 */

%package%

import org.apache.log4j.Logger;
```

Example 11-2. file-template-java (continued)

```
/**
 * [Documentation Here!]
 *
 * @author  %author%
 * @version $Id: ch11,v 1.8 2004/12/01 01:52:45 free1 Exp jamie $
 *
 **/
public class %class% {

    /**
     * Provides access to the CVS version of this class.
     **/
    public static final String VERSION =
        "$Id: ch11,v 1.8 2004/12/01 01:52:45 free1 Exp jamie $";

    /**
     * Provides hierarchical control and configuration of debugging via
     * class package structure.
     **/
    private static Logger log =
        Logger.getLogger(%class%.class);

}
```

The template system shown in Example 11-3 causes an attempt to find a nonexistent Java source file within this project hierarchy (for example, via **C-x C-f src/com/ mycorp/util/FooManager.java**) to result in the prompt Start with template file? (y or n) in the minibuffer, and if you answer **y**, you'll see your FooManager.java buffer start out with contents in the following example.

Example 11-3. FooManager.java

```
/* FooManager.java
 * Created on Sun Nov  9 20:56:12 2003
 *
 * (c) 2004 MyCorp, etc. etc.
 */

package com.mycorp.util;

import org.apache.log4j.Logger;

/**
 * [Documentation Here!]
 *
 * @author  Jim Elliott
 * @version $Id: ch11,v 1.8 2004/12/01 01:52:45 free1 Exp jamie $
 *
 **/
public class FooManager {
```

Example 11-3. FooManager.java (continued)

```
/**
 * Provides access to the CVS version of this class.
 **/
public static final String VERSION =
    "$Id: ch11,v 1.8 2004/12/01 01:52:45 free1 Exp jamie $";

/**
 * Provides hierarchical control and configuration of debugging via
 * class package structure.
 **/
private static Logger log =
    Logger.getLogger(FooManager.class);

}
```

The template has been used to populate the buffer with the standard project header comments and a basic Java class skeleton, with proper contextual values filled in (such as the current time, the person creating the file, the file and class name, and so on). Even the Java package statement has been inferred by examining the directory path in which the source file is being created. The Logger declaration will look familiar to anyone who uses the excellent *log4j* system to add logging and debugging to their Java projects. (The strange version numbers in "$Id" strings are managed by the CVS version control system and will be updated to the proper file and version information when it's checked in. This topic is discussed in Chapter 12.)

To make this work, the template system needs to be able to do a couple of things:

- Intercept the user's attempt to find a nonexistent file.
- Check whether there is an appropriate template file somewhere in a parent directory.
- If so, offer to use it, and populate the buffer with the contents of the template file.
- Scan the template file for special placeholders (such as %filename%) and replace them with information about the file being created.

Let's look at the source code that makes this all happen! (As always, if you don't want to type the code listed in Example 11-4 yourself, you can download it from this book's web site.*)

Example 11-4. template.el

```
;;;;;;;;;;;;;;;;;;;;;;;;;;;;; -*- Mode: Emacs-Lisp -*- ;;;;;;;;;;;;;;;;;;;;;;;;;;;;
;; template.el --- Routines for generating smart skeletal templates for files.
```

---

* The version presented in this example is simplified for reasons of space and clarity. The full version, which adds the ability to insert templates for function definitions and process arbitrary Emacs Lisp functions within template files, is also available for download.

Example 11-4. template.el (continued)

```elisp
(defvar template-file-name "file-template"
  "*The name of the file to look for when a find-file request fails. If a
file with the name specified by this variable exists, offer to use it as
a template for creating the new file. You can also have mode-specific
templates by appending \"-extension\" to this filename, e.g. a Java specific
template would be file-template-java.")

(defvar template-replacements-alist
  '(("%filename%" . (lambda ()
                     (file-name-nondirectory (buffer-file-name))))
    ("%creator%" . user-full-name)
    ("%author%" . user-full-name)
    ("%date%" . current-time-string)
    ("%once%" . (lambda () (template-insert-include-once)))
    ("%package%" . (lambda () (template-insert-java-package)))
    ("%class%" . (lambda () (template-insert-class-name)))
    )
  "A list which specifies what substitutions to perform upon loading a
template file. Each list element consists of a string, which is the target
to be replaced if it is found in the template, paired with a function,
which is called to generate the replacement value for the string.")

(defun find-template-file ()
  "Searches the current directory and its parents for a file matching
the name configured for template files. The name of the first such
readable file found is returned, allowing for hierarchical template
configuration. A template file with the same extension as the file
being loaded (using a \"-\" instead of a \".\" as the template file's
delimiter, to avoid confusing other software) will take precedence
over an extension-free, generic template."
  (let ((path (file-name-directory (buffer-file-name)))
        (ext (file-name-extension (buffer-file-name)))
        attempt result)

    (while (and (not result) (> (length path) 0))
      (setq attempt (concat path template-file-name "-" ext))
      (if (file-readable-p attempt)
          (setq result attempt))
      (setq attempt (concat path template-file-name))
      (if (file-readable-p attempt)
          (setq result attempt))
      (setq path (if (string-equal path "/")
                     ""
                   (file-name-directory (substring path 0 -1)))))))
    result))

(defun template-file-not-found-hook ()
  "Called when a find-file command has not been able to find the specified
file in the current directory. Sees if it makes sense to offer to start it
based on a template."
  (condition-case nil
      (if (and (find-template-file)
```

Example 11-4. template.el (continued)

```
            (y-or-n-p "Start with template file? "))
        (progn (buffer-disable-undo)
          (insert-file (find-template-file))
          (goto-char (point-min))

          ;; Magically do the variable substitutions
          (let ((the-list template-replacements-alist))
            (while the-list
              (goto-char (point-min))
              (replace-string (car (car the-list))
                      (funcall (cdr (car the-list)))
                      nil)
              (setq the-list (cdr the-list))))
          (goto-char (point-min))
          (buffer-enable-undo)
          (set-buffer-modified-p nil)))
   ;; This is part of the condition-case; it catches the situation where
   ;; the user has hit C-g to abort the find-file (since they realized
   ;; that they didn't mean it) and deletes the buffer that has already
   ;; been created to go with that file, since it will otherwise become
   ;; mysterious clutter they may not even know about.
   ('quit (kill-buffer (current-buffer))
     (signal 'quit "Quit"))))

; Install the above routine
(or (memq 'template-file-not-found-hook find-file-not-found-hooks)
    (setq find-file-not-found-hooks
          (append find-file-not-found-hooks '(template-file-not-found-hook))))
)

(defun template-insert-include-once ()
  "Returns preprocessor directives such that the file will be included
only once during a compilation process which includes it an
abitrary number of times."
  (let ((name (file-name-nondirectory (buffer-file-name)))
     basename)
    (if (string-match ".h$" name)
    (progn
      (setq basename (upcase (substring name 0 -2)))
      (concat "#ifndef _H_" basename "\n#define _H_" basename
          "\n\n\n#endif   /* not defined _H_" basename " */\n"))
      "" ; the "else" clause, returns an empty string.
    )))

(defun template-insert-java-package ()
  "Inserts an appropriate Java package directive based on the path to
the current file name (assuming that it is in the com, org or net
subtree). If no recognizable package path is found, inserts nothing."
  (let ((name (file-name-directory (buffer-file-name)))
     result)
    (if (string-match "/\\(com\\|org\\|net\\)/.*/$" name)
    (progn
```

Example 11-4. template.el (continued)

```
        (setq result (substring name (+ (match-beginning 0) 1)
                    (- (match-end 0) 1)))
        (while (string-match "/" result)
          (setq result (concat (substring result 0 (match-beginning 0))
                    "."
                    (substring result (match-end 0)))))
        (concat "package " result ";"))
      "")))

(defun template-insert-class-name ()
  "Inserts the name of the java class being defined in the current file,
based on the file name. If not a Java source file, inserts nothing."
  (let ((name (file-name-nondirectory (buffer-file-name))))
    (if (string-match "\\(.*\\)\\.java" name)
    (substring name (match-beginning 1) (match-end 1))
      "")))

(provide 'template)
```

You'll notice that this code makes heavy use of the regular expression facilities, which is no surprise. The first section sets up some variables that configure the operation of the template system. **template-file-name** determines the file name (or prefix) that is used to search for templates; the default value of **file-template** is probably fine. **template-replacements-alist** sets up the standard placeholders, and the mechanism by which they get replaced by appropriate values. Adding entries to this list is one way to extend the system. Each entry consists of the placeholder to be replaced, followed by the Lisp function to be executed to produce its replacement. The way this function can be stored in a list and executed when appropriate later is one of the great things about Lisp and is discussed in more depth in the calculator mode example in the next section. The placeholders supported are:

%filename%
> Gets replaced by the name of the file being created.

%creator%, %author%
> These are synonyms; both get replaced by the name of the user creating the file.

%date%
> Turns into the current date and time when the file is created.

%once%
> Expands into boilerplate code for the C preprocessor to cause a header file to include itself only once, even if it's been included multiple times by other header files. (This sort of thing has been taken care of in more modern environments like Objective C and Java but can still be handy when working with traditional C compilers.)

%package%

Is replaced by the Java package which contains the file being created (assuming the file is a Java class). This package is determined by examining the directory structure in which the file is being placed.

%class%

Becomes the name of the Java class being defined in the file, assuming it's a Java source file.

The first function, **find-template-file**, is responsible for searching the directory hierarchy above the file being created, looking for a file with the right name to be considered a file template (if **template-file-name** has been left at its default value, this looks for either a file named *file-template* or *file-template-ext* where *ext* is the extension at the end of the name of the file being created). It just keeps lopping the last directory off the path in which it's looking, starting with the location of the new file, and seeing if it can read a file with one of those names in the current directory, until it runs out of directories.

The function **template-file-not-found-hook** is the "main program" of the template system. It gets "hooked in" to the normal Emacs **find-file** process, and called whenever **find-file** doesn't find the file the user asked for (in other words, a new file is being created). It uses **condition-case** (a mechanism similar to exception handling in C++ and Java) to make sure it gets a chance to clean up after itself if the user cancels the process of filling in the template file. It checks whether the template file can be found, asks users if they want to use it, and (if they do) loads it into the new buffer and performs the placeholder substitutions. For an explanation of the list manipulation and **funcall** code that makes the substitutions work, read the discussion of Calculator mode in the next section. Finally, it jumps to the beginning of the new buffer and marks it as unchanged (because, as far as users are concerned, it's a brand new buffer on which they've not yet had to expend any effort).

Immediately after the function definition is the chunk of code that hooks it into the **find-file** mechanism. The **file-not-found-hooks** is a variable that Emacs uses to keep track of things to do when a requested file is not found. (Giving you opportunities to change or enhance normal behavior through "hooks" is a wonderful trait of Emacs that is discussed in more depth following the Calculator mode example later in this chapter.) Our code checks to make sure it's not already hooked up (so you don't end up having it run twice or more if you re-load the library file during an Emacs session), and then installs our hook at the end of the list if it's not there.

The rest of the file is helper functions to handle the more complex placeholders. **template-insert-java-package** figures out the value that should replace %package%, while **template-insert-class-name** figures out the Java class name that replaces %class%.

The last function call in the file, (provide 'template), records the fact that a "feature" named "template" has been loaded successfully. The **provide** function works with **require** to allow libraries to be loaded just once. When the function (`require 'template`) is executed, Emacs checks whether the feature "template" has ever been provided. If it has, it does nothing, otherwise, it calls **load-library** to load it. It's a good practice to have your libraries support this mechanism, so that they can be gracefully and efficiently used by other libraries through the **require** mechanism. You'll find this pattern throughout the Emacs library sources.

Programming a Major Mode

After you get comfortable with Emacs Lisp programming, you may find that that "little extra something" you want Emacs to do takes the form of a major mode. In previous chapters, we covered major modes for text entry, word processor input, and programming languages. Many of these modes are quite complicated to program, so we'll provide a simple example of a major mode, from which you can learn the concepts needed to program your own. Then, in the following section, you will learn how you can customize existing major modes without changing any of the Lisp code that implements them.

We'll develop Calculator mode, a major mode for a calculator whose functionality will be familiar to you if you have used the Unix *dc* (desk calculator) command. It is a Reverse Polish (stack-based) calculator of the type made popular by Hewlett-Packard. After explaining some of the principal components of major modes and some interesting features of the calculator mode, we will give the mode's complete Lisp code.

Components of a Major Mode

A major mode has various components that integrate it into Emacs. Some are:

- The *symbol* that is the name of the function that implements the mode
- The *name* of the mode that appears in the mode line in parentheses
- The *local keymap* that defines key bindings for commands in the mode
- *Variables* and *constants* known only within the Lisp code for the mode
- The special *buffer* the mode may use

Let's deal with these in order. The mode symbol is set by assigning the name of the function that implements the mode to the global variable **major-mode**, as in:

```
(setq major-mode 'calc-mode)
```

Similarly, the mode name is set by assigning an appropriate string to the global variable mode-name, as in:

```
(setq mode-name "Calculator")
```

The local keymap is defined using functions discussed in Chapter 10. In the case of the calculator mode, there is only one key sequence to bind (**C-j**), so we use a special form of the **make-keymap** command called **make-sparse-keymap** that is more efficient with a small number of key bindings. To use a keymap as the local map of a mode, we call the function **use-local-map**, as in:

```
(use-local-map calc-mode-map)
```

As we just saw, variables can be defined by using setq to assign a value to them, or by using **let** to define local variables within a function. The more "official" way to define variables is the **defvar** function, which allows documentation for the variable to be integrated into online help facilities such as **C-h v** (for **describe-variable**). The format is the following:

```
(defvar varname initial-value "description of the variable")
```

A variation on this is defconst, with which you can define constant values (that never change). For example:

```
(defconst calc-operator-regexp "[-+*/%]"
  "Regular expression for recognizing operators.")
```

defines the regular expression to be used in searching for arithmetic operators. As you will see, we use the **calc-** as a prefix for the names of all functions, variables, and constants that we define for the calculator mode. Other modes use this convention; for example, all names in C++ mode begin with c++-. Using this convention is a good idea because it helps avoid potential name clashes with the thousands of other functions, variables, and so on in Emacs.

Making variables local to the mode is also desirable so that they are known only within a buffer that is running the mode.* To do this, use the **make-local-variable** function, as in:

```
(make-local-variable 'calc-stack)
```

Notice that the name of the variable, not its value, is needed; therefore a single quote precedes the variable name, turning it into a symbol.

Finally, various major modes use special buffers that are not attached to files. For example, the **C-x C-b** (for **list-buffers**) command creates a buffer called *Buffer List*. To create a buffer in a new window, use the **pop-to-buffer** function, as in:

```
(pop-to-buffer "*Calc*")
```

There are a couple of useful variations on **pop-to-buffer**. We won't use them in our mode example, but they are handy in other circumstances.

switch-to-buffer

> Same as the **C-x b** command covered in Chapter 4; can also be used with a buffer name argument in Lisp.

---

* Unfortunately, because such variables are defined before they are made local to the mode, there is still a problem with name clashes with global variables. Therefore, it is still important to use names that aren't already used for global variables. A good strategy for avoiding this is to use variable names that start with the name of the mode.

set-buffer

Used only within Lisp code to designate the buffer used for editing; the best function to use for creating a temporary "work" buffer within a Lisp function.

More Lisp Basics: Lists

A Reverse Polish Notation calculator uses a data structure called a *stack*. Think of a stack as being similar to a spring-loaded dish stack in a cafeteria. When you enter a number into a RPN calculator, you *push* it onto the stack. When you apply an operator such as plus or minus, you *pop* the top two numbers off the stack, add or subtract them, and push the result back on the stack.

The *list*, a fundamental concept of Lisp, is a natural for implementing stacks. The list is the main concept that sets Lisp apart from other programming languages. It is a data structure that has two parts: the *head* and *tail*. These are known in Lisp jargon, for purely historical reasons, as **car** and **cdr** respectively. Think of these terms as "the first thing in the list" and "the rest of the list." The functions **car** and **cdr**, when given a list argument, return the head and tail of it, respectively.* Two functions are often used for making lists. **cons** (construct) takes two arguments, which become the head and tail of the list respectively. **list** takes a list of elements and makes them into a list. For example, this:

```
(list 2 3 4 5)
```

makes a list of the numbers from 2 to 5, and this:

```
(cons 1 (list 2 3 4 5))
```

makes a list of the numbers from 1 to 5. **car** applied to that list would return 1, while **cdr** would return the list (2 3 4 5).

These concepts are important because stacks, such as that used in the calculator mode, are easily implemented as lists. To push the value of x onto the stack **calc-stack**, we can just say this:

```
(setq calc-stack (cons x calc-stack))
```

If we want to get at the value at the top of the stack, the following returns that value:

```
(car calc-stack)
```

To pop the top value off the stack, we say this:

```
(setq calc-stack (cdr calc-stack))
```

Bear in mind that the elements of a list can be anything, including other lists. (This is why a list is called a *recursive* data structure.) In fact (ready to be confused?) just about everything in Lisp that is not an atom is a list. This includes functions, which

---

* Experienced Lisp programmers should note that Emacs Lisp does not supply standard contractions like cadr, cdar, and so on.

are basically lists of function name, arguments, and expressions to be evaluated. The idea of functions as lists will come in handy very soon.

The Calculator Mode

The complete Lisp code for the calculator mode appears at the end of this section; you should refer to it while reading the following explanation. If you download or type the code in, you can use the calculator by typing **M-x calc-mode Enter**. You will be put in the buffer *Calc*. You can type a line of numbers and operators and then type **C-j** to evaluate the line. Table 11-7 lists the three commands in calculator mode

Table 11-7. Calculator mode commands

Command	Action
=	Print the value at the top of the stack.
p	Print the entire stack contents.
c	Clear the stack.

Blank spaces are not necessary, except to separate numbers. For example, typing this:

```
4 17*6-=
```

followed by **C-j**, evaluates (4 * 17) - 6 and causes the result, 62, to be printed.

The heart of the code for the calculator mode is the functions **calc-eval** and **calc-next-token**. (See the code at the end of this section for these.) **calc-eval** is bound to **C-j** in Calculator mode. Starting at the beginning of the line preceding **C-j**, it calls **calc-next-token** to grab each *token* (number, operator, or command letter) in the line and evaluate it.

calc-next-token uses a **cond** construct to see if there is a number, operator, or command letter at point by using the regular expressions **calc-number-regexp**, **calc-operator-regexp**, and **calc-command-regexp**. According to which regular expression was matched, it sets the variable **calc-proc-fun** to the name (symbol) of the function that should be run (either **calc-push-number**, **calc-operate**, or **calc-command**), and it sets tok to the result of the regular expression match.

In **calc-eval**, we see where the idea of a function as a list comes in. The **funcall** function reflects the fact that there is little difference between code and data in Lisp. We can put together a list consisting of a symbol and a bunch of expressions and evaluate it as a function, using the symbol as the function name and the expressions as arguments; this is what **funcall** does. In this case, the following:

```
(funcall calc-proc-fun tok)
```

treats the symbol value of **calc-proc-fun** as the name of the function to be called and calls it with the argument tok. Then the function does one of three things:

- If the token is a number, **calc-push-number** pushes the number onto the stack.

- If the token is an operator, **calc-operate** performs the operation on the top two numbers on the stack (see below).
- If the token is a command, **calc-command** performs the appropriate command.

The function **calc-operate** takes the idea of functions as lists of data a step further by converting the token from the user directly into a function (an arithmetic operator). This step is accomplished by the function **read**, which takes a character string and converts it into a symbol. Thus, **calc-operate** uses **funcall** and **read** in combination as follows:

```
(defun calc-operate (tok)
  (let ((op1 (calc-pop))
        (op2 (calc-pop)))
    (calc-push (funcall (read tok) op2 op1))))
```

This function takes the name of an arithmetic operator (as a string) as its argument. As we saw earlier, the string tok is a token extracted from the *Calc* buffer, in this case, an arithmetic operator such as + or *. The **calc-operate** function pops the top two arguments off the stack by using the **pop** function, which is similar to the use of cdr earlier. **read** converts the token to a symbol, and thus to the name of an arithmetic function. So, if the operator is +, then **funcall** is called as here:

```
(funcall '+ op2 op1)
```

Thus, the function + is called with the two arguments, which is exactly equivalent to simply (**+ op2 op1**). Finally, the result of the function is pushed back onto the stack.

All this voodoo is necessary so that, for example, the user can type a plus sign and Lisp automatically converts it into a plus function. We could have done the same thing less elegantly—and less efficiently—by writing **calc-operate** with a **cond** construct (as in **calc-next-token**), which would look like this:

```
(defun calc-operate (tok)
  (let ((op1 (calc-pop))
        (op2 (calc-pop)))
    (cond ((equal tok "+")
           (+ op2 op1))
          ((equal tok "-")
           (- op2 op1))
          ((equal tok "*")
           (* op2 op1))
          ((equal tok "/")
           (/ op2 op1))
          (t
           (% op2 op1)))))
```

The final thing to notice in the calculator mode code is the function **calc-mode**, which starts the mode. It creates (and pops to) the *Calc* buffer. Then it kills all existing local variables in the buffer, initializes the stack to nil (empty), and creates the local variable **calc-proc-fun** (see the earlier discussion). Finally it sets Calculator mode as the major mode, sets the mode name, and activates the local keymap.

Lisp Code for the Calculator Mode

Now you should be able to understand all of the code for the calculator mode. You will notice that there really isn't that much code at all! This is testimony to the power of Lisp and the versatility of built-in Emacs functions. Once you understand how this mode works, you should be ready to start rolling your own. Without any further ado, here is the code:

```
;;    Calculator mode.
;;
;;    Supports the operators +, -, *, /, and % (remainder).
;;    Commands:
;;    c         clear the stack
;;    =         print the value at the top of the stack
;;    p         print the entire stack contents
;;

(defvar calc-mode-map nil
  "Local keymap for calculator mode buffers.")

; set up the calculator mode keymap with
; C-j (linefeed) as "eval" key
(if calc-mode-map
    nil
  (setq calc-mode-map (make-sparse-keymap))
  (define-key calc-mode-map "\C-j" 'calc-eval))

(defconst calc-number-regexp
  "-?\\([0-9]+\\.?\\|\\.\\)[0-9]*\\(e[0-9]+\\)?"
  "Regular expression for recognizing numbers.")

(defconst calc-operator-regexp "[-+*/%]"
  "Regular expression for recognizing operators.")

(defconst calc-command-regexp "[c=ps]"
  "Regular expression for recognizing commands.")

(defconst calc-whitespace "[ \t]"
  "Regular expression for recognizing whitespace.")

;; stack functions
(defun calc-push (num)
  (if (numberp num)
      (setq calc-stack (cons num calc-stack))))

(defun calc-top ()
  (if (not calc-stack)
      (error "stack empty.")
    (car calc-stack)))

(defun calc-pop ()
  (let ((val (calc-top)))
    (if val
```

```
      (setq calc-stack (cdr calc-stack)))
   val))

;; functions for user commands:
(defun calc-print-stack ()
  "Print entire contents of stack, from top to bottom."
  (if calc-stack
      (progn
        (insert "\n")
        (let ((stk calc-stack))
          (while calc-stack
            (insert (number-to-string (calc-pop)) " "))
          (setq calc-stack stk)))
    (error "stack empty.")))

(defun calc-clear-stack ()
  "Clear the stack."
  (setq calc-stack nil)
  (message "stack cleared."))


(defun calc-command (tok)
  "Given a command token, perform the appropriate action."
  (cond ((equal tok "c")
         (calc-clear-stack))
        ((equal tok "=")
         (insert "\n" (number-to-string (calc-top))))
        ((equal tok "p")
         (calc-print-stack))
        (t
         (message (concat "invalid command: " tok)))))

(defun calc-operate (tok)
  "Given an arithmetic operator (as string), pop two numbers
off the stack, perform operation tok (given as string), push
the result onto the stack."
  (let ((op1 (calc-pop))
        (op2 (calc-pop)))
    (calc-push (funcall (read tok) op2 op1))))

(defun calc-push-number (tok)
  "Given a number (as string), push it (as number)
onto the stack."
  (calc-push (string-to-number tok)))


(defun calc-invalid-tok (tok)
  (error (concat "Invalid token: " tok)))

(defun calc-next-token ()
  "Pick up the next token, based on regexp search.
As side effects, advance point one past the token,
and set name of function to use to process the token."
  (let (tok)
```

```
     (cond ((looking-at calc-number-regexp)
            (goto-char (match-end 0))
            (setq calc-proc-fun 'calc-push-number))
           ((looking-at calc-operator-regexp)
            (forward-char 1)
            (setq calc-proc-fun 'calc-operate))
           ((looking-at calc-command-regexp)
            (forward-char 1)
            (setq calc-proc-fun 'calc-command))
           ((looking-at ".")
            (forward-char 1)

            (setq calc-proc-fun 'calc-invalid-tok)))
     ;; pick up token and advance past it (and past whitespace)
     (setq tok (buffer-substring (match-beginning 0) (point)))
     (if (looking-at calc-whitespace)
       (goto-char (match-end 0)))
     tok))


(defun calc-eval ()
  "Main evaluation function for calculator mode.
Process all tokens on an input line."
  (interactive)
  (beginning-of-line)
  (while (not (eolp))
    (let ((tok (calc-next-token)))
      (funcall calc-proc-fun tok)))
  (insert "\n"))

(defun calc-mode ()
  "Calculator mode, using H-P style postfix notation.
Understands the arithmetic operators +, -, *, / and %,
plus the following commands:
    c   clear stack
    =   print top of stack
    p   print entire stack contents (top to bottom)
Linefeed (C-j) is bound to an evaluation function that
will evaluate everything on the current line. No
whitespace is necessary, except to separate numbers."
  (interactive)
  (pop-to-buffer "*Calc*" nil)
  (kill-all-local-variables)
  (make-local-variable 'calc-stack)
  (setq calc-stack nil)
  (make-local-variable 'calc-proc-fun)
  (setq major-mode 'calc-mode)
  (setq mode-name "Calculator")
  (use-local-map calc-mode-map))
```

The following are some possible extensions to the calculator mode, offered as exercises. If you try them, you will increase your understanding of the mode's code and Emacs Lisp programming in general.

- Add an operator ^ for "power" (**4 5 ^** evaluates to 1024). There is no built-in power function in Emacs Lisp, but you can use the built-in function expt.
- Add support for octal (base 8) and/or hexadecimal (base 16) numbers. An octal number has a leading "0," and a hexadecimal has a leading "0x"; thus, 017 equals decimal 15, and 0x17 equals decimal 23.
- Add operators \+ and * to add/multiply *all* of the numbers on the stack, not just the top two (e.g., **4 5 6 \+** evaluates to 15, and **4 5 6 *** evaluates to 120).*
- As an additional test of your knowledge of list handling in Lisp, complete the example (Example 5) from earlier in this chapter that searches **compilation-error-regexp-alist** for a match to a compiler error message. (Hint: make a copy of the list, then pick off the top element repeatedly until either a match is found or the list is exhausted.)

Customizing Existing Modes

Now that you understand some of what goes into programming a major mode, you may decide you want to customize an existing one. Luckily, in most cases, you don't have to worry about changing any mode's existing Lisp code to do this; you may not even have to look at the code. All Emacs major modes have "hooks" for letting you add your own code to them. Appropriately, these are called *mode-hooks*. Every built-in major mode in Emacs has a mode hook called *mode-name*-**hook**, where *mode-name* is the name of the mode or the function that invokes it. For example, C mode has **c-mode-hook**, shell mode has **shell-mode-hook**, etc.

What exactly is a hook? It is a variable whose value is some Lisp code to run when the mode is invoked. When you invoke a mode, you run a Lisp function that typically does many things (e.g., sets up key bindings for special commands, creates buffers and local variables, etc.); the last thing a mode-invoking function usually does is run the mode's hook if it exists. Thus, hooks are "positioned" to give you a chance to override anything the mode's code may have set up. For example, any key bindings you define override the mode's default bindings.

We saw earlier that Lisp code can be used as the value of a Lisp variable; this use comes in handy when you create hooks. Before we show you exactly how to create a hook, we need to introduce yet another Lisp primitive function: **lambda**. **lambda** is very much like **defun** in that it is used to define functions; the difference is that

---

* APL programmers will recognize these as variations of that language's "scan" operators.

lambda defines functions that don't have names (or, in Lisp parlance, "anonymous functions"). The format of **lambda** is:

```
(lambda (args)
   code)
```

where *args* are arguments to the function and *code* is the body of the function. To assign a lambda function as the value of a variable, you need to "quote" it to prevent it from being evaluated (run). That is, you use the form:

```
(setq var-name
      '(lambda ( )
          code))
```

Therefore, to create code for a mode hook, you could use the form:

```
(setq mode-name-hook
      '(lambda ( )
          code for mode hook))
```

However, it's quite possible that the mode you want to customize already has hooks defined. If you use the setq form, you override whatever hooks already exist. To avoid this, you can use the function add-hook instead:

```
(add-hook 'mode-name-hook
      '(lambda ( )
   code for mode hook))
```

The most common thing done with mode hooks is to change one or more of the key bindings for a mode's special commands. Here is an example: in Chapter 7 we saw that picture mode is a useful tool for creating simple line drawings. Several commands in picture mode set the default drawing direction. The command to set the direction to "down," **picture-movement-down**, is bound to **C-c .** (**C-c** followed by a period). This is not as mnemonic a binding as **C-c <** for **picture-movement-left** or **C-c ^** for **picture-movement-up**, so let's say you want to make **C-c v** the binding for **picture-movement-down** instead. The keymap for picture mode is, not surprisingly, called **picture-mode-map**, so the code you need to set this key binding is this:

```
(define-key picture-mode-map "\C-cv" 'picture-movement-down)
```

The hook for picture mode is called **edit-picture-hook** (because **edit-picture** is the command that invokes picture mode). So, to put this code into the hook for picture mode, the following should go into your *.emacs* file:

```
(add-hook 'edit-picture-hook
      '(lambda ( )
          (define-key picture-mode-map "\C-cv" 'picture-movement-down)))
```

This instruction creates a **lambda** function with the one key binding command as its body. Then, whenever you enter picture mode (starting with the next time you invoke Emacs), this binding will be in effect.

As a slightly more complex example, let's say you create a lot of HTML pages. You use HTML mode (see Chapter 8), but you find that there are no Emacs commands that enter standard head and title tags, despite the fact that the help text reminds you of their importance. You want to write your own functions to insert these strings, and you want to bind them to keystrokes in HTML mode.

To do this, you first need to write the functions that insert the tag strings. The simplest approach would just be to insert the text:

```
(defun html-head ( )
  (interactive)
  (insert "<head></head>"))

(defun html-title( )
  (interactive)
  (insert "<title></title>"))
```

Remember that the calls to (interactive) are necessary so that Emacs can use these functions as user commands.

The next step is to write code that binds these functions to keystrokes in HTML mode's keymap, which is called **html-mode-map**, using the techniques described in Chapter 10. Assume you want to bind these functions to **C-c C-h** (head) and **C-c C-t** (title). **C-c** is used as a prefix key in many Emacs modes, such as the language modes we saw in the last chapter. Again, this is no problem:

```
(define-key html-mode-map"\C-c\C-h" 'html-head)
(define-key html-mode-map"\C-c\C-t" 'html-title))
```

Finally, you need to convert these lines of Lisp into a value for **html-mode-hook**. Here is the code to do this:

```
(add-hook 'html-mode-hook
     '(lambda ( )
        (define-key html-mode-map"\C-c\C-h" 'html-head)
        (define-key html-mode-map"\C-c\C-t" 'html-title)))
```

If you put this code in your *.emacs* file, together with the earlier function definitions, you get the desired functionality whenever you use HTML mode.

If you try using these functions, though, you'll find they have some noticeable drawbacks compared to the other tag insertion commands in HTML mode. For one thing, while the other helper commands leave your cursor in between the opening and closing tags, our insertions leave the cursor after the closing tag, which is not only inconsistent, but it's much less helpful. Also, while the other tags you insert can be customized in terms of your preferred capitalization, or wrapped around existing content in the document, our simple-minded **insert** calls give us no such capabilities.

Luckily, it's not hard to add the smarts we want. It turns out that HTML mode is defined in the file *sgml-mode.el* (we learned this by applying help's handy **describe-function** command, **C-h f**, to the mode-defining function HTML mode. Armed with this knowledge, it was an easy matter to pull up and study the Lisp code that makes it work using the **find-library-file** utility shown in "A Treasure Trove of Examples" earlier in this chapter. A little quick hunting to find a parallel example revealed that the tag support is implemented using a skeletal function generator. Without going into too much detail, it turns out that the code we want to use is this:

```
(define-skeleton html-head
  "HTML document header section."
  nil
  "<head>" _ "</head>")

(define-skeleton html-title
  "HTML document title."
  nil
  "<title>" _ "</title>")
```

The define-skeleton function sets up the skeletal HTML code to be inserted, and it does this by writing a Lisp function based on the template you pass it. Its first argument is the name of the Lisp function to define, and the next is a documentation string for that function explaining what it inserts. After that comes an optional prompt that can be used to customize the content to be inserted. We don't need any customization, so we leave it as nil to skip the prompt. Finally comes the list of strings to be inserted, and we mark where we want the cursor to end up with "_". (To learn more about the way this skeleton system works, invoke **describe-function** on **insert-skeleton**.)

With these changes, our new commands work just like the other insertion tools in HTML mode. Even more than the specific Lisp code that came out of this example, the *technique* we used to create it is worth learning. If you can develop the skills and habits involved in tracking down an example from the built-in libraries that is close to what you want, and digging into how it works just enough to come up with a variant that solves your problem, you'll be well on your way to becoming the friendly Emacs Lisp guru your friends rely on when they need a cool new trick.

Here is a third example. Let's say you program in C, and you want a Lisp function that counts the number of C function definitions in a file. The following function does the trick; it is somewhat similar to the **count-lines-buffer** example earlier in the chapter. The function goes through the current buffer looking for (and counting) C function definitions by searching for { at the beginning of a line (admittedly, this simplistic approach assumes a particular and rigid C coding style):

```
(defun count-functions-buffer ()
"Count the number of C function definitions in the buffer."
  (interactive)
  (save-excursion
    (goto-char (point-min))
    (let ((count 0))
      (while (re-search-forward "^{" nil t)
        (setq count (1+ count)))
      (message "%d functions defined." count))))
```

The **re-search-forward** call in this function has two extra arguments; the third (last) of these means "if not found, just return `nil`, don't signal an error." The second argument must be set to `nil`, its default, so that the third argument can be supplied.*

Now assume we want to bind this function to **C-c f** in C mode. Here is how we would set the value of **c-mode-hook**:

```
(add-hook 'c-mode-hook
    '(lambda ()
        (define-key c-mode-map "\C-cf" 'count-functions-buffer)))
```

Put this code and the function definition given earlier in your *.emacs* file, and this functionality will be available to you in C mode.

As a final example of mode hooks, we'll make good on a promise from the previous chapter. When discussing C++ mode, we noted that the commands **c-forward-into-nomenclature** and **c-backward-into-nomenclature** are included as alternatives to **forward-word** and **backward-word** that treat *WordsLikeThis* as three words instead of one, and that this feature is useful for C++ programmers. The question is how to make the keystrokes that normally invoke **forward-word** and **backward-word** invoke the new commands instead.

At first, you might think the answer is simply to create a hook for C++ mode that rebinds **M-f** and **M-b**, the default bindings for **forward-word** and **backward-word**, to the new commands, like this:

```
(add-hook 'c++-mode-hook
    '(lambda ()
        (define-key c++-mode-map "\ef"
          'c-forward-into-nomenclature)
        (define-key c++-mode-map "\eb"
          'c-backward-into-nomenclature)))
```

(Notice that we are using **c++-mode-map**, the local keymap for C++ mode, for our key bindings.) But what if those keys have already been rebound, or what if **forward-word** and **backward-word** are also bound to other keystroke sequences (which they usually are anyway)? We need a way to find out what keystrokes are bound to these functions, so that we can reset *all* of them to the new functions.

Luckily, an obscure function gives us this information, **where-is-internal**. This function implements the "guts" of the **where-is** help command, which we will see in Chapter 14. **where-is-internal** returns a list of keystroke atoms that are bound to the function given as an argument. We can use this list in a **while** loop to do all of the rebinding necessary. Here is the code:

```
(add-hook 'c++-mode-hook
    '(lambda ()
        (let ((fbinds (where-is-internal 'forward-word))
```

---

* The second argument to **re-search-forward**—and other search functions—gives a bound to the search: if given an integer value *n* don't search past character position *n*. A value of `nil`, the default, means don't give the search a bound.

```
          (bbinds (where-is-internal 'backward-word)))
        (while fbinds
          (define-key c++-mode-map (car fbinds)
            'c-forward-into-nomenclature)
          (setq fbinds (cdr fbinds)))
        (while bbinds
          (define-key c++-mode-map (car bbinds)
            'c-backward-into-nomenclature)
          (setq bbinds (cdr bbinds)))))))
```

The two lines in the top of the **let** statement get all of the key bindings of the commands **forward-word** and **backward-word** into the local variables **fbinds** and **bbinds**, respectively.

After that, there are two **while** loops that work like the **print-stack** function of the calculator mode shown earlier in this chapter. This use of **while** is a very common Lisp programming construct: it iterates through the elements of a list by taking the first element (the **car**), using it in some way, and deleting it from the list ((setq *list* (cdr *list*)). The loop finishes when the list becomes empty (nil), causing the **while** test to fail.

In this case, the first **while** loop takes each of the bindings that **where-is-internal** found for **forward-word** and creates a binding in C++ mode's local keymap, **c++-mode-map**, for the new command **c-forward-into-nomenclature**. The second **while** loop does the same for **backward-word** and **c-backward-into-nomenclature**.

The surrounding code installs these loops as a hook to C++ mode, so that the rebinding takes place only when C++ mode is invoked and is active only in buffers that are in that mode.

One final word about hooks: you may have noticed that some of the mode customizations we have shown in previous chapters include hooks and others do not. For example, the code in the previous chapter to set your preferred C or C++ indentation style included a hook:

```
(add-hook 'c-mode-hook
    '(lambda ()
        (c-set-style "stylename")
        (c-toggle-auto-state)))
```

whereas the code that sets an alternative C preprocessor command name for the **c-macro-expand** command did not:

```
(setq c-macro-preprocessor "/usr/local/lib/cpp -C")
```

Why is this? Actually, the correct way to customize any mode is through its hook—for example, the preceding example should really be:

```
(add-hook 'c-mode-hook
    '(lambda ()
        (setq c-macro-preprocessor "/usr/local/lib/cpp -C")))
```

If you merely want to set values of variables, you can get away without a hook, but a hook is strictly required if you want to run functions like **c-set-style** or those used to bind keystrokes. The precise reason for this dichotomy takes us into the murky depths of Lisp language design, but it's essentially as follows.

Variables that are local to modes, like **c-macro-preprocessor**, do not exist if you don't invoke the mode in which they are defined. So, if you aren't editing C or C++ code, then **c-macro-preprocessor** doesn't exist in your running Emacs, because you haven't loaded C mode (see below). Yet if your *.emacs* file contains a **setq** to set this variable's value, then you call the variable into existence whether or not you ever use C mode. Emacs can deal with this: when it loads C mode, it notices that you have already set the variable's value and does not override it.

However, the situation is different for functions. If you put a call to a mode-local function like **c-set-style** in your *.emacs* file, then (in most cases) Emacs complains, with the message `Error in init file`, because it does not know about this function and thus cannot assume anything about what it does. Therefore you must attach this function to a hook for C mode: by the time Emacs runs your hook, it has already loaded the mode and therefore knows what the function does.

These examples of hooks are only the briefest indication of how far you can go in customizing Emacs's major modes. The best part is that, with hooks, you can do an incredible amount of customization without touching the code that implements the modes. In exchange, you should remember, when you do write your own modes, to think about useful places to put hooks so others can take advantage of them.

Building Your Own Lisp Library

After you have become proficient at Emacs Lisp programming, you will want a library of Lisp functions and packages that you can call up from Emacs at will. Of course, you can define a few small functions in your *.emacs* file, but if you are writing bigger pieces of code for more specialized purposes, you will not want to clutter up your *.emacs* file—nor will you want Emacs to spend all that time evaluating the code each time you start it up. The answer is to build your own Lisp library, analogous to the Lisp directories that come with Emacs and contain all of its built-in Lisp code. After you have created a library, you can load whatever Lisp packages you need at a given time and not bother with the others.

Creating a library requires two simple steps. First, create a directory in which your Lisp code will reside. Most people create a *elisp* subdirectory of their home directory. Lisp files are expected to have names ending in *.el* (your *.emacs* file is an exception). The second step is to make your directory known to Emacs so that when you try to load a Lisp package, Emacs knows where to find it. Emacs keeps track of such directories in the global variable **load-path**, which is a list of strings that are directory names.

The initial value for **load-path** is populated with the names of the Lisp directories that come with Emacs, e.g., */usr/local/emacs/lisp*. You will need to add the name of your own Lisp directory to **load-path**. One way to make this addition is to use the Lisp function **append**, which concatenates any number of list arguments together. For example, if your Lisp directory is *~<yourname>/lisp*, you would put the following in your *.emacs* file:

```
(setq load-path (append load-path (list "~yourname/lisp")))
```

The function **list** is necessary because all of the arguments to **append** must be lists. This line of code must precede any commands in your *.emacs* file that load packages from your Lisp directory.

When you load a library, Emacs searches directories in the order in which they appear in **load-path**; therefore, in this case, Emacs searches its default Lisp directory first. If you want your directory to be searched first, you should use the **cons** function described earlier instead of **append**, as follows:

```
(setq load-path (cons "~yourname/lisp" load-path))
```

This form is useful if you want to replace one of the standard Emacs packages with one of your own. For example, you'd use this form if you've written your own version of C mode and want to use it instead of the standard package. Notice that the directory name here is not surrounded by a call to **list** because **cons**'s first argument can be an atom (a string in this case). This situation is similar to the use of **cons** for pushing values onto stacks, as in the calculator mode described earlier.

If you want Emacs to search the directory you happen to be in at any given time, simply add nil to **load-path**, either by prepending it via **cons** or by appending it via **append**. Taking this step is analogous to putting . in your Unix PATH environment variable.

After you have created a private Lisp library and told Emacs where to find it, you're ready to load and use the Lisp packages that you've created. There are several ways of loading Lisp packages into Emacs. The first of these should be familiar from Chapter 10:

- Type **M-x load-library Enter** as a user command; see Chapter 10.
- Put the line (load *"package-name"*) within Lisp code. Putting a line like this into your *.emacs* file makes Emacs load the package whenever you start it.
- Invoke Emacs with the command-line option **"-l *package-name*"**. This action loads the package *package-name*.
- Put the line (autoload *'function "filename"*) within Lisp code (typically in your *.emacs* file), as described in Chapter 10. This action causes Emacs to load the package when you execute the given *function*.[*]

---

[*] There is also the option **"-f *function-name*"** which causes Emacs to run the function *function-name* at startup, with no arguments.

Byte-Compiling Lisp Files

After you have created your Lisp directory, you can make loading and running your Lisp files more efficient by *byte-compiling* them, or translating their code into *byte code*, a more compact, machine-readable form. Byte-compiling the Lisp file *filename.el* creates the byte code file *filename.elc*. Byte code files are typically 40 to 75 percent of the size of their non-byte-compiled counterparts.

Although byte-compiled files are more efficient, they are not strictly necessary. The **load-library** command, when given the argument `filename`, first looks for a file called *<filename>.elc*. If that doesn't exist, it tries *<filename>.el*, that is, the non-byte-compiled version. If that doesn't exist, it finally tries just *<filename>*. Thus, you can byte-compile your *.emacs* file, which may result in faster startup if your *.emacs* is large.

You can byte-compile a single function in a buffer of Lisp code by placing your cursor anywhere in the function and typing **M-x compile-defun**. You can byte-compile an entire file of Lisp by invoking **M-x byte-compile-file Enter** and supplying the filename. If you omit the *.el* suffix, Emacs appends it and asks for confirmation. If you have changed the file but have not saved it, Emacs offers to save it first.

Then you will see an entertaining little display in the minibuffer as the byte-compiler does its work: the names of functions being compiled flash by. The byte-compiler creates a file with the same name as the original Lisp file but with c appended; thus, *<filename>.el* becomes *<filename>.elc*, and *.emacs* becomes *.emacs.elc*.

Finally, if you develop a directory with several Lisp files, and you make changes to some of them, you can use the **byte-recompile-directory** command to recompile only those Lisp files that have been changed since being byte-compiled (analogously to the Unix **make** utility). Just type **M-x byte-recompile-directory Enter** and supply the name of the Lisp directory or just press **Enter** for the default, which is the current directory.

CHAPTER 12
Version Control

The Uses of Version Control

If you write either large programs or long documents, you have probably been caught at least once in a situation where you've made changes that turned out to be a bad thing, only to be confused and stymied because you weren't sure exactly how to reverse them and get back to a known good state. Or, perhaps you've released a program or document to someone else, then gotten a bug fix or a comment that you couldn't integrate properly because you couldn't recover the old version that person was working with. Perhaps you're a member of a development or documentation team and have felt the need for some way to keep change histories, indicating who was responsible for each change.

These common kinds of problems can be addressed with a *version control system*. A version control system gives you automated help at keeping a change history for a file or group of files. It allows you to recover any stage in that history, and it makes getting reports on the differences between versions easy.

Today a variety of version control systems are widely available on machines that run Emacs. Some are commercial, but there are a wealth of free, open, and powerful choices, and it seems appropriate for our discussion to focus on these. Historically, Emacs evolved largely in a Unix environment alongside the SCCS and RCS systems, and its built-in support for version control reflects their approach and terminology. Today the most popular by far is CVS (which builds on RCS, giving it more flexibility and power), and there is a new system called Subversion that is starting to catch on. Preliminary support for working with Subversion shipped with Emacs 21.3.5; its documentation suggests you check the Subversion site, *http://subversion.tigris.org/*, for updates.

Given that when you need version control, you generally need it very badly (and you have enough other challenges to occupy your mind), it's not surprising that most integrated development environments today offer automated support for these tools. And if any other IDE does it, by now you can certainly predict that Emacs does too!

In this chapter, we'll introduce you to the Emacs facility called VC, an Emacs Lisp minor mode that makes using version control systems very easy. VC runs all version control commands for you (using Emacs' subprocess facilities in the same way that compiler modes do). VC hides almost all the details of their interfaces from you; instead, you can trigger most basic version control operations with a single command, with Emacs correctly deducing what needs to be done next.

As noted above, the VC architecture was designed with the behavior of RCS in mind. So as we explain VC, we'll explain the RCS terminology and behavior as Emacs presents it. Where needed, we'll point out key differences in the way CVS behaves. Subversion, in turn, is being designed as a more modern version of CVS, and acts like CVS with respect to its interactions with Emacs.

Version Control Concepts

Each file under version control has a change history that consists of an *initial version* and a series (or sometimes a branching tree) of subsequent *revisions*.

To make a file version-controlled, you must *register* it; that is, you must tell the version control system to treat the file contents you're starting with as an initial version and begin maintaining a change history for it.*

To change a registered file, in the old days you'd have to *check out* the file. Doing so notifies the version control system that you're modifying it. Under SCCS and RCS, this would lock the file so that no one else could check it out until you were done (anyone else could still look at it, though). This limitation was one of the major motivations for the development of CVS, the Concurrent Versions System, which doesn't make locks. Instead, it tries to reconcile any concurrent changes at the time that they are committed, as described below. Even so, some developers prefer to configure CVS to keep files locked at the OS level until they consciously decide they want to make changes to one of them; this largely mimics the RCS experience, albeit on a voluntary basis.

In a system like SCCS or RCS that uses locking, you may sometimes find that you can't check out a file because someone else has it locked already. Perhaps that person checked it out and wandered away, so that the lock is stale. You may want to *steal the lock*—that is, seize control of the work file with whatever changes the other person has made and take responsibility for checking in a clean set of changes yourself. (It's bad practice to do this casually!) Again, this hasn't generally been an issue since CVS made concurrent edits a practical option—recall that the "C" in CVS stands for "concurrent."

---

* You don't need to have registered a file from VC to use VC on it. VC works just fine on a preexisting tree of version-controlled files.

While making changes to your *work file* (the working copy you've checked out) and experimenting with them, you may decide at any time to *revert* the work file—that is, to throw away your changes and undo the check-out operation. After you've made changes to your file that you want to keep, you must *check in* those changes. Doing so adds them permanently to the saved change history as a new revision of the file. Under RCS and SCCS, it also removes the lock on your work file, so that other people can check it out and edit it. Under CVS and Subversion, the file was never locked; instead, the version control system tries to reconcile your changes with any other changes that might have been made since check-out time and yells for help (manual intervention) if it finds conflicts. Because you never really checked the file out in a concurrent system, the standard term for integrating your changes back into such a repository is *commit* rather than *check in*. The CVS interface also allows you to call it checking in, to accommodate people who are used to older systems, and that's what Emacs calls it too.

The register, check-out, revert, and check-in operations are the basic ones. But you may want to do other things as well. You can also retrieve any saved revision, get a difference report between any two saved versions or any saved version and your (possibly modified) work file, or even completely remove saved revisions that you want to throw away (though this is rare).

If conflicts are reported during a check-in operation, Emacs offers to help you resolve them by launching an Ediff session (described at the end of this chapter). If you decide against Ediff, you will see the conflicts as represented within the file by the version control system and you can address them manually or use whatever other tools you find convenient. If you later decide you do want help from Ediff after all, you can use **M-x vc-resolve-conflicts Enter** while you're editing the conflicted file.

Most version control systems (and all the ones we're talking about here) associate *change comments* with each revision. So each time you check in a registered file, you can add an explanation of the change to the change history, which won't be part of the file itself. Each revision has a *revision number*, which identifies its place in the history. The base revision in SCCS, RCS, and CVS is 1.1. If the history is a linear sequence of changes (which is typical for small projects), sequence numbers are two numeric fields separated by a dot. Subversion uses a simpler revision numbering scheme with which you're undoubtedly familiar: The first revision is numbered 1, the one that comes after it is 2…subtle, eh?

It is possible to start branches so that variant versions of files can be maintained in parallel. In such cases, the main trunk still has two-field revision numbers, but branches have more fields. The exact naming conventions for branches are arcane and different between SCCS and RCS or CVS; if you need to know about them in detail, consult the documentation for your version control system. Once again, this is a whole lot simpler in Subversion, which versions the entire source tree as a unit and supports efficient copies of parts of the tree. In Subversion, a branch is just another directory. There is a lot more to know about version control systems than we go into here, and two excellent O'Reilly books on the topic are: *Essential CVS* by Jennifer Vesperman and *Version Control with Subversion* by Ben Collins-Sussman, Brian W. Fitzpatrick, and C. Michael Pilato.

How VC Helps with Basic Operations

Historically, you had to know three or four different shell commands to do the basic operations of version control (registration, check in, check out, and revert), and you had to do each one outside your editor (or in an editor subshell). This procedure was complicated and annoying, or at best a distraction from the flow of working on your code and changes.

VC's interface is much simpler. The simplicity comes from noticing that whatever state your version-controlled file is in, there is normally just one logical thing to do next. Here are the rules:

- If your file isn't under version control, the next logical thing to do is register it and (where relevant) check out a modifiable copy for you.

- If it's registered, but not checked out by anyone, the next thing you generally want to do is check it out so you can edit it (again, where relevant, such as if you're using CVS in a "keep files read-only unless I say I want to edit them" mode).

- If you have made changes to the file, the next logical thing is to check it back in, which may involve reconciling your changes with those made by someone else.

- Much more rarely, if you're using one of the pre-CVS systems, if someone else has a file checked out, you may want to steal the lock (notifying the lock owner that you've done so).

Indeed, VC mode has just one basic command: **C-x v v** (for **vc-next-action**), which you can think of as "do the next logical thing to this file" or, more precisely: "take the currently visited file to the next normal version control state." It follows the arrows in Figure 12-1, which describes the traditional version control cycle.* This command is available in every Emacs since 19; when you invoke it, it automatically fetches the rest of VC and does its job.

There's a little more to it than that, of course. For one thing, when you check in a set of changes to a file, VC pops up a buffer for you to enter a change comment. Similarly, if you're in an older version control environment, when you steal a lock, VC pops up a buffer requesting an explanation. This explanation is mailed to the lock owner.

---

* Minor tricky detail: your very first **vc-next-action** on a new work file normally takes you from "unregistered" through "registered, unlocked," and then to "locked, editable." Why make you do two commands for those two steps when one will cover the typical case? If you want to register a file but not check it out, use **C-x v i** (for **vc-register**). With the advent of CVS, this point becomes largely moot as you'll see in Figure 12-2.

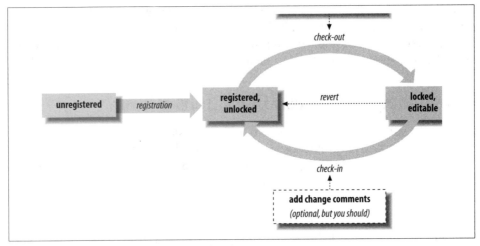

Figure 12-1. The traditional version control cycle

VC gives you a revert operation as well: **C-x v u** (for **vc-revert-buffer**). Actually, the function that implements **vc-next-action** checks to see if the buffer is unmodified since check-out time; if so, it offers to revert the buffer and unlocks the work file rather than checking in an empty change.

Although it's worth understanding this traditional flow because it's how VC is designed, working with today's concurrent version control systems is slightly different. Luckily, it's even a little simpler. Because there is no need to obtain a lock in order to edit a document, one of the VC steps is missing (or, if you prefer, you can think of it as implicit). This is illustrated in Figure 12-2.

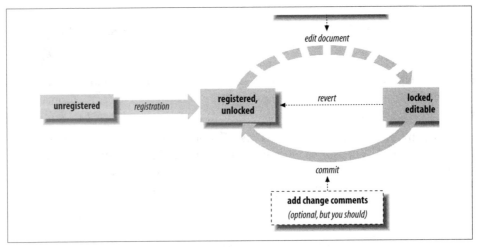

Figure 12-2. The concurrent version control cycle

The transition from the unmodified state to the modified state (with respect to the version in the repository) is shown as a dotted line, because you no longer perform a VC operation here. You just start editing the file you want to work with. Whenever you tell VC you want the "next action" it's able to tell whether the document is modified or not. If it is, the current version is committed ("checked in," if you will) and you're prompted for the change comments. If the file is registered but unmodified, VC simply displays a message in the minibuffer telling you that the buffer is up to date.

If you prefer to configure CVS to give you read-only versions of files until you explicitly choose to edit them, your workflow will remain that of Figure 12-1.

Editing Comment Buffers

In VC mode, three operations typically pop up a buffer to accept comment or notification text: check in, lock stealing, and (under circumstances to be explained later in the chapter) file registration. In each case, the operation is on hold until you type **C-c C-c** to commit the comment buffer. You can enter a comment right away and finish the operation, or you can go off and do something else. VC waits patiently to commit until you are ready. If you delete the pop-up buffer, the operation is quietly scrubbed.

The comment buffer is a plain-text buffer. However, each time you commit a comment buffer, the contents are saved to a new slot in a ring of comment buffers. You can cycle backwards in the ring with **M-p** and forward with **M-n**, or you can search for text backwards in the ring with **M-r** and forward with **M-s**. By design, these are the same keys you can use to navigate an Emacs minibuffer command history. By far the most commonly used of these commands is **M-p**. Being able to recall and edit the last change comment is often useful since it's common to make a series of related changes.

VC Command Summary

To give you the flavor of the other things VC can do for you, Table 12-1 provides a summary of VC commands. Each one will be explained in detail, but you can probably guess some of their actions from the command names.

Table 12-1. VC commands

Keystrokes	Command name	Action
C-x v v	vc-next-action	Go to the next logical version control state.
C-x v d	vc-directory	Show all registered files beneath a directory.
C-x v =	vc-diff	Generate a version difference report.
C-x v u	vc-revert-buffer	Throw away changes since the last checked-in revision.
C-x v ~	vc-version-other-window	Retrieve a given revision in another window.
C-x v l	vc-print-log	Display a file's change comments and history.

Table 12-1. VC commands (continued)

Keystrokes	Command name	Action
C-x v i	vc-register	Register a file for version control.
C-x v h	vc-insert-headers	Insert version control headers in a file.
C-x v r	vc-retrieve-snapshot	Check out a named project snapshot.
C-x v s	vc-create-snapshot	Create a named project snapshot.
C-x v c	vc-cancel-version	Throw away a saved revision.
C-x v a	vc-update-change-log	Update a GNU-style ChangeLog file.

These commands are ordered in the table roughly by decreasing frequency of use. This is also the order in which we'll describe them in the following sections. All VC commands have the common prefix **C-x v**. Your fingers will learn this prefix quickly, and all you usually have to remember is the single command suffix. Two minor commands, **vc-rename-file** and **vc-clear-context**, are not bound to keys. They are explained later on.

VC Mode Indicators

VC grabs a bit of the mode line for each buffer visiting a registered file and tries to use it to keep you informed of the version control state of that file. You'll notice that when a buffer is visiting a version-controlled file, the mode tags part of the mode line (shown in parentheses) shows the name of your version control system and a revision number for the file.

When those two parts are separated by a dash, the file is not yet checked out; when they're separated by a colon, the file has been checked out, and the revision number is the one the file had when you checked it out. Note that since most people use concurrent version control systems these days, in which you don't check files out or obtain locks, you can think of the dash as meaning unmodified, while the colon means there have been changes that are not yet committed to the repository.

If you don't see these indicators, the file isn't registered yet. These three states are illustrated in Figure 12-3.

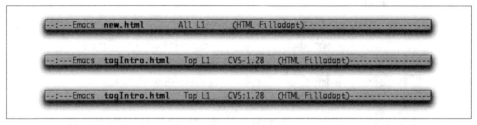

Figure 12-3. Mode lines showing a file that is not under version control, one that is unchanged with respect to the repository, and one that has had changes saved but not yet committed.

Which Version Control System?

We said earlier that VC uses any of a number of version control systems (more may be added in the future). It chooses which to use for any given file by looking for a corresponding *master file*—that is, a file containing a change history.

If you're using RCS, each of your project directories usually has a subdirectory in which RCS masters live. If you're using SCCS, there are *SCCS* subdirectories. CVS is a little trickier; your project directory has a *CVS* subdirectory with control information in it, but CVS masters are typically kept in one central repository directory, the location of which is typically given by the CVSROOT environment variable, and will likely be on another machine completely, using the pserver network protocol. Subversion, too, uses a separate server machine to store the revision repository; it generally uses WebDAV over HTTP for its transactions. Your local Subversion master files are kept in a subdirectory named *.svn*.

If VC can't find a master in any of these special directories, it looks for a master in the same directory as your work file (so you don't have to create SCCS or RCS directories if you don't mind your work directories being cluttered with masters). VC checks each of these possibilities (so you can actually use more than one system in the same directory, although we don't recommend it).

If VC can't find a master anywhere, it looks for an *RCS, SCCS, CVS,* or *.svn* directory. The order in which these are attempted is controlled by the variable **vc-handled-backends**, described in "Customizing VC" later in this chapter. The first one it finds tells it which version control system to register new files with. If it can't find any of these directories, and you tell it to register a file, it assumes you want to use RCS and creates the master right alongside your work file.

To find out which of SCCS, RCS, CVS, or Subversion is available on your system, simply execute the commands **comb**, **rcs**, **cvs**, and **svn** respectively, with no arguments. If you see an error or usage message, the corresponding system is ready to use; if you see command not found, it's not.

Individual VC Commands

We've already explained what the main command, **vc-next-action**, does. Now we'll describe each of VC's other commands in detail. We have chosen the order of these descriptions to take you from frequently used and simpler commands to rarer and more complex ones.

You can, accordingly, read to the end of chapter or bail out at any point if you think you've learned all you need to. But try to persevere because you may find that the descriptions of the less common commands give you some new ideas about how to track and organize your project files.

Working with Groups and Subtrees of Files

Usually, the projects you want to put under version control have more than one file; it's normal for them to contain all the files under a specific directory and subdirectory. Therefore, seeing a list of all version-controlled files beneath the current working directory is often useful. Being able to perform an operation on all of them *en masse* is even more useful.

VC mode supports this directly. The command **C-x v d** (for **vc-directory**) puts you in a buffer running a customized Dired (directory editing) mode, which lists all registered files under the current directory, indicating which, if any, are checked out and who has locked them. The status field in this listing is automatically kept up to date by check-in and check-out operations.

If you mark several files in this Dired buffer (with the ordinary Dired mark command described in Chapter 5) and then perform either a **vc-next-action** or **vc-revert-buffer**, VC performs that operation on all the marked files. The most common case in which you'll perform this procedure is when you want to check in changes to several files simultaneously. VC helps you out: it pops up a buffer for only one change comment, which it then applies to every revision the check-in creates.

The **vc-revert-buffer** design is a bit more conservative; normally, it prompts you once for each file to make sure you really want to discard its changes.

Some Dired commands are rebound in VC Dired to run version-control commands. The = keystroke, for example, runs **vc-diff** on the current file rather than a Dired **diff**. And **g** refreshes all the VC status fields in the directory.

Difference Reports

Earlier, we mentioned that version control systems help you generate difference reports between versions. VC's command for this is **C-x v =** (for **vc-diff**). This command normally shows you the difference between your work file and the last revision you checked in so that you can see exactly what changes you'll be committing if you check in again.

If you give this command a prefix argument, **C-u C-x v =**, it prompts you for a file name and two revision numbers and reports the difference between those revisions of the file. If the older revision number is empty (that is, you simply press **Enter** at that prompt), it defaults to the last checked-in revision. If the newer revision is empty, it defaults to the work file. So pressing **Enter** twice compares the work file with what was last checked in to the repository, a very common task.

It's also possible to get a difference report for a whole tree of project files. If the filename you give **C-u C-x v =** is actually a directory, you'll see the differences between your specified versions for every registered file underneath that directory.

By design, such a difference report can be shipped and mechanically applied as a patch using Larry Wall's **patch** utility (available on all modern Unixes). This is a tremendous help when you're cooperating on a software project by email; you can download sources, register them, make modifications—and then, with one command, generate a complete patch set of your changes to mail to your collaborators.

The exact format of these reports varies somewhat between version control systems because VC uses each system's native difference reporter.* Generally, the output resembles that of the Unix **diff** command. We'll see how to customize the report later in this chapter. Finally, the last section of the chapter introduces Ediff, an alternate and powerful way to compare and resolve differences between multiple files or versions.

Retrieving Old Revisions

You can use the command **C-x v ~** (for **vc-version-other-window**) to retrieve any saved revision of a file. The revision is retrieved into a work file with the same name as your file, except for a suffix that identifies its revision number (the suffix is actually a dot, followed by a tilde, followed by the revision number, followed by another tilde). So you can retrieve several revisions, and they won't step on each other. This command is useful when you want to eyeball the entire old version of a file, as opposed to just its changes from previous versions or its differences from later ones.

The version suffix format is very close to what Emacs generates for saved versions if you set the global Emacs Lisp variable **version-control** (which VC has made pretty much obsolete). For example, if you're visiting a file named *foo.html* and you retrieve version 1.3 by typing **C-x v ~ 1 . 3 Enter**, you will now be visiting a file named *foo.html.~1.3~* (and because it ends with a tilde, Dired's command to flag backup files will mark it, as discussed in Chapter 5).

Viewing Change Histories

If you use **C-x v l** (for **vc-print-log**) on a registered file, VC pops up a buffer containing that file's change history. This command is most useful for viewing the change comments associated with each revision.

Registering a File

Normally, registering a file for version control with **C-x v v** (for **vc-next-action**) with a nonconcurrent version control system also checks out an editable copy. Occasionally it's useful to be able to just register a file without checking it out. The command **C-x v i** (for **vc-register**) does this. With modern concurrent version control systems, this distinction is fading away.

---

* This is a slight oversimplification. VC actually has its own script as a wrapper around SCCS's **sccsdiff**, in order to give it a calling sequence more like RCS's **rcsdiff**.

Inserting Version Control Headers

Most version control systems encourage you to embed in your file one or more magic strings that get automatically updated at check-in, check-out, and revert time. The purpose of these strings is to carry automatically inserted information about the current revision number of the file, who last modified it, and when it was last checked in.

These header strings largely duplicate within the file the version information that VC puts on the mode line—and the rest of that information you can get with **C-x v l** (for **vc-print-log**). This feature might not seem very useful, but (in particular) embedding a version string can make it possible to mine version-control information out of a compiled binary program.

Further, you may frequently view version-controlled files through something other than Emacs. If so, you won't have an Emacs mode line displaying version control information, and there is some value in having the magic headers visible in the file. Accordingly, VC provides you with a command to insert them. (Note that what VC inserts are correctly formatted placeholders for the headers; the actual values get filled in by the underlying version control system each time you commit the file.)

If you type **C-x v h** (for **vc-insert-headers**) while visiting a registered and editable file, VC tries to determine from the syntax of the file how to insert the version control header(s) as a comment and then do so. VC knows about C and Java code, and **nroff/troff/groff** code especially, and can usually deduce the right thing from Emacs' **comment-start** and **comment-end** global variables (set by each major mode) so it can insert HTML comments, for example. It falls back to **#-to-\n** comments (like those used by shell, awk, Perl, tcl, and many other Unix languages) if it can't figure out anything better to do. This command is also smart enough to notice if you already seem to have version control headers present in the file and will ask you for confirmation before inserting a redundant set.

One special behavior with respect to C code is worth mentioning. C files don't actually get version headers put in comments by default. Instead, Emacs generates a string initialization for a static dummy variable called **vcid**. This action is taken so the header will actually be generated into the corresponding object file as a string, and you can use the *strings* command (if you've got a Unix-like environment) to see which versions of its sources a binary was generated from.

Making and Retrieving Snapshots

A *snapshot* of a project is a set of revisions of the project files treated as a unit. Typically, releases are associated with points at which the project's product goes to a customer or other outside evaluator.

When you're working with a subtree of project files and want to define a release of a document or program, you may find it tedious to have to do it by remembering or storing long lists of file revision numbers. Accordingly, most version control systems give you the ability to associate a symbolic release name with all the revisions that make up a release, and then to use that symbolic name later on when naming revisions for retrieval or difference reports.

Bare RCS and CVS both provide this capability. Bare SCCS does not, but VC includes code to simulate it under SCCS. In practice, the difference between native symbolic names and VC's is next to invisible. The only drawback of VC's simulation is that the SCCS tools won't know about symbolic names when you call them outside VC. (Note that this concept doesn't really apply to Subversion, because in that environment *every* revision is a snapshot of the files and directories comprising the entire module.)

The **C-x v s** (for **vc-create-snapshot**) prompts you for a symbolic name. VC then associates this name with the current revision level of every registered file under the current directory.

The symbolic names you create with **vc-create-snapshot** are also valid arguments to any other VC command that wants a revision number. Symbolic names are especially useful with **vc-diff**; it means you can compare named releases with each other or with your checked-out work files. The **C-x v r** (for **vc-retrieve-snapshot**) command takes a symbolic name and checks out every registered file underneath the current working directory at the revision level associated with the name.

Both the snapshot commands will fail, returning an error and not marking or retrieving any files, if any registered file under the current directory is checked out by anyone. The **vc-create-snapshot** command fails in order to avoid making a snapshot that, when retrieved later, won't restore the current state completely. It also fails in order to avoid stepping on your work file changes before you've had the chance to check them in or revert them out.

Updating ChangeLog Files

The command **C-x v a** (for **vc-update-change-log**) helps VC work with some project-management conventions used by the Free Software Foundation. FSF projects generally have in each directory a file called *ChangeLog* that is supposed to contain timestamped modification comments for every file in that directory. The *ChangeLog*, historically, provided the change history, or audit trail, for which VC uses change comments.

Rather than make you enter every change comment twice (!), VC provides a hook that copies recent change comments out of masters beneath the current directory and appends them to a *ChangeLog* in the approved format.

Renaming Version-Controlled Files

Renaming version-controlled files can be tricky. In RCS or SCCS, you have to rename not just the work file but its associated master. Under CVS, for reasons too arcane to go into here, it's hard to do at all without breaking something.

The **vc-rename-file** tries to insulate you from the details and to catch and inform you about various error conditions that can arise. It simply prompts for old and new filenames, tries to do the right thing, and tells you if it cannot.

 Renaming interacts badly with the simulated symbolic-name feature under SCCS. This is one of the better reasons to use RCS or CVS. And, actually, if you think you might need to rename or move files, you're best off investigating Subversion since one of its major design goals was to be the first version control system in which this task is straightforward.

When VC Gets Confused

The filesystem operations required to determine a file's version control state can be expensive and slow, especially in an NFS or other networked environment. VC goes to some pains to compensate (unless, as we'll see later on, you tell it not to).

It has two major methods: (1) caching per-file information (such as the locking user and current revision number) in memory rather than running version control utilities to parse it out of the relevant master every time, and (2) assuming that it can deduce a registered file's version control state from its write permissions. Specifically, VC assumes that a registered file that is writable is in the checked-out-and-locked state and that a registered file that is *not* writable is *not* a checked-out version being edited.

Multiuser environments being what they are, VC's cached information and assumptions about permissions occasionally lead it down the wrong path. This situation almost always occurs because someone has manually changed a file's permissions behind VC's back.

If you think that this situation has occurred, call **vc-clear-context**. This command forces VC to throw away all its cached-in-memory assumptions about the version control state of the files you are working with.

It is also theoretically possible for VC to get confused by a race condition between two or more VCs, or between VC and someone running the bare SCCS, RCS, or CVS utilities. This is not just a VC problem; the same sort of race is possible (though less likely) between two or more people running the bare utilities. However, this kind of race is very rare even in VC; the authors haven't heard of any instance in hundreds of thousands of programmer-hours in which it's known to have happened.

If you're concerned about this issue, the VC source code (*vc.el* in your Emacs Lisp source directory) includes a comment giving a careful and extensive analysis of potential multiuser conflict and race situations. VC is exactly as safe from them as the underlying utilities can be.

Customizing VC

Some of the rules we've described earlier in the chapter for VC's behavior can be changed by setting certain Emacs variables related to VC mode. We'll go over a few of the most important here.

vc-handled-backends

> This variable controls the set of version control systems used by VC, and the order in which they are found in the list controls the order in which they are attempted. It defaults to (RCS CVS SVN MCVS SCCS). If you remove values from the list, they won't be considered valid version control systems to use. If the list is empty, VC is disabled entirely.

vc-display-status

> This variable displays a file's revision number and status on the mode line of each buffer visiting it, if this is non-**nil**. To avoid expensive queries of the master file, you may want to turn this variable off if you are running VC over very slow network links.

vc-*backend*-header

> These variables provides lists of the headers to be inserted by **vc-insert-headers** when using the specified version control system. For example, the headers for CVS are in the variable **vc-cvs-header**. You can customize these lists if you like a different format for your version number headers.

vc-keep-workfiles

> Normally, VC leaves a read-only copy of the work file in place whenever it performs a check-in. This feature is convenient because it means **make** and other tools always find work files where they expect to. If you're very tight on disk space, you can turn it off, but then you have to execute an explicit check-out every time a tool other than VC needs the work file. (Emacs itself knows about version control through a piece of VC code that's always resident; its visit commands perform a check-out if necessary, without locking the file.)

vc-mistrust-permissions

> This variable is normally **nil**. Make it **t** to tell VC not to trust a file's permissions or ownership as indicators of its version control state. This change slows VC down a lot, but it may be necessary if (for example) your development group is working in several different directories and accessing work files via symbolic links. In such a case, the permissions and ownership of the link convey nothing about the state of the work file.

vc-suppress-confirm

This variable defaults to **nil**. If it is non-**nil**, it suppresses the confirmation prompt **vc-revert-buffer** normally gives you before discarding changes.

vc-initial-comment

Most version control systems allow (but do not require) you to enter an initial comment when you register a file—a lead-off for the change history. If this variable is non-**nil**, VC pops up a buffer for this comment at registration time just as it normally does for change comments at check-in time.

diff-switches

The Emacs *diff.el* mode takes command-line switches from this global variable to pass to **diff** when generating a change report. VC uses it the same way. It defaults to the single switch **-c** to force **context-diff** format; **-u** for **unified-diff** format is also fairly popular.

A number of other, less important global variables are fully documented in the Emacs online help system.

Extending VC

VC was designed from the beginning to be usable as a front-end for multiple version control systems. The code that actually runs the version control tools is carefully isolated from the user-level package logic in such a way that plugging in new systems is not very hard. VC's author originally wrote it to handle SCCS and RCS; CVS support was added later, by a different person, without much difficulty, and Subversion support was an even simpler variant of the CVS code.

There are a couple of extensions to Emacs for users of ClearCase, a popular commercial project-management system. Whether this code is accepted into the GNU Emacs distribution, considering the FSF's hostile attitude towards non-freeware, is another question. So far they have not been, but you can obtain the packages over the internet. At the time of this writing, the best choice appears to be *clearcase.el*. The author of the first implementation, *VC-ClearCase*, has even stated that he's switched over to *clearcase.el*. The current download site is *http://members.verizon.net/~vze24fr2/ EmacsClearCase/*. If it's moved by the time you read this, hopefully a Google search will steer you in the right direction.

By the time you read this book, then, your VC may well handle additional systems besides the ones we have described here (though CVS and Subversion are likely to remain the most popular ones for the foreseeable future). If you are a skilled Emacs Lisp programmer (or would like to become one) and have your own favorite version control system, by all means hack the source code—extend VC to use it, and share your results so that everyone benefits.

What VC Is Not

VC is not a total solution to the project-management problem. Although it assists single-author programming or document maintenance greatly and can give vital help on small- to medium-scale projects involving several developers, it's not necessarily adequate by itself for large multiple-component, multiple-directory projects. The following are some of its more obvious deficiencies for larger projects:

- It is not integrated with a change request or problem-report system.
- Its only way of grouping project files is by directory subtree. This limitation may create problems for large, multiple-directory projects, especially when two or more need to share a common library or subtree.

You can work around these deficiencies on small projects. Variant versions might be handled with compile-time conditions, like **#ifdef**s in C code. Change requests can be kept separately in some kind of database (such as the FSF's GNATS system, or Mozilla's Bugzilla). Programmers can carry around in their heads the state needed to do renames without disruption.

As projects scale up in size and intricacy, however, such *ad hoc* measures increasingly fail to prevent damaging friction and lead to death by accumulated details. Complexity control for very large projects requires a fundamentally stronger (and, unfortunately, more constraining and complex) support environment that goes beyond version control—a full project-management system.

For more on the design issues in project-management systems, see the latter half of the book *Applying SCCS and RCS* by Don Bolinger and Tan Bronson (O'Reilly).

Using VC Effectively

We urge those of you with prior version control experience to heed the following maxim: *to use VC effectively, check in your changes early and often!* Of course, when you are working as part of a team of developers, you do need to take care to check in only a consistent and working set of files each time. There's nothing quite equal to the frustration of discovering that you can no longer compile and test your own code because someone else has checked in a fragmentary or broken piece of theirs.

If you're used to version control interfaces that are as clumsy and difficult as bare SCCS, RCS, or—to a lesser extent—CVS, your reflexes may prevent you from getting the most leverage out of VC. You probably won't commit often; you're not used to being able to instantly get status reports on a whole subtree of files.

It's worth a little thought and effort to reeducate yourself. You'll find that, instead of being an irritating minor chore, version control under VC can be tremendously liberating. By checking changes in often, you'll find you can afford to experiment more, because you'll know how to revert to a known good state quickly if need be.

Comparing with Ediff

In working with any version control system, you sometimes want to compare differ-ent revisions of a file. Often you're interested in what's changed in the current work-ing revision, but sometimes you're after more historical information. The most challenging situation arises when an optimistic strategy like CVS is proved wrong, and you need to merge incompatible changes made by multiple developers to the same section of a file.

We've already described **vc-diff**, VC's built-in facility for helping with these tasks. We would be remiss, however, if we did not introduce you to Ediff, an even more powerful facility that is available in current releases of GNU Emacs. Ediff is extremely rich; it almost feels like another program that "takes over" your Emacs ses-sion for a while. Full coverage would require an entire chapter, or perhaps even its own handbook, but this introduction will get you started and point you at the built-in manual if you want to delve deeper.

Starting Ediff

For the most part, you launch Ediff as an independent entity rather than having it invoked automatically by the version control interface. The exception (as mentioned above) is if you ask Emacs for help resolving conflicts when they occur during a check-in operation or manually invoke **vc-resolve-conflicts** while visiting a buffer containing such conflicts.

If you want to use Ediff to compare two nonconflicting revisions of a file, choose Tools → Compare (Ediff) → File with revision, or type **M-x ediff-revision Enter**. Ediff prompts you for the file you'd like to compare (defaulting to the file associated with the current buffer), and the revision(s) you'd like to compare, defaulting to the ver-sion last checked in and the current state of the buffer. (Ediff can also be used for many tasks outside the context of version control systems; you might want to explore the options on the Compare (Ediff) menu on a rainy day.)

The first time you invoke Ediff, you will probably find it disorienting. In addition to the expected pair of buffers showing you the two files or revisions being compared, it pops open a small "control window" (see Figure 12-4) in which you type com-mands. In its default configuration, this is a separate operating system window (or what Emacs refers to as a "frame"). For Ediff commands to work, this window must have keyboard focus (must show as being the currently active window as far as the operating system is concerned). This is different from almost any other situation in Emacs, in that you're looking at and manipulating content in one frame while a sec-ond frame has focus.

In its default configuration, the control window is designed to be small enough not to get in the way on smaller displays. The problem is that you might not even notice

Figure 12-4. The Ediff control window in its default state (Mac OS X)

it, let alone realize what it's for! In addition to being the place you type Ediff commands, this small window shows you where you are in the difference list (in this case, before the first of seven differences), and reminds you that you can type **?** to get some more help. As a new Ediff user, we strongly recommend that you type **?** each time you fire it up to expand the control window into the larger, Quick Help mode, shown in Figure 12-5.

```
 ●●●                            Ediff
█   Move around      |    Toggle features     |       Manipulate
================|=======================|======================
p,DEL -previous diff |   | -vert/horiz split  |a/b -copy A/B's region to B/A
n,SPC -next diff     |   h -hilighting        | rx -restore buf X's old diff
    j -jump to diff  |   @ -auto-refinement   |  * -refine current region
   gx -goto X's point|                        |  ! -update diff regions
  C-l -recenter      |  ## -ignore whitespace |
  v/V -scroll up/dn  | #f/#h -focus/hide regions | wx -save buf X
  </> -scroll lt/rt  |   X -read-only in buf X | wd -save diff output
    ~ -swap variants |   m -wide display      |
================|=======================|======================
    R -show registry |   = -compare regions   | M  -show session group
    D -diff output   |   E -browse Ediff manual| G  -send bug report
    i -status info   |   ? -help off          | z/q -suspend/quit
----------------------------------------------------------------
For help on a specific command:  Click Button 2 over it; or
                                 Put the cursor over it and type RET.
-- *Ediff Control Panel*   At start of 7 diffs      Quick Help
```

Figure 12-5. The Ediff control window showing Quick Help (Mac OS X)

In addition to the control window, you'll see the differences between the files you're comparing inside the frame you were previously using for editing. If you're looking at a large file, none of the differences might be visible initially. You can jump to the first difference by typing **n** or pressing the space bar, as suggested by the quick help window. (Remember that for any of the Ediff commands to work, the control/quick help window *must* have keyboard focus.) The displayed differences will look something like Figure 12-6.

Ediff centers the difference regions within each buffer, and marks the changed lines with color, further emphasizing the specific portions of the lines which have changed to help attract visual attention to the differences. This is much more helpful than the traditional diff mode, making it worthwhile learning the strange new interface.

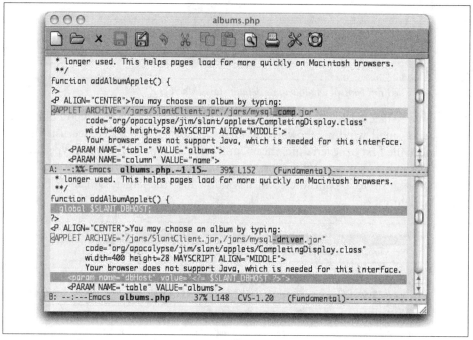

Figure 12-6. Differences displayed by Ediff

Using Ediff

The basic way to use Ediff is to scroll through the buffers, seeing what has changed between them. The normal Emacs "browsing" keys (**Space** to move forward, **Del** to move backward) are bound in the control window to take you through the differences one by one. Pressing **n** (next) and **p** (previous) has the same effect. If you want to go to a specific difference, you can type a number followed by **j** (jump) to move immediately to that difference. To scroll up or down by pages rather than by differences you can use **v** to move forward and **V** to move backward. If your buffers contain wide lines, you can also type < and > to scroll left and right. If you'd like to view the buffers side by side rather than one above the other, type | (vertical bar). Typing this a second time returns to showing the buffers vertically. To reduce the need to scroll horizontally, you can make the comparison window as wide as possible by typing **m** (this is also a toggle; typing it again returns the window to its previous width). This command might cause the control window to lose focus, forcing you to click back into it before issuing the next Ediff command. (See "Recovering from Confusion" later in this chapter.) Important commands available in Ediff are summarized in Table 12-2.

Table 12-2. *Ediff commands*

Keystrokes	Command name	Action
Space or **n**	**ediff-next-difference**	Move to the next difference between the files.
Del or **p**	**ediff-previous-difference**	Move to the preceding difference between the files.
j	**ediff-jump-to-difference**	Go to the difference specified as a numeric prefix argument.
v or **C-v**	**ediff-scroll-vertically**	Move forward one page in both buffers.
V or **M-v**	**ediff-scroll-vertically**	Move backward one page in both buffers.
<	**ediff-scroll-horizontally**	Scroll each buffer to the left.
>	**ediff-scroll-horizontally**	Scroll each buffer to the right.
| (vertical bar)	**ediff-toggle-split**	Switch between viewing the buffers one above the other and side-by-side.
m	**ediff-toggle-wide-display**	Toggle between normal frame size and making it as wide as possible.
a	**ediff-copy-A-to-B**	Copy the version of the current difference found in buffer A to buffer B.
b	**ediff-copy-B-to-A**	Copy the version of the current difference found in buffer B to buffer A.
r a or **r b**	**ediff-restore-diff**	Restore the current difference in buffer A (or B) to the way it was before copying from the other buffer.
A or **B**	**ediff-toggle-read-only**	Switch the specified buffer into (or out of) read-only mode.
g a or **g b**	**ediff-jump-to-difference-at-point**	Recenter the comparison buffers on the difference nearest to your current location (point) in the specified buffer.
C-l	**ediff-recenter**	Restore the comparison display so that the highlighted regions of all buffers being compared are visible; useful if you've been doing something else and want to get back to comparing.
!	**ediff-update-diffs**	Recalculate and redisplay the highlighted regions; useful if you've manually made extensive changes to a buffer.
w a or **w b**	**ediff-save-buffer**	Save the specified buffer to disk.
E	**ediff-documentation**	Open the manual for Ediff.
z	**ediff-suspend**	Close the Ediff control window, but leave the session active so you can resume it later.
q	**ediff-quit**	Close the Ediff window and end this comparison session.

Making Changes

In addition to simply viewing the differences between files, you will sometimes want to resolve or merge them (especially if you've entered Ediff as the result of conflicts that occurred while checking in a file revision). Several commands help with this, and they generally require you to choose which buffer you want to work from. As you might have noticed in Figure 12-5, Ediff assigns each file or revision buffer a letter to identify it: A, B and sometimes C if you are comparing three things. A number of

Ediff commands work with these buffer identifiers—the letter X is used to stand for these labels in the quick help window for most commands that use them.

To copy the version of the current difference found in one buffer to the other buffer, type the letter assigned to the buffer with the "right" version. For example, to copy A's version to B, type **a**. Ediff makes this change but keeps track of the old value in the buffer you changed. Following along in our example, if after changing buffer B like this, you change your mind and want to restore its old state, you can type **r b** (for "restore buffer B"). These changes are kept track of on a difference-by-difference basis, so you don't have to change your mind right away; you can jump back to that difference and restore it at a later time, as long as you're still in the same Ediff session.

Of course, to make changes to a buffer, it cannot be in read-only mode. If you are comparing a current file with a historical revision, the buffer representing the older version is read-only because you can't change the past. If you want to avoid accidentally changing a file while browsing differences, you can cause its buffer to become read-only by typing **Shift** and the buffer's letter label. (**Shift-b** to make buffer B read-only). This is a toggle, so doing it again makes a read-only buffer editable. If you do this to a buffer representing a historical revision, although Emacs will then let you edit the buffer, you're not actually affecting the revision within the version control system. So unless you're *trying* to confuse yourself, we'd suggest avoiding this practice.

If you're whipping through the buffers, making many changes by selecting appropriate versions to use within the Ediff control window, you may find yourself wanting to save one or the other of your difference buffers. While you can certainly click over to the difference window, move into that buffer, and use the standard **C-s** command to save, Ediff offers a more convenient alternative. Simply press **w** (write) followed by the buffer's letter label to save that buffer without leaving the control window.

Quitting Ediff

When you're done comparing the files, the quickest way to close the control window and get back to the "normal" Emacs world is to type **q** to quit your Ediff session. After confirming that you really want to do this, Ediff closes the control window and cleans up after itself. You can also suspend the session temporarily by typing **z** for suspend. This closes the Ediff control window, but Ediff remembers that you were in the middle of a session, to which you can return later whenever you'd like. The easiest way to do this is to view the list of active Ediff sessions by choosing Tools → Ediff Miscellanea → List Ediff Sessions. When you actually quit an Ediff session, it no longer appears in this list.

Recovering from Confusion

If you've been cruising along in Ediff and suddenly find your commands aren't working, you've probably accidentally clicked on the differences window and are typing in one of the buffers directly, or perhaps you used an Ediff command that switched the window focus on you unexpectedly. Make sure to undo the stray characters you've typed into the comparison buffer, then click on the control window and start issuing commands again.

Of course, you may want to intentionally jump over to edit one of the buffers as you notice changes you'd like to make. You can do that at any time; just remember to switch back to the control window when you want move to other differences or use other Ediff commands. If, after editing one of the comparison buffers for a while, you'd like to return to viewing differences, starting with the difference nearest to your edit location, click in the control window and type **g** followed by the letter assigned to the buffer in which you're interested (as discussed earlier in "Making Changes").

If you've made substantial changes by editing the buffer directly, you may find that the difference region highlights have drifted out of synch with the actual location of differences. To fix this, once the control window has focus, type **!** to cause Ediff to recalculate and redisplay the differences.

If you've reconfigured the buffers you're looking at (perhaps you wanted to look up some help text, or engage in a side task, which Emacs certainly encourages) you can restore the window configuration for Ediff by clicking on the control window and typing **C-l** (recenter). This sets up the comparison window to display the files you're comparing and centers the current difference in each buffer. You may find that it also causes the comparison window to get keyboard focus, so be sure to click on the control window if necessary before you try to issue any Ediff commands.

Learning More

As noted, there is a whole lot more to Ediff than we can discuss here. When you want to explore it, a good starting place is the built-in Ediff manual. You can get to this by typing **E** (**Shift-e**, the capitalization matters) in the Ediff control window. If you're not already inside Ediff, you can choose Tools → Ediff Miscellanea → Ediff Manual, or you can invoke Info, the Emacs documentation browser, by typing **C-h i**, and choose Ediff from the main menu of topics. (Typing **m** for menu, followed by **e d Enter** is enough to complete "Ediff" and jump to its manual.)

For more task-specific help, you can click on any of the commands in the quick help window using your middle mouse button to get help describing what it does. (If you lack a three button mouse, you can click on the command with your regular mouse button and then press **Enter**.)

Customizing Ediff

By now it should come as no surprise that you can change many details about the way that Ediff works so it better fits your way of thinking and working. After you've got a good grasp of the basics, you can use the Custom facility described in Chapter 10 to tweak the way Ediff works by choosing Tools → Ediff Miscellanea → Customize Ediff. If the use of a separate operating system window (frame) for the control window is driving you batty, you can toggle that behavior right away by choosing Tools → Ediff Miscellanea → Toggle use of separate control buffer frame.

Invoking Ediff Automatically

If Ediff is so powerful, why isn't it the default mode used by the **vc-diff** command? The most likely explanation is historical; **vc-diff** has been around longer than Ediff, and it would have been disruptive to long-standing users of Emacs if a strange new interface was unexpectedly foisted on them. It seems people are writing patches to integrate Ediff more tightly with VC, but they are not (yet?) part of the Emacs distribution. If you're interested in the current state of any of these efforts, try a Google search for "vc ediff."

CHAPTER 13

Platform-Specific Considerations

In this chapter, we describe installing Emacs on Unix, Mac OS X, and Windows as well as some of the subtleties of running Emacs on the latter two platforms.

Emacs 21 runs on free Unix systems including Linux and BSD variants as well as on commercial Unix versions such as AIX, Solaris, SunOS,' and Ultrix. It runs on Mac OS X (currently a separate fork, but due to be folded into the main distribution starting with 21.4). It runs on Windows and even on MS-DOS. You can still get ports for Mac OS 8/9 and Amiga (to name only a few). Emacs is truly a multiplatform editor.

We cover installing Emacs on Unix, Mac OS X, and Windows. For Windows and Mac OS X, prebuilt binaries are available. You may want to build Emacs from source in order to obtain the latest version. However, we have found up-to-date binaries online for Windows and Mac OS X; you just have to scout around on the Net to find them. By the time you read this, the sources for the binaries that we cite may be out of date. Check out this book's web site for updated links in that case (*http://www.oreilly.com/catalog/gnu3*).

A related issue is where to get Emacs. The Free Software Foundation (FSF) is the official source for Emacs, but like most software organizations, official releases are few and far between. Often, building Emacs from CVS sources is the best way to get a leading-edge version. Only you can decide whether you would rather have the latest features—along with some bugs—or download the tried-and-true version from the FSF's site.

Emacs and Unix

Emacs was originally built on a Unix system and continues to run on the multitude of Unix variants out there. We're going to download the latest source and show you how to build Emacs from scratch. It's not really that hard and it has the salutary effect of keeping you up-to-date with future releases.

Where to Get Emacs?

If you can't wait, the primary source for downloading Emacs is *http://ftp.gnu.org/pub/ gnu/emacs/*. Alternatively, you can use CVS to nab the absolute latest build. But more on that in a minute.

Downloading Emacs from the Web

You can get Emacs from any one of many sites—as long as your Internet connection is fast enough to transfer a 20 MB file easily. You must also have at least 120 MB of disk space free; this number will certainly grow in future Emacs releases.

The Free Software Foundation maintains a definitive list of all mirror sites. The FSF is the principal sponsor of the GNU Project and it is housed at their site. If you want to look around a bit, *http://www.gnu.org/* is the place to start. Or as mentioned earlier, you can just jump directly to the directly listing for Emacs at *http://ftp.gnu.org/ pub/gnu/emacs/*. You should see a list similar to Figure 13-1.

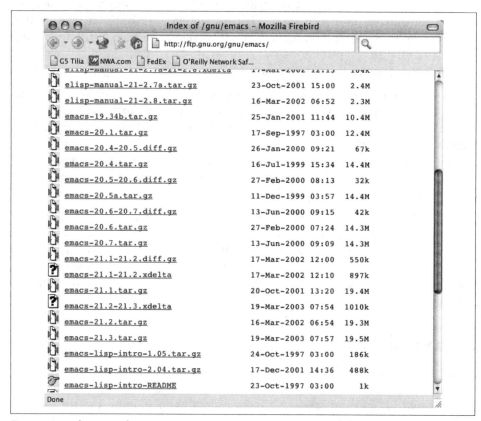

Figure 13-1. The emacs directory at gnu.org

Look for the latest version of Emacs (21.3 in Figure 13-1) and download it.

Where to Put Emacs?

Regardless of where you go to get the source, where you put the files you download is really up to you. For our Unix-based systems, we downloaded everything into */usr/local/install*. This is a fine place to start, but if you have a favorite download/development area, feel free to use that. In fact, you can even put everything in your home directory while you're building things.

The only thing to remember is that the build process involves a lot of files that you won't need after everything's done. Make sure you put things somewhere that's easy to clean up when all is said and done.

As for the final destination of the executable, that's also up to you. Most Unix systems (including Mac OS X) will do well to use the */usr/local* hierarchy. That directory is both common and the default choice in the build scripts. If you're not on a machine that you have complete control over, though, you can certainly install Emacs into your home directory (or a subdirectory you keep for you own software).

One quick note on using your home directory for the executable version of Emacs: it does make it easy to back up Emacs or transfer it to another machine if you upgrade your system (we know from experience!). However, it can limit who has access to Emacs. If another user works on the same machine and you both want to use Emacs, installing to a common directory (like */usr/local*) is definitely the way to go.

Uncompressing and Unpacking

Now that you have the file, you need to do two things to it before you can actually build Emacs: uncompress and unpack. You can use the **tar** command to do both. Make sure you are in the directory where you downloaded the Emacs file. Type the following command (changing the *n* to the version number that matches the file you downloaded), and you will see a list of files.

```
$ tar xvzf emacs-21.n.tar.gz
x emacs-21.3, 0 bytes, 0 tape blocks
x emacs-21.3/AUTHORS, 77854 bytes, 153 tape blocks
x emacs-21.3/FTP, 8950 bytes, 18 tape blocks
x emacs-21.3/INSTALL, 42841 bytes, 84 tape blocks
x emacs-21.3/README, 4046 bytes, 8 tape blocks
x emacs-21.3/BUGS, 1042 bytes, 3 tape blocks
x emacs-21.3/move-if-change, 129 bytes, 1 tape blocks
x emacs-21.3/ChangeLog, 161418 bytes, 316 tape blocks
x emacs-21.3/Makefile.in, 25461 bytes, 50 tape blocks
. . .
```

This list of created files goes on for quite a while—over 2500 files for Emacs 21.3. If you don't want to see the list, omit the **v** (**verbose** option) from the **tar** command. When this command completes, you have all of the files for Emacs.

Now that any necessary preparations are out of the way, you can go through the steps to build and install Emacs itself.

Downloading Emacs from CVS

As we mentioned earlier, you can also use **CVS** to pull the source files. The big advantage with CVS is that you get the absolute latest version.

1. Create or switch to a directory where your Emacs build can remain. Don't do this in a temporary directory unless you don't plan on keeping Emacs around. Once there, set up the **CVS_RSH** environment variable:

   ```
   % setenv CVS_RSH ssh
   ```

   If the **setenv** command is not recognized, you're probably running **bash** instead of a **csh**-derived shell. In that case, use the following command for the environment variable.

   ```
   $ export CVS_RSH="ssh"
   ```

2. Use the **cvs** command to grab the source code.

   ```
   % cvs -z3 -d:ext:anoncvs@savannah.gnu.org:/cvsroot/emacs co emacs
   The authenticity of host 'savannah.gnu.org (199.232.41.3)' can't be established.
   RSA key fingerprint is 80:5a:b0:0c:ec:93:66:29:49:7e:04:2b:fd:ba:2c:d5.
   Are you sure you want to continue connecting (yes/no)?
   ```

3. Verify that the public key matches this key:

   ```
   80:5a:b0:0c:ec:93:66:29:49:7e:04:2b:fd:ba:2c:d5
   ```

   That just makes sure you actually got connected to the right system and aren't being fed some malicious alternative.

4. If the keys match, type **yes** and press **Enter**.

   ```
   Warning: Permanently added 'savannah.gnu.org,199.232.41.3' (RSA) to the list of known hosts.
   cvs server: Updating emacs
   U emacs/.cvsignore
   U emacs/AUTHORS
   U emacs/BUGS
   U emacs/COPYING
   U emacs/ChangeLog
   U emacs/FTP
   U emacs/INSTALL
   ...
   ```

You'll see thousands of filenames flying by. If you have a slow network connection, this process could take a while. Hang in there, though—you're on your way to building the absolute latest version of Emacs!

Building Emacs

Unless you get a prebuilt version of Emacs that is right for your system, you will need to build and install the many executable components of Emacs from source code before you can use it. At this point, it doesn't matter how you got the source code (HTTP or CVS), you just need to compile it! Here is some information to get you started on this task.

Your source code has a top-level directory with a name like *emacs-21.3*. In this directory, you will find files called *INSTALL* and *README*. Examine *README* first; it contains useful general information as well as last-minute release notes that may be important for you to read before proceeding. Then read *INSTALL*, which gives step-by-step instructions for building Emacs. Even if you aren't a Unix expert, you should be able to follow these instructions. (For convenience, we provide a procedure you can follow later in this section.)

The FSF's standard installation procedure gets more comprehensive and bulletproof all the time. Still, the actual ease of building Emacs depends primarily on what combination of hardware and software you have. The FSF's installation script includes a program called **configure** that examines your system, figures out what hardware and software you are running, and configures Emacs accordingly.

configure is likely to guess correctly if you have a popular combination (such as a Sun SPARC CPU and a recent release of Solaris). If this is true, you should be able to build Emacs without lots of tweaking or technical expertise. However, if you have an unusual setup—a wildly obsolete computer or operating system version, an unusual hardware/software combination, or unconventional system configuration—then you will have no choice but to tweak the software. That's beyond the scope of this book, but those *README* and *INSTALL* files that come with the source distribution are a great place to start when dealing with uncommon setups.

Here's a procedure for building Emacs that you can use as a guide:

1. Change to the directory where you uncompressed and unpacked Emacs. For example, if you placed it in the */usr/local/install* directory:

   ```
   $ cd /usr/local/install/emacs-21.3
   ```

2. Run the configure utility.* You should see quite a bit of output that shows what parts of the system the build script is looking for.

   ```
   $ ./configure
   creating cache ./config.cache
   checking host system type... sparc-sun-solaris2.9
   checking for gcc... gcc
   checking whether the C compiler (gcc  ) works... yes
   ```

---

* Depending on your system and its permissions, you may have to switch to the root user using **su** to install Emacs. In that case, you won't need to preface the final **make** command with **sudo**.

```
checking whether the C compiler (gcc  ) is a cross-compiler... no
checking whether we are using GNU C... yes
checking whether gcc accepts -g... yes
checking whether ln -s works... yes
checking how to run the C preprocessor... gcc -E
```

3. If **configure** is successful, you should see a handy summary message similar to the following:

```
Configured for `sparc-sun-solaris2.9'.

  Where should the build process find the source code? /usr/local/install/emacs-21.3
  What operating system and machine description files should Emacs use?
        `s/sol2-5.h' and `m/sparc.h'
  What compiler should emacs be built with?                gcc -g -O2
  Should Emacs use the GNU version of malloc?              yes
  Should Emacs use a relocating allocator for buffers?     yes
  Should Emacs use mmap(2) for buffer allocation?          no
  What window system should Emacs use?                     x11
  What toolkit should Emacs use?                           LUCID
  Where do we find X Windows header files?                 Standard dirs
  Where do we find X Windows libraries?                    Standard dirs
  Does Emacs use -lXaw3d?                                  no
  Does Emacs use -lXpm?                                    yes
  Does Emacs use -ljpeg?                                   no
  Does Emacs use -ltiff?                                   no
  Does Emacs use -lungif?                                  no
  Does Emacs use -lpng?                                    no
  Does Emacs use X toolkit scroll bars?                    no
```

If the configuration process fails for any reason, you'll want to go back and consult the *INSTALL* document. It has several tips and tricks for particular systems and situations.

4. If everything is properly configured, you can go ahead and compile Emacs with the **make** utility. This may take a while, so start it before you head out for lunch.

```
$ make
if [ ! -f /usr/local/install/emacs-21.3/lisp/abbrev.elc ]; then \
  make  bootstrap; \
fi
cd lib-src; make all  \
  CC='gcc' CFLAGS='-g -O2' CPPFLAGS='' \
  LDFLAGS='' MAKE='make'
gcc -DHAVE_CONFIG_H -I. -I../src -I/usr/local/install/emacs-21.3/lib-src -I/usr/
local/install/emacs-21.3/lib-src/../src   -g -O2 -o test-distrib /usr/local/install/
emacs-21.3/lib-src/test-distrib.c
./test-distrib /usr/local/install/emacs-21.3/lib-src/testfile
gcc -DHAVE_CONFIG_H -I. -I../src -I/usr/local/install/emacs-21.3/lib-src -I/usr/
local/install/emacs-21.3/lib-src/../src   -g -O2 /usr/local/install/emacs-21.3/lib-
src/make-docfile.c -lsocket -lnsl -lkstat -o make-docfile
...
```

5. When that completes, the *INSTALL* document recommends testing your newly built Emacs with the following command:

```
$ src/emacs -q
```

Emacs should run and you should get an introduction screen similar to
Figure 13-2.

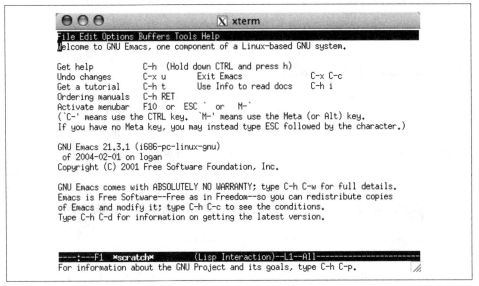

Figure 13-2. Emacs test after building on a Linux system

6. If you see the Emacs splash screen,* you're in good shape, so go ahead and install
   it:

```
$ sudo make install
```

or, if you *su*'d to root earlier, simply:

```
$ make install
```

You'll be prompted for your password. After the install completes, you should
be all set to use Emacs. Congratulations!

Emacs and Mac OS X

As you may have picked up reading other parts of this book, we treat Mac OS X as a
Unix variant for many tasks. We do that with good reason, of course. Mac OS X is
based on Unix. For example, you could more or less follow the CVS and Unix build
instructions in the previous sections and come away with a full installation of Emacs.†

---

* One of the authors was not able to see the splash screen, but the install worked fine nonetheless. We say
  forge ahead even if you don't see it.

† We say "more or less" because at the time we went to press, you still needed to grab the source from a separate site. That difference should eventually disappear as well.

However, as you know, Mac OS X can be a little different in some ways; it doesn't have all the Unix utilities by default (see the section on installing Ispell for one example of this). This section covers installing Emacs on Mac OS X as well as other issues such as running Emacs from the command line, changing the location of your Meta key, and installing Ispell. And if you do want to build Emacs from scratch using CVS, we have a few notes on that, too.

"But I Already Have Emacs"

Mac OS X comes with a version of Emacs installed: 21.2.1 with Panther (10.3.2) and 21.1.1 with Jaguar (10.2.8). To start this version, use the Terminal application in your *Utilities* folder (which is inside the *Applications* folder) and just type **emacs**.

Figure 13-3 shows the built-in Emacs running in the Terminal application.

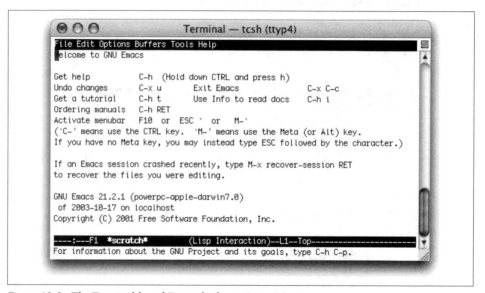

Figure 13-3. The Terminal-based Emacs built into Mac OS X

But you should be aware that although it is built-in and certainly the easiest to start using, this version of Emacs has a few shortcomings:

1. It runs, well, you know, in a Terminal.

2. It does not have any of the graphical user interface features such as icons or expected mouse behavior.

3. The Terminal application often supercedes Emacs when handling things like the scrollbars and some key bindings.

If you can live with those restrictions—or have no choice—then feel free to skip the next section on installing Emacs and get on with using the version you have. The vast majority of information in this book still applies.

Installing Prebuilt Emacs on Mac OS X

What if you want the latest version of Emacs but don't want to build it yourself? After all, not every Mac OS X user is an old Unix hack! Mac systems made a name for themselves by providing some of the best user interface conventions around in a single, good-looking package. That hasn't changed. If you're not a big fan of do-it-yourself application building, you can download a nifty application bundle and just drag-and-drop your way to a recent build of Emacs.

Downloading Alex Rice's application bundle of Emacs 21.3.5

Most Mac users will want to grab a prebuilt binary version of Emacs that's all ready to go. Alex Rice created just such a build. It can be found online (for free!') at: *http://mindlube.com/products/emacs/index.html*. You can download directly from that page, but be sure to grab the correct version. You can pick from the Jaguar (Mac OS X 10.2) version or the Panther (Mac OS X 10.3) version.

You'll be downloading a *.dmg* file which is the Mac disk image format. It should automatically unpack and mount itself, but if it doesn't for some reason, just double-click on the *.dmg* file after it is completely downloaded.

As it launches, you'll need to read and agree to the license. After you do that, you should have a new "disk" mounted and you'll see the Emacs application all ready to drag and drop. (See Figure 13-4.)

Drag the big gnu to your *Applications* folder and off you go. That really is all there is to it. Many, many thanks to Alex Rice and Mindlube! (And feel free to eject the mounted image once you have copied Emacs to your hard drive.)

Building Emacs from Source on Mac OS X

While Mac OS X is based (very squarely) on Unix, as of build 21.3.5, your best bet for building Emacs is still to go with a slightly modified build process. (The Mac build should join up with the normal build in version 21.4.) Until 2004, that separate process was maintained by Andrew Choi and made available to the public at *http://members.shaw.ca/akochoi-emacs/*. Fortunately, it is still available there, although Andrew is no longer the Mac maintainer.

---

* A donation to defray hosting costs would certainly be appreciated; the site includes a link for contributions.

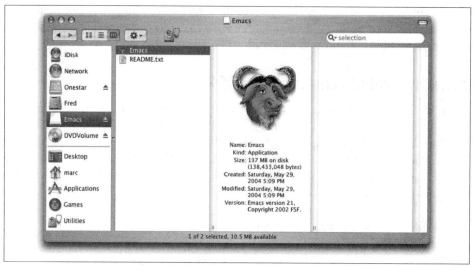

Figure 13-4. The mounted disk image for Emacs on Mac OS X (Panther)

 Full instructions on the build can also be found at Andrew's site. While the build is essentially the same as it is for other Unix systems (you run **configure** and then **make**), retrieving the source code is best done through CVS to get the latest version. If you have installed the Mac Developer Tools CD, you'll have CVS. If you haven't installed the Mac Developer Tools (usually available on a separate CD that came with your Mac or with your copy of Mac OS X), you must; the Developer Tools are required to build version 21.3 from source.

Before you build

For the 21.3 build, Andrew Choi has posted the steps required to retrieve and build Emacs at *http://members.shaw.ca/akochoi-emacs/stories/obtaining-and-building.html*.

If you plan to go this route on Panther (Mac OS X 10.3), just follow Andrew's instructions. Alternatively, you can follow the Unix build instructions from the previous section. If you're still running Jaguar, you'll need to do a bit of preparatory work. Read on.

Jaguar (Mac OS X 10.2) preparation. The first of the extra notes is that you should upgrade to Panther (10.3) if you aren't there already. Seriously. There are lots of benefits. But if that's just not in the cards for you, you do need to take a small detour before installing Emacs.

Mac OS X 10.2 lacks a piece of software required for Emacs: **texinfo**. (That tool comes preinstalled on 10.3.) It's not hard to install; you just have to remember to do it. You basically install the **texinfo** package as you would if any other Unix package. You can look back at the previous section for more details, but here are the basics.

You'll need to perform these commands from the Terminal application. By default, Terminal starts you out with a C-Shell variant, so we'll use the % character for the prompt in the commands for this section.

1. Pull the **texinfo** package from the */pub/gnu/texinfo* folder at *ftp.gnu.org*. The compressed archive file will be called something like *texinfo-4.7.tar.gz*. Grab the latest version available.

2. Unpack the archive.

   `% tar xvzf texinfo-4.7.tar.gz`

   If you downloaded **texinfo** through a browser, chances are the browser uncompressed it for you. Some of them might even have unpacked it as well. If you have a *.tar* file sitting on your desktop, you can unpack it like this:

   `% tar xvf texinfo-4.7.tar`

3. Move to the *texinfo-4.7* directory and configure your build.

   `% ./configure`

4. Assuming that all goes well, you can build everything:

   `% make`

5. And assuming that went well, you can install it. But you'll have to do that as an administrator. Fortunately that's easy to do in the Terminal window. Just run this command:

   `% sudo make install`

You'll be prompted for your password. Type it in and everything should go well. If you aren't allowed to administer your own machine, you'll need the help of someone who does have admin privileges.

Now that you've installed **texinfo**, you'll need to download, unpack, and install Emacs, either by following Andrew Choi's instructions or ours in the "Emacs and Unix" section earlier in this chapter.

Your Mac build should end up creating a double-clickable icon that you can drag and drop into your *Applications* folder just like the prebuilt download.

Starting Emacs from the Command Line on Mac OS X

On Mac OS X, you have Emacs preinstalled, but as we know, it is an older version of Emacs. Let's say that you have installed the graphical version and want to start it with some command-line arguments. For example, you might want to run **emacs --debug-init** to debug your *.emacs* file. The Mac OS X Gnu icon certainly should be a permanent fixture on your Dock, but at times the command line is the way to go.

We learned this trick from Andrew Choi's Mac OS X FAQ, and we share it here, slightly tweaked, for convenience. Check out his page at *http://members.shaw.ca/akochoi-emacs/stories/faq.html*.

Essentially, you replace the binary that comes with Mac OS X with a shell script that runs the new version of Emacs you installed. You might want to simply rename the old binary so that you can on occasion use it instead.

Here's the procedure.

1. To be sure which Emacs runs when you type **emacs**, type **which emacs** in the Terminal application.

   ```
   % which emacs
   /usr/bin/emacs
   ```

2. Rename or delete */usr/bin/emacs*.

   ```
   % sudo mv /usr/bin/emacs /usr/bin/oldemacs
   ```

   You'll be prompted for your password.

3. Create a file called *emacs* with the following two lines:

   ```
   #!/bin/sh
   /Applications/Emacs.app/Contents/MacOS/Emacs "$@"
   ```

   If you installed Emacs into a different folder, adjust the second line accordingly.

4. Move the file you created to */usr/bin*:

   ```
   % sudo mv emacs /usr/bin
   ```

5. Change */usr/bin/emacs* to be executable by the world:

   ```
   % chmod +x /usr/bin/emacs
   ```

   Now you can invoke graphical Emacs from the terminal window simply by typing **emacs**, with or without command-line arguments.*

Mac OS X and the Meta Key

This book has mentioned using the **Command** key for **Meta** on Mac OS X. By default, the **Command** key (sometimes called the **Open Apple** key, or more simply ⌘) is **Meta**. But in fact you have a choice. The variable **mac-command-key-is-meta** can be used to select which key you want to use.

As the variable name implies, setting **mac-command-key-is-meta** to **t** means that you use ⌘ as the **Meta** key. So you can type the **M-x** combination as ⌘**x**.

The alternative (setting **mac-command-key-is-meta** to **nil**) sets the **Option** (or **Alt**) key to be your **Meta** key. You might do this if you want to continue using the **Command** key for Mac functions or if you find that **Option** is simply easier to reach. Of course, it's not quite that simple. Emacs still traps the **Command** key. That trapping is supposed to be turned off with one more variable: **mac-pass-command-to-system**, but to be honest, we never got that to work.

---

* You can still run this new Emacs as a plain Terminal app with the **-nw** command-line argument (type emacs –nw.)

Installing Ispell

As mentioned in Chapter 3, Emacs uses Ispell for its spell-checking functionality. However, despite voluminous hooks to it, the Ispell executable is not part of Emacs and is not installed by default on Mac OS X. You must therefore install Ispell to get spell-checking to work properly.

We took the easy path to doing this: downloading and installing Fink (see *http://fink. sourceforge.net* for instructions). Fink is an all-purpose Mac OS X installer that enables you to install Unix software on your Mac easily.

After installing Fink, installing Ispell was completely painless:

```
% fink install ispell
```

Just one further step is required so that Emacs finds Ispell without tweaking. Create a symbolic link between the location where Fink installs Ispell (*/sw/bin/ispell*) and where Emacs expects Ispell to be (*/usr/bin/ispell*).[*]

```
% sudo ln -s /sw/bin/ispell /usr/bin/ispell
```

Voilà. Emacs spell-checking with Ispell now works as described in Chapter 3.

Emacs and Windows

You can also download and install Emacs 21.3 for the various Windows platforms (Win95, Win98, Win2K, WinXP, and so on). As most Windows machines do not ship with the tools required to build Emacs from scratch, we'll look at downloading and installing prebuilt executables.[†]

Installing Emacs

As with all platforms, you have choices when installing Emacs on Windows. You can install a binary hosted by the FSF (likely to be older, but certainly stable). You can find a more recent binary online (we'll point you to the one we prefer). You could also build Emacs from CVS, but if you're doing that on Windows, chances are you are not reading this book. Windows comes with no default compilers.

Installing the latest binaries: Nqmacs

Our source for the latest binaries is Nqmacs (*http://sourceforge.net/projects/nqmacs/*). This is simply a build of the latest version of GNU Emacs from CVS sources, not a sepa-

---

* We found this hint on John Schneider's web page called "Getting Mac OS X.3 to Behave Almost Like My Linux Boxes" (*http://www.eecs.wsu.edu/~schneidj/mac-os-x-10.3.html*).

† Okay, okay. If you want to build it on Windows, you certainly can. We suggest grabbing the various development tools like **make** and **gcc** from the Cygwin project (*http://www.cygwin.com*) and then following the Unix build instructions.

rate version of Emacs as the name may imply. Windows binaries are posted here on a regular basis, giving Windows users access to the latest version without having to build it themselves.

To install on Windows, simply download the latest binaries, unpack into a new folder using WinZip or Windows own decompression utilities, go to the *bin* sub-folder and double-click on *runemacs.exe*. By right-clicking on the icon, you can send a copy of the icon to the desktop.

Installing Emacs from the FSF

As we mentioned, the binaries at the FSF are stable but generally older. For example, at this writing, the Nqmacs site provides binaries built on 7/25/04 while the FSF's site provides binaries from 3/10/2004.

To download Emacs from the FSF, simply point your browser at *http://ftp.gnu.org/pub/gnu/emacs/*. Scroll down to find the *windows* folder. In there, you should find several downloads. The binaries come in three flavors:

- **bare** (barebin)—the bare minimum you need to get going
- **standard** (bin)—what most folks need to get running
- **full** (fullbin)—the full meal deal; everything and then some

Grab the one you want and download it. You can use WinZip (*http://www.winzip.com*) to unpack it. If you have the Cygwin utilities installed, you can also use **gunzip** and **tar** as we discussed in the Unix installation section.

 Be careful! The *README.W32* file notes that you may run into some small problems if you unpack your Emacs distribution into a path where one or more of the directory names contains spaces. For example, don't unpack Emacs in the *Program Files* directory. If you don't like adding things directly to your C: drive, create an *Applications* folder or something similar and unpack Emacs in that folder.

After that's unpacked, you're 99 percent of the way there. The latest versions of Emacs need nothing else, actually; you just double-click on *runemacs.exe* (in the bin directory of your Emacs folder) and off you go! If you like, you can create shortcuts in your Start menu or on the desktop. Just point them at *runemacs.exe* and you should be set.

Where to Put Your .emacs File

Probably the single biggest Windows consideration is the location of the *.emacs* file. This file goes in your "home" directory. We use quotes there because the Windows world doesn't have a strictly defined home directory the way some other operating systems like Unix and Mac OS X do. By default, Emacs assumes that the C:\ folder is your home directory. You can put your *.emacs* file there, but you can also modify your home directory using the Windows environment variable called HOME. To change this environment variable on Windows XP, select System from the Control Panel. A System Properties window displays. Choose the Advanced tab, then choose Environment Variables. HOME is probably not listed; click on New, then type HOME and the path to your desired home directory. Emacs will now look for the *.emacs* file in this directory.

Because of naming compatibility issues, older Windows versions of Emacs used the *_emacs* file rather than the *.emacs* file for customization and configuration. This file is still a valid option. However, if both *_emacs* and *.emacs* are found in the home directory, only *.emacs* is used.

Starting Emacs from the Command Line

The Emacs *bin* folder includes two related files, each sporting a Gnu icon: *emacs.exe* and *runemacs.exe*. Typically you'll use *runemacs.exe*; this runs Emacs graphically without opening a console window. The other file, *emacs.exe*, can be used to run Emacs from the command line as described next.

To run Emacs from the command line, **cd** to the directory where you installed Emacs and type **emacs -nw** (or whatever command-line argument you wanted to use; **-nw** runs Emacs in the console window). You can also do this by choosing Start → Run, then selecting Browse to locate *emacs.exe*. Add any command-line arguments you wish, and then click **OK** to invoke Emacs using these arguments.

Making Emacs Act like Windows: CUA Mode

CUA stands for common user access, a standard originally developed by IBM. CUA mandates that certain keys should always perform certain functions. In Windows, for example, **C-c** copies and **C-v** pastes from one application to another. As you know, Emacs uses these key bindings for its own purposes.

That's where Kim Storm's CUA mode comes in. This mode was so popular that it is now part of Emacs.* It allows standard Windows key bindings, like **C-x** for cut and **C-v** for paste, to work properly within Emacs. It's quite clever—these keys cut and paste only when an active selection exists. That leaves the normal functionality of multistroke commands like **C-c C-f** in fine shape.

To turn on CUA mode, select C-x/C-c/C-v cut-and-paste (CUA) from the Options menu. If you decide you want to use CUA mode for multiple sessions, select Save Options to have Custom (discussed in Chapter 10) automatically add it to your *.emacs* file.

As you can see from the option name, in this mode, **C-x** is used for cutting text, **C-c** is used for copying text, and **C-v** is used for pasting text. What is not so apparent is that

---

* If you are running an older version of Emacs and want this functionality, visit *http://www.cua.dk/emacs.html* to download and install CUA mode.

C-z runs undo rather than minimizing the window (in CUA mode, you can minimize using **C-x C-z**).

What if you're used to confirming a region before you cut it using **C-x C-x**? You can type **C-c C-x C-x** in this case. This works in part because **C-c** cancels the active region. Remember that **C-x** would normally cut.

Strictly speaking, **C-x C-x** doesn't immediately cut text, if you type it fast enough. Cut is really bound to **C-x <timeout>**. In other words, Emacs is watching to see if you type something else really quickly. If you have a region highlighted and type **C-x C-s** to save the buffer, Emacs does the right thing. But if you pause after **C-x**, you'll cut text. This is true of **C-c** as well. If you immediately type another sequence after **C-c**, Emacs uses **C-c** as a prefix. If you pause, it copies the highlighted text.

CUA mode has a few other interesting behaviors. It has highly advanced rectangle support. (Rectangle editing is described in Chapter 7.) It also has the common behavior of replacing highlighted text. If you select a region and start typing, the highlighted text is replaced. Taking this one step further, you can do a quick and dirty search and replace in this way. Let's say that the text you typed over is just the first of several identical instances where you want to replace text. Typing **M-v** (for **cua-repeat-replace-region**) replaces the next instance. Repeat this command to continue making replacements. If there is no string to replace, **M-v** does nothing.

For example, let's take our classic Dickens passage and replace the word *times* with *rhymes*:

Highlight the word *times*.

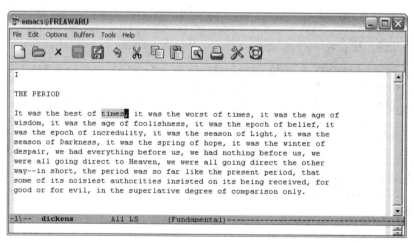

The word *times* is highlighted.

Type: **rhymes**

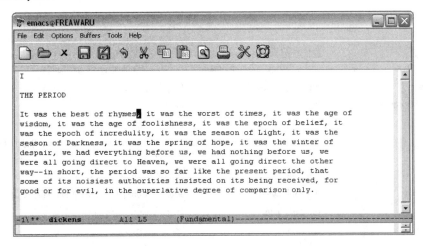

Emacs replaces *times* with *rhymes*.

Type: **M-v**

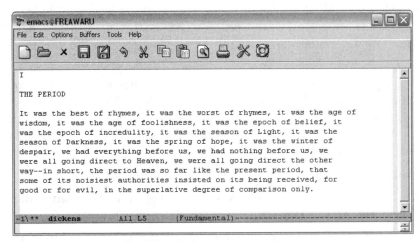

Emacs replaces the next instance of *times* with *rhymes*.

You may love CUA mode or you may hate it; the only way to see if your fingers are ready for this option is to try it out. If you've used Emacs for years, you may find CUA mode keeps doing unexpected things. Your finger habits are set to Emacs's ways. On the other hand, it's hard to move back and forth between applications and change your finger habits all the time. If you have not yet gotten used to the Emacs key bindings, you may well love CUA mode, as many people do.

Table 13-1 lists CUA mode commands.

Table 13-1. CUA mode commands

Keystrokes	Command name	Action
C-c C-x C-x	cua-exchange-point-and-mark	Exchange location of cursor and mark.
C-c	copy-region-as-kill	Copy the region.
C-x *or* C-w *or* S-Delete	kill-region	Delete the region.
C-v *or* C-y *or* S-Insert	cua-paste	Paste most recently killed or copied text.
M-v	cua-repeat-replace-region	After highlighting and replacing a string, find the next string and replace it the same way.
PgUp	cua-scroll-up	Scroll up one page (or to the beginning of the buffer).
PgDown	cua-scroll-down	Scroll down one page (or to the end of the buffer).
M-y	cua-paste-pop	After **C-v**, pastes earlier deletion.
C-z *or* C-x u	cua-undo	Undoes the last change.
C-x C-z	iconify-frame	Minimize the current frame (what **C-z** does outside CUA mode).

Installing Ispell

Installing Ispell on Windows can be tricky. Emacs 20 and beyond includes features like Flyspell and earlier versions of Ispell won't handle that functionality. Many Windows users do not compile their own software, and even if they did, the very newest Ispell also doesn't work with Emacs.

We found the version we describe here in a post by Raymond Zeitler (*http://lists. nongnu.org/archive/html/help-emacs-windows/2004-06/msg00023.html*), and we thank him heartily for it. The only downside to this version is that it is designed for English speakers. It may well work with other languages, but you'd have to find the *<language>.hash* file appropriate for your language.

The first step is to download a Windows binary of Ispell 3.1.20.[*]

Open a command window. On Windows XP, you open it using Start → Run, then typing **command** and clicking **OK**.

Create a temporary directory and move there (you can substitute another name for *tmp*).

```
C:\> mkdir tmp
C:\> cd tmp
```

FTP to **gatekeeper.dec.com**.

```
C:\tmp> ftp gatekeeper.dec.com
```

---

[*] This binary is also available from this book's web site, *http://www.oreilly.com/catalog/gnu3*.

Type anonymous as your username and your email address as your password.

Move to the */pub/GNU/windows/emacs/contrib* directory.

```
C:\tmp> cd /pub/GNU/windows/emacs/contrib
```

Type **bin** to change to binary mode.

```
C:\tmp> bin
```

Download *ispell.zip*.

```
C:\tmp> get ispell.zip
```

Type **bye** to close your ftp session, then **exit** to close the MS-DOS window.

Unzip the archive with WinZip or Windows' own decompression utility. We need to move a few files around to make Ispell work properly with Emacs.

Move *ispell.exe* to Emacs' *bin* folder. For example, if you called the folder where you installed Emacs *nqmacs*, you would place the file in *nqmacs\bin*.

Move *english.hash* to your home directory (either **C:** or the one you defined earlier as the location for your *.emacs* file). Now copy *english.hash* to *american.hash* (both files must exist for Ispell to work properly). We suspect but cannot verify that this would not be necessary for users of systems expecting British English dictionaries.

There's a lot more to the world of Emacs in Windows. We encourage you to check out the frequently asked questions and documentation available online at *http://www.gnu.org/software/emacs/windows/*.

CHAPTER 14

The Help System

Emacs has the most comprehensive help facility of any text editor—and one of the best such facilities of any program at all. In fact, the Emacs help facilities probably cut down the time it took for us to write this book by an order of magnitude, and they can help you immeasurably in your ongoing quest to learn more about Emacs.

In this chapter, we describe Emacs help in the following areas:

- The tutorial.
- The help key (**C-h**) and Help menu, which allow you to get help on a wide variety of topics.
- The help facilities of complex commands like **query-replace** and **dired**.
- Navigating Emacs manuals and using the **info** documentation reader.
- *Completion*, in which Emacs helps you finish typing names of functions, variables, filenames, and more. Completion not only saves you time and helps you complete names of functions you know about but can help you discover new commands and variables.

Using the Tutorial

If you are just starting out with Emacs, check out the tutorial by typing **C-h t** (for **help-with-tutorial**), which deletes all extra windows (leaving just one) and starts up a learn-by-doing tutorial. Actually, it displays a file called *TUTORIAL* in the window. The tutorial is currently available in 21 languages. The tutorial provides an introduction to the following Emacs features:

- Basic cursor motion
- Delete and yank
- Visiting and saving files
- Buffers
- Text and auto-fill modes

- Incremental search
- Basic help commands

You might want to use the tutorial along with Chapters 1 and 2. The tutorial is helpful, but of necessity it covers only the most basic information.

Help Commands

Emacs has many help commands, which are available as standard Emacs commands or as options to the **C-h** help key. They can be used to find information about commands, keystrokes, variables, modes, and various things about Emacs in general. The most basic help command is **C-h C-h** (**help-for-help**). **C-h ?** also invokes **help-for-help**. This command causes Emacs to open a *Help* buffer in a window with descriptions of all the help commands. You can type any one of these help keys, or, if you press **Space**, the *Help* window scrolls down as if you pressed **C-v**. Any other key aborts the whole process. If you scroll to the bottom of the help documentation, you can type a help key or any other key to abort.

The keys listed in the *Help* are those that, when appended to your help key, run Emacs help commands at any time. Help commands fall into two general categories: those that provide answers to specific questions and those that give general information about Emacs.

You will find the help commands in the former category to be invaluable after you have become comfortable with Emacs. Because it is so large and functionally rich, there will be times when you need to look up a detail such as a keystroke or command name or when you need to do something with Emacs that you don't know exactly how to do. As we've repeated again and again throughout this book, Emacs probably does what you want; you just need to figure out how. The help commands let you find these things out immediately, without leaving Emacs and without being a slave to your reference manual (or even this book).

Detail Information

Let's start with the help commands that are useful when you need to look up a specific detail. You'll probably use the commands listed in Table 14-1 most often.

Table 14-1. Detail information help commands

Keystrokes	Command name	Question answered
C-h c	describe-key-briefly	What command does this keystroke sequence run?
C-h k *Help → Describe →* *Describe Key*	describe-key	What command does this keystroke sequence run, and what does it do?

Table 14-1. Detail information help commands (continued)

Keystrokes	Command name	Question answered
C-h f *Help → Describe →* *Describe Function*	**describe-function**	What does this function do?
C-h v *Help → Describe →* *Describe Variable*	**describe-variable**	What does this variable mean, and what is its value?
C-h m *Help → Describe →* *Describe Buffer Modes*	**describe-mode**	Tell me about the modes the current buffer is in.
C-h b *Help → Describe →* *List Key Bindings*	**describe-bindings**	What are all the key bindings for this buffer?
C-h w	**where-is**	What is the key binding for this command?
C-h s	**describe-syntax**	What is the syntax table for this buffer?
C-h l	**view-lossage**	What are the last 100 characters I typed?
C-h e	**view-echo-area-messages**	What messages have appeared in the minibuffer during this session?

What if you press the wrong key, and something happens to your buffer—but you're not sure what? Usually, the safest thing to do is to press **C-_** or **C-x u** (**undo**). But sometimes this command won't help, for example, a runaway **replace-string**. If you remember what you typed, you can use **C-h c** (for **describe-key-briefly**) to see what command was run; just retype the offending keystroke(s) at the prompt, and Emacs responds with the name of the command bound to the key(s) in the minibuffer. If the command name alone doesn't help, **C-h k** (for **describe-key**) pops up a *Help* window with a description of the command as well as its name and key binding. (**C-h k** and **C-h c** also help you find out what command a toolbar icon or menu item runs.)

However, if you don't know what keys you pressed, you can type **C-h l** (for **view-lossage**). This pops up a *Help* window showing the last 100 keystrokes you typed; the offending ones are likely near the end, and you can use **C-h c** or **C-h k** with those keystrokes.

Now suppose you want information on a command that isn't bound to keystrokes. Type **C-h f** (for **describe-function**) and enter the name of the command at the prompt; Emacs responds with a *Help* window containing the documentation for that command. If you remember the name of a command but forget its binding, type **C-h w** (for **where-is**). This is the "opposite" of **C-h c**; it shows the key binding for a given command in the minibuffer, or the message *command-name* is not on any keys if the command has no binding.

You may forget a detail that involves the value of a variable. For example, will Emacs respect or ignore case during a search (the variable **case-fold-search**)? How often are my buffers being auto-saved (the variable **auto-save-interval**)? If you type **C-h v** (for **describe-variable**) followed by the name of the variable, Emacs puts its value as well as its documentation in a *Help* window. **C-h f**, **C-h w**, and **C-h v** all allow you to use completion when typing command or variable names. **C-h f** and **C-h v** are also especially useful to Emacs Lisp programmers; note that **C-h f** gives you information on *all* functions, not just those bound to keystrokes as commands.

Another common help situation arises when you use a special mode, such as shell mode or a mode for a programming language or text processor, and you forget a command specific to that mode or some other characteristic such as indentation conventions. If you type **C-h m** (for **describe-mode**) in a buffer running the mode, Emacs pops up a *Help* window showing the mode's documentation. Documentation for a mode usually includes all of its local key bindings (for example, all the commands special to the mode and their associated keystrokes), customization variables, and other interesting characteristics.

What if you want to find out all the keyboard commands available in a given mode? **C-h b** (for **describe-bindings**) gives you a *Help* window showing *all* key bindings active in the current buffer, including local (buffer-specific) as well as global ones. It also lists all bindings for mouse actions, menu options, and function keys.

C-h b produces quite a lot of output. If you want to limit this output to only those key bindings with a particular prefix, type that prefix followed by **C-h**. For example, typing **C-x C-h** produces a *Help* window listing all key bindings that begin with **C-x**.

C-h s (for **describe-syntax**) is a more specialized command, designed for Lisp programmers. It produces a *Help* window with a description of the *syntax table* (see Chapter 9) active in the current buffer.

Apropos Commands

Another type of help command applies when you want Emacs to do something, but you're not sure exactly what command to use or what variable to set. These are **apropos** commands, which resemble a rudimentary information retrieval system of the type found at many libraries. The **apropos** command has several forms, shown in Table 14-2.

Table 14-2. Apropos commands

Keystrokes	Command name	Question answered
C-h a *Help → Search Documentation →* *Find Commands by Name*	**apropos-command**	What commands include this word?
(none) *Help → Search Documentation →* *Find Options by Name*	**apropos-variable**	What variables include this regular expression?

Table 14-2. Apropos commands (continued)

Keystrokes	Command name	Question answered
(none) *Help → Search Documentation →* *Find Options by Value*	apropos-value	What variables are set to this regular expression?
(none) *Help → Search Documentation →* *Search Documentation Strings*	apropos-documentation	Where is this regular expression mentioned in the documentation?
(none) *Help → Search Documentation →* *Find Any Object by Name*	apropos	What functions and variables involve this regular expression?

All **apropos** commands prompt for regular expressions (an ordinary text string will work, but you can create more powerful searches using regular expressions; see Chapter 11 for details). When you type **C-h a** followed by a regular expression, Emacs finds all the commands that match it; it displays their key bindings (if any) and the first lines of their documentation in an *Apropos* window that is in Apropos mode. This mode displays hyperlinked help. If you click on a bolded item using your middle mouse button or move the cursor there and press **Enter**, Emacs displays more information.

As always, if you are leery of using regular expressions, use regular search strings as long as you stick to nonspecial characters. For example, if you want to know what replace commands Emacs supports, press **C-h a** and then type **replace**; Emacs displays a list of information on the following commands:

- dired-do-query-replace
- ebrowse-tags-query-replace
- ethio-replace-space
- map-query-replace-regexp
- query-replace
- query-replace-regexp
- query-replace-regexp-eval
- replace-buffer-in-windows
- replace-rectangle
- replace-regexp
- replace-string
- tags-query-replace

If you have ever used an information retrieval system, you already know that some skill is needed to use such a system effectively. You need to choose your concepts (search strings) carefully, so that they aren't too general (too much output to wade through) or too specific (too little output, making it less likely that you get the information you want). This problem is compounded when you use the **apropos** command, which is the same as **apropos-command** except that it reports on *all* functions (including internal Emacs functions) and variables as well as commands.

If you type in a search string that is too general, Emacs produces an enormous buffer of help information. For example, invoking **apropos-command** with the argument "buffer" results in output listing well over two hundred Emacs commands. In general, you may have to invoke the **apropos** commands a few times to get the information you want (in terms of size as well as relevance).

The **apropos** command itself is usually overkill, unless you are a Lisp programmer who needs information on noncommand functions (see Chapter 11 for details on this use of **apropos**). Use a more specific command when possible. For example, to get information on variables, use **apropos-variable**. To find out about variables related to auto-saving, type **M-x apropos-variable Enter auto-save Enter**. Emacs responds with information about the variables **auto-save-default**, **auto-save-file-format**, **auto-save-file-name-transforms**, **auto-save-interval**, **auto-save-list-file-prefix**, **auto-save-timeout**, **auto-save-visited-file-name**, and **delete-auto-save-files**. To find the value and full description of one of these variables, move to the *Apropos* window and either click with the middle mouse button or move to the desired variable and press **Enter**.

Help with Complex Emacs Commands

Many of the more complicated Emacs commands include their own sets of help keystrokes. These commands often have their own help functionality, but help is invoked with ? rather than the standard help key. Here is a summary of some popular complex commands and what ? does within each of them:

dired *(C-x d)*
You see a list of the most frequently used commands in the minibuffer. *This list is far from complete.* Type **C-h m** (for **describe-mode**) for more comprehensive documentation and **C-h b** (for **describe-bindings**) for all the key bindings available to you.

query-replace *(M-%)*
You see a *Help* window listing the available commands. Typing **C-h** does the same thing. This also works with **query-replace-regexp**.

save-some-buffers *(C-x s)*
Behavior is similar to **query-replace** just described.

list-buffers *(C-x C-b)*

You see a **Help** window giving information on buffer menu mode. This command has the same effect as typing **C-h m** (for **describe-mode**).

Completion

When you are responding to a minibuffer prompt with the name of something on which Emacs can do completion, typing **?** at any time gives you a **Completions** window with the choices available at that point. Completion is explained in detail later in this chapter.

Navigating Emacs Documentation

Once upon a time, to get access to Emacs documentation, you ordered manuals from FSF. You can still do so if you like printed documentation (as we do) and would like to support the FSF, but most of the documentation you will ever want or need is at your fingertips right in Emacs.

Using Info to Read Manuals

Most GNU documentation (including Emacs documentation) is in texinfo format and designed to be read in the Info documentation reader. Typing **C-h i** (for **info**) puts you at the top-level of the Info tree. You'll see that Emacs is just one choice of many. In Info, documentation is organized as *trees* of information called *nodes*. If you want information on a topic, you can select its tree; the nodes of the tree contain information on subtopics, subsubtopics, etc., organized hierarchically.

When you type **C-h i**, you see a read-only buffer containing the *directory node* of the **Info** system in a window in Info mode. If you press **h** while in **Info**, you get a tutorial on **Info** analogous to the one described earlier for basic Emacs commands.

You're probably better off typing **C-h r**, which sends you directly to the Emacs manual.

Type: **C-h r**

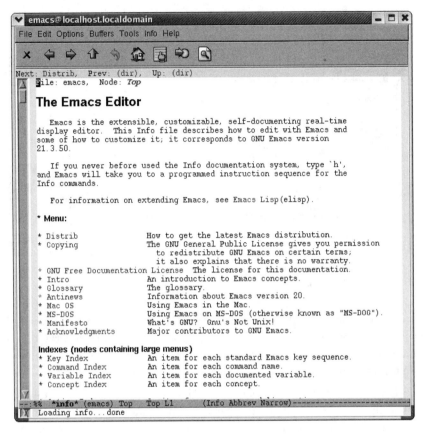

Emacs displays the table of contents for the Emacs manual.

Note that the icons are almost completely different in Info mode. Later in this section, Table 14-3 lists them, along with the keystrokes needed for navigating in this mode.

Info is relatively simple, yet complex enough to have its own tutorial. Typing **h** sends you through a tutorial to acquaint you with the main commands.

To select a menu option (you see a * next to these), move to that option. Obviously, moving with the mouse is one method; you then select the option using the middle mouse button. Alternatively, move to the option by pressing **Tab**, and then press **Enter**.

Move to Minibuffer (you'll need to scroll down), and then press **Enter**.

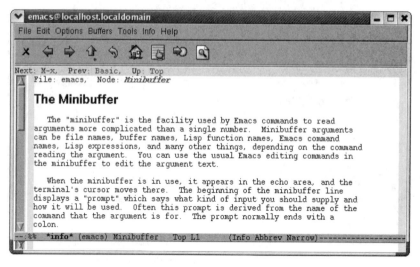

The Minibuffer topic appears.

If you want to read through the whole topic, you can press **Space** to scroll down. **Space** is helpful for continuous reading because after you complete a topic, it moves you to the next node at this level. If you read all of this topic, you'll learn more about the minibuffer than you ever thought possible.

If you press **u** twice (to move up a level), you'll move back to the Emacs table of contents. The up arrow icon on the toolbar does the same thing. To accomplish this with a single keystroke, type **t** (for **Info-top-node**) or click on the house toolbar icon. That command takes you to the top level in one move, no matter how far down the Info tree you've traveled.

To search for a particular topic, type **i** or click on the toolbar icon that shows a finger pointing at a piece of paper.

Type: **i**

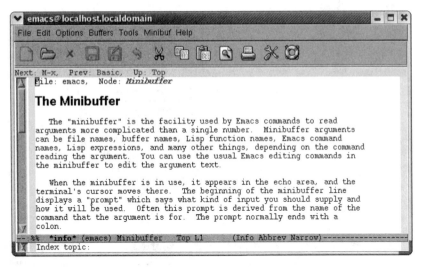

Emacs prompts for an index topic.

Type: **macro Enter**

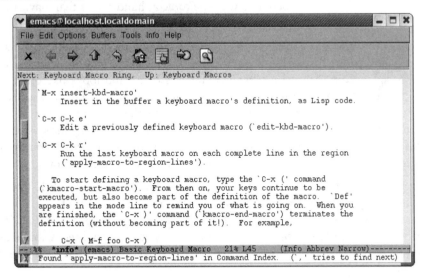

Emacs brings up the first topic related to macros.

Type a comma: ,

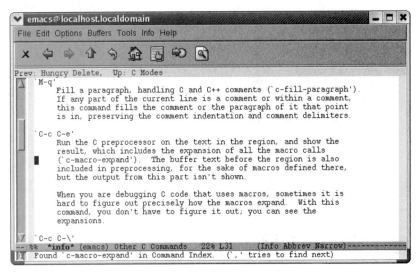

Emacs moves to the next macro-related topic in the index.

As you step through index entries in this way, it's helpful to look at the top of the screen to see what topic you're in. You might want to move up a node (or to the previous or next node) to get a better view of the topic at hand rather than navigating to the next index entry by typing another comma.

Navigating through Info can take some practice. For example, one might think that the command **p** (for **Info-prev**)* would behave rather like a web browser back button (especially given that the toolbar icon for this command looks like one). Previous in this case means relative to the Info documentation tree, not to your session (though it may appear that way sometimes). It means that you want to move to the previous item at this level. To move back to the previous screen in your session, use **l** (for **Info-last**), shown on the toolbar with a curved arrow icon (like the icon for undo in other modes). This command behaves like a web browser back button.

The commands **C-h F** (for **Info-goto-emacs-command-node**) and **C-h K** (for **Info-goto-emacs-key-command-node**) let you use **Info** in a more focused way. They are essentially the **Info** equivalents of **C-h f** (for **describe-function**) and **C-h k** (for **describe-key**), respectively: they start up the **Info** system and go directly to the documentation for the command (for **C-h F**) or the keystroke(s) (for **C-h K**) you give as an argument.

---

* These command names are case-sensitive. For example, completion won't find them if you type them with a lowercase i.

Table 14-3. Info commands

Keystrokes	Toolbar icon	Command name	Action
Tab		Info-next-reference	Move to the next menu item or cross-reference.
Space		Info-scroll-up	Scroll the screen; move to the next topic at this level when finished.
Del *or* PgUp		Info-scroll-down	Scroll backward.
p		Info-prev	Move to the previous topic at this level (not like a browser back button). If there is no previous topic, move up a level.
u		Info-up	Move up a level.
n		Info-next	Move to the next topic at this level.
i		Info-index	Search the index for a topic.
,		Info-index-next	Go to the next topic in the index.
m		Info-menu	Select a menu item through the keyboard.
q		Info-exit	Quit info.
s		Info-search	Search for a regular expression.
g		Info-goto-node	Go to a specified node.
t		Info-top-node	Go to the top node.
l		Info-last	Go to the last node you visited (like a browser back button).
h		Info-help	Start the info tutorial.

FAQ, News, and Antinews

To display the Frequently Asked Questions (FAQ) file, type **C-h f**. This file is in Info format.

Perhaps the most important of the remaining Emacs help commands for hard-core users and customizers is **C-h n** (for **view-emacs-news**), which visits the *NEWS* file that comes with Emacs. This file contains a history of changes made to Emacs since the last major version; for example, all changes in Version 20.1 and following up to the latest minor version (which in our case is Version 21.3.5, though the file says 21.4). This can be a very long file if there have been several minor releases since the last major version—in our case, the file is 12,886 lines long. If you want to look through it for changes to a specific aspect of Emacs, use an appropriate search command. But if you just want to skim it, note that this file was intended for use with outline mode: topics are introduced on lines beginning with *, and subtopics are introduced on lines beginning with **. Use outline mode commands to skim the file; see Chapter 7 for information. The outline mode command **hide-body** displays the main topics and hides the text; **show-all** redisplays all the text as well.

An entertaining approach to learning about the latest release is Antinews. This file takes the viewpoint that Emacs has been downgraded, in our case from 21.4 to 21.3. It takes you through all the features that have been ripped from Emacs 21.4 to create Emacs 21.3. Antinews is a menu item on the first page of the Emacs manual you reach via **C-h r**.

Table 14-4 summarizes commands relating to reading documentation, getting general information about Emacs, and language encoding issues.

Table 14-4. Documentation, general information, and encoding options

Keystrokes	Command name	Action
C-h t *Help → Emacs Tutorial*	**help-with-tutorial**	Run the Emacs tutorial.
C-h i	**info**	Start the Info documentation reader. If prefaced with **C-u**, reads an Info file of your choice.
C-h r *Help → Read the Emacs Manual*	**info-emacs-manual**	Opens the Emacs manual.
C-h F *Help → More Manuals → Find Command in Manual*	**Info-goto-emacs-command-node**	Start Info documentation reader at the node that discusses this command.
C-h K *Help → More Manuals → Find Key in Manual*	**Info-goto-emacs-key-command-node**	Start Info documentation reader at the node that discusses this key sequence.
C-h n *or* C-h C-n *Help → Emacs News*	**view-emacs-news**	View news about recent changes in Emacs.
C-h C-f *Help → Emacs FAQ*	**view-emacs-FAQ**	View a file of frequently asked questions and their answers about Emacs.
(none) *Help → Search Documentation → Emacs Terminology*	**search-emacs-glossary**	Open a glossary of Emacs terms.
(none) *Help → Search Documentation → Look Up Subject in User Manual*	**emacs-index-search**	Search the index of the Emacs user manual.

Table 14-4. Documentation, general information, and encoding options (continued)

Keystrokes	Command name	Action
(none) *Help → Search Documentation → Look Up Subject in ELisp Manual*	**elisp-index-search**	Search the index of the Emacs Lisp manual.
C-h Enter *Help → More Manuals → Ordering Manuals*	**view-order-manuals**	Displays information about ordering print manuals.
C-h p	**finder-by-keyword**	Invoke a menu that lets you get information about Emacs Lisp packages available on your system.
C-h C-c *Help → Copying Conditions*	**describe-copying**	View the General Public License (GPL).
C-h C-d *Help → Getting New Versions*	**describe-distribution**	View information on ordering Emacs from FSF.
C-h C-p	**describe-project**	View information on the GNU project. (See the Preface.)
C-h C-w *Help → (Non)Warranty*	**describe-no-warranty**	View the (non-)warranty for Emacs. Emacs doesn't provide a warranty, hence the name here.
C-h C-t	**view-todo**	If you're a programmer looking to contribute to the Emacs code base, use this command to view a list of what needs to be done.
C-h C-e *Help → Emacs Known Problems*	**view-emacs-problems**	Displays the *PROBLEMS* file, which includes a list of known problems.
C-h h	**view-hello-file**	View the *HELLO* file, which displays the word "hello" in numerous languages.
C-h L *Help → Describe → Describe Language Environment*	**describe-language-environment**	Prompts for either default (current environment) or lists possible completions. Menu option shows these choices.
C-h I *or* **C-h C-** *Help → Describe → Describe Input Method*	**describe-input-method**	Shows current input method (the default) or, with completion, a list of possible input methods.
C-h C *Help → Describe → Describe Coding System*	**describe-coding-system**	Shows current coding system (the default) or, with completion, lists all available coding systems.

Completion

We saw an example of Emacs's completion facility in Chapter 1. Completion is more than just a feature: it is a general principle in the design of Emacs. It can be articulated as follows:

> If you have to type in the name of something, and that name is one of a finite number of possibilities, Emacs should figure out what you mean after the smallest possible number of keystrokes.

In other words, you can type in the *shortest unambiguous prefix* and tell Emacs to figure out the rest of the name. By "shortest unambiguous prefix," we mean "enough of the name, starting from the beginning, to distinguish it from the other possibilities." Several important things in Emacs have names that are chosen from a finite number of possibilities, including the following:

- Commands
- Files in a given directory
- Buffers
- Emacs variables

Most of the time, completion is available when you are prompted for a name of something in the minibuffer. While you are typing in the name, you can use three keys to tell Emacs to help complete it for you: **Tab**, **Space**, and question mark (?). Their functions are shown in Table 14-5.

Table 14-5. Completion keys

Keystroke	Action
Tab	Completes the name as far as possible.
Space	Completes the name out to the next punctuation character.
?	Lists the choices at this point in a *Completions* window.

You will probably find **Tab** to be the most useful.

As a running example, assume you have typed **C-x C-f** to visit a file, and the file you want to visit is a C program called *program.c*. Let's say you type **pro** and press **Tab**; Emacs responds by completing the name to the full *program.c*. If you press **Space**, Emacs completes only as far as *program*. After Emacs completes the name, you can press **Enter** to visit the file.

How much of the name do you need to type in before you can use completion? That depends on the other possible choices in the given situation. If *program.c* were the only file in your directory, you could just type **p** and press **Tab**.* If there were other files in your directory and none of them has a name beginning with **p**, you could do the same thing. But if you had a file called *problem.c*, you would have to type **prog** before you pressed Tab; in this case, **prog** is the shortest unambiguous prefix. If you just type in **pro** and press **Tab**, Emacs responds with a *Completions* window containing a list of the completion choices, in this case *program.c* and *problem.c*, and returns your cursor to the minibuffer so that you can finish typing the filename. The

---

* You can't just press **Tab** without typing the **p** because the current and parent directories, named . and .., respectively, are also file choices. Normally, Emacs runs **dired** when you visit a file that's a directory.

same thing happens if you typed a question mark instead of **Tab**. At this point, you can type **g** and press **Tab** again; Emacs completes the name to *program.c*.

As another example, let's say you have documentation for your C program in the file *program.txt*, and you want to visit it. You press **C-x C-f** and type **prog** at the prompt, followed by **Tab**. Emacs completes out to *program.*. At this point, you can type **t** and press **Tab** again; Emacs completes the entire *program.txt*. In other words, you can use completion repeatedly when specifying a name.

Finally, let's say you also have a file in your directory called simply *program*, which is the result of compiling your C file, but you still want to visit the documentation file. You type **prog** and press **Tab**; Emacs completes out to *program.* (including the period). At this point, **Tab** and **Space** do different things. If you press **Tab** again, Emacs responds with the message [Complete, but not unique] in the minibuffer, but if you press **Space**, Emacs assumes you aren't interested in the file *program* and attempts to complete further. Because you have the files *program.c* and *program.txt*, Emacs only completes out to *program.*, and you have to type **t** and press **Tab** again.

Completion works the same way with buffer names, for example, when you type **C-x b** to switch to another buffer in the current window. It also works with command names when you type **M-x**—but with one added feature. Notice that when you specify a file or buffer name, it is possible that the file or buffer you want doesn't yet exist (for example, when you want to create a new file). In this case, of course, you must type in the entire file or buffer name and press **Enter**. But when you type **M-x** for a command, there is no possibility of the command not existing. Therefore, Emacs automatically attempts to do completion on command names when you press **Enter**.

For example, if you want to put a buffer for a text file in auto-fill mode (see Chapter 2), you can type **M-x auto-f** and press **Enter** instead of typing the entire **M-x auto-fill-mode**. If you type in a nonunique (ambiguous) prefix of a command name—for example, if you type **M-x aut**—and press **Enter**, then **Enter** acts just like **Tab**; in this case, it completes out to **auto**. If you press **Enter** again, Emacs responds with a *Completions* window listing the choices. To get **auto-fill-mode**, you have to type **f** and press **Enter** again.

Completion on command names with **Enter** is *very* convenient. After you have used Emacs for a while, you will become familiar with the shortest unambiguous prefixes for commands you use often, and you can save a considerable amount of typing by using these prefixes instead of the full names.[*]

Emacs can also do completion on the names of Emacs variables. In Chapter 2, and elsewhere, we saw how you can use **M-x set-variable** to change the values of Emacs variables. The **Enter** feature just described works on variables as well as commands;

---

[*] For example, if you make changes to your *.emacs* file regularly, you will appreciate that **M-x eval-c** is an acceptable prefix for **M-x eval-current-buffer**.

therefore, you can use completion, including **Enter**, when doing **M-x set-variable**. Actually, commands and variables are both special kinds of Emacs Lisp *symbols*, and Emacs can do completion with **Enter** on all kinds of Lisp symbols. Completion on Lisp symbols comes in handy when you are using some of the help commands described earlier in this chapter.

Customizing Completion

If you have read Chapter 10 and are comfortable with setting Emacs variables, you should know that a few variables can customize the way Emacs does completion. The variable **completion-auto-help** determines whether a *Completions* window automatically appears when you try to use **Space** or **Tab** on an ambiguous prefix. Its default is **t**, meaning that such windows automatically appear. If you set it to **nil**, instead of a *Completions* window appearing, Emacs just displays the message [Next char not unique] for a couple of seconds in the minibuffer.

If you are a programmer or if you use text formatters like LATEX, you will create files that are not meant for humans to read, such as object files created by compilers and print files created by text formatters. Ideally, you wouldn't want Emacs to bother with these files when you are doing completion; for example, if you have the files *program.c* and *program.o* (object-code output from the compiler), you want Emacs to recognize only the former. Emacs does have a feature that deals with this; indeed, you may already have noticed that in this kind of situation, if you type **program** and press **Tab**, Emacs ignores *program.o* and completes out to *program.c*. The variable **completion-ignored-extensions** controls this; it is a list of filename suffixes that Emacs ignores during filename completion. By default, the list includes tilde (~) for Emacs backup files, .o for programmers, various suffixes for users, .elc (byte-compiled Emacs Lisp) for Emacs customizers, and others. (Of course, if you really want to look at these files, you can type their names manually.)

You can add your own "ignored" suffix to the list by putting a line of this form in your *.emacs* file:

```
(setq completion-ignored-extensions
      (cons "suffix" completion-ignored-extensions))
```

For example, let's say you are doing text processing with a printer that prints Post-Script, and your text processor produces print files with the suffix *.ps*. If you don't want to look at these files, put the following line in your *.emacs* file:

```
(setq completion-ignored-extensions
      (cons ".ps" completion-ignored-extensions))
```

Finally, you can tell Emacs to ignore case distinctions when doing completion by setting the variable **completion-ignore-case** to **t** (or any value other than **nil**). Its default value is **nil**, meaning that Emacs respects case distinctions.

Emacs Variables

This appendix lists some Emacs variables. We chose them for their general useful-
ness and for their applicability to subjects in this book.

The variables below are grouped by category, and their default values are shown
(where practical to do so). For more details on specific variables, see the chapters
referred to at the beginning of each table. For information on variables used in programming language modes, see Chapter 9.

Table A-1. Backups, auto-save, and versioning (Chapters 2, 12)

Variable	Default	Description
make-backup-files	t	If **t**, create a backup version of the current file before saving it for the first time.
backup-by-copying	nil	If **t**, create backup files by *copying* rather than *renaming* the file being saved to a backup version. The default is renaming, which is more effi- cient. Copying can yield different results, especially when you're editing files owned by another user, and in operating systems that allow "hard links" to files (alternate names that are associated with the physical file). There are a raft of variables that can tweak this behavior based on con- text; check the online help for **make-backup-files** for the details.
version-control	nil	If **t**, create numbered versions of files as backups (with names of the form *filename~N~*). If **nil**, only do this for files that have numbered ver- sions already. If **'never** (note the leading single quote), never make numbered versions.
kept-new-versions	2	Number of latest versions of a file to keep when a new numbered backup is made.
kept-old-versions	2	Number of oldest versions of a file to keep when a new numbered backup is made.

Variable	Default	Description
delete-old-versions	nil	If **t**, delete excess versions (not those kept according to the above variables) without asking for confirmation first. If **nil**, ask for confirmation first. If any other value, don't delete excess versions.
auto-save-default	t	If **t**, do auto-saving of every file visited.
auto-save-visited-file-name	nil	If **t**, auto-save to the file being visited rather than to a special auto-save file.
auto-save-interval	300	Number of keystrokes between auto-saving; if 0, turn off auto-saving.
auto-save-timeout	30	Length of time of inactivity after which Emacs auto-saves. If **nil** or 0, turn off this feature.
delete-auto-save-files	t	Non-**nil** means delete auto-save files whenever the "real" file is saved.
buffer-offer-save	nil	Non-**nil** means offer to save the current buffer when exiting Emacs, even if the buffer is not a file.
vc-handled-backends	(RCS CVS SVN SCCS Arch MCVS)	Version control systems used with the **vc** package. The order in which they appear in this list controls the order in which they will be attempted when working with a new file.
vc-display-status	t	If non-**nil**, display the version number and the locked state in the mode line.
vc-keep-workfiles	t	If non-**nil**, do not delete work files after you register changes with the version control system.
vc-mistrust-permissions	nil	If non-**nil**, do not assume that a file's owner ID and permission flags reflect version control system's idea of file's ownership and permission; get this information directly from version control system.
vc-suppress-confirm	nil	If non-**nil**, do not ask for confirmation before performing version control actions.
vc-initial-comment	nil	If non-**nil**, prompt for an initial comment when registering a file with version control system.
vc-make-backup-files	nil	If non-**nil**, make standard Emacs backups of files registered with version control.
diff-switches	-c	Command-line switches used to control the format of change reports by VC as well as *diff.el*.

Table A-2. Searching and replacing (Chapter 3)

Variable	Default	Description
case-fold-search	t	If non-**nil**, treat upper- and lowercase letters as the same when searching.
case-replace	t	If non-**nil**, preserve the original case of letters when doing replaces (even if **case-fold-search** is on).
search-upper-case	'not-yanks	If non-**nil**, uppercase letters in search strings defeat **case-fold-search** (i.e., force search to be case-sensitive). The symbol **'not-yanks** means convert uppercase letters in yanked text to lowercase.

Table A-2. Searching and replacing (Chapter 3) (continued)

Variable	Default	Description
search-exit-option	t	If non-**nil**, any control character other than those defined in incremental search (**Del**, **C-j**, **C-q**, **C-r**, **C-s**, **C-w**, **C-y**) exits search.
search-highlight	t	If non-**nil**, highlight partial search matches.
query-replace-highlight	t	If non-**nil**, highlight matches in query-replace mode.

Table A-3. Display (Chapters 2, 4)

Variable	Default	Description
next-screen-context-lines	2	Retain this many lines when scrolling forward or backward by **C-v** or **M-v**.
scroll-step	0	When moving the cursor vertically out of the current window, scroll this many lines forward or backward. If 0, scroll enough lines to place the cursor at the center of the window after scrolling.
hscroll-step	0	When moving the cursor horizontally out of the current window, scroll this many columns left or right. If 0, scroll enough lines to place the cursor at the center of the window after scrolling.
tab-width	8	Width of tab stops; when set, it becomes local to the current buffer.
left-margin	0	Number of columns to indent when typing **C-j** in fundamental mode and text mode.
standard-indent	4	The number of columns to indent when using commands that increase or decrease margins.
truncate-lines	nil	If non-**nil**, do not wrap long lines; instead, truncate them and use arrows to show that the line continues off-screen. (Nongraphical versions of Emacs use $ instead to show where the line extends.)
truncate-partial-width-windows	t	If non-**nil**, truncate long lines (as above) in all windows that are not the full width of the display.
window-min-height	4	Minimum allowable height of windows (in lines).
window-min-width	10	Minimum allowable width of vertically split windows (in columns).
ctl-arrow	t	Non-**nil** means display control characters using ^X, where X is the letter being "controlled." Otherwise, use octal (base 8) ASCII notation for display—for example, **C-h** appears as \010 in octal.
display-time-day-and-date	nil	If non-**nil**, **M-x display-time Enter** will also show the day and date.
line-number-mode	t	If non-**nil**, display the line number on the mode line.
line-number-display-limit	nil	Maximum size of buffer (in characters) for which line numbers should be displayed. A value of **nil** means no limit.
column-number-mode	nil	If non-**nil**, display the column number on the mode line.
visible-bell	nil	If non-**nil**, "flash" the screen instead of beeping when necessary.
track-eol	nil	If non-**nil**, whenever the cursor is at the end of the line, "stick" to the end of the line when moving the cursor up or down; otherwise, stay in the column where the cursor is.

Table A-3. Display (Chapters 2, 4) (continued)

Variable	Default	Description
blink-matching-paren	t	If non-**nil**, blink matching open parenthesis-type character when a corresponding close parenthesis is typed.
blink-matching-paren-distance	25600	Maximum number of characters to search through to find a matching open parenthesis character when a close parenthesis is typed.
blink-matching-delay	1	Number of seconds to pause when blinking a matching parenthesis.
echo-keystrokes	1	Echo prefixes for unfinished commands (e.g., **C-**) in minibuffer after user pauses for this many seconds; 0 means don't do echoing at all.
insert-default-directory	t	If non-**nil**, insert the current directory in the minibuffer when asking for a filename.
highlight-nonselected-windows	nil	If non-**nil**, highlight regions in windows other than the one currently selected; applies to GUI displays and others that support highlighting.
mouse-scroll-delay	0.25	Delay, in seconds, between screen scrolls when mouse is clicked and dragged from inside a window to beyond its borders. 0 means scroll as fast as possible.
mouse-scroll-min-lines	1	Scroll at least this many lines when mouse is clicked and dragged up or down beyond a window.

Table A-4. Modes (Chapters 2, 5, 7)

Variable	Default	Description
major-mode	fundamental-mode	Default mode for new buffers, unless set by virtue of the filename; when setting this variable, remember to precede the mode name with a single quote (the value is a *symbol*).
default-major-mode	fundamental-mode	The major mode for new buffers.
auto-mode-alist	(*see Chapter 10*)	List of associations between filenames and major modes.
interpreter-mode-alist	(*see Chapter 9*)	A list similar to **auto-mode-alist**, but for interpreted languages like Perl and Python.
indent-tabs-mode	t	If non-**nil**, allow the use of tab characters (as well as spaces) when indenting with **C-j**. This can really drive other developers mad, so you should probably disable this if you are working on a team.
dired-kept-versions	2	When cleaning a directory in Dired, keep this many versions of files.
dired-garbage-files-regexp	"\\.\\(?:aux\\\|bak\\\|dvi\\\|log\\\|orig\\\|rej\\\|toc\\)\\'"	Defines what file types are marked when selecting garbage files in Dired.
dired-listing-switches	"-al"	Options passed to the **ls** command for generating **dired** listings; should contain at least "-l".
dired-view-command-alist	(*see Chapter 10*)	Defines helper applications for Dired to invoke when opening certain types of files.

Table A-4. Modes (Chapters 2, 5, 7) (continued)

Variable	Default	Description
shell-file-name	*varies*	Filename of shell to run with functions that use one, such as **list-directory**, **dired**, and **compile**; taken from value of the Unix environment variable **SHELL**.
load-path		List of directories to search for Lisp packages to load (see Chapter 11); often set to *lisp* subdirectory of directory where Emacs source code is installed on your system.
lpr-switches	**nil**	Defines command-line options to pass to **lpr**
calendar-week-start-day	0	Day defined as first day of the week. 0 is Sunday, 1 is Monday and so on.
picture-tab-characters	"!-~"	Characters interpreted as tab stops in picture mode if they appear on a line of their own.

Table A-5. Text editing (Chapters 2, 3, 7, 8)

Variable	Default	Description
sentence-end	*(see Chapter 13)*	Regular expression that matches ends of sentences.
sentence-end-double-space	t	If non-**nil**, do not treat single spaces after periods as ends of sentences.
paragraph-separate	"[\t\f]*$"	Regular expression that matches beginnings of lines that separate paragraphs.
paragraph-start	"\f\\\|[\t]*$"	Regular expression that matches beginnings of lines that start or separate paragraphs.
page-delimiter	"^\f"	Regular expression that matches page breaks.
tex-default-mode	'latex-mode	Mode to invoke when creating a file that could be either TEX or LATEX.
tex-run-command	"tex"	Character string used as a command to run in a subprocess on a file in mode.
latex-run-command	"latex"	String used as a command to run LATEX in a subprocess.
slitex-run-command	"slitex"	String used as a command to run SliTEX in a subprocess.
tex-dvi-print-command	"lpr -d"	Character string used as a command to print a file in tex mode with **C-c C-p**.
tex-alt-dvi-print-command	"lpr -d"	Command to direct *.dvi* files to a secondary printer.
tex-dvi-view-command	(if (eq window-system 'x) "xdvi" "dvi2tty * | cat -s")	Character string used as command to view a *.dvi* output file with **C-c C-v**; this expression yields *xdvi* on X Window systems, and a terminal-based alternative on others. This will only work if a Unix-like operating environment is present (such as Mac OS X, or Cygwin under Windows).
tex-offer-save	t	If non-**nil**, offer to save any unsaved buffers before running TEX.
tex-show-queue-command	"lpq"	Character string used as command to show the print queue with **C-c C-q** in Tex mode.
tex-directory	"."	Directory for TEX to put temporary files in; default is the current directory.

Table A-5. Text editing (Chapters 2, 3, 7, 8) (continued)

Variable	Default	Description
outline-regexp	"[*\f]+"	Regular expression that matches heading lines in outline mode.
outline-heading-end-regexp	"\n"	Regular expression that matches ends of heading lines in outline mode.
selective-display-ellipses	t	If **t**, display "..." in place of hidden text in outline mode; otherwise don't display anything.

Table A-6. Programming (Chapter 9)

Variable	Default	Description
compile-command	"make -k"	Default compilation command to use when compiling files via Emacs language modes. For example, to set ant as the default compilation tool, set this to **"ant -emacs"**.
compilation-error-regexp-alist	(*very long regular expression*)	Regular expression designed to match error messages from all the compilers supported by Emacs.
comment-column	32	The column at which Emacs should insert comments. If code reaches this column, inserts comment one space beyond code.
comment-multi-line	nil	If **t**, continue comment on the next line. If **nil**, start a new comment on the next line.
c-style-alist	(*see Chapter 9*)	The code indentation style to use. Many are available; see Chapter 9.
debug-on-error	nil	If non-**nil**, emacs will go into debug mode when an error occurs in evaluating Lisp code. This can be handy when you're trying out a new function, but you probably want to read the debugger's help first to learn your way around.
c-macro-preprocessor	"/lib/cpp -C"	Defines which command is used to invoke C preprocessor when you type **C-c C-e**.
stack-trace-on-error	nil	If non-**nil**, Emacs displays a stack trace when an error occurs in evaluating Lisp code. This is useful in similar situations as **debug-on-error** and might give you enough information without having to learn the debugger interface.

Table A-7. Completion (Chapter 14)

Variable	Default	Description
completion-auto-help	t	If non-**nil**, provide help if a completion (via **Tab** or **Enter** in minibuffer) is invalid or ambiguous.
completion-ignored-extensions	(*see Chapter 14*)	List of filename suffixes Emacs ignores when completing filenames (for example, ~).
completion-ignore-case	nil	If non-**nil**, ignore case distinctions when doing completion.

Table A-8. Miscellaneous

Variable	Default	Description
kill-ring-max	**60**	Keep *n* pieces of deleted text in the kill ring before deleting oldest kills.
require-final-newline	**nil**	If a file being saved is missing a final newline: **nil** means don't add one; **t** means add one automatically; otherwise ask whether to add a newline.
next-line-add-newlines	**nil**	If non-**nil**, **next-line** (**C-n** or down arrow) inserts newlines when at the end of the buffer, rather than signaling an error.
undo-limit, undo-strong-limit	**20000, 30000**	These two variables jointly control how much space Emacs is willing to allocate to supporting the **undo** command. If you ever find yourself wanting to undo more than past what Emacs remembers, you might want to investigate increasing these limits; with today's memory sizes they can probably comfortably be much larger.
mac-command-key-is-meta	**t**	If **t**, the Mac **Command** key is used for **Meta**; if **nil**, the **Option** key is **Meta** instead.

Emacs Lisp Packages

The tables in this appendix list the most useful Lisp packages that come with Emacs. All Lisp packages are typically located in the directory *emacs-source/lisp*, where *emacs-source* is the directory in which you placed the Emacs source distribution. We have omitted all of the packages that provide "basic" Emacs support; likewise, we have omitted many packages whose functionality is obsolete or unspeakably obscure.

While some of these packages are described in some detail in this book, most aren't; you will have to rely on GNU Emacs' help for precise descriptions of what the package does. See Chapter 14 for details about help; the most important help commands you will need for finding out about the functionality of Lisp packages are **C-h p** (for **finder-by-keyword**), **C-h f** (for **describe-function**), and **C-h m** (for **describe-mode**).

C-h p is especially helpful. It lets you navigate through a hierarchy of information about all packages available on your system, from general areas of functionality, like those in the tables in this appendix, to the **C-h m** information about each individual mode. Unfortunately, the detailed information is sometimes incomplete and also lists many packages that could not possibly be interesting to anyone other than hard-core Emacs customizers.

Wherever it is reasonable, the tables in this appendix give commands that "start" the package. This startup information has the following meanings:

- If the package implements a major mode, the startup command is the function that puts Emacs into this major mode.

- If the package implements a major mode that is automatically loaded when you visit a file with a certain suffix, we list "suffix *suffixname*" in addition to the startup command.

- If the package implements a minor mode, the startup command is the function that puts Emacs into this minor mode.

- If the package implements a set of general-purpose functions, we've tried to pick the most "typical" of these functions. For example, the **studly** package implements three commands. We arbitrarily picked **studlify-region** as one way to invoke this package. If there isn't any reasonable choice, we list "many."

Finally, a word on using the packages. Some packages are automatically loaded when Emacs starts; some are loaded when you visit a file with the appropriate suffix (such as many of the modes for programming languages); some are automatically loaded whenever you give the appropriate command (for example, **M-x shell Enter** loads the package *shell.el* for **shell-mode**); and some are never automatically loaded. So how do you know which is which?

You don't really have to concern yourself with this issue. In the tables, the Startup column tells you what command (or commands) put the package to work. Start Emacs, and give this command (**M-x *startup-command* Enter**). If Emacs complains **no match**, the package wasn't loaded automatically and you need to load the package "by hand." To do so during an Emacs session, use the command **M-x load-library** *name* **Enter**, where the package's "name" is given in the first column of the table. You can also tell Emacs to load packages automatically at startup time by putting lines in your *.emacs* file that have this form:

```
(load-library "name")
```

Finally, if you're interested in looking at the source code of the libraries, which can be a great way to pick up techniques as you develop skills in programming Emacs Lisp, check out the **find-library-file** function presented in Chapter 11.

Now, without further ado, here are the tables of Lisp packages.

Table B-1. Support for Java, C, and C++ programming

Package	Description	Startup
cc-mode	Major mode for editing Java, C, C++ and Objective-C source files	**java-mode, c-mode, c++-mode, objc-mode**, suffixes *.java, .c, .h, .y, .lex, .cc, .hh, .C, .H, .cpp, .cxx, .hxx, .c++, .h++*
cmacexp	Function for using cpp to expand macros in C source code	**c-macro-expand**
hideif	Minor mode for hiding code within C preprocessor commands	**hide-ifdef-mode**
cpp	Major mode for highlighting and hiding code within C preprocessor conditionals; takes advantage of graphical displays	**cpp-parse-edit**

Table B-2. Support for Lisp programming

Package	Description	Startup
lisp-mode	Major modes for Lisp, Emacs Lisp and Lisp interaction	**lisp-mode, emacs-lisp-mode, lisp-interaction-mode**, suffixes *.l, .lisp, .lsp, .ml, .el,* and others[a]
scheme	Major mode for editing Scheme source files	**scheme-mode**, suffixes *.scm, .stk, .ss, .sch, .oak*

Table B-2. Support for Lisp programming (continued)

Package	Description	Startup
cl	Functions and macros for Emacs Lisp compatibility with Common Lisp	many
debug	Major mode for debugging Emacs Lisp programs	**debug**, automatically invoked if an error occurs running code when **debug-on-error** is not **nil**
edebug	Emacs Lisp debugging functionality, implemented as a minor mode	**edebug**
disass	Function to disassemble compiled Emacs Lisp code	**disassemble**
elp	Code profiler for Emacs Lisp	**elp-instrument-package**, **elp-instrument-function**
trace	Produces function call traces for Emacs Lisp	**trace-function**

a Emacs Lisp mode is also invoked for files named *.emacs* or *_emacs*. In the default configuration, Lisp Interaction mode is used by the initial *scratch* buffer.

Table B-3. Support for other programming tasks and languages

Package	Description	Startup
gud	Major mode for working with many different debuggers including *jdb*, *gdb*, *sdb*, *dbx*, *xdb*, *perldb*, *pdb* (Python), and *bash*	**jdb**, **bashdb**, **gdb**, and many others
perl-mode	Major mode for working with Perl source	**perl-mode**, suffixes *.pl*, *.pm*, *.perl*, *.al*, and capitalized variants
cperl-mode	Major mode for working with Perl source, which many prefer to the older Perl mode	**cperl-mode**, suffixes *.pl*, *.pm*, *.perl*, *.al*, and capitalized variants
python	Major mode for editing Python source files	**python-mode**, suffix *.py*
tcl	Major mode for editing TCL source files	**tcl-mode**, suffixes *.tcl*, *.exp*, *.itcl*, *.itk*
sql	Major mode for editing SQL queries	**sql-mode**, suffix *.sql*
ada-mode	Major mode for editing Ada source files	**ada-mode**, suffixes *.ada*, *.adb*, *.ads*, *.adb.dg*, *.ads.dg*
pascal	Major mode for editing Pascal source files	**pascal-mode**, suffixes *.p*, *.pas*
modula2	Major mode for editing Modula-2 source code	**modula-2-mode**
fortran	Major mode for editing Fortran source files	**fortran-mode**, suffixes *.f*, *.F*, *.for*
f90	Major mode for editing source code in the Fortran 90 dialect	**f90-mode**, suffixes *.f90*, *.f95*
asm-mode	Major mode for editing assembly language source code	**asm-mode**, suffixes *.s*, *.S*, *.asm*
awk-mode	Major mode for editing awk code	**awk-mode**, suffix *.awk*
m4-mode	Major mode for editing m4 macro source	**m4-mode**, suffixes *.m4*, *.mc*
ps-mode	Major mode for editing PostScript code	**ps-mode**, suffixes *.ps*, *.eps*, with any capitalization
compile	Major mode for compiling programs (often through **make** or **ant**) and allowing easy access to the source lines on which errors are reported	**compile**

Table B-4. Support for Text Processing

Package	Description	Startup
text-mode	Major mode for editing unprocessed text files	**text-mode**, suffixes *.txt, .text, .article, .letter*, and files starting with */tmp/Re, Message* and a digit (mail), */tmp/fol* (news)
sgml-mode	Major mode for editing structured documents (including HTML and XML)[a]	**html-mode, xml-mode, sgml-mode**, suffixes *.htm, .html, .shtml, .xml, .xsl, .dtd, .sgm, .sgml*
tex-mode	Major mode for editing TEX and LATEX files	**tex-mode, latex-mode**, suffixes *.tex, .ins, .TeX, .ltx, .sty, .cls, .clo, .bbl*
bibtex	Major mode for editing bibliography files	**bibtex-mode**, suffix *.bib*
refbib	Convert bibliography files in **refer** format to **bibtex** format	**r2b-convert-buffer**
nroff	Major mode for editing **nroff** and **troff** text files	**nroff-mode**, suffixes *.mm, .me, .ms, .man*, or any digit following a period (manual page source)
scribe	Major mode for editing Scribe text files	**scribe-mode**, suffix *.mss*

a See Chapter 8 for an extensive discussion of working with markup languages in Emacs.

Table B-5. Emulations for other editors

Package	Description	Startup
vi	Major mode for emulating the **vi** editor	**vi-mode**
vip	Another major mode for emulating **vi**	**vip-mode**
edt	Function to set key bindings to emulate the VAX/VMS **EDT** editor	**edt-emulation-on**

Table B-6. Interfaces to operating system utilities[a]

Package	Description	Startup
shell	Major mode for interacting with the command-line shell.	**shell-mode**
find-dired	Run the **find** command and use **dired** on the resulting list of files.	**find-dired**
tar-mode	Access files inside a **tar** archive through a **dired**-like interface.	**tar-mode**, suffix *.tar*
arc-mode	Access files in several other archive formats through a **dired**-like interface.	**archive-mode**, suffixes *.arc, .zip, .lzh, .zoo, .ear, .jar, .war*, as well as capitalized variants; *.sxd, .sxm, .sxi, .sxc, .sxw*
lpr	Print the contents of a buffer or region.	**lpr-buffer, print-buffer, lpr-region, print-region**
sort	Sort the contents of a buffer.	**sort-columns, sort-fields, sort-lines, sort-numeric-fields, sort-paragraphs, sort-regexp-fields**
spell, ispell	Various tools for checking spelling.	See Chapter 3
diff, ediff	Tools to help in comparing files.	See Chapter 12

a Some of these will be useful on Windows only if you've installed a Unix compatibility package like Cygwin (see *http://www.cygwin.com*).

Table B-7. Networking support

Package	Description	Startup
ange-ftp	Provides transparent access to remote files via FTP	most standard file-handling commands
url	Functions for retrieving the contents of documents through URLs	Invoked from Lisp code, not interactively
quickurl	Functions for looking up and adding URLs to documents	many commands beginning with **quickurl**
talk	A multi-user talk package that runs in Emacs	**talk-connect**
eudc	A unified directory client for looking up address information from LDAP, BBDB, CCSO PH/QU and other directory servers	**eudc-mode**
net-utils	Provides access to common network utility programs (ping, traceroute, netstat, etc.	**ping**, **traceroute**, **netstat**, etc.

Table B-8. Games and amusements

Package	Description	Startup
animate	Draws animated text.	**animate-birthday-present**
blackbox	Major mode to play the Blackbox game.	**blackbox-mode**
decipher	Major mode to cryptanalyze monoalphabetic substitution ciphers (break simple codes).	**decipher**
dissociate	Randomly scramble text.	**dissociated-press**
doctor	Major mode for playing the famous "psychoanalyst" game.	**doctor**
dunnet	Major mode for playing an adventure game.	**dunnet**
gomoku	Major mode for playing Gomoku.	**gomoku**
hanoi	Solve the Towers of Hanoi puzzle for you.	**hanoi**
life	Explore cellular automata using John Conway's "life" game rules.	**life**
mpuz	Generate a random multiplication puzzle.	**mpuz**
snake	Steer an animated snake towards food without hitting yourself or the walls.	**snake**
solitaire	Play the peg solitaire game.	**solitaire**
studly	Randomly capitalize letters for that polished, professional look.	**studlify-region**
tetris	Guide falling tiles to complete rows.	**tetris**
yow	Print a random quotation from Zippy the Pinhead.	**yow**
zone	Rearrange your buffer in a hypnotic way.	**zone**

Again, this is only a sampling of some available packages, to give you a sense of the breadth and depth of capabilities that ship with Emacs. The list isn't close to complete even with respect to what's available at this time, and new features are always being added. Your best bet is to explore for yourself using the tools mentioned at the beginning of this appendix. And don't forget to search the Web for nonstandard additions that might be just what you need for your own environment and projects!

APPENDIX C
Bugs and Bug Fixes

There are no perfect programs. GNU Emacs is very thoroughly debugged, but it is certainly possible to find things that don't work correctly.

The Free Software Foundation (FSF) welcomes problem reports. However, they need to be real problem reports; simple differences of opinion about how something should work are not bugs. If you think that a certain command should work differently, remember that Emacs has been around for a long time and has many users; it can't be changed to satisfy a single user. (On the other hand, in most cases, you could write some Lisp to change it yourself.) In the *GNU Emacs Manual*, the FSF publishes some excellent guidelines for reporting bugs, which we'll summarize very quickly:

- Before you report a bug, see if it's on the list of known problems. You can view this list by typing **C-h C-e**.

- You most certainly have a bug if you run into some kind of system error (Emacs dumps core, terminates with a segmentation fault, crashes, hangs, or does something else antisocial).

- When reporting bugs, be as specific as possible. A few commands will help you report exactly what was happening when things went awry. **C-h l** (for **view-los-sage**) reports the last 100 or so keystrokes you made; **M-x open-dribble-file** *file-name* saves every keystroke you type in the specified *filename*.

- The FSF discourages you from trying to interpret bugs in the bug report. "I did thus-and-such and this happened" is useful, particularly if the problem is repeatable; "I think there's a problem with font handling" doesn't give any useful information at all.

- Always report which version of Emacs you are using. The command **M-x emacs-version** gives you the relevant information.

- Always report the contents of the file you were editing (if it makes a difference), the contents of your *.emacs* file, which mode you were in, and any Lisp libraries (custom or otherwise) that you have to load in order to create the problem.

We will add one very important guideline:

- Although we have taken every effort to write a book that is accurate, we are far from perfect. With that in mind, please *do not* cite this book as an authority when reporting a bug. Although we haven't asked, the Free Software Foundation would be completely justified in rejecting any bug reports based on a third-party publication. If you suspect a bug, use the *GNU Emacs Manual* or the help facility to find out what the command that's giving you trouble is really supposed to do. In doing so, you may find out that this book is incorrect; if you do, please report the problem to *booktech@oreilly.com*.

If you do have a bug to report, type **M-x report-emacs-bug** to send it from within Emacs. You'll be prompted for a subject line and dropped into Emacs' interface for sending mail. If mail from Emacs isn't set up properly, you can email *emacs-pretest-bug@gnu.org* using your preferred mail client. Be sure to include an informative subject line that summarizes the problem.

APPENDIX D

Online Resources

This appendix includes some helpful Emacs web sites. Some of those listed describe add-on packages for Emacs. In some cases, the sites have been stable for years and are likely to remain that way. In other cases, web sites come and go and URLs change. If you find errors in this list or have suggestions for additions, please email us at *booktech@oreilly.com*.

Table D-1. Emacs web sites

Web site	URL
The Free Software Foundation	*http://www.fsf.org/*
The official web site for GNU Emacs	*http://www.gnu.org/software/emacs/*
The GNU General Public License	*http://www.gnu.org/copyleft/gpl.html*
The web site for this book	*http://www.oreilly.com/catalog/gnu3/*
The very unofficial dotemacs home (great collection of *.emacs* files to aid you in creating your own)	*http://www.dotemacs.de/*
Dotfiles.com (includes dot files for other applications as well as Emacs)	*http://www.dotfiles.com/*
The Emacs Wiki	*http://www.emacswiki.org/cgi-bin/wiki /*
Emacs Haiku	*http://www.dina.dk/~abraham/religion/haiku-2.txt*
Emacs implementations	*http://www.finseth.com/~fin/emacs.html*
David Wheeler's essay arguing for a GPL-compatible license for open source projects	*http://www.dwheeler.com/essays/gpl-compatible.html*

Table D-2. Platform and accessibility-related web sites

Web site	URL
FSF's download site for Emacs for Unix and Windows	*http://ftp.gnu.org/pub/gnu/emacs/*
Andrew Choi's Mac OS X FAQ and build instructions	*http://members.shaw.ca/akochoi-emacs/*
	http://members.shaw.ca/akochoi-emacs/stories/obtaining-andbuilding.html

Table D-2. Platform and accessibility-related web sites (continued)

Web site	URL
Alex Rice's Mac OS X build	*http://mindlube.com/products/emacs/index.html*
Fink, a Unix software installer for Mac OS X	*http://fink.sourceforge.net/*
John Schneider's "Getting Mac OS X.3 toBehave Almost Like My Linux Boxes"	*http://www.eecs.wsu.edu/~schneidj/mac-osx-10.3.html*
Nqmacs, a Windows Emacs binary	*http://sourceforge.net/projects/nqmacs /*
Cygwin: Unix commands for Windows	*http://www.cygwin.com/*
Ngai Kim Hoong's page relating to Emacs and Cygwin (even Emacs and Palm Pilots)	*http://www.khngai.com/emacs/*
Kim Storm's CUA mode	*http://www.cua.dk/emacs.html/*
Emacspeak (an audio interface to Emacs)	*http://emacspeak.sourceforge.net/*

Table D-3. Text-related sites

Web site	URL
Ispell FAQ	*http://www.kdstevens.com/~stevens/ispell-faq.html*
Raymond Zeitler's post pointing to the right version of Ispell for Windows	*http://lists.nongnu.org/archive/html/help-emacs-windows/2004-06/msg00023.html*
Eric Pement's "Understanding GNU Emacs and Tabs" page	*http://www.student.northpark.edu/pemente/emacs_tabs.htm*
Eric Pement's awk scripts for converting to outline mode outlines to classical outline formats	*http://www.student.northpark.edu/pemente/awk/outline_classic11.awk.txt*
	http://www.student.northpark.edu/pemente/awk/outline_numbered11.awk.txt
ASCII art (fun with picture mode)	*http://www.ascii-art.de/*

Table D-4. Programming languages, version control, and customization sites

Web site	URL
CPAN (the Comprehensive Perl Archive Network)	*http://www.cpan.org/*
Collection of Emacs Development Environment Tools (CEDET)	*http://cedet.sourceforge.net/*
JDEE site	*http://jdee.sunsite.dk/*
PHP mode	*http://sourceforge.net/projects/php-mode/*
Subversion	*http://subversion.tigris.org*
Clearcase extensions (*clearcase.el*)	*http://members.verizon.net/~vze24fr2/EmacsClearCase/*

Table D-5. Markup language-related sites

Web site	URL
psgml mode	*http://www.lysator.liu.se/projects/about_psgml.html*
psgml setup instructions from OpenACS	*http://openacs.org/doc/openacs-5-0-0/psgml-mode.html*
Norm Walsh's DocBook site	*http://www.docbook.org/*
TEI Emacs (also includes JDEE for Linux and Windows)	*http://www.tei-c.org/Software/tei-emacs/*
Jim Clark's nxml mode	*http://thaiopensource.com/download/*
Nxml mode mailing list	*http://groups.yahoo.com/group/emacs-nxml-mode/*
RELAX NG	*http://www.relaxng.org/*
HTML helper mode	*http://www.nongnu.org/baol-hth/*
HTMLModeDeluxe	*http://www.emacswiki.org/cgi-bin/wiki/HtmlModeDeluxe/*
Darren Brierton's Emacs WebDev Environment	*http://www.dzr-web.com/people/darren/projects/emacs-webdev/*

APPENDIX E
Quick Reference

This quick reference is arranged topically, in roughly the same order as the commands were treated in the text. Unfortunately, it's impossible to be both "quick" and thorough, particularly with an editor as large and comprehensive as GNU Emacs. We've tried to take a middle road between completeness and quickness; we'll confess that, if we've erred, we've erred on the side of quickness.

Table E-1. File-handling commands (Chapter 1)

Keystrokes	Command name	Action
C-x C-f *File → Open File*	**find-file**	Find file and read it in a new buffer.
C-x C-v	**find-alternate-file**	Read an alternate file, replacing the one read with **C-x C-f**.
C-x i *File → Insert File*	**insert-file**	Insert file at cursor position.
C-x C-s *File → Save (current buffer)*	**save-buffer**	Save file.
C-x C-w *File → Save Buffer As*	**write-file**	Write buffer contents to file.
C-x C-c *File → Exit Emacs*	**save-buffers-kill-emacs**	Exit Emacs.

Table E-2. Cursor movement commands (Chapter 2)

Keystrokes	Command name	Action
C-f	**forward-char**	Move *forward* one character (right).
C-b	**backward-char**	Move *backward* one character (left).
C-p	**previous-line**	Move to *previous* line (up).
C-n	**next-line**	Move to *next* line (down).
M-f	**forward-word**	Move one word *forward.*
M-b	**backward-word**	Move one word *backward.*
C-a	**beginning-of-line**	Move to beginning of line.

Keystrokes	Command name	Action
C-e	end-of-line	Move to *end* of line.
M-e	forward-sentence	Move forward one sentence.
M-a	backward-sentence	Move backward one sentence.
C-v	scroll-up	Move forward one screen.
M-v	scroll-down	Move backward one screen.
M-<	beginning-of-buffer	Move to beginning of file.
M->	end-of-buffer	Move to end of file.
(*none*)	goto-line	Go to line *n* of file.
(*none*)	goto-char	Go to character *n* of file.
M-*n*	digit-argument	Repeat the next command *n* times.
C-u *n*	universal-argument	Repeat the next command *n* times (four times if you omit *n*).

Table E-3. Deleting, yanking, region, and clipboard commands(Chapter 2)

Keystrokes	Command name	Action
C-d	delete-char	Delete character under cursor.
Del	delete-backward-char	Delete previous character.
M-d	kill-word	Delete next word.
M-Del	backward-kill-word	Delete previous word.
C-y *Edit → Paste Most Recent*	yank	Restore what you've deleted.
C-w *Edit → Cut*	kill-region	Delete a marked region (see next section).
C-@ *or* C- Space	set-mark-command	Mark the beginning (or end) of a region.
C-x C-x	exchange-point-and-mark	Exchange location of cursor and mark.
C-w	kill-region	Delete the region.
C-y	yank	Paste most recently killed or copied text.
M-w	kill-ring-save	Copy the region (so it can be pasted with **C-y**).
C-x h	mark-whole-buffer	Mark buffer.
M-y	yank-pop	After **C-y**, pastes earlier deletion.
(*none*)	clipboard-kill-region	Cut region and place both in kill ring and on system clipboard.
(*none*)	clipboard-yank	Paste text from clipboard.
(*none*)	clipboard-kill-ring-save	Copy text to clipboard.

Table E-4. Text filling and reformatting commands (Chapter 2)

Keystrokes	Command name	Action
(none) *Options → Word Wrap in Text Modes*	**auto-fill-mode**	Toggle auto-fill mode, in which Emacs formats paragraphs as you type them.
M-q	**fill-paragraph**	Reformat paragraph.
(none) *Edit → Fill*	**fill-region**	Reformat individual paragraphs within a region.

Table E-5. Stopping and undoing commands (Chapter 2)

Keystrokes	Command name	Action
C-g	**keyboard-quit**	Abort current command.
C-x u	**advertised-undo**	Undo last edit (can be done repeatedly).
C-_ *Edit → Undo*	**undo**	Undo last edit.
(none)	**revert-buffer**	Restore buffer to the state it was in when the file was last saved (or auto-saved).

Table E-6. Search and replace commands (Chapter 3)

Keystrokes	Command name	Action
C-s *Edit → Search → Incremental Search → Forward String*	**isearch-forward**	Start incremental search forward; follow by search string. Also, find next occurrence (forward) of search string.
C-r *Edit → Search → Incremental Search → Backward String*	**isearch-backward**	Start incremental search backward; follow by search string. Also, find next occurrence (backward) of search string.

Table E-7. Regular expression search commands (Chapter 3)

Keystrokes	Command name	Action
C-M-s Enter *Edit → Search → Regexp Forward*	**re-search-forward**	Search for a regular expression forward.
C-M-r Enter *Edit → Search → Regexp Backwards*	**re-search-backward**	Search for a regular expression backward.
C-M-s *Edit → Search → Incremental Search → Forward Regexp*	**isearch-forward-regexp**	Search incrementally forward for a regular expression.
C-M-r *Edit → Search → Incremental Search → Backward Regexp*	**isearch-backward-regexp**	Search incrementally backward for a regular expression.
C-M-% *Edit → Replace → Replace Regexp*	**query-replace-regexp**	Query-replace a regular expression.

Table E-8. Spell-checking commands (Chapter 3)

Keystrokes	Command name	Action
(*none*) *Tools → Spell Checking →* *Spell-Check Buffer*	**ispell-buffer**	Check spelling of the buffer.
(*none*) *Tools → Spell Checking →* *Spell-Check Comments*	**ispell-comments-and-strings**	Checks spelling of comments and strings in a program.
(*none*) *Tools → Spell Checking → Automatic* *Spell-Checking (Flyspell)*	**flyspell-mode**	Enter the flyspell minor mode, in which incorrectly spelled words are highlighted.
(*none*)	**flyspell-buffer**	Spell-check the current buffer, underlining all misspelled words. Use middle mouse button to correct.

Table E-9. Buffer commands (Chapter 4)

Keystrokes	Command name	Action
C-x b *Buffers → Select Named Buffer*	**switch-to-buffer**	Move to the buffer specified.
C-x → *Buffers → Next Buffer*	**next-buffer**	Move to the next buffer in the buffer list.
C-x ← *Buffers → Previous Buffer*	**previous-buffer**	Move to the previous buffer in the buffer list.
C-x C-b *Buffers → List All Buffers*	**list-buffers**	Display the buffer list.
C-x k	**kill-buffer**	Delete the buffer specified.
(*none*)	**kill-some-buffers**	Ask about deleting each buffer.

Table E-10. Windows and frames (Chapter 4)

Keystrokes	Command name	Action
C-x 2 *File → Split Window*	**split-window-vertically**	Divide current window into two windows, one above the other.
C-x 3	**split-window-horizontally**	Divide current window into two side-by-side windows.
C-x o	**other-window**	Move to the other window; if there are several, move to the next window.
C-x 0	**delete-window**	Delete the current window.
C-x 1 *File → Unsplit Windows*	**delete-other-windows**	Delete all windows but this one.
C-x 4 f	**find-file-other-window**	Find a file in the other window.
C-x 4 b	**switch-to-buffer-other-window**	Select a buffer in the other window.

Table E-10. Windows and frames (Chapter 4) (continued)

Keystrokes	Command name	Action
(none) *Tools → Compare (Ediff) →* *This Window and Next Window*	**compare-windows**	Compare this window with the next window and show the first difference.
C-x 5 o *Buffers → Frames*	**other-frame**	Move to other frame.
C-x 5 0 *File → Delete Frame*	**delete-frame**	Delete current frame.
C-x 5 2 *File → New Frame*	**make-frame**	Create a new frame on the current buffer.
C-x 5 f	**find-file-other-frame**	Find file in a new frame.
C-x 5 r	**find-file-read-only-other-frame**	Finds a file in a new frame, but it is read-only.
C-x 5 b	**switch-to-buffer-other-frame**	Make frame and display other buffer in it.

Table E-11. Shell mode commands (Chapter 5)

Keystrokes	Command name	Action
(none)	**shell**	Enter shell mode.
C-c C-c *Signals → BREAK*	**comint-interrupt-subjob**	Interrupt current job; equivalent to **C-c**.
C-c C-z *Signals → STOP*	**comint-stop-subjob**	Suspend or stop a job; **C-z** in Unix shells.
M-p *In/Out → Previous Input*	**comint-previous-input**	Retrieve previous commands (can be repeated to find earlier commands).
M-n *In/Out → Next Input*	**comint-next-input**	Retrieve subsequent commands (can be repeated to find more recent commands).
Enter	**comint-send-input**	Send input on current line.
Tab	**comint-dynamic-complete**	Complete current command, filename, or variable name.

Table E-12. Dired commands (Chapter 5)

Keystrokes	Command name	Action
C-x d *File → Open Directory*	**dired**	Start Dired.
C *Operate → Copy to*	**dired-do-copy**	Copy file.
d *Mark → Flag*	**dired-flag-file-deletion**	Flag for deletion.
D *Operate → Delete*	**dired-do-delete**	Query for immediate deletion.
f	**dired-advertised-find-file**	Find (so you can edit).

Table E-12. Dired commands (Chapter 5) (continued)

Keystrokes	Command name	Action
g *Immediate → Refresh*	**revert-buffer**	Reread the directory from disk.
m or * m *Mark → Mark*	**dired-mark**	Mark with *.
Q *Operate → Query Replace in Files*	**dired-do-query-replace**	Query replace string in marked files.
R *Operate → Rename to*	**dired-do-rename**	Rename file.
s	**dired-sort-toggle-or-edit**	Sort the Dired display by date or by filename (toggles between these).
t *Mark → Toggle Marks*	**dired-toggle-marks**	Toggle marks on files and directories; pressing t once marks all unmarked files and directories; pressing t again restores original marks.
u *Mark → Unmark*	**dired-unmark**	Remove mark.
+ *Immediate → Create Directory*	**dired-create-directory**	Create a directory.
* ! or M-Del *Mark → Unmark All*	**dired-unmark-all-files**	Remove all marks from all files.

Table E-13. Macro commands (Chapter 6)

Keystrokes	Command name	Action
C-x (	**kmacro-start-macro**	Start macro definition.
F3	**kmacro-start-macro-or-insert-counter**	Start macro definition. If pressed while defining a macro, insert a counter.
C-x)	**kmacro-end-macro**	End macro definition.
F4	**kmacro-end-or-call-macro**	End macro definition (if definition is in progress) or invoke last keyboard macro.
C-x e	**kmacro-end-and-call-macro**	Execute last keyboard macro defined. Can type e to repeat macro.
C-x C-k n	**name-last-kbd-macro**	Name the last macro you created (before saving it).
C-x C-k e	**edit-kbd-macro**	Edit a keyboard macro by typing C-x e for the last keyboard macro defined, M-x for a named macro, C-h l for lossage, or keystrokes for a macro bound to a key.
C-x C-k Enter	**kmacro-edit-macro**	Edit the last keyboard macro.

Table E-14. Outline mode commands (Chapter 7)

Keystrokes	Command name	Action
(none)	outline-mode	Toggle outline mode

Table E-14. Outline mode commands (Chapter 7) (continued)

Keystrokes	Command name	Action
C-c C-t *Hide → Hide Body*	hide-body	Hide all body lines.
C-c C-a *Show → Show All*	show-all	Show everything that's hidden.

Table E-15. Compilation mode commands (Chapter 9)

Keystrokes	Command name	Action
C-x `	**next-error**	Move to the next error message and visit the corresponding source code.
M-n	**compilation-next-error**	Move to the next error message.
M-p	**compilation-previous-error**	Move to the previous error message.
C-c C-c	**compilation-goto-error**	Visit the source code for the current error message.

Table E-16. Basic indentation commands (Chapters 7 and 9)

Keystrokes	Command name	Action
C-M-\	**indent-region**	Indent each line between the cursor and mark.
M-m	**back-to-indentation**	Move to the first nonblank character on the line.
M-^	**delete-indentation**	Join this line to the previous one.

Table E-17. C motion commands (Chapter 9)

Keystrokes	Command name	Action
M-a	**c-beginning-of-statement**	Move to the beginning of the current statement.
M-e	**c-end-of-statement**	Move to the end of the current statement.
M-q	**c-fill-paragraph**	If in comment, fill the paragraph, preserving indentations and decorations.
C-M-a	**beginning-of-defun**	Move to the beginning of the body of the function surrounding the point.
C-M-e	**end-of-defun**	Move to the end of the function.
C-M-h	**c-mark-function**	Put the cursor at the beginning of the function, the mark at the end.
C-c C-q	**c-indent-defun**	Indent the entire function according to indentation style.
C-c C-u	**c-up-conditional**	Move to the beginning of the current preprocessor conditional.
C-c C-p	**c-backward-conditional**	Move to the previous preprocessor conditional.
C-c C-n	**c-forward-conditional**	Move to the next preprocessor conditional.

Table E-18. SQL mode commands (Chapter 9)

Keystrokes	Command name	Action
C-c C-c	sql-send-paragraph	Send the paragraph the cursor is on. A paragraph is defined by the particular database client. For the **sql-mysql** process, for example, a paragraph begins with a statement like select or update and ends with a semicolon. Any number of lines can intervene.
C-c C-r	sql-send-region	Send the marked region.
C-c C-b	sql-send-buffer	Send the entire buffer.

Table E-19. Lisp commands (Chapter 9)

Keystrokes	Command name	Action
C-M-b	backward-sexp	Move backward by one S-expression.
C-M-f	forward-sexp	Move forward by one S-expression.
C-M-t	transpose-sexps	Transpose the two S-expressions around the cursor.
C-M-@	mark-sexp	Set mark to the end of the current S-expression; set the cursor to the beginning.
C-M-k	kill-sexp	Delete the S-expression following the cursor.
(none)	backward-kill-sexp	Delete the S-expression preceding the cursor.
C-M-n	forward-list	Move forward by one list.
C-M-p	backward-list	Move backward by one list.
C-M-d	down-list	Move forward and down one parenthesis level.
(none)	up-list	Move forward out of one parenthesis level.
C-M-u	backward-up-list	Move backward out of one parenthesis level.
C-M-a	beginning-of-defun	Move to the beginning of the current function.
C-M-e	end-of-defun	Move to the end of the current function.
C-M-h	mark-defun	Put the cursor at the beginning of the function, put the mark at the end.

Table E-20. VC commands (Chapter 12)

Keystrokes	Command name	Action
C-x v v	vc-next-action	Go to the next logical version control state.
C-x v d	vc-directory	Show all registered files beneath a directory.
C-x v =	vc-diff	Generate a version difference report.
C-x v u	vc-revert-buffer	Throw away changes since the last checked-in revision.
C-x v ~	vc-version-other-window	Retrieve a given revision in another window.
C-x v l	vc-print-log	Display a file's change comments and history.
C-x v i	vc-register	Register a file for version control.
C-x v h	vc-insert-headers	Insert version control headers in a file.
C-x v r	vc-retrieve-snapshot	Check out a named project snapshot.
C-x v s	vc-create-snapshot	Create a named project snapshot.
C-x v c	vc-cancel-version	Throw away a saved revision.
C-x v a	vc-update-change-log	Update a GNU-style ChangeLog file.

Table E-21. Ediff commands (Chapter 12)

Keystrokes	Command name	Action
Space or n	ediff-next-difference	Move to the next difference between the files.
Del or p	ediff-previous-difference	Move to the preceding difference between the files.
j	ediff-jump-to-difference	Go to the difference specified as a numeric prefix argument.
a	ediff-copy-A-to-B	Copy the version of the current difference found in buffer A to buffer B.
b	ediff-copy-B-to-A	Copy the version of the current difference found in buffer B to buffer A.
r a or r b	ediff-restore-diff	Restore the current difference in buffer A (or B) to the way it was before copying from the other buffer.
A or B	ediff-toggle-read-only	Switch the specified buffer into (or out of) read-only mode.
g a or g b	ediff-jump-to-difference-at-point	Recenter the comparison buffers on the difference nearest to your current location (point) in the specified buffer.
!	ediff-update-diffs	Recalculate and redisplay the highlighted regions; useful if you've manually made extensive changes to a buffer.
w a or w b	ediff-save-buffer	Save the specified buffer to disk.
z	ediff-suspend	Close the Ediff control window, but leave the session active so you can resume it later.
q	ediff-quit	Close the Ediff window and end this comparison session.

Table E-22. CUA mode commands (Chapter 13)

Keystrokes	Command name	Action
C-c C-x C-x	cua-exchange-point-and-mark	Exchange location of cursor and mark.
C-x *or* C-w *or* S-Delete	kill-region	Delete the region.
C-v *or* C-y *or* S-Insert	cua-paste	Paste most recently killed or copied text.
C-c	copy-region-as-kill	Copy the region.
M-v	cua-repeat-replace-region	After highlighting and replacing a string, find the next string and replace it the same way.
M-y	cua-paste-pop	After C-v, pastes earlier deletion.
C-z *or* C-x u	cua-undo	Undoes the last change.
C-x C-z	iconify-frame	Minimize the current frame (what C-z does outside CUA mode).

Table E-23. Help commands (Chapter 14)

Keystrokes	Command name	Question answered
C-h k Help → Describe → Describe Key	describe-key	What command does this keystroke sequence run, and what does it do?
C-h f Help → Describe → Describe Function	describe-function	What does this function do?

Table E-23. Help commands (Chapter 14) (continued)

Keystrokes	Command name	Question answered
C-h v *Help → Describe → Describe Variable*	**describe-variable**	What does this variable mean, and what is its value?
C-h m *Help → Describe → Describe Buffer Modes*	**describe-mode**	Tell me about the modes the current buffer is in.
C-h b *Help → Describe → List Key Bindings*	**describe-bindings**	What are all the key bindings for this buffer?
C-h a *Help → Search Documentation → Find Commands by Name*	**apropos-command**	What commands include this word?
(none) *Help → Search Documentation → Find Options by Name*	**apropos-variable**	What variables include this regular expression?
(none) *Help → Search Documentation → Find Any Object by Name*	**apropos**	What functions and variables involve this regular expression?

Table E-24. Documentation help commands (Chapter 14)

Keystrokes	Command name	Action
C-h t *Help → Emacs Tutorial*	**help-with-tutorial**	Run the Emacs tutorial.
C-h i	**info**	Start the Info documentation reader. If prefaced with **C-u**, reads an Info file of your choice.
C-h r *Help → Read the Emacs Manual*	**info-emacs-manual**	Open the Emacs manual.
C-h K *Help → More Manuals → Find Key in Manual*	**Info-goto-emacs-key-command-node**	Start Info documentation reader at the node that discusses this key sequence.
(none) *Help → Search Documentation → Look Up Subject in User Manual*	**emacs-index-search**	Search the index of the Emacs user manual.
C-h p	**finder-by-keyword**	Invoke a menu that lets you get information about Emacs Lisp packages available on your system.

Table E-25. Important modes

Mode	Function
fundamental-mode	The default mode
text-mode	Major mode for writing text (Chapter 2)
outline-mode	Major mode for writing outlines (Chapter 7)
picture-mode	Major mode for creating ASCII drawings using the keyboard (Chapter 7)
html-mode	Major mode for writing HTML (Chapter 8)

Table E-25. Important modes (continued)

Mode	Function
sgml-mode	Major mode for writing SGML and XML (Chapter 8)
latex-mode	Major mode for formatting files for TEX and LATEX (Chapter 8)
c-mode, c++-mode	Major mode for writing C and C++, and Java programs (Chapter 9)
java-mode	Major mode for writing Java programs (Chapter 9)
perl-mode, cperl-mode	Major modes for writing Perl programs (Chapter 9)
sql-mode	Major mode for interacting with databases using SQL (Chapter 9)
emacs-lisp-mode	Major mode for writing Emacs Lisp functions (Chapters 9 and 11)
lisp-mode	Major mode for writing Lisp programs (Chapters 9 and 11)
lisp-interaction-mode	Major mode for writing and evaluating Lisp expressions (Chapters 9 and 11)
auto-fill-mode	Minor mode that enables word wrap (Chapter 2)
overwrite-mode	Minor mode that replaces characters as you type instead of inserting them (Chapter 2)
flyspell-mode	Minor mode for flyspell spell-checker (Chapter 3)
flyspell-prog-mode	Minor mode for spell-checking programs with flyspell (Chapter 3)
abbrev-mode	Minor mode for word abbreviations (Chapter 3)
artist-mode	Minor mode for creating ASCII drawings using the mouse (Chapter 7)
font-lock-mode	Minor mode for highlighting text in colors and fonts (Chapter 9)
vc-mode	Minor mode for using version control systems (Chapter 12)

Glossary

abbrev mode

A mode in which you define abbreviations that are automatically replaced when you type them. You might define abbreviations for phrases, long words, or common misspellings. Emacs' abbreviation facility, also found in vi, is similar to, but significantly predates, features like auto-text in Microsoft Word. For more information on abbrev mode, see Chapter 3.

ange-ftp mode

An easy-to-use interface to the file transfer protocol (FTP) written by Andy Norman. Use the **find-file** command to find files and directories on the Internet or other networks as if they were on the local system. To specify a remote file, just type */user@systemname:/pathtofile/fi lename*. The slash at the beginning and the colon between the system name and path are easy to forget, and ange-ftp mode won't work without them. If you omit the path and filename, Emacs uses Dired to display the top directory on the remote system (if the remote system permits directory listings). Rather than using FTP commands to retrieve files, you can display them or copy them using Dired commands. Ange-ftp mode, then, is useful for looking at files as well as downloading them. However, like FTP itself, it is highly insecure.

auto-fill mode

A minor mode in which Emacs does word wrap. When you reach the end of a line and auto-fill mode is on, you can keep typing and Emacs breaks lines appropriately. Auto-fill mode is off by default.

auto-save file (*#file#*)

Emacs periodically saves your buffer in a temporary file called an auto-save file. Emacs also saves files in an auto-save file if a session is terminated abnormally. For example, if you are working on a file called *budget* and the system goes down, look for an auto-save file called *#budget#* when the system is back up. For more information on auto-save files, see Chapter 2.

backup file (*file~*)

When you tell Emacs to save a file, it first copies the current version to a file of the same name followed by a tilde (~). For example, if you save the file *budget*, Emacs moves the previous version to *budget~*. If you later decide you don't want the changes you saved, you can use the backup file. For more information on backup files, see Chapter 2.

body

In outline mode, there are headers (the skeleton of the outline) and paragraphs of text, which form the body.

bookmark

A named location in a file. Finding a file always brings you to the beginning; moving to a bookmark opens the file and brings you to a particular location. Bookmarks are helpful for marking places in online documentation and other files you read or refer to as well as for specifying where you left off when working on a file. For more information on bookmarks, see Chapter 4.

buffer

The work area in which Emacs displays a copy of a file or a blank area in which you can type. When you edit a file, Emacs copies the file into a buffer of the same name; the file on disk remains unchanged. When you save a buffer, Emacs copies the changes you have made into the file on disk. In addition to buffers for working with files, Emacs creates its own specialized buffers for processes, such as working with the command line, using the calendar feature, and displaying help, for example.

byte-compile

A method for compiling Emacs Lisp files, whose names end in *.el*. After you byte-compile a file, its name ends in *.elc*. Byte-compiling Emacs Lisp functions makes them load more efficiently.

calendar

An Emacs facility that allows users to work with a calendar. When you type **M-x calendar**, Emacs displays a three-month calendar at the bottom of the screen with the cursor on the current date. You can mark dates with diary entries and view holidays from the calendar. For more information about the calendar, see Chapter 5.

clipboard

An interprogram storage area. Text cut in one application can be pasted in another. Commands such as **clipboard-yank** specifically deal with the clipboard rather than the kill ring, which is the storage area for cut or copied text in Emacs. See Chapter 2 for more details and *see also* kill ring.

comment

Text that is ignored by a programming language or text formatting program.

Emacs inserts comment syntax appropriate for the mode you are in when you type **M-;**. In some general modes, such as text mode and fundamental mode, no comment syntax is defined.

completion

A shortcut feature that allows you to type the first few letters of a command, variable, or filename and press **Tab**. Emacs either completes it (if it's unique) or lists possibilities in a *Completions* buffer.

copyleft

An agreement that software should be shared freely with others and that those others in turn must be able to share it. A copyright restricts usage of information whereas a copyleft is designed to guarantee its continued free availability to all. The term copyleft is also used to refer to the GNU General Public License. You can view the GPL by typing **C-h C-c**.

CUA

Common User Access. A standard originally set by IBM that dictates that certain key sequences should run certain commands, including **C-c** to copy, **C-x** to cut, and **C-v** to paste. CUA mode allows Emacs users to use CUA key sequences. See Chapter 13.

cursor

The cursor indicates where you are in the buffer. Emacs often refers to the cursor as point. Technically, point is located between two characters: the cursor and the previous character.

customization

By default, Emacs behaves in a given way. Through customization you tailor that behavior to your needs and preferences. You customize Emacs using Custom, the interactive customization interface, or directly by changing the *.emacs* file. Customization is discussed in detail in Chapter 10.

cut

To kill text so that it can later be yanked (pasted).

default

The normal value for a variable or option. For example, by default, auto-fill mode is not turned on.

default direction

Normally when you type, text appears from left to right. In picture mode, it's possible to move in eight different directions. When you start picture mode, the default direction is right. You can specify a different direction, like up, down, northwest, southeast, and so on, which then becomes the default direction. **C-c C-f** to move forward and **C-c C-b** to move backwards are relative to the default direction.

delete

To omit text and not store it in the kill ring for later retrieval.

diary

An Emacs feature that allows you to make notes about certain dates. Emacs then displays a reminder on the date you've marked. Diary entries can be set for a given date, a block of dates, or periodically (biweekly, for example). For more information on the diary, see Chapter 5.

directory

A data structure for organizing files. Synonymous with folder.

Dired

The directory editor. Using Dired, you can perform various operations on files and directories, such as moving, compressing, deleting, copying, and byte-compiling. For more information on Dired, see Chapter 5.

.emacs file

The initialization file where you change Emacs default behavior. The commands in this file run when you start Emacs. However, Emacs does not need this file in order to run. Throughout the book, we suggest lines you can add to your *.emacs* file to change some aspect of Emacs behavior. Custom, the interactive customization interface, modifies *.emacs* when you use it to modify options and save your changes.

emacsen

The generic term for various versions of Emacs.

file

A storage area on disk. When you find a file in Emacs, it copies the file into a buffer, a working area in memory. When you save changes, Emacs copies the changes in the current buffer and overwrites the file on disk.

fill prefix

In text mode and auto-fill mode, a fill prefix is a string of characters you define that Emacs inserts at the beginning of each line of a paragraph. Fill prefixes could be a string of spaces (this is an easy way to indent text) or a simple greater-than sign (>), often used in email to differentiate text being quoted from a previous message.

frame

A window in which Emacs buffers are displayed. By default, users have one frame, but they can create more. When there is one frame, the system's name appears as the title. When there are multiple frames, the frames are titled by buffer name. In common usage, what Emacs calls a frame is called a window. However, in Emacs, a window is a portion of a frame or a split screen. For more information on windows and frames, see Chapter 4.

global abbreviations

Abbreviations you have defined that work in every major mode. By contrast, local abbreviations work only in the mode in which you define them. Global abbreviations, then, are good when you always want Emacs to make automatic replacements; local abbreviations are good for replacements you want in text mode, for example, but not in C mode. For more information on abbreviations, see Chapter 3.

GNU

An acronym for "GNU's Not Unix."

header

1. The beginning of a file, such as a LATEX file, that defines certain characteristics about the document's format. 2. Version control information embedded in a file that is automatically updated at check-in, check-out, and revert time.

home directory

Your personal directory. On a Unix system, often */home/username*. On Windows, either *C:* or a directory specified by the HOME environment variable.

incremental search

A search that Emacs launches as soon as you type the first character of the search string.

initialization file

See .emacs file

kill

To delete and store text in the kill ring.

kill ring

The area where Emacs holds deletions. By default, the kill ring holds the last 60 deletions or kills. Note that deletion commands (such as **C-d** to delete a character) do not store deleted text in the kill ring; see Chapter 2 for details.

local abbreviations

Abbreviations you have defined that are specific to (or "local to") a given mode. You might want different abbreviations in text mode and in C mode, for example. For more information on abbreviations, see Chapter 3.

macros

A sequence of recorded keystrokes. For information on creating macros, see Chapter 6.

major mode

Emacs's way of adapting its behavior to the primary task at hand. Text mode is a major mode designed for writing text; C mode is for writing C programs. Different modes have different commands that make sense in that mode, in addition to

global commands that work in every mode.

mark

A secondary pointer that, along with the cursor, is used to define the boundaries of a region. Regions can be deleted, moved, or copied. In GNU Emacs, the mark is not displayed.

minibuffer

An area at the bottom of the screen into which the user enters certain information. For example, when you write a file by typing **C-x C-w**, Emacs asks for the filename in the minibuffer. Emacs also displays messages in this area.

minor mode

Features that can be turned on and off independent of the major mode you are in. Auto-fill mode, which does word wrap automatically, is a minor mode.

mode

Emacs's way of adapting its behavior to the task at hand. There are major modes, that define the primary task at hand, and minor modes, options that you turn on and off within a major mode. For example, text mode is a major mode; auto-fill mode, which enables word wrap, is a minor mode.

mode line

The last line of an Emacs window, often displayed in reverse video or in another color. The mode line tells what buffer you are editing, the major and minor modes you have turned on, and where you are in the buffer. Optionally, the mode line provides other information, such as the time of day.

output groups

In shell mode, an output group consists of a shell command and its output. An output group provides a convenient way to move between commands in shell mode since the output of any given command may be several screens long.

overwrite mode

A minor mode that allows users to type over existing text. To start overwrite mode, type **M-x overwrite-mode Enter.**

paragraph formatting

See auto-fill mode.

paste

To insert text that has been stored in the kill ring or on the system clipboard. The Emacs term for *paste* is *yank*.

path

The location of a given file or folder. For example, the *.emacs* file is usually stored in a user's home directory. On some Unix systems, the path to this file is */home/user-name/.emacs*.

pause

A macro feature that stops a macro temporarily to allow user input. The user then restarts the macro by typing **C-M-c**. For more information, see Chapter 6.

picture mode

A major mode designed for creating simple drawings using keyboard characters. See Chapter 7 for more information.

point

The cursor position. To be precise, point is considered to be between the character under the cursor and the previous character. In practice, you can usually consider the cursor and point synonymous. Knowing precisely where point is, however, can help you understand the workings of certain commands better (such as yanking or transposition commands).

query

A macro feature that allows the user to decide whether to continue a macro or to stop it.

query-replace

A search and replacement feature that allows users to decide, on a case-by-case basis, whether a given replacement should be done.

read-only

A file or buffer that can be viewed but not modified. You can copy text from a

read-only buffer and paste it into another buffer.

read-write

A file or buffer that can be viewed (read) and changed (written to).

rectangle editing

Using rectangles, you can rearrange and edit columns of information. For more information on using rectangles, see Chapter 7.

region

The area between the cursor (also called point) and the mark. Regions can be cut, moved, or copied. The region currently defined is highlighted on some displays. If it isn't, you can press **C-x C-x** (for **exchange-point-and-mark**) to see the region's boundaries.

registers

Areas in which you store rectangles, cursor positions, or text. Similar to the kill ring, but registers are given single-character names for easy (and often repeated) retrieval of information.

regular expression

A feature that allows sophisticated and flexible matching of strings. Emacs supports regular expression searches and regular expression replacement. See Chapters 3 and 11.

search and replace

See query-replace.

search string

In a search, the text that is being searched for.

setup file

See *.emacs* file.

shell buffer

An Emacs-created buffer for working with the command line, allowing you to use Emacs editing commands and features, such as completion, while interacting with the operating system. To start a shell buffer, type **M-x shell**.

variable

Emacs provides hundreds of features that you can tailor by setting variables. You can set variables for a single session by typing **M-x set-variable** *variablename* or permanently using the *.emacs* file or Custom, the interactive customization interface. See Chapter 10.

window

An area of the screen in which a buffer is displayed. By default, Emacs has one window. Many features, including help, automatically break the screen into two windows. You can set up horizontal windows (the most frequently used kind) and vertical or side-by-side windows. It is possible to have multiple windows on one buffer. GUI windows are referred to as frames.

word search

A search facility that ignores line breaks and punctuation. If you can't find some text that you know is there with other searches, such as incremental-search, chances are there is a line break that incremental-search interprets as a character. Try word search instead.

word wrap

See auto-fill mode.

yank

Paste text that has been cut or killed.

Index

* (asterisk)
    buffers and, 97
    Dired, 130
    in mode line, 10
\# (comment mark), annotations, 111
$$ (dollar signs) in LaTeX, 258
% (percent sign)
    buffers and, 97
? (question mark), Dired, 130
~ (tilde)
    backup files and, 43
    buffers and, 100

A

abbrev mode, 4, 487
abbreviations, 487
    capitalization and, 80
    defining, 77
    disabling, 80
    Flyspell, 73, 74
        deleting, 78
    global, 77
    local, 77
active buffers, checking, 84
alternation operators, regular expressions in
        functions, 363
ange-ftp mode, 487
annotations, bookmarks, 110, 111
apropos command, help, 443
argument codes, Lisp interactive
        functions, 352
artist mode, 4
    commands, 216
    drawing with mouse, 213
asterisk (*)
    Dired, 130
    mode line, 10
atoms (Lisp), 346
    syntax, 346
auto complete, 13
auto-fill mode, 4, 21, 47, 487
automatic template system, building, 374
auto-newline, C programming language
        mode, 281
auto-save files, 487
    creation, 44
    Dired, 132
    recovering text from, 44
    variables, 457
auto-save mode, 4

B

backups
    files, 43, 487
        Dired, 126
        overwriting original with, 43
    numbered backups, 43
    variables, 457
backward movement of cursor, 23
binding, 10
    macros to keys, 160
blank lines in picture mode, 209
bookmarks, 106, 487
    annotations, 110
    commands, 112
    deleting, 108

We'd like to hear your suggestions for improving our indexes. Send email to *index@oreilly.com*.

jumping to, 107
list, 109
   commands, 110
   display, 109
moving to, 107
renaming, 108
setting, 107
text insertion and, 108
Boolean syntax (Lisp), 347
braces ({ }) in LaTeX, 258
buffer highlighting, 331
buffer list
   commands, 101
   saving buffers, 100
   symbols, 98
   window, moving to, 99
   (see also buffers)
buffers, 3, 488
   * (asterisk), 97
   % (percent sign), 97
   ~ (tilde) and, 100
   active, 84
   annotations, # (comment mark), 111
   built-in functions, 359
   commands, 100
   comment buffer, VC mode, 403
   cycling through, 87
   default directory, 14
   deleting, 87
   displaying, windows, 88
   editing multiple in separate windows, 92
   frames, 84
   Help, 17
   internal, names, 84
   Ispell and, 64
   listing, 98
      by major mode, 86
   major modes, 84, 381
   marks, 89
   Messages, 84
   minibuffer, 10
   mode line, 17
   modes and, 3
   multiple, 85
      displaying, 100
   names
      mode line, 96
      named same, 96
      renaming buffers, 96
   number of, 84
   read-only, 97
      toggling status, 97

reverting from files, 42
saving
   buffer list, 100
   multiple, 95
scratch, 10
shell commands, output, 118
status, 100
switching between, 85
windows and, 84
(see also shell buffers)
Buffers menu, 84
bug reports, 470
built-in functions, 358
   buffers, 359
   locating, 372
   regions, 359
   regular expressions, 360
      match portions, 365
      operator context, 364
      operators, 361, 368
      operators, grouping, 363
   text, 359
byte-compiling Lisp files, 397, 488

C

C language mode, 266
C++ language mode, 266
C++ mode/C mode comparison, 283
C motion commands, 276
C programming language mode
   auto-newline, 281
   hungry-delete key, 281
C programming language, support, 275
C++ programming language, support, 275
calculator mode, Lisp, 384
   code, 386
calendar, 488
   display, 142
   holiday commands, 148
   holiday display, 144
   movement commands, 143
   navigating, 142
   week start day, 142
canceling commands, 41
canceling searches, 52
capitalization, 40
capitalization commands, 40
capitalization in abbreviations, 80
carriage return, picture mode, 211
case-fold-search variable, 62
Case-Insensitive Search option, 61
case-replace variable, 62

case-sensitivity in searches, 50, 61
C-c commands, 11
cc mode, 3
CEDIT (Collection of Emacs Development
    Environment Tools),
    installation, 286
centering, 186
  display, 26
  line-by-line, 187
C-h command, 16
change comments, version control, 400
ChangeLog files, version control, 409
changes
  recovering, 44
  undoing, 41
character encoding
  HTML helper mode, 238
  HTML mode, 224
characters
  regular expressions, 62
  syntax (Lisp), 346
  variables, 339
ClearCase, VC and, 412
clipboard, 37
  commands, 38
  pasting from, 38
  text
    placing in, 37
    retrieving, 38
colons, tab stops and, 173
color
  automatic, 331
  changing, 332
  cursor, 333
color-enriched text, saving, 333
columns, editing (see rectangle editing)
command pairs, LaTeX mode, 259
command-line
  Emacs startup
    Mac OS X, 431
    Windows, 435
  options, 342
commands, xvii, 10
  artist mode, 216
  bookmark list, 110
  bookmarks, 112
  buffer list, 101
  buffer manipulation, 100
  C commands, 11
  C motion commands, 276
  calendar movement, 143
  canceling, 41

capitalization, 40
C-c, 11
C-h, 16
clipboard, 38
compilation mode, 265
Ctrl, 23
Ctrl key and, 11
CUA mode, 438
cursor movement, 22, 23, 26
C-x commands, 11
deletion commands, 31
diary, 148
digit-argument, 26
Dired, 137
Ediff, 416
enriched mode fonts, 334
file-handling commands, 18
find-file, 15
Flyspell, 73
help commands, 441
  apropos, 443
  complex commands, 445
holiday commands, 148
HTML helper, 239
HTML mode, 228
incremental searches, 53
indentation, 181, 185
Info commands, 451
Ispell, 73
keyboard access, 27
keystrokes, 10
kill commands, 29
killing, 31
LaTeX mode, 261
M commands, 11
macro commands, 169
Meta, 23
nxml mode, 252
outline mode, 193
picture mode, 212
printing commands, 140, 141
programming language codes, 271
rectangles, 201
redoing, 42
reformatting commands, 22
regions, 37
repeating, 26, 58
search commands, 54
searches, regular expressions in, 63
S-expressions (LISP), 299
shell commands, Dired, 128
shell mode, 115, 122

commands (*continued*)
  stopping, 43
  tab commands, 176
  TeX mode, 261
  text filling, 22
  transposition, 40
  undoing changes, 43
  VC mode, 401, 403
    difference reports, 406
    groups, 406
    subtrees, 406
  windows, 90, 105
  write-file, 15
  yanking text, 31
comment buffer, VC mode, 403
comments, 488
  change comments, version control, 400
  copying, macro for, 166
  Custom interface, 313
  Lisp mode, 302
  markup languages, 219
  programming language mode, 269
  syntax and, 268
comparing files
  between windows, 105
  Dired, 128
compatibility mode, xvi
compilation mode, 3, 5
  commands, 265
  error message parser, 266
  error messages, 265
  JDEE and, 292
compilation, programming language
      modes, 264
compile package, 266
compilers, interface, 264
completing words, Ispell, 69
completion, 13, 488
  Custom interface variables, 324
  customization, 456
  HTML helper mode, 237
  keys, 453
  variables, 463
compressing files, Dired, 127
conditional expressions, Lisp functions, 358
constants, major modes, 381
context operators, regular expressions in
      functions, 364
control structures, Lisp functions, 355
copying files, Dired, 126
copying text, 35, 36
  comments, macro, 166

CUA and, 46
  marking, 32
  search strings, 53
copyleft, 488
CPerl mode, 4, 294
Ctrl commands, 23
Ctrl key, commands and, 11
CUA (Common User Access), 46
CUA mode
  commands, 438
  Emacs on Windows, 435
  rectangle mode, 202
cursor, 6, 488
  color, 333
  editing and, 28
  picture mode, 209
  windows, 89
cursor movement, 22
  backward one word, 23
  to beginning of file, 59
  commands, 23, 26
  end of file, 25
  forward one word, 23
  screen by screen, 25
  scrolling, 25
  sentence by sentence, 24
Custom interface, 306, 307
  comments, 313
  .emacs file and, 326
  erasing customization, 309
  font customization, 332
  navigation, 307
  options, 308
  resetting, 308
  session settings, 308, 312
  State button, 311
  variable location, 324
  word abbreviation mode and, 313–317
customization, 45
  auto-mode and, 341
  completion, 456
  Custom interface, 306, 307
    erasing customization, 309
    navigation, 307
    options, 308
    State button, 311
  cut commands, 45
  Ediff, 420
  erasing, 309
  fonts, 332
  key bindings, 335
  keyboard, 45, 47

Lisp and, 306
modes, 389–395
online resources, 473
Options menu, 306, 317
    Dired and, 318
paste commands, 45
special keys, 338
toolbar, hiding/showing, 46
VC mode, 411
Customize Emacs option, Options
        menu, 318
cut commands, customizing, 45
cutting, CUA and, 46
cutting text, encoding and, 38
CVS, Emacs
    building, 425
    downloading, 424
C-x commands, 11
cyclic diary entries, 146
cycling through buffers, 87

D

debugging
    bug reports, 470
    JDEE and, 293
    programming language modes, 264
default
    direction, 489
    tabs, 171
default directories, 14
defining macros, 151
deleting
    bookmarks, 108
    buffers, 87
    commands for, 31
    files, Dired, 126, 132
    frames, 95
    kill ring and, 31
    lines of text, 29
    in picture mode, 211
    recovering, 36
    regions, 34, 35
    text, 27
    undoing, 35
    windows, 92
deleting text, marking for, 32
diary, 489
    adding entries, 146
    blocks of dates, marking, 146
    cyclic entries, 146
    entry display, 147
    file creation, 145

dictionary, Ispell, 65
difference reports, VC mode, 406
digit-argument command, 26
directories, default, 14
Directory Editor (see Dired)
Dired, 123
    * (asterisk), 130
    ? (question mark), 130
    colors, 124
    commands, 137
    comparing files, 128
    compressing files, 127
    copying files, 126
    customization, Options and, 318
    deleting files, 126
    display, 124
        sorting, 124
    editing files, 125
    file groups, 134
    files
        auto-save, 132
        backups, 126
        selecting, 132
    marking files, 132
    navigating directories, 136
    permissions, 124
    query-replace, 136
    renaming files, 126
    selecting files by type, 133
    selecting files with regular
            expressions, 133
    shell commands, 128
    sorting, 130
    uncompressing files, 127
    viewing files, 125
disabling abbreviations, Flyspell, 80
display, 6
    calendar, 142
    centering, 26
    diary entries, 147
    variables, 459
distribution of Emacs, xii
Document Type Definition (see DTD)
documentation of Emacs, navigating, 446
downloading Emacs
    CVS, 424
    Unix and, 422
drawings, 204
    artist mode, 213
    picture mode, 204
DTD (Document Type Definition), XML
        and, 218

dynamic abbreviations, Flyspell, 74

E

Ediff, 414
    commands, 416
    customization, 420
    launching, 414
    leaving, 418
editing
    capitalization, 40
    columns (see rectangle editing)
    cursor and, 28
    files, Dired, 125
    hidden text, 191
    introduction, 20
    JDEE and, 290
    macros, 157
    multiple buffers, separate windows, 92
    picture mode and, 208
    recovering edits, 44
    rectangles and, 194
        CUA mode and, 202
    recursive, 60
    transpositions, 39
    undoing edits, 41
editing mode, SQL, 298
ELisp library, JDEE installation, 286
Emacs
    CVS and
        building Emacs, 425
        downloading, 424
    documentation, navigation, 446
    history of, xi
    integration, 2
    introduction, 1
    Mac OS X, 427
        building Emacs from source code, 429
        command line startup, 431
        Ispell installation, 433
        Jaguar, 430
        Meta key, 432
        prebuilt Emacs, 429
    popularity, 1
    quitting, 15
    starting, 5
    Unix, 422
        downloading, 422
        location, 423
        uncompressing, 423
        unpacking, 423
    versions, 18, 428
    Windows and

command line startup, 435
    CUA mode, 435
    Emacs installation, 433
    FSF installation, 434
    Ispell installation, 438
.emacs file, 489
    Custom interface and, 326
    error messages on startup, 48
    Lisp and
        editing files, 329
        sample file, 328
        saving files, 330
    Lisp functions and, 327
    location, 434
    statements, 327
    word abbrevations, 78
Emacs Lisp mode, 4
encoding, cutting and pasting, 38
enlarging windows, 104
enriched mode, 5
    fonts, commands, 334
enriched text, saving, 334
enriched-mode library, 334
error message parser, compilation mode, 266
error messages
    compilation mode, 265
    .emacs files changes, 48
etags, 263, 272
executing macros, 152, 161
    regions, 167
expressions
    conditional, Lisp functions, 358
    regular, functions, 360
Extensible Markup Language (see XML)
extensions, filename, 4

F

faces (fonts), 330
FAQ file display, 451
file-handling commands, 18
filenames, 4
    extensions, 4
files, 3
    adding lines, 45
    auto-save, 487
        creating, 44
        Dired, 132
    backups, 43, 487
        Dired, 126
        numbered backups, 43
        overwriting original, 43
    buffers, reverting from, 42

comparing
    between windows, 105
    Dired, 128
compressing, Dired, 127
copying, Dired, 126
deleting, Dired, 126
diary, creation, 145
editing, Dired, 125
groups, Dired, 134
inserting in other files, 14
Lisp, byte-compiling, 397
marking, Dired, 132
opening, 11
reading wrong file, 13
renaming
    Dired, 126
    version controlled, 410
saving, 15
selecting
    Dired, 132
    with regular expressions, Dired, 133
selecting by type, Dired, 133
uncompressing, Dired, 127
version controlled (see version control)
viewing, Dired, 125
file-template-java file, 374
fill mode, word wrap and, 45
fill prefixes, 183, 489
find-file command, 15
find-library file, 370
finger habits, 2
first line of paragraph, indents, 177
floating point number syntax (Lisp), 346
Flyspell, 70
    abbreviations, capitalization and, 80
    commands, 73
    dynamic abbreviations, 74
    highlighting, 71
    word abbreviation mode, 75
    word abbreviations, 73, 74
        defining, 77
        deleting, 78
        disabling, 80
Flyspell mode, 4
Flyspell prog mode, 4
font lock mode, 5, 220, 274
font-enriched text, saving, 333
fonts
    changing interactively, 330
    Custom interface, 332
    enriched mode, commands, 334
    faces, 330

Isearch and, 331
    programming language modes, 274
FooManager.java file, 375
formatting paragraphs, troubleshooting, 48
Fortran language mode, 266
forward movement of cursor, 23
fragments, Lisp, 304
frames, 489
    buffers and, 84
    creating, 93
    deleting, 95
    minimizing, 95
    moving between, 95
    names, 94
    sizing, 93
    windows comparison, 82
FSF (Free Software Foundation), xi
    bug reports, 470
    downloading Emacs and, 421
    Emacs installation, 434
functions
    built-in, 358
        buffers, 359
        locating, 372
        regions, 359
        text, 359
    Lisp, 346
        argument codes, 352
        conditional expressions, 358
        control structures, 355
        converting to Emacs
            commands, 351–353
        defining, 347–351
        primitive, 353
        regular expressions and, 371
        return values, 346
        statement blocks, 354
        syntax, 346
Fundamental mode, 3

G

games, xvi
games and amusements, Lisp packages, 468
global abbreviations, 489
    Flyspell, 77
grouping operators, regular expressions in
        functions, 363
groups
    output, 490
    VC mode, 406
groups of files, Dired, 134
GUI windows (see windows)

H

headers
  HTML mode, 222
  version control, 408
help
  buffer, 17
  commands, 441
    apropos, 443
    complex commands, 445
  details, 441
  point, 17
  tutorial, 440
Help menu, 16, 17
hidden text, editing, 191
hiding/showing
  HTML tags, 223
  text, 190
  toolbar, 8, 46
highlighting
  automatic, 331
  buffer highlighting, 331
  Flyspell, 71
  searches and, 51
holiday commands, 148
holidays, displaying in calendar, 144
horizontal windows, 89
HTML helper mode, 220, 230
  character encoding, 238
  commands, 239
  completion, 237
  prompting, 238
  starting, 231
  templates, 231
HTML (hypertext markup language), 218
  ISO accents mode, 225
  writing in, 220
HTML mode, 3, 220
  accented characters, 226
  character encoding, 224
  commands, 228
  headers, 222
  hiding/showing tags, 223
  hyperlinks and, 222
  key bindings, 222
  punctuation, 228
  starting, 221
  symbols, 228
  XHTML and, 223
HTMLModeDeluxe, 220
hungry-delete-key, C programming language
    mode, 281
hyperlinks, HTML mode, 222

I

hypertext markup language (see HTML)

icons, toolbar, 7
  troubleshooting, 18
IDEs (integrated development
    environments), 264
incremental regular expression searches, 50
incremental searches, 49, 51
  commands, 53
  regular expressions, 63
  starting, 51
Indented text mode, 3, 176
indents, 176
  commands, 181, 185
  Lisp mode, 301
  paragraphs, 177
    filling, 178
    first line, 177
  programming language modes, 270, 278
    commands, 271
  regions, 179
  tips, 181
Info commands, 451
Info mode, 5
inserting files in other files, 14
installation
  Emacs on Mac OS X
    building from source, 429
    prebuilt, 429
  Emacs on Unix, 421
  Emacs on Windows, 433
  Ispell
    on Mac OS X, 433
    on Windows, 438
  JDEE, 287
integer syntax (Lisp), 346
integration, 2
interactive functions, argument codes, 352
interactive mode, SQL, 297
internal buffers, names, 84
Isearch mode, 4
  fonts and, 331
ISO accents mode, 5
  HTML, 225
Ispell
  buffer, 64
  commands, 73
  completing words, 69
  dictionary, inserting words, 65
  Mac OS X installation, 433
  replacing words, 69

single word checking, 69
skipping words, 67
Windows installation, 438

J

Java mode, 4, 284
Java tools registration, 289
JDEE (Java Development Environment for
      Emacs), 284, 285
    CEDET installation, 286
    Code Generation menu options, 292
    compiling and, 292
    debugging and, 293
    editing with, 290
    ELisp library, installation, 286
    installation, 287
    JDK (Java Development Kit)
        registration, 289
    resources, 294
    running and, 292
jumping to bookmarks, 107

K

key bindings
    customization, 335
    defining, 11
    HTML mode, 222
    psgml mode, 256
    unsetting, 339
keyboard
    binding macros to, 160
    command access, 27
    commands, 10
    cursor movement and, 22
    customization, 45, 47
    macro input pauses, 162
    menu access, 8
    regions, marks, 32
    remapping keys, 47
keymaps, 11
keystrokes, macro definition, 152
kill commands, 29
kill ring, 31, 490
    recovering deletions and, 36
killing, commands for, 31

L

LaTeX, 218
    $$ (dollar signs), 258
    braces, 258
LaTeX mode, 3

command pairs, 259
commands, 261
paragraphs, 259
printing in, 260
quotation marks, 259
libraries
    enriched mode, 334
    Lisp, building, 395
    source code, 465
lines of text, deleting, 29
Lisp
    atoms, 346
    calculator mode, 384
        code, 386
    customization and, 306
    .emacs and
        editing files, 329
        sample file, 328
        saving files, 330
    files, byte-compiling, 397
    fragments, 304
    functions, 346
        argument codes, interactive
            functions, 352
        conditional expressions, 358
        control structures, 355
        converting into commands, 351–353
        defining, 347–351
        .emacs file and, 327
        primitive, 353
        return values, 346
        statement blocks, 354
    introduction, 345
    libraries, building, 395
    line evaluation commands, 304
    lists, 383
    packages, 464
        C support, 465
        C++ support, 465
        games and amusement, 468
        Java support, 465
        Lisp programming support, 465
        networking support, 468
        text processing, 467
    S-expressions, commands, 299
    stacks, 383
    variables, 346
Lisp interaction mode, 4, 304
Lisp language mode, 266
Lisp mode, 4, 298
    comments, 302
    differences, 303
    indentation, 301

Lisp packages, 340
Lisp programming, xvi, 344
Lisp statements, 45
listing
    bookmarks, 109
        commands, 110
        display, 109
    buffers, 98
        by major mode, 86
        symbols, 98
        (see also buffer list)
lists, Lisp, 383
literal tabs, 174
local, abbreviations, 490
local keymap, major modes, 381
locked files, version control, 399
lpr-buffer command, 140
lpr-region command, 140

M

Mac OS X
    Emacs, 427
        building from source code, 429
        command-line startup, 431
        Ispell installation, 433
        Jaguar, 430
        Meta key, 432
        prebuilt, 429
    troubleshooting commands, 149
macro ring, 160
macros
    binding to keys, 160
    commands, 169
    defining, 151
    editing, 157
    example
        business letter with pauses, 162
        comment copying, 166
        indentation marks, 167
        references buffer creation, 155
        transposition macro, 152
    execution, 152, 161
    introduction, 150
    naming, 161
    pausing for keyboard input, 162
    queries, adding, 165
    regions, 167
    repeating, 153
    saving, 161
    writing tips, 154
major modes, 3, 490
    buffers, 84

listing by, 86
minor mode dual position, 5
programming, 381
    calculator, 384
    components, 381
make utility (UNIX), 264
manpages, reading, 141
margins, 182
marking files in Dired, 132
marking sections, Outline mode, 192
marking text, 32
    paragraphs, 35
    regions, 35
marks, 490
    buffers, 89
    regions, 32
markup languages
    comments, 219
    DTD (see DTD)
    font-lock mode, 220
    HTML (see HTML)
    LaTeX (see LaTeX)
    online resources, 473
    TeX (see TeX)
    WYSIWYG tools, 219
    XML (see XML)
menu bar, 8
menus, 9
    Buffers, 84
    Help, 17
    keyboard access, 8
    mouse and, troubleshooting, 19
    pop-ups, 8
    text-based, option selection, 9
Messages buffer, 84
Meta commands, 23
Meta key
    Mac OS X, 432
    placement of, xvii
    using, 11
    versus Esc, xvii
minibuffer, 10, 490
    absent, 19
    troubleshooting, 19
minimizing frames, 95
minor modes, 4, 490
    outline, 192
    refill mode, 20
mmm (multiple major modes) mode, 220
mode line, 9, 490
    * (asterisk) in, 10
    buffer name, 96

buffers, 17
troubleshooting, 19
modes, 3
  abbrev, 4
  artist, 4
  auto-fill, 4, 21, 47
  auto-mode and, 341
  auto-save, 4
  cc mode, 3
  compatibility, xvi
  compilation, 3, 5
  Cperl, 4
  customizing, 389–395
  Emacs Lisp, 4
  enriched, 5
  Flyspell, 4
  font-lock, 5, 220
  fundamental, 3
  HTML helper, 220, 230
    character encoding, 238
    commands, 239
    prompting, 238
    starting, 231
    templates, 231
  HTML mode, 3, 220
    character encoding, 224
    commands, 228
    hiding/showing tags, 223
    key bindings, 222
    starting, 221
  HTMLModeDeluxe and, 220
  Indented text mode, 3
  Info, 5
  Isearch, 4
  ISO accents, 5
  Java, 4
  LaTeX mode, 3
  Lisp, 4
  Lisp interaction, 4
  major modes, 3
    buffers, 84
    programming, 381–389
  minor modes, 4
  mmm (multiple major modes), 220
  nxml, commands, 252
  Outline, 3, 4, 187, 189
    marking sections, 192
  overwrite, 4, 41
  paragraph indent text, 3, 4, 22
  Perl, 4
  picture mode, 3, 204
    editing in, 208

programming language modes, 263
psgml, 220, 253
Refile, 4
Refill, 20
SGML, 3
  writing XML, 244
sgml mode, 220
SGML name entity, 4
shell, 3, 118
SQL, 4
text, 3
  default, 47
variables, 460
VC, 5
view mode, 3
mouse
  drawing, artist mode, 213
  menu access, troubleshooting, 19
  text selection, 37
moving
  between windows, 90
  to bookmarks, 107
  text, 35
    marking, 32
  windows, buffer list, 99
multiple buffers, 85
  displaying, 100
  saving, 95

N

names
  bookmarks, renaming, 108
  buffers
    named same, 96
    renaming buffers, 96
  frames, 94
  macros, 161
  major modes, 381
navigation
  calendar, 142
  Custom interface, 307
  Dired, 136
  Emacs documentation, 446
  windows, 103
Nqmacs, 433
numbered backups, 43
nxml mode
  commands, 252
  writing XHTML, 246

O

online resources, web sites, 472
opening files, 11
operators
    regular expressions, 368
        alternation functions, 363
        context, 364
        functions, 361
        grouping functions, 363
Options menu, 317
    customization and, 306
    Customize Emacs option, 318
    Dired and, 318
    Save Options option, 318
    Show/Hide option, 317
Outline minor mode, 192
Outline mode, 3, 4, 187
    commands, 193
    demoting sections, 192
    marking sections, 192
    promoting sections, 192
    starting, 189
output groups, 121, 490
overwrite mode, 4, 41, 491

P

packages, Lisp, 340, 464
    C support, 465
    C++ support, 465
    games and amusement, 468
    Java support, 465
    Lisp programming support, 465
    networking support, 468
    text processing, 467
paragraph indent text mode, 3, 4, 22
paragraphs
    centering, 186
    formatting, troubleshooting, 48
    indents, 177
        filling, 178
    LaTeX mode, 259
    marking, 35
parentheses, syntax and, 268
paste commands, customizing, 45
pasting text, 36
    from clipboard, 38
    CUA and, 46
    encoding and, 38
pausing macros for keyboard input, 162
Perl mode, 4, 266, 294
permissions, Dired display, 124

PgUp command, troubleshooting, 19
PgUp key, with text-based menu options, 9
picture mode, 3, 204
    blank lines, 209
    blank space, blocks, 212
    carriage return and, 211
    commands, 212
    cursor motion, 209
    deletion, 211
    drawing in, 204
    editing in, 208
    tabs, 212
    text mode comparison, 211
platform-specific considerations, 421–439
point, 6, 491
    Help, 17
    (see also cursor)
pop-up menus, 8
prefixes, fill prefixes, 183
primitive functions, Lisp, 353
printing, 140
    commands for, 140, 141
    LaTeX mode, 260
programming
    Lisp (see Lisp programming)
    major modes, 381
        calculator mode, 384
        components, 381
    modes for, xvi
    variables, 462
programming language modes, 263
    C, 266, 275
        commands, 276
    C++, 266, 275
    code indentation, 278
    comments, 269
    compiling in, 264
    CPerl, 294
    debugging in, 264
    fonts, 274
    indentation, commands, 271
    indents, 270
    Java, 266, 284
    Lisp, 266
        comments, 302
        indentation, 301
        Lisp interaction mode, 304
    Lisp modes, 298
    Perl, 266, 294
    Scheme, 266
    SGML, 266
    Simula, 266

SQL, 266, 296
   editing mode, 298
   interactive mode, 297
  syntax, 268
programming languages, online
     resources, 473
prompting, HTML helper mode, 238
psgml mode, 220, 253
  bindings, 256
punctuation, 39
  HTML mode, 228
  syntax and, 268

Q

queries, macros, 165
query-replace, 50, 56
  Dired, 136
  recursive editing and, 60
  regular expressions, 63
  repeating, 58
  responses, 56
question mark (?), Dired, 130
quitting Emacs, 15
quotation marks, LaTeX mode, 259

R

reading files, wrong file, 13
reading manpages, 141
read-only buffers, 97
  toggling status, 97
recovering deletions, 36
recovery
  from auto-save files, 44
  changes, 44
rectangle commands, 201
rectangle editing, 194
  CUA mode and, 202
recursive editing, 60
redoing commands, 42
refill mode, 4, 20
reformatting commands, 22
regions, 22, 491
  built-in functions, 359
  centering, 186
  commands for, 37
  defining, 32
  deleting, 34, 35
  indents, 179
  macros, 167
  marking, 35
  marks, keyboard, 32

registering files, version control and, 399
registers, 491
regular expression replace, 50
regular expression searches, 50
regular expressions, 491
  built-in functions
    operator context, 364
    operators, 368
  characters in, 62
  file selection, Dired, 133
  functions, 360, 371
    match portions, 365
    operators, 361
    operators, grouping, 363
  incremental searches, 63
  query-replace, 63
  search and replace and, 62
  searches, commands, 63
remapping keys, 47
renaming
  bookmarks, 108
  files
    Dired, 126
    version controlled, 410
renaming buffers, 96
repeating
  commands, 26, 58
  macros, 153
  query-replace, 58
replacing (see search and replace)
reporting bugs, 470
resetting, Custom interface and, 308
resources, web sites, 472
return values, functions (Lisp), 346
returns, picture mode, 211
Reverse Polish Notation calculator, 383
reverting buffers from files, 42
revision number, version control, 400
revisions, retrieving (VC mode), 407

S

Save Options option, Options menu, 318
saving
  buffers
    buffer list, 100
    multiple, 95
  files, 15
    scratch buffer, 15
  macros, 161
scratch buffer, 10, 15
screen by screen movement, 25
scrolling, 25

search and replace
  canceling searches, 52
  Case Insensitive Search, 61
  case-fold-search variable, 62
  case-replace variable, 62
  case-sensitivity, 50, 61
  copying to search string, 53
  direction of search, 50, 52
  etags and, 272
  highlighting, 51
  incremental regular expression
      searches, 50
  incremental searches, 49, 51
    commands, 53
    starting, 51
  operations, 55
  query-replace, 50, 56
  regular expression replace, 50
  regular expression searches, 50
  regular expressions, commands, 63
  regular expressions in, 62
  search commands, 54
  simple search and replace, 50
  simple searches, 49, 53
  special characters, 63
  troubleshooting, 81
  variables, 459
  word searches, 49, 54
search icon, toolbar, 54
security, shell mode and, 122
selecting files
  by type in Dired, 133
  with regular expressions, Dired, 133
selecting text, 36
  mouse, 37
send commands, SQL, 298
session settings, Custom interface, 308, 312
S-expressions (LISP), commands, 299
SGML mode, 3
  writing XML, 244
sgml mode, 220
SGML name entity mode, 4
shell buffer, 114, 491
  history commands, 120
  multiple, 121
  output groups, 121
  starting, 118
shell commands
  Dired, 128
  history commands, 120
  output to buffer, 118

shell mode, 3, 118
  commands, 115, 122
  security and, 122
  troubleshooting, 149
Show/Hide, Options menu, 317
shrinking windows, 104
side-by-side windows, 102
simple search and replace, 50
simple searches, 49, 53
  commands, 54
sizing
  frames, 93
  windows, 19, 104
    limits, 105
sorting, Dired and, 130
source code, Emacs, Mac OS X and, 429
spaces, changing to/from tabs, 176
special characters
  conventions, 337
  search and replace, 63
special keys, customization, 338
spelling
  Flyspell, 70
  Ispell
    buffer, 64
    completing words, 69
    single word, 69
splitting windows, 89
  vertically, 102
SQL mode, 4
SQL (Structured Query Language), 296
  editing mode, 298
  interactive mode, 297
  send commands, 298
stacks, Lisp and, 383
Stallman, Richard, xi
starting Emacs, 5
Stat button, Custom interface, 311
statement blocks, Lisp functions, 354
statements, .emacs, 327
status, buffers, 100
stopping commands, 43
strings
  syntax and, 268
    Lisp, 347
  variables, 339
switching between frames, 95
switching between windows, 90
switching buffers, 85
symbols
  buffer list, 98

HTML mode, 228
major modes, 381
syntax (Lisp), 347
variables, 339
syntax
atoms (Lisp), 346
functions (Lisp), 346
highlighting (see font-lock mode)
programming language modes, 268

T

tab commands, 176
tabs, 170
colons at tab stops, 173
converting to spaces, 176
default, 171
literal tabs, 174
picture mode, 212
spaces, 175
tab stops, changing, 172
width, 175
TEI (Text Encoding Initiative) Emacs, 246
Template.el file, 376
templates
automatic template system, 374
FccManager.java file, 375
file-template-java file, 374
HTML helper mode, 231
TeX, 218
TeX mode commands, 261
text
built-in functions, 359
centering, 186
clipboard
placing text in, 37
retrieving from, 38
color-enriched, saving, 333
copying, 35, 36
deleting, 27
recovering, 36
regions, 35
editing hidden, 191
enriched, saving, 334
fill prefixes, 183
font-enriched, saving, 333
hidden, editing, 191
hiding/showing, 190
indents, 176
paragraph first line, 177
paragraphs, 177, 178
inserting, bookmarks and, 108
lines, deleting, 29

margins, 182
marking, 32
paragraphs, 35
regions, 35
moving, 35
online resources, 473
outline mode, 187
overwriting, 41
pasting, 36
regions, 32
deleting, 35
marking, 35
selecting, 36
mouse, 37
tabs, 170
uppercase, 40
text editing, variables, 461
text filling commands, 22
text mode, 3
centering lines, 186
default, 47
picture mode comparison, 211
word abbreviations, 77
word wrap and, 45
Text Properties menu, font changes, 330
text-based menus, option selection, 9
tilde (~), buffers and, 100
toolbar, 7
customizing, 45
hiding/showing, 8, 46
icons, 7
troubleshooting, 18
search icon, 54
transposition commands, 40
transpositions, 39
troubleshooting
menu access, 19
minibuffer, 19
mode line, 19
paragraph formatting, 48
PgUp, 19
search and replace, 81
shell mode, 149
toolbar icons, 18
tutorial for help system, 440
typos
flyspell mode and, 70
transpositions, 39
word abbreviation mode, 75

U

uncompressing files, Dired, 127

undoing, 35
    backup files and, 43
    changes, commands for, 43
    edits, 41
Unix, 421
    Emacs, 422
        downloading, 422
        location, 423
        uncompressing, 423
        unpacking, 423
    make utility, 264
uppercase text, 40

V

variables
    auto-save, 457
    backups, 457
    case-fold-search, 62
    case-replace, 62
    characters, 339
    completion, 463
    display, 459
    Lisp, 346
    location, Custom interface, 324
    major modes, 381
    miscellaneous, 463
    modes, 460
    programming, 462
    search and replace, 459
    setting, 339
    strings, 339
    symbols, 339
    text editing, 461
    versioning, 457
VC mode, 5
    change histories, 407
    ChangeLog files, 409
    ClearCase and, 412
    commands, 401, 403
        difference reports, 406
        groups, 406
        subtrees, 406
    comment buffer, 403
    customization, 411
    extensions, 412
    file registration, 407
    indicators, 404
    snapshots, 408
version control
    change comments, 400
    ChangeLog files, 409
    changes to files, 417

    checked-out files, 410
    Ediff and, 414
    file registration, 407
    files, registering, 399
    headers, 408
    locked files, 399
    online resources, 473
    renaming files, 410
    revision number, 400
    revisions, retrieving, 407
    snapshots, 408
    system selection, 405
    uses, 398
    work files, 400
    (see also VC mode)
version, Emacs, x
versioning, commands, 457
vertical windows, 102
View mode, 3
viewing files, Dired, 125

W

web sites, 472
whitespace, syntax and, 268
windows, 492
    buffer display, 88
    buffer list, moving, 99
    buffers and, 84
    commands, 90, 105
    cursors, 89
    deleting, 92
    enlarging, 104
    files, comparing between, 105
    frames comparison, 82
    horizontal, 89
    moving between, 90
    multiple buffers in separate windows, 92
    navigating, 103
    shrinking, 104
    side-by-side, 102
    sizing, 104
        limits, 105
    splitting, 89
        vertically, 102
    startup and, 90
    vertical, 102
Windows and Emacs
    command line startup, 435
    CUA mode, 435
    installation, 433, 434
    Ispell installation, 438
word abbreviation mode

Custom interface and, 313–317
Flyspell, 75
word abbreviations, Flyspell, 73, 74
word searches, 49, 54
word wrap, 45
words
   searching by, 492
   syntax and, 268
work files, version control, 400
workspace, 6
write-file command, 15
writing
   in HTML, 220
   XHTML, nxml mode and, 246
   XML, 243
      SGML mode, 244
writing macros, tips for, 154
WYSIWYG (what you see is what you get)
      tools, 219

X

X Window System
   minibuffer, missing, 19
   mode line, missing, 19
   window, size problems, 19
XHTML
   HTML mode and, 223
   writing, nxml mode, 246
XML (Extensible Markup Language), 218
   DTD and, 218
   psgml mode, 253
   TEI Emacs, 246
   writing, 243
      SGML mode, 244

Y

yanking text, commands for, 31

About the Authors

Debra Cameron is the president of Cameron Consulting. In addition to her love for Emacs, Deb researches emerging technologies and their applications. Her book *Optical Networking: A Wiley Tech Brief* (2002) describes applications ranging from a grassroots neighborhood network in Sweden to Canada's optical Ethernet. Deb also writes and presents videos on computer security topics. Deb frequently edits for O'Reilly and others, working on titles such as *DNS and Bind*, *TCP/IP Network Administration*, and *HTML and XHTML: The Definitive Guide*, as well as numerous Java tomes. After using a variety of operating systems from CP/M onward, her coauthors Jim and Marc converted her to her platform of choice, Mac OS X.

James Elliott is a senior software engineer at Berbee, with over 15 years of professional experience as a systems developer. Thanks to some clever and helpful colleagues at his first internship, he's benefited from Emacs that entire time. A decade before starting that career, he cultivated his involvement and fascination with computers. He has a passion for building and sharing high-quality tools and frameworks to simplify the tasks of other developers, and Emacs is a great foundation. After a globe-trotting childhood, Jim earned his bachelor's degree in computer science at Rensselaer Polytechnic in upstate New York, and his master's degree at the University of Wisconsin-Madison, with some interesting stints at Bell Laboratories (in Murray Hill, birthplace of C and Unix). Although he succumbed to the allure of the real world shortly after completing his Ph.D. qualifying exams, he was happy to find interesting work in Madison, where he lives with his partner Joe Buberger and two challenging cats.

Marc Loy is a senior-level programmer with over two decades of programming experience. He has played with Java since the alpha days and can't find his way back to C. He received his master's degree in computer science at the University of Wisconsin-Madison. He is currently digging into the world of digital video but still makes time to churn out the occasional coding project.

Eric Raymond is an observer-participant anthropologist in the Internet hacker culture. His research has helped explain the decentralized open source model of software development that has proven so effective in the evolution of the Internet. His own software projects include one of the Internet's most widely used email transport programs. Eric is also a science fiction fan, a musician, an activist for the First and Second Amendments, and a martial artist with a Black Belt in Tae Kwon Do. His home page is at *http://www.catb.org/~esr*.

Bill Rosenblatt is the president of GiantSteps/Media Technology Strategies, a consulting firm in New York City. Before founding GiantSteps, Bill was CTO of Fathom, an online content and education company associated with Columbia University and other scholarly institutions. He has been a technology executive at McGraw-Hill and Times Mirror and head of strategic marketing for media and publishing at Sun Microsystems. Bill was also one of the architects of the Digital

Object Identifier (DOI), a standard for online content identification and digital rights management.

Colophon

Our look is the result of reader comments, our own experimentation, and feedback from distribution channels. Distinctive covers complement our distinctive approach to technical topics, breathing personality and life into potentially dry subjects.

The animal on the cover of *Learning GNU Emacs,* Third Edition is a gnu (or wildebeest). Gnus are African antelopes that inhabit the Serengeti Plains. Male gnus (bulls) reach up to 52 inches in height and 500 pounds inweight, and have the most lethal horns of any of the antelopes. Bulls are very territorial and tend to remain alone. The females and young generally live in small herds. However, they may congregate in the tens of thousands during migration. Gnus are the favorite prey of lions.

Jamie Peppard was the production editor and proofreader for *Learning GNU Emacs* Third Edition. Nancy Reinhardt was the copyeditor . Adam Witwer and Claire Cloutier provided quality control. Mary Agner provided production assistance. Johnna VanHoose Dinse wrote the index.

Edie Freedman designed the cover of this book using a 19th-century engraving from the Dover Pictorial Archive. Clay Fernald produced the cover layout with Quark Express 4.1 using Adobe's ITC Garamond font. Emma Colby produced the Quick Reference card with Adobe InDesign CS using the fonts Linotype Birka and Adobe Myriad Condensed.

Melanie Wang designed the interior layout, based on a series design by David Futato. This book was converted by Julie Hawks to FrameMaker 5.5.6 with a format conversion tool created by Erik Ray, Jason McIntosh, Neil Walls, and Mike Sierra that uses Perl and XML technologies. The text font is Linotype Birka; the heading font is Adobe Myriad Condensed; and the code font is LucasFont's TheSans Mono Condensed. The illustrations that appear in the book were produced by Robert Romano and Jessamyn Read using Macromedia FreeHand MX and Adobe Photoshop CS.

Better than e-books

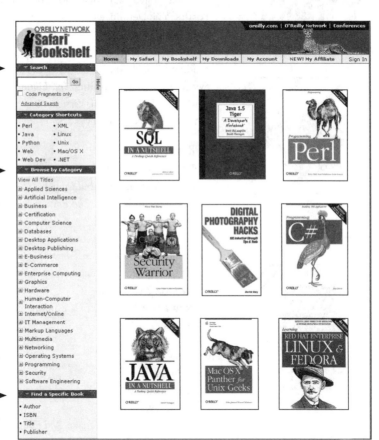

Search
inside electronic versions of thousands of books

Browse
books by category. With Safari researching any topic is a snap

Find
answers in an instant

Read books from cover to cover. Or, simply click to the page you need.

Search Safari! The premier electronic reference library for programmers and IT professionals

Related Titles Available from O'Reilly

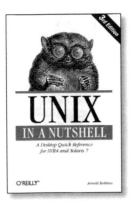

Unix Administration

CVS Pocket Reference, *2nd Edition*
DNS & BIND, *4th Edtion*
DNS & BIND Cookbook
Essential CVS
Essential System Administration, *3rd Edition*
Essential System Administration Pocket Reference
Postfix: The Definitive Guide
qmail
sendmail, *3rd Edition*
sendmail Cookbook
System Performance Tuning, *2nd Edition*
The Unix CD Bookshelf, *Version 3.0*
Unix Backup & Recovery

Unix Basics

GNU Emacs Pocket Reference
Learning GNU Emacs, *2nd Edition*
Learning the bash Shell, *2nd Edition*
Learning the Korn Shell
Learning the Unix Operating System, *5th Edition*
Learning the vi Editor, *6th Edition*
sed & awk Pocket Reference, *2nd Edition*
sed & awk, *2nd Edition*
Unix in a Nutshell, System V Edition, *3rd Edition*
Using csh & tcsh

Unix Tools

BSD Hacks
Effective awk Programming, *3rd Edition*
lex & yacc, *2nd Edition*
Managing Projects with make, *2nd Edition*
Practical PostgreSQL
The Complete FreeBSD, *4th Edition*
Unix Power Tools, *3rd edition*
Writing GNU Emacs Extensions

Keep in touch with O'Reilly

1. Download examples from our books

To find example files for a book, go to:

www.oreilly.com/catalog

select the book, and follow the "Examples" link.

2. Register your O'Reilly books

Register your book at *register.oreilly.com*

Why register your books?
Once you've registered your O'Reilly books you can:

- Win O'Reilly books, T-shirts or discount coupons in our monthly drawing.
- Get special offers available only to registered O'Reilly customers.
- Get catalogs announcing new books (US and UK only).
- Get email notification of new editions of the O'Reilly books you own.

3. Join our email lists

Sign up to get topic-specific email announcements of new books and conferences, special offers, and O'Reilly Network technology newsletters at:

elists.oreilly.com

It's easy to customize your free elists subscription so you'll get exactly the O'Reilly news you want.

4. Get the latest news, tips, and tools

www.oreilly.com

- "Top 100 Sites on the Web"—PC Magazine
- CIO Magazine's Web Business 50 Awards

Our web site contains a library of comprehensive product information (including book excerpts and tables of contents), downloadable software, background articles, interviews with technology leaders, links to relevant sites, book cover art, and more.

5. Work for O'Reilly

Check out our web site for current employment opportunities:

jobs.oreilly.com

6. Contact us

O'Reilly & Associates
1005 Gravenstein Hwy North
Sebastopol, CA 95472 USA

TEL: 707-827-7000 or 800-998-9938
(6am to 5pm PST)

FAX: 707-829-0104

order@oreilly.com
For answers to problems regarding your order or our products. To place a book order online, visit:

www.oreilly.com/order_new

catalog@oreilly.com
To request a copy of our latest catalog.

booktech@oreilly.com
For book content technical questions or corrections.

corporate@oreilly.com
For educational, library, government, and corporate sales.

proposals@oreilly.com
To submit new book proposals to our editors and product managers.

international@oreilly.com
For information about our international distributors or translation queries. For a list of our distributors outside of North America check out:

international.oreilly.com/distributors.html

adoption@oreilly.com
For information about academic use of O'Reilly books, visit:

academic.oreilly.com

O'REILLY®

Our books are available at most retail and online bookstores.
To order direct: 1-800-998-9938 • *order@oreilly.com* • *www.oreilly.com*
Online editions of most O'Reilly titles are available by subscription at *safari.oreilly.com*